A Devotional Study
of the Pauline Epistles.

# *Revealing Heaven's* Secrets

Warren Henderson

All Scripture quotations are from the New King James Version of the Bible, unless otherwise noted. Copyright © 1982 by Thomas Nelson, Inc. Nashville, TN

*Revealing Heaven's Secrets – A Devotional Study of the Pauline Epistles*

By Warren Henderson
Copyright © 2024

Cover Design: Ben Bredeweg

Photo by: Brent Rawlings

Editing/Proofreading: Mercer Armstrong, Marilyn MacMullen, and Dan Macy

Published by Warren A. Henderson Publishing
1025 Iron Cap Dr.
Stevensville, MT 59870

Perfect Bound ISBN: 978-1-939770-74-5
eBook ISBN: 978-1-939770-75-2

Copies of *Revealing Heaven's Secrets* are available through various online retailers worldwide. Our website address is: warrenahendersonpublishing.com

# Table of Contents

Preface ................................................................... 1

Romans .................................................................. 5

1 Corinthians ........................................................ 97

2 Corinthians ...................................................... 185

Galatians ............................................................ 241

Ephesians ........................................................... 277

Philippians ......................................................... 337

Colossians .......................................................... 371

1 Thessalonians .................................................. 399

2 Thessalonians .................................................. 421

1 Timothy .......................................................... 435

2 Timothy .......................................................... 471

Titus ................................................................... 493

Philemon ........................................................... 513

Endnotes ............................................................ 517

# Preface

The Christian community has a vast library of various Bible study resources. Though profitable, many of these resources tend to condition their readers into embracing a particular systemized thinking without the benefit of exploring and discovering the Truth for themselves. As each believer has an anointing from the Holy Spirit to rightly discern truth and error (1 Jn. 2:20, 27), it is important for each Christian to rightly discern the meaning of Scripture (2 Tim. 2:15). It is good for us to remember that human commentary is not inspired and thus will include some amount of error.

Though teachers are supplied by Christ to affirm and apply truth for the benefit of the Church, it is evident that their ministry is to equip believers for *the work of the ministry* (Eph. 4:11-12). Hence, each Christian has a responsibility to study and learn sound doctrine for himself or herself. To this end the Word of God and the Spirit of God are sufficient to guide any true seeker of truth Heavenward.

The following abbreviations are used herein: "O.T." = Old Testament, "N.T." = New Testament, "ch." = chapter, "v." = verse, and "vv." = verses. "Church" is capitalized when speaking of the universal Church, the body of Christ, but is lowercase when addressing local church topics. Simple outlines for each of the epistles are provided to convey main themes and subjects.

Besides being with the Lord, one of the great mysteries of Heaven will be that all believers will come into the unity of the faith (Eph. 4:13). A moment after the trump of God calls us home, we will all be most profoundly grateful to have all of our doctrinal imperfection forever removed. May the Lord give each one of us grace and wisdom to understand the vast truth of His Word and live it out in faithful love.

— Warren Henderson

# The Pauline Epistles

Paul is credited with writing thirteen of the twenty-one New Testament epistles. He may also be the author of the Epistle to the Hebrews. Paul's writing style is logical in construction and draws precedents from Old Testament Scripture to establish and defend New Testament doctrine; this is especially true in Romans and Galatians. Generally speaking, Paul's epistles are to Gentile believers. This may explain why the epistle of Hebrews, if Paul did write it, is quite different in style. Paul, being disdained by Jewish orthodoxy, chose to begin the epistle with an exaltation of God instead of his normal introduction in order to win over a stubborn and uncommitted audience.

The foreword portions of many of the Pauline epistles provide the doctrinal basis to compel believers to live for the Lord Jesus Christ. Paul generally uses *identification* truth (i.e., the believer's *position* with Christ) to implore Christians to *practically* live for Christ. *Relationships* are established by acts (e.g., birth, adoption, a marriage covenant, etc.), but *fellowship* is dependent upon right behavior. God regenerates and adopts a believer into His family, but God's fellowship with a believer is contingent upon his or her continuing in righteous conduct.

The Pauline epistles were likely written in the following order: Galatians, 1 and 2 Thessalonians, 1 and 2 Corinthians, Romans, Ephesians, Colossians, Philemon, Philippians, 1 Timothy, Titus, and 2 Timothy. Galatians was written after Paul and Barnabas' first missionary journey, while 1 and 2 Thessalonians were penned during his second foreign outreach effort with Silas. Letters were sent to the Church at Corinth and to the Roman believers during Paul's third missionary journey. Ephesians, Philippians, Colossians, and Philemon were penned during Paul's first Roman imprisonment (i.e., his fourth missionary journey). His epistles to his spiritual sons, Timothy and Titus, were written in the final two or three years of his life; Paul was again a prisoner of Rome when he wrote 2 Timothy, his final epistle.

The following table organizes the thirteen Pauline epistles in order of theme, focus and study content.

| Epistle | 1 & 2 Thessalonians | Romans, 1 & 2 Corinthians, Galatians | Ephesians, Philippians, Colossians, Philemon | 1 & 2 Timothy, Titus |
|---|---|---|---|---|
| Theme | One Hope | One Faith | One Love | One Church Order |
| Focus | Christ & His Second Coming | Christ & His Cross | Christ & His Church | Christ & His Congregations |
| Study Content | Eschatological | Soteriological | Christological | Ecclesiological |

# Romans

## Background

It is unknown how the gospel message had reached Rome; Scripture does not record Paul or any other missionary traveling there. The best explanation is that Christians, many of whom were being persecuted for their faith, were faithfully sharing the message of eternal life wherever they went and with whomever they came in contact. This epistle is rightly placed as the first epistle in the canon of N.T. Scripture as it thoroughly addresses the paramount subject of what the gospel message is: What is God's only means of forgiving, justifying, and sanctifying sinners unto His eternal glory? The answer is through the gospel message of Jesus Christ.

## Theme(s)

The *Gospel of God* (Rom. 1:1) or the *Gospel of His Son* (Jesus Christ; Rom. 1:9) is the main theme. In the first eight chapters of the book, we learn that condemned sinners must be justified in Christ to be saved and then sanctified in Christ to please God. God's sovereign dealings with the nation of Israel in relationship to the Old Covenant and the New Covenant is the subject matter of chapters 9-11. The practical applications of living out the gospel of Jesus Christ are addressed in the last five chapters of the Epistle. The key verses relating to the book's theme are Romans 1:16-17. Romans provides a reasonable and logical basis for the Christian faith and ensures that the foundational doctrines of Christianity are known to the believers in Rome.

## Keywords and Phrases

Keywords and phrases include: "righteous/righteousness," "justification/justify/justified/just," "salvation," "believing/believes," "faith," "everyone" (not just Jews, but Gentiles also), "power," and "live/life." Consider that "righteousness" occurs 92 times in the New Testament and is found 36 times in Romans and that various forms of the word "justify" are found 22 times in Romans compared with only 27 times in all the other epistles. The key phrase "the righteousness of God" is found eight times in the epistle.

## Date
Since Paul acknowledged that the gift from the believers in Achaia to the poor saints in Jerusalem was now ready, and that the directions for the collection of this gift were previously conveyed (1 Cor. 16; 2 Cor. 8 and 9), the Epistle of Romans was obviously written subsequent to the Corinthian Epistles. The fact that Paul refers to Cenchrea (the Corinth port; Rom. 16:1) and that he was only at Corinth for three months at the close of his third missionary journey dates the writing between late 56 A.D. and early 57 A.D.

## Outline
I. Introduction and Theme (1:1-17).
II. The Righteousness of God in judging those who disobey revealed truth (1:18-3:20).
III. The Righteousness of God in justifying those who trust God's Word (3:21-5:21).
IV. The Righteousness of God in sanctifying those who are justified in Christ (6:1-8:39).
V. The Righteousness of God in dealing with the nation of Israel (9:1-11:36).
VI. The Righteousness of God as demonstrated in the sanctified life of a believer (12:1-16:27).

# Romans Chapter 1

## Introduction (vv. 1-9)

The Latin root of Paul's name means "little" and Paul's strenuous service to the Lord was characterized by lowliness in demeanor. He considered himself as "the least of all saints" (Eph. 3:8). Paul refers to himself as both a bondservant and as an apostle in verse 1. According to the Mosaic Law, a Hebrew slave was to be released after six years of service, or at the fifty-year Jubilee if occurring before the six-year tenure was served, unless the slave desired to remain with his master for life (Lev. 25:39-42). If this was the slave's choice, he was taken to a doorpost, his ear was placed next to the wood, and the master pushed or pounded an awl through the slave's ear. The resulting hole marked him as a bondservant for life. Hence, Paul often referred to himself as a bondservant to express his own love for and lifelong commitment to the Lord Jesus Christ.

Paul was also an apostle, or "sent one," of Jesus Christ; Paul was a minister of "the gospel of God," which was also "the gospel of His Son" (v. 9). At his conversion in Acts 9, the Lord immediately informed Paul of his divine calling, which he later confirmed: He was "separated" from among men to be an apostle to the Gentiles (Eph. 3:8). The other apostles also recognized the uniqueness of Paul's ministry to declare the riches of God's grace to Gentiles (Gal. 1:15-16).

The words "to be" in front of "an apostle" were added by the translators to improve readability, but are not found in the Greek text and, in fact, should not be added to the English text. Paul was not called "to be" an apostle; he was *an* apostle. Apostles were personally appointed by Christ for ministry (a preliminary office in the Church). However, "apostle" was not a title in the Church, except when Christ assumes the title to speak of His incarnation and work of reconciliation assigned to Him by His Father (Heb. 3:1). Consequently, we never read of the Apostle Paul or Pastor "…" or Elder "…" or Deacon "…" in Scripture; rather, we read of men being appointed and commissioned as foundational leaders and ministers within the New Testament Church. There are no titles of status for believers in the New Testament, just ministries to perform. Accordingly, all titles of exaltation are reserved for Jesus Christ – He is *"the Apostle and High Priest of our confession"* (Heb. 3:1).

Verse 2 informs us that the gospel, literally, the good news of God in Christ, was not new revelation, but rather the fulfillment of numerous Old Testament prophecies. Through the prophets, God painted a predictive portrait, so that Israel would recognize her Messiah when He arrived. He would be born of a virgin (Isa. 7:14), from the tribe of Judah (Gen. 49:10), the seed of David (v. 3; 2 Sam. 7:12-13), and in Bethlehem of Ephrathah (Mic. 5:2), but would live in Egypt for a time (Hos. 11:1), before being raised in Nazareth in Zebulun (Isa. 9:1; Matt. 2:23). Jesus Christ did fulfill each of those prophecies, and dozens more, to emphatically prove that He was Israel's Messiah and the Savior of the world.

The additional phrase *"according to the flesh"* (v. 3) is not necessary to affirm Christ's humanity but is used here to infer that Christ is much more than a mere descendant of King David, as the next verse explains. Through the power of the Holy Spirit, the incarnate Son of God was born of the virgin Mary to be Israel's Messiah. After providing propitiation for human sin at Calvary, the Lord Jesus died and was buried. Then He was raised from the dead three days later through the power of the Holy Spirit. Paul states that Christ's resurrection affirmed His deity and that His Father was completely satisfied with His redemptive work (v. 4).

Having received the grace of God through Christ, Paul was committed to fulfilling his divine calling as an apostle of Jesus Christ to the Gentiles (v. 5). In fact, all those justified in Christ are called of God and, having answered His invitation, have a call of service, a "work of ministry" (Eph. 4:12), to complete (v. 6). The calls of God to salvation in Christ, to sanctification in Christ, and to service for Christ are all connected by the sovereign purposes of God for our lives.

Paul addresses his letter to all the beloved of God in Rome. In Romans 16 we learn that there were several local churches in Rome. Because these believers had been justified in Christ (i.e., they had been declared positionally righteous in Christ by God; 4:21-25), Paul refers to them as "saints" (v. 7). Obviously, Paul is addressing living people on earth, and not the deceased who had been given some special heavenly status by humanized religion. In short, all who have trusted Christ and have been regenerated by the Holy Spirit have an eternal and righteous standing before God (2 Cor. 5:21). Thankfully, Christ and the Holy Spirit continue to make intercession for all those justified in Christ, His saints (Rom. 8:27, 34). Scripture often refers to Christians as "saints" (Col. 1:12; Jude 3); accordingly, Paul typically addressed his epistles to the saints gathered together at some particular locale (e.g., 1 Cor. 1:2; Eph. 1:1; Phil. 1:1).

Continuing his salutation to the believers in Rome, Paul declares *"grace to you and peace from God our Father and the Lord Jesus Christ"* (v. 7). This statement affirms the divine equality of God the Father and His Son – the grace we desperately need comes from both. Although Paul adds "mercy" between "grace" and "peace" when writing to his spiritual sons Titus and Timothy, this same opening greeting is generally found in his other epistles. The order is intentional; God's grace is always the forerunner to enjoying God's peace. Peace in our hearts is positive proof that God's grace has been at work in our lives. It is impossible for the Lord to give peace to those who have not given over their lives to Him (John 14:27).

The believers at Rome had already experienced God's grace by believing the gospel message; they were at peace with God. However, they must continue depending on God's grace to enjoy the peace of God (i.e., the peace which surpasses all understanding; Phil. 4:7), to properly serve Him. Throughout our earthly sojourn, we must have God's grace working in us to enjoy His peace.

Paul often began his epistles by expressing what he appreciated about his readers. Hence, Paul commends the saints at Rome for their tenacious testimony of following Christ. Their faithfulness was being talked about throughout the Roman Empire (v. 8). For that reason, Paul was compelled to continue praying for them, and God could attest to the fact that Paul delighted in his spirit to offer up fervent, believing prayers on their behalf (v. 9).

## Yearning to Visit Believers in Rome (vv. 10-13)

The apostle then mentioned that he longed to visit them in Rome, that is, if God permitted him to come (v. 10). The goal of such a trip would be to impart to them a spiritual gift that would build them up in their faith and better equip them to serve God; Paul was referring to the ministry of God's Word (v. 11; 1 Cor. 14:1-3). God alone bestows spiritual gifts from Himself to believers at their conversion (12:3-8; 1 Cor. 12:4-11); apostles did not engage in this ministry. In the case of young Timothy, Paul merely affirmed (announced) the gift and calling which Timothy had already received from God (2 Tim. 1:6).

If God permitted Paul to come to Rome, Paul knew that it would be a mutually beneficial trip for everyone. The believers at Rome would be built up in their faith and he would be encouraged by their fellowship and faithfulness (v. 12). This is a good reminder for believers not to forsake the assembling of themselves together – we need each other to be stronger in the Lord (Heb. 10:25)! Paul then mentioned that he had often planned to come to Rome but had been hindered (v. 13). Paul did not identify the hindrance. Perhaps the pressing needs of believers in Achaia or elsewhere had kept Paul from coming to Rome (Rom. 15:20-29), or possibly satanic opposition limited Paul's movements (1 Thess. 2:18), or the Holy Spirit may have constrained Paul from traveling to Rome at that present time (Acts 16:6-7).

## Under Obligation to Share the Gospel (vv. 14-17)

Although what had kept Paul from coming to Rome was not identified, the desired outcome of such a future visit was – productive gospel ministry (v. 13). He would confirm the outworking of the gospel in the minds of believers and also confront those opposing the gospel message that would surely lead some to salvation in Christ (Phil. 1:7). Paul's past opposition to Christianity, the unmerited forgiveness he had received in Christ, and his divine calling to be an apostle to the Gentiles put Paul under compulsion to share the gospel with those who desperately needed to heed it, including those at Rome (v. 14).

For this reason, Paul felt that he was a debtor to the unregenerate; he was under obligation to share the only remedy for sin and death with anyone who would listen to him. He also was burdened to ensure that the saints in Rome understood the full ramifications of the Gospel. Hence, he was "ready" with as much strength as he possessed to preach the gospel in Rome also (v. 15). The word rendered "ready" (*prothymos*) in verse 15 means "willing" or "eager." This is the type of zeal Paul had for preaching the only message on earth that could change lives forever.

In verse 16, Paul declares his unwavering allegiance to share God's gospel message to a lost world. He was more afraid of displeasing the Lord than of the consequences of being disobedient. The fear of God is truly the death of all other fears and liberates the believer to serve God without being hindered by threatening shadows (Heb. 2:15). Paul understood that *"the gospel of Christ ... is the power of God to salvation for everyone who believes"* (v. 16).

Salvation itself is a three-part reality consisting of a process of God sandwiched between two acts of God. Salvation begins when an individual believes the gospel of Jesus Christ and is, consequently, regenerated (born again) by the Holy Spirit (John 1:12-13; Tit. 3:5). The soul is saved at this time and eternal life with God is received. After this act of God, the long process of sanctification begins – this process morally transforms us to act and think as Christ does (Rom. 8:29). Salvation concludes with glorification, an act of God which transforms the believer's lowly body and makes it holy and fit for Heaven (1 Cor. 15:51-52).

Despite the hostility that sometimes accompanies sharing the gospel, may we follow Paul's example of declaring God's message of love and truth to those who urgently need to hear it. Sadly, many Christians today want to be "Raptured" away from responsibility. God will not hold us guiltless if we withhold His words of life (Ezek. 33:6-7)!

Paul then declares that the good news message of Christ reveals *"the righteousness of God from faith to faith"* (v. 17). The righteousness of God is the theme of Romans. As this is the first time that the word "righteousness" appears in the epistle, we pause to discern how this word is used in Scripture. This knowledge will aid our understanding of what Paul meant by the phrase "faith to faith."

The word *righteousness* meaning "purity, justness or correctness" and is used to convey three separate ideas in Scripture. First, God's character is holy and faultless; He is without wrong or dishonor. Second, righteousness speaks of God's method for justifying sinners through the substitutionary judgment of His righteous Son for the unrighteous. Third, righteousness speaks of the believer's standing before God after believing on His Son alone for salvation. Since the idea of "faith to faith" is followed by the affirmation *"the just shall live by faith,"* the likely meaning of the verse is that the believer's salvation is completely founded in faith from start to finish. We must believe that God is righteous, His means for salvation is righteous, and that those justified by faith are fully equipped to live righteously for God. Nothing that we possess in Christ was earned; it was all obtained by grace through faith (Eph. 2:8)!

*"The just shall live by faith"* is a quotation from Habakkuk 2:4. Initially, the prophet Habakkuk did not understand why God was not punishing His corrupt and idolatrous people. The prophet suffered from tunnel vision; that is, he was judging the affairs of God from his narrow slice of time and limited perception. After he learned that God did have plans to punish and refine His covenant people, the prophet was perplexed how God could use a wicked nation like Babylon to accomplish His agenda. The Lord informed His servant that Babylon would be judged also for their wickedness and brutality. God's exhortation to Habakkuk is that "the just shall live by faith." Man cannot understand all that God is achieving or is destined to accomplish; therefore, it is best to trust Him and believe that He will do what is best. This brought great joy to the prophet's soul, and will to ours also, if we put the verse into practice.

Habakkuk 2:4 is quoted three times in the New Testament to explain enjoying spiritual life in Christ through faith (v. 17; Gal. 3:11; Heb. 10:38). Romans emphasizes that those justified in Christ should be characterized by "just" behavior. The Galatian reference focuses on pleasing God by "living" in the resurrection power of Christ's life. The writer of Hebrews reminds us of the necessity of genuine "faith" to progress in the Lord's work and that the believer's faith and hope are tied together. Both aspects have their culmination in Christ's coming for His Church: *"For yet a little while, and He who is coming will come and will not tarry. Now the just shall live by faith"* (Heb. 10:37). The phrase "faith to faith" then indicates that the believer's salvation, from start to finish, must be based on faith in God and His Word alone.

## Creation Demands a Creator (vv. 18-23)

Before Paul reveals the mystery of God's righteousness in justifying sinners, he must first address the unrighteousness of man. Court is now in session. A divine tribunal putting all of humanity on trial begins in verse 18 and concludes in Romans 3:20. In this imaginary court scene, God is the Judge, Paul the prosecuting attorney, and humanity is the defendant.

The premise for prosecuting humanity is expressed in verse 18: *"For the wrath of God is revealed from Heaven against all ungodliness and unrighteousness of men, who suppress the truth in unrighteousness."* When God reveals something of Himself to man, He then holds man accountable for obeying it; if dismissed by man, then God's judgment is deserved. In Romans 1:18-32, Paul, addressing the pagan world, provides the first of three arguments to prove that mankind is inherently sinful and deserves divine retribution: creation demands a Creator. Romans 2 contains the remaining two arguments detailing human rebellion against revealed truth: the guilty human conscience and disobedience to God's written Law.

The first particular revelation of God to humanity is identified in verse 20: *"For since the creation of the world His invisible attributes are clearly seen, being understood by the things that are made, even His eternal power and Godhead, so that they are without excuse."* To look at the order and sophistication of life and say there is no Designer is to reject what God has displayed about Himself. But natural man has not only rejected the notion that he is accountable to a Creator, but he also made and worshiped images of the very creatures that God offered as evidence of His intellect: *"Professing to be wise, they became fools, and changed the glory of the incorruptible God into an image made like corruptible man – and birds and four-footed animals and creeping things"* (1:22-23). Sadly, many in our modern culture view themselves as the ones in control of their own destinies, thus revering themselves above God. An idol is anything that displaces our proper reverence for our Creator – it does not necessarily have to be an image of gold or silver. Mankind reveals his spiritual ignorance when he worships the creature instead of the Creator (Acts 17:30).

## The Consequences of Worshiping Creation (vv. 24-32)

Those choosing to worship creation rather than the Creator are given over to a reprobate mind: *"Therefore God also gave them up to uncleanness, in the lusts of their hearts, to dishonor their bodies among themselves"* (vv. 24-25). Paul states that because natural man rejected creation truth (i.e., did not want to retain God in their knowledge), God "gave them up" to uncleanness (v. 24), to vile passions (v. 26), and to a debased (reprobate) mind (v. 28). Similarly, because of the idolatrous tendencies of the Israelites, God gave them over to worship the host of Heaven (Acts 7:42). The farther man strays from God, the worse he behaves. This perverse progression has been witnessed in Western Culture in recent years – the sexual revolution of the 1960s and 1970s led to the homosexual revolution, which has culminated in the transgender revolution at this present time.

Without the Holy Spirit's conviction and enlightenment, the worst of man's depraved condition becomes apparent; consequently, these idolaters indulged all sorts of social offenses, moral impurities, and sexual perversions (vv. 26-31). Such sexual behavior is an abomination to God (Lev. 20:13). It is rebellion against His creation order for the genders and His design for marriage – a covenant between a man and a woman until death separates them (Matt. 19:4-6). When God gives people up to their erotic appetites because of rebellion, it results in a terrible personal cost, says William MacDonald:

> Women became lesbians, practicing unnatural sex and knowing no shame. Men became sodomites, in total perversion of their natural functions. Turning away from the marriage relationship ordained by God, they burned with lust for other men and practiced homosexuality. But their sin took its toll in their bodies and souls. Disease, guilt, and personality deformities struck at them like the sting of a scorpion. This disproves the notion that anyone can commit this sin and get away with it.[1]

Those abusing sex (i.e., behaving contrary to God's revealed will for marriage) do so because they do not retain reverence for God in their thinking (v. 28). As a result, God gives them over to "a debased mind." The

Greek word *adokimos*, rendered "a reprobate" (KJV) or "a debased" (NKJV) mind, literally means "a cast out" mind. When man thumbs his nose at God's efforts to draw him to Himself and then willfully engages in behavior which affronts God, God honors that decision by giving man over to a cast-out mind. Without God's assistance, the worst of man will be evident in such a spiritual condition. Without God, the darkened conscience will never understand its need for Christ.

Creation provides an adequate testimony that a Creator exists! The Bible declares that God is the Creator. This fact presents man with a crucial test: Will we grasp the evidence by faith or reject it? *"By faith we understand that the worlds were framed by the word of God, so that the things which are seen were not made of things which are visible"* (Heb. 11:3). To summarize, Paul explains that suppressing creation's evidence of the Creator results in four inescapable realities:

- Rejection of the Creator, as evidenced by immoral living and idolatry, leads to divine judgment (vv. 18-21).

- Rejecting the Creator leads to the worship of creation (including self-worship; vv. 22-23).

- Worshiping creation results in immoral and vile behavior (vv. 24-27).

- Those who pervert sex (vv. 24-27) and engage in the listed sins (vv. 29-31) inherently know that they deserve God's judgment (v. 32).

May believers remember that any idolatry (thoughts unworthy of God or misplaced affections) is insulting to God. Additionally, God will judge, not only those engaging in abhorrent behavior, but also those who observe it with approval (e.g., watching it on a screen; v. 32).

Paul began his case against humanity (primarily he is addressing heathen Gentiles) by stating that God's wrath actively abides on those who reject His revealed truth. Paul then showed that natural man has rejected the testimony of creation by a Creator and opted rather to worship creation. These are condemned, not because of knowledge that they did not have, but for rejecting the truth they did possess. Having snubbed the Creator, God withdraws from those under judgment and leaves them to themselves. Without God's influence upon the human mind, the worst of the sin nature inherited from Adam becomes quickly evident in man's behavior. Turning away from God always leads to more sin, sorrow, and His condemnation.

# Romans Chapter 2

### The Moralizer Is No Better Than the Pagan (vv. 1-6)

Having shown that natural man is guilty before God for revering creation and not the Creator, Paul turns his attention to the self-righteous moralizer. Certainly, many listening to Paul's condemnation of the heathen world would have agreed with his assessment, and heartily added, "We agree with you, Paul, but that is not us. We deplore such pagan tendencies." The moralizer, that Paul is now addressing, justifies himself before God by comparing himself to the behavior of others instead of to God's standard of morality. The standard to guide behavior which resides within his human spirit. By comparing himself to others, the moral pagan believes he will escape God's wrath, but Paul states that because he does not consistently do what he knows is right, he is no different than those he judges unfit for Heaven (v. 1).

The moral pagan is therefore no different than the natural pagan, as both fall short of perfectly obeying the truth that God has revealed to them (v. 2). Paul reminds the religious moralizer that he cannot avoid God's judgment, for God is completely aware of his offenses and he cannot escape divine jurisdiction. Those trying to justify themselves before God by comparing their behavior to others will receive a guilty verdict in God's courtroom and be sentenced to an inescapable judgment (v. 3).

God's good and forbearing nature granted an opportunity for the moralizer to consider the moral law planted within his human spirit. But instead of reckoning personal failure according to God's standard, the religious pagan sought to justify himself by performing self-reckoned good deeds (vv. 4-5). Man cannot *rejoice in iniquity* (i.e., compare himself to other sinners in order to feel good about his own self-imagined uprightness). Anything less than perfection is sin and will be judged by God. Anyone (Jew or Gentile) ignoring God's revealed righteousness in this way will be reserved for His judgment in a coming day.

John informs us that all those not divinely justified in Christ will be held accountable to Christ at the Great White Throne Judgment, which occurs directly after the Kingdom Age is complete (Rev. 20:11-15). At this time, God's Law (the truth) and the past deeds of each unregenerate soul will be compared and shown to be wanting. No one can earn God's favor by doing so called *good deeds*, especially while disobeying the standard of behavior inherently placed within them by God. Accordingly, God will render to each one according to his deeds (v. 6), and we all have done bad deeds (3:23).

## The Hypothetical Argument (vv. 7-10)

In this section, Paul is emphasizing the point that man apart from God cannot *perfectly* do good deeds to please God. In fact, God declares that the *sum total* of man's self-working to accomplish good is putrid in His sight (Isa. 64:6). From a naturalistic perspective, all mankind, no matter what the religious bias or social backdrop, suffers the same moral ill; we cannot continue in well-doing even when we try our best, a fact to which our conscience bears witness.

Hence, those seeking eternal life, glory, honor and immortality (i.e., God's approval) by doing good works (v. 7) are no better equipped to inherit Heaven than those who are self-seeking and blatantly disobedient to God's truth (v. 8). In fact, God determines tribulation and anguish against everyone who does evil, but glory, honor, and peace to those who obey His moral law (vv. 9-10). The more people rebel against revealed truth, the more judgment is secured against them. But their standing before God is not improved by attempting to do good. F. B. Hole explains why good deeds cannot negate the offense of sin.

> Some read verse 7, and say, "There! So, after all, you have only got to keep on doing good and seeking good, and eternal life will be yours at the end." We have only to read on a little further, however, and we discover that no one does good or seeks good, except the one who believes in Christ. The ground of judgment before God is *our works*. If anyone does truly believe in the Savior, he experiences salvation, and hence has power to do what is good and to continue in it. Moreover, the whole object of his life is changed, and he begins to seek glory and honor and that state of incorruptibility which is to be ours at the coming of the Lord. On the other hand, there are all too many who, instead of obeying the truth by believing the Gospel, remain slaves of sin. The works of these will receive well-merited condemnation in the day of judgment.[2]

Paul's main point in this passage is that no one can continue in well-doing, whether one tries his best or not. The fact that we feel guilt, even one time, proves that we are disobedient to the moral law God placed within us. The human conscience monitors our behavior and when it determines that

God's moral programming has been violated, a guilt alarm sounds in our mind. How we respond to our wounded conscience is what is important to God – will we own our guilt and seek God's forgiveness or ignore it and reap His wrath?

## Moral Law and the Human Conscience (vv. 11-16)

Why do we feel guilt after engaging in certain behaviors which no written law forbids? We have a moral law implanted within us which forces its way into our reasoning process. This is why world cultures, even isolated societies, generally agree that it is morally wrong to kill, to steal, to commit adultery, to lie, to be disrespectful to parents, etc. Why is there a uniform code of ethics that spans the globe and is observed to be independent of time and culture? The answer is that the One who designed us has integrated a moral code of ethics within our being to beckon each person to look inward for evidence of a Creator.

Adam became a living soul after God breathed into him a spirit (Gen. 2:7); Adam was created in God's own image, which meant he was a spiritual being with moral reckoning (Gen. 1:27). Everyone coming from Adam, including Eve, has this same spirit, which gives everyone God-consciousness and an inherent moral compass to guide God-honoring behavior. The Creator is commanding each of us to behave in one perfect way – there is no partiality on this matter, nor will He show partiality on the day of judgment (v. 11). Unfortunately, none of us behaves perfectly – that is, as God does. *"For all have sinned and fall short of the glory of God"* (3:23). We cannot continue in well-doing, whether in disobedience to God's written Law, or to the moral law He has placed deep within us (v. 12). If you have ever felt guilt after doing something, then you know this to be true. Consequently, our own guilty consciences prove to us that we fall below the standard of perfection needed to enter Heaven and that we deserve God's condemnation (v. 13).

Our consciences produce feelings of guilt when we transgress the moral law God placed within us. *"Therefore, to him who knows to do good and does not do it, to him it is sin"* (Jas. 4:17). Natural man cannot identify the source of these intense feelings of guilt. What can be done to quiet the deafening indictment of a wounded conscience? Pondering his loathsome situation, man rationalizes, "If doing something I know to be wrong induces mental anguish, then doing what I know to be right should ease my guilty pangs." As a result, except for biblical Christianity, the religions of the world are founded on the "need of doing" to obtain a supernatural blessing or to gain spiritual enlightenment and enhancement. Works-based religion is a natural product of a depraved human conscience trying to ease its own grieving. The fact that we feel guilt is evidence to us that we did not continue in well-doing; we did not obey what we instinctively knew was right behavior (v. 15).

Biblical Christianity declares that you cannot "do" something to earn your way to Heaven – you could never do enough, and what is necessary to gain entrance has already been "done" at Calvary. The world's religion cries "do," while biblical Christianity declares "done." Hence, we must realize that every aspect of our being has been affected adversely by sin, and only through Christ and the power of the Holy Spirit can the matter be resolved. My guilty conscience bears witness to me that I need a Savior! Accordingly, all those not trusting the gospel that Paul was preaching (the good news of Jesus Christ) will receive eternal condemnation when all the secrets of men will be judged (v. 16).

## The Jews Had the Law and Its Condemnation (vv. 17-24)

Having successfully prosecuted the natural man and the religious moralizer, Paul introduces God's case against His covenant people. The Jews had an advantage that the two previous guilty defendants did not have. Namely, they had direct exposure to God's written Law and His glory (vv. 17-18). The glory here speaks of the supernatural feats accomplished during the Egyptian exodus, the wilderness experience that followed, and then the conquest of Canaan – the entire nation regularly witnessed God's awesome power.

The Jews thought that they were a special people because they had God's written Word. But on the contrary, God wanted His Word to have them – God wanted a holy people as a testimony of Himself to the world. Indeed, the Jews possessed God's Law, but because the religious leaders had humanized its teachings, they had blindly guided others away from the truth (vv. 19-20). For example, they rightly taught that the Law forbids stealing, adultery, and idolatry (these were sins against others, themselves, and God), yet, secretly they were committing these offenses (vv. 21-22).

To have God's truth and ignore it (like the natural man did with the evidence of creation) would certainly result in God's condemnation. But to assume a pompous spirituality of knowing and teaching God's Law after rejecting and changing it was deeply offensive to God; consequently, His name was being blasphemed among the nations (vv. 23-24).

The Jewish nation was supposed to represent Jehovah to the Gentiles as a holy, unique people, but their testimony of not obeying what they taught caused the nations to not take them seriously and to ridicule their God. The

Jews sought to establish their own righteousness by following their human traditions rather than obeying God's righteous Law (10:1-3). In God's judicial economy, accountability to Him increases in proportion to responsibility given (Luke 10:12, 12:48). Greater responsibility means greater reward for faithfulness or greater judgment for failure. The Jews had been given much more divine revelation than the Gentiles and therefore had much greater accountability to God. L. M. Grant suggests an application of this truth for those of us in the Church Age to consider:

> But let *everyone* who has the Word of God take warning from this. For if we (Gentiles) have the further revelation and advantage of the New Testament, are not the same perverting evils becoming more glaring amongst ourselves? Who is he who boasts of an open Bible, yet calmly ignores and disobeys its plain injunctions? Can we dare to flatter ourselves that the sin of Christendom is less atrocious than that of Israel under law? Indeed not; for the abuse of the doctrines and privileges of the manifested grace of God is greater evil than disobedience of the law of God.[3]

## The Circumcision That God Desires (vv. 25-29)

Circumcision was a "token" of Abraham's righteous standing gained by faith in God's promise (Gen. 15:6), not by the act of circumcision itself. The "token" of circumcision was given by God after Abraham's exercise of faith. Abraham was justified by faith before he was circumcised at the age of ninety-nine (4:11). However, as a perpetual sign of His covenant with Abraham, the Lord required Abraham and his male descendants to also be circumcised (Gen. 17:1-14). This command was later reiterated and incorporated into the Mosaic Law (Lev. 12:3).

Over time, the Jews wore male circumcision like a badge that identified them as God's chosen people destined for blessing because of God's promise to Abraham. In other words, the sign of the covenant became more vital than living out the morality linked with the sign (v. 25). It would be similar to a married man boasting of his beautiful gold wedding ring, but then surreptitiously committing adultery. By breaking his wedding vow, the husband is mocking the symbol of his vow to his wife. Paul informed his countrymen that by failing to keep their covenant with God, they mocked the outward symbol of that covenant – circumcision. Consequently, their circumcision had become uncircumcision in God's eyes.

Likewise, when an uncircumcised man (inferring a Gentile man) commits himself to obey God's Law, his uncircumcision becomes the badge of circumcision to God (v. 26). If a married man is faithful to his wife, even though he has lost his wedding band, his covenant with her is still maintained. So, if the Gentiles observed the Law, their behavior condemned the Jews who possessed and had transgressed the Law. A true Jew, in spirit, was one whose heart was circumcised to God – such a person received the praise of God. Of course, this was only a possibility after a Gentile has been born again in Christ, but Paul's emphasis here is to condemn the rebellious behavior of the Jews, by comparing them to Gentiles who were choosing to obey less precise moral revelations from God.

The Jews' faithfulness to God was much more important to Him than merely bragging about their circumcision (i.e., flashing their wedding ring, so to speak, as a show of allegiance). Their unfaithfulness to God had mocked their circumcision, in the same way a married man mocks his wedding ring by committing adultery (v. 27). Their circumcision, the wedding band, was to be a reminder of their covenant with Him and nothing more! Consequently, physical circumcision itself had no spiritual value to God other than it tested the sincerity and faith of His covenant people.

Besides being a symbol of God's covenant, male circumcision had a much deeper spiritual meaning that Paul wanted his audience to understand. By stripping away the foreskin from the organ that best identified an individual as a male, God was symbolizing the stripping away of an old identity and the need to rely on God for a new way of life. Male circumcision would be a constant reminder to have no confidence in the flesh (Phil. 3:3).

It is the same for believers today; in Christ we become a new creation with a new identity in Him (2 Cor. 5:17). Yet, our new identity in Christ demands that we live the "circumcised life," which is the "cutting off" or "putting to death" of the desires and the will of our flesh. In doing so, Gentiles could experience God as spiritual Jews and achieve what the Jewish nation had not been able to do through superficial obedience to the circumcision command (v. 28).

Accordingly, Paul declares that it is the circumcision of the heart God wants in a believer's life, not an outward show of spirituality (v. 29). The Jews were mocking their circumcision through spiritual adultery and religiosity. It is not circumcision itself that is important, but what it stands for: a reliance on God and not the flesh. Depending on a physical mark to confirm spirituality and neglecting the spiritual meaning of the mark is foolishness. A true believer of God (a true Jew in this case) will endeavor to obey the truth that God has revealed and live the circumcised life.

# Romans Chapter 3

### The Jewish Objector Is Silenced (vv. 1-8)

Paul, God's prosecutor of humanity, has concluded the evidence against natural man, the religious moralizer, and the Jews. Before God proclaims His verdict, a fictitious Jewish objector is permitted to challenge Paul in a back-and-forth rhetorical manner, which further serves to affix guilt to the Jewish nation. Israel deserved greater condemnation than the Gentiles.

Responding to Paul's statement that a true Jew, one who had God's approval, had a circumcised heart (2:29), the objector wonders then what profit there actually was in being a Jew or being physically circumcised (v. 1). Paul states that the Jewish people had special privileges not bestowed on the Gentiles. For example, they were the only people on earth to personally receive God's written Law (v. 2). The Jews knew exactly what was expected of them and would be blessed if they obeyed. Sadly, as a nation they failed to exercise faith in God's Word; they were not circumcised in their hearts.

The objector then admits that many Jews did fail to keep God's Law, but what about the faithful remnant? Would the unfaithfulness of some prevent God from fulfilling His promises to the Patriarchs concerning their ancestors (v. 3)? Referring to David's statement in Psalm 51:4, Paul concisely affirms that God is always right and always true to His word regardless of what man does or says (v. 4). In fact, if every person on earth agreed on something, while God affirmed otherwise, God's testimony would trump the integrity of all humanity. God's purposes and promises cannot be thwarted by human failure! Human sin only serves to prove the reliability of God's Word and His sovereign control over His creation.

The objector's next statement illustrates the ridiculous attempts of the guilty to avoid divine accountability. If that is true, and our unrighteousness causes God's righteousness to shine more brilliantly, why does God judge us (v. 5)? In other words, why is God judging those who make Him look good? Paul states that such a statement is not worthy of consideration, for how can God judge those in the world fairly if He is not a righteous Judge (v. 6). A holy God must judge sin; therefore, God is not unrighteous for glorifying Himself by judging all those who do not obey His Law.

Lastly, the objector suggests that he should lie (sin) even more in order to better vindicate God's righteous judgment against him and add to God's glory (v. 7). His point being, how can a righteous God find fault with a sinner, who is effectively adding praise to His glory by experiencing His wrath? This is obviously circular logic, for the revelation of divine truth preceded human disobedience. Thus, the ramifications of sin must be dealt with according to God's revealed will; God will honor Himself despite what man does or does not do. As F. F. Bruce explains, Paul interrupts the objector to point out that some had wrongly accused him and other Christians of propagating such heresy:

> "As a matter of fact," says Paul, "that is precisely what some people say my gospel amounts to; but their charge is not only slanderous, it stands self-condemned because it is such a contradiction in terms." The gospel of justification by faith, apart from *works of righteousness*, has always called forth this criticism, but the criticism is amply refuted by the fact that the same gospel insists unequivocally on *the fruits of righteousness* which must follow justification.[4]

Therefore, the suggestion that someone should do evil to bring God more glory deserves condemnation (v. 8). Anyone not living to please God deserves His wrath – eternal judgment.

## All Are Under Sin (vv. 9-20)

The objector's final statement is found in the beginning of verse 9 and begs the question as to whether the pagan Gentiles were in a better situation than the Jews (i.e., are the Jews worse off than the Gentiles because they have greater accountability with God concerning His Law; v. 9). While some will be under greater condemnation for rejecting greater opportunity to please God, Paul affirms that there is no difference between Jew and Gentile on the matter of guiltiness before God – all men are spiritually dead. All those born of Adam are under the power of sin and prove it by their behavior – there are none righteous before God (v. 10).

Having silenced the objector and finished describing how the natural man, the religious moralizer, and the Jews had utterly failed to obey the righteousness of God revealed to them (1:18), Paul is ready to declare God's verdict against all humanity. The apostle refers to Psalm 14:2-3 in order to reinforce the conclusion: *Naturally speaking*, no one seeks after God, understands His righteousness, or can continue in well-doing (vv. 10-12). All are guilty before God – no one completely follows God's revealed truth; hence, all are guilty before God and deserve His judgment.

Allegorically speaking, God performs a medical examination of the human race to further corroborate His assessment of humanity's deplorable spiritual condition (vv. 13-18). Man's throat is an open tomb full of deceitful and corrupt speech, his tongue is venomous, and his mouth is full of curses. His feet are swift to murder, and he leaves behind misery and destruction wherever he goes because he does not know how to make peace. Humanity has no regard for God. Rather, men live as if He does not exist; thus, naturally speaking, mankind is completely unprofitable to God. In man's natural state, the human heart, mind, and will are completely depraved and controlled by sin!

In verses 19-20, Paul reveals why God gave His covenant people His Law at Mount Sinai long ago. The purpose of the Law was to convince them that no matter how hard they tried, they could never perfectly keep God's Law. Consequently, no one can ever hope to approach God through personal effort of doing good. Even if someone had a perfect day without sin, what would make up for offenses against God for all the other days? The purpose of the Law was to show man his sin, to cause him to acknowledge his guilt before God, and then to point him to God's only solution for sin – to be justified in Christ by faith (Gal. 3:24).

## Justified by God's Grace Through Faith (vv. 21-28)

Paul begins the second major section of Romans in verse 21 – *God's Righteousness in Justifying Sinners*. The main idea of this segment is that justification is received by faith, not by doing good works. Obviously, the Law is righteous, for it reveals the standard of behavior God expected His covenant people to obey. But the Jews could not keep the Law and therefore stood condemned before God (v. 23). Knowing this would happen, God foretold through the Old Testament prophets that a New Covenant would declare God's righteous means of saving sinners. The Old Covenant which the Jews could not keep had been replaced with a unilateral covenant that God would honor despite their failings. The writer of Hebrews explains that this New Covenant had been secured through Christ (Heb. 8:7-13).

Jeremiah says that this would be an everlasting covenant resulting in eternal blessing to the Jews (Jer. 32:40). This promise is understood to be literal, for God will erect an eternal city where the Jewish remnant will dwell (Isa. 48:2, 52:1). The prophet Ezekiel refers to the New Covenant as a *"Covenant of Peace"* with the Jewish nation (Ezek. 34:25). Isaiah proclaimed that through this covenant, *"Israel shall be saved in the Lord with an everlasting salvation"* (Isa. 45:17). Why was the New Covenant needed and how did it secure such blessing for Israel?

The writer of Hebrews informs us that this covenant was sealed by

Christ's blood and would accomplish what the Old Covenant could not – propitiation for sins (Heb. 8:8). The Old Covenant was conditional in nature; the Jews had to keep God's Law in order to receive God's blessing (Ex. 19:5-8; Heb. 8:9). The New Covenant would be unconditional in nature and would be the means by which God would honor His covenant with Abraham, which was instituted by two immutable things – God's Word and His oath (Heb. 6:13-18), neither of which can fail. Consequently, in a future day, after repenting of their sins and turning to Christ at the conclusion of the Tribulation period, the entire Jewish nation will be saved (11:25-29).

God ratified and sealed the New Covenant with the blood of His own Son. The Lord Jesus Christ said on the eve of His death, *"This cup is the new covenant in My blood, which is shed for you"* (Luke 22:20). By punishing His Son for the sins of the people, God could righteously extend forgiveness and blessing to them though they deserved neither. At Calvary, God demonstrated all aspects of His holy character and attributes in the matter of saving sinners: His need for justice and righteousness, His desire to be merciful, gracious, loving, compassionate, longsuffering, and His sovereign, all-knowing, all-powerful, unchanging, eternal essence.

The New Covenant, which was made with the house of Judah and Israel (Heb. 8:8), would end the dispensation of the Law and usher in the age of grace – the Church Age. The blessings of this covenant are received through faith in Christ, and in Him alone. Thankfully, the Gentiles are a second benefactor of this covenant (Eph. 2:11-3:6). The gospel message of Jesus Christ (that a righteous substitute was judged in the place of sinners) is how God's righteousness is revealed to the world today (v. 21)!

Paul then explains the main aspects of the New Covenant – God's means of saving sinners: Salvation is received by faith in the finished work of Jesus Christ (v. 22). *"Faith is the substance of things hoped for, the evidence of things not seen"* (Heb. 11:1). Faith stretches the soul to believe that which cannot be fully based on sensory information or reason. Those trusting in Christ alone for salvation are redeemed by the shed blood of Christ and are freely justified by God's grace (v. 24). Redemption has the idea of delivering or making something free by paying a price. Justification means "to be declared righteous," even though we are not righteous in practice; this is a positional term meaning that believers have a perfect standing of righteousness before God. Grace is receiving God's unmerited favor, or **G**od's **R**iches **A**t **C**hrist's **E**xpense.

This salvation is possible because Christ, at Calvary, successfully offered propitiation to God through His own blood (v. 25). Animal blood atonement offered previously under the Law pictured God's ultimate means of propitiation which would be achieved through the sacrifice of His Son. Propitiation refers to the means by which complete satisfaction is obtained – God's anger over human sin has been once-for-all-time dealt with at Calvary (Heb. 2:9; 1 Jn 2:2). This means that those who trust Christ alone will never pay the penalty for their sin (8:1), for Christ has already been judicially punished for all of our sins. God would be unrighteous to judge a second time what has already been completely judged through the suffering and death of His Son. This is why, just before His death, the Lord Jesus triumphantly declared, *"It is finished"* (John 19:30).

The New Testament epistles provide further details about how justification is accomplished. Paul informs us that a believer is justified freely by God's grace (3:24), by Christ's blood (5:9), and by faith (5:1). Speaking of Abraham, James declares another astounding fact pertaining to justification: *"You see then that a man is justified by works, and not by faith only"* (Jas. 2:24). Humanly speaking, this may seem confusing. How can justification be so complicated if God accredited Abraham a righteous standing for simply exercising faith in His promise to him (Jas. 2:23)?

Using your God-given imagination for a moment, envision a huge reservoir in the upper elevations of a mountain range. Water from melting snow from mountain grandeurs gently streams down into bubbling brooks, which, in turn, fill this reservoir to capacity. An enormous dam holds back this vast resource except for the water rushing from its base into a deep channel. This channel conveys the water a great distance away to a collection pool in the plains below. As individual headgates about this collection pool are opened, the vital blessing of the reservoir is applied to parched farm fields already sown with seed. Thus, the immense reservoir so far above in the mountains is responsible and necessary for an abundant harvest to follow below. Justification is, from a biblical sense, depicted in this imaginary scene. The reservoir pictures God's vast oceans of grace waiting to be bestowed from heavenly realms. The channel represents the means by which God's grace is conveyed to mankind – through the blood of Jesus Christ. The act of opening the headgates symbolizes an individual trusting in the gospel message and, thus, receiving God's manifold grace through the blood of Christ. The harvest of good works that follows is the practical demonstration of a justified soul (Jas. 2:17).

Thus, a believer is justified by grace, through Christ's blood, by personal faith, and his faith is evidenced by good works. True faith produces good deeds, including obedience. A soul that has been declared righteous by God should seek to live righteously. Those who have been justified in Christ should live to show Christ to others by their actions.

Paul offers further insight as to how God dealt with the sins of believers in Old Testament times (v. 25). God could righteously forebear to judge Old Testament sins until propitiation was offered at Calvary, because these saints were *covered* by the shed and applied blood of animals on altars. Old Testament believers trusted God and obeyed His commands to sacrifice innocent, unblemished animals as a temporary substitution for wrongs committed – this pictured the future and final offering of Christ where God would once, and for all time, judicially punish His perfect, sinless Son for all human sin (1 Jn. 2:2).

The gospel of Jesus Christ is how God is demonstrating His righteousness to the world today (v. 26). He upheld His just and holy nature by judging His Son in the place of the condemned, that He might be able to justify those exercising faith in His means of salvation – trusting in the finished work of Christ alone. Therefore, as condemned criminals (v. 23) we cannot boast before God of our good deeds or law-keeping to justify ourselves; we must exercise faith in Jesus Christ alone to receive God's gift of salvation (vv. 27-28).

## Whosoever Will May Be Justified by Faith (vv. 29-31)

Having described the only means by which a person may stand justified before God and become a child of God (John 1:12-13), Paul affirms that both Jew and Gentile can take advantage of God's gracious offer. As the apostle will further explain in chapter 9, this was God's foreordained plan to fulfill His promise to Abraham that all the families of the earth would be blessed through one of his descendants (Gen. 12:3).

No doubt some of the Jews in Paul's audience were wondering if the New Covenant (established by Christ) was in contradiction to Old Testament Law (v. 31). Paul claims that the gospel message not only agrees with Old Testament prophecies, but it also fulfills them. The central theme of the Bible is God's *Good News* message of love to the world: Salvation is freely granted to those trusting alone in Christ's redemptive work (John 3:16).

When the Lord looks down from His heavenly throne to examine humanity, He finds that there is no one who perfectly does what is right, and that most are unconcerned about their spiritual condition before Him. Paul rightly concludes, *"We all have sinned and fallen short of the glory of God"* (v. 23). If man could keep God's Law, he would be justified before God (2:11-13), but it is self-evident that no one can approach God this way; rather, as Paul has just explained, man must be justified through faith in the One who did meet all the demands of the Law – Christ.

# Romans Chapter 4

Abraham Was Justified by Faith (vv. 1-5)
   In the previous chapter, Paul introduced the method by which God could righteously save guilty sinners by justifying them in Christ. When an individual exercises faith in the gospel of Jesus Christ, God responds by imputing a standing of righteousness to that person. Through the divine act of regeneration, the new believer is made alive in Christ and becomes one with Him forever. Through this blessed union, a believer not only receives spiritual life, but shares with Christ all the blessings of His station as Lord of lords and King of kings. Thus, all believers are destined to rule and reign with Christ forever (8:17; 2 Tim. 2:12). By the divine act of justification, a repentant sinner trusting Christ for salvation is declared positionally righteous before God. Only perfect people can dwell with God in Heaven. In Christ, those who are not perfect are imputed a standing of perfection.
   There can be little doubt that the teaching of justification by faith was a completely new idea to Paul's Jewish audience of staunch Law-keepers. In this chapter, Paul uses two Old Testament figures every Jew could identify with, Abraham and David, to show that justification is received by faith, not by good works or by Law-keeping. To further explain how justification is accomplished, Paul employs one Greek word, *logizomai*, eleven times in this chapter. *Logizomai* is an accounting term, which is usually rendered in the English language as "accredited," "accounted," "counted," "reckoned," or "imputed." For example, if someone legitimately credits your bank account with funds, that money becomes your possession.
   The apostle begins by mentioning that the key Jewish patriarch of the Old Testament, Abraham, was not justified before God by the things he did in the flesh (v. 1). Because Abraham was justified solely by exercising faith in God's Word, the patriarch could not brag to God of his accomplishments (v. 2). Later, Paul informs us that there is nothing we can do in the power of our flesh to impress God (8:8). By quoting Genesis 15:6, Paul was emphasizing that God's past dealings with Abraham declared how He would save sinners throughout time: *"Abraham believed God, and it was accounted to him for righteousness"* (v. 3).
   Genesis 15 records the interaction between God and Abraham on the

day God ratified His covenant with Abraham. Previously, God affirmed His commitment to Abraham (Gen. 12:1-3) but performed no signs and wonders to prompt Abraham's trust in what He had promised to do. God's Word was good enough for him – Abraham simply trusted God and believed. God responded to Abraham's faith in Genesis 15 by accrediting a standing of righteousness to his account. Obviously, God wanted no confusion on this matter as to how He would save sinners, for the words "believe," "counted," and "righteousness" all occur for the first time in the Bible in Genesis 15:6. This foundational verse then appears three times in the New Testament: Romans 4:3, Galatians 3:6, and James 2:23. In Abraham's case, what preceded imputed righteousness? His faith. His good works, the outcome of true faith, were demonstrated in Genesis 22, by his willingness to offer up his son Isaac as a burnt offering in accordance with God's command.

Paul then summarizes the two options by which descendants of Adam may approach God, by works or by faith (vv. 4-5). In the first way, a person attempts to impress God by doing good works in order to earn His favor and a good standing. However, the consequence is that God's grace is not received, and that person's sin debt is not forgiven. The second means by which a person may approach God is through faith in God's revealed truth. God responds by forgiving that individual's sin debt, redeeming him by the blood of His Son, and bestowing on him or her the gift of positional righteousness in Christ. Charles Stanley gives this example of how redemption provides a new status of positional freedom:

> What is redemption? The emancipation, or redemption, of all the slaves in the West Indies, some years ago, will illustrate what redemption is. A vast sum was given, voted by the English government, for the complete redemption of the slaves. They were, so to speak, redeemed forever – forever emancipated, delivered from the wretchedness of slavery.[5]

## David Was Justified by Faith (vv. 6-8)

The apostle then quotes David (Ps. 32:1-2) to illustrate that David understood that he was undeserving of Heaven, but that through faith in God's Word and personal repentance, God did have a righteous means of forgiving him (vv. 6-8). God had made unilateral promises to David, which David reckoned that God would keep, despite his sins of adultery and murder. The Law demanded David's death for these offenses, but David knew God would have to keep His word to him. Hence, there had to be a pathway of restoration by faith beyond what the Law required at that time.

## Justification Is Not Received Through Ordinances (vv. 9-12)

In the remaining verses of this chapter, we learn why Paul specifically chose Abraham and David as examples of justification by faith. Besides being esteemed men of faith in Jewish history, the dynamics of when they were justified by God is of particular interest to Paul. For example, Abraham was justified by God in response to his faith (Gen. 15:6) before he was circumcised in response to God's later command (Gen. 17:24). Clearly, Abraham was justified by faith in God's Word and not by the act of circumcision (vv. 9-10).

Abraham received circumcision as a token of the covenant God had made with him. In obedience to God's command, ninety-nine-year-old Abraham and all the males of his house were circumcised that very day (Gen. 17:26-27). The descendants of Abraham continue to perform this symbolic ritual to honor God and to acknowledge His covenant with them. Paul tells us that circumcision was *"a seal of the righteousness of the faith which he had yet being uncircumcised"* (v. 11). Circumcision was a "token" or a "sign" of Abraham's righteous standing that was gained by his faith in God's promise.

The means by which Abraham obtained a righteous standing before God is the same way God would offer salvation to both Jews and Gentiles (v. 12). Consequently, Abraham is referred to as *"the father of all those who believe."* Although the Jews and several other people groups sprang from Abraham's loins, anyone following Abraham's example of exercising faith in God's promises is, spiritually speaking, a child of Abraham.

## Justification Is Not Received Through the Law (vv. 13-25)

God had revealed to Abraham certain details concerning His future glorious kingdom (Heb. 11:10-16). By faith, Abraham knew that he and all the redeemed would dwell with God in this future heavenly city whose foundations God had established. Obviously, Abraham received these promises related to his justification prior to the giving of the Law to Moses at Sinai (v. 13).

Furthermore, the Law promised God's presence and blessing to His covenant people on earth only if they obeyed it (v. 14). The Law did not offer them a heavenly inheritance; its purpose was to show His covenant people that they were guilty sinners before God and thus needed a Savior. Anyone not continuing to keep all the Law was considered a Law-breaker and stood condemned before the Law-Giver (Gal. 3:10-12).

Because no one could completely keep God's Law, the Law declared that no one was righteous before God, but rather deserved God's wrath (v. 15). All sin disappoints God, but transgression is the specific act of violating God's commands. One may feel guilty about driving 100 MPH down a road with no posted speed limit, but a speeding ticket cannot be issued for such foolish behavior. However, if a sign posts the speed limit, then a speeding ticket is justified, because there has been a transgression of the law. The speed limit sign, so to speak, had been posted for the Jewish nation, and they deserved punishment for breaking God's Law.

The good news was that Law-breakers could be forgiven of their offenses and escape God's wrath if they exercised faith in God's gracious remedy, as Abraham and David did. Abraham was promised a seed (a people) from his loins, but he and his wife Sarah were old and could not naturally produce children (v. 16, 19). Yet, later, because of their faith, God granted the miracle of life, and Isaac, the promised child, was born. In the same way, every son and daughter of Adam is born spiritually dead (5:12) but can experience spiritual birth by following Abraham's example of exercising faith in God's revealed Word (v. 17, 20-22). In this way, Abraham is indeed the father of nations (the meaning of his name; v. 18). The spiritual seed resulting from his faith is being reproduced through countless individuals (both Jews and Gentiles) throughout the world.

Paul concludes the chapter by affirming that anyone in the Church Age can be justified by faith before God, just as Abraham was (vv. 23-24). Abraham was not shown all that his Savior would later accomplish on his behalf, but he did firmly believe that God would honor all the promises made to him, and that pleased the Lord. What is the message that we must believe today to be justified in Christ and become a spiritual descendent of Abraham? That Jesus Christ *"was delivered up because of our offenses, and was raised because of our justification"* (v. 25; 1 Cor. 15:3-4).

Paul purposely chose Abraham and David from Old Testament history to better explain the dynamics of justification. Abraham was justified by faith prior to being circumcised and before the Law was given to Moses. David was justified by faith years after being circumcised as a baby and centuries after the Law had been received. Thus, Paul proves that neither Law-keeping, nor physical circumcision were the basis of justification; God's grace was extended to both Abraham and David on the basis of their faith in God's Word and His holy character. Likewise, this is the only means by which God can righteously forgive sinners and usher them into Heaven today!

# Romans Chapter 5

## The Blessings of Justification (vv. 1-11)

In this chapter, Paul explains the blessings of our justification (vv. 1-11) and then the basis for our justification (vv. 12-21). Paul begins by identifying a number of eternal blessings for those who have been justified through faith (i.e., declared righteous in Christ by trusting in His gospel message). First, the believer has "peace with God" (v. 1). The Greek word translated "peace" is *eirene* which means to "be made at one again." This understanding is directly reflected in Acts 7:26 (KJV) when Moses sought to make two quarreling brothers at *"one again." Eirene* in this verse is rendered "to reconcile" in the New King James Version of the Bible. The idea is that a believer is no longer estranged from God, and, more importantly, God no longer views the believer an enemy that opposes Him (v. 10). Relationship-wise, God and the believer are one.

The second benefit of justification mentioned is that believers have "access to God" (v. 2). A justified person is invited to boldly approach God's throne in prayer to receive help in time of need (Heb. 4:14-16).

The third benefit identified is the ability to "rejoice in hope of the glory of God" (v. 2). A justified person can have present joy in the promise of the Lord's coming (Tit. 2:13). Joy is delighting in Christ with confidence, and hope exercises joy in God's future promises.

The fourth benefit of justification is that believers can glory in their tribulations (v. 3). Children of God understand that no personal hardship is permitted that does not have their heavenly Father's approval. Trusting Him through life's trials brings God glory and permits Him to build our endurance and refine our character (v. 4; Jas. 1:2-3).

The fifth blessing of those justified in Christ is that we receive the opportunity to experience the abundant love of God (v. 5). The believer understands God's parental love through the indwelling Holy Spirit and permits us to cry out to Him with intimate passion (8:15).

The sixth benefit of justification is that believers are saved from future wrath (v. 9). The justified person will never come under God's judicial wrath (for Christ bore God's wrath for sin once for all time), rather he or she looks for the coming of Christ to escape the Tribulation period when

God's wrath will judge the world (1 Thess. 1:10, 5:9; Rev. 3:10).

The seventh blessing of justification that the apostle speaks of is having joy in God (v. 11). As a result of reconciliation with God, a justified person has unspeakable joy in life, with full appreciation for the Lord Jesus Christ who made it all possible. The Lord Jesus did not promise that believers will be happy during their earthly sojourn (John 15:18-20), but they can enjoy God's peace by resting in Him despite their circumstances (John 16:33).

The idea of someone dying to save the life of a good person is a reasonable concept to our minds, if the one giving his or her life loves the person to be saved (v. 7). But who, in their right mind, would be willing to die for a wicked and vile person? Yet, that is what the love of God prompted Him to do; He sent His righteous Son to die in the place of His enemies, who were destined for destruction (v. 6). The righteous dying for the unrighteous gave the opportunity for those having no strength before God to be saved.

Accordingly, the blood of Christ is the foundation of the believer's acceptance with God (v. 9). Through the blood of Christ, God can righteously justify condemned sinners who believe on His Son. Likewise, the applied blood of Christ is the basis of the sinner's confidence that he or she can draw near to a holy God and experience His goodness, with no future threat of coming under His wrath. As a child of God, believers should expect God's parental discipline for personal sin; this correction is an expression of His immense love for His own children (Heb. 12:4-9). God knows that we will never be more joyful and fruitful than when we are in communion with Him.

Thankfully, those justified in Christ are saved from God's future wrath when He will judge those in rebellion against Him. God knows those who are His and marks a difference between His children and the children of the devil, who are appointed to wrath (Eph. 2:2-3). This point is a strong argument for the position that believers will be removed from the earth before the wrath of God is poured out on the inhabitants of the earth during the Tribulation period (1 Thess. 1:10, 5:9).

Through the redeeming blood of Christ, God is able to extend forgiveness to those who are dead in trespasses and sins. C. H. Mackintosh warns believers not to let justification through Christ's blood alone slip from our doctrinal foundation:

> *It is all through the blood of Jesus* – nothing less – nothing more – nothing different. *"It is the blood that makes an atonement for the soul."* This is conclusive. This is God's simple plan of justification. ... From

Genesis 3 to the close of Revelation, I find the blood of Christ put forward as the alone ground of righteousness. We get pardon, peace, life, righteousness, all by the blood, and nothing but the blood. The entire book of Leviticus is a commentary upon the doctrine of the blood.[6]

May each believer never forget the tremendous significance God the Father ascribes to His own Son's blood – we are redeemed and cleansed by the blood of Christ alone!

The work of redemption was accomplished by Christ in His death on the cross and has in view the payment of the price demanded by a holy God for the deliverance of the believer from the bondage and burden of sin. In redemption the sinner is set free from his condemnation and slavery to sin.

– John F. Walvoord

## Death, Sin, and Transgression (vv. 12-14)

Though "the flesh" sometimes refers to the human body in Scripture, the term, especially in the New Testament epistles, is used to refer to the fallen, independent nature which allows sin its opportunity within us. Paul states that through the fall of Adam, sin and spiritual death entered the world (v. 12). Every individual coming from Adam's line is born with his inherited fallen nature (Ps. 51:5, 58:3); that is, we are born sinners and separated from God. Therefore, John states that those who reject Christ's offer of salvation *"are condemned already"* (John 3:18); we are all born in that desperate spiritual condition. On this point, Warren Wiersbe writes:

Each of us is racially united to Adam, so that his deed affects us. The fallen angels cannot be saved because they are not a race. They sinned individually and were judged individually. There can be no representative to take their judgment for them and save them. But because you and I were lost in Adam, our racial head, we can be saved in Christ, the Head of the new creation.[7]

Some would question God's fairness in condemning the human race because Adam, our federal head, disobeyed God's prohibition of eating fruit from the tree of the knowledge of good and evil (Gen. 3:1-7). There are several important considerations in pondering the *fairness* of God on this matter.

First, God had previously told Adam that he would die if did not heed this commandment, so the fact that God has not wiped humanity from the face of the earth is an act of tremendous mercy.

Second, because we are all descendants of Adam, if individually tested as Adam was, each of us would have eventually followed Adam's example. The writer of Hebrews uses this same principle to confirm that the priestly tribe of Levi, while still in the loins of Abraham, paid tithes to the priest Melchizedek. This argument proves that Christ's priesthood, typified by Melchizedek, is superior to the Levitical priesthood. Likewise, Adam's sin was truly an act of the people.

Third, it was necessary for God to create Adam as a moral being with free choice to ensure humanity did not robotically honor God. Adam was created innocent (Eccl. 7:29), but still had the potential to disobey God. If there is no real choice to obey or not to obey, then genuine love cannot be demonstrated. God foreknew that when solicited to sin by the devil, Adam would choose wrongly, but this also would allow God to accomplish His predetermined plan of redemption in order to restore those who wanted to be justified in Christ (1 Pet. 1:19-20).

> We desperately need to understand something of the magnitude of sin, of evil, and of gross wickedness in this world if we are to appreciate our redemption. God's love, grace, and mercy shine all the brighter against the awful reality of evil. Indeed, the very existence of evil is a powerful proof of God's existence and holiness.
>
> – Dave Hunt

Until the Law was given to the Jews, God had on rare occasions revealed His will to individuals in the form of a charge or a call, but at Mount Sinai, He spelled out His code of ethics in intricate detail. In this respect, the Jews had an advantage over all other nations. Yet, privilege and responsibility are yoked together, meaning that the Jews had greater accountability to God for their actions than the other nations did. Obedience would be rewarded, but disobedience against God's Law would be reckoned as transgression against God: *"The law brings about wrath; for where there is no law there is no transgression"* (4:15), and *"For until the law sin was in the world, but sin is not imputed when there is no law"* (v. 13).

All of mankind was condemned in Adam and through Adam all humanity received a fallen nature which opposes God. Sin and death, therefore, have continued in the world, but from the time of Adam until the time of the Law, sin was not imputed as transgression. This does not mean that human sin during this time did not offend God – all sin offends God – but rather, sin was not explicitly regarded as transgression against God. Adam's sin was imputed as transgression because he disregarded the one divine prohibition issued to him in Eden (v. 15). On this point, F. B. Hole writes:

> Adam sinned against a definite commandment; hence his sin was a transgression. After that some 2,500 years had to roll away before the law of Moses was given, when once more transgression became possible. Between those points there was no transgression, for there was no law to transgress. Yet there was sin universally, as proved by the universal reign of death. The practical difference lay here, that sin is not "imputed" when there is no law: that is, it is not put to our account in the same way.[8]

During this long interim (from Eden to Sinai), the human conscience experientially proved to one's own soul that he or she had an imbedded code of ethics which could not be perfectly obeyed no matter how hard one tried (2:15). Internal feelings of guilt meant only one thing – sin had been committed. Now that the Law of God had been revealed, ignorance would no longer be an excuse; the Jewish nation was directly responsible to God and sin would be accounted as transgression against Him.

The good news is that just as God condemned humanity for Adam's transgression (Adam being the federal head of humanity), God could also offer salvation to all humanity through the obedience of the Last Adam (the spiritual head of redeemed humanity), Christ. Throughout the remainder of this chapter Paul compares and contrasts the sorrows caused by Adam and the blessings accomplished by Christ in relationship to the human race.

## Death in Adam, Justification and Life in Christ (vv. 15-21)

Paul contrasts what Adam brought on humanity through rebellion with what Christ offers humanity through obedience. In verse 15, Adam's offense is contrasted with Christ's free gift. In verse 16, Adam's condemnation is compared with Christ's offer of acquittals. In verse 17, Adam's behavior brought spiritual and physical death upon humanity, but Christ's work at Calvary allows God to offer eternal life to the repentant. In verse 18, Adam's transgression prompted God's judgment, but Christ's obedience permits God to justify those exercising faith in His Son.

This contrast between Adam's and Christ's activities is used to explain why it was beneficial for God to condemn the whole world based on

Adam's sin (vv. 19-21). By condemning Adam (the fountainhead of humanity) for disobedience, God could also offer salvation to all of humanity through one perfect man's obedience (speaking of Christ – the fountainhead of spiritual life). This understanding lays the foundation for the identification truths presented in the next chapter (i.e., how the believer is positionally identified *with Christ* from God's perspective).

Through Adam's sin, death passed down to all his descendants, but through Christ *"grace reigns through righteousness unto eternal life"* (v. 21). When you consider God's righteous plan of salvation, man has much more in Christ now than Adam had in Eden before the fall. The believer has the implanted life and Spirit of God within. The believer will rule and reign with Christ, and inherit all things in Christ (8:17; 2 Tim. 2:12; Rev. 21:7). The believer is justified before God (a standing of righteousness which cannot be lost) and by spiritual rebirth and adoption becomes a child of God with a promised inheritance (John 1:12-13; 8:15). While still in innocence, Adam enjoyed fellowship with God in paradise, but he had none of these blessings of salvation in Christ.

John informs us that Satan will be bound in the bottomless pit during Christ's future reign on earth (Rev. 20:1-8). However, at the end of that time he will be released to again test man's resolve to follow God. Even after one thousand years of peace and prosperity, the devil will successfully deceive the nations of the earth to rebel against Christ. One might ask, "Why would God allow Satan to lead such a rebellion against His own Son? Why not just destroy Satan and be done with wickedness?" Unfortunately, wickedness would not expire with the end of Satan, for his rebel spirit entered into the world in Eden and intruded into humanity (1 Jn. 2:16).

Death and rebellion have been passed down to every generation since that time (v. 12). Summarizing the state of the human heart, the prophet Jeremiah wrote, *"The heart is deceitful above all things, and desperately wicked; who can know it? I, the Lord, search the heart, I test the mind, even to give every man according to his ways, according to the fruit of his doings"* (Jer. 17:9-10). Before destroying Satan, God will allow him to test the human heart's desire for godliness, and find it lacking.

While enjoying God's fellowship in a perfect environment, both the first man (Adam) and the last humans on earth before it is destroyed (Rev. 20:11; 21:1; 1 Pet. 3:10), are shown to be incapable of pleasing God when tempted to sin against Him. Man, left to himself, will always go his own way; he will turn away from God (Isa. 53:6). Thankfully, God provided a righteous solution for human rebellion by judging His Son Jesus Christ in our place and giving those who trust in Him eternal life.

# Romans Chapter 6

### Sanctified in Christ (vv. 1-10)

Having discussed God's righteousness in condemning sinners (1:18-3:20) and also in justifying them through faith in Christ (3:21-5:21), Paul begins the third major section in Romans – *God's Righteousness in Sanctifying Those Justified in Christ* (6:1-8:39). What God redeems, He sets apart for His use and honor. This is why justification must precede sanctification, for we must have Christ's life before we can live for Christ's glory.

J. Oswald Sanders' outline of Romans 6 conveys progressive warnings for us to be mindful of, so that God's work of sanctification in our lives is not hindered:

>   Vv. 1-11:    You cannot continue in sin.
>   Vv. 12-14:   You need not continue in sin.
>   Vv. 15-19:   You must not continue in sin.
>   Vv. 20-23:   You had better not continue in sin.[9]

Paul's focus in Romans 3:21-5:21 had been on "sins" (humanity's sin collectively beginning with Adam), but in Roman 6:1 he speaks of "sin" to introduce a new subject matter. The topic is no longer how God has dealt with human sin by punishing His Son, but the believer's responsibility to personally judge sin and yield to God through Christ's resurrection power. Some might think that, since they have been justified in Christ and have been forgiven of their sin debt, they can live any way they want, but that way of thinking is an affront to God (vv. 1-2). Believers are sanctified in Christ to live for and to serve God, not themselves, and certainly not their vile flesh. The believer's union and oneness with Christ should motivate him or her not to sin, lest we make Christ privy to our sin.

Romans 6 is a premier portion of Scripture which speaks of God's desire for sanctification in the believer's life. In this chapter, Paul itemizes several identification truths before addressing the practical side of sanctification: Positionally speaking the believer was crucified with Christ (v. 6), died with Christ (vv. 3, 8), was buried with Christ (v. 4), was made alive with Christ

(v. 8) and was raised up with Christ to walk in the newness of His life (v. 4). When Christ was crucified, God saw all believers positionally crucified with Him. When Christ died, God saw all believers die with Him…etc. Paul wants Christians to understand that their complete oneness with Christ is in itself motivation to refrain from sin.

The Greek verb *baptizo* is rendered "baptism" in verse 3 and means to be dipped into or immersed into something. Spiritual baptism at Pentecost (Acts 2; 1 Cor. 12:13) created the Church (the Body of Christ). Since that time believers are immersed in the Body of Christ and made one with Him by the power of the Holy Spirit. There is no water mentioned in this text; the entire context of the passage is the believer's spiritual identity and union with Christ. Believer's baptism is a personal act of obedience to Christ's command to identify with Him through water baptism (e.g., 1 Cor. 1:17). Spiritual baptism is connected with what God does in response to a new believer's faith; water baptism is what a believer does in response to God's Word (Matt. 28:19-20). There is no example of anyone in the Church Age being baptized prior to professing Christ as Savior. Spiritual baptism and water baptism are completely different subjects.

Paul tells us that "the Old Man" was crucified and died when Christ died, so that we are no longer slaves to sin (v. 6). At Calvary, the Old Man (i.e., what we were in Adam by nature before being justified in Christ), the man who was dominated and controlled by the flesh – that man died with Christ. The Old Man does not speak of what we have done, but who we were in Adam. Paul conveys the practical aspects of this positional truth to the believers at Galatia: *"Those who are Christ's have crucified the flesh with its passions and desires"* (Gal. 5:24). The believer has been positionally crucified with Christ so that his or her flesh nature will lose its controlling influence as he or she matures in Christ. It is not that the flesh nature diminishes in strength, but rather that the Holy Spirit within the believer overpowers it. What originated in the world cannot compete with that which is supernatural; thus, a yielded life cannot be overcome by the flesh nature.

> Some sins we have committed,
> Some we have contemplated,
> Some we have desired,
> Some we have encouraged;
> In the case of some we are innocent only because we did not succeed.
>
> – Lucius Annaeus Seneca

Paul's point is that a dead person is freed from any bondage to the former life and may now serve a new master, God, in the newness of life. The Greek word translated "freed" in verse 7 is a *perfect* tense verb, meaning that this liberation from the power of death and sin has been accomplished forever. Because Christ rose from the grave, those trusting in Him receive eternal life in Him and the ability to overcome sin through the power of the Holy Spirit (8:13; John 3:16). The Greek verb translated "live" in verse 8, is a *future* tense verb indicating that those who have positionally died with Christ, not only live in Christ now, but will live with Him for eternity. Since Christ will never die again and the believer is in spiritual union with Christ, then the believer also can never die in the spiritual sense. Since Christ will never die again, believers in Christ shall live forevermore in Him!

A number of years ago, I was speaking to a younger believer about the security of his salvation. He expressed some doubt that his salvation could be forever. I asked him, "Right now are you in Christ or out of Christ?" He said, "I am in Christ." I expressed my joy to hear that, as there are only two groups of people on earth today – "saints" and "ain'ts" (i.e., those justified in Christ and those who are not). I then asked my brother, "Is Christ ever going to die again for the judgment of sin?" He said, "Absolutely not." and then referred to Hebrews 10:12-18 as justification for his answer. I said, "Correct, so if you are in Christ now, and He will never die again, how could you ever die with Him again, that is, if you could somehow lose your salvation?" I then explained, "All believers died with Christ once at Calvary…we will never die with Him again because He will never die again, which means once in Christ – forever in Christ!" My younger brother was relieved to comprehend this identification truth.

Paul told the believers at Ephesus that because they had heard and learned Christ (i.e., believed in Him), they had the ability to put off the former conduct of the *Old Man* and live as a *New Man* in Christ (Eph. 4:22-24). Positionally speaking, the Old Man is what we were in Adam and the New Man is what we are in Christ. This is why Scripture does not refer to those justified in Christ as "sinners" (in the positional sense) after their conversion; rather, they are alive to love and serve God. C. H. Mackintosh explains God has much more for us than just escaping death; He wants us to experience His love and newness of life – and live as a "New Man":

> It is a very common error to view the Lord Jesus rather as the averter of God's wrath, than as the channel of His love. That He endured the wrath of God against sin is most preciously true. But there is more than this. He

has come down into this wretched world to die upon the cursed tree, in order that, by dying, He might open up the everlasting springs of the love of God to the heart of poor rebellious man.[10]

May those in Christ live out His life and not behave as if they were still dead in trespasses and sins. The Old Man is dead – the New Man is alive!

## Delivered From Sin and Death to Serve God (vv. 11-23)

In verse 11, the subject transitions from identification truth (i.e., how God sees us "with Christ") to practical sanctification (i.e., our personal responsibility of holiness to God because of our identification with Christ). Ultimately, complete freedom from the pull of sin within us will be achieved at glorification. Until then, consistent mortification of sin within our members must be an ongoing exercise of all believers (vv. 11-12). Only by yielding to the life of Christ within us are we able to *"make no provision for the flesh, to fulfill its lusts"* (13:14).

Gratification and mortification are the only two things the flesh understands. The danger is that if we choose to gratify the flesh, even a little, it will want more the next day because the flesh is never satisfied – *"The eye is not satisfied with seeing, nor the ear filled with hearing"* (Eccl. 1:8; KJV). The only spiritual recourse to deal with the lusting of the flesh is to deal it a deadly blow and to keep on mortifying it day after day – this is God's will for every believer.

> Abide in the Lord Jesus, the sinless One – which means, give up all of self and its life, and dwell in God's will and rest in His strength. This is what brings the power that does not commit sin.
>
> – Andrew Murray

Paul uses four key verbs in Romans 6 to convey how a believer can have a God-pleasing life. First, the verb "know" is mentioned three times in verses 1, 6, and 9. A believer must understand his or her identification with Christ, that is, how God sees him or her positionally in Christ.

Second, Paul says each believer must personally "reckon" (v. 11) these identification truths: "I was crucified with Christ." "I died with Christ." "I was buried with Christ." "I am alive with Christ." "I am seated with Christ in heavenly places right now" (Eph. 2:6). This is how God sees the believer at present. Though physically many are still serving Christ on earth, positionally all believers are with Christ in heavenly places. This is why Paul refers to believers as "ambassadors for Christ" (2 Cor. 5:21). Our citizenship is in Heaven, but we have the opportunity today to represent Heaven's interests on earth (Phil. 3:20).

Third, the verb rendered "present" or "yield" indicates the appropriate response of a believer who has acknowledged their complete identification in Christ – they are to be living sacrifices for Him. When we say "no" to the flesh and "yes" to what Christ commands, we have offered up to God a sacrifice that reminds Him of His Son. A sacrifice is not a sacrifice unless it costs something, and submitting to God's will costs us our selfish desires.

Fourth, the verb "obey" (used four times in various ways in verses 16 and 17), ensures that we can only offer up pleasing sacrifices to God if we know and obey His word. Scripture informs us what behavior pleases God. We demonstrate love for God by doing what He approves of and abstaining from what does not (John 14:15).

Paul then identifies some of the blessings of experiencing the life of Christ (v. 22): First, through the Holy Spirit, the believer gains power over besetting sin. Second, the believer becomes a servant of God, instead of sin. Third, the believer is now able to please God through doing good works. Fourth, the believer has everlasting life in Christ.

Paul summarizes his main point concerning sanctification in verse 23: *"For the wages of sin is death, but the gift of God is eternal life in Christ Jesus our Lord"* (Rom. 6:23). This verse is often used in presenting the gospel to the lost, but in its context here, Paul is presenting a general principle: Sin causes us to be spiritually separated from God – this is referred to as "death" in Scripture. Positionally, we all were born into the world separated from God by Adam's sin, but it is also true that when believers sin (practice sin), broken fellowship with God occurs. Even after being born again, our sin still separates us from enjoying God and experiencing His goodness! Broken fellowship results when a child offends his parents, but the relationship remains unbroken. Sin always results in some type of separation from God, either in relationship (caused by original sin) or in fellowship (caused by personal sin after regeneration).

> A sight of Christ death, if it is a true sight, is the death of all love of sin.
>
> – Charles Spurgeon

We choose our sin, but it is God who chooses the consequences of our sin and offers consoling grace for those who regret and repent of their sin (1 Jn. 1:9). God's infinite grace and forgiving heart ensure that failures are never final unless we choose to wallow in self-pity rather than finding a joyful refuge in His grace.

# Romans Chapter 7

## United With Christ – the New Husband (vv. 1-6)

In this chapter, Paul describes his personal struggles to obey God's Law apart from divine power. For this reason, forty-one "I," "me," and "myself" pronouns appear in Romans 7. He begins the discussion by reminding his audience that the Law has dominion only over living people. The Jews were not accountable to obey the Law once they were deceased (v. 1). He cites the Levitical Law governing marriage to emphasize this point: A wife was bound to her husband by a marriage covenant as long as he was alive; if he died, she was released from the commitment and could remarry (v. 2). The Levitical Law did not permit wives to divorce their husbands, so the only way out of her obligation was her husband's death; if she married another man while her husband was alive, she would be considered an adulteress and under the condemnation of the Law (v. 3).

In verse 4, it is obvious that a reversal of this analogy is being presented: Those in Christ are compared to the wife, and the Law to her husband. In the illustration, it was the husband who died, however in application, it was not the Law that perished (it still lives), but believers who have positionally died with Christ. Thus, the Law's claims upon them have been severed. Death ends obligation to commitments! Death means that believers are no longer under the Law's demands and condemnation, but are free to be married to (united with) Christ and to serve Him in the newness of His life.

Just as a wife could not have two husbands, a believer cannot be bound to the Law and to Christ at the same time. Law and grace cannot be mixed in matters of salvation, nor in service to the Lord. And as J. G. Bellett explains, having died with Christ, believers have no obligation to live in the flesh as Law-keepers:

> The apostle entertains the claims of the law upon the believer, and shows that they also have been disposed of. He does this very simply; he says that the authority of the law addresses itself only to a living man, that is, a man in the flesh. It is the flesh or man as born of Adam, that the law was given to; but the believer has ceased in this sense to be a living man, has ceased to be of Adam, inasmuch as he has died and risen

again; and consequently, being a dead and risen man, and not a living man, the law does not address its claims to him, he is not the object for the law.[11]

It is important to understand that Paul is not teaching on marriage per se. Rather, he is using the Law governing marriage to stress a point – since Christ has paid the judicial penalty of the Law on our behalf (Heb. 2:9, 10:10-18), the Law has no judicial hold on believers any longer. The Law is not dead – it still represents the righteousness of God to guide conduct, but believers are dead to the Law's sting (1 Cor. 15:56) because they are united with Christ (in His death and in His life). Thus, believers *"are not under the Law, but under grace"* (6:14).

Although, technically speaking, the Gentiles were never under the Law to begin with, the Law still showed humanity's sinfulness and need of a Savior (3:20; Gal. 3:24). The Law arouses the sinful impulses of our flesh nature, that is, we want to do even more what we are told not to do (v. 5). For believers, the Law had served its purpose by causing us to be aware of our sin, moving us to repentance and confession of Christ as the only possibility for forgiveness and restoration to God. Accordingly, the believer is not bound to live in the power of the flesh while attempting to be good Law-keepers (v. 6). Rather, because the believer has died with Christ and now lives in Christ, the old order of things has been put away. Believers are now one with Christ (i.e., a new Husband) and have the opportunity to serve God through Him.

## The Flesh

Paul reminds us that our flesh wants to do what our conscience knows is wrong to do (v. 5). Knowing what God does not want us to do just makes us want to do it more. As soon as we notice a sign "Do not touch – wet paint" hanging on a nearby park bench, we naturally want to ignore the sign and touch the bench to see if the paint has dried or not.

Because the apostle repeatedly refers to "the flesh" in chapters 6, 7, and 8, we pause to understand Paul's meaning. There are several connotations of the word "flesh" in Scripture, most of which have no ethical overtones. For example, flesh may speak of the material substance of the body, whether of animals or of men (1 Cor. 15:39), or it may relate to the human body (Phil. 1:22) or to humanity in general (John 1:13). Though there are various ways the word "flesh" is used in Scripture there are two main meanings which have important theological implications.

First, the flesh may speak of our physical bodies, the whole material part of man. God created Adam's body out of the dust of the ground (Gen. 2:7, 21, 23) with a number of mechanisms which would maintain the body's health and promote self-preservation (e.g., we desire water when thirsty, food when hungry, rest when weary, and children through procreation, etc.). Centuries later, Christ came to the earth and was born of a virgin birth to be made manifest *in flesh* (1 Tim. 3:16). In this sense, "the flesh" speaks of created, natural bodily impulses which are common to all humans. In Christ, all of those impulses were under His perfect control. However, in fallen humanity, such impulses often go unchecked.

The second major use of the word "flesh" pertains to human behavior rather than human form. It refers to man's fallen nature, which is controlled by the power of sin. It is the evil quality which intruded into man, became a resident traitor within him, and is now in league with the devil. Consequently, everything God says about the flesh is *negative.* In the flesh there is *no good thing* (v. 18). The flesh profits *nothing* (John 6:63). A Christian is to put *no confidence* in the flesh (Phil. 3:3). He is to make *no provision* for the flesh (13:14). A person who lives for the flesh is living a negative life. This is why, as Charles Ryrie observes, the phrase "the flesh" has an overwhelmingly negative connotation in Scripture:

> It [the flesh] refers to our disposition to sin and to oppose or omit God in our lives. The flesh is characterized by works that include lusts and passions (Gal. 5:19-24; 1 Jn. 2:16); it can enslave (Rom. 7:25); and in it is nothing good (Rom. 7:18). Based on this meaning of the word "flesh," to be carnal means to be characterized by things that belong to the unsaved life (Eph. 2:3).[12]

The flesh, governed by the fallen nature, is never satisfied; it wants more than what is reasonable or lawful. Instead of drinking *"a little wine for [one's] stomach's sake"* (1 Tim. 5:23), the flesh longs to be drunk with wine (Eph. 5:18). This is because when a person is intoxicated, the restraining influence of reason is lost, and it becomes easier for the flesh to rule the moment. Accordingly, those who want to serve God must not act in the wisdom and power of the flesh, but in the newness of life achieved through their spiritual union with Christ – the new Husband.

## The Law Awakens and Condemns Sinfulness (vv. 7-14)

Some might think that Paul was being critical of the Law (v. 7), but that was not the case; the Law is not sinful; rather, *"the Law is holy, just, and good"* (v. 12). The Law shows man his sinfulness (v. 7, 3:20) and points him to the solution – Christ the Savior (Gal. 3:24).

The Law ensured that Paul was not ignorant of his depravity anymore. If the Law had not stated that coveting, lusting for what is outside of God's will, was sin, Paul would not have felt guilty about his thought life. However, living with this awareness was worse than his life in ignorance (v. 8). The Law had caused Paul to be conscious of his coveting but gave him no ability to do anything about it, except feel guilty – consequently, he "died" to thoughts of being alive and holy through Law-keeping (v. 9).

Not only did Paul have no ability to control the very behavior he now knew was offensive to God, but he also realized that he just wanted to do what displeased God even more (v. 10). The apostle likens his continuing failure to do what he knows is right to experiencing the pangs of death – the Law spiritually slayed him (v. 11). He realized that it was not the Law's fault; it was good and spiritual and represented the righteousness of God. The Law permitted Paul to see himself as God did – a guilty sinner with no opportunity to live for God (vv. 12-13). Paul knew he was carnal and sold under sin with no hope of escaping its ongoing control (v. 14).

## The Strife Between the Law of God and Sin (vv. 15-25)

Although the expression "sin nature" is not found in the Bible, Christians often use the phrase to describe the self-seeking disposition of our fallen state that Paul alludes to in verses 15-20. Unchecked, the lusts of our flesh and the desires of our minds lead us into sin. In our natural state we cannot help but sin; we are born with a deep-seated malice against God. Paul refers to this disposition as *"the law of sin"* or *"the sin that dwells in me"* throughout this passage (vv. 17, 20, 21, 23, 25). The other law he refers to is "the law of God." His human spirit accurately conveyed the law of God to his mind; that is, Paul knew how God wanted him to behave (vv. 22, 23, 25).

Paul understood that there was nothing in his flesh nature that would naturally want to honor the Lord. Instead of eating what is necessary to maintain a fit body, the flesh engages in gluttony (Prov. 23:21, 28:7). Scripture exhorts us to dress modestly, to refrain from flaunting our bodies before others (1 Tim. 2:9; 1 Pet. 3:3), and not to seek to be the center of attention (Luke 14:8), but the flesh wants to be noticed and admired by others. The marriage covenant protects the sexual relationship between a husband and a wife, but unchecked cravings lead to fornication, which is a great offense against God (1 Thess. 4:3; Eph. 5:5-6) and against one's own body (1 Cor. 6:18).

Paul spoke of a law within his members – the law of Sin (v. 23) which continued to oppose the law of God in his mind (i.e., his understanding of what God demanded of him). The law of sin was an abiding evil presence within himself. There is no need to put a pre-conversion or post-conversion label to the latter portion of Romans 7; an unregenerate person and a believer not walking in the Spirit will both struggle as Paul describes. Every believer must realize that there is nothing in his or her flesh, naturally speaking, that can please God. It is only when a believer yields his or her body to God's Word and Spirit as a consecrated vessel that he or she can do anything to please God (this is the subject matter of the next chapter).

As J. N. Darby notes, Paul is explaining the nature of things within himself that govern his behavior:

> With the mind Paul himself serves the law of God, but with the flesh the law of sin. This is not a question of deliverance, or of success, or of failure, but the natural and characteristic tendency of the new and of the old man. In Heaven we shall not have the old nature, the flesh; in Christ we are delivered from its power and are no longer under law, having died in Him.[13]

After stating that all men, including himself, were incapable of continued moral correctness through natural efforts, Paul ponders this hopeless condition: *"O wretched man that I am! Who will deliver me from this body of death?"* (v. 24). Paul then proclaims the answer, *"I thank God – through Jesus Christ our Lord! ... There is, therefore, now no condemnation to them which are in Christ Jesus"* (8:1). Although man does not have the natural wherewithal to obey what he understands of God's law, there is a solution – the Lord Jesus Christ! Instead of being condemned in Adam, our position in the crucified and risen Christ is that we are dead to sin and alive unto God without condemnation (5:16, 18). Thus, while we know that we still have the law of sin in our members and nothing good in our flesh, we can rest in the assurance that God does not view us in the flesh (8:9).

Though we still have a nature within us that opposes God, we are not condemned for having it once we are in Christ. Wrong attitudes and thoughts will still be present in us, but our responsibility in Christ is neither to pursue nor to fulfill them, but to yield to His work of sanctification (Gal. 5:16). The work of sanctification begins in the believer's life immediately after he or she answers the call of salvation. God begins to fashion the new believer into a holy vessel and each believer is exhorted to cooperate in the working out of what God is working into his or her life (1 Thess. 5:23).

Ultimately, God will conform all believers to the moral image of Christ

(8:29). We are not to resist God's working in our lives, but instead to yield to it by surrendering to Him. God promises to chasten those who choose not to submit to Him in order that they may become broken before Him and experience sanctification (Heb. 12:6). Accordingly, sanctification in a practical sense is occurring in all believers, but some are more serious about it than others and, therefore, will reap the greater blessing of being further refined now. The limiting factor in this process is how much we allow our flesh to stand in the way.

Paul understood that only Jesus Christ could deliver him from this ongoing warring in his members. Paul was either speaking of his physical death, for he knew that he would then be present with Christ in Heaven (2 Cor. 5:8), or of his glorification at the Day of Christ (13:11; Phil. 1:6, 23). When Christ comes to the air, all His saints will be resurrected from their graves and all those living will be instantly changed to receive an immortal body, a Christ-like body, free from sin (1 Cor. 15:51-52; Phil 3:21; 1 Thess. 4:13-18). Either way, Paul was assured of complete deliverance from "this body of death."

## The Inner or Inward Man

Though Paul's inner man (i.e., his spirit) desired to obey God, he found no natural ability to do so. Yet, as a believer, it is this spiritual part of our essence which must govern our thinking and our actions (2 Cor. 4:16). Before we can understand how this is possible, we need a better understanding of how God created us.

God, who is triune, created man in His image. Man is not God, nor triune, but is tripartite. God is three distinct persons (Father, Son, and Spirit), while man is one person with three parts (spirit, soul, and body). The Holy Spirit acknowledges that each of us possesses a spirit, a soul, and a body (1 Thess. 5:23). These human components are interrelated but are exclusive in their properties.

The body is "world-conscious," the soul is "self-conscious," and the spirit of man is "God-conscious." The spirit is the noblest part of man and refers to the innermost area of our being – the "inner man." The body is the lowest portion of our existence and forms the outermost being. Between these two components dwells the soul. The soul comprises our intellect, our emotions, our personality, and our will. The soul links with the physical realm through the five senses, and through the spirit the soul connects with God. The soul is a bridge between the body and the spirit. When a believer is in fellowship with God, the Holy Spirit has the freedom to commune with man's spirit, which transmits godly thoughts to the soul. This in turn exercises the body to conform to the Spirit's control.

Before the fall of man, Adam's soul was completely under the control of his spirit. But the spirit cannot act directly on the body; it cannot bypass the soul (the mind). Thus, man has the will to choose to ignore his spirit and follow the desires of the flesh. God created the soul of man to stand between the body and the spirit in order to exercise power over the whole of man. It has the ability to consider spiritual things and render decisions other than what natural reason would endorse.

God's Spirit expresses His mind to the unseen human spirit – the inner man. The unregenerate are warned of coming judgment and are called to repentance (John 16:7-11), while the saved are further enlightened regarding the things of God (1 Cor. 2:10-13). In his fallen state, man is spiritually dead (i.e., separated from God) and cannot understand the things of God unless supernatural illumination is provided (1 Cor. 2:14); this is the only means by which those inflicted by satanic blindness may understand the truth (2 Cor. 4:4). God's communication to the unregenerate is not unidirectional, but more like a beacon which is warning ships of dangerous shoals. Only through trusting the gospel message can a human spirit directly commune with God the Father. This is accomplished through the intercession of His indwelling Spirit (8:26) and the mediatorship of His Son (1 Tim. 2:5).

The human soul is the window between the physical and the spiritual worlds and this is where the decision whether or not to exercise faith in divine truth is rendered. The inner man speaks of the human spirit, which longs to be one with the Creator again. After regeneration, the Spirit of God indwells the believer and has direct communion with the inner man. The believer's inner man is strengthened to pursue the things of God through spiritual exercises such as the study of Scripture, prayer, submission to truth, sincere repentance, and confession of personal sins (Eph. 3:16).

> Prayer is the acid test of the inner man's strength. A strong spirit is capable of praying much and praying with all perseverance until the answer comes. A weak one grows weary and fainthearted in the maintenance of praying.
>
> – Watchman Nee

# Romans Chapter 8

### The Holy Spirit Accomplishes What the Flesh Cannot (vv. 1-4)

Paul now answers the question he posed at the end of Romans 7: How can believers escape the problem of indwelling sin? He begins by stating three things that the Holy Spirit does for the believer. First, through regeneration and becoming one with Christ, the believer is no longer condemned, despite still possessing a nature that wants its own way (v. 1).

Second, Paul explains that the believer has received a new nature and that through the power of the Holy Spirit, this nature can control the believer so that his or her flesh nature (the big bully within) no longer rules his or her life: *"For the law of the Spirit of life in Christ Jesus has made me free from the law of sin and death"* (v. 2). This results in a new war within each believer, a war between the old and new natures. *"Let us cleanse ourselves from all filthiness of the flesh and spirit, perfecting holiness in the fear of God"* (2 Cor. 7:1). Thankfully, this is a battle in which the believer can be victorious, for the power of the Holy Spirit is now *available* to overcome his or her inherent depravity. Some have taught that the flesh nature is eradicated at conversion, but clearly Paul stated that there would be an ongoing war between these two natures within the believer; the flesh and the new nature are completely opposed to each other and both compete for control of an individual's mind (Gal. 5:16-17).

Paul writes: *"For what the law could not do in that it was weak through the flesh, God did by sending His own Son in the likeness of sinful flesh"* (v. 3). The same Greek word *homoioma*, translated as "likeness" in this verse, is also used in Philippians 2:7, which states that Christ *"was made in the likeness of men."* The word "likeness" in both verses means "resemblance" or "form." Humanly speaking, Christ's form was that of a man, but He was more; He also possessed a divine nature. The Lord looked like everyone else, but He did not act like them. His life was unique for *"in Him is no sin"* (1 Jn. 3:5), He *"knew no sin"* (2 Cor. 5:21), and He *"did no sin"* (1 Pet. 2:22).

Therefore, God sent His Son into the world in the likeness of sinful flesh (i.e., he looked like everyone else born of Adam) to be judged for all in Adam and all that had been done in the flesh. Clearly then, there was nothing worth saving in man's corrupt state. The fallen nature is selfish and self-promoting. Even its purest motives taint what we might consider to be a good work – from God's perspective, there is nothing good in man's disposition towards Him to be saved. Rather man and all his deeds had to be condemned.

Third, the Spirit of God speaking through man's spirit is in direct opposition to the lusts of the body and mind. The Holy Spirit speaks, convicts, draws, and chastens us, but He does not force the believer to do what is right. The decision is left to us: To whom will we listen and who will we obey? If we listen to the Spirit (walk in the Spirit), then we enjoy spiritual fruitfulness that could never occur in the flesh (v. 4).

## The Flesh Nature and the Holy Spirit Are in Conflict (vv. 5-13)

All those born in the flesh naturally follow the impulses of the flesh, but those born of God who live after the Spirit of God do what pleases Him (v. 5). Living after the flesh is death (i.e., results in separation with God) because the flesh is not subject to God. For the believer, this break in fellowship (not relationship) voids the opportunity to please God (v. 7). In contrast, yielding to the new spiritual nature received at regeneration results in a life that pleases God (v. 6). Those choosing the latter way of life are enabled by the Holy Spirit to enjoy God's peace and be fruitful for Him.

John refers to this new nature as a righteous seed implanted within a new believer at his or her spiritual birth. This seed cannot choose sin or lead the believer away from what pleases God: *"No one who is born of God practices sin, because His seed abides in him; and he cannot sin, because he is born of God"* (1 Jn. 3:9; NASB). "Born of God" and "born again" are equivalent terms with the washing of regeneration (Tit. 3:5). It is only by the conviction of the Holy Spirit and the power of God's Word resounding in our minds that we are enabled to repent, choose Christ, and receive eternal life in Him. Until then we are simply dead corpses marching in cadence with Satan, performing his rebel agenda, and coming ever nearer to his final destination – Hell (Eph. 2:1-3). Once we trust Christ, we become a New Man in Him, and receive His nature through the Holy Spirit; what we positionally were in Adam (the Old Man) is gone, but we still have his old nature within us.

There are many things for which our flesh can lust: social status, fame, food, vices, sexual pleasures, money, beauty, etc. If we allow our flesh to lust for what it wants we must expect our behavior to adversely affect our spiritual vitality. Peter recognizes that a believer cannot live according to the flesh and be in the will of God (1 Pet. 4:2).

Clearly, when the believer is in the flesh, he or she cannot please God; this is a practical truth (v. 8). Thankfully, once individuals have been regenerated in Christ and become new creations, God does not, positionally speaking, see them in the flesh any longer (v. 9). The Father sees all true believers in His Son; they have the Spirit of Christ within them and are one with Christ forever. The Holy Spirit who raised up Christ from the dead also indwells believers and gives them resurrection power to live for Christ in righteousness (vv. 10-11).

What was dead in sin and corrupted by a rebellious nature has been transformed by the Holy Spirit to be profitable to God. Though the original nature still remains within, the Holy Spirit provides believers the opportunity and the power to no longer yield to it, but rather to the will of God. Given the immense suffering that the flesh has caused humanity, the believer has no reason to ever serve it again; to do so would result in death (separation from God's goodness; v. 12). Rather, believers must be on high alert and be willing to instantly mortify any observed fleshly thoughts or impulses; otherwise, those who are God's cannot live for Him (v. 13).

The Greek verb translated "put to death" or "mortify" in verse 13 is in the present tense and active voice, meaning that believers are to be on active duty to mortify the deeds of the flesh in real time. If your flesh nature raises its ugly head – you are to inflict a mortal blow against it. The only way to deal with lusting flesh is to put it to death; no pity, no mercy, and no procrastination.

Mortification or gratification are the only two things the flesh understands, but if we choose to gratify the flesh, even a little, it will want more the next day because the flesh is never satisfied. The only spiritual recourse in dealing with the lusting of the flesh is to deal it a deadly blow and to keep on mortifying it day after day – this is God's will for every believer. Consistent mortification of the flesh ends the power of the carnal mind that causes the believer to lose spiritual fellowship with the Savior.

Death and dying are not pleasant topics of conversation. There is a finality associated with death that our flesh loathes, because it ceases to function. But from God's standpoint, as Paul reminds the Galatians, Christians have already died positionally with Christ, and should therefore live out this truth: *"Those who are Christ's have crucified the flesh with its passions and desires"* (Gal. 5:24). The purpose of crucifixion was to end a life, though death would occur sometime after the victim was crucified. Thus, the cross ensures that as time moves on, there will be less of the believer's flesh and more of Christ apparent in his or her life. Eradication of the flesh nature will ultimately occur at glorification. Until that time, there should be a diminishing control of the old nature in the believer's life as he or she matures in Christ. It is not that the flesh nature within us wanes in strength, but rather that through the power of the Holy Spirit it is overcome.

## The "New Nature" or "New Man"

Prior to trusting Christ as Lord and Savior, people do not have the ability to please God; in fact, their old nature directly opposes God in thought and in deed (5:10, 8:5-7). The believer needs a new nature that longs to please God and to perform His will (Eph. 4:24). This "new nature" or "new man" is received from God at conversion through an act of the Holy Spirit called regeneration (Tit. 3:4-5). The Holy Spirit washes us by bringing us to see the wrong in our sinful attitudes and desires. He makes us feel their uncleanness, and leads us to repent of and repudiate them.

Peter refers to the new nature received as a divine nature: *"By which have been given to us exceedingly great and precious promises, that through these you may be partakers of the divine nature, having escaped the corruption that is in the world through lust"* (2 Pet. 1:4). Regeneration is the implantation of a new life and a new order of living. This is why a regenerated person is referred to as a "new man" in Colossians 3:10; he received a new disposition which is to govern his thinking and behavior. John refers to the new nature received by those "born of God" as a righteous seed implanted within a new believer (1 Jn. 3:9).

Before the one-time act of regeneration, the believer was spiritually dead, but through rebirth he or she is made spiritually alive! Imagine for a moment a peach seed placed within a coffin containing a rotting corpse. The seed contains life, while the coffin contains nothing but death. In time, the seed will sprout and grow into a fruit-bearing tree. Through the power of the Holy Spirit, God implants life within a repentant sinner – that which was once dead now lives to bear fruit to God (John 15:1-5).

## The Believer – a Son and Heir of God (vv. 14-17)

Paul emphasizes that the believer's position in Christ has a responsibility attached to it: True sons of God are led by the Spirit of God (v. 14). Willing submission and obedience are proof of sonship and love for the Lord Jesus (Luke 6:46). When believers follow the Spirit, He responds by infusing them with inner peace and giving them a sense of security as a child of God (v. 15). The Holy Spirit bears witness with the believer's spirit that he or she really is a child of God (v. 16). No one has the authority to assure someone else that he or she is a child of God (i.e., have salvation in Christ). That is the role of the Holy Spirit. We may declare the truth of the gospel with authority, but only God accurately knows whether saving faith resides in the human heart. For those who have been born again, the Holy Spirit enables us to cry out to "Abba," our heavenly Father, with confidence and with expectation of His help and care.

As God's children, all believers are heirs of God and joint heirs with Christ (v. 17). In a coming day, true believers will inherit all that Christ has (Rev. 21:7). All believers are sons and have the Spirit of adoption (not the spirit of bondage as a servant). All believers have the Holy Spirit indwelling them and He guarantees their co-heirship with Jesus Christ. Given this hope, all sons should reveal God's glory as Christ did, while waiting for the manifestation of glory to come.

It is understood that this eternal inheritance can be realized only after a season of suffering during our earthly sojourn. Those who are Christ's will gladly live for Him; this invites the world's hatred and persecution (John 15:18-20). Later, Paul told his spiritual son Timothy that all who live godly for Christ would suffer persecution for doing so (2 Tim. 3:12). But the apostle also explains that the joy, the fellowship in Christ, and the purification that results through righteous suffering more than compensate for all the ills endured in this world for Him.

Every believer will enjoy the Lord in eternal bliss and glory, but some will appreciate the heavenly experience more than others. Paul knew the tie between suffering for Christ now and reigning with Him later. When Paul weighed all his troublesome experiences against his future with Christ, he concluded: *"For I consider that the sufferings of this present time are not worthy to be compared with the glory which shall be revealed in us"* (v. 18).

Our school days on earth are toilsome and often agonizing, but our righteous groaning is not a useless thing in God's kingdom. Paul compares these to a woman in the travail of childbirth. Her suffering ends when her child is born. Likewise, one day we shall be delivered from the presence of sin and all its ugliness to experience the wonders of Christ's presence. Until that day, may we stay true to our calling in Christ and keep toiling for Him – it will be worth it all when we see Christ! As shown through Christ's own example, suffering must precede glory (1 Pet. 2:21-24).

> No condemnation now I dread; Jesus, and all in Him, is mine;
> Alive in Him, my Living Head, and clothed in Righteousness Divine.
> Bold, I approach the eternal throne,

And claim the crown, through Christ my own.

– Charles Wesley

## Sin's Consequences Are Vanquished (vv. 18-25)

Having thought about how believers are destined to rule and reign with Christ in His future kingdom, Paul assures his audience that their sufferings at this present time are not even comparable to the glory that will be realized in them later. He wrote something similar to the saints at Corinth, *"For our light affliction, which is but for a moment, is working for us a far more exceeding and eternal weight of glory"* (2 Cor. 4:17). The Lord is watching and He knows the quality of our work and will reward it appropriately and abundantly in a coming day (Heb. 6:10-12).

Paul then explains that the revelation of the Son of God and the restoration of man to God is what the entire planet is waiting for (vv. 19-22). At Christ's Second Advent to the earth, the redeemed will be established at His side. The devastation caused by sin will be reversed. Originally, man was created to rule over the earth so as to represent the image and likeness of God (Gen. 1:26; Heb. 2:6-8). When man sinned, God could not have an imperfect head ruling over a perfect creation, so God cursed the earth and made it a fitting habitation for a condemned race to suffer in their sin. Yet, in a coming day, as prophesied by Isaiah (Isa. 4), the Lord will completely repair the damage that resulted from sin and then everyone on the earth and creation itself will rejoice!

Believers can look forward not only to the restoration of creation to full fruitfulness, but also to when they will receive the full rights of their adoption in God's family (v. 23). Adoption represents the ultimate goal of the believer's salvation, that is, to be fully son-placed in order to receive the full inheritance and governing authority as an adult son (Col. 3:24). Christ has already fully purchased the souls and bodies of those who have trusted the gospel message (1 Cor. 6:20), but these will not gain all the privileges of an heir until after their bodies have been redeemed. This event, the glorification of all saints on earth, is often referred to as *the Rapture of the Church* (1 Thess. 4:13-18).

Paul states that those who have been born again have already received the blessings of salvation which the Holy Spirit possesses (v. 23), and therefore can continue in hope of being with the Lord and fully son-placed. Hope is the ability to have present joy in the future promises of God and the believer's "blessed hope" is the appearing of Christ in the clouds to call His people off the earth to ever remain with Him (vv. 24-25; Tit. 2:13).

## The Indwelling Divine Intercessor (vv. 26-27)

The Holy Spirit helps us in our weaknesses (v. 26). The Greek word translated "weaknesses" is *astheneia* and may speak of any kind of physical, emotional, or spiritual disability. But it is not just assistance in our weaknesses that is promised; the Holy Spirit also offers intercession on our behalf before the throne of grace when we do not even know what to pray for or how to adequately express ourselves in prayer (v. 27).

During times of deep distress or tragic grief it may be hard to formulate words while praying; it is at these times that the Holy Spirit perfectly expresses our needs to our High Priest in Heaven without any audible sound. When we groan, the Holy Spirit also groans with spiritual ministry. This is not the speaking in tongues as some teach, because the ministry the Holy Spirit engages in is literally without sound.

The English expression of action, "makes intercession," is derived from a Greek verb with a present tense, meaning that the Holy Spirit *keeps on interceding* on our behalf. We never need to worry about the Holy Spirit being unaware of our troubles and sorrows, or that He gets tired of groaning when we groan, or that some matter is not worthy of His attention. He is within us and before the throne in Heaven to help us in all our weaknesses, which He understands better than we do. He continues to make ongoing intercession for us anytime we are in need. This enablement should cause the believer to be victorious over his or her flesh nature.

## God's Purposes Are Good and Cannot Fail (vv. 28-39)

Paul closes his discussion on the topic of the believer's sanctification by highlighting that God's sovereign control of our lives guarantees that everything that happens will bring about a greater blessing to those who love him and more honor to His name (v. 28). On a personal level, there may be a perceived loss at any moment in time, but in the eternal picture God is working everything for good.

Paul's promise is to those "who love God." If one truly loves the Lord, submitting to His precepts will be a delight. Love for the Lord is a stronger motive for obedience than the fear of consequences: *"There is no fear in love; but perfect love casts out fear, because fear involves torment. But he who fears has not been made perfect in love"* (1 Jn. 4:18). A believer motivated by love for Christ can venture into each and every day with confidence that God has his or her best in mind; he or she need not fear eternal retribution for every misstep.

Without God, suffering would be a most miserable experience! It is only through Him that our human misery can have a foreknown and profitable outcome. God ensures that the result of our suffering accomplishes a greater good, such as conforming us into the moral image of Christ (v. 29). He is the One of status among His brethren – "the Firstborn" (Heb. 2:11-12). And all saints are "predestined" to be conformed to His moral image; this is the ultimate goal of the believer's sanctification – to think, to speak, to behave as Christ does. The believer is at present being conformed to the moral image of Christ and at glorification this supernatural transformation will be abruptly completed – the believer will then reflect the moral glory of Christ forever (1 Cor. 15:51-52).

> Many men owe the grandeur of their lives to their tremendous difficulties.
> — C. H. Spurgeon

There are times where Paul refers to positional truths which are works of God's sovereign power and grace beyond the constraints of time which hold us. For example, we read in 1 Corinthians 12:13, *"For by one Spirit we were all baptized into one body."* This baptism by the Holy Spirit relates to the formation of the body of Christ (i.e., *"the one body"*) in which all true believers compose a part – this mysterious Body called the Church was formed on the Day of Pentecost (Acts 2:2-4, 15-18). It is a positional truth which stands apart from the constraints of time – the Church is an eternal reality.

The personal blessings of the Spirit's baptism become apparent in time when a repentant soul experiences regeneration and partakes of the benefits of that baptism. This is why Paul states that all those answering the call of salvation have been justified and glorified in Christ now (v. 30). In time, justification occurs when one trusts the gospel message, but glorification is a future reality for all those saints living on earth at present. But positionally speaking, because Christ has been glorified and sits at God's right hand in Heaven, God views all believers as glorified and seated beside Him in Heaven already (Eph. 2:6). God created time and therefore He is not subject to it, but rather works His purposes in time. The point Paul now explains in further detail is who is going to be able to remove a believer from that privileged location on the throne of God in Heaven?

Indeed, God is for those who love Him, and the benefit of resting in Him during trials is that *"we are made more than conquerors through Him who loved us"* (v. 37). Truly, *"if God is for us, who can be against us?"* (v. 31). God will defend His own. The fact that He did not spare His own Son to satisfy our need of salvation shows that God will continue to supply whatever we need freely (v. 32). How can anyone bring a charge against God's elect (i.e., those in Christ), for they were justified by God (v. 33)? Who could ever condemn a believer, for God has already judged Christ for his or her offenses and Christ is now alive in Heaven to intercede on behalf of those who are His (v. 34)?

Paul mentions the love of the Lord three times in the final verses of this chapter to encourage believers forward in the process of their sanctification (vv. 35, 37, and 39): First, the believer cannot be separated from the love of God. Second, through Christ's love already demonstrated at Calvary, we know ultimate victory is assured over temporal foes. Third, the love of God is active and continually comes to us through Christ.

The apostle presents two lists of things and circumstances that some might think could separate us from God, but cannot. In verse 35, we learn that no earthly or physical reality can sever the believer's union with Christ; thus, all in Christ will continue to experience the love of God. In verse 38, the same truth is conveyed concerning all spiritual realities and even time itself. All believers are secure as God's children forever. No one (natural or supernatural) nor anything (natural or supernatural) has the power to separate the believer from Christ! Believers are safe in God's everlasting grip (John 10:28-29)!

> Nothing in the afterlife of the believer adds in the smallest degree to his title of favor with God, nor to his perfect security. Through faith alone this standing before God is conferred, and before Him the weakest person, if he be but a true believer on the Lord Jesus Christ, has precisely the same title as the most illustrious saint.
>
> – C. I. Scofield

> Where does your security lie? Is God your refuge, your hiding place, your stronghold, your shepherd, your counselor, your friend, your redeemer, your savior, your guide? If He is, you don't need to search any further for security.
>
> – Elisabeth Elliot

# Romans Chapter 9

## Paul's Burden for Israel (vv. 1-3)

In Romans chapters 9-11, Paul transitions from God's righteousness in sanctifying believers in Christ to God's past, present, and future dealings with the nation of Israel. The Jews were a religious people (10:1-3), but Paul knew they were spiritually lost and yearned for them to seek righteousness in Christ and be saved (vv. 1-2).

His immense sorrow for his countrymen over their rejection of God's only means of salvation, Christ, was so great that if it were possible, he was willing to be eternally condemned on their behalf for them to be saved (v. 3). Paul's deep affection for them was akin to that of Moses, who prayed, *"I pray, blot me out of Your book"* when God threatened to wipe out the Israelites after the golden calf incident (Ex. 32:32). We understand these statements as hyperbolic aspirations for emphasis, as no one can be taken from God's salvation grasp (John 10:28-29), and no one but Christ can substitute for Hell-bound sinners to offer salvation. Yet, Paul's sincere declaration does convey the serious nature of gospel work and the burden each of us should have for the lost. Without Christ, our neighbors, coworkers, friends, and family members are heading to a horrible eternity in the Lake of Fire (Rev. 20:15).

## Israel's Privileges (vv. 4-5)

This disheartening reality had not resulted because of a lack of revealed truth, but because the nation of Israel had largely rejected the truth. In fact, the Israelites enjoyed special privileges that no other people on the planet had, but these benefits also made them more accountable to God for their actions. What were these privileges? To adequately answer this question, Paul prefaces his response with the question: *"Who are the Israelites?"* He then lists a number of unique privileges that the Jews had received, that is, special revelation from God that the Gentiles were not given (vv. 4-5):

- They were an adopted nation, a special people for God (Ex. 4:22; Deut. 7:6).

- They witnessed God's glory as connected with the tabernacle and later with the temple (Ex. 40:35).

- God made certain covenants with Israel which He will honor.

- God gave the Jews the Mosaic Law (Ex. 19:5, 31:13).

- They were given a special service towards God: to worship Him at the tabernacle/temple (Ex. 19:6).

- God made specific promises to Jewish individuals and the Jewish nation (Josh. 1:2).

- They had patriarchs: Abraham, Isaac, Jacob, etc.

- They were given Christ as their Messiah (2 Cor. 5:16).

## Israel's National and Spiritual Legacies Are Different (vv. 6-13)

But despite all of Israel's privileges as God's covenant people, they failed to receive the rich blessings that God promised them. Hence, some might ask, "Did God's plan for Israel fail?" The short answer to this is, "No, God's plans never fail." The Jews lost God's blessings for a time because of unbelief, but ultimately God will keep all His promises to Israel.

God chose the Jewish nation to be a testimony for Him among the nations (Ps. 67:1-7), but they failed miserably (2:24). Paul continues to show that the basis of being a true Israelite is related to spiritual, not physical, birth (vv. 6-7). True Israelites are the spiritual offspring of Abraham, those who follow his example of exercising faith in God's Word alone. Thus, anyone following Abraham's example of trusting God's Word by faith will be imputed a righteous standing in the same way that Abraham was declared righteous (Gen. 15:6). In the spiritual sense, these individuals become children of Abraham and also of God.

Accordingly, those who are the spiritual offspring of Abraham (i.e., the children of the promise, just as Isaac had been a child of promise) may not be physical descendants of Abraham (v. 8). Paul applies three examples from the Old Testament to illustrate God's sovereign will and mercy at work. We began by recalling that God's offer of salvation is universal. He legitimately desires that no one should perish, but that all should take advantage of the salvation He offers (Tit. 3:11; 2 Pet. 3:9).

Although God chose Isaac and not Ishmael as the seed of Abraham (the child of promise), this does not mean that Ishmael was denied God's blessing or did not have an opportunity to serve God. Ishmael, the first son of Abraham, was greatly blessed by God (Gen. 17:19-21), but he was not the one through whom God chose to fulfill His covenant with Abraham. Ishmael was the product of human reasoning (the flesh) which resulted from Abraham's doubt in God's Word. God didn't cause Ishmael to return to pagan Egypt and stay there after knowing who the one true God was.

The Lord Jesus told the Pharisees, who were physical descendants of Abraham, that they were children of the devil and not of Abraham because they did not believe the truth which He was declaring to them (John 8:44). It is also evident that if the promises of God made to Abraham were received just through natural birth alone, then the Ishmaelites, Midianites, and Edomites would have them too, and not just those in the lineage of Isaac.

Paul presents a second example to show that God's spiritual calling is different than what would occur in nature. Although Esau was older than his twin-brother Jacob and should have received the birthright blessing, that was not God's plan (vv. 9-13). Esau was a carnal man governed by his fleshly appetites. Esau despised his birthright, which represented his "spiritual heritage." Hence, the writer of Hebrews declares him to be a "profane" person (Heb. 12:16-17) because he did not value spiritual matters (the blessing) over temporal desires (food). Esau pictures the natural man's propensity to be lured by his own lusts and worldliness – to value things seen and not the promises of God. He is not mindful of the future, but when the future arrives, he is remorseful concerning the consequences of past actions, yet still not repentant. Esau was also blessed by God, but God did not force Esau to disobey his parents and marry pagan women, who caused him to turn away from worshiping Jehovah.

Our world is full of people like Esau. It is no wonder that God declared, *"Jacob have I loved, but Esau have I hated"* (v. 13). We understand this statement to be in the "comparative" sense and not an "absolute" declaration, for God loves all men, but hates their behavior (Matt. 10:37; Luke 14:26). Even though Esau's behavior grieved the Lord, He still promised to bless him (Gen. 27:38-40). While it is true that God had pre-selected Jacob for His eternal purpose in time (v. 12), He did not force Esau to be faithless and rebellious in character. Nor did He coerce Jacob to value the birthright.

## A Sovereign God Determines His Mercy (vv. 14-24)

Paul apparently sensed that some in his audience might take issue with God's sovereign purposes and even suggest that God was not being fair (v. 14). The apostle emphatically proclaims that God's dealings with man are completely righteous, just, and appropriate to ensure that God can show the most mercy to humanity. An unjust and unrighteous God is unimaginable and any argument advanced otherwise must be rejected. While making intercession for Sodom in Genesis 18, Abraham confirmed this truth: *"Shall not the judge of all the earth do right?"* (Gen. 18:25). Indeed, He shall, for if God was unrighteous, how shall He judge the world (3:6)!

The Jews in Paul's audience knew this assessment to be true. However, that God would exercise His sovereign right to choose to bless the Gentiles while setting aside the majority of Israel, to them was unthinkable. Paul confronts the objector head on by quoting Old Testament Scripture, which the Jews possessed and could not deny. The apostle affirms that God has the right to extend mercy or withhold it; that is His prerogative. Israel deserved complete judgment for their rejection of Christ, yet God would deal with them in such a way as to bring the Jewish nation to repentance so He could extend compassion and mercy to Israel. Paul's point is that man cannot make demands on God's mercy; it is freely bestowed according to the sovereign goodness of God (vv. 15-16).

As a third example of God's sovereignty at work, the apostle submits God's dealings with Pharoah during the time of the Exodus. At this time, Moses was pronouncing plagues on Egypt to secure the release of the enslaved Jewish nation. Between Exodus 4 and 14, Pharaoh's heart is mentioned twenty times: On ten occasions it is the king's stubbornness at work, and ten times it is God who hardens his heart to accomplish His will. Clearly, at times God hardened Pharaoh's heart to accomplish His will, but Pharaoh's heart was not entirely hardened by God, for he hardened it himself afterwards.

Pharaoh maintained free choice in his overall decision-making. James confirms that it would have been impossible for God to cause Pharaoh to lie, for a holy God does not tempt anyone to sin; such behavior would be an affront to His righteous character (Jas. 1:13-14). Pharaoh had free choice in whom he would choose to revere. God did not force Pharaoh to worship Egyptian gods or to do evil.

God would have been perfectly just to destroy a pagan like Pharaoh, but instead He designed ten specific plagues to prove to Pharaoh that He was superior to the Egyptian gods. Pharaoh rejected this revelation and hardened his own heart against the Lord – Pharaoh prepared himself to be a vessel of wrath fit for destruction (vv. 17-22). God raised Pharaoh up to the pinnacle of human authority and power to demonstrate His superiority over man and to bring the most glory to Himself in the deliverance of His people from Egypt. God brought glory to His name by incorporating Pharaoh's foreknown rebellion and stubborn disposition into His plans.

This example shows how human responsibility and sovereign design ensure that God will receive all the glory in every situation. God has a will, which He exercises as He pleases, and no one can successfully resist it. When challenged, the righteousness of God shall be demonstrated at the conclusion of His ways. Indeed, some people have better spiritual opportunities than others and some people benefit more from the same opportunities than others do, but everyone has been exposed to some opportunity to know God. Paul's point is that all are guilty before God, and therefore, no one has a claim on His grace. This means that no one can say God is unfair when some receive His grace and others do not, for if it is justice that is being demanded, all would be condemned by God.

Man has no choice in being a part of God's plan, but as a moral and a conscious being, he has every choice in how he will answer God's call and be used within God's unfolding design. Whether or not we yield to His call, God will be glorified through our choices; He will use us either as vessels of mercy prepared for glory, or as vessels of wrath fit for destruction (v. 23). God prepares yielded vessels (both Jews and Gentiles in Christ) for glory and rebellious vessels (those outside of Christ) to receive His wrath (v. 24).

A vessel is used to hold or to transport something – it is what a vessel *does* and not what it *is* that is important. Consequently, Scripture refers to individuals as vessels and states that God will use both the yielded and the rebellious vessels to work His eternal purposes and to uphold His glory.

## Israel's Blindness – Mercy to Gentiles Was Foretold (vv. 25-33)

Paul now quotes or refers to several Old Testament prophecies to show that Israel's initial rejection of Christ was foreknown, and as a result God always planned to offer the Gentiles the blessings Israel failed to receive. This is how God would ultimately fulfill His promise to Abraham that through his Seed all the families of the earth would be blessed (Gen. 12:3). Thus, Paul, quoting Hosea (Hos. 2:23), states that God would both call and love a people (the Gentiles) who were not His covenant people (v. 25). Hosea declares (Hos. 1:10) that these who were not His people would be called "sons of the living God" (v. 26).

Did this mean that God was finished with the nation of Israel? To answer this question Paul quotes Isaiah (Isa. 10:22-23) to affirm that a remnant of Israel will be refined and saved in the future, but most of the Jewish nation would suffer God's judgment. Despite Israel's unfaithfulness to Jehovah, the Old Testament prophets inform us that the Lord will be moved with compassion and mercy to restore the Jewish nation to a place of special intimacy with Him in a future day.

God has not abandoned His adulterous wife, His covenant people of old (Ezek. 16:32, 38); He has an agenda for restoring the nation of Israel to a position of honor and blessing. Isaiah foretold that God's Servant-Messiah would accomplish this feat in two ways: First, He would *"bring Jacob back to Him, so that Israel is gathered to Him"* (Isa. 49:5). Second, He would also be *"a light to the Gentiles, that You should be My salvation to the ends of the earth"* (Isa. 49:6).

The Gentiles were not His people by covenant and therefore were without hope (Eph. 2:11). Yet, Paul affirms that God will restore Israel to Himself and will also extend mercy to the Gentiles (vv. 25-26). In fact, God would use believing and blessed Gentiles to provoke Israel to jealousy and draw them back to Himself (11:11). Jehovah would call a people His children who were not His people, and then He would rebuild the Jewish nation to become a beacon of divine truth among the nations (Amos 9:11-12). Thankfully, through Christ, all men can experience God personally.

In verse 30, the apostle returns to the questions that prompted his dialogue: "Is God unfair in His sovereign designs?" and "Did God's plan for Israel fail?" The answer to both questions is "No" – God is not unjust and Old Testament prophecy affirms that His plan for Israel has not failed. The reason that the Gentile believers were now receiving God's favor was because they had trusted in Christ for salvation and been declared righteous by God (v. 30). In contrast, Israel had rejected Christ and crucified Him, and sought to justify themselves through Law-keeping (vv. 31-32). This was a direct fulfillment of Psalm 118:22. The Jewish nation stumbled over Christ, the Rock of Offense, and the blessings that God had placed in their hands fell into the laps of the Gentiles who were not expecting it. Truly *"whoever believes on Him will not be put to shame."*

Mysterious are God's ways! How is it that He can incorporate both human submission and rebellion into His sovereign design, causing all events to bring about His glory? Before creation, God looked down the corridors of time, considered all the possible permutations of natural cause and effect as well as the future choices of cognitive beings, and made sovereign choices to bless humanity in time and to glorify His name throughout time and eternity. As only a triune God existed when the plan of redemption was devised, the plan is solely His – it originated in His mind and He deserves all the glory for it. God's choices ensure that humanity will receive the greatest possible blessing and that He will obtain the most glory as a result.

# Romans Chapter 10

### Israel's Failure Prompts Opportunity for All (vv. 1-13)

Having addressed God's dealing with Israel in the past, Paul speaks to the Jewish nation's present situation. About half of this chapter is composed of direct quotations from the Old Testament. The use of prophecy is to again prove that a sovereign God is not surprised or hindered by the poor spiritual condition of His covenant people.

Israel had zeal for God, but not according to revealed truth; the nation was ignorant of God's righteousness and, consequently, of their need to be declared righteous by Him (vv. 1-3). E. J. Young summarizes the reality of Israel's spiritual state: "Israel hated the holiness God had demanded"[14]; rather, they sought to establish their own righteousness before God through zealous Law-keeping and self-reckoned good works.

For centuries, the Jewish people had nonchalantly engaged in religious charades void of love and devotion; they practiced traditions and pious forms without even knowing that they were angering the Lord. Many professing Christ today continue this practice of identifying with Christ through religious rote without knowing Him personally as Savior (Matt. 7:21-23). Worship and service that pleases God must emerge from a willing heart that is illuminated by the Holy Spirit in accordance with revealed truth (John 4:24, 16:13). If what we say or do is neither true nor Spirit-led, it does not honor God; it is mere form, religious fanfare, and has no eternal value.

Paul then quotes Moses to show that receiving God's approval by faith in Christ rather than trying to earn a righteous standing by Law-keeping is not a new concept (v. 4). Even the Law-giver, Moses, stated that the righteousness of the Law could be achieved only if someone kept all the Law (v. 5). This was obviously an impossibility and was to cause Israel to realize their need for a Savior – that they could not save themselves.

Some search for the means to earn Heaven their entire lives, but God has made the message of salvation in Christ readily available to all (vv. 6-7). As we have already witnessed, creation demands a Creator, the human conscience instinctively reckons what is right and wrong, and the entirety of God's Word points mankind to God's Savior – Christ. There is the testimony of miracles and of radically changed lives, such as the life of Paul, which provides evidence of the validity of the gospel message. God is searching out man, to seek and to save the lost through revealed truth. Man does not need to explore the heights of Heaven or the depths of the abyss to find out how to please God. Those who truly search for the truth in order to know God will be readily met by a seeking Savior (Jer. 29:13).

To ensure that there would be no confusion on the matter, Paul again states what truth must be acted on in faith to receive a righteous standing before God in the Church Age: *"If you confess with your mouth the Lord Jesus and believe in your heart that God has raised Him from the dead, you will be saved"* (v. 9). Paul and Silas stated the matter this way: *"Believe on the Lord Jesus Christ, and you will be saved"* (Acts 16:31).

For Jesus Christ to be "Lord" means that He is not only alive (thus affirming His resurrection), but that He also has a position and rule over all things. This means that He is also God and deserves our loyalty, service and worship. Obviously, new converts do not fully understand what the Lordship of Christ means to them personally, but clearly true believers would never think that they could receive Christ as a Savior and reject Him as Lord. The Holy Spirit is responsible for convicting sinners of their sinful state and prompting them to believe God's Word concerning their need for a Savior (John 16:8; 1 Cor. 2:14, 12:3). Those who truly believe this truth in their hearts will gladly confess Christ with their mouths (v. 10).

Paul then cites both Isaiah (Isa. 49:23) and Joel (Joel 2:32) to affirm that anyone, Jew or Gentile, who calls upon the Lord Jesus Christ will be saved; those doing so will not be ashamed in God's presence (vv. 11-13). In verse 11, Paul slightly modifies Isaiah's words *"They shall not be ashamed who wait for Me"* to *"Whoever believes on Him will not be put to shame"* to ensure his Jewish audience understood that even Gentiles could be blessed by God in Christ also.

Like Peter on the day of Pentecost, Paul also quotes Joel's prophecy here to substantiate the gospel message's validity and power to transform the lives of all who believe it. The only explanation for Jewish believers speaking in different tongues (languages) on the day of Pentecost was the coming of the Holy Spirit to accomplish exactly what Joel said would happen when the Holy Spirit was poured out on those in Israel. This meant that a new age had come; a new opportunity now existed for all (Jews and Gentiles; v. 12) to call upon the name of the Lord to be saved (v. 13).

Clearly, some people in the world are exposed to more revelation of the truth than others, which then puts them under more accountability – this is why Israel was harshly judged by the Lord Jesus. But Paul was ensuring that his audience knew that during the Church Age, both Jews and Gentiles who called on the name of the Lord Jesus in faith would be saved!

Having acknowledged this truth, three questions are then posed to spur on worldwide evangelistic outreach ministry in verse 14: *"How shall they call on Him in whom they have not believed?" "How shall they believe in Him of whom they have not heard?" "How shall they hear without a preacher?"* Fred Stallan summarizes the meaning of these questions:

> "And how shall they believe in him of whom they have not heard?" The RV correctly deletes "of." The thrust of the verse is not hearing about the Lord but hearing Him, which no doubt means through the preachers. Christ speaks through His servants but if there is no preacher (Paul's third question), then the Lord is not heard. The original gives a participle here, "how shall they hear without one preaching?" The people depended on hearing the voice of God through preachers and if there was no one preaching then there was nothing for men and women to consider.[15]

Paul's main point in verse 14 is that no one can have the privilege of personally knowing the Savior without first hearing Him (through others sharing His Word) and then trusting in Him. Abel, Abraham, David, etc. were justified before God because they each obeyed the revelation God presented to them, yet they did not know Christ personally or what God would accomplish by Him. These Old Testament saints believed in the types of Christ without actually understanding the reality that each represented. No one can come to God but through the finished work of Christ (Acts 4:12), and no one can have the personal blessing of knowing and serving Christ without first understanding who He is and what He has done and continues to do. This necessitates the sending of believers throughout the world to inform all people groups about the "gospel of peace" (v. 15).

Nahum 1:15 is then quoted to indicate God's delight with those who will take the message of Christ worldwide. Because missionaries move their feet to go where Christ needs to be proclaimed, God considers them to have beautiful feet. Obviously, not everyone will heed their message (v. 16), but believers are not accountable to make the unregenerate believe their report; rather, they are to be witnesses for Christ (Acts 1:8). Witnesses share with others what they know to be true.

> Any method of evangelism will work, if God is in it.
>
> – Leonard Ravenhill

The Holy Spirit is the One responsible for working in the hearts of those who hear God's Word. Yet, an individual cannot repent and receive Christ as Savior without first understanding the Word of God, for *"faith comes by hearing, and hearing by the word of God"* (v. 17). It is absolutely necessary, then, for the lost to hear the gospel message to experience rebirth. But only the Holy Spirit can enlighten the unregenerate soul to the truth and power of the gospel message (1 Cor. 2:9-14).

> It is clear you don't like my way of doing evangelism. You raise some good points. Frankly, I sometimes do not like my way of doing evangelism. But I like my way of doing it better than your way of not doing it.
>
> – D. L. Moody

Thankfully, even in Paul's day, believers were proclaiming the gospel message of Jesus Christ throughout the Roman Empire and beyond (v. 18). No one would know God if He did not choose to reveal Himself, and God desires to show Himself to all who will pursue Him in true humility. Paul declares that in the Church Age, God is reaching out to the Gentiles (no longer to Israel primarily) through the worldwide proclamation of the gospel. God would empower and bless Gentile believers in such a way that Israel would be jealous over what they were missing by disbelief (v. 19).

Paul then quotes Isaiah (Isa. 65:1) to show how God was using the Gentiles to provoke the Jews to consider their present condition before the Lord: *"But Isaiah is very bold and says: 'I was found by those who did not seek Me; I was made manifest to those who did not ask for Me'"* (v. 20). W. E. Vine explains the Hebrew meaning of Isaiah 65:1 which permitted Paul to rightly apply the verse to the Gentiles:

> The original has the past tenses, as in the RV margin: "I was inquired of (or rather, I was discernible) by them that asked not for Me (i.e., who refused to turn to God and seek Him); I was found (to be found) by them that sought Me not." God was ever ready to reveal Himself, had there been a heart to approach Him in humble desire to walk in His ways.[16]

Sadly, God had stretched His hands out towards Israel, *"a disobedient and contrary people,"* for a long time, but they would not receive His offer to be justified in Christ to receive His blessing (v. 21). But all is not lost. As Paul explains in the next chapter, God will restore Israel to Himself and richly bless the Jewish nation in a coming day.

# Romans Chapter 11

### A Spiritual Jew Has Salvation in Christ (v. 1)

In this chapter, Paul will use the testimony of five witnesses to verify that God has a future plan for the Jewish nation of Israel: Paul himself (v. 1), Elijah (vv. 2-10), the Gentiles (vv. 11-15), Abraham (the root; vv. 16-24), and finally, God Himself (vv. 25-36).

God's unilateral and eternal covenant recorded in Genesis (35:10-12) pertains to Abraham's physical lineage. While the Church enjoys much blessing in Christ because of the Abrahamic covenant, the Church has no specific promise of land – Abraham's descendants through Isaac and Jacob do. For example, the prophet Ezekiel informs us that land allotments running north and south of the millennial temple in Jerusalem will be inherited by each Jewish tribe in the Kingdom Age (Ezek. 47:13-48:35). Thus, it is important to understand that the Bible speaks of two peoples descending from Abraham: a physical people or *seed* (the Jews) with the promise of physical blessings on earth, and a spiritual people or *seed* (the Church) with spiritual blessings secured in Heaven.

Paul acknowledged that he was physically born a Jew, *the seed of Abraham* (v. 1), but had become a spiritual child of Abraham by trusting in the gospel message of Jesus Christ. Paul had undergone spiritual birth. He had been justified in Christ and was enjoying the resurrection power and fellowship of Christ's life. The nation of Israel will not obtain this blessing until after the Church Age is complete and the Tribulation period draws to a close (vv. 25-27).

In the Church Age, all who follow Abraham's example of trusting in the divinely revealed truth of the gospel are called *"Abraham's seed"* (Gal. 3:26-29). Accordingly, Abraham is *"the father of all them that believe, though they be not circumcised"* (4:11). The Church is not the Jewish nation, but a spiritual body of Jews and Gentiles who have trusted the gospel message of Jesus Christ. As God promised Abraham, all families of the earth would be blessed in him (Gen. 12:3). This has been fulfilled because Christ, the Messiah, is a descendant of Abraham (Matt. 1:1-17). The nation of Israel, the physical seed of Abraham, and the spiritual seed of Abraham, those justified in Christ by faith, have different promises and blessings.

Acknowledging the rare enigma of a zealous Jew, a Pharisee of Pharisees, renouncing Judaism to be justified in Christ, Paul suggests his own salvation proves that God is not finished with the Jewish people (v. 1). Paul later informed Timothy that his own salvation was a preview of God's plan for the Jewish nation in the future (1 Tim. 1:16).

Reviewing Paul's conversion story recorded in Acts 9:1-6 illustrates Paul's meaning. Israel's future conversion at the end of the Tribulation period occurs when the remnant of Israel who survive the Tribulation see Christ's Second Advent to the earth (Zech. 12:10-13:1, 14:4; Rev. 1:7). Likewise, while on the road to Damacus, Paul actually saw Christ at his conversion. Paul's conversion pictures Israel's future acceptance of Christ as their Messiah, when He appears to rescue them from the Antichrist.

## God Reserves a Faithful Remnant in Israel (vv. 2-6)

Paul's second witness to show that God was not finished with Israel is Elijah. Elijah thought that all of his countrymen had strayed away from Jehovah and that he was the only true believer remaining in Israel (vv. 2-3). However, God informed him at Mount Sinai that He had maintained a pure remnant of 7,000 faithful Jews who had not committed idolatry (v. 4).

Paul then affirmed that God has always and will always maintain a remnant of faithful Jews until national restoration occurs (v. 5). During the Church Age, this Jewish remnant is composed of individual Jews who have received God's grace through trusting in Jesus Christ alone for salvation, not in their good works (v. 6). Humanized religion (doing good works to impress God) cannot be mixed with God's message of salvation by grace through faith in Christ alone (Eph. 2:8).

## Israel Set Aside, but Not Forever (vv. 7-12)

Only those Jews who trust Christ (i.e., the chosen or elect in Christ) obtain the goodness that God promised them through Abraham. As a nation, because they had ignored the pleading voice of God's Son, Israel has been given over to a state of spiritual blindness (v. 8) and darkness (v. 10) until God's work in redeeming Gentiles during the Church Age is finished (v. 25). This means that although individual Jews might come to Christ during the Church Age, the nation in general is marked by insensitivity and dullness to the spiritual truths necessary to understand to be saved. During this interim, God considers Israel as "fallen" (v. 11), "lost" (v. 12), and "cast away" (v. 15). Nationally speaking God has put them on the shelf, while He is wooing a largely Gentile Bride for His Son called the Church.

Paul quotes Psalm 69:22-23, to show that David foretold that Israel would initially reject their Messiah and that God would turn the table of blessing He set before them in Christ into *"a snare and a trap, a stumbling block and a recompense to them"* (v. 9). Because Israel stumbled over Christ, the Jewish nation would lose out on all the privileges and blessings that God purposed in Christ to give them.

However, Paul is quick to highlight three important points concerning Israel's future in verses 10-11: First, the Jewish nation had not fallen from God's favor forever. Second, through the failure of Israel, God brought salvation to the nations. Third, God would abundantly bless the Gentiles in Christ to make His covenant people jealous and draw them back to Himself. In fact, seeing how God keeps His promise to bless the Gentiles will cause the Jewish nation to yearn for God to keep His promise to restore and bless Israel too (9:25-26; Jer. 31:35-37)!

## Israel's Temporary Blindness Benefits the Gentiles (vv. 13-25)

Paul employs two analogies in Romans 11 to reveal God's plan to ultimately restore the Jewish nation and to also bless the Gentiles through the Abrahamic covenant: the lump of dough offering (v. 16), and the olive tree (vv. 16-25). The latter illustration also serves to warn Gentile believers to learn from God's dealing with the Jews and avoid repeating their mistakes (vv. 20-22; 1 Cor. 10:6, 11).

God's covenant with Abraham which promised blessing to all families of the earth is both the lump of dough and the root of the olive tree. When the first part of the dough was ceremonially offered to God, it symbolized that the entire lump belonged to the Lord (Num. 15:17-21). Similarly, when the priest waved the firstfruits sheaf before the Lord, it affirmed that the entire harvest to follow was also His (Lev. 23:9-14). Christ was the portion of dough offered to God, and through Him, all taking advantage of God's covenant with Abraham through faith are sanctified in Christ (Gal. 3:14).

Christ is also represented in the olive tree (Jer. 11:16-17) that draws up blessing from its root (i.e., God's covenant with Abraham). It would be natural for the blessings of the root to pass through the tree to nourish its branches (picturing the two houses of Israel and Judah), but these were cut off by disbelief. God then grafted in a wild olive tree, the Gentiles collectively speaking, to receive the blessings of Christ during the Church Age. Such grafting is an intervention in the natural growth of the tree which highlights the nature of the illustration. Later, God will graft the original branches back into the tree when the Jewish nation comes to faith after the conclusion of the Church Age, signaled by the Rapture of the Church. This also signals "the fullness of the Gentiles" (v. 25) which is the point in time when the last Gentile is saved through the gospel of the grace of God and when that gospel ceases to be preached. All the goodness God intends for us and Israel comes through Christ – our blessed Olive Tree.

"The times of the Gentiles" identified in Luke 21:20-24 and Revelation 11:1-2 should not be confused with "the fullness of the Gentiles" (v. 25). With respect to the relationship between Israel and "the times of the Gentiles,' the nation of Israel will not be restored to God until the latter part of the Tribulation period when the Gentiles overrun and control Jerusalem. Before the Kingdom Age commences, the Lord Jesus will descend to the earth to war against the Antichrist and his armies in the Megiddo Valley. His victory will deliver Jerusalem from the Antichrist's invading armies (Zech. 14). All those following the Antichrist will be immediately killed (Rev. 19:20-21). After the Battle of Armageddon, the nations will be gathered and judged (Matt. 13:47-50, 25:31-46). Those who did not take his mark will be allowed to enter Christ's kingdom on earth – this will conclude *"the time of the Gentiles."*

The national blindness referred to by Paul in this chapter will continue until the last Gentile believer is added to the Church; this will conclude the Church Age, *"the fullness of the Gentiles."* This term speaks of God's grace to the Gentiles, while "the times of the Gentiles" refers to the oppression of Israel by Gentiles. The latter began with Nebuchadnezzar's sacking of Jerusalem and Judah's deportation to Babylon in 605 B.C. and will conclude when Christ returns to establish His kingdom and fulfill all the promises of the Abrahamic Covenant as pertaining to Israel.

The analogy of the olive tree shows us that God will restore Israel to Himself. The fact that the Jews (the natural branches) could be, and indeed will be, grafted back into the olive tree indicates that the focus of the illustration is not eternal salvation per se, but rather the blessings that God desires to share with those who exercise faith in Him. Gentile believers (the wild tree) are a second benefactor of the New Covenant and thus are permitted to share in the blessing of the spiritual salvation promised to Israel (Eph. 2:11-3:7). Gentiles are grafted into the olive tree, indicating the blessings of Christ rooted in God's covenant with Abraham. The New Covenant permits individual Jews to be saved now and the Jewish nation to be reconciled to God after the Church Age ends.

Since Christ's rejection, the Jewish nation remains in spiritual blindness (v. 7) and cut off from the blessings God desired for them in Christ. If God so severely judged His covenant people (the natural branches) for their willful idolatry and wickedness, why would He hesitate to punish those who were not natural branches for the same offenses (the Gentiles; vv. 21-22)?

This is not a warning to individual Gentiles, but rather a rhetorical statement speaking of the Gentiles collectively (i.e., it is not the wild branches grafted into the good olive tree, but one wild tree). Paul is simply stating that if the Jewish majority rejected Christ and lost the blessing that God promised to Abraham's descendants, certainly the Gentiles who were merely a second benefactor of the spiritual blessings of the Abrahamic Covenant could more readily lose the same opportunity. The exhortation to the Gentiles is this: You should esteem the unusual opportunity God has bestowed upon you, remain humble before God, and faithful to Him. Whether Israel or Gentiles, willful sin and pride result in a loss of God's blessing to those He loves.

## Repentant Israel Will Be Saved by God's Deliverer (vv. 26-32)

Paul's last witness to testify of Israel's blessed future is the best of all, God Himself. Quoting what God spoke through the prophet Isaiah, the apostle affirms: First, God foretold and controls the timing of Israel's salvation (v. 25). Second, God made covenants and promises to Israel. Those promises which have been fulfilled prove that God will keep His Word pertaining to the remaining ones (vv. 26-28). Third, God cannot lie; His very nature ensures that He is providing accurate testimony of Israel's future restoration (v. 29). Fourth, God is a gracious and forgiving God, as past evidence shows (vv. 30-32).

While the Gentile nations are subject to the wrath of God in the Tribulation, a primary purpose of the Tribulation period is the advancement of God's program for Israel. Daniel's seventy-week prophecy paused (not abandoned) after sixty-nine weeks with the rejection by Israel of their Messiah in His first advent. The remaining week, which will be the seven years of the Tribulation is the recommencement of God's program for Israel and the outpouring of God's wrath is designed to discipline Israel to the point that she cries out to God for deliverance and believes in her Messiah in His Second Coming. Thus, Jews who survive the Tribulation will be gathered from throughout the earth (Ezek. 20:33-34; Matt. 24:31) to the wilderness of the people (Ezek. 20:35). There God will conduct business with the remnant. They will pass under the rod (Ezek. 20:37) before they can enter and possess the full extent of the land and blessings promised to Abraham (Ezek. 20:35-44).

As a result, Paul's grand conclusion is that "all Israel will be saved." We understand that Paul is speaking of "all believing Israel" – the future refined and restored Jewish nation. Verse 26 indicates that "all unbelieving Israel" will perish during the Tribulation period. This incredible plan to save Israel was destined to occur because *"the gifts and the calling of God are irrevocable"* (v. 29).

## God's Matchless Wisdom (vv. 33-36)

As Paul contemplates God's wisdom and longsuffering love to Israel and the grace He extends to undeserving Gentiles, he is moved to close the chapter with a doxology (vv. 33-36). God's judgments are unsearchable and His ways past finding out (v. 33). No created being can know the mind of God or offer Him counsel (v. 34). Nor is God indebted to any part of creation; His gifts are founded in grace; therefore, He is not obligated to show mercy to anyone (v. 35). Because all the wisdom, the knowledge, and the judgments of God are infallible and all things are under His control and for His glory, Paul had great hope for Israel's future in Christ (v. 36).

Paul poses another rhetorical question in verse 35, *"Or who has first given to Him and it shall be repaid to him?"* which he answers in verse 36. No one has ever put God in a situation where God is indebted to man or even needed man's assistance to accomplish His purposes. This is not to say that God is not unmindful to respond in grace to those who cheerfully give to Him as an expression of thankfulness for what they have received in grace (2 Cor. 9:7). But that is not Paul's point here. Rather, the apostle is declaring that God has never been dependent on any created being – no one has a position of equality with God. All creation is dependent upon Him; He is the Author, Originator, and Sustainer of all things which are for His glory – end of story! This means that God is never surprised by anything and that there is no possibility that God will lose control of any part of His creation.

All these high contemplations of God caused Paul to close the chapter with lofty praise. Who but God could have ever devised such a just and merciful plan to transform rebels into redeemed and rewarded worshippers? Although the world is a dark place, the believer's future in Christ is very bright, for nothing can separate us from the love of God in Christ (8:35-39).

Fred Stallan observes that verse 35 contains the third of Paul's four doxologies in the Epistle. The third doxology pertains to Israel's preservation: "Having considered God's ways with Israel and the future He has in store for that nation, Paul records here, *'For of him, and through him, and to him, are all things: to whom be glory forever. Amen.'*"[17]

Verses 33-36 represent the climax of the Epistle! In the next chapter, the apostle descends from this mountaintop view of God's sovereignty in action to the plain of human obligation. Realizing all that God has accomplished on our behalf, how should we live to please Him? The remainder of the Epistle is full of practical helps to assist believers to do just that.

# Romans Chapter 12

## Unwavering Dedication and Service to God (vv. 1-2)

Considering the matchless wisdom and mercies of God just mentioned and all that He secured in Christ on the believer's behalf, the apostle begs those at Rome to live acceptably before God as consecrated priests (v. 1). Each Christian is a believer-priest and is called on to be a continual, living sacrifice to God. Through the power of the Holy Spirit, this may be accomplished in various ways: rejecting the desires of the flesh that are beyond God's will (8:13), offering up praise to God (Heb. 13:15), supporting the Lord's work through gifts (1 Cor. 16:2), and frequently remembering the Lord Jesus by observing the Lord's Supper (1 Cor. 11:22-33). Above all, the fragrant aroma of Christ's character is to be evident in all that we do (2 Cor. 2:14).

The Greek word rendered "present" in verse 1 is translated in the same way in Romans 6:13. Both verses speak of the believer's ability to be a living sacrifice – "to offer up" to God what is pleasing to Him. To do what God wants us to do means that we have to say "no" to what we want; in other words, it costs us something to give to God what pleases Him. This is what it means to offer up to God an acceptable sacrifice, and it is our priestly duty.

Additionally, Paul suggests that one of the ways that believers worship the Lord is to reject the world's philosophies and attractions by renewing our minds on what is true and spiritual (v. 2). This is accomplished by yielding to God's Word to avoid conformity to the world. Worldliness is a system of values which excludes Christ's authority and ignores God's standards of wholesomeness.

In this chapter, Paul addresses how believer-priests representing God on earth are to express love to God by service (vv. 1-8) and how priests are to express His love to other believers (vv. 9-16) and to the lost (vv. 17-21).

## Spiritually-Enabled Priestly Service (vv. 3-8)

Speaking through the grace that was given to him as an apostle, Paul reminds his audience that there is nothing in the gospel message that makes them superior to anyone else (v. 3). Christ is the Head of the Body and all believers have equal status within the Body, though not the same calling, gift, or giftedness. Understanding this should cause believers to behave appropriately in desiring to serve Christ by using their spiritual gift(s).

This means that no believer is to have an exaggerated idea concerning his or her importance in the Body or the application of his or her spiritual gift in the Body of Christ. A spirit of humility is necessary for the Holy Spirit to enable believers to use their abilities and spiritual gifts in a way that will benefit the Church. Believers who exaggerate the benefit of their gifts and diminish the importance of other gifts do not understand the reason God gives spiritual gifts – to build up the Body of Christ, not to induce pride. Each believer is a unique trophy of God's grace and each believer has a unique function in the Body of Christ to perform. Everyone is needed for the work of ministry of building up the Body (Eph. 4:12).

Additionally, there is no room for being envious of other saints' spiritual gifts or giftedness. God chooses the calling of each believer in the Body and then equips him or her to fulfill their assigned ministry (v. 6; 1 Cor. 12:11). Believers who ignore their place in the Body of Christ and pursue ministry that they are not equipped for will do more damage than good – it is only what God energizes that will benefit the Church. Hence, believers are to use spiritual discernment in the application of their gift(s). If you receive joy in a particular ministry and others are clearly blessed by it, then continue doing what God is blessing. However, if what you are doing is drudgery and there appears to be no benefit to anyone, then seek the Lord on the matter. Obtain godly counsel, pray for wisdom, and wait until the Lord reveals a different type of ministry to explore. We must rely on God's wisdom and grace, and then by faith draw upon the full measure of strength He supplies.

The human body has many unique *members* (i.e., organs and functional parts) that depend on each other for the welfare of the entire body. Similarly, the Body of Christ also has many unique members with important roles to be performed if the Church is to function as Christ desires it to (vv. 4-6). Only when all believers are in fellowship with the Lord and enabled by the Holy Spirit to use their spiritual gifts in full measure that God gives will the Church profoundly represent Christ in the world. We need each other and each other's abilities in the Body. Paul describes seven spiritual gifts which equip believers to fulfill their priestly ministry (vv. 6-8).

*Prophesying* (v. 6) has several meanings: to speak with divine inspiration, which may include foretelling future events, or simply to utter divine truth that has already been revealed through God's written Word. In the apostolic age, prior to the canonization of Scripture, God spoke directly through the apostles and prophets to convey truth to His people. Today we understand that a modern-day "prophet" would be *forthtelling* truth and not *foretelling* the future (1 Cor. 13:8-10). God's prophets were rarely tactful or soft-spoken mouthpieces for God; rather they were forthright and no-nonsense. Prophets keenly felt God's anger when His character had been affronted by His wayward people and that displeasure was reflected in their ministry. Today, the gift of prophecy might be evident when an individual, having properly discerned the spiritual disparity between the Church's behavior and God's Word, bluntly sets the matter straight.

Paul speaks of two more spiritual gifts bestowed in grace to believers in verse 7: *ministry* (or serving) and *teaching*. Those with the gift of ministry were to focus on what God had called them to do; likewise, those given a teaching gift were to be diligent in using it.

God gives to some believers a servant's heart. Observation finds two broad variations of this gift, *helps* and *service*. Believers with the gift of *helps* will be people-oriented; they enjoy rubbing shoulders with others as they serve. Not only do these saints get things done for others in need, but they also provide an emotional component that is therapeutic for the soul. Other believers are more focused on getting things done that need to be done, without human interaction. They are happy to clean the church building or paint someone's house, even when no one else is nearby. These saints are task-driven, where the former are people-driven; both these aspects of ministry in the Body are much needed.

It should be understood that the title "minister" is not biblically applied to those in church leadership; in fact, the term is applied in a variety of ways in the New Testament: it is spoken of as a spiritual gift (v. 7), and is applied to those in civil authority (13:1-4), to different believers as they serve Christ in various capacities (1 Cor. 3:5, 4:1; 2 Cor. 6:4, 11:15) and to Christ, who is a minister of the truth to the Jews (15:8). It is never used as a title before a proper name anywhere in Scripture. In summary, every believer is a minister and should function in the Body of Christ according to the ministry he or she has been called by the Lord to do.

A teacher is able to rightly discern the meaning of Scripture and then is able to effectively explain and apply it for the benefit of his or her audience. The priest Ezra was a scribe, an instructor of the Law. His passion as a teacher is recorded in Ezra 7:10: *"Ezra had prepared his heart to seek the Law of the Lord, and to do it, and to teach statutes and ordinances in Israel."* Ezra spent time in God's Word to understand it. He obeyed what he knew to be true, and he desired others to know God's Word also. Effective teachers do what they teach others to do.

The apostle identifies four more gifts in verse 8: *exhortation, giving, administration*, and *mercy*. God knows that we need both encouragers (like Barnabas) and exhorters in our lives. The Greek verb *protrepomai* is rendered "encouraged" in Acts 18:27 (RV): *"The brethren encouraged him [Apollos]."* The first portion of this word, *protrepo,* literally implies "to urge forward." When God's people do well, especially in areas in which they tend to struggle, believers should add energy to the right behavior with praise and encouragement in order to reinforce it.

Encouragement is not the same thing as *exhortation*, the gift Paul identifies in verse 8. Believers need constant exhortation to serve the Lord properly: *"Exhort one another daily"* (Heb. 3:13). "To exhort" is translated from the Greek word *parakaleo*, which means "to call near and invoke." If a believer has lost his direction, those with maturity are to draw near in love and redirect his path. We are to literally "come alongside and turn." Exhortation is for small course changes, whereas admonishing and rebuke are for correcting more serious matters of foolishness and sin, respectively. Exhortation is most effective when the receiver knows that the exhorter loves them. Genuine love for another removes the opportunity for jealously and pride to interfere with profitable exhortation.

The spiritual gift of *giving* provides astute perception of those in need, how to best supply those needs, and a compassionate burden to do so. People with this gift joyfully and liberally offer what they have, often beyond their means to alleviate someone's lack or to support a ministry.

The spiritual gift of *administration* enables individuals to organize people and activities in such a way that an efficient, orderly, and effective outcome is realized. These gifted organizers have a special knack for getting things done and getting the most out of the time they have.

Those with the spiritual gift of *mercy* have a God-given ability to aid and comfort those in distress. While this may include meeting a distressed person's necessities, mercy supplies a cheerful component that settles one's anxiety and infuses hope for the future: "All is not lost…you will get through this…I will do whatever I can to help you through this trial."

God distributes differing spiritual gifts according to His will and then gives us whatever strength and ability is needed to use what He has given. As believer-priests properly use the spiritual gifts they have received, a testimony of God's grace is made available for all to witness (1 Pet. 4:10).

## Love Without Hypocrisy Within the Church (vv. 9-16)

Perhaps one of the most neglected ministries within the Church is genuine hospitality (vv. 9-13). Some believers decline to use their homes in ministry because they do not believe they have the ability to do so. Others set their expectation so high they feel inadequate. Yet, there is nothing in Scripture that suggests that hospitality is a specific spiritual gift per se, or that there is some standard to which we must comply. Hence, Peter exhorts his audience *"to use hospitality one to another without grudging"* (1 Pet. 4:9). Every believer should be given to hospitality. The home is a lovely setting in which to console the grieving, refresh the weary, exhort the erring, and reach the lost with the gospel. It is a means of showing honor, respect, appreciation, and kind affection to one another.

Our English word "hospitality" is translated from the Greek noun *philoxenos* or verb *philonexia*, which together only occur five times in the New Testament. Hospitality literally means to be "fond of strangers" (or guests). Paul, John, and Peter urge their audiences to engage in hospitality and also identified hospitality as an act of genuine love towards others.

This is why Paul exhorts the believers at Rome to: *"Love without hypocrisy... [be] given to hospitality"* (vv. 9, 13). Thankfully, God's love towards us is not hypocritical; He has intimates, but no favorites (Acts 10:34). Consequently, James warns *"if you show partiality, you commit sin"* (Jas. 2:9). Hospitality is a means for enhancing Christian fellowship, especially toward those with whom you may feel uncomfortable or with whom you are not prone to interact. We are not to be respecters of persons but are to attempt to have profitable love-relationships with those believers with whom we are associated. This means giving preference to other believers by voicing our appreciation, engaging in genuine acts of charity, and joyfully praying for them (vv. 10-13).

In verses 14-16, Paul exhorts believers as to how they should consider and treat each other. Having the same mind does not mean that all believers are to think alike, but that we should have the mind of Christ (v. 16; Phil. 2:1-5). This type of thinking is not being proud of my opinions and doings, but rather elevates the interests of others above our own and sees the good of the Body as a higher objective than personal gain. Our fallen nature craves the pampered life and the recognition of others, but Paul says to associate with the humble and do not seek high status. This is how Christ lived while on the earth and expects us to live during our sojourn also.

Our tendency is to rub shoulders with those of status, those who are well-to-do and to snub those of humble estate. We tend to avoid identifying and associating with those who are burdened, persecuted, and suffering. But all believers are one in Christ; we all are members of His Body, of His Church, and we are His Bride. When one member of the Body suffers – all its members suffer. This spiritual reality must compel us to have the same care for one another that Christ would have for us (1 Cor. 12:25-26). Indeed, we are to weep with those who weep, bless those who persecute, and rejoice with those who rejoice.

## Overcoming Evil With Good (vv. 17-21)

Having addressed how believer-priests should behave towards fellow believers, the apostle now gives instruction on how believers should interact with the lost. In short, Paul says that believers should uphold "good things" (i.e., what God considers to be righteous) in all that they do and live peacefully with all men as much as is possible (vv. 17-18). This means that Christians are not to return "evil for evil" or hold grudges against those who have wronged them. Repaying evil for evil is the way of the world, but if believers want the unregenerate to search beyond this world for answers, they must see behavior that is out of this world.

Moses also reminded the Israelites, before they entered the Promised Land, that vengeance and recompense for wrongdoing was the Lord's business (Deut. 32:35). Paul quotes Moses' command in verse 19, but then adds further instructions for believers in the Church Age. Christians have the indwelling Holy Spirit and are commanded to fulfill the greater intention of the Law – to love selflessly (13:8-10). Recognizing God's righteous standard is the focus of keeping the Law, but demonstrating His irresistible love in righteousness is paramount in fulfilling the Law – and this we must do to win the lost to Christ!

Christians, therefore, should more fervently desire to pluck lost souls out of hellfire than they desire to get even for wrong done to them. Paul exhorts us to show the love of God to those who oppress us, even giving our enemies food and drink if they are hungry and thirsty. In so doing we heap coals of fire on their heads, so to speak (v. 20). William MacDonald explains Paul's idiom: "If the live coal treatment seems cruel, it is because this idiomatic expression is not properly understood. To heap live coals on a person's head means to make him ashamed of his hostility by surprising him with unconventional kindness."[18]

The "heap coals of fire" expression may refer to the ancient Egyptian custom of carrying coals of fire in a vessel on one's head as an expression of kindness to a neighbor that one desired to be reconciled with. Starting household fires for cooking and heat was problematic in those days, so a gift of burning coals was a gesture of goodwill. In a coming day, the Lord will set right all that has been wrong. Until then, may we endeavor to show love when we've been wronged that the lost might recognize that there is something beyond just being right.

# Romans Chapter 13

### The Christian and Government (vv. 1-7)

Shifting from how believers should behave towards the unregenerate, Paul now speaks to how Christians should relate to civil authorities: *"Let every soul be subject to the governing authorities. For there is no authority except from God, and the authorities that exist are appointed by God"* (v. 1). God instituted human government in the days of Noah to teach humanity submission to His authority. Accordingly, when those who are representing Him become corrupt, His retribution is severe because His character has been blasphemed (e.g., Ezek. 34:16-22).

No authority exists unless God permits it; therefore, disobedience to home (Gen. 3:16), civil (Gen. 9:1-17), and church (Heb. 13:17) authority is rebellion against God's rule. The only exception to this would be if the authority over us is acting contrary to God's revealed mandates. At such times we should obey God and willingly suffer the consequences for doing so (e.g., Acts 4:19-20, 5:29). The fear of God's judgment is a sobering deterrent against defying those who represent Him, who are being used by Him to teach us submission and to bless us.

To summarize, there are only two authority structures in the world: God's and Satan's, and they stand completely opposed to one another. After Lucifer rebelled against God (Isa. 14:12-15), he injected his own proud and selfish spirit into the world (1 Jn. 2:16). This independent thinking and rebel spirit then caused humanity to fall. God's authority is supreme, while Satan's authority is tolerated within boundaries, until God's purposes have been served. God allows Satan to test man's moral resolve. Thus, we honor God by obeying those He has placed in authority over us; compliance is rendered to win not the esteem of men, but the approval of God.

Whether it is home, civil, or church authority, no divinely instituted form of government is perfect on this side of Christ's rule in the Kingdom Age. Regardless, we are accountable to God to obey those in authority over us (if they are not disobeying God) or be judged by Him (v. 2). Sometimes, this authority becomes corrupt, but as much as possible we are "to salute the uniform" so to speak and not the person or establishment that may be wearing the uniform dishonorably.

Those representing God's authority in government are to uphold His righteousness in executing their responsibilities (v. 3). This means that we do not need to fear God's ministers if we do well; rather, we will have their praise. But if we engage in evildoings, then His ministers are to execute judgment to right the wrong (v. 4). Believer-priests would do well to ask themselves if they are attempting to undermine or side-step God's authority in any way. Service for God must be carried out within His authority structures. The flesh nature despises authority – it wants its own way. The flesh does not want to be ruled by anyone – it is rebellious in nature. God's power and blessing can only be conferred through personal submission and obedience to His authority.

The centurion in Matthew 8:5-13 understood this truth. After thinking about the authority that was over him, which gave him authority over others, he understood that the Lord Jesus was also under authority and thus had God's authority to bless others. Consequently, the one in authority did not need to be present to serve others. Likewise, God's power can be known in a personal way only by submitting to His authority in our lives – only then will we be able to bless others.

In verse 5, Paul suggests two reasons for obeying the authority that God has placed over us. First, those who resist God-established authority resist the One who originated it (v. 2). Second, our conscience tells us that we should obey God's authority over us (1 Tim. 1:5). Just as children instinctively know that it is proper to submit to the authority of their parents, we all know that it is appropriate to submit to the church elders and civil officials that He has placed over us. Those in positions of authority are ideally God's ministers for accomplishing good and promoting justice. For this reason, we are to render to them reasonable financial support for their service (i.e., pay our taxes) and respect them as being under God's authority (vv. 6-7).

## Love Fulfills the Law (vv. 8-10)

Having addressed the relationship of believers to governing authorities, Paul provides further help in how to show God's love to one's fellow-man – your neighbor, so to speak. The Christians in Rome were instructed to *"Owe no one anything except to love one another, for he who loves another has fulfilled the law"* (v. 8). Some godly servants, such as Hudson Taylor serving the Lord in China and the renowned preacher Charles Spurgeon, took this verse to mean that they should remain, financially speaking, debt-free.

Personal conviction pertaining to this command will vary, but clearly believers are to pay all their debts and as soon as they are due. This means that Christians must choose a lifestyle that permits them to live within their means and be diligent to maintain that course of action when tempted to do otherwise. Much debt occurs because of a lack of self-denial. There may be reasons where securing a loan is a necessity, but indebtedness should not characterize the believer's livelihood.

While this idea is a good personal application of the passage, Paul's admonition more fully focuses on the spiritual matter of believers delighting God's heart by fulfilling the Law. But what is the difference between the phrases *keeping the Law* and *fulfilling the Law*?

Previously, the apostle informed his audience that the purpose of the Mosaic Law was to show that man was sinful and needed a Savior – Christ (3:20-25). If someone stole something, it proved that he or she could not "keep" the law and was guilty before God. The law declares God's holiness and man's depraved state. But once the Holy Spirit indwells a believer, he or she becomes able to "fulfill" the law. When one chooses not to steal, that is keeping the law; but fulfilling the law is not just *not stealing* from another – it is *giving to* that person. When one chooses not to commit adultery, that is keeping the law; but fulfilling the law is not just *not committing adultery* with another's spouse – it is *giving to* that marriage relationship so it can thrive. This type of righteous and selfless giving expresses God's love and we are indebted to God to share His love with others. F. B. Hole puts the matter this way:

> Verse 8 extends the thought, of rendering what is due, far beyond governments to all men. The Christian is to be free of all debt, except the debt of love. *That* he can never fully pay. The object of infinite love himself, his attitude is to be love in this unloving world. In so doing he fulfills the law though he is not put under it, as we saw so clearly in chapter 6.[19]

God's holiness is reflected in *keeping the law*, but His gracious character is represented in *fulfilling the law*. Through the power of the Holy Spirit, the believer conveys the love of God to others in a supernatural way. It is not natural to love our enemies, to do good to those who persecute us, to bless those who curse us, or to withhold vengeance when it is just. Only by the power of the Holy Spirit in our lives are we able to demonstrate the love of God in such ways. This is how you love your neighbor as yourself – *"love is the fulfillment of the Law"* (v. 10).

## Cast Off Evil Works and Put on Christ (vv. 11-14)

This chapter concludes with an exhortation to holy living. Believers are to awake from spiritual slumber by putting off works of darkness such as drunkenness, lewdness, strife, lusting, envy, and by putting on Christ to reflect His light (i.e., the righteousness of His character; vv. 11-13). What is the motivation for this behavioral change? Paul says, *"for our salvation is nearer than when we first believed"* (v. 11). Obviously, Paul was already a believer when he wrote this epistle, so if our salvation is received by trusting in Christ as our Savior, then what is verse 11 talking about?

Glorification occurs at the Rapture of the Church; this is when the believer's body will be transformed into a Christ-like body and be saved from the presence of sin. An individual's soul is eternally saved when he or she trusts the gospel message; however, his or her body will be eternally saved (made holy and immortal) at Christ's return (1 Cor. 15:51-52). As John notes, living each and every day as if the Lord is returning for His Church has a purifying effect on our behavior (1 Jn. 3:2-3). No true believer wants to be indulging in sin or lusting after what is abhorrent to Christ when He suddenly appears to take His Church home to Heaven.

Hence, Paul concludes that believer-priests must, *"Put on the Lord Jesus Christ, and make no provision for the flesh, to fulfill its lusts"* (v. 14). Levitical priests were given the skins of the animals they sacrificed to make clothes to wear for daily life (Lev. 7:8). A priest leaving the tabernacle would have been wearing the skin of the sacrifice – thus not the priest, but the means of his atonement was being publicly displayed.

Similarly, our position of righteousness secured by God's sacrifice for sin should cause us to, practically speaking, "shine out" Christ during daily priestly service to Him. In our day-to-day life, others should not see us, but the "sacrifice" – the glory of the Lord Jesus. The inherent beauty of the bride of Christ in Revelation 19:7-9 is the glory of Christ seen in the bride. Not only does she have a position of righteousness, but the works of righteousness Christ has done through her are spectacular and these will radiate the glory of Christ forever!

> Man's thought is always of the punishment that will come to him if he sins. God's thought is always of the glory man will miss if he sins. God's purpose for redemption is glory, glory, glory!
>
> – Watchman Nee

# Romans Chapter 14

## Christian Liberty and Handling Debatable Things (vv. 1-9)

In contrast to the Mosaic Law, the Church has been given few commandments to obey. Through the new covenant established by Christ's blood we live in *the Age of Grace*. God allows us much freedom in working out the questionable things of our salvation (Phil. 2:12). God knows that love is a better motive to inspire service to Him than the fear of judgment alone (1 Jn. 4:18).

Interestingly, the Lord Jesus taught more often about what was wise and foolish than concerning what was blatantly right and wrong. It is obviously wise to do what God requires us to do and to abstain from what He forbids; doing otherwise would be foolish. Christian liberty, however, pertains to the realm of debatable things and personal preferences, not to issues of evil or sin. Accordingly, Paul exhorts us to not judge one another in matters of liberty, but *"let every man be fully persuaded in his own mind"* (v. 5), *"for whatever is not of faith is sin"* (v. 23).

In verses 1-3, Paul provides three principles that should guide our liberty (i.e., our freedom in Christ) in relationship to others. First, we are to accept those weaker in the faith. This means that we will not burden them with quarrels about areas of Christian liberty. It is not profitable to persuade those young in the faith into a particular way of thinking about questionable matters before they have the maturity and time to work through the matter before the Lord themselves.

Second, we are to forbear with each other in the realm of Christian liberty. We realize that godly believers will not think the same way on questionable matters and we are willing to accept these non-doctrinal differences with patience and tolerance to ensure that Body life is not needlessly impacted negatively.

Third, Paul reminds us that only a master judges his own servants. Servants have no authority to judge one another. Our Master is quite capable of judging the motives and convictions of all who are His! Believers undermine the authority of their Master (Christ) when they seize the role which He alone has been given by His Father (John 5:22).

Hence, a warning is given in verse 4 to servants judging other servants on questionable things. Only Christ is worthy and able to properly judge His servants. Only He knows the motivation of His servants and the value of their service. Therefore, believers should heed scriptural limitations in judging others. Our tendency is to be critical, and it is doubtful that any servant of the Lord would successfully pass our biased scrutiny (v. 10).

With this said, clearly there are some matters that believers must judge in order to diminish the influence of sin among God's people. For example, we are permitted to judge those identifying with Christ who are committing immoral acts (1 Cor. 5) or embracing false doctrine (2 Thess. 3:6, 14). Judgments must be rendered in such cases to encourage those in sin to repent and to limit the influence of their sin on others. Hence, those walking with the Lord are to have no fellowship with those who are not (1 Cor. 5:11, 15:33). If an individual is out of fellowship with the Lord, it is impossible for that person to enjoy Christ's fellowship with other Christians.

However, there are other aspects pertaining to those professing Christ that believers are not to judge because only the Lord knows the integrity of the heart. We are not to judge in the area of liberty (v. 3). This speaks of questionable activities not specifically prohibited by Scripture, which permits believers to have differing opinions on what is acceptable conduct. The motives of others are not to be judged (Matt. 7:1-5), nor the effectiveness of their ministry (1 Cor. 4:1-4). Paul knew that the flesh was biased, and, therefore, he did not even judge the value of his own ministry; this is the Lord's responsibility. Lastly, we are not to judge the salvation of others, though there may be reason to be concerned for their souls. Only the Lord knows who are truly His (John 5:21-24). We do not know what resides in the hearts of others, but the Lord does, which means that only He can render accurate judgment in these matters.

Paul also forbade Christians from legislating special days, feast days, or Sabbaths and then forcing their personal convictions on others (v. 6; Col. 2:16). Rather Paul says, *"Let every man be fully persuaded in his own mind"* about such things (v. 5). Let us remember that Scripture endorses only one special day for the Church to regard; everything else originated with man. The early Church dedicated the first day of the week for corporate worship and service (Acts 20:7). Moreover, it is wise to rest the body one day out of seven, which follows the pattern exemplified by God in the first workweek (Gen. 2:1-3). In the Church Age, there are no biblical holidays to observe. In fact, most of the traditional holidays that believers are absorbed with today are rooted in heathen practices and regrettably distract from honoring the Lord Jesus as He has requested in Scripture.

Christians are to judge the behavior and doctrine of other professing

Christians, but we are not to judge fellow believers in the areas of personal liberty, nor their motivation for or profitability of ministry, or whether they are actually saved; only the Lord knows the genuineness of their faith. Jesus Christ bought us with a great price, His own blood, and was raised from the dead to share His life with us (v. 9). Hence, believers are dead to self; they are not to be driven by human traditions or selfish desires, or to issue egocentric judgments of others, but rather to behave in such a way that pleases their Savior, Jesus Christ: *"If we live, we live to the Lord; and if we die, we die to the Lord...we are the Lord's"* (vv. 7-8).

## The Believer's Works Will Be Judged by Christ (vv. 10-12)

Paul quotes Isaiah 45:23 in verse 11 to show that everyone, saved and lost, will answer to God (v. 12). To honor His Son, God the Father will permit the Lord Jesus Christ to perform this judicial duty in a coming day (John 5:27). The Lord Jesus will pay a fair wage to those who reject His salvation, but unfortunately, the wages of sin is death (Rom. 6:23) – eternal separation from God in the Lake of Fire. This condemnation will ultimately occur at the Great White Throne judgment (Rev. 20). The godly preacher, Robert Murray McCheyne, was passing out gospel tracts one day and handed one to a well-dressed lady. She gave him a snooty look and said, "Sir, you must not know who I am!" The kind McCheyne replied, "Madam, there is coming a day of judgment, and on that day, it will not make any difference who you are!"[20]

Besides judging the wicked, the Lord will also reward believers for serving Him faithfully in accordance to revealed truth, rather than by obeying the traditions of men (10:2-3). Paul affirms that every believer will stand before the Lord to give an account of how he or she lived for Him (v. 10). This is called the *Judgment Seat of Christ*. As every believer stands before the Lord Jesus to be examined, we will realize that it is not what we have done for Christ that matters as much as why and how we served Him.

The *Judgment Seat of Christ* is not a judgment of salvation, but one of works. Good works will be amply rewarded and everything else will be burned up and we will be glad to see it go (1 Cor. 3:11-15)! What was done in truth for Christ (1 Cor. 3:11), done willingly (1 Cor. 9:17), done for the Lord with right motives (Col. 3:23-25), while not seeking the praise of others (Matt. 6:1-5) will be rewarded. The *Judgment Seat of Christ* occurs immediately after the Church is raptured into Heaven (1 Thess. 4:17). The Lord will have His reward with Him when He returns to the air for His Church (Rev. 22:12). In John's vision of things to come, we find the twenty-four elders (representing the redeemed from the earth) on thrones and wearing crowns (having already been rewarded for faithful service) before God's throne in Heaven (Rev. 4:4).

The *Judgment Seat of Christ* is also referred to as *the Day of Christ*, or *the Day of the Lord Jesus* which believers are to long for (1 Cor. 1:8, 5:5; Phil 1:6, 10, 2:16). *The Day of Christ* is not to be confused with *the Day of the Lord*, an Old Testament term that speaks of divine judgment on the earth and is used in the New Testament to speak of the Tribulation period through the millennial reign of Christ, the destruction of the earth, and the Great White Throne Judgment (1 Thess. 5:1-11; 2 Pet. 3:10). Paul clarifies both terms in 2 Thessalonians 2:1-10.

## Liberty in Christ at Work (vv. 13-23)

As believers, it is often difficult to work out the *gray* areas of our liberty. This may be a permissible activity, but is it wise for me to engage in it? The tenor of the Testaments is quite different on this subject. The Old Testament contained hundreds of laws that could never be fully obeyed, for the purpose of showing sin (Gal. 3:10-12, 24). In the New Testament, grace reigns on behalf of the believer; hence there are very few "dos and don'ts" levied. God desires that love and not fear would motivate our service to Him (1 Jn. 4:18).

Christian liberty is freedom from sin, not freedom to sin.

– A. W. Tozer

Obviously, what God says to do, we should do, and what God says that we should not do, we should avoid doing. But, what about all those facets of living in which Scripture is silent? The Lord desires us to work out our salvation (i.e., sanctified living) with fear and trembling before Him (Phil. 2:12). He desires us to be holy priests. The task then is to reduce the gray area of our liberty into appropriate personal conduct that neither offends our conscience or the edicts of Scripture and yields to the counsel, warnings, guidelines, and lessons learned (the failures of others) as preserved in Scripture. The believer is not to live in a fog of unclear notions, but to become fully persuaded in his or her mind as to what behavior is wise and what is foolish (vv. 14, 22-23).

To this end, Paul provides a number of good principles in the remaining verses of this chapter to guide believers in questionable matters. These are posed as questions to ask ourselves to determine whether or not we should engage in some debatable activity.

- Will this activity stumble a weaker brother in the Lord (vv. 13, 20-21)?

- Will this activity unnecessarily cause a lack of peace (v. 19a)?

- Will this activity promote the spiritual growth of other believers (v. 19b)?

- Do I have complete faith that this activity is permissible (vv. 22-23)?

Paul's main point in this section is service to Christ that is acceptable to God. Hence the apostle reminds his audience that *"The kingdom of God is not eating and drinking, but righteousness and peace and joy in the Holy Spirit"* (v. 17). Believers who serve Christ in these things will have God's approval and that of men also (v. 18). The evangelist Charles Stanley writes:

> If God reigns in our hearts, there will be consistency, that which is consistent with the holy position we are in. *"Let us therefore follow after the things that make for peace, and things wherewith one may edify another"* (v. 19). This will lead us to do nothing, whether in eating flesh or drinking wine, whereby a brother may be stumbled (vv. 20-21). This must not, however, lead us to compromise the gospel. Had Paul also refused to eat with the Gentiles lest he should offend Peter, that would not have been for edification, but would have compromised the gospel.[21]

Christians are not to dabble in debatable activities which will promote disunity and strife, or stir inappropriate passions, or have the appearance of evil. Rather, we are to endeavor to maintain peace with others as much as possible in peaceful, joyful, and righteous harmony with the Holy Spirit.

It may be technically permissible for me to walk across the kitchen floor wearing muddy boots, but it certainly will not make for peace with my wife. It may be permissible for me to drink a glass of wine, but to do so in front of a newly saved alcoholic only serves to plant doubts in his or her mind about my own maturity and my actions may cause him or her to resume a behavior that could lead them back into addiction and misery. Only the Holy Spirit can create an atmosphere of peace and unity in a Christian home or in a gathering of God's people, but we are to work hard to keep intact what the Holy Spirit has labored to achieve (Eph. 4:3).

# Romans Chapter 15

## Christian Liberty Should Benefit Others (vv. 1-3)

The opening three verses of this chapter provide a summary of Paul's instructions and exhortations posed in the previous chapter. Those mature in the Christian faith should sacrifice their liberty so as to not stumble those younger in the faith (v. 1). The mature should behave in a way that would edify the weak as they develop and grow in their faith (v. 2). Mature saints who have settled their liberty in matters where Scripture is indifferent should be willing to absorb the objections of weaker brethren and patiently assist them to grow in Christ. This attitude follows the example of Christ, who came to earth not to please Himself, but to suffer in our place and be a ransom for us (v. 3). The Lord Jesus never complained about sacrificing Himself on our behalf. Likewise, we should not complain about sacrificing our liberty in Christ for the good of those He loves.

## Jews and Gentiles Are One in Christ (vv. 4-7)

Paul informs his audience that Old Testament Scripture has been preserved so that believers in the Church Age might learn to hope in God through experiencing the patience and comfort found in His Word (v. 4).

Throughout much of Israel's biblical history, we find only brief periods in which the entire nation was benefitting from God's presence among them. The conquest of Canaan, under Joshua's leadership, and the reigns of King David and King Solomon are a few of these special times of blessing and prosperity. However, most of Israel's history is marred by spiritual complacency, or idolatry and carnality, such that God's presence was not enjoyed by His people.

But God loved His covenant people too much to allow them to go their own way, so He chastened them to make them realize that they would never be happier or more prosperous than remaining in communion with Him. These eras of discipline caused much misery, and even resulted in the dispersion and death of many Jews. Paul did not want the Church of Jesus Christ to repeat Israel's past mistakes! Believers must remain near to Christ, remain like-minded and unified in Him to effectively represent Him to a lost world (v. 5). The oneness of believers honors God the Father and His Son, the Lord Jesus Christ, for it displays the eternal unity that the Godhead enjoys (John 17:21-23). Sadly, a lack of love, pride, elevating one's rights, and selfishness cause harmful divisions within the Body of Christ.

After proclaiming the necessity of unity in the work of the Lord, Paul exhorts the believers at Rome to *"Therefore receive one another, just as Christ also received us, to the glory of God"* (v. 7). There were to be no exclusive cliques or religious sects within the Body of Christ. All believers were to love each other and walk as far as they could with other believers, that is, to the extent that sound doctrine and sound morality permitted. It is important that believers be in fellowship with the Lord, so that they can enjoy fellowship with each other. This is especially true for those gathering together as an assembly of believers in a particular location.

Biblically speaking, believers, including new converts, relocating Christians, and traveling workers, who desired to be a part of a local church were added to the fellowship in various ways. For example, we read that Barnabas provided a word of testimony to the saints in Jerusalem on Paul's behalf so that he would be received by them (Acts 9:27). New converts, after being water baptized, were received into church fellowship (Acts 2:41-42). As believers moved from one location to another, they carried with them letters of introduction from their home church meetings in order to be received into the fellowship of other assemblies (Acts 18:26-27; Rom. 16:1; Col. 4:7-8). Yet, a believer who was widely known to have a good testimony, such as Paul, would not need a letter of introduction to be received, as he would already be known by the church (2 Cor. 3:1-2).

Letters not only introduced believers to other meetings, but affirmed their faithfulness and their moral integrity (e.g., Phoebe, 16:1-2; Apollos, Acts 18:27). Those with letters of introduction could be welcomed into the family life of the assembly without reservation. This biblical practice safeguards the assembly against wolves who want to secretly enter the meeting and also provides information as to how incoming believers have been used previously to bless God's people.

The Greek word translated "receive" in verse 7 is a verb in the present tense, middle voice, and imperative mood. Believers are commanded to actively receive those who desire to be added to the local fellowship unless there is a good reason not to (e.g., he or she does not have a sound profession of Christ, or is not sound in doctrine or in life). The middle voice tells us that it is good for us to readily receive other believers into the body-life of the local church. We should desire everyone to be plugged into the privileges and responsibilities of church family life.

## The Ministry of Christ to the Gentiles (vv. 8-13)

The key word in the remainder of this chapter is "ministry," as rendered in verses 8, 16, 25, 27, and 31. The idea of "ministry" is sacrificially serving others without concern for one's self. To explain this selfless concept of service, the apostle identifies three types of ministries: First, Jesus Christ sacrificing Himself that the gospel could be offered to the Gentiles (vv. 8-13). Second, Paul bringing the gospel message and teachings of Christ to the Gentiles (vv. 14-24). Third, the Gentiles providing aid to the poor believers in Jerusalem (vv. 25-33).

The ministry of Christ to the Gentiles would cause them to glorify God for His mercy (v. 8). In verses 10-12, the apostle quotes Psalm 18:49, 117:1, Deuteronomy 32:43, and Isaiah 10:1, 10 to prove that the work of Christ to permit Gentiles to receive salvation was foretold. As a result, the Gentiles would sing praises to Jehovah's name and rejoice with His covenant people over the One from the root of Jesse who would reign over them and give them hope for the future. The sacrificial ministry of Jesus Christ was a direct fulfillment of Old Testament Scripture and shows that it was always God's intention to save Gentiles through the death, burial, and resurrection of His Son.

## The Ministry of Paul to the Gentiles (vv. 14-24)

Although Paul had not met the believers in Rome, he had heard of their goodness and sound doctrine and was confident that they would receive his admonitions willingly and thus be better equipped to admonish others also (vv. 14-15).

The apostle describes the various attributes of his present ministry among the Gentiles: It was received in God's grace (vv. 14-15). It centered in the gospel message of Jesus Christ (v. 16). It was done for God's glory (v. 17). It was accomplished by God's power through answered prayer (vv. 18-19). It was completely arranged according to God's sovereign plan (vv. 20-24).

In fulfilling his calling to serve the Gentiles, Paul was eager to venture to regions where the gospel had not been preached before (v. 20). Paul even notes that he had fully preached the gospel message from Jerusalem to Illyricum (v. 19). Although it would be easier for him to build on the foundations of others, he felt compelled to engage in pioneering evangelism. Paul viewed those Gentiles responding to the gospel, those sanctified by the Holy Spirit, as his acceptable offering of praise to God (v. 16). Thank the Lord for all those who are faithful to share the gospel message where it has never been heard before!

*Revealing Heaven's Secrets*

Paul had wanted to visit the believers in Rome for many years, but did not have the opportunity to do so because of the ministry to the Gentiles that he just described (vv. 22-23). However, that situation had changed; Paul sensed that his pioneering work in the region (speaking of Achaia) had been successful and would permit others to continue building on the foundation that he had laid. Paul also desired to visit Spain, so he planned to briefly visit the saints in Rome whenever he traveled westward (v. 24). That proposed trip did not materialize; there is no record of Paul reaching Spain, and no evidence that he went to Rome until taken there later as a prisoner.

## The Ministry of Gentiles to the Saints in Jerusalem (vv. 25-33)

Rather than journeying to Rome, Paul was heading in the opposite direction to take a collection to the poor saints in Jerusalem (v. 25; 2 Cor. 8-9). Understanding the plight of their Jewish brethren in Jerusalem, the Gentiles in Macedonia and Achaia sent gifts of money to assist them (vv. 26-27). After completing this task, the apostle hoped to visit Rome with all *"the fullness of the blessing of the gospel of Christ"* while on his way to Spain (vv. 28-29). Paul yearned for the mutual blessing of Christ's fellowship that would be shared during his time with them.

In verse 27, Paul emphasizes that those who had been spiritually blessed by ministry had "a duty" to support those who blessed them. The gospel message had originated in Jerusalem and had been brought to the Gentiles by Jewish believers. Therefore, the Gentile believers had "a duty" to reciprocate a blessing to encourage the believers in Jerusalem. This realization should squelch any thoughts of Anti-Semitism within the Church today – we Gentiles have the opportunity to hear the gospel and be saved today because Christian Jews obeyed the Great Commission long ago.

The New Testament indicates that Church workers were employed by the Lord, not by local churches. Serving the Lord is not a career to be chosen, but a heavenly calling to be fulfilled! God enables the ministry of His workers and is responsible for supporting them financially (Phil. 4:10-19; Col. 4:17). The Lord most often accomplishes this through His people. Examples would include the support of: the evangelist (1 Cor. 9:14), a teaching elder (1 Tim. 5:17-18), a teacher in general (Gal. 6:6), and a commended worker (1 Cor. 9:4). Christian love is to be circulated within the Church; if we have been blessed by someone, we should desire to bless them also in whatever way the Lord has equipped us.

# Romans Chapter 16

## Closing Remarks and Personal Greetings (vv. 1-23)

In the previous chapter, the apostle spoke of Christ's ministry to the Gentiles, his own ministry to the Gentiles, and the Gentiles' ministry to the saints in Jerusalem. In this chapter, Paul highlights the ministry of other saints to him. Most of the individuals listed were Gentiles, but a few Jewish believers are also identified as ministering to Paul.

Because sending dispatches was expensive and slow going, it was customary for the one writing a letter in Paul's day to pass along greetings to others known to the recipient(s) and, in closing, to allow those known by the sender to do the same. Consequently, the last chapter of Romans contains the names of a number of serving saints associated with Paul's ministry; their names preserved in Scripture attest to their faithfulness to the Lord and to His people. It is remarkable that Paul is able to personally address nearly thirty people and also to greet several local churches in Rome without having ever been there.

Paul begins this roster of names by mentioning a faithful sister named Phoebe (vv. 1-2). The apostle tells the believers in Rome to receive her into their fellowship as she was coming to them from the church in Cenchrea, the seaport of Corinth. Phoebe was a helper of many, including Paul. As Phoebe was traveling to Rome, it is quite possible that she was carrying the very letter we are reading to the saints at Rome on Paul's behalf.

Paul refers to her as a "servant," the feminine form of the Greek word *diakonos* translated "deacon" in 1 Timothy 3:8-13 which speaks of a particular office within the local church. Deacons in the church had to be males (the husband of one wife); their wives also had to be faithful to the Lord. Phoebe was a female who served the Lord. There is nothing in Scripture to suggest that she was an officer in the church, as apostles, elders, and deacons had to be masculine to represent God's authority in the Church. God is spirit, but masculine in His presentation of authority (1 Cor. 11:7).

If you had Priscilla and Aquila's (vv. 3-5) names in your address book, you would have many blotted out entries for them – they were on the move in the Lord's work. Many Jews settled in Greece after being expelled from Rome by the decree of Claudius in 49 A.D. Jewish immigrants from Rome,

*Revealing Heaven's Secrets*

such as Aquila, born in Pontus, and his wife Priscilla settled in Corinth (Acts 18:2-3). Paul first arrived in Corinth in the spring of 51 A.D. during his second missionary journey. He apparently lived with Priscilla and Aquila much of the time he was in Corinth, as they were fellow tent-makers by trade. After one and a half years, Paul set sail for Syria and took Priscilla and Aquila with him as far as Ephesus. They remained behind while Paul went back to the assembly at Antioch to give a report (Acts 18:18-22).

Paul returned to Ephesus in the spring of 53 A.D. (his third missionary journey). While in Ephesus, he wrote the believers at Corinth and passed on greetings from Priscilla and Aquila, who were still in Ephesus and had a church meeting in their home (1 Cor. 16:19). Claudius died about this time, so Priscilla and Aquila returned to Corinth, possibly accompanying Apollos (Acts 18:27). In about 57 A.D., Paul addresses Priscilla and Aquila, his *"fellow workers,"* who were then in Rome. Paul praises their faithfulness to him: *"who risked their own necks for my life, to whom not only I give thanks, but also all the churches of the Gentiles"* (v. 4). Early Church workers were not sedentary; the Lord's servants were mobile, versatile, and available to serve in whatever ministry they were led to engage in by the Holy Spirit. We learn in verse 5 that they hosted another church meeting in their home. This was a normal practice early in the Church Age (Col. 4:15).

Epaenetus, the first convert in Achaia and a beloved brother of Paul, is mentioned next (v. 5). He must have belonged to the household of Stephanas (1 Cor. 16:15). Mary was a faithful servant not only to Paul, but to the entire missionary team (v. 6). Paul mentions Andronicus and Junia, likely Jews, who had come to Christ before he did. These men had been fellow prisoners with Paul at some point in his ministry (v. 7). They were notable apostles (or "sent ones") which likely refers to their evangelistic commissioning early in Church history. These men had obviously been faithful witnesses of Christ for many years.

The names of several saints are then mentioned, about whom we know nothing other than they were beloved servants with a connection to Calvary: Amplias, Urbanus, Stachys, Apelles, Herodion, Tryphena, Tryphosa, Rufus, Asyncritus, Phlegon, Hermas, Patrobas, Hermes, Philologus, Julia, Nereus, and Olympas (vv. 8-15). Paul also sent greetings to the saints who belonged to Aristobulus and to Narcissus. These households likely including slaves, yet Paul knew them personally. Salutations also went to the brethren gathered with those named in verse 14 and then again to those named in verse 15. Apparently, Paul was aware of two more house churches in Rome in addition to one identified in verse 5. Speaking of her loving care, Rufus' mother had been like a mother to Paul also. This long roster of names indicates that many in the Body of Christ served Paul in various capacities for which he was tremendously thankful.

In verse 16, and three more times in other Epistles, Paul exhorts believers to greet each other with a "holy kiss." "Holy" is translated from the Greek adjective *hagios*, which is normally translated "holy" or "saint(s)." The Greek noun *philema*, which is derived from the verb *phileo* which means "a brotherly love," is translated "kiss." *Philema* can be any personal greeting which is used to express genuine brotherly love in a wholesome (holy) way. Accordingly, "a holy kiss" is only one of many types of personal gestures that may express brotherly love across various cultural norms. What the apostle is encouraging is that saints freely express Christ's love to each other in a manner that is pure and blameless, and which conveys hearty affection. This might be accomplished by many types of gestures depending on the social customs of the day: a kiss, a hug, a pat, a handshake, or a nod.

Paul exhorts the saints at Rome to deal properly with those causing division in their ranks: *"Now I urge you, brethren, note those who cause divisions and offenses, contrary to the doctrine which you learned, and avoid them"* (v. 17). Paul gives similar instruction elsewhere: the disorderly (2 Thess. 3:11, 14, 15) or factious (Tit. 3:10-11) are to be *avoided* completely (Acts 20:28-31). These behaviors are often associated with those not sound in doctrine. The purpose of shunning is to help another person see that he or she is out of fellowship with God, and therefore out of fellowship with His people. A believer engaging in gross sin and who has rejected biblical reproof should be dealt with by *excommunication* (1 Cor. 5:11-13). This has the effect of delivering the rebellious person to Satan for buffeting, possibly ending in that person's death (1 Cor. 5:5; 1 Tim. 1:20).

In verses 19-20, Paul employs unusual imagery borrowed from a story in the book of Joshua to encourage believers to stand strong in the Lord against evil and false teachers. Joshua is a strong type of Jesus Christ. Even the meaning of both their names is the same – "Jehovah's salvation." After a spectacular military victory over the five armies of southern Canaan, it was time for their leaders to be judged. Joshua commanded that the five kings be brought out of their cave prison; then he addressed his captains: *"'Come near, put your feet on the necks of these kings.' And they drew near and put their feet on their necks. Then Joshua said to them, 'Do not be afraid, nor be dismayed; be strong and of good courage, for thus the Lord will do to all your enemies against whom you fight'"* (Josh. 10:24-25). After Joshua's captains stepped on the necks of the kings, Joshua slew all five kings with a sword and had their bodies hung on five trees as a public testimony of their defeat. The pressing of one's foot on the neck of an enemy was an Eastern custom to demonstrate complete victory. Spiritually speaking, Christ allows His followers to share in the victory that is only possible through Him. Likewise, it was Joshua, not the captains, who actually slew the enemy with his sword!

The overall picture before us has its prophetic origin in Genesis 3:15, which foretold that Christ would bruise the serpent's head. In Eden, God had said to the serpent (Satan), *"And I will put enmity between you and the woman, and between your seed and her Seed* [Christ]; *He shall bruise your head, and you shall bruise His heel"* (Gen. 3:15). The Lord Jesus fulfilled this prophecy at Calvary (John 12:31-33). At Calvary, Satan was defeated by the seed of the woman.

Paul may be referring to Christ's future victory over Satan and the wicked at His second advent to the earth (Rev. 19:17-20:3) or he may be speaking of the victory that a believer can have over evil today in Christ. Paul's exhortation is to study God's Word in order to know how He expects us to live before Him, and then seek to live a simple life which shuns evil and worldly pleasure. As saints rely on God's grace to realize holy living, the victory is won through Christ, and the devices of Satan are spoiled.

Having passed along hellos to various saints in Rome, Paul includes greetings from those who were with him in Corinth at that time: Timothy, Lucius, Jason, Sosipater, Tertius, Gaius, Erastus, and Quartus (vv. 21-23). Timothy, Paul's spiritual son in the faith, was Paul's faithful coworker. Gaius not only was Paul's host, but he also hosted a church in his home (this is the fourth reference in this chapter to a church meeting gathering in a home). Tertius was Paul's scribe and had written the epistle for him.

Verse 23 contains a lovely picture of the common love and position in Christ that all believers enjoy. Paul includes the greeting of Erastus, the treasurer of the city, and that of Quartus, a brother in the Lord. At the time this epistle was written, about half of the Roman Empire was composed of slaves. Quartus (meaning the number *four*) was likely a believing slave, and yet Paul treats him with the same respect as the wealthy city official.

## The Benediction (vv. 24-27).

Paul reminds the saints at Rome that God reveals Himself and His will for our lives primarily by studying His Word and being illuminated by the Holy Spirit to understand its meaning (v. 25). God reveals His will for us in Scripture to test the validity of our faith (v. 26). Obeying God's Word demonstrates true faith; genuine faith is evident if we do what God asks us to do and avoid doing what He prohibits (Jas. 2:17).

# 1 Corinthians

## Background

The city of Corinth was situated some 50 miles west of Athens in southern Achaia. At the time of Paul's writing, Corinth likely had a population of at least 500,000 people, the majority of whom were slaves. Slaves were needed to transport merchandise and supplies between two busy seaports: Lechaeum 1.5 miles to the west of Corinth and Cenchreae 6 miles to its east. (Corinth was situated on a four-mile strip of land between these two ports.) Cargo was often transferred from port to port; at times ships and all were transported overland. This port arrangement made Corinth the main thoroughfare of commerce in southern Greece, and Cenchreae (Corinth's seaport on the Aegean Sea) one of three major Aegean seaports (Thessalonica and Ephesus being the other two).

Because Corinth was an immense center for international commerce, it naturally became a hotbed for the most immoral forms of paganism. During the time of Paul's writing, approximately one thousand prostitutes associated with the temple of Aphrodite were roaming the streets of Corinth. Consequently, "Corinth" became a byword for what was lewd, indecent, and sensual.

Paul first came to Corinth in the spring of 51 A.D. during his second missionary journey and stayed for one and a half years. While at Ephesus (during his third missionary trip), Paul wrote an epistle to the Corinthians which the Holy Spirit did not retain as part of the inspired Word of God (5:9). Apollos was in Corinth at this time, sent there by the brethren in Ephesus (Acts 18:27). After Paul learned of misunderstandings and additional problems (1:11, 16:17), he wrote a second letter from Ephesus, which is titled *1 Corinthians* in our Bibles. Paul threatened to come with a rod if the Corinthians did not correct particular problems (4:18-12). Later, he did sail directly from Ephesus to Corinth for this purpose. He later refers to this visit as "a painful trip" (2 Cor. 2:1).

After arriving back at Ephesus, Paul wrote a third letter, which "pained" him (2 Cor. 2:3-4); this letter was not divinely preserved for us in Scripture. After the riot in Ephesus, Paul traveled to Macedonia where he met Titus returning from Corinth. Titus gave a good report on the Corinthian

Christians, but some still questioned Paul's apostleship (2 Cor. 2:13, 6:5-6). Paul responded by composing a fourth epistle, *2 Corinthians*. He made a third trip to Corinth, likely during the winter of 56-57 A.D. and remained there for three months (Acts 20:2-3).

## Theme(s)
Paul wrote to transform the behavior of a disorderly group of believers into that which would honor God. Paul affirmed that Christ was their head, that moral integrity was expected of believers, and that they needed to honor Christ by obeying revealed truth concerning Church order and doctrine. Main themes are Christian Conduct, Church Order, and Church Body Life.

## Keywords
Keywords and phrases include: "judgment," "glory," "temple," "body," "wise/wisdom," "member," "tongue," "head/authority," "power," "spiritual," "to know," "do you not know," and "to judge."

## Date
Likely written in the latter portion of Paul's three-year stay at Ephesus during his third missionary journey: 55-56 A.D.

## Outline
I. Introduction and Affirming Christ's Lordship (1:1-9).
II. Addressing Disorderly Conduct in the Church (1:10-6:20).
III. Answering Questions (7:1-14:40).
IV. Affirming the Importance of Christ's Resurrection (15:1-38).
V. Miscellaneous Counsel and Closing (16:1-24).

## Theological Value
Jack Hunter identifies the *theological value* of 1 Corinthians, by listing ten key doctrines that are included in the epistle.

1. **Doctrine of the Godhead**. This is implied in passages where more than one Person is mentioned: e.g., 1:1, 3; 8:6; 12:4–6.

2. **Doctrine of God**. The following passages refer to God the Father as distinct from the Lord Jesus Christ and the Holy Spirit: the will of God (1:1); the faithfulness of God (1:9); the wisdom of God (1:21); the sovereignty of God (1:27); the power of God (2:5); the source of revelation (2:10); the giving God (2:12); the knowledge of God (3:20);

the rule of God (4:20); the headship of God (11:3); the energy of God (12:6); the grace of God (15:10).

3. **Doctrine of Christ**. Christ is: our Lord (1:2); the Son of God (1:9); the power of God (1:24); the wisdom of God (1:24); the believers' wisdom, righteousness, sanctification and redemption (1:30); the foundation of the local assembly (3:11); the judge of the servant (4:4); our passover (5:7); the rock (10:4); the head of every man (11:3); the firstfruits (15:23); the Last Adam (15:45); the Second Man (15:47).

4. **Doctrine of the Holy Spirit**. The Spirit is presented as: the medium of revelation (2:10); the divine Searcher (2:10); the Spirit of the knowledge of God (2:11); the indwelling Spirit (2:12); the Teacher (2:13); the Giver (12:8).

5. **Doctrine of the Church**. Paul describes the Church at Corinth as: the Church of God (1:2); God's husbandry (3:9); God's building (3:9); God's temple (3:16); body of Christ (12:12, 27).

6. **Doctrine of Salvation**. To Paul the doctrine of salvation has: its center in Christ (15:3–4); its central theme in the cross (1:18; 2:2); its demonstration in the power of God (1:18); it is set forth in the preaching (1:21).

7. **Doctrine of the Scriptures**. Note the recurring expression of the phrase, "It is written." This to Paul was final and authoritative. Therein lay the only court of appeal: see 1:19, 31; 2:9; 3:19–20; 7:10–11; 9:9–10; 10:7–11, 26; 14:21; 15:32, 45, 54–55. There are other passages where he refers to the Scriptures without using the formula, "It is written."

8. **Doctrine of Demons**. This interesting subject is touched upon by Paul in chapters 8 and 10, and is also referred to in 12:2.

9. **Doctrine of the Resurrection**. This is expounded very fully in chapter 15. He deals with the resurrection of Christ and the terrible consequences if He had not risen, then goes on to deal in a most illuminating way with the resurrection of the saints (vv. 42–49).

10. **Doctrine of the Coming of the Lord**. This is specifically referred to in 15:23–28, then in vv. 51–57.[22]

## Paul's Missionary Trips, Epistles, and Visits to Corinth

| Trip | Letters | | | Visits to Corinth | | Date |
|---|---|---|---|---|---|---|
| | Number | Known As | Where Written | Number of Visit | Length of Time | |
| 2nd | | | | 1st (Acts 18:1-18) | 18 Months (Acts 18:11) | 51-52 A.D. |
| 3rd | 1st (1 Cor. 5:9) | Lost | Ephesus (Acts 19:1-41, 20:31) | | | 54-57 A.D. |
| | 2nd | 1 Corinthians | Ephesus (1 Cor. 16:8-9,19) | | | |
| | | | | 2nd – Stern Trip (2 Cor. 2:1, 12:14, 13:1-2) | Short | |
| | 3rd (2 Cor. 2:3-4, 7:8, 12) | Lost | Ephesus | | | |
| | 4th | 2 Corinthians | Macedonia/ Met Titus there (2 Cor. 2:13, 7:2-16) | | | |
| | | | | 3rd (Acts 20:1-4; 2 Cor. 12:14, 13:1) | 3 Months in Greece including some time in Corinth (Acts 20:1-4) | 56-57 A.D. |

# 1 Corinthians Chapter 1

## Introduction (vv. 1-9)

Paul was directly called by the Lord Jesus on the road to Damascus to be an apostle (i.e., a sent one) to the Gentiles (v. 1; Acts 9:1-16). A brother named Sosthenes was with Paul in Ephesus at the time of this writing, so Paul included his name in the salutation. Had the ruler of the synagogue in Corinth, who was badly beaten by the Greeks during Paul's second missionary journey, come to Christ and then traveled to Ephesus to be with Paul? This seems unlikely, but certainly within the realm of possibility.

It is significant that the apostle addresses his letter to *"the church of God which is at Corinth"* and not the "Corinthian Church" (v. 2). When writing to a group of believers, Paul acknowledges the composite nature of the Body of Christ which was gathering at different locations. To assign an individualized name would have worked to divide the homogenous identity of all believers being one in Christ. It is His *ekklesia* (i.e., a called-out company) at Corinth, not the Corinthian Church. All those in Christ, no matter where they reside, are set apart to enjoy oneness in Him. This idea sets the stage for the apostle's exhortation for the saints at Corinth to rally around their Head, rather than to other servants of the Lord or ideologies. All those calling on the name of the Lord Jesus are positionally sanctified in Christ and are to submit to God's work of sanctification in their lives.

Continuing his salutation, Paul declares *"grace to you and peace from God our Father and the Lord Jesus Christ"* (v. 3). This is Paul's trademark greeting and is word for word how he saluted the Romans also (Rom. 1:7). *Grace* was a greeting that the Greeks commonly used, while Jewish believers traditionally referred to the blessing of *peace* to convey a how-do-you-do. The statement in verse 3 affirms the divine equality of God the Father and His Son – the grace we desperately need comes from both. The order of grace and peace is purposeful; God's grace received is always the forerunner of enjoying God's peace.

If you had been an apostle in the early days of the Church Age and you wanted to transform a group of believers that were carnal, divided, and out of order into a Christ-honoring gathering of saints, how would you go about doing it? This was Paul's challenge with the church at Corinth. Instead of immediately tackling issues, he chose to uphold the Head of the Church, the Lord Jesus Christ, before the Corinthians. Paul knew that if believers held Him in utmost esteem, most of their problems would be resolved.

Six times in the opening ten verses, Paul uses the word *kurios*, which is normally translated as "Lord" in the New Testament, to speak of Christ's supremacy over them. In fact, this is the highest concentration of *kurios* in any equivalent passage in the New Testament. Its linguistic root *kuros* means "supreme in authority," and normally refers to God the Father or God the Son, as in this text. Some might think that Paul went a little overboard with his usage of *kurios*, but that is not the case. When God's people let divine headship slip, they soon devalue God's order to follow their own carnal ways. The end result is sin and the loss of God's blessing. Through Paul, the Holy Spirit affirmed this warning to the Corinthians and to us too!

The believers were glorying in all sorts of things besides Christ, which was causing disunity and division in the assembly. Some were promoting their favorite preachers to the point of spurning others (v. 12). Some saints were so enamored with their spiritual gifts that they were promoting themselves instead of selflessly serving others in grace. Paul states that the Corinthians had been amply bestowed with spiritual gifts (vv. 4-7). Their testimony of Christ was enhanced with: *"all utterance and all knowledge"* (v. 5). *Utterance* refers to the outward expression (likely including the use of tongues) of the inward *knowledge* that had been given them by revelation. The fact that they had these spiritual gifts meant that they had trusted in Christ and that He had responded by saving them and equipping them to serve Him (v. 6). However, the Corinthians had to learn that possession of spiritual gifts and true spiritual maturity were vastly different matters.

Rather than being occupied with their spiritual gifts and promoting themselves, the saints at Corinth should be enthralled with the Giver of the gifts they had received – Christ. He is the One who promised to preserve them blameless until He returns to take them (His Church) from the earth (v. 8). It is in Christ alone that God was able to bring us into fellowship with Himself (v. 9). Hence, all believers are to eagerly wait for the day of His coming, the moment when He will be personally revealed to His Church (v. 7). This event, which includes the *Judgment Seat of Christ*, is referred to by Paul as *"the Day of our Lord Jesus Christ"* or *the Day of Christ*, or *the Day of the Lord Jesus* (5:5; Phil 1:6, 10, 2:16). *The Day of Christ* is not to be confused with *the Day of the Lord*, an Old Testament term that speaks of divine judgment on the earth and used in the New Testament to speak of the Tribulation period and the millennial reign of Christ, the destruction of the earth, and the Great White Throne Judgment (1 Thess. 5:1-11; 2 Pet. 3:10).

Although all believers are positionally blameless in Christ by the divine act of justification, we are not without fault. After our glorification, Christ's examination of our deeds, words, and motives will reveal this to be true. On *the Day of Christ* (at Christ's Judgment Seat) our works will be judged for eternal reward (3:11-15). Given this future day, let us live for Christ today!

## Man's "Isms" Cause Schisms (vv. 10-17)

Paul had received information from the house of Chloe concerning a number of divisive issues that were hindering unity in the church at Corinth (vv. 10-11). William MacDonald suggests that Paul is laying down an important principle of Christian conduct by mentioning his information source: "We should not pass on news about our fellow believers unless we are willing to be quoted in the matter. If this example were followed today, it would prevent most of the idle gossip which now plagues the church."[23] To highlight their spiritual union, Paul refers to them as "my brethren" and then implores them to speak the same thing and to be joined together in unity by having the same mind – the mind of Christ. Paul will specifically address these concerns over the next five chapters (1:10-6:20).

The apostle begins by rebuking the unnatural divisions that were forming in the church particularly around the heroizing of gifted men; Paul, Apollos, and Cephas (Peter) are specifically named (v. 12). Additionally, some at Corinth believed that they had a special relationship with Christ that other saints did not share – *"I am of Christ."* But Paul emphatically declares that Christ is not divided, that all saints are one in Him and have equal status (v. 13). It was Christ who had died for them and purchased their souls by His own blood – they were all His and one in Him.

To stress this point, believer's baptism is referred to as an example of something all believers must do to identify their oneness with Christ and that they are under His headship. Believers were not baptized in the name of anyone else, but unto Christ and in His name (v. 14; Matt. 28:19-20). To further substantiate this point, Paul notes that while he was with them, he actually baptized only a few people – so few, in fact, that he can quickly list those he did baptize: Crispus, Gaius, and the household of Stephanas (vv. 14-16). These were not baptized in Paul's name, but in the name of Christ. The baptizer was insignificant to the baptism activity. Rather, it was the One to whom the believers were proclaiming their loyalty to who was important – Christ.

The exhortation is straightforward: Do not boast in people or heroize fellow servants of Christ. Rather, we are to glory in the Lord Jesus and follow Him. He who baptizes is nothing; Paul did not want people to follow the one baptizing new converts or to associate salvation with baptism, thus making the gospel message of Jesus Christ void. Verse 17 is one of the best verses in the New Testament to show that water baptism is not the same as spiritual baptism. What a believer does in the physical realm does not somehow force God to bestow some spiritual favor. There is no association in Scripture between water baptism and the granting of salvation. Water baptism is an act of obedience to Christ's command, and spiritual baptism is an act of God in response to an individual trusting in Christ alone for salvation. Paul states that water baptism is not part of the gospel message, which in itself, is the power of God unto salvation (v. 17; Rom. 1:16).

The believers at Corinth were glorying in all sorts of things besides Christ, which was causing disunity and division in the assembly. By glorying in their favorite preachers or in their newfound liberty, they were actually robbing Christ of honor. Paul reminds them that every part of their salvation, including their sanctification, was in Him: *"you are in Christ Jesus."* Thus, all their bragging and glorying should be in Him. Most of the Corinthian believers would have been Greeks, and the Greeks love human wisdom and the sayings of their philosophers. In the next verse, Paul implies in a roundabout way that the problems in the church at Corinth were because they were pursuing human wisdom and not the simplicity of truth in Christ.

## Human Wisdom in Contrast With Divine Wisdom (vv. 18-25)

The message (*logos*) of the cross is foolishness to those who are perishing; there was nothing appealing about shame and death to the Greek mind. However, those who had embraced the gospel knew otherwise, as they had experienced the transforming power of God in their lives (v. 18). Human wisdom and secular philosophies will never lead sinners to humble themselves and receive the message of the cross for salvation.

Worldliness is any sphere from which the Lord Jesus is excluded. This is why James says anyone who is *"a friend of the world makes himself an enemy of God"* (Jas. 4:4). Worldliness opposes God, and God hates it. Being worldly-minded is a system of thinking which is in direct opposition to the teachings of Christ. Ponder for a moment how the world's standard of wisdom is in direct opposition to what the Lord Jesus taught:

*The world* wants to be served, but Christ says humble yourself and serve others.
*The world* says save your life, but the Lord says lose your life to gain a life worth living.
*The world* exclaims "live for the moment," but Christians are to live for eternity.

*The world* says live for self, but the Lord says lose your life for Him.
*The world* is into power, but the Lord uses weak things to confound the mighty.
*The world* permits greed to rule distribution, but Christians are to give according to need.
*The world* says acquire wealth, but God teaches us not to seek to be rich.
*The world* uses money and power to rule, but Christians are to pray and to use Scripture in love to serve others.
*The world* says retaliate and get even, but the Lord teaches us to repay evil with good and be forgiving.
*The world* uses violence, but Christians are to turn the other cheek.

Human wisdom will always be in opposition to Jesus Christ and His message, because God's wisdom poses an opposite way of thinking that is foolish to the world. Paul quotes Isaiah 29:14, to show that God, through the cross of His Son, will ultimately test the inhabitants of the earth (vv. 19-20). Those who humbly accept this seemingly implausible message in faith will be saved. On judgment day the message of the cross that seemed to be foolish by man's reckoning will be proved valid by God (v. 21).

Paul then reminded his audience that the Greeks were intellectuals who prided themselves on pursuing wisdom, while the Jews were sign-seekers (v. 22). But neither man's wisdom nor man's prove-it-to-me attitude would bring a guilty sinner to a place of experiencing the wisdom and power of God. Rather, these limiting mindsets cause men to stumble over the gospel message of Jesus Christ (vv. 23-24). Regardless of what people do with the gospel message now, ultimately they will know that God's wisdom and power are much greater than anything that humanity could produce (v. 25).

## The Corinthians Lacked True Wisdom (vv. 26-31)

Paul then challenged the Corinthians to take a quick inventory of the assembly. How many of them were intellectuals, philosophers, wealthy and influential? He infers that not many of them were noble. God had reached them through the simple message of the cross and not by high-sounding rhetoric or fanciful gimmicks (v. 26). The foolish and weak had responded to the gospel, and God would use these to further declare His glory by confounding the wise and powerful (vv. 27-28). What was naturally foolish and weak would be made wise and strong in Christ (v. 30). God works this way so that no flesh will glory in His presence, which means He will get all the glory (v. 29). Paul then reminds them of a truth witnessed throughout Scripture: *"He who glories, let him glory in the Lord"* (v. 31).

# 1 Corinthians Chapter 2

## No Reliance on Human Wisdom (vv. 1-8)

The apostle reminds the Corinthian believers that when he first met them, he did not resort to hifalutin speech or high-sounding philosophical arguments to validate his message (v. 1). Rather, he felt timid, anxious, and weak as he preached the simplicity of the gospel message to them (vv. 2-3). As Hamilton Smith explains, Paul was not natural Paul when he came to Corinth to share the gospel message:

> Moreover, the preacher himself was among them in a *condition* that was humiliating to the pride of man. He did not come as a self-confident orator. Conscious of his own weakness, realizing the deep need of those to whom he preached, and the gravity of his message, he was amongst them in fear and much trembling.[24]

The Lord had taught Paul that in gospel ministry only two things mattered: the accurate sharing of God's Word and the power of the Holy Spirit to convict the hearer of its meaning. Therefore, he had not resorted to human tactics that would have appealed to the Corinthians such as fanciful and intellectual arguments or brow-beating speech to compel them to receive his message (v. 4). This also meant that there was nothing inherently special about Paul, hence, none of them should place him on some pedestal of admiration – Christ was the one to be appreciated in gospel work. This is why Paul uses the plural pronoun "we" extensively in this chapter. He includes himself with all those who sincerely preach the gospel message.

It was not the influence of human wisdom that caused the Corinthians to repent and to turn to Christ, but a powerful work of God (v. 5). Only those experiencing this type of divine illumination of the truth would value Paul's message as wise (v. 6). Certainly, the unregenerate would not be able to understand or appreciate what Christ accomplished at Calvary, nor would those young in the Lord, until they had gained spiritual understanding from above. Previously, this good news message had been a mystery, that is, a truth tucked away deep in the vast recesses of God's mind before time began, but now it had been revealed at the appropriate time in accordance with God's sovereign purposes (v. 7).

Paul's example of gospel ministry is a good one for us to follow. Salvation is completely God's business; therefore, we should never resort to intellectual arguments, enticing words, or gimmicks to cause people to profess Christ as their Savior. Rather, we must rely on the power of God's Word and His Spirit. We win people to what we win them with! True conversion comes from God, not by a humanized message that He hates. Hence, God told Jonah: *"Preach ...the message that I tell you"* (Jonah 3:2).

Next, the apostle explains that the gospel message of Jesus Christ had not been fully revealed prior to the Church Age (v. 8). If Satan (who influences worldly leaders to do evil) had understood what God was going to accomplish through Christ's death and resurrection, Satan would not have crucified the Lord Jesus. The main theme of the entire Bible centers on the person and work of Jesus Christ: *"For God so loved the world that He gave His only begotten Son, that whoever believes in Him should not perish but have everlasting life"* (John 3:16). *"For the testimony of Jesus is the spirit of prophecy"* (Rev. 19:10). *"For all the promises of God in Him* [Christ] *are Yes, and in Him Amen"* (2 Cor. 1:20). Yet, God kept the plan of salvation in Christ a mystery until after His resurrection.

The Old Testament contains hundreds of messianic types and prophecies to convey the truth of Christ, but these are scattered in Scripture in such a way that full understanding of the events and benefits of Calvary would not be understood from just one text. For this reason, most of the Old Testament pictures of Christ are concealed in abstract symbols, reclusive narratives and statements, mysterious people and names, and unusual events. All these Old Testament gems were once concealed from human comprehension. However, these accentuate Christ and His work when illuminated by the light of New Testament revelation.

## Spiritual Truth and Discernment Come From God (vv. 9-16)

God has revealed Himself and His mysterious ways to humanity in a variety of ways through the ages (e.g., creation, conscience, miracles, etc.). Of special benefit is God's Word to us through the prophets of old and through the apostles in the infancy of the Church Age. Paul quotes Isaiah 64:4 to impress this point upon his audience: *"Eye has not seen, nor ear heard, nor have entered into the heart of man the things which God has prepared for those who love Him"* (v. 9). This verse is often quoted to verify the future incomprehensible wonders of Heaven, but that is not the context in which Paul uses it. Rather, as F. B. Hole explains, his focus is on what *"God has revealed"* to us.

To this verse the Apostle Paul referred in 1 Corinthians 2:9, showing that though in ordinary matters men arrive at knowledge by the hearing of the ear – **tradition** – or by the eye – **observation** – or by what we may call **intuition**, these things can only reach us by **revelation** from God by His Spirit. Isaiah knew that there were things to be revealed. Paul tells us that they have been revealed, so that we may know them.[25]

So, while it is true that God's heavenly abode will be more spectacular than we could ever imagine, that is not what Paul is calling our attention to. Rather, he is speaking of the wonderful truths that God has newly revealed: *"But God **has revealed them** to us through His Spirit. For the Spirit searches all things, yes, the deep things of God"* (v. 10). What the Corinthians could have never understood through their senses or intellect had now been revealed to them (and us too) by the Holy Spirit. We call this divine *revelation*. What was not revealed to Israel concerning salvation has been disclosed to the Church, who, through the indwelling Holy Spirit, has the opportunity to understand the deep things of God.

The *revelation* of God was conveyed to us through divine *inspiration* given to the apostles (v. 10) by the Holy Spirit: *"These things we also speak, not in words which man's wisdom teaches but which the Holy Spirit teaches, comparing spiritual things with spiritual"* (v. 13). The latter phrase means that the Holy Spirit is communicating spiritual meanings by spiritual words. Then, as we read that which has been divinely inspired (Scripture), the Holy Spirit gives us *illumination* to understand what we read: *"But the natural man does not receive the things of the Spirit of God, for they are foolishness to him; nor can he know them, because they are spiritually discerned"* (v. 14).

The Holy Spirit teaches us spiritual truth as we compare the truth of Scripture with Scripture. This is called *"rightly dividing the word of truth"* (2 Tim. 2:15) and poses a fundamental rule of biblical hermeneutics – Scripture interprets Scripture. Truth cannot contradict itself, so when we compare all of Scripture with itself and come to a homogeneous understanding, only then have we laid hold of God's truth. Those who discern spiritual truth in this way cannot be judged by those who have not yet known God's truth. Neither the unregenerate nor carnal believers can discern truth correctly (v. 15).

Paul concludes that it is a complete waste of time to explain God's grand program of salvation to someone who does not have the indwelling Holy Spirit. Such an effort would be like trying to teach theoretical physics to a stone monument of Albert Einstein. The monument may be in Einstein's image, but there is nothing within to respond to the teachings of Einstein. Though man was made in God's image, because of sin there is nothing within him that will naturally understand what is important to God. What was dead and unresponsive to God must be first made alive by the Spirit of God to be able to understand the things of God. Many believers waste time appealing to the intellect of the unregenerate instead of sharing God's Word in order to reach down into their conscience. Without conviction of sin, lost sinners will never understand their need of salvation.

Paul again quotes Isaiah to emphasize his conclusion: *"Who can know the mind of the Lord that He may instruct Him?"* (v. 16; Isa. 40:13). This question is really a statement – God cannot be known through any human means. Ontological reasoning will never find God. However, because God chose to reveal Himself through His inspired Word and has given believers illumination to accurately understand Scripture, we may know Him and may learn about the mysteries of grace being extended to us through Christ. As a result, we not only have the opportunity to know God, but also to learn the mind of Christ and think on things in the same way that He does (v. 16).

Hence, we can approach God, not through human knowledge or wisdom, but rather through divine revelation, which the Holy Spirit enables us to understand. Man's knowledge is based on comparison, observation, and demonstration. God is unique, eternal, and spiritual; He cannot be compared to anything else in creation, nor be grasped. Paul's main point in this chapter is that God cannot be understood through disciplines of science or human reasoning, so Paul did not resort to these means. Rather, he expressed only what God had deemed necessary to reveal of Himself.

The pre-conversion ministry of the Holy Spirit gives illumination to the carnal mind as to the meaning of God's Word and then causes the unregenerate to feel the weight of their rebellion against it. Feelings of guilt, the need to be right with God, and the fear of impending judgment are what a sinner experiences before trusting Christ as Savior (Rom. 2:15; Heb. 9:14). It is only the Spirit of God who can accomplish this type of ministry in the unregenerate heart (John 16:8). Man cannot learn of God or approach God through any other agency than what He has revealed to us and enables us to understand. This reality supplies a test for every person – will an individual rely on human wisdom and reasoning to impress God, or will he or she humbly trust in the revealed wisdom of God to be saved by Him?

For believers, the divine agencies of the Word of God and the Spirit of God continue to work in us to both reveal and accomplish God's purposes. May the Holy Spirit continue to illuminate our minds that we might discover the vast riches of Christ, God's Truth, in Scripture (John 14:6)!

# 1 Corinthians Chapter 3

### A Poor Spiritual Diet Promotes Carnality (vv. 1-4)

After conversion, Christians should be governed, not by the law of sin within them, but rather by the Spirit of God (Rom. 8:13). Moderation and self-control are a testimony to others that God is the One controlling a believer's actions (Phil. 4:5). Regrettably, many in the church at Corinth were being controlled by their lusting flesh and did not have such a testimony. Apparently, their motto for life was now: "Since Christ was punished for all of our sin – let's party and enjoy whatever we can!"

Paul does not mince words; he tells them three times that they are "*carnal*." The normal Greek word translated "flesh" in the New Testament is *sarx*, and Paul uses this word as a modifier (*sarkikos*) to describe their carnal behavior; they were "fleshly" (v. 1). Their flesh was governing their behavior within the assembly, and, as a result, the testimony of the church was suffering because their communion with Christ was being hindered.

There were various doctrines of the faith that Paul wanted to teach the Christian believers, but they lacked the spiritual maturity to understand and appreciate the deeper things of God (v. 2). Paul likens them to babes that can only digest spiritual milk (i.e., the elementary aspects of the Christian faith). They had no desire to mature in the faith in order to digest meatier doctrine. The writer of Hebrews addresses a similar problem of spiritual lethargy among believers (Heb. 5:12-14). The Lord Jesus affirmed the necessity of internalizing (feeding on) God's Word to better live for Him (Matt. 4:4). This means that believers should never be satisfied with their spiritual maturity, but should be constantly studying God's Word to gain a deeper understanding of Him and His desire for us.

Clearly, those who profess Christ as Savior will require tender care and regular feedings of the sincere milk of the Word (i.e., the rudiments of Christian doctrine; 1 Pet. 2:2) to encourage their growth. Spiritual maturity must be the goal. Maturity is evidenced by a deepening devotion to Christ, being a more faithful witness for Him in character and actions, spending time in Bible study and prayer, repenting and forsaking sin, and faithfully attending church meetings. Regrettably, many of the Corinthians were apathetic towards their spiritual diet, which meant they were more active in their carnal indulgence. As a result, the assembly was characterized by strife, envy, disunity, and hero-worship, and sadly appeared no different to outsiders than other people in the world (vv. 3-4).

> However sweet the word may sound, any sectarian boasting is but the babbling of a babe. The divisions in the Church are due to no other cause than to lack of love and walking after the flesh.
>
> — Watchman Nee

## God Determines the Service of Believers (vv. 5-10)

The believers at Corinth were carnally touting their favorite preachers in a divisive way; they had forgotten the bigger picture of ministry altogether. It is not the particular laborer (e.g., Paul or Apollos) that matters in the work of the Lord, but rather that the Lord is laboring with His people. To confront this dangerous sectarianism, Paul reminds them that all believers are servants of God and are important and equipped to serve God.

Paul uses an illustration from horticulture to emphasize this point (vv. 5-8). God uses some believers to till, others to plant, others to water, and others to reap, but it is He who gives the harvest; the laborers alone cannot produce anything. Believers are tools in God's hands. Saints labor for the Lord, but it is He who blesses their efforts to further His purposes.

It is natural for us to boast of our temporal accomplishments, but this is not profitable for eternity. May we remember that if the Lord is not in the work, we are wasting our time and resources! Conversely, when we are in the will and strength of God, *"we are more than conquerors through Him who loved us"* (Rom. 8:37). We do not labor alone or in vain for the kingdom, for it is Christ's work, and He labors with us to achieve it. We are His eyes to discern the needs of others and His hands to serve them: *"We are God's fellow workers"* (v. 9). Being yoked with Christ ensures that all God wants us to achieve for the honor of His Son's name is doable!

Through the horticulture example, Paul showed that all servants are to work together under God's authority in gospel ministry, for He alone gives the increase. Paul transitions to an example from construction to show that God's servants are also responsible for the character of their work while building up the local assembly (God's Temple). Paul acknowledged his part in this effort – he had been chosen to lay the initial foundation through pioneering work (v. 10). This was all accomplished in grace, so Paul claimed no bragging rights about what God had achieved in Corinth. He was just one of many workers (like Apollos) that God would use to raise up a testimony for Christ in that city. But he does issue a warning that any teachers coming after him should take heed as to how they build on the foundation he had laid. Paul knew that the Corinthians were being influenced by false teachers, so he issues a warning to them – God will judge anyone spreading false doctrine in the assembly (v. 17).

## One Foundation: Two Kinds of Building Materials (vv. 11-23)

Paul hoped that sincere workers would follow after him and build enduringly with gold, silver, and precious stones on the foundation of Christ that he had laid in Corinth (vv. 11-12). These lasting works speak of Spirit-led and Spirit-equipped ministry that was fostered in truth for the edification of the Body. However, the apostle again warns those who would harm the Corinthian believers by building with wood, hay, and straw upon the solid foundation that had been established. These works speak of spreading false doctrine and self-promoting ministries performed in the flesh. What is seen above the ground to appeal to men (wood, hay, and stubble) has no value to God, but His unseen spiritual work in the human heart (represented by the gold, silver, and precious stones buried in the ground) is profitable to Him.

Paul informed the saints at Rome that all believers will stand before Christ at His Judgment Seat in a future *Day* (i.e., the Day of Christ) to have their works evaluated (Rom. 14:10-12). The Judgment Seat of Christ is not a determination of salvation (those in Christ are His forever), but it is an evaluation of works that believers have done in Christ's name. If believers choose to build on the foundation of truth and engage in Spirit-equipped ministry motivated by love for Christ, then those works will stand Christ's scrutiny and believers will receive an appropriate reward (vv. 13-14).

However, if believers build on the pure foundation works promoting personal glory, carnality, false doctrine, and humanism, these works will be shown to be worthless and will be abruptly incinerated by the brilliance of Christ's holy presence (v. 15). Being in glorified bodies then, we will all be delighted to see such offenses to our Savior go up in smoke! At the Judgment Seat of Christ, the Lord Jesus will honor all who have honored Him with their lives (2 Cor. 5:10). Some believers may lose most or all of what they have labored for their entire lives because it had no value for eternity; yet, Paul notes that their souls are safe from the fire of God's wrath.

The rewards that are earned for service during this lifetime provide the believer with a greater appreciation for the Lord, a greater capacity to worship Him throughout eternity, and, indeed, a greater capability to enjoy Heaven (Rev. 4:11). Paul clearly taught that some believers will shine more brilliantly than others in their eternal glorified bodies; this earned radiance

*1 Corinthians*

is a reflection of Christ's glory (15:40-42). What is truly done for Christ now translates into an eternal weight (or measure) of glory (2 Cor. 4:17).

Every Christian is part of God's vast spiritual house called the Church that He is assembling one soul at a time. Through the Church, the unregenerate witness the awesome nature of God and His capacity to do the unbelievable in His people. Paul also speaks of the local assembly as God's sacred temple in verse 16. Because the Holy Spirit indwelt the saints, they became a special house of worship when they gathered in one place.

In verse 17, Paul describes the accountability that preachers and teachers of God's Word have to the Lord (e.g., Jas. 3:1). The apostle was especially concerned that wolves posing as sheep might slip into the church at Corinth to spread false doctrine and thereby corrupt the meeting. Paul warns that anyone who defiles the temple of the Lord (i.e., ruins the testimony of the local assembly) will be eternally destroyed by God.

Accordingly, the believers at Corinth should beware of anyone promoting human wisdom in their midst. Such people must humble themselves by coming to the cross of Christ for salvation. Consequently, they will know the truth and be able to build wisely into the Church (v. 18). Secular philosophies and skepticism are foolishness to God and therefore have no place in the church meetings (v. 19). The best wisdom that humanity has to offer is utter foolishness to God – it is completely futile (v. 20). Therefore, believers should never permit what is worthless to Christ to govern the affairs of His Church.

May we remember that we build into the Church what we build into our own lives. Base living and carnal ideas defile the Church and exalting men instead of Christ causes divisions in the Church; such nonsense supplants the headship of Christ (vv. 21-22). Workers are given by Christ to the Church (Eph. 4:11) – they belong to the Church. Believers do not belong to them; therefore, there should be no heroizing of people within the Church.

In this chapter, Paul's concern for the Corinthian believers has been twofold: First, that their spiritual growth had been limited by an apathetic spiritual appetite for God's Word. Second, their immaturity made them vulnerable to the sway of false teachers and of their own flesh, either of which could ruin the assembly's testimony. The apostle concludes his appeal for their spiritual growth and unity by reminding the Corinthians of their union with Christ. Because they were one with Christ, they were one with God, which meant that everything was theirs in Christ (v. 23). No believer or religious group holds an exclusive claim to Christ – all are His.

# 1 Corinthians Chapter 4

## The Believer's Stewardship Is Judged by Christ (vv. 1-7)

In the previous chapter, we learned that all believers are to serve Christ – we are His ministers. Paul encourages the Corinthians to maintain this view of himself and of other apostles; elevating them beyond this common ministry that all believers shared would cause division in the Church.

Paul had been divinely tasked with a special ministry of revealing the hidden mysteries of God being accomplished through Jesus Christ (v. 1; Acts 20:24). He was accountable to the Lord to complete his assignment to the best of his ability, for stewards must be found to be faithful (v. 2).

In a coming day, each of us will have to give a stewardship account to the Lord. How did we use our time, resources, and spiritual gifts to further His kingdom? Were we faithful to the tasks assigned to us, including the little things? Here are some ideas to improve our stewardship:

1. Sacrifice the *Fluff of Life* – purge meaningless activities that are robbing time. The permissible must not replace the best, or even the good.

2. Prioritize and Cut – stick to your calling, learn to say "no," and put boundaries on new activities in order to stay effective in ministry.

3. Minimize Travel Time – accomplish as much communication as possible through electronic means rather than traveling, which expends much time and resources.

4. Do Not Waste Time Entertaining Goats – Christ's teachings are to be committed to faithful believers who will in turn teach others (2 Tim. 2:2). New converts require special care, but there should be fruitfulness in time. If Satan can keep us busy attending his people, he will.

5. Improve Organization – develop an efficient filing system of storing past emails, messages, letters, studies, spreadsheets, receipts, etc. This will reduce time in tax preparations, in responding to questions already answered previously, or in future ministry and study development.

6. Develop Teaching Materials – if you are a teacher, completely develop electronic copies of both questions and answers for your students so that repeat studies in the future will require minimal preparation.

7. Minimize Social Media, Unnecessary Phone Calls, and Messaging – These means of communication can waste a lot of time when a brief email or text message could have sufficed. We really do not need to know what our friends ate for lunch – stick to what information is pertinent to serve.

8. Limit Distractions – set aside study time without distractions (the early morning hours are a great time of the day to spend time with the Lord).

Each believer will give an account of his or her stewardship within the Church at the Judgment Seat of Christ. Only the Lord can accurately judge the value of our ministry and why we served Him as we did. Knowing how biased the flesh is in such matters, Paul did not even judge the value of his own ministry (v. 3). He was not aware of any negligence in serving the Lord, but he realized that only the Lord could perfectly judge his doings and only He, as his Master, had the authority to do so (v. 4; Rom. 14:4). Only the Lord knows the hidden things of the heart – what actually motivated us to serve Him (v. 5). Those serving in the power of the Holy Spirit with proper motives will be rewarded by God; those being found faithful will be praised by God. If the apostle did not feel it was appropriate or that he was able to accurately judge the spiritual benefit of his own stewardship, what business do we have in judging what others do for the Lord?

As previously discussed, the Corinthian believers had a tendency to heroize certain teachers within the assembly and also itinerant preachers (1:10-13). This practice of favoring certain ministers and being critical of others was rooted in pride, so the result was disunity in the church. What is of the flesh will always work to undermine God's best for His people!

Paul offered a simplified illustration involving him and Apollos to ensure the Corinthians understood his point (vv. 6-7). He then reminded them that he and Apollos, and indeed every minister of Christ, received their ability and calling from God. Both were given a specific ministry to fulfill and the divine enablement to perform it. Since different teachers were given various abilities and ministries according to God's will, why should we compare God's servants, especially to their detriment? If all we have comes from God, who are we to question what He gives or why He gives it or how others use what He has given?

Our carnal flesh yearns to compare what we have to what others have in order to prompt dissatisfaction with what God has given us. We compare the abilities, the assets, and the ministries of other people to suggest that God showed better wisdom with one person than another person. We are to compare what we do to Scripture in order to align our lives with God's will, but comparing believers' giftedness or the ministries they have been chosen for is demeaning to God. We should be thankful for what He does give, instead of complaining about what He does not!

Without Christ, the believer is nothing, has nothing, and can do nothing for God. But in Him we inherit all things (Rom. 8:17), rule over all things (2 Tim. 2:12), and can do all things that God endorses (Phil. 4:13). Let us maintain this big-picture reality and not squabble about distinctions that have no bearing on furthering the cause of Christ. *"He who glories, let him glory in the Lord"* (1 Cor. 1:31).

## The Apostolic Example of Humility and Faithfulness (vv. 8-17)

Because the apostles were abiding by Christ's callings for their lives, they often suffered: hunger, thirst, inadequate clothing, homelessness, ridicule, and various persecutions including beatings (vv. 10-13). Hence, worldlings considered them to be the scum of the earth – worthy to be condemned to death (v. 9). The Greek word translated "spectacle" in verse 9 conveys the idea of *a theatre*. Paul is picturing himself being thrown into an arena with wild beasts for the purpose of entertaining others by this deadly sport. As fools for Christ, all eyes were on them – even the heavenly angels were witnessing their plight as they faithfully served Christ.

Because the apostles had fully identified with Christ in their ministry, they were considered weak and foolish by worldlings who hated, dishonored, and persecuted them for their testimony. The Lord Jesus warned His disciples that the world would hate them because it hated Him, and that the world would persecute them because of their identification with Him, whom the world also persecuted (John 15:18-20). Paul and those with him could attest to the truthfulness of the Lord's statement.

In contrast, many of the Corinthian believers were rich, full, and prospered as kings because they were not submitting to Christ's calling for their lives (v. 8). There will be a future day when all believers will enjoy ruling and reigning with Christ in His kingdom (Paul looked forward to that reality), but now was not the time for such things. They were to be Christ's representatives in the world, not to enjoy the world's pleasantries by neglecting their calling in Christ.

The Greek word for Church is *ekklesia*, which means "called out ones." The Church is a company of believers who are *kaleo* (called) – *ek* (out of or from something). But what are God's people called out from? Randy P. Amos explains, and may we live accordingly:

- They are called *out of* the world's thinking and system (John 15:19).
- They are called *out of* the perishing nations (Acts 15:14).

- They are delivered *from* this present age (Gal. 1:4).
- They are delivered *from* the power of Satan's darkness (Col. 1:13).
- They will be physically delivered *out of* this world into Heaven (Rev. 3:10).
- They are commanded to come *out of* wicked Babylon (Rev. 18:4).[26]

While the Corinthian believers lived like kings above the humiliation of identifying with Christ, the apostles labored with their hands to provide for their own needs and relied on the Lord to provide for the ministry (v. 12; Acts 18:3; Phil. 4:15-19). Paul had no interest in shaming them into a lifestyle of cross-bearing, but wanted to warn them that now was not the time to reign as kings. Rather, they had an opportunity to labor for and to suffer for Christ to obtain an eternal reward in His Kingdom (v. 14). Reigning as worldlings in a world condemned to destruction could not be compared with reigning with Christ in His future kingdom. Hence, the Corinthians were to be a living testimony of Christ, not of the world.

Paul's tone softens and becomes more appealing in verse 14. He had brought them the gospel message which had saved their souls. Being the one who had shown them the way of life, he considered himself their spiritual father; thus, he pleaded with them to follow his example of living for Christ (vv. 15-16). For this purpose, Paul was sending Timothy to teach them *"my ways in Christ, as I teach in everywhere in every church"* (v. 17). The necessity of fully identifying with Christ and His teachings was what Paul taught all believers everywhere. There was no variation of doctrines that Paul taught to various groups of believers; there was one embodiment of Church truth taught to all the churches (v.17, 7:17, 11:16, 16:1).

## Paul's Authority as an Apostle (vv. 18-21)

Apparently, some accused Paul of hiding behind a stern letter instead of being willing to come personally to rebuke them (v. 18). Paul's response to his critics was that in the Lord's will he would come to them, either in love (if they responded well to this letter) or with a rod (if they did not; v. 21). In short, he was not afraid to visit them, but the demeanor in which he would come depended on their response to his correction in this epistle.

Paul then reminded his audience that the kingdom of God is not concerned with mere words, but with the spiritual working of God's power (vv. 19-20). The point is that high-sounding men rarely speak for the Lord. But humble and obedient individuals are the vessels God uses to declare His glory. If Paul came to them carrying a rod, then the Corinthians would learn the hard way that his words were accompanied by God's power.

# 1 Corinthians Chapter 5

### Indifference to Sin in the Church Rebuked (vv. 1-2)

The house of Chloe had informed Paul of an ongoing immoral situation within the church at Corinth: a man was having sexual relations with his father's wife (i.e., stepmother; v. 1). Not only was the sin public, but the Corinthian believers were boasting about the matter; it was an example of the kind of freedom that they believed was permissible in grace (v. 2). But Paul sharply rebukes their actions; they should be mourning over the sin and should have removed the sinning man from their church fellowship.

### Sin in the Church Must Be Dealt With (vv. 3-8)

Paul did not need to hear any more details about the matter. He was with them in spirit and was able to judge the matter as if he were present with them (v. 3). The subject behavior was offensive to God (Lev. 18:8). They gathered under Christ's authority and in that authority the assembly should put the sinning man out of the church fellowship (vv. 4-5; i.e., he must be excommunicated to uphold Christ's dignity and headship). Church discipline of this type is for the purpose of isolating an errant believer from all the privileges of local church body-life, so that he or she can fully experience the full detriment of not being in fellowship with Christ.

There is much confusion today concerning the meaning of the word "discipline" as we normally associate it with the administration of "pain." The concept that "pain" and "discipline" are synonymous falls miserably short of the biblical meaning of discipline. Biblical discipline (training) includes a number of tools which can be used in order to affirm good behavior or to correct wrong or undesired behavior.

There is *instruction* by which God's truth is communicated in an understandable way so that God's people are not ignorant of God's will. There is *encouragement* which rewards and reinforces right behavior, especially in areas where the recipient tends to struggle. There is *exhortation*, which means "to come alongside and turn" – all believers need course corrections by those who love them. When someone becomes insubordinate or troublesome, he must be admonished by God's Word. *Admonition* literally means "to put in mind" and calls attention to a subject by giving a mild rebuke.

Not every behavior will require stern reproof. *Correction*, a milder form of calling attention to foolish or improper behavior, will be employed much more often. The Greek word translated "correction" in 2 Timothy 3:16 means to "straighten up again." A believer who is unruly is to be warned to yield to the church elders (1 Thess. 5:14). When believers transgress known or obvious boundaries, there should be a *rebuke*. Rebuke has the thought of "putting honor upon something" and is used often in the Gospels to describe the Lord's sharp reproof of a wrong attitude, often in a stressful situation.

The disorderly (2 Thess. 3:11, 14, 15) and those who are divisive (v. 17) or factious (Titus 3:10-11) are to be *avoided* completely (Acts 20:28-31). These behaviors are often associated with those not sound in doctrine. The purpose of shunning is to help another person see that he or she is out of fellowship with God, and therefore out of fellowship with His people. As in the case before us, a believer engaging in gross sin and who has rejected Biblical reproof should be dealt with by *excommunication* (vv. 5, 11-13). This form of discipline was not imposed by any individual or by individuals in the church, but by the collective body of saints in the church fellowship. The "you" (v. 4) and "yourselves" (v. 13) are derived from plural pronouns and speak of the local church. Paul instructs the assembly as to what must be done, but the act of discipline itself was not under apostolic authority.

Excommunication has the effect of delivering the rebellious to Satan for buffeting (v. 5; 1 Tim. 1:20). Hopefully, this will cause the wayward to repent and be restored to the Lord and His people. However, if willful sin continues, it is possible that God will not tolerate the defaming testimony against His Son and might even remove the rebel child from the earth through death. John refers to such a divine act *"as sins unto death"* (1 Jn. 5:16). Although Paul states that a true believer's soul is saved in such situations, the shame of appearing before God in Heaven in this manner is unimaginable (v. 5). In the Lord's presence, such wayward believers will be forced to ponder the dishonor they brought on His name (1 Jn. 2:28).

All acts of correction and discipline must be accomplished with genuine love for the recipient and with the end goal of his or her full restoration to fellowship with God and His people. Discipline motivated by insincerity prompts God's displeasure and will result in more damage than good. The narrative of Judges 20 illustrates this point. God permitted the deaths of 40,000 soldiers on the correct side of righteousness because they did not have the proper attitude in correcting those on the wrong side of righteousness. Not only is the purity of Christ to be upheld in the local assembly, but the beauty of His character must be revealed too.

The Corinthian believers should not be boasting in this brother's sin. Rather, to correct the matter they must uphold Christ's holiness and authority. Paul tells them that they were erroneously "puffed up" over the matter (v. 2). This is what leaven in a lump of dough does – it "puffs up" the dough. Likewise, leaven in us causes us to glory in what offends God.

Leaven, in Scripture, speaks of sin, corruption, or evil doctrine (Matt. 13:33). The first mention of leaven in Scripture describes the simple meal Lot's wife prepared for the two visiting angels (Gen. 19:3). The unleavened bread stood in sharp contrast to Lot's "leavened" life (i.e., his failure to separate from the world). The next reference to leaven in the Bible relates to the unleavened bread which was to be a part of the Passover Feast and the celebration of Unleavened Bread that followed (Ex. 12). Those Jews eating the Passover Lamb to escape God's wrath in Egypt had to maintain an unleavened life. Those partaking of Christ for salvation in the Church Age are also to live a consecrated life to Him – for *"Christ, our Passover, was sacrificed for us"* (v. 7). Redemption demands sanctification, not pride! The believer's life is likened to the festival of Unleavened Bread. Just as this feast followed the death of the Passover Lamb, our newness of life in Christ, which gives power over sin, follows the death of Christ at Calvary.

Paul warns the Corinthians to not have any fellowship with anyone identifying with Christ but who was at the same time willfully engaging in sin. Just as a little leaven leavens the whole lump of dough, false doctrine and ongoing sin have a cascading effect that can spread throughout the entire assembly if unchecked (vv. 6, 8). If sin in the Church is not dealt a deadly blow by God's people, it will thoroughly corrupt all who do not esteem holiness as necessary for maintaining fellowship with Christ.

## Gathered in Christ's Name

The early Church met to hear God's Word, to pray together, to keep the Lord's Supper and for fellowship (Acts 2:42). Believers gathered in the name of the Lord Jesus, hence, in the authority of that Name. Paul ensured that the church at Corinth understood this fact: *"In the name of our Lord Jesus Christ, when you are gathered together"* (1 Cor. 5:4). Whenever God's people meet together, they do so in Christ's name and to be with Him.

Whether it is a simple feast of bread and wine to remember Him and to publicly proclaim the value of His death, or to be in His Word to learn His mind, or to be before His mercy seat to tell Him of our needs and to request grace to better serve Him – we meet with Him and in His name. The Lord and His presence alone draws us to all the church meetings. I want to be at every meeting because the Lord will be at every meeting. When a believer justifies careless absenteeism, in effect he or she is casting a vote to close down the assembly and remove Christ's name from the community!

The Lord gave this promise to His disciples: *"For where two or three are gathered together in My name, I am there in the midst of them"* (Matt. 18:20). Paradise is wherever the Lord is (Luke 23:43), meaning that the closest experience of Heaven itself on this side of glory is to be with other believers in the presence of the Lord Jesus. The gathering of the local assembly should be treasured, for it is a visible exhibition to the world that Christ has a record of Himself here – a testimony (a lampstand) in the world.

## In the World, but Not of the World (vv. 9-13)

Paul's edict to the assembly at Corinth in how to handle the sinning brother reflects God's passion for holy living – *"Put away from yourselves the evil person"* (v. 13). All sin grieves God, but the devastating nature of sexual immorality is why the fornicating man at Corinth was to be excommunicated. Furthermore, the Corinthians were not to have any casual contact with any professing Christian who was unrepentant in sin (vv. 11-12). Yet, Paul is careful to ensure that the Corinthians do not misunderstand his application: This clause did not apply to the unregenerate, but rather to professing Christians engaged in immorality, greed, idolatry, railing (the use of abusive language against others), drunkenness, extortion, etc. (vv. 9-10).

Previously, Paul had warned the Corinthians about having close contact with those in sin, as they could easily become influenced by it and lose their testimony. However, Paul did not want the believers at Corinth to wholly isolate from the lost, for how else would they be able to see and hear the gospel message? It was desirable for them (and for us too) to influence the lost for Christ without being corrupted by their sinful ways. This was the example of the Lord Jesus during His earthly ministry (Matt. 9:10-12). However, if someone identifies himself or herself as a Christian, but is engaged in willful, unrepentant sin, believers are not to have close association with that person at all. This becomes difficult to implement when the one in sin is a close family member, but the command is valid regardless. Embracing a wayward believer, as if there is nothing wrong, endorses his or her sin, which works to strengthen sin's hold.

Fellowship with other believers should be determined on the basis of sound doctrine and sound morals, meaning that believers must be judging each other in these areas of life to protect the testimony of Christ in the Church (v. 12). Concerning the unregenerate, it is God who will judge them; but believers must judge themselves to maintain a proper testimony of Christ that will draw the lost to the Savior (v. 13).

# 1 Corinthians Chapter 6

### Do Not Permit the Unrighteous to Judge the Righteous (vv. 1-8)

The house of Chloe had apparently informed Paul of another issue in the church at Corinth – believers were publicly suing each other. How could believers be unified in worship when the church assembled together given that some saints were injuring each other in civil court? Paul's opening question conveys his utter shock on hearing this heart-breaking news.

Under the Law, no Jew having a controversy or an offense to be judged would have ever brought it before a Gentile tribunal. Rather, it was to be heard by the priests and appointed judges of Israel (Deut. 16:18-22). Jehovah was in the midst of His people. It would have been insulting to Him for His people to ask Gentile pagans, who did not know Him or His Law, to judge their grievances.

Paul affirms a similar procedure for saints in the Church Age. Christians were not to take each other into Gentile courts to resolve their disputes; rather, they were to submit to the judgment of the wise among them, which should include the elders of the church (vv. 1-5). The apostle is not speaking in a derogatory manner of those in judicial offices, but rather stating that believers are held to a higher standard of holy conduct that is becoming of Christ; unregenerate judges uphold only the laws of the land. God's Laws are absolute and do not change, but human standards of morality are constantly changing and are often contrary to God's justice. Hence, even those lightly esteemed in the church for their wisdom would be better judges of spiritual matters, than a civil judge with no spiritual wisdom (v. 4).

Paul's sarcasm in verse 5 was "a shame on you" tactic that affirmed that there were wise believers in the church who could resolve disagreements among them. The Corinthians should keep the big picture in view – it would be much better for the cause of Christ for someone to be willfully defrauded by another believer (to lose temporary things) rather than to demand one's rights and cause public disdain to the Lord's name in secular courts (vv. 6-8). It would be better for believers to suffer a brief financial loss than to forfeit eternal reward at the Judgment Seat of Christ.

To further his point, the apostle reminds his brethren at Corinth that in a coming day they will "judge the world" and "judge the angels" (vv. 2-3).

Why then would they want to take each other to a secular court for judgments when the unregenerate judges hearing their cases were destined to be judged by them with Christ in a future day? Furthermore, at the Great White Throne judgment, all of the wicked will be judged by Christ and cast in the Lake of Fire. Evil angels will be eternally condemned at that time also. Believers will be with Christ as He judges all that affronts Him.

Believers have a bright future in Christ! Besides having the opportunity to praise and worship the Lord with unhindered affections and strength, believers also rule and reign with Christ, judge the wicked with Christ, and inherit all things with Christ (Rev. 21:7). Therefore, any legal disagreements among believers today would be minuscule in comparison to the eternal matters they would judge under Christ's authority in the future.

## Believers Must Flee Fornication (vv. 9-18)

In chapters 5 and 6, Paul addresses three sins in the assembly that were grieving God: outrageous sin, litigation among believers, and the desecration of God's sanctuary by fornication. Any sexual relation other than between a husband and wife is referred to as fornication in the Bible. This is why Paul says *"to avoid fornication, let every man have his own wife"* (7:2). Fornication then includes adultery, pre-marital relationships, homosexuality (e.g., sodomy), beastiality, etc. Under the Law, any Jew engaging in these sexual sins was to be put to death (Lev. 20:10-13), except for those engaging in pre-marital sex who were to marry (Deut. 22:29).

When it comes to God's standard of purity, nothing has changed in the New Testament; the only difference is that immediate punishment for sexual sin is not demanded by God. Such sins are still offensive to God and will be punished, but not by immediate death. To say that the New Testament does not condemn fornication is absurd (vv. 13, 18; 1 Thess. 4:5). Paul and John both confirm that those engaging in such sin will not go to Heaven, but will be cast in the Lake of Fire (Eph. 5:3-5; Rev. 21:8). God is offended when people exchange divinely revealed truth for a lie; He responds by turning them over to their own reprobate thinking. For example, homosexuality was a primary behavior that resulted after God removed His convicting influence from people who had rejected Him (Rom. 1:21-28).

Some at Corinth had been saved out of all kinds of sinful behaviors including gross immorality associated with paganism (vv. 9-10). Being new creations in Christ meant that they could not continue in sin (1 Jn. 3:9), thus Paul says, *"such were some of you"* (v. 11). The Greek verb translated *"were washed"* is in the middle voice meaning that the Corinthians freely chose to trust in the gospel message and be washed clean by the blood of

Christ. The verbs rendered "sanctified" and "justified" are in the passive voice, meaning that God responded to their free expression of faith by doing what only He can do – justifying them in Christ and setting them aside for His glory. Praise the Lord!

Through Christ, grace is extended to believers to work out the questionable areas of life with fear and trembling before the Lord (Phil. 2:12). Scripture refers to this privilege and responsibility as Christian "liberty." Believers are to heed the guidelines and warnings of Scripture, glean from the good examples of godly saints in Scripture, and also learn to avoid the mistakes and failures of those who missed the mark. Obviously biblical commands are nonnegotiable (such as abstaining from fornication); we must do what God commands and avoid doing what He prohibits.

Paul reminds the Corinthians that though there were many permissible activities (the idea behind "all things"), not all are profitable for them to engage in (v. 12). In fact, some could enslave them. It would be far better never to start what you cannot stop later. Addictions often begin with the gullible desire to feel good, but in time, one continues the behavior to not feel bad. Addiction is often referred to as "substance abuse," but in reality, it is the person who is abused by the debilitating situation, not the substance.

Many believers today are also mastered by activities which are not inherently evil, but they have become enslaved by them nonetheless: gaming, social media, amusements, sports, education – the list is endless. Sadly, our time, resources, and affections are wasted on what has no value for eternity. The Christian's only goal in life is to give our Savior honor and glory through complete submission to His will (Eph. 1:12). To achieve this goal, the believer must be liberated from all controlling hindrances.

Apparently, some at Corinth were justifying gluttony because of their newfound liberty in Christ: *"Foods for the stomach and the stomach for foods"* (v. 13). But Paul declares that both will be eventually destroyed by God. The point is that believers should not live for what is temporary but serve the Lord with our bodies which He has purchased. We need food, but we are not to live for food by engaging in gluttony. Similarly, our bodies are designed for procreation, but we are to live for the Lord, not for sexual pleasure outside of God's will (i.e., outside of marriage). We are more than a physical body and immorality injures the whole person (v. 18). As all believers are in union with Christ, and destined to be raised up in resurrection power to be with Him forever, why would any believer want to make Christ privy to such an offensive and damaging sin now (vv. 14-15)?

The temple of Aphrodite in Corinth may have had more than a thousand temple prostitutes to seduce worshipers with immoral pagan practices.

Clearly, some believers in the assembly had been fornicators and idolaters before coming to Christ (v. 9), so Paul was rejecting the notion that believers could still engage in that putrid lifestyle. Becoming one flesh with a harlot does immense damage to one's soul (Prov. 6:32). God designed the sexual bonding of a husband and wife to be much more than just a physical act. Those who think that they can lightly engage in fornication and not be emotionally and spiritually impacted are deceived. Such sin adversely affects the entire person and so, for the sake of the Body of Christ, believers must *"flee sexual immorality"* (vv. 16-18).

## Desecrating God's Holy Temple (vv. 19-20)

Except for the Church Age, and as long as the earth exists, Jerusalem is the place God has chosen to place His name (i.e., the formal place to worship God; 1 Kgs. 11:32; Jer. 3:17). At present, all believer-priests compose the temple of God and lift up worship and living sacrifices to God wherever and whenever they desire (Rom. 12:1; 1 Pet. 2:5, 9; Rev. 1:6). Having two temples to honor God on earth at the same time would be confusing, so after the Church is removed from the earth, and after the Tribulation period is over, a gigantic temple will be built in Jerusalem during the Kingdom Age (Ezek. chs. 40-47).

In order to exhort the saints at Corinth to holy living, Paul reminds them that they are a part of God's holy temple: *"Do you not know that your body is the temple of the Holy Spirit who is in you, whom you have from God, and you are not your own? For you were bought at a price; therefore, glorify God in your body and in your spirit, which are God's"* (vv. 19-20).

Sometimes all believers in the Body of Christ, the Church, are spoken of in Scripture as His living temple on earth (1 Tim. 3:15; 1 Pet. 2:5). At other times the temple of the Lord refers to the testimony of believers gathered at one location – the local church (3:16-17). Each assembly is to be a lampstand (a testimony) for God to the lost in the world (Rev. 2:5). Additionally, in verses 19-20, Paul exhorts individual believers to understand that their bodies are temples of the Holy Spirit and that they should pour out their whole self in consecrated service for the glory of God.

Our bodies and souls have been purchased by the blood of Christ; therefore, we are to give ourselves fully to the cause of Christ. We are to be holy living temples that offer worship to God through our thoughts, words, and deeds. Although the Lord has yet to return to redeem what He has already purchased, our bodies, we are nonetheless completely His. Until then, may we all live for the praise of His glory by surrendering our will for His – full consecration can occur only when we surrender all to God!

# 1 Corinthians Chapter 7

Marriage and Singleness in the Lord (vv. 1-9)

Having addressed various problems in the assembly of which the house of Chloe had made him aware, the apostle shifts to answering a list of questions he had received from the church. The first inquiry pertained to the appropriate attitude toward marriage and singleness. Apparently, some had adopted a form of self-denial that claimed a married couple should live as if they were not married: *"It is good for a man not to touch a woman"* (v. 1).

Some insight into the Greek word rendered "touch" will be helpful in understanding this statement. *Haptomai* means to "attach to" or "cling to." The middle voice is used to convey the idea, "You don't have to seek a wife for yourself." While Paul does not affirm their asceticism, he does say that there are valid reasons for believers to remain single (vv. 2, 7, 26). In Paul's mind, there was a distinct advantage to being single in order to concentrate more fully on ministry without being distracted by family responsibilities. But he realized that marriage, and not singleness, was God's intention for most men and women. Hence, in marriage, a man should have his own wife, and a wife her own husband; this stipulation prohibited polygamy (v. 2).

It would be wise for men and women to follow God's design of marriage to preclude lust that leads to fornication. The "one flesh" or the "one person" relationship in marriage is to be a wonderful experience of full disclosure, security, and intimacy (Gen. 2:23-24). This means that husbands and wives are to "render" to each other in such a way that the sexual needs of both spouses are satisfied; this would preclude sexual sin outside of marriage (v. 3; Ex. 21:10). The Greek word translated "render" is an imperative mood verb (i.e., a command), and therefore conveys the meaning "you must give to your spouse what is due to him or her." Sex is never to be weaponized or abused in a marriage, but for mutual enjoyment.

God designed the sexual union between a husband and wife to be a satisfying experience that would enrich the marriage covenant. Hence, it would be offensive to God for sex to be used for selfish gain or unnatural pleasure. Neither party was to deprive the other of this marital responsibility, unless it was mutually agreed to do so for a brief time in order to be more fully given to prayer and fasting (vv. 4-5). Yet, it would be wise to limit these durations to prevent the devil from exploiting an open door of temptation. While the matter of God's design for marriage was not open to debate, Paul states that his counsel on when to refrain from sexual relations and how long to do so was offered as guidance, and not a command (v. 6).

The idea of husbands and wives abstaining from marital relations for a time of spiritual exercise is not a new concept. In preparation to meet the Lord at Mount Sinai, the Israelites were to consecrate themselves by washing their clothes and refraining from sexual relations for a three-day period (Ex. 19:14-15). This restriction highlighted the solemn nature of the upcoming event and the need for complete devotion in preparation to meet Jehovah.

Paul desired that everyone would be as he was, single, so that believers could be fully given to ministry without the distractions of marital and family responsibilities (vv. 7-9). Yet, God designed marriage with the goal of producing godly offspring for Himself, so Paul realized that it was God's will for most saints to marry (Mal. 2:15). Furthermore, Paul realized that those called to a life of singleness to serve the Lord would also receive a "gift" to equip them to do so. Those struggling with ongoing natural lust for the opposite gender obviously had not been given this gift and should marry in the will of the Lord, to preclude fornication. The Greek word rendered "gift" is *charisma*, and is derived from the root word *charis*, which means "grace." God always gives His servants sufficient grace to accomplish what He has purposed for them to do!

## Regulations for Married Believers (vv. 10-16)

Corinth was a vile seaport city, known for its lascivious excesses. Pagan ritualistic immorality and polygamy were commonplace. Some who had turned to Christ were wondering if they should remain with their unsaved spouses; others were inquiring about what to do if deserted by a spouse (believing and unbelieving). In this section, Paul labors to reorient new believers to God's original design for marriage and how to honorably handle these real-life situations that some saints in Corinth were now facing.

Paul begins by affirming God's original design for marriage in the Garden of Eden, prior to the fall of humanity: one man and one woman committing themselves to each other by a marriage covenant until death separates them (v. 10). The idea of divorce, the result of a sinful heart rebelling against God's design for marriage, came later and was permitted by the Mosaic Law. However, the Lord Jesus said that divorce was permissible only for the sin of adultery, as unfaithfulness to one's marriage vows breaks the marriage covenant (Matt. 5:31-32, 19:9). It seems unlikely that the Lord is referring only to the Jewish betrothal period in which a groom learned that his espoused wife was not a virgin. First, the situation is quite specific to be addressed so thoroughly, and second, Jehovah divorced His wife Israel because of her adultery (spiritual unfaithfulness; Ezek. 16:20, 32, 38; Jer. 3:8). God's own actions indicate that divorcing an unfaithful spouse is warranted if efforts to bring repentance and restoration have failed.

Having affirmed what Scripture taught about God's design for marriage, Paul affirmed the high standard that believing couples were to maintain, lest they bring dishonor on the name of Christ (v. 11). Christian couples should strive to be reconciled when difficulties arise, but if restoration is not possible, living separated lives (as if single) from each other was permitted.

A civil divorce should not be sought in such situations unless it is the only means remaining to ensure the safety or financial integrity of the individuals involved. This should be viewed as a civil formality to insulate a believer from possible financial loss and physical harm. (Divorce often leads to remarriage and thus should be avoided if at all possible.) Furthermore, if there are no scriptural grounds for divorce (adultery), a civil divorce does not dissolve the marriage covenant in God's eyes. Restoration, not divorce, is a testimony of God's grace; therefore, God places a higher standard of behavior on married believers, which is why Paul did not mention the exception clause found in Matthew's Gospel.

Next, Paul turns his attention to an existing marriage in which one of the spouses had become a Christian. Paul's counsel was that a believer should honor their marriage covenant and remain with their unbelieving spouse, if possible (vv. 12-14). The testimony of Christ in the believing spouse may lead the unregenerate spouse to salvation. In this situation, the unsaved spouse is literally "sanctified" by the believing spouse, that is "set apart" to see and to hear the gospel message in a special way.

If, however, the new believer is deserted by the unsaved spouse, the believer is loosened from the marriage covenant (v. 15). This assumes that the unsaved spouse has entered a new relationship and has broken his or her marriage covenant by committing adultery. A believer in this situation should refrain from civil divorce and remarriage until the door of opportunity has been closed for restoration (i.e., the offending spouse divorces the believing spouse and remarries someone else). Although this is not God's best intention for marriage, a deserted believing spouse is not under obligation to reconcile with the former spouse any longer and would be free to marry another believer. Requiring a believing spouse to remain single for life, because of being abandoned by an unbelieving spouse would be an unbearable burden for most people, given what Paul said in verse 9;

therefore, remarriage was permitted for this situation to make for peace.

Not only can a believing spouse be used of God to lead his or her unsaved spouse to the Lord, but unbelieving children are also given a special blessing from the Lord to hear the gospel message from a believing parent (v. 14). In this sense, the children are "holy," meaning that they are "set apart" to hear the gospel message in the same way an unsaved spouse is. This does not guarantee the salvation of the children, as some teach, but rather highlights the divine privilege they have that many do not receive.

## Remain in Your Calling (vv. 17-24)

Apparently, the Corinthians were in a quandary as how to live for Christ after being delivered from their pagan culture. Should they fully isolate from the lost to avoid worldliness and temptations to sin? As sanctified believers in Christ, did God require them to radically change things such as their marital status, occupations, location, etc.? Paul had already encouraged believers to remain with their unbelieving spouses, so that they could be further exposed to the gospel message; now he addresses other practical aspects of the believer's calling in Christ.

The main exhortation was that believers should serve God faithfully wherever He has placed them and in accordance with whatever calling He has equipped them for (v. 17). This was not just a truth Paul was conveying to the church at Corinth; it was a valid teaching for all believers to heed. It is not one's ethnicity, social status, or particular vocation that matters, but how believers serve and represent Christ in all their doings (v. 20).

Whether born a Greek or a Jew does not matter. If believers obey God's plan for their lives, they will enjoy Christ's life to the full (vv. 18-19). Consequently, even if one was a slave when regeneration occurred, he or she could live a full and fruitful life for Christ as a slave and not miss out on anything (v. 21). If free, believers should realize that they were enslaved to Christ, so their freedom was not anything to be proud of (v. 22). The fruit of the Spirit was available to all believers to pursue and enjoy, so a believer's location, profession, ethnicity, etc. could not restrain this mutual spiritual reality.

We have been redeemed by Christ to serve Him freely and completely no matter what our circumstances. Therefore, we should not become enslaved to secular traditions and human philosophies (v. 23). Slaves cannot serve two masters; only Christ is to be the believer's Master. Nor should believers engage in some revolutionary agenda that would isolate them from the unregenerate and thereby remove them from the divine calling that God desires for them (v. 24).

## Counsel to the Unmarried (vv. 25-40)

Given the escalating persecution against Christians at the time Paul penned this letter to the Corinthians (vv. 26, 29), the apostle offers the following counsel to the unmarried, and also how to behave if you were already married. Paul offers the following guidance:

- If married, stay married; if not married, do not seek to be (v. 27).

- If a single person decides to marry, it is not a sin (v. 28).

- Facing martyrdom will be emotionally easier without family responsibilities (v. 28).

- A spouse should not hinder the other from serving the Lord (v. 29).

- If married, realize that attending to the needs of a spouse and family will reduce one's ability to serve others outside the home (vv. 32-34).

- An individual is a steward of his own virginity; anyone desiring to marry and to have a family, should do so before becoming too old; choosing to marry is not a sin (vv. 36-38).

- Widows may remarry, but only in the Lord (v. 39).

Given the severity of persecution against the Church at that time, and the reality that marriage, commerce, property, food, clothing, etc. would all pass away in due time, Paul was exhorting the believers to live for eternity.

Most English translations of verses 36-38 have confused Paul's directives (the JND translation offers clarity). The noun rendered "virgin" in verse 34 is feminine and relates to an unmarried female in contrast to a married woman. However, the nouns and inferred pronouns in verses 36-38 are all masculine. It is not a father's marital intentions for his virgin daughter that is the topic, but a man's intentions concerning his "virginity" – should he marry or not. To do so was not a sin, but do not wait too long to marry.

The Law did not allow a wife to divorce her husband, which Paul affirms in verse 38, but if a believer's husband had died, she was free to marry in the Lord. However, Paul suggests that she should consider remaining single to better serve the Lord unhindered by domestic responsibilities (v. 39). Paul concludes this section on a note of irony, *"and I think I also have the Spirit of God"* (v. 40). His point being, he was an apostle, and no one in Corinth had a monopoly on the Holy Spirit. This meant that the commands and the counsel just given on the subject matters of marriage and singleness were inspired by God and should be heeded.

# 1 Corinthians Chapter 8

## A Brother Is More Important Than Food (vv. 1-13)

Paul addresses another question posed by the Corinthians concerning meat offered to idols. Before answering the specifics, he first teaches them about sacrificing their personal liberty (choosing wise behavior in permissible things) for the good of other believers. He begins by saying "we" (i.e., believers) know that an idol is nothing; it is merely a figment of man's fallen imagination, for there is only one God (v. 1). The heathen boast of various "so-called gods" in Heaven and on earth, but believers understand that there is only one God, the Creator of all things who is in authority (vv. 5-6). The Corinthians knew this to be true, but they had various opinions on how to honor God in the matter of eating meat that had been offered to idols.

The particular situation that the apostle is addressing pertains to the marketplace practices in cities like Corinth which were also the sites of pagan temples. Idols do not eat much, so good quality meat offered to idols was sold in the market at a reduced price. So, a frugal believer, understanding that there is only one God and that meat was not tainted by what is not real, could buy this high-quality low-cost meat with a good conscience (v. 4). But in such matters, truth alone is insufficient to guide one's behavior (v. 2). Truth must lead others to God, which means the application of truth must be prompted by love. This type of love will seek a behavior that will bless and edify others, because the believer loves God and wants to exalt Him (v. 3). Such individuals are known by God, that is, they are known with favor by God – they have God's appreciation and praise.

This means that our frugal believer should be conscious of a scenario in which serving meat offered to idols might be offensive to a *weak* believer who witnesses or hears about the matter (v. 9). William MacDonald describes what a "weak" believer means in this passage:

> The expression weak here does not mean physically weak or even spiritually weak. It is a term describing those who are unduly scrupulous in matters of moral indifference. For instance, as far as God is concerned, it is not wrong for a believer to eat pork. It would have been

wrong for a Jew to do so in the Old Testament, but a Christian is at perfect liberty to partake of such food. However, a Jew converted to Christianity might still have scruples about this. He might feel that it is wrong to eat a roast pork dinner. He is what the Bible calls a weak brother. It means that he is not living in the full enjoyment of his Christian liberty.[27]

Returning to our illustration, the weak believer might be a new convert freshly saved out of idolatry or Judaism, but is not yet capable of forming sound spiritual decisions in questionable areas of life. Such believers would have preconceived ideas about meat offered to idols, but have not yet come to appreciate their liberty in Christ (v. 7). Mature believers should be alert to situations which might stumble those younger in the faith. The safe course of action would be not to serve meat offered to idols to the weaker brother in question. Neither should they boast about their practice of liberty to him, or to others, to prevent him from hearing about it indirectly.

Whether a person eats the meat offered to an idol or not is not the essential matter that Paul is addressing, for *"food does not commend us to God"* (v. 8). The Lord Jesus said that it was not what goes into a man's mouth, but what comes out of his mouth that defiles him (Matt. 15:11). Whatever we eat before the Lord is sanctified and is made acceptable by giving thanks to Him for it (1 Tim. 4:15). This means that we can eat the food before us with a clear conscience: *"I know and am convinced by the Lord Jesus that there is nothing unclean of itself; but to him who considers anything to be unclean, to him it is unclean"* (Rom. 14:14). However, whatever the believer's persuasion might be on the matter of a proper healthy diet, or economical purchases, it should be understood to be an area of liberty. Such liberties are to be forfeited, if need be, to avoid unnecessarily offending others who do not understand such things (v. 9).

Paul is teaching us that truth alone is insufficient to guide our behavior; we need to show each other the love of Christ while still holding on to the truth. Love without truth is hypocrisy and truth without love is brutality; both virtues must guide what we do. We need to follow the Lord Jesus' example who was full of grace and truth in all He did (John 1:14).

In chapter 5, the Corinthians had love without truth; they showed tolerance to a brother in gross sin and were "puffed up" about it. Paul now warns them that just having the truth without love will cause them to be "puffed up" in pride also. This is what leaven does: It puffs up, and acting in truth without love (i.e., doing what we know will not benefit others) carries with it the stench of pride. Our self-promotion, especially at the expense of others, has the stench of pride to God.

If a man has a spot of skin cancer on his arm, a surgeon could remove the entire arm or the surgeon could skillfully remove only the malignant part. Both actions remove the dangerous threat, but the repercussions of the former action will leave the patient disabled for life. Executing truth at any cost is disguised cruelty! This means we do not cause division by promoting our dietary convictions among those who see things differently, especially younger believers who, because of a heightened sensitivity to the ills of their past, choose safety over knowledge (Rom. 14:1-3).

With maturity an older child may choose to use a crosswalk to safely cross a busy street. However, it would be wrong to force a younger child, who sees nothing but danger, to cross the street on their own or to shame him for not being willing to do so. Paul's point is that our mealtimes should be marked by thanksgiving and joyful fellowship, not unprofitable opinions or uncaring behaviors rooted in pride.

We should gladly yield our liberty (the right to act as we deem fit) if there is the potential for stumbling someone by our eating and drinking (v. 9). If our behavior causes other believers to think evil of us, or to act against their conscience, we have sinned against them and against Christ (vv. 10-12). Paul says it would be better not to eat what is questionable ever again, rather than risk stumbling a fellow believer in the Lord (v. 13).

With this said, notice that one must be walking forward before there is potential to stumble over something. In application, if a professing Christian is not obeying the Lord (not living out sound doctrine), perhaps less urgency to sacrificing our liberty is warranted. If someone is spiritually stagnant (i.e., not walking with the Lord), stumbling over a particular area of another's Christian liberty is not likely, and would not be the crucial matter needing to be dealt with in any case.

The dietary laws issued to the Jews were specific to them; these were to accentuate their need for holiness in all areas of life, for holy Jehovah resided with them. Under the Law, non-compliance with these specific "dos and don'ts" would be sin. However, in the Church Age, the matter of what we eat is not a moral issue, but rather one of wisdom. Believers would be wise to eat what is good for the body and likewise foolish to consume or drink what is harmful. Believers would also be wise not to eat or drink what might offend others who are of a differing conviction. A brother or sister in Christ is much more significant to the Lord than what we eat!

Let us remember that nothing of eternal significance is achieved without personal sacrifice. God's own actions demonstrate that genuine love begins with self-sacrifice (e.g., John 3:16).

# 1 Corinthians Chapter 9

### Paul Vindicates His Apostleship (vv. 1-3)

Paul begins to vindicate his apostleship by posing four consecutive questions, all of which demanded an affirmative response. Some at Corinth did not believe Paul was a legitimate apostle or at least considered him to be inferior to those who had been Christ's original disciples. Paul dispels this thinking by stating three claims. First, his apostleship did not come by human authority – he was directly sent by the Lord (v. 1). Second, like the other apostles, he had seen the risen Savior; Paul had a personal encounter with Him on the road to Damascus. Third, the proof or "seal" of his apostleship was evident in the Corinthians themselves. If they were saved, it was because Christ had endorsed and empowered his ministry among them (vv. 2-3). Paul will repeat this same defense again in a later letter to the Corinthians (2 Cor. 3:2).

### Paul Was Entitled to Financial Support as an Apostle (vv. 4-10)

Having asserted his authority as a true apostle of Christ, Paul launches into a lengthy proof that he was also entitled to monetary support as an apostle, though he did not demand that right from the Corinthians. The apostles in Jerusalem lived quite differently than Paul and Barnabas did as itinerant workers. The apostles in Jerusalem were apparently married, had homes, and were well supported financially (vv. 4-5). The lives of Paul and Barnabas, on the other hand, could not be characterized by these features. Because of this ministry and lifestyle disparity, some in Corinth doubted their apostleship and therefore declined to support them.

Although Paul did receive gifts from various individuals and churches, he was a tentmaker by trade, and at times had to withdraw from ministry to labor in order to support himself (v. 6). Some of the Corinthians believed that this behavior proved that Paul was not really an apostle; otherwise, the Lord would support his ministry, such that he would not need to suspend it to labor with his hands.

However, Paul corrects their thinking by saying that he and Barnabas had the right to receive support, to marry, to have a family, but had chosen not to exercise these privileges lest their ministry suffer for doing so. They were itinerant preachers who regularly suffered rejection, harsh living conditions, various persecutions, and were under the constant threat of death for preaching Christ. Would that be a good living situation for a wife and children? To ensure that their motives for ministry were not questioned by those they were serving, lest the preaching of the gospel be hindered, they chose not to demand any compensation. They deserved recompense for their ministry, just as a soldier who wars, a man who plants a vineyard, and a shepherd caring for sheep deserved wages, fruit, and milk, respectively (vv. 7-10). If it is appropriate for these earthly occupations to receive just compensation, how much more so for the Lord's servants who engaged in eternal service for God.

Paul quotes Moses to offer an additional example of this principle. Moses had stressed the fair and kind treatment of beasts of burden: *"You shall not muzzle an ox while it treads out the grain"* (Deut. 25:4). An ox that was serving its master by trampling stalks of grain on the threshing floor in preparation for winnowing should be permitted to eat some of the stalks. Likewise, those laboring for the kingdom of God were worthy of financial support from those who had benefitted from their preaching (vv. 9-10).

## Determined Not to Hinder the Gospel (vv. 11-15)

As laboring apostles of Christ, Paul and Barnabas deserved financial support from the church at Corinth, but to ensure that their motives for preaching would not be questioned, they did not demand compensation for their ministry (vv. 11-12). It was more important to the apostles that the gospel message be shared blamelessly in Corinth, than to know where their next meal was coming from.

Paul and Barnabas worked for the Lord and He was therefore responsible to provide for their needs. Just as the Lord provided a well-set table for His serving priests in the temple, Paul was confident that their needs would be met by the Lord also (v. 13). In the next chapter, Paul explains that under Levitical Law, the Lord's altar was His table for His servants. Priests derived their sustenance from the sacrifices and offerings received from the people. The Lord knows how to set a table for His own anywhere (Ps. 23:5, 78:19). Although Paul and Barnabas deserved their support, if the Corinthian believers were not prompted to supply their necessities, the Lord would move others to do so in order that the work of spreading the gospel message would continue (v. 14).

As shown from the apostles' example, there will be occasions that require us to sacrifice our liberty in Christ in order to remain blameless, lest the unregenerate are hindered from hearing the gospel message (10:33). Whether the matter is sacrificing our Christian liberty or living in a way that defies the Lordship of Christ, the unregenerate are watching. We should not do anything that would prevent the lost from hearing the good news message, or even worse, cause them to blaspheme the One who entrusted us with sharing it with them. So, Paul was determined to preach the gospel without charge. He states that he would rather die than not boast in the Lord's ability to support His work without appealing for human support (v. 15). In fact, there is no biblical record of New Testament workers engaging in fund raising campaigns or soliciting others for support; they labored for the Lord and He was able to care for His own dear servants.

## Fulfill Your Calling No Matter the Cost (vv. 16-18)

Christ had assigned Paul the task of preaching the gospel message to the Gentiles, and because of that stewardship, he was going to serve to the best of his ability through the grace supplied him (v. 16). Paul was under divine compulsion to preach, but if he willingly yielded to his calling out of love for Christ, then he would be rewarded for his service (v. 17). Paul believed that no one should boast in what he or she had been commanded to do by the Lord; rather, it was a privilege to serve the One who had died for them.

However, if he neglected his calling, he knew that there would be divine consequences: *"Woe is me if I do not preach the gospel."* Because of this inescapable accountability, Paul was determined not to charge for his service, but to rely on the Lord to supply all his needs. He knew the best way to fulfill his calling and not suffer loss at the Judgment Seat of Christ was to remain blameless (v. 18). Because Paul's calling came from God, Paul would not ask for ministry funding. Hence, Paul was compelled to continue preaching the gospel message, even if no financial support was received from the Corinthians.

God likewise equips believers today with the resources needed to worship and serve Him. First of all, the Christian is indwelt by the Holy Spirit (6:19), who leads and guides us. Second, in Christ we possess all spiritual blessings in heavenly places (Eph. 1:3), which enables us to manifest the character of Christ to the world. A believer can, by faith, lay hold of all the love, grace, and peace he or she needs to exhibit Christ in his or her life. Third, God supplies physical resources to those who desire to willingly serve Him.

Yet, as Paul's resolve demonstrates, it is not the lack of time or financial backing that hinders our ability to serve God, but, rather, our commitment to serve the Lord instead of ourselves. Paul had placed all of his time and resources at the Lord's disposal. He felt that his ministry was so critical to saving lost souls from hellfire that he did not reserve his time or his resources: *"And I will very gladly spend and be spent for your souls; though the more abundantly I love you, the less I am loved"* (2 Cor. 12:15). We may be ready to pray, but not to labor, or labor and not pray, but Paul teaches us that we really cannot serve as we should until all that we have is at the Lord's disposal.

## Becoming All Things to All Men (vv. 19-23)

Because Paul viewed himself as a servant to all men and he had liberty to serve Christ without human interference, he pursued a versatile preaching ministry (v. 19). He was keenly aware that though the gospel message could not be altered, the method of presenting it to different audiences should vary. His goal: *"I have made myself a servant to all, that I might win the more."* Paul had a passion for winning souls to Christ and knew it was wise to do so (Prov. 11:30).

Paul notes three ways that he had *become all things to all men*. First, to the Jew, he became a Jew (v. 20). Although Paul was a Jew by birth, and was highly trained in the Law, in Christ, he was no longer bound to the ceremonies or traditions of Judaism. Yet, we see Paul observing certain Jewish rituals, honoring the Patriarchs, speaking in Hebrew, and quoting the Old Testament to gain an audience with his brethren.

Second, to those without the Law (the Gentiles), he became a Gentile. Paul approached them differently; he dressed like them, ate with them, and went where they gathered – the Law did not permit a Jew to act this way (v. 21). At the Areopagus in Athens, he spoke to a group of Greek intellectuals about the shrine they had erected "TO THE UNKNOWN GOD" (Acts 17:23). Paul informed them of God's name, revealed His divine attributes, and the message that their Creator wanted them to know concerning Christ.

Third, to the weak, he became weak, likely a reference to slavery (v. 22). Although Paul was a free man who had privileges as a Roman citizen, he willingly put aside his civil rights to reach slaves for Christ. About half of the Roman Empire was enslaved at this time, meaning there were many people to reach who had nothing and no reason to live. For example, Quartus (meaning *four*) was likely a believing slave (Rom. 16:23).

Why would Paul continue in gospel ministry without soliciting financial support and why did he become all things to all men in that ministry? Paul had relinquished his own rights and his own will for his Christ-directed ministry so that the work of the gospel could continue unhindered. His life's ministry was the fellowship of the gospel. Consequently, Paul knew that he would be able to share in the triumphs of the gospel in a future day (v. 23).

## Running for the Prize (vv. 24-27)

Paul affirms consecration in the Christian life by using the imagery of a foot race. The Corinthians would have been familiar with both the Greek Olympic Games and their own Isthmian Games. Though there were many runners, there was only one winner. So, Paul exhorts all believers to *run* hard in order to *obtain* the prize. There is no automatic connection between running and winning, but the opportunity is there for all believers to be winners. Warren Wiersbe explains this athletic illustration:

> An athlete must be disciplined if he is to win the prize. Discipline means giving up the good and the better for the best. ... There is nothing wrong with food or fun, but if they interfere with your highest goals, then they are hindrances and not helps. The Christian does not run the race in order to get to Heaven. He is in the race because he has been saved through faith in Jesus Christ. Only Greek citizens were allowed to participate in the games, and they had to obey the rules both in their training and in their performing. Any contestant found breaking the training rules was automatically disqualified.
>
> In order to give up his rights and have the joy of winning lost souls, Paul had to discipline himself. ... If we want to serve the Lord and win His reward and approval, we must pay the price. The word *castaway* (1 Cor. 9:27) is a technical word familiar to those who knew the Greek games. It means "disapproved, disqualified." At the Greek games, there was a herald who announced the rules of the contest, the names of the contestants, and the names and cities of the winners. He would also announce the names of any contestants who were disqualified. Only one runner could win the olive-wreath crown in the Greek games, but *every* believer can win an incorruptible crown when he stands before the Judgment Seat of Christ. This crown is given to those who discipline themselves for the sake of serving Christ and winning lost souls. They keep their bodies under control and keep their eyes on the goal.[28]

Paul viewed his spiritual calling as a footrace to be won (v. 24). The finish line was his death or the Rapture of the Church (1 Thess. 4:13-18; 2 Tim. 4:6-8). The reward (the crown) for finishing the race well would be given at the Judgment Seat of Christ (v. 25). Paul's chief competitor was his own flesh; he was not racing other believers (vv. 26-27).

By God's grace, Paul was determined to keep his flesh from ruling his behavior, lest he lose his testimony and become unprofitable in ministry.

*1 Corinthians*

Paul didn't shadow-box his own flesh; he landed the blows. He knew drastic measures were required to keep his internal bully under wraps. Paul was in a long, grueling race, but he was not competing against other Christians – he was competing against himself. His goal was to keep one stride ahead of his flesh nature in order to finish well.

Paul was determined that his inner man, and not his flesh, would govern his actions. He knew that if he achieved this objective, he would receive an incorruptible crown at the Judgment Seat of Christ, as would all believers who competed with the same spiritual tenacity. All runners have the same motive: whatever we do during this race must ultimately be for God's glory.

Believers do not compete against each other, for God has given each believer a specific calling to fulfill and that will not be finished until the race is over. We do not race against each other; the competition is within ourselves. None of us was born with discipline. Discipline in the Christian life is learned through trials, various experiences, and accomplishments which God uses to shape us into Christ-likeness. Love for the Savior precedes a discipline life. Only a deep appreciation for Christ will keep us pressing forward and upward in our higher calling. There are so many ways to be disqualified in the Christian race. There are so many reefs of temptation to shipwreck our lives on, but love for Christ and the light of His Word guides us safely homeward. As we willingly place ourselves in subjection to Christ and the authority of His Word, we learn tenacity, temperance, and self-control. Discipline causes us to align our wants with what God wants most for us and then going on with Him to achieve it.

> Discipline, for the Christian, begins with the body. We have only one. It is this body that is the primary material given to us for sacrifice. We cannot give our hearts to God and keep our bodies for ourselves.
>
> – Elisabeth Elliot

In the Christian race we don't want to burn out or rust out; we want to last out for Christ. The goal is to maintain a consistent, God-honoring life to maximize our capacity to serve Him and to finish the race well. Paul knew what his flesh nature was capable of doing and that he had to maintain a disciplined life to finish well, else he would be sidelined because of sin. Anytime that we allow the flesh to rule our behavior, we become disqualified to run for Christ: *"Those who are in the flesh cannot please God"* (Rom. 8:8). We are either moving forward with the Lord to win His praise and admiration or we are backsliding way from Him to earn His disapproval and correction.

# 1 Corinthians Chapter 10

### Learning From Israel's Past Failures (vv. 1-15)

Paul now uses an example of Israel's past foolishness as an object lesson to teach the Corinthian believers the necessity of faithfulness to the Lord. He warns them (and us too), *"now these things were our examples"* (v. 6, 11). The application is clear; Christians should learn from the mistakes of Israel: *"For whatever things were written before were written for our learning"* (Rom. 15:4). Human history inevitably repeats itself when man fails to acquire wisdom from his past failures. For this reason, Paul chose this historical illustration to *"admonish"* (v. 11) the church to *"not lust after evil things as they also lusted"* (v. 6). May we heed God's disciplinary dealings with Israel who lusted for what was outside of God's will for them, lest we also invite God's chastening hand for our own carnality.

The apostle begins by listing some of the common blessings that the Israelites shared as a community of redeemed people. Notice the repeated used of the word "all" in verses 1-4 to show that God's goodness was uniformly received by all the Israelites. *All* received shade and direction during the day from the cloud overhead. *All* passed through the Red Sea to be delivered from Pharaoh and his army. *All* ate the bread of life (the manna) which came down from Heaven. *All* drank water from the life-giving rock which Moses struck in the wilderness on their behalf.

The significance of the rock in the wilderness as a type of Christ's future work at Calvary was highlighted. Christ was struck by Jehovah's rod at Calvary, such that anyone drinking of Christ through faith would have rivers of living water flowing out of him (John 7:37-38). In fact, all the other notable blessings that Israel had received in the wilderness also pictured what would be later secured through Christ (e.g., Christ is the bread of life which came down from Heaven; John 6:35). All the blessings that Israel enjoyed in the wilderness prophetically came through Christ, just as all the spiritual blessings in heavenly places are now available to all Christians today in Christ (Eph. 1:3).

How did Israel respond to God's loving care and goodness? The Jewish nation lusted after things outside of God's will for them, murmured and complained against God, and broke His Law by committing idolatry. As a result, *"God was not well pleased"* with them and caused His covenant people to wander thirty-nine more years in the wilderness, until the older unfaithful generation had perished, excluding Joshua and Caleb (v. 5).

To further admonish the saints at Corinth to learn from Israel's past failures, Paul mentions another dark day in Israel's history as recorded in Exodus 32. Moses lingered long with the Lord on Mount Sinai. Fearing that Moses had died, the people asked Aaron to make them a god who could take them back to Egypt. Aaron fashioned a golden calf about which the people played, to the extent that many engaged in licentious behavior (v. 7). Through Moses, God brought swift retribution against them for breaking His Law and 3,000 died by the sword in one day (Ex. 32). Later, 23,000 of them died in one day by a plague after committing idolatry and fornication with the Midianites through Balaam's counsel (v. 8; Num. 25).

Two more brief examples of Israel's past failures and God's disciplinary response are mentioned (vv. 9-10): First, Israel had murmured against God's wilderness provisions for them, so the Lord sent fiery serpents among them to teach them a life-and-death lesson – their satisfaction in life was to be in the Lord and not in what they ate (Num. 21:5-6). Second, the rebellion of Korah, Dathan, and Abiram with 250 princes against Moses and Aaron, God's appointed leaders for the nation, resulted in the deaths of all the rebels (some were burned by fire from the Lord; others the earth swallowed alive).

The application for the Corinthians was straightforward: The self-indulgence of God's people is always an affront to God's holiness and goodness and He must punish such behavior. As witnessed with our first parents in Eden, unchecked lust eventually results in doubting God's Word and goodness. Paul was pleading with the Corinthians not to invite Christ's correction by engaging in such behavior. Committing idolatry or fornication, or rebelling against God's appointed leaders, or murmuring against the Lord always prompts a painful response! They should be completely satisfied in Christ and not desire anything or do anything that does not have His approval.

To ensure the Corinthians were being thoroughly warned not to repeat Israel's past failures (v. 11), Paul identifies three specific patterns of behavior to be avoided in verses 12-14. First, they must be aware of self-confidence (v. 12). Without Christ the believer can do nothing for God (John 15:5). It in the flesh the believer can do everything that God hates (Rom. 8:8). Hence, it is not the believer's self-discipline that will restrain the sinful impulses of the flesh, but rather yielding to the Spirit of God and God's Word (Rom. 8:13).

This warning seems to be directed at older believers, who might think that because of their spiritual maturity, they could dabble in self-gratifying behaviors and not be adversely affected. You may possess great agility and balance, but why walk on the edge of a cliff, when keeping a safe distance is warranted? What if a sudden gust of wind or earthquake occurred? Might one stumble over an unseen object or become suddenly light-headed and faint? Satan does not send believers a postcard, an email, or a text message as to how he is going to attack; it usually comes in an area of life that we have not fortified because we are not expecting him to attack there. So, why allow personal pride to prompt thrill-seeking, flesh-motivated behavior which puts a believer at risk of stumbling into sin.

Second, the Corinthians were to rely on God's grace during arduous times. God will not test the believer beyond what he or she is able to bear, without providing ample grace to overcome the trial, rather than being overcome by it. All believers are invited to come before God's throne of grace at any time through prayer to receive whatever is needed to prevail triumphantly in Christ (Heb. 4:14-16). Recalling God's promises is a great defense against being overcome by despair: For example, the Lord has promised to never leave nor forsake the believer (Heb. 13:5).

Third, saints should flee things that rob our affections for the Lord. As shown by Israel's past failures, idolatry must be completely avoided at all times. Anything that supplants Christ's supremacy in our hearts is a form of idolatry. In verse 15, Paul poses a rhetorical question to indicate that he knew that the Corinthians, being wise, would be in full agreement with his conclusions.

## Believers Must Remain at the Lord's Table (vv. 16-22)

*The Lord's Table* is an expression that is used in both the Old and New Testaments to convey divine provision and fellowship (9:13; Ps. 23:5, 78:19; Mal. 1:7, 12). Both the Levitical priests through the provisions gained at the altar (Lev. 6:16, 26, 7:6, 31-32) and believer-priests under the new covenant of grace (1 Cor. 10:20-21) have been invited to abide at the Lord's Table.

In the New Testament, the expression "the Lord's Table" (i.e., the spiritual abode where believers receive blessing and commune with Christ; vv. 16-22) is often confused with the term "the Lord's Supper" (which refers to a physical remembrance meeting of the local church; 1 Cor. 11:17-34). Many in Christendom refer to the Lord's Supper by the non-scriptural term "the communion service." There is *communion with Christ* at His table, but more specifically, there is a *remembrance of Christ* at every Lord's Supper – the value of His death is proclaimed afresh.

## Similarities of the Lord's Table and the Lord's Supper

| | |
|---|---|
| Both speak of a bread and a cup. | |
| Both are the Lord's: The Lord's Supper doesn't belong to any special sect of Christianity. | |
| Invited by the Lord to participate in both. | |
| Both confer a privilege, but also demand responsibility. | |

| Differences | The Lord's Table (1 Cor. 10:16-22) | The Lord's Supper (1 Cor. 11:17-34) |
|---|---|---|
| The Term | "Table" | "Supper" |
| Term Usage | Used in Old and New Testaments (1 Cor. 9:13; 10:18; Mal. 1:7; 12). In O.T., the altar was the Table of the Lord (Lev. 6:16-26; 7:6-32; Ezek. 41:22). | Used only in New Testament (for the Church). Specific: used to describe when Christians gather to remember Christ. |
| Context of Usage | "Communion," "partakers," "fellowship" | "Remembering the Lord, proclaiming His death" |
| Who Gathers | A believer is already there (no steps necessary); it is a personal reality. | "When you gather together" (vv. 18, 20). It is a corporate reality when God's people come together. |
| Compared to other Tables | Yes, Table of Israel (Mal. 1:12) and Lord's Table (1 Cor. 10:20-21) are compared to the Table of demons. | Not compared with another Table (it is a memorial supper). |
| Occurrence of Participation | No mention of "coming together," provisions are continually provided after rebirth (Heb. 4:16). At any time. | *"For as often as you"* (v. 26). Acts 20:7 indicates that the early Church kept weekly on Sunday. |
| View | Invisible to the world | Visible to the world |
| Participation | Provisions provided as needed/desired | Commanded by the Lord |
| Spread by | God for His people | God's people for God |
| Exclusion from Participation | "He who comes unto Me, I in no way cast out" (John 6:37). "Come unto Me, all you that labor and are heavy laden, and I will give you rest" (Matt. 11:28). God is Sovereign over His Table. | The Lord invites all believers to the Lord's Supper. Those in sin (1 Cor. 5:3-5) or holding false doctrine (Titus 3:10, 2 Thess. 3:6, 14) should not participate. |
| Order of Symbols | Cup is first – speaks of the common redemption of all believers. Bread is second – speaks of the communion all believers have in Christ (as His body – the Church). | Bread is first – speaks of the "physical" body of the Lord being broken for us. Cup is second – speaks of the Lord's blood shed for the remission of sins. |
| Warnings | About "living" unworthily | About "eating" unworthily |
| Second Coming | No mention – because believers will always receive provisions from Christ. | Observed until Christ comes for the Church; then we will no longer need a reminder, will have the reality (the Lord). |

The Lord's Table is spiritual and is set by Him, whereas the table at the Lord's Supper is physical and is set by us; at the former we receive provisions from the Lord, but at the latter we remember and worship Him. This is why the normal emblems of the Lord's Supper are reversed in order and are ascribed different meanings when referring to the Lord's Table.

Earlier, Paul highlighted the blessings of God's presence in the wilderness that "all" the Israelites received. Now he shows the same truth in the Church Age. All true believers have the opportunity to "partake" of the Lord (vv. 17, 18) and to have "fellowship" with the Lord (v. 20) as they enjoy "communion" with him (vv. 16, 17). The Lord's Table speaks of the sum total of the spiritual blessings we have in Christ, while the Lord's Supper refers to the remembrance meeting of the Church.

In the sense that the souls of believers are refreshed through Spirit-led worship, the Lord's Table would include the Lord's Supper, but the distinct terminology and significance of each should not be lost. It is a great privilege to remember the Savior and to refresh the heart of God during the Lord's Supper. Likewise, it is a blessing to the heart of all believers to commune with and receive from the Savior at His Table. May we never choose to leave His presence!

Apparently, some of the Corinthians were still participating with unsaved family members and friends in social rituals and feasts honoring pagan gods. To do so meant that they had departed from the Lord's Table to partake from the table of demons. So Paul sternly warns them:

> *You cannot drink the cup of the Lord and the cup of demons; you cannot partake of the Lord's table and of the table of demons. Or do we provoke the Lord to jealousy? Are we stronger than He?* (vv. 21-22).

This was the same offense Israel had committed against God long ago, the only difference being that their table was set before them in the wilderness, while believers have a spiritual table in Heaven to enjoy today. Regardless, God's presence and blessing were at both tables. Paul thus exhorts the believers at Corinth not to remove themselves from the Lord's Table to celebrate fictitious rituals, to partake of the world's trifles, and to engage in self-indulgent behavior. As Jack Hunter explains, to do so is to fellowship with demons and that would be offensive to the Lord Jesus!

> Paul ... now draws attention to the fact that sacrifices offered to idols are really offered to demons, and not to God (see Deut. 32:16–17). He reveals the terrible existence of evil spirits, hostile to God, master-

minded by Satan. For a Christian to sit at a table to partake with the ungodly in a feast dedicated to a pagan god was to acknowledge and share in that worship, to have fellowship with what was really an evil spirit. Such conduct was totally incompatible for a believer in the Lord Jesus.[29]

Regrettably, many believers today, often in ignorance, engage in religious holiday fanfare and social festivities that actually demean Christ and honor pagan deities. Those purchased by His own blood are His, not the world's possession. Given Christ's sacrificial love demonstrated at Calvary, how could we ever think His love would not resent our wandering affections and unfaithfulness. His jealousy over us is proof of His enduring love for us!

At Calvary, Christ died and passed out of this world. Three days later His body was raised from the grave. The Lord Jesus was then highly exalted by His Father to the right hand of the majesty on high (Heb. 1:3). The world crucified His Son, and thus Christ is no longer in the world – to enjoy spiritual life with Him, we must by faith come along to where He is.

As Paul has just informed us, believers have a great privilege to sit with Christ at His table, to receive from and to commune with Him there. How offensive it must be to the Lord Jesus for believers to desert Him in order to party in the world with demons. Christian liberty did not permit the Corinthians to commit idolatry – what they were doing was sin against God!

## Drinking and Eating Without Offense (vv. 23-33)

Having reproved the participation of the Corinthians in various social customs involving things which did not honor the Lord, such as idol feasts, the apostle transitions to the subject of Christian liberty which he introduced in chapter 8. The emphasis of the former discussion was that a brother is more important than meat; therefore, mature believers should gladly set aside their Christian liberty to not needlessly stumble a weaker believer.

In the closing verses of this chapter, Paul provides a list of guidelines and principles to assist believers in discerning their response to questionable activities which Scripture does not specifically address. Each principle is posed as a question. Believers should ask themselves such questions before engaging in something that might be foolish to do:

- Does this activity benefit my spiritual growth (v. 23)? Many things are permissible to do, but are these profitable and helpful to me? Will watching secular programming, or listening to worldly music, or reading sensual novels enhance my spiritual growth or cause me to accept behaviors and thought-patterns which offend Christ?

- Does this activity put the well-being of others before my own interests (v. 24)? Does this activity show a genuine concern for others? Will my behavior promote the spiritual growth of others?

- Could this activity needlessly stumble other believers (v. 28)? Does claiming my liberty cause a weaker believer to think evil of me or to do something against his or her conscience?

- Does this activity glorify God (v. 31)? Does this area of conduct have God's full approval or is it an affront to His holy character? Will this activity cause others to praise God?

- Could this activity hinder the unsaved from receiving the gospel (vv. 32-33)? Since the lost have their own customs and preconceived notions about Christians, would engaging in this activity reduce witnessing opportunities?

To further assist believers in discerning wise conduct in questionable matters, the apostle also offers counsel for two real-life scenarios that the Corinthians might encounter. First, if you find a good deal on meat at the market, do not ask if the meat was being discounted because it was offered to idols (v. 25). The earth and all its abundance are God's and available to bless us, and meat offered to idols does not change the meat (v. 26).

Second, if invited to the home of an unbeliever for dinner, you are free to go, but do not ask if the meat was offered to idols (v. 27). Rather, give thanks for the food that God has provided for you and eat it gratefully. However, if another believer attending the same meal states that the meat was offered to idols, then do not partake of the meat, lest you offend the one who made you aware of the matter (v. 28). Although you have given thanks for the meat and your conscience is free to eat it, you do not want to offend or even judge the conscience of another believer who does not have the same freedom (vv. 29-30).

The commands of Scripture determine our conduct on moral matters of right and wrong. The warnings, guidelines, lessons learned, and principles contained in Scripture, the counsel of godly saints, and the leading of the Holy Spirit enable us to discern what would be wise or foolish to do. If we lack wisdom in such things, we are to ask the Lord for discernment and James says that He will provide help liberally (Jas. 1:5). May all that we do be for the honor and the glory of God (v. 31).

# 1 Corinthians 11

## Follow My Example (v. 1)

The apostle's request in verse 1 for the Corinthians to imitate him, just as he imitates Christ, serves as a capstone to the previous section. Paul was determined to set aside personal liberties gained in Christ in order to benefit others. Similarly, the believers at Corinth should not be boasting of and parading their new liberties in Christ, but rather selflessly serving others through them. Their behavior should neither stumble a weaker brother, nor impede the lost from considering the gospel message.

## A Salute to Divine Order (vv. 2-16)

The believers at Corinth were largely following the biblical traditions (i.e., divinely inspired commands; 2 Thess. 2:15) conveyed to them by the apostle; this conduct prompted Paul's praise (v. 2). However, there were still areas of Church order and doctrine that they were compromising. Paul does not praise the assembly for this conduct. The remainder of the epistle addresses these matters. Paul begins by addressing the practice of head covering among the genders during times of spiritual exercise.

What does God desire from the Church during her earthly sojourn? The answer is to reveal *"the manifold wisdom of God ... to the principalities and powers in the heavenly places"... "to the praise of His glory"* (Eph. 1:13, 3:10). Believers are to make God look good by magnifying Christ in every situation (Phil. 1:20). Consequently, we must realize that much of God's order for the Church is for the purpose of revealing something about Himself. For example, God instituted masculine plural leadership in the Church (first Apostles, then church elders) to reveal that He is masculine in representation and plural in personage. While some may view God's design for the Church as nonessential, we must recognize that some decrees are right (because they agree with our conscience), but other commands are simply right because God commands them (these test our conscience).

We live in days in which the devil is relentlessly trying to undermine the rudiments of God's creation order in Genesis 1: What is life? What is the origin of life? What is gender? What is marriage? What is work?

Unfortunately, many identifying with Christ today are falling prey to the undercurrent of humanized religion which craves to erode God's purposes. Paul commences the subject of the head covering practice by addressing divine order (v. 3). God the Father and God the Son are equals, but the Son submits to the Father's authority. In creation order, God created the man first and then the woman, thus, the man is the head of the woman (i.e., the man is to exercise authority over her). Intrinsically, God views men and women as equals but with different roles in executing His authority (v. 11).

While discussing creation order, Paul explains that what is created by another becomes the glory of the originator (v. 7): God created man from the dust of the ground, thus man represents God's glory. God created the woman (the gender) from the side of the first man, thus the woman symbolizes man's glory; and the woman's long hair originates from her and is hence her glory (v. 15). What originates from another should not rule over the originator, but rather should honor it in representation (1 Tim. 2:13-14). In God's economy of order, it would be as wrong for a woman to rule the man, as it would be for the woman's hair to control her actions.

Some have wrongly linked 1 Corinthians 11:3 (ESV) to male headship in marriage only, but Eve was created as a woman; she later became Adam's wife. While the Greek word *gune* may be translated "wife," the context of creation order in the verse requires that the better rendering is "woman." Paul is referring to God's design for each gender when He created male (to lead) and female (to help). Given our depraved nature, humanity will naturally devalue God and His purposes, but He has given believers a reminder, a reoccurring visible symbol, to prevent us from doing so.

Paul often uses military illustrations to explain spiritual truths. We will likewise consider such an example to reflect on Paul's teaching of headship and the head-covering practice (vv. 4-7). If a commanding officer were to suddenly enter a room filled with subordinates, each soldier would be expected to stand at attention and to salute their superior without saying a word. The soldiers' silence and salute demonstrate respect and willing submission to the authority over them. When addressing the group, the commander would speak directly to the highest-ranking officer while the remaining outranked soldiers remained silent. That officer would then carry out his orders by directing the activities of the other soldiers.

The idea of believers visibly saluting God's authority and demonstrating audible order when they come into His presence is the subject matter of 1 Corinthians 11 and 14, respectively. The same verses that command *the what* of the head-covering practice also provide *the when*: when believers enter the Lord's presence to pray (Heb. 4:14-16) and when the Lord draws near to us to express His Word (i.e., through prophecy/teaching; vv. 4-7). Church Order in 1 Corinthians 11 is not specifically referred to until verses 17-34 when the subject changes to the Lord's Supper. In this portion, Paul clearly states, *"when you come together in one place ... as a church"* (vv. 11: 17, 18, 20). Thus, restricting the visible salute to only church meetings is contrary to the "when" commanded in the Creation Order section (vv. 2-16). Anytime that we come into God's intimate presence to talk to Him or He comes into our presence to communicate His Word to us, as subordinates to the Lord, we all should give Him a visible salute: men should have uncovered heads and women should have covered heads.

As sisters willingly cover themselves (man's glory) and their hair (their glory), all glories competing with God's glory (as symbolized in the uncovered heads of the brothers) are removed. This scene reflects God's heavenly throne room where angelic beings such as Cherubim and Seraphim use their own wings to cover their intrinsic glories, so that only God's glory is seen by all (Isa. 6:2; Ezek. 1:11). Any visible portion of these creatures (such as their differing faces) that is described reflects the glory of Christ and is hence recorded for our appreciation. The covering behavior of these heavenly creatures ensures that even a woman's hands covering her head during times of impromptu prayer is an acceptable salute to God. May all believers be increasingly aware of God's holiness and glory when we speak to Him or for Him!

Some have suggested that a woman can speak in the church if her head is covered based on verse 6, but this interpretation would clearly contradict the command for women to be silent in such meetings. To ensure that this injunction was understood, Paul added, *"for it is shameful for women to speak in church"* (14:35). This is not because women have nothing valuable to say (many of our beloved hymns prove otherwise), but rather it would be inappropriate for women to usurp God's appointed authority in the church.

The basis of biblical hermeneutics is that the truth is in the whole of Scripture, and therefore Scripture interprets Scripture. How then should we understand the head-covering offenses identified in verses 5-6? First, we realize that Paul is speaking about the head-covering practice in chapter 11 and appropriate audible ministry in the church in chapter 14. Many in the Church at Corinth had adopted a license mentality (i.e., all is permissible under grace); part of the resulting chaos was that some sisters had removed their head coverings.

Second, notice that Paul identifies two offenses that a woman can commit concerning the head-covering practice. Each offense carries a different penalty to illustrate the seriousness of each infraction (vv. 5-6). If a woman is not covered when prayer and teaching are occurring (the single offense), then she is to be shorn, but if she is speaking and uncovered (a double offense), then she is to be shaved. *Figuratively speaking*, Paul is saying that if a woman wanted to act like a man – she should look like a man to her shame. To infer that she can speak if covered is to twist the corrective tone of the text and contradict what Paul writes in chapter 14.

The Greek verb *katakalypto* is rendered "let her be covered" in verse 6. The preposition *kata* means "down" and *kalypto* means "to hide or to veil." The verb is in the imperative mood (i.e., a command), but in the middle voice (i.e., the woman is to cover her head on her own behalf). As the head covering itself is a symbol of submission, it would be mockery of the sign to force men to be uncovered or women to be covered during times of prayer without personal conviction of the truth. The head-covering practice is commanded, but we are not commanded to constrain others to obey the Lord's commands (e.g., we do not force others to be baptized or to break bread; believers must have submitted hearts in such matters).

Two different Greek words are employed to show the difference between cutting a woman's hair short or shaving her head bald. The latter action would remove her glory and leave her in a shameful state. Just as it is wrong to exceed the speed limit while driving, it is doubly wrong to speed through a red light; the double violation has a more severe penalty. Paul does not address the equally wrong offenses of a man's head being covered during times of prayer and teaching or the double offense of speaking for God while his head was covered because the Corinthian men were not doing this. As the devil proved in Eden, those dissatisfied with God's best for them usually work to cause others to spurn God's best also.

The audible ministry within church meetings must be done by men, as they represent God in the meeting (14:33-35). When men and women gather for spiritual exercise, both genders are to salute the Lord as He commands (vv. 4-7). The head-covering practice is tied with the activities of prayer and prophesying (or teaching), not church meetings exclusively. When speaking for God, men must speak the truth as energized by the Holy Spirit or suffer judgment (Jas. 3:1). As worship and prayer come from the heart, everyone is to be actively engaged in both when gathered (Acts 4:23-31) – what God enables from a pure heart rises up to Him as sweet incense (Ps. 141:2).

In the Lord's Supper, for example, the Holy Spirit uses a male speaker to align everyone's thoughts on the same thing. Although the brother's words do not rise above the ceiling, all that precipitates from Christ-loving hearts does! God is looking beyond spoken words into each worshiper's heart for something of lasting value to refresh His own heart. When a sister hears a brother publicly share her own secret meditations, it verifies to her that God is listening to her heart and also that the brother speaking is being led by the Holy Spirit. It is thrilling to hear my wife or one of my daughters say to me or to another brother, "Thanks for sharing my thought during the Lord's Supper." Through such a simple testimony, what was spoken by a brother was validated by God through a sister! This is why all believers should come to the Lord's Supper with hearts full of adoration and then seek to worship the Lord together. Our God is a God of perfect order and peace (14:33). Seeing that God has intimately tied His own glory to the practices of the Church, may we seek to honor Him in the way He deems best and thereby enjoy His approval and His peace.

To summarize, Paul supplies five reasons as to why men should be uncovered and women should be veiled when public praying and teaching are occurring: First, it shows agreement with divine order for creation (vv. 3-6). The head covering itself is "a sign of authority" (v. 10); therefore, the uncovered heads of men and the covered heads of women are to be a visible salute to God's authority. Second, the glory of God is properly manifested by the uncovered heads of men and when the sisters cover competing glories (themselves and their hair; v. 7). Third, the angels are watching and learning about submission and order (v. 10; 1 Pet. 1:12). Paul states that God is using the Church to teach the angels (Eph. 3:10). Fourth, nature itself teaches the significance of the glories (vv. 13-15). God created women to naturally have long hair. Observation indicates that while women often experience thinning hair with age, many men experience balding or baldness in their autumn years. Fifth, the Church at Corinth would be unusual compared to other gatherings of believers. The Greek text of verse 16 is the most difficult to translate in this section. But given the context of the preceding fourteen verses, it would seem that Paul was saying, "If you Corinthians do not submit to the head-covering practice, you will be quite peculiar, as other churches are following the symbolic headship custom." Paul taught one embodiment of Church Truth to all the local churches and we, just like the Corinthians, are accountable to God to obey it (4:17; 7:17).

## The Lord's Supper (vv. 17-34)

Interestingly, Paul discusses three different symbols in this chapter: the veil (a symbol of submission to authority), the bread (symbolizing the broken body of the Lord Jesus at Calvary), and the cup (containing wine to symbolize Christ's redeeming blood that was shed on the cross on our behalf). Clearly, symbolic truth has its place in meetings of the Church for it calls our attention to things that are important to God.

We read of four times that the Lord personally met with Paul to convey to him vital doctrine; one such event was to ensure that the Lord's Supper was not changed into something that He did not institute. The Corinthians were guilty of doing this, so Paul corrects two issues pertaining to the Lord's Supper. First, they had inserted the Lord's Supper into a *love feast* in which drunkenness, gluttony, and social preferences were occurring. Second, they were not judging themselves before partaking of the remembrance feast.

In the previous verses, Paul appealed to creation order to teach the Corinthians about the importance of the head-covering practice. However, in verse 17, the subject matter transitions to focus on church gatherings. Five times in the latter portion of the chapter, Paul refers to the saints "coming together" as a local church gathering (vv. 17, 18, 20, 33, 34).

Paul scolds and reproves this local assembly of believers about several ongoing problems: First, there were cliques, factions, and schisms in the church, which were undermining the unity of believers that should characterize meetings of the church (v. 18). Second, there were doctrinal errors and heresies within the church that were causing division; these would increase until it was evident who was doctrinally correct, as living sound doctrine promotes peace among God's people (v. 19). Third, the Corinthians had perverted the purpose of the Lord's Supper by their love feasts which promoted drunkenness, gluttony, and selfishness (vv. 20-23).

The latter offense earned a sharp rebuke from the apostle. If they wanted to eat and drink in such an unworthy manner, they should do it in their own homes, not when the church gathers to worship the Lord (vv. 22, 33-34). What they were doing was not in keeping with the Lord's intentions for His supper. The apostle then conveys the two main purposes of keeping the Lord's Supper: to remember the work and the person of the Lord Jesus Christ and to publicly declare the value of His death (vv. 23-27).

On the eve of His crucifixion, the Lord Jesus instructed His disciples to keep the Lord's Supper often and as He had prescribed it. When they did gather to break bread, they were to maintain the feast's intended purpose of remembering Him. Paul reiterates the words of the Lord to the Corinthians: *"'Take, eat; this is My body which is broken for you; do this in remembrance of Me.' In the same manner He also took the cup after supper, saying, 'This cup is the new covenant in My blood. This do, as often as you drink it, in remembrance of Me'"* (vv. 24-25). "As often as" means every time it is kept. Believers are to keep the Lord's Supper often, in the way specified, but no specific regularity was stated. The first Lord's Supper was not held in a church building; in fact, the Church did not exist at that time. The first Christians obeyed the Lord's command by continuing steadfastly in the breaking of the bread (Acts 2:42), and they did so often from house to house (Acts 2:46). Christians were meeting informally and often to remember the Lord (not just on Sundays or as a local assembly).

Years later, the practice of the local church gathering together on Sundays to break bread became the standard pattern of the Church. For example, on one occasion, Paul waited a week in Troas to break bread with the saints there on Sunday (Acts 20:7). However, because Paul preached long, they actually did not break bread until the wee hours on Monday morning and that was completely acceptable.

To summarize, *the commands* for the Lord's Supper are to do it often and to preserve its protocol and purpose. The *developed pattern* of the Church was that saints gathered together in local assemblies each Sunday to break bread together. The latter point is a scriptural observation, which means there is no prohibition in Scripture preventing saints from remembering the Lord on other days of the week or in smaller groups. While following the scriptural pattern is safe for guiding our behavior, not following what is observed should never negate what is commanded. So, no matter what our circumstances might be, let us follow the Lord's command and remember Him the best possible way that we can!

While it is true that the Lord Jesus invites all believers to participate in the Lord's Supper, a local assembly of God's people should not welcome just anyone into their midst to break bread. It is not that the Lord's Supper needs to be protected per se, but rather that we do not want to grieve the Holy Spirit by allowing the unregenerate, those in sin, or those who are embracing false doctrines to participate as if they were sanctified believer-priests fit for worship (1 Pet. 2:5, 9).

Who should participate in the Lord's Supper? First, only those who have a sound profession of Christ should participate; the Lord's Supper was given by the Lord to His disciples as a memorial feast (Luke 22:19). Second, those who partake must be doctrinally sound (2 Thess. 2:6, 3:14; 2 Jn. 9-10) and, third, morally sound (5:1-5, 11, 13). If these aspects are not met, those individuals are welcome to observe, but they should not partake of the bread and wine, nor participate audibly.

Letters were used to validate these priestly qualities in believers journeying from one church to another (Acts 18:26-27; Rom. 16:1; Col. 4:7-8). These letters enabled visiting believers to be received into another local church fellowship with joy and to all the privileges and responsibilities of a believer-priest (Rom. 15:7). To preclude the Lord's discipline, only believer-priests who exhibit His life should partake of the wine and the bread. This is why all believers are commanded to examine themselves before partaking of the emblems (v. 27). This self-examination is not meant to exclude us from participating in the Lord's Supper, but to enable us to do so! This means that each of us must ensure that our sins have been confessed to the Lord and cleansed by Him (1 Jn. 1:9) and that our hearts are pure towards Him and those with whom we are gathering to worship (Matt. 5:24-24). Believer-priests who come together to remember the Lord in the beauty of His holiness with hearts full of adoration should always be welcome.

With this observation in mind, C. H. Mackintosh notes the importance of believers continually keeping the Lord's Supper today:

> We are anxious to impress the seriousness of neglecting to eat the Lord's Supper ... it is dangerous ground for any to attempt to set aside this positive institution of our Lord and Master. It argues a wrong condition of soul altogether. It proves that the conscience is not subject to the authority of the word, and that the heart is not in true sympathy with the affections of Christ. Let us therefore see to it that we are honestly endeavoring to discharge our holy responsibilities – that we celebrate it according to the order laid down by God the Holy Spirit.[30]

Indeed, any professing Christian who can carelessly ignore the Lord's dying request to remember Him suffers from acute spiritual heart disease!

Besides preparing for the Lord's Supper through self-examination, every believer should come to the remembrance feast with carefully arranged thoughts of worship from Scripture, which have been in preparation since the last offering to the Lord. The Lord's Supper is not a sharing time, a teaching time per se, or a time to petition God with personal prayer requests – it is a special gathering to remember and worship the Lord.

> The believer's authority to worship is not the traditions of men, nor reasonings of human wisdom, but the clear revelation of God's Word.
>
> – A. P. Gibbs

Paul informed the Corinthians that some of them were weak, sick, and had died because they were not keeping the Lord's Supper as commanded by the Lord (vv. 30-32). They had not honored the Lord by their actions; therefore, in holy love, He had severely chastened them. The Lord knows that believers will be happiest and most fruitful when we are in the center of His will; hence, He disciplines us to achieve that outcome (Heb. 12:6-9).

The Church is to maintain the regular observance of the Lord's Supper until the Lord returns to gather up His Bride to Heaven (v. 26; Luke 22:18). Then we will enjoy the marriage supper of the Lamb with Him (Rev. 19:9).

# 1 Corinthians Chapter 12

### Turning From Dumb Idols to Serve Christ (vv. 1-3)

Paul addresses another question posed to him by the Corinthians concerning spiritual gifts, though the word "gifts" is not found in the Greek text in verse 1. The Greek word *pneumatikos* rendered "spiritual" is in the plural, which is why many translators add the word "gifts" behind "spiritual" as this is clearly the main topic of the chapter. However, spiritual "things" or "realities" is what Paul speaks about initially in verses 1-3.

The Corinthians were reminded that they had been delivered from aimlessly following after dumb idols by responding to the gospel message of Jesus Christ (v.v. 1-2). The Holy Spirit illuminated their minds and convicted them of their sin and their need for a Savior. Consequently, anyone having the Holy Spirit will live to exalt Christ as Lord, but those who do not have the Holy Spirit (i.e., not born again), will have no genuine regard for the Lordship of Jesus Christ (v. 3). True believers are identified by their consistent love and obedience to the Lord Jesus.

Before discussing the proper use of spiritual gifts in ministry, Paul encourages the believers in Corinth to listen to and obey the leading of the Holy Spirit just as they did in coming to Christ. Previously, they were under the control of demonic spirits and their sinful flesh, but spiritual gifts are to be used in the power and wisdom of the Holy Spirit, not for carnal purposes!

### Believer-Priests Are Given Spiritual Gifts (vv. 4-11)

In many ways, the former Levitical priesthood typifies with astonishing precision the eternal realities realized in believer-priests by the Holy Spirit today. As each believer-priest serves with pure motives and is infused with divine power, the Lord Jesus is honored and God Himself is refreshed. What is freely offered in sacrifice on earth through Christ fills the throne room of Heaven with a sweet aroma of our Lord. In this spiritual sense, Christ is our Golden Altar of Incense in which we can offer to God what He appreciates and we can do so at any time and on any day.

Just as the Levitical priests were anointed with oil at their consecration, the Holy Spirit anoints believers at their conversion also. Each believer is anointed and called to serve the Body of Christ as a priest to God. Not only does this separate out believers to accomplish God's purposes, but this anointing actually provides divine discernment of the truth, which enables believers to follow after God's will in their ministry (1 Jn. 2:20). It is through this provision of the Holy Spirit that a new believer becomes part of a holy priesthood which is *"to offer up spiritual sacrifices, acceptable to God by Jesus Christ"* (1 Pet. 2:5) forever.

Levitical priests were also completely equipped by the Lord with all the necessary implements and clothing to fulfill the office of priest. Similarly, the Holy Spirit distributes spiritual gifts to believer-priests in the Church Age *"as He wills"* (v. 12). The number of these spiritual gifts per believer will vary (v. 4), but each will receive at least one spiritual gift (v. 7). Also, the manner in which these gifts will be used will differ (v. 5), and the beneficiaries (those who receive the spiritual ministry) will vary (v. 6). For example, let us consider the versatility of the spiritual gift of teaching.

There are many flavors of teaching: counseling, instructive, exhortative, expositional, illustrative, encouraging, prophetic, academic, etc. Some will receive a five-star teaching gift and others a one-star enablement, yet each believer is to be faithful to whatever ability God has bestowed on them. The intended beneficiaries of the spiritual gift of teaching will also vary widely. Some will provide marriage and family counseling to those in need. Some will speak from pulpits, others in classrooms, others at the kitchen table leading Bible studies, and still others will engage in itinerant ministries. There are women who shepherd other women, while other sisters long to teach children. Each spiritual gift is multi-dimensional in nature and purpose, which makes ascribing one particular name to a received gift from the Holy Spirit problematic.

Using one's gift(s) with wisdom as enabled by the Holy Spirit is what is important, not having a name for the spiritual gift itself. Pursuing ministry which has not been enabled by the Holy Spirit will cause more damage than good to the Body of Christ. This is why it is important to understand what your spiritual gift is and how the Lord wants you to serve others. If what you are doing is genuinely blessing others and you are not burdened by the ministry, but rather enjoy doing it – then keep on doing it and see if the Lord opens the door to further opportunities to serve.

Besides 1 Corinthians 12, only two other portions of Scripture specifically address the giving of spiritual gifts to believers, Romans 12 and Ephesians 4. In Romans 12, God the Father bestows gifts (seven are mentioned) to equip believers for priestly ministry. In Ephesians 4, it is Christ who provides His Church with gifted individuals (five types of

*1 Corinthians*

ministries are listed), so that believers will be better equipped to accomplish the work of ministry that each has been assigned. In 1 Corinthians 12, it is the Holy Spirit who distributes spiritual gifts (nine are named) to believers which assisted in proclaiming and protecting the truth in the early Church (v. 11). In all, nineteen spiritual gifts and ministries are identified in Scripture. Clearly, the Lord has fully equipped believers for the priestly service that He has called us to perform, and it is a joy to serve Him in the way that we know will please Him.

The spiritual gifts listed in verses 8-10 are often referred to as "sign gifts." The Jews especially desire God's Word to be accompanied by supernatural signs (1:22). On the day of Pentecost, Peter explained that God had given the Jews a sign; the prophecy of Joel had been partially fulfilled as evidenced by the hearing of several distinct foreign languages in the temple (Acts 2:15-21). Paul confirms that the gift of tongues was not meant for use in Church ministry, but was marked for use in gospel ministry, especially as a warning to Israel to repent and receive Christ before it was too late (14:21-22). But Israel did not repent and suffered wide-sweeping judgment by the Romans in 70 A.D. The temple was destroyed, and the remaining remnants of the Levitical priesthood were put away.

The history of the New Testament Scripture verifies a diminishing use of these gifts just before the Jewish nation was judged. There are no references to the use of the sign gifts after about 60 A.D., and over half the New Testament was written after that time.

Before discussing the gifts mentioned, it is helpful to notice that two different Greek words are translated "another" in verses 8-10. The most common word is *allos* which is normally rendered "other," "another," or "some" in Scripture. The other word *eteros* is less common and conveys a more specific thought of something "of a different kind or sort." *Eteros* appears twice in verses 8-10 between the second and third gifts and the seventh and eighth gifts. This creates three distinct categories of gifts.

*The word of knowledge* and *the word of wisdom* worked cooperatively in declaring divine truth and then applying it in wisdom. These gifts were much needed in the early days of the Church Age, as the New Testament Scripture was not available to believers at that time.

*Faith* is the first gift mentioned in the second group of gifts. This supernatural enabling to trust God is not connected with salvation but is associated with the gifts of *healings* and *the working of miracles*. Besides blessing others, these spectacular manifestations of God's power confirmed that the apostles were continuing the ministry of the Lord Jesus and were under His authority (Acts 2:22; Heb. 2:4). Likewise, the gifts of *prophecy* and *discerning spirits* were necessary in the early days of the Church Age, as it required many years for the apostles to write the divinely inspired books that became the canonized Word of God (Heb. 2:3). Therefore, these gifts were important to accurately guide saints into the truth and protect them from false doctrine (14:29-32).

The third set of gifts included *speaking in tongues* and the *interpretation of tongues*. Tongues is always associated with speaking a discernable language in Scripture; it is not vocalized gibberish (Acts 8-11; 14:10-12). These gifts warned the lost (mainly the nation of Israel) that judgment was coming if they did not repent and receive the truth. This is how speaking in tongues is consistently used in the Old Testament (Deut. 28:49; Isa. 11:28; Jer. 5:15) and in the New Testament (14:22).

Notice that some saints received the gift of tongues, yet others received the interpretation of tongues, so not being able to speak in tongues cannot be a test of salvation, as some claim. These gifts were given at regeneration (Acts 10:44-46), so the idea that *a second blessing* of the Holy Spirit is needed for believers to receive the gift of tongues is foreign to Scripture.

It was possible that the same believer might have both gifts (14:5), but in meetings of the church, the gift of tongues was not to be used, unless there was someone with the spiritual gift of interpretation (14:28). This was not just the natural ability to interpret a language but the divine ability to convey the spiritual meaning of the utterance also. This is why if no one with the spiritual gift of interpretation was present, the one desiring to communicate a message in tongues was to pray for the interpretation (14:13). If the individual already had the gift of interpretation, then he would not need to pray for God to grant him the ability to interpret his message. The prayer is not for the receipt of a new spiritual gift, but for a special help for this unique situation.

## All Parts and Functions of the Body Are Important (vv. 12-31)

All believers, whether Jew or Greek, male or female, free or slave, have become one in Christ through the baptism of the Holy Spirit (vv. 12-13; Gal. 3:28). Spiritual baptism was the act of Christ through the Holy Spirit that placed believers into the Body of Christ at Pentecost and created the Church (Mark 1:8); this particular event will not be repeated. However, the positional truth of baptism, becoming one with Christ, becomes effectual when, over the course of time, individual sinners trust Christ for salvation and become spiritually unified with Christ (Acts 11:16-17; Rom. 6:3).

This means that the Church is composed of all believers from all different ethnic backgrounds over the entire Church Age. This spiritual temple, the Body of Christ, is still being constructed today and consists of many members, all of whom have designated roles in the Body, and therefore all believers are important to the proper functioning of the Body. This means every believer is to strive to exercise and develop his or her spiritual gift(s) without striving with each other. The Church can only represent Christ to the unregenerate when the Body is behaving with edifying love as its Head desires. Paul tells us what good body life in the Church should look like:

First, no believer should disdain his or her spiritual gift, or another's spiritual gift, or value one spiritual gift above another, as all gifts are important to body life of the Church (vv. 15-16).

Second, understanding the many diverse operations necessary for a healthy Body, God has placed each member in the Body to accomplish a specific purpose (vv. 17-18). In fact, the Body cannot function as it should without this diversity of working parts; this means that every member of the Body is needed and should be functional (vv. 19-20).

Third, the Body is composed of many members, while some members are weaker than others, they are still important to the Body (vv. 21-25). An arm is stronger than the liver, but the liver is vital to the human body. A foot is tougher than an eye, but without the eye the foot would suffer injury.

Fourth, some members are not attractive or elegant (such as a heart, for example), but still deserve respect for their critical function in the body (vv. 23-24). These members of our body are covered with clothing or skin so that they become less noticeable and are protected from exposure to shame and ridicule. However, other members of the body must remain visible and are therefore more vulnerable. Jack Hunter applies Paul's teaching to the local assembly: "When the members who can be seen publicly are functioning, carrying out the responsibilities of preaching, etc., and the members not fitted in that way are doing their work, quietly and out of the public eye, then the whole appearance is one of godly order and spiritual beauty."[31]

Fifth, all members are different, but all are needed to allow the body to function as the Head, the Lord Jesus Christ, desires (v. 27). In his expanded translation of the New Testament, Kenneth Wuest renders verse 27 as follows: "And as for you, you are Christ's body and members of it individually." Believers are not part of "a" body, or even "the" body (the definite article is not in the Greek text); we are Christ's Body – we are to manifest His life – we are Him in the world. For this reason, each member should care for other members of the Body (v. 25). There should be no division. When one member hurts, the entire Body hurts, and when one member does well, the whole body rejoices (v. 26). When there are divisions and factions within the Church, the testimony of Christ is marred, the Spirit is quenched, and fruitfulness ceases.

From a practical standpoint, one way of identifying spiritual gifts is to observe how believers react in stressful situations. Their first impulse will often indicate how God has equipped them to serve the Church. For example, picture the following scene. A church is gathered to remember the Lord on Sunday morning by keeping the Lord's Supper. While one man named Tony passes the tray of cups across the aisle to another man, Frank, it drops, and the cups and their contents spill out on the floor. Obviously, this is a stressful situation which provides an opportunity for different believers to use their spiritual gifts. A sister with the gift of helps quickly rises from her seat and hurries to the kitchen to retrieve a damp rag and some towels to clean up the mess. Another sister with the gift of mercy pats Tony on the shoulder and says, "Don't worry about it; I drop things all the time." "Frank, you did not receive a cup, I was considering not partaking anyway, so please take mine," says a brother with the gift of giving. The teacher says, "If you would have held the tray with two hands while passing it, you would not have dropped it." A brother with the gift of administration stands up and asks a believer to retrieve the tray and refill the cups while the sister with the gift of helps is cleaning up the mess; he then informs everyone that the Lord's Supper will continue as soon as the tray is refilled. This situation probably does not occur often in your assembly, but it does show how the Lord equips various believers to serve.

All the spiritual gifts in your local church are important and all need to be identified, exercised, and developed. There is no need to ascribe names to what people do, but rather believers should be encouraged to keep ministering in ways that bring them joy and bless the Church. If you are weary of serving or are harming the Body – stop what you are doing!

In the final four verses of the chapter, Paul brings the subject of spiritual gifts to a crescendo in order to preface the important subject of the next chapter – spiritual gifts must be used in love to edify others, not to promote oneself! This is why the apostle wrote, *"But earnestly desire the best gifts. And yet I show you a more excellent way"* (v. 31).

There are three lists of spiritual gifts (including individuals given a role or spiritual enablement) in this chapter. Notice that tongues and interpretation of tongues is last in all three lists. For example, in verse 28, Paul lists the gifts according to rank and value to the Church and then in verses 29-30 he repeats the same idea by addressing the importance of roles in the Church. Paul had a clear message for the Corinthians who were engrossed with their sign gifts to the detriment of Bodily edification. They were especially enamored by the gift of tongues and were showcasing their abilities to the neglect of profitable teaching in the assembly. Paul provides some specific safeguards in chapter 14 to remedy this situation.

In verse 28, Paul purposely lists the most important gifts for edifying the Church first: there were individuals who provided foundational help to the Church (first apostles, second prophets, and third teachers). The "first apostles" speaks of the original disciples commissioned by Christ and later a few others that were "sent ones" having also heard Christ's teachings and witnessed His resurrection (Acts 1:2-3, 21-22). All this to say, not all believers are "the apostles" as some teach.

Next, Paul identifies supportive and sign gifts, with the gift of tongues being mentioned last. As previously stated, the same hierarchical format is used again in verses 29-30 when speaking of specific roles in the Body-life of the Church. That is, the apostles were listed first and those speaking in other languages or interpreting other languages were again listed last. Paul was not slighting anyone's spiritual gift by using this order, but rather was emphasizing that any ability received from God could become a liability to His work, if not used with wisdom and in love.

Paul summarizes the main message of the chapter with his closing charge: *"But earnestly desire the best gifts. And yet I show you a more excellent way"* (v. 31). Given that the Holy Spirit expresses sovereign wisdom in bestowing spiritual gifts to believers at regeneration and then energizes those gifts for the edification of the Body of Christ, what does Paul mean by the charge, "earnestly desire the best gifts"? The idea is not that believers should be desiring different or more spiritual gifts than what they have received in grace, but rather that they should earnestly desire that God would raise up believers in the local assembly who already possess the most helpful gifts to edify others. Paul has just taught the Corinthians that these gifts would center in the accurate declaration, teaching, and application of God's Word, namely *prophecy* (v. 1). This exhortation also served as a warning not to magnify lesser gifts (such as speaking in tongues) which did not edify the body as prophecy did.

The Corinthians were glamorizing the use of tongues as being the most important gift in the assembly, which diminished the preaching of apostolic truth that was necessary to build up believers in their faith. So, Paul will teach them "a more excellent way" in the next chapter – the way of love! The believer's supreme motive of using spiritual gifts must be genuine love for other saints and not self-love. Only then will we be able to honor God in what we do.

# 1 Corinthians Chapter 13

### Serving Without Love Is Meaningless (vv. 1-3)

The subjects of 1 Corinthians chapters 12 and 14, respectively, are Church body life and Church order. Paul sandwiches the subject of sharing God's love in the Church between these two topics for a specific reason: Biblical love should govern the use of spiritual gifts and ministry in the local assembly. The Corinthian believers were being selfish and self-focused in the use of their spiritual gifts. The gift of tongues was being overemphasized by some to the detriment of the assembly body-life.

Whether you waxed eloquent in some human language or even spoke with the authority of angels, if what was said did not genuinely profit others, you might as well have whacked a cymbal or banged a brass gong (v. 1). If a prophet could expound all the mysteries of God, or if someone else with extraordinary faith could move mountains, or if another one gave all their wealth to the poor, or yet another suffered a martyr's death, it would profit nothing unless accomplished in a spirit of sacrificial love (vv. 2-3).

Paul is not stating that the gift of tongues is some kind of celestial language that angels speak that is gibberish to men. When Scripture records angels speaking, they were always understood by humans (Gen. 19:1; Dan. 10:11; Luke 1:26). By using these hyperbolic examples of speaking (v. 1), intellect (v. 2), and devotion (v. 3), Paul is stating that speech or service of any kind is not profitable unless given with selfless care for others.

True love is fostered in a humility that seeks the welfare of others. Love seeks the best for others above one's own interest. Biblical love always begins with personal sacrifice – *"For God so loved the world that He gave His only Son"* (John 3:16). In the first three verses of this chapter, Paul resolutely states that what we do for the Lord, even martyrdom, means nothing, if not motivated by genuine love from God. Hence, speaking publicly in a language that no one else can understand is selfish and is inconsiderate of others; it is not an act of humility, but of personal pride.

### What Love Is and What Love Is Not (vv. 4-7)

Paul begins by describing what selfless love looks like, then moves to what love is not, before concluding with what genuine love is. In all, he shares eight characteristics of what love is and what love is not:

| **What love is:** | **What love is not:** |
| --- | --- |
| Suffers long – it is patient | Does not envy – rejoices when others are honored |
| Kind – tender and compassionate | Does not boast of self – quiet about one's accomplishments |
| Centers in the truth – rejoices in it | Not proud – all abilities come from God |
| Bears all things – commitment based | Keeps no list of wrongs – releases offenses |
| Believes the positive possibility first | Does not seek self-interest above others |
| Hopes – rejoices in God's promises | Not easily provoked to anger |
| Endures – longsuffering of offenses | Does not rejoice in sin or failures of others |
| God's love is inexhaustible/eternal | Does not think evil – thinks positively or gives the benefit of the doubt |

Because the source of true love is God, all that His love motivates will reflect the fruit of the Holy Spirit. Biblical love is sacrificial in nature: *"For God so loved the world that He gave His only begotten Son"* (John 3:16). The only way that we can love others as God loves is to experience His selfless, sacrificial love: *"We love because He first loved us"* (1 Jn. 4:19).

## What Fails and What Will Not Fail (vv. 8-9)

In verse 8, we learn that prophecy, tongues, and knowledge (revelations) from God will all cease, but love will continue forever. The three gifts mentioned in verse 8 are representative of all three categories of gifts discussed in 1 Corinthians 12:8-10, thus representing all the sign gifts. The Greek verbs used in verse 8 to describe how each gift will cease enables us to better understand the meaning of "that which is perfect" in verse 10.

*Katargeo* is a future tense verb in the passive voice which describes the "putting out of action" of the gifts of prophecy and knowledge. The passive voice means that God Himself will act to cause these two gifts to cease in the future. However, the Greek verb associated with tongues ceasing is *pausontai*, also in the future tense, but in the middle voice. This indicates that the gift of tongues would "be stilled" on their own. This is why verse 9 only mentions the gifts of prophecy and knowledge. These gifts were for the edification of believers and will cease when God brings about that which is perfect – Scripture, the ultimate expression of truth and knowledge that believers are to understand in the Church Age (v. 10). However, tongues, which were for reaching the lost (14:22), will vanish on their own.

In general, prophecy (foretelling or forthtelling the truth), speaking in tongues, and revelations all concluded at the end of the apostolic age; however, we will be recipients of God's love for eternity. The evidence within Scripture indicates that gifts such as tongues, healings, and miracles generally ceased by approximately 60 A.D. The majority of the N.T. was written after this date with no recorded use of such gifts; afterwards these gifts were referenced in the past tense (1 Tim. 1:18, 4:14; Heb. 2:3-4; 2 Pet. 2:19-21) or were not available when needed. For example, in about 64 A.D. Timothy is told to drink a little wine to settle his ongoing stomach issues (1 Tim. 5:23) and Paul could not heal Epaphroditus of a sickness that nearly took his life in about 60 A.D. (Phil. 2:25-30).

Why would the sign gifts of prophecies and knowledge cease? At the dawn of the Church Age, believers did not have the canon of Scripture to guide them, so expressions of prophecy through various individuals to guide Christians into deeper truth were necessary. But once what was perfect had been received, then these individual declarations would not be necessary. This is why the book of Acts reveals a clear historical transition from "apostles" to "apostles and elders" to just "elders" (local church leaders) – the apostles died and were not replaced. What God wants the Church to know has been revealed through the inspiration of Scripture.

## That Which Is Perfect Has Come (vv. 10-13)

Paul acknowledges that at that present time, believers only *"know in part and we prophesy in part"* (v. 9). They were waiting for a time when what was perfect would come (v. 10). Some have suggested that Paul is referring to the coming of the *perfect* One (Christ) to snatch up His Church and return to Heaven. However, the Greek word rendered "perfect" is in the neuter gender, so Paul is talking about a subject of non-personage.

Others have suggested that the phrase "that which is perfect" may refer to our complete understanding of the *Faith* once believers are in Heaven. However, it is blatantly obvious that spiritual gifts would cease once believers are in Heaven and therefore it would not be necessary to state that fact. Such an idea would mean that new revelations would be continuing throughout the Church Age. Hence, Christ would be required to judge His Church to varying degrees of revealed truth at His Judgment Seat, instead of one embodiment of truth for the entire Church Age. Jesus Christ desires His Church, His Temple, to be built on one foundation of truth (Matt. 16:18; 3:11). The idea of progressive revelation would result in division and chaos within the Church. Both grammar and reason indicate that the "perfect" must relate to something received before the Church is glorified with Christ in Heaven.

Given the construction of the Greek text in verses 8 and 9, it seems apparent that Paul is speaking about something that makes prophesying and knowledge (declaring and knowing the truth) in part not necessary anymore. God causes "declaring in part" to cease, because He has provided the whole truth that the Church is to understand at this time (in Heaven there will be more for us to learn; Eph. 2:7). What is perfect then speaks of the completed canon of Scripture in the Apostolic Age (Heb. 2:3-4; Jude 3). On completion God would then cause the gifts of prophecy and knowledge to cease.

God revealed to the apostles what He desired humanity to know during the Church Age. That said, complete "unity of the faith" (i.e., full understanding by the saints of what has been revealed in Scripture) will not occur until the Church is in Heaven (Eph. 4:12-13). No wonder Paul described himself and other believers at that time as mere children beholding something that could not be fully understood and appreciated. It was if they were looking at a dim reflection in a mirror to discern the fuller truth that was coming into focus.

Paul speaks of progressing from childhood to adulthood (speaking of spiritual maturity, not heavenly perfection). Again, he was looking into "a mirror dimly" waiting for clearer understanding of truth that would be seen "face to face" (v. 11). This describes Paul's situation when he was writing to the Corinthians. He was looking forward to receiving the full revelation of Scripture to gain maturity in understanding truth.

The language of verse 11 is reminiscent of God's declaration to Aaron and Miriam concerning how He revealed truth to His servant Moses:

*If there is a prophet among you, I, the Lord, make Myself known to him in a vision; I speak to him in a dream. Not so with My servant Moses; He is faithful in all My house.* ***I speak with him face to face, even plainly, and not in dark sayings****; and he sees the form of the Lord* (Num. 12:6-8).

Because of His close personal relationship with the Lord, Moses received "face-to-face" revelation from God that was completely clear to him. While it is true that when we see the Lord "face to face" we will have perfect understanding of revealed truth, that is not what Paul is speaking of. Rather, he was eagerly waiting for God to reveal all that He wanted the Church to know through Scripture. Church history gives this view credence, for, as previously mentioned, prophecy, speaking in tongues, and revelations of knowledge concluded towards the end of the Apostolic Age.

With this said, God is God and He will do whatever will honor Himself and bring the most blessing to humanity. It would be wrong for any human to try to limit God's sovereignty. For example, at this present moment, many Muslims coming to Christ have reported having dreams which called their attention to the loveliness of Christ.[32] In fact, we would expect God to continue revealing Himself through mysterious forms of communication. However, if and when divine visions and dreams do occur today, they would be of a localized nature with individual benefit and would not impart new revelation for the Church to heed. There is one embodiment of truth for the Church to obey in the Church Age and that is contained within Scripture.

From a practical standpoint, what does this mean for us today? The New Testament records the direct and specific calls of the disciples to ministry. So, should Christians today expect to receive a personal visit from God to call them into service? Should we expect a voice from Heaven, a vision, or a prophetic utterance to confirm God's calling for us? During the early days of the Church Age, prophets were given to the Church as a check against false teachers – they confirmed the oral transmission of the Word of God by the apostles before it was available in written form. Since believers have a divine anointing to understand truth (1 Jn. 2:20, 27) and the Word of God is now complete (Jude 3), modern Christians should not presume personalized directives from God. He may use visions, dreams, confirming signs, and etc. to direct our way, but such phenomena will not contradict Scripture.

Notice that while the gifts of prophecy and knowledge (revelation of truth to the Church) and tongues (declaring truth to the lost) will cease, love will endure forever. This is why love is greater than faith and hope (Rom. 13:13); once we are in Heaven, the latter two virtues will have served their purpose, but believers will bask in the inexhaustible love of God forever.

Paul concludes the chapter with a lovely summary: *"Now abide faith, hope, love, these three; but the greatest of these is love"* (v. 13). Faith takes God at His Word without sensory or intellectual confirmation. Hope rejoices in God's future promises. Love is the unselfish, sacrificial goodness of God to us. Hope and faith will cease when the Lord returns for His Church – faith gives way to sight and hope is complete, but in God's presence, we will experience His boundless and pure love forever.

# 1 Corinthians Chapter 14

## Prophecy Is the Superior Gift (vv. 1-22)

Building on the foundation laid in the previous chapter, Paul exhorts the believers to desire and to use their spiritual gifts to edify each other. The gift of prophecy was especially profitable for this goal (i.e., the accurate teaching of God's Word; v. 1). The motivation of those speaking in an unknown language during the meetings of the church was to showcase their ability and build themselves up rather than edify others (vv. 2, 4). Without an interpreter, only God would understand the mysteries being spoken.

Some have suggested that Paul is speaking of a *prayer tongue*, which enables believers to better pray to God. However, the context of Paul's exhortation relates to public ministry in a known language that will edify, exhort, and encourage others, rather than a private prayer ministry in an unknown tongue (v. 3). Furthermore, the Holy Spirit, who resides within all true believers offers up perfect, inaudible intercession on behalf of believers, even when we do not know what to pray (Rom. 8:26).

Paul is not being negative towards the gift of tongues (i.e., the speaking of various human languages; v. 10). Rather, he was concerned with how the gift was being used in the meetings of the church. Paul, himself, had the ability to speak in tongues, but did not use this gift when conveying doctrine to God's people (v. 18). This was to ensure that everyone understood what he was saying (v. 6). Because tongues equipped the saints to convey the gospel message to the lost, especially to Israel (v. 22), he wanted them to use the gift in the way God intended (v. 5).

The apostle then referred to some inanimate objects, three musical instruments, to advance his main point (vv. 7-9). Unless the flute and the harp provide a distinct sound when played, their unique tones and qualities will not be appreciated by the hearer. If a trumpet is blown to sound an alarm, but its unique sound is garbled, how can it successfully be used to rally soldiers for battle? Additionally, there are many distinct languages in the world; all are significant, but a message is only intelligible to those who understand the language in which it is spoken. What is said is meaningless to those who do not understand that language (vv. 10-11).

Likewise, it is unprofitable for those speaking in unknown languages to do so in the meetings of the church because no one can be spiritually edified by hearing what they cannot understand (v. 12). If a believer receives a message from the Lord, it should be conveyed in a language that everyone understands. One should not speak in another language unless he has prayed that God would provide an interpreter to translate the message into a language discerned by the hearers and God has answered that prayer (v. 13).

Verse 14 seems to indicate that the gift of tongues bypasses the mind to supernaturally convey truth in such a way that even the one speaking does not understand what he is saying. Similarly, it is doubtful that Balaam's donkey knew anything about the words coming out of its mouth when God used it to reprove the pagan prophet of his behavior (Num. 22:28).

It would be more beneficial for everyone, whether words were spoken in the spirit of prayer or while singing or teaching, that what is said be in a discernable "learned" language (vv. 14-15, 17). The apostle then adds, how else will the saints know whether to add their "Amen" to indicate approval and agreement with what the speaker said? The congregation must understand what was spoken to do so (v. 16).

Regrettably, this unifying aspect of congregational affirmation of the truth is often ignored today. Everything that is sung, prayed, and taught in the meetings of the church should be intently evaluated by all believers. If what was heard is discerned to be truthful and accurate, then it should be affirmed by voicing a hearty "Amen." This was practiced throughout the Old Testament when the Lord's people came together for prayer, worship, or teaching (e.g., Deut. 29; Neh. 5:13, 8:6; 1 Chron. 16:8-36; Ps. 106:48). As Paul notes, this congregational practice continued in church meetings (v. 16). Collectively and continually affirming truth builds unity and protects the local church against the intrusion of false doctrine.

There is no definite article in the phrase "in the church" in verse 19. Paul had ample ability to speak in unknown languages, but he refrained from doing so "in church" meetings to ensure the edification of others; he would rather speak five beneficial words of understanding than 10,000 words that no one else could understand (vv. 18-29).

The previous verses were leading up to the apostle's exhortation in v. 20: *"Brethren, do not be children in understanding; however, in malice be babes, but in understanding be mature."* The Corinthians were not to be like children captivated by the dazzling exhibition of tongues. Rather, they should show maturity by focusing on ministry that would benefit others. The admonition *"in malice be babes"* has a similar connotation. Malice is *congealed* anger that holds a grudge and babes have a simple understanding of evil. The idea is that the Corinthians did not need to know everything about something to know that it was evil – deep down they knew that promoting themselves through flashy display in the church meetings was not honoring to Christ or beneficial to His people.

By quoting Isaiah 28:11-12, Paul confirmed that God's intended use for the gift of tongues (speaking other languages) in the Church Age was consistent with how tongues were used in the Old Testament – to warn the wayward to repent. The application was mainly to the nation of Israel. When they heard a language that they did not know, it meant God was going to use foreign invaders to punish them (e.g., Deut. 28:49; Jer. 5:15). Paul therefore concludes that tongues were to be a sign to the lost (i.e., a warning of imminent judgment), but prophecy spoken with words of understanding was required to edify the Body of Christ (v. 22).

## The Church at Corinth Is Called to Order (vv. 23-40)

Throughout this epistle we have been learning of the various problems within the church in Corinth. In this section, we get a better idea of just how chaotic the church meetings had become. Paul continues to labor to bring the assembly back into God's order so that they would enjoy God's peace, and the Gentiles would not think that they were wacky (v. 23). Proper order in the affairs of life, including our worship, is exceedingly important to God, *"for God is not the author of confusion but of peace"* (v. 33) and He desires that *"all things be done decently and in order"* (v. 40). Satan is the author of deception and confusion (John 8:44), but God sets in place standards of proper order to confound Satan's attempts to pervert divine truth and obscure the testimony of His Son within us.

It is important to understand that the regulations that are supplied by Paul in this section pertain to meetings of the Church and not to informal gatherings of believers. Paul is addressing when *"the whole church comes together in one place"* (v. 23). Again, the N.T. pattern of corporate meetings follows the example of the O.T. gatherings of the Lord's covenant people: both young and old, gathering for the public preaching of Scripture, for prayer, for confession of sin, and for worship. In fact, there are no examples in Scripture of separate meetings for children or for women.

If the unity of God's people is a manifestation of God's glory on earth, as the Lord Jesus states in John 17:20-23, why would local churches willingly splinter and hinder the body life of the local assembly? The sense of oneness and family life is critical for each gathering. Every believer needs to know and to appreciate the communal love and mutual respect that is enjoyed in family life. The local church is a living body, a family of believers, and we should be careful of any activity that hinders its unified communion with Christ.

The apostle's synopsis of the church meetings in Corinth is that they were characterized by chaos (vv. 23-26). Believers were simultaneously sharing various teachings, prophecies, and psalms (perhaps singing), much of which was spoken in an unknown tongue without an interpreter. Paul says that such disorder will likely deter a lost person who might visit their gathering from considering the gospel message. The purpose of prophecy was to bring about conviction, but how could the unsaved be brought to a place of receiving salvation in Christ when they could not understand what was being said (vv. 24-25)? Rather than benefitting from the experience, the unregenerate would leave the meeting thinking, "Those people are absolutely nuts – I am never going back there again" (v. 23). What is said in the church meetings should be for the edification of others (v. 26).

To remedy the situation, Paul supplies rules to govern the audible ministry during church meetings. This was necessary to ensure God-honoring order and the edification of believers. Given all that Paul has said previously, it is obvious that he is discouraging the use of tongues in the church meetings, but he was not forbidding their use (v. 39). From a rational perspective, even if what was spoken in tongues was true and the interpretation was correct, it would take twice as long as simply speaking plain, understandable words. Regardless, if the Corinthians were going to publicly address the saints during meetings of the church, they should follow these rules to ensure that the experience would be as profitable as possible for everyone:

First, if the Corinthians chose to speak in tongues, there were to be no more than three who did so, and those who did had to do so one at a time and use an interpreter (v. 27). Second, if there was no interpreter, the person desiring to speak in an unknown tongue should be silent (v. 28). Third, the ministry of the prophets was to follow the same protocol as speaking in tongues (v. 29). Fourth, if a prophet received a fresh word from the Lord, the one speaking was to be silent and give way to the prophet who has just received new revelation (v. 30). Fifth, the prophetic ministry in the church should be given by one speaker at a time, then checked and verified by other prophets (vv. 31-32). Sixth, women were not to speak publicly in the church meetings, but to learn from their husbands at home (vv. 34-35).

Why was Paul imposing these specific criteria for the church meetings at Corinth? Because, *"God is not the author of confusion but of peace, as in all the churches of the saints"* (v. 33). The devil is working diligently to cast doubt on the person and work of Christ and to mar the testimony of those who represent Him. As discussed in chapter 11, one of the ways he accomplishes this is to undermine God's creation order established in Genesis 1. Paul has already taught the Corinthians that male gender represents God's glory, while the female gender symbolizes man's glory (11:7). Therefore, God desires that the male gender represent His authority in the Church. Males are to assume leadership roles in its meetings, including the audible ministry. The sisters are not to have a leading voice in Church meetings. Rather, they are entrusted with visual ministry to ensure that there are no competing glories in the meetings. When men and women behave as God desires, the local assembly is a picture of God's heavenly abode in which only His glory and authority are evident (11:2-7).

The Greek verb translated "keep silent" in verses 28, 30, 34 is *sigao* which means "to keep secret" or literally to speak within oneself or under one's breath without impeding another person's speech (e.g., Luke 18:39). Hence, anyone publicly speaking was to yield (keep silent) if someone had received a prophetic word. Paul then applies *sigao* to preclude women from speaking publicly in the church meetings in the same way (v. 34). In church meetings, women are to *sigao* (i.e., have no singular, leading voice). However, *sigao* does not mean total silence, because everyone should participate in singing and congregational *amens* (14:16; Col. 3:16).

When the local church is gathered in one place, women are not to have a distinct leading voice but are to "keep silent." This means that a woman is not to disrupt the male speaker in any fashion. In other words, there should never be a time during any part of the church meeting that someone might think that a sister was leading the meeting.

Sensing that some would have difficulty with these restrictions, Paul affirms his apostleship and that the commandments he had delivered to them came directly from the Lord (vv. 36-37). The prophets in their midst could validate this statement to be true. Paul was the one who brought the Word of God to them originally; their response to his message then confirmed that he had been sent to them by the Lord. This meant that spiritually-minded individuals would continue to obey the teachings of Christ revealed through him. Anyone operating in ignorance of these truths did so willfully, because Paul had just explained the matter (v. 38).

Verses 39-40 provide a concise summary of chapter 14. All things in the church meetings should be orderly and honor God's authority. Paul does not encourage speaking in tongues during the church meetings, as this tends to cause disorder and to puff up those speaking. With this said, he does not prohibit the use of tongues either, that is, if his rules of conduct are followed. Paul does encourage the saints to pursue sound teaching which edifies all believers gathered in the name of Christ.

# 1 Corinthians Chapter 15

The Fact of Christ's Resurrection (vv. 1-11)

False teachers were trying to convince the Corinthians that Jesus Christ had not risen from the dead; His remains were still in a tomb somewhere near Jerusalem. This entire chapter is offered by the apostle to attest to the fact that Christ did rise from the grave. He also explains the necessity of His resurrection to the Christian faith, and that all believers must experience resurrection to receive a body fit for Heaven. Because Satan was defeated at the cross by Christ's work of propitiation (John 12:31-32) and then again by resurrection power at His exaltation (Eph. 1:20-21), the devil will always attempt to undermine these truths. However, Paul affirms that these main elements of the gospel message were foretold in the Old Testament:

> *Moreover, brethren, I declare to you the gospel which I preached to you, which also you received and in which you stand, by which also you are saved, if you hold fast that word which I preached to you – unless you believed in vain. For I delivered to you first of all that which I also received: that Christ died for our sins according to the Scriptures, and that He was buried, and that He rose again the third day according to the Scriptures* (vv. 1-4).

The Greek verbs rendered "declare," "preached," and "received" in verse 1 are all present tense verbs, which meant that Paul's message preached to the Corinthians and what they had believed to be saved had not changed – he was still preaching the same gospel. The verb translated "stand" is a perfect tense verb, meaning that the Corinthians had an eternal standing in Christ because they had believed the message of Christ crucified, that He had died for their sins, and then He was raised from the dead, showing God's satisfaction with His Son's redemptive work.

Paul's statement *"unless you believed in vain"* in verse 2 is not an assertion that the Corinthians might not be saved, but rather, if they were saved, it was because they had believed on the true gospel message, the one that Paul had initially preached to them. This message included the resurrection of Christ; hence, the Corinthians were not to slip from believing this fundamental truth. There is no soul-saving, life-changing power in any message other than Christ's crucifixion, death, and resurrection.

Perhaps this illustration will help the reader understand why Christ had to both die and be brought back to life on the believer's behalf. Picture yourself visiting a terminally ill friend in a hospital. While you are talking to your friend, she gets drowsy, closes her eyes, stops breathing, and a few moments later quietly passes into eternity. If you could raise your friend from the dead, would she be any better off? No, she has a fatal disease and would just die again. If you could somehow instantly heal her disease, would she be any better off? No, she would just be a healthy dead person. Your friend needs both life and healing from her disease. The Lord Jesus dealt with the deadly disease called sin at Calvary, and because He was raised from the dead, believers can not only be forgiven of their sins, but they, in Him, receive His life. The Lord Jesus gave up His life that we might live out His life now. This is why the Lord said, *"I give them eternal life, and they shall never perish; neither shall anyone snatch them out of My hand"* (John 10:28). In Christ there is life; outside Christ there is only death! In Christ, we are much more than just forgiven sinners!

> On what does the Christian argument for immortality really rest? It stands upon the pedestal on which the theologian rests the whole of historical Christianity – the resurrection of Jesus Christ.
>
> – Henry Drummond

There have been many skeptics who have tried to disprove the resurrection of Christ, but in the process became convinced themselves of its validity: Frank Morrison, Josh McDowell, Lee Strobel, and C. S. Lewis, to name a few. The evidence for Christ's resurrection is overwhelming, and Paul wants his audience to understand this. He then lists five eyewitness accounts of Christ's resurrection prior to His ascension (vv. 5-7).

In total, Scripture records five eyewitness accounts of seeing Jesus Christ alive on resurrection day (in order: John 20:11-18; Matt. 28:8-10; 1 Cor. 15:5; Luke 24:13-32; 24:36-43) and then at least five more eyewitness accounts over the next forty days before His ascension into Heaven (in order: John 20:26-31; vv. 6-7; John 21; Acts 1:2-12). Not only did Christ appear alive to Peter (Cephas), to His own half-brother James, and then to the original disciples, Paul states that Christ showed Himself at one time to over 500 people (perhaps this was on a mountain in Galilee; v. 6; Matt. 28:16-20).

> I went to a psychologist friend [before Strobel's conversion] and said, If 500 people claimed to see Jesus after he died, it was just a hallucination. He said hallucinations are an individual event. If 500 people have the same hallucination, that's a bigger miracle than the resurrection.
>
> – Lee Strobel

The last witness that Paul refers to is himself. He personally saw the Lord Jesus on the road to Damascus which led to his conversion (vv. 8-9; Acts 9:1-16). This event happened after Christ's ascension to Heaven and provides a testimony in addition to the ten eyewitness accounts of Christ's resurrection before His ascension.

Paul's own conversion from a Pharisee of Pharisees persecuting the Church to an apostle sent by Christ to the Gentiles highlights the validity of the resurrection of Christ. Likewise, each of the original disciples were transformed from common laborers to zealous men who thought nothing of losing their lives for Christ – they saw, heard, and felt the risen Savior and never got over that experience. They willingly hazarded their lives in obedience to Christ's command to be His witnesses throughout the world.

In God's timing, Paul was saved and he became an apostle by the grace of God (v. 10). Because he persecuted the Church before his conversion, Paul considered himself the least of the apostles and his conscience was under deep obligation to share the gospel (v. 9; Rom. 1:14). He concludes this first section by stating that if anyone was saved at Corinth, it was because he or someone else had shared a complete gospel message with them, a message which included the resurrection of Christ (v. 11).

## The Necessity of Christ's Resurrection (vv. 12-19)

Did Christ really rise from the dead? Ronald Gregor Smith summarizes the world's answer to this question: "So far as historicity is concerned ... it is necessary to explain: We may freely say that the bones of Jesus lie somewhere in Palestine, but the Christian faith is not destroyed by this admission."[33] Contrary to this statement, the Apostle Paul claims in this section of holy text that the Christian faith stands or falls on the resurrection of Jesus Christ. It is through the resurrected life of Christ that the Church has spiritual life and power, and the hope of glorification.

Paul understood that the resurrection of the dead was more than just an "I hope so" crutch to get the believer through tough times; it was an essential part of the believer's salvation. Without resurrection there is no salvation! *"For if the dead do not rise, then Christ is not risen. And if Christ is not risen, your faith is futile; you are still in your sins!"* (vv. 16-17). Furthermore, if there is no resurrection of the dead, *"then also those who have fallen asleep in Christ have perished. If in this life only we have hope in Christ, we are of all men the most pitiable"* (vv. 18-19). Paul stated that if the resurrection of Christ did not occur, then we would still be spiritually dead even though we had trusted in Christ for salvation.

The apostle asserts the following arguments to substantiate the necessity of Christ's Resurrection. First, Christ foretold His own resurrection (Matt. 17:22-23). "Is Christ a liar?" (v. 12). The obvious answer to this question, is "no"; Christ could not be a liar and still be God's perfect, sinless Lamb of sacrifice offered for the sins of the world (1 Jn. 2:2). The Lord Jesus declared to the Pharisees that His resurrection would be a sign to them and would set Him apart from anyone else who ever lived (Matt. 12:39-40).

Second, if there is no resurrection, then there is nothing special about Jesus Christ; He is dead just like everyone else who is dead (v. 13). Yet, Scripture declares that Christ's resurrection proves that He is the only begotten Son of God and the firstfruits of the First Resurrection (Rom. 1:4; Heb. 1:5; Rev. 20:6).

Third, if Christ is not risen from the grave, then the gospel message has no power to save (v. 14). If Christ were still in the grave, it would mean that God the Father was not satisfied with His Son's redemptive work. On the contrary, as foretold in Scripture (Ps. 16:9-11), the Father raised His Son from the dead to declare His complete acceptance of Christ's propitiatory sacrifice for human sin (Acts 2:30-32). God the Father is a reliable witness of His Son's resurrection, which consummated the utter defeat of the devil who tried to prevent it from happening (Eph. 1:19-21).

Fourth, Paul and the other apostles would be false witnesses if Christ had not risen from the dead (v. 15). But since the gospel had such a powerful effect on the Corinthians, it was evident that the message Paul preached to them (including the reality of Christ's resurrection) was approved by God.

Fifth, if there were no such thing as bodily resurrection, then Christ would still be in the grave. If Christ were still in the grave, then all believers, including the Corinthians, would still be in their sins (vv. 16-17). This meant that their faith was futile because they had believed a message that was not true. Even if they could receive forgiveness of sins through the cross of Christ without His resurrection, believers would have no resurrection power to overcome the sin within them (i.e., the carnal impulses of flesh nature). Believers would just be forgiven spiritually dead people.

Sixth, if there is no resurrection from the dead, Paul states that they would be the most pitiable people on earth – they were suffering persecution for preaching a message that offered no hope (vv. 18-19). This meant that believers who had already died would not have life after death – they had perished forever! Why suffer now, if there is no hope for a better future?

## The Order of Resurrections (vv. 20-28)

Next, Paul explains the order of bodily resurrections. The first person to experience glorification in resurrection was Christ (vv. 20-21). The next individuals (i.e., those born condemned in Adam) to be glorified are those who are Christ's at His coming (vv. 22-23). This speaks of the Rapture of the Church from the earth to Heaven (1 Thess. 4:13-18). The next phase of the *First Resurrection* is that Tribulation saints and the Jewish Remnant will be raised up at Christ's second coming to the earth (Rev. 20:4; Ezek. 36:21-28). Old Testament saints will likely be raised up at this time (Dan. 12:1-3) but may experience resurrection prior to the Tribulation period when the Church is raptured (Heb. 11:39-40).

During the millennial reign of Christ, He shall have all rule and authority (vv. 24-25). The enemy of God, Satan, and the enemy of man, death, shall both be destroyed at the end of the Millennial Kingdom (vv. 26-27; Rev. 20). Christ must "put an end to" before He can "deliver" up the kingdom to God. Acceptance of the Kingdom by the Father from His Son is the confirmation and demonstration that Christ's work to redeem humanity and restore all creation to perfection is complete (v. 28). In the eternal state God is all in all and there will be no sin, no enemies, and no curses, just the glory and the goodness of God.

Natural law governs us while we are on earth, but that is not true in the spiritual realm of the afterlife. Whether one spends eternity in Heaven or in Hell, everyone will undergo bodily resurrection. This ensures that everyone will have a body suited for his or her final destination. Christ taught that He, as the Son of God, created all life and that all life was in Him (John 1:3-4).

The Lord also stated in John 5:24-29 that at His command all the deceased would be resurrected (i.e., all disembodied souls would be joined to an eternal body). There are only two types of resurrection mentioned by Christ in this passage: a resurrection of the just to enable eternal residence in Heaven and a resurrection of the condemned to be punished for eternity in the Lake of Fire (Rev. 20:10, 15). The Lord Jesus has received authority from His Father to initiate both of these resurrections. Scripture informs us that the first resurrection (i.e., of the just) occurs in several stages, as Paul has just confirmed. The resurrection of the condemned happens all at once at the Great White Throne Judgment.

## The Moral Value of the Resurrection (vv. 29-34)

Paul then refers to the moral value of the resurrection, that is, that all believers must give an account of themselves to the Lord in a future day (2 Cor. 5:8). But how would that be possible if there were no resurrection from the dead? Furthermore, what benefit is there in preaching the gospel and baptizing new converts, in perpetuating a message that promises tribulation and possible death in this life, if there is no life beyond the grave?

Based on verse 29, some religious groups practice baptizing people in the place of those who have died, but who were not baptized while alive. But Paul was not authorizing this bizarre religious practice. Rather, he was emphasizing that there was no practical reason to suffer the perilous repercussions of living for Christ if there were no hope of resurrection in the future (v. 30). Having watched previous Christians being martyred for the faith, why would we baptize anyone, if death is all there is to look forward to – life might as well be lived according to personal choice. Thankfully, new generations of disciples were being baptized in Christ's name because they did believe in their future resurrection.

Because bodily resurrection was assured for every believer, Paul was willing to expose himself to the threat of death daily, just as he rejoiced over the believers at Corinth daily (v. 31). The apostle then shares an example of this perspective. He recounts the fierce persecution he had experienced in Ephesus for the cause of Christ (Acts 19:23-41). This grim situation was apparently indelibly marked in Paul's memory as he likely refers to the situation again in a later letter to the Corinthians (2 Cor. 1:8-9).

In recalling the situation Paul says, *"We had the sentence of death in ourselves"* (1 Cor. 1:9); in other words, the missionary team believed their time on earth had come to an end. Why was Paul willing to suffer the threat of death day after day? Because he knew that the doctrine of resurrection was true; he had seen the Lord Jesus personally after His death. If he did not believe in a bodily resurrection, he would be much better off in this life to adopt the adage, *"Let us eat and drink, for tomorrow we die"* (v. 32). In other words, why not live for today if there is no hope for tomorrow? Paul chose not to live by this motto. Rather, his life's ambition was *"to live Christ, and to die gain"* (Phil. 1:21).

For the believer to live for eternity instead of the here and now meant that the Christians would have to guard who they allowed to influence them, because *"Evil company* [companions] *corrupt good habits* [morals]*"* (v. 33). Paul was indicating that there were wolves in sheepskins among them and that these false teachers needed to be purged from their ranks. They were not to permit their assembly to be corrupted by false doctrine.

Notice that we become like those we spend time with. If we closely associate with an angry person – we will become angry as well (Prov. 22:24-25). If we walk with the wise, we will be wise, but if our companions are fools, we will also become foolish (Prov. 13:20). Similarly, spending time with false teachers does not increase one's wisdom, but rather prompts spiritual and moral compromise leading us into sin.

## The Resurrection of the Body (vv. 35-53)

Have you ever wondered what kind of body believers will have in Heaven? There were some in Paul's day who were asking this question too. Regrettably, some even began to question the teaching of resurrection because they could not understand how a physical body could exist in Heaven (v. 35). Paul uses a horticultural example to explain this difficulty.

Just as a seed must fall into the ground and die in order to bring forth life, we must die to experience resurrection (v. 36). Our future resurrected bodies will draw characteristics from our earthly bodies, in the same way a corn plant acquires its characteristics from the kernel of corn that was sown in the ground (vv. 36-38). The plant is not the seed per se, but what it is was drawn from the seed. This seems to indicate that the individuality of our human soul will be maintained in Heaven, though our visible form will be quite different in expressing who we are.

Paul then observes that not all flesh is the same; people, animals, fish, and birds have differing bodies, yet each possesses life from God (v. 39). By comparing the glories of terrestrial bodies with celestial ones in verse 40, Paul is inferring that our glorified bodies are much more spectacular than our present, earthly bodies. Then, in a roundabout way, Paul addresses how saints in their glorified bodies will appear in Heaven in verses 41-44. While all believers in the Church have been positionally declared righteous in Christ, each believer has the opportunity to labor in righteousness for Christ today. Those things which are done in accordance with revealed truth and in the power of the Holy Spirit have eternal value; these righteous acts are the believer's adornment in eternity. In Heaven, the bride of Christ must have righteous attire; she is *"arrayed in fine linen, clean and bright, for the fine linen is the righteous acts of the saints"* (Rev. 19:8).

The Lord Jesus rebuked the Church at Laodicea with these words: *"You are wretched, miserable, poor, blind, and naked – I counsel you to buy from Me gold refined in the fire, that you may be rich; and white garments, that you may be clothed, that the shame of your nakedness may not be revealed; and anoint your eyes with eye salve, that you may see"* (Rev. 3:17-18).

Those in the Church at Laodicea were not living for Christ; consequently, God's righteousness was not displayed in their lives.

Paul explains in verses 40-42 that after the resurrection, some saints will shine forth the glory of God more brightly than others, just as some stars in the nighttime sky are brighter than other stars. This acquired glory directly reflects the righteous acts (good works) that are done for Christ by His strength in this present life. Eternal glory, evidently, has a weight to it; in other words, its quality is measurable (2 Cor. 4:17) and can be earned by believers through selfless service for Christ now.

Thus, to be appropriately dressed for eternity, believers should secure for themselves a covering of eternal glory, which consists of righteous acts. Though saved, a believer may still appear to be spiritually naked in Heaven (i.e., personal acts of righteousness on earth provide believers with varying reflections of God's glory in Heaven; Rev. 3:18). Without being justified in Christ, no one can enter Heaven, and only by doing righteous acts for Him and by His power do believers contribute to their eternal attire of glory.

Paul says that our present, natural bodies are weak and perishable, but after death, our new spiritual bodies will be raised up in power and be incorruptible (vv. 42-44). The natural (earthy) reality which caused failure is revealed first and then the heavenly (spiritual) solution to human failure is revealed second (vv. 45-46) – just as Adam was revealed first and fell, and then Christ (the last Adam) came with the spiritual solution to sin to offer forgiveness and life (vv. 47-49).

This follows the pattern by which God issues grace and mercy throughout Scripture: the natural choice to bless man is first shown as a failure, to be followed by the unnatural solution to achieve what the first could not. For example, the natural choice of a clan head was the firstborn male in a family, but God often chose to bless others by the unnatural choice (not the firstborn male) instead. Hence, Seth, not Cain, was chosen; Isaac, not Ishmael, was chosen; Jacob, not Esau, was chosen; and Joseph not Reuben was chosen, etc. Our natural bodies often dishonor the Lord, but that will be an impossibility in our glorified bodies – there is no flesh nature within the glorified body that will rebel against the Lord (v. 50).

Presently believers do not have physical bodies fit for Heaven. However, Paul reveals a wonderful mystery in verses 51-53 that will thrill the heart of every true Christian. In a coming day, the Lord Jesus will return to the air for His Church and in the twinkling of an eye, at the last trump, all believers in Christ will either be raised up from their graves with glorified bodies, or, if living, will instantly experience glorification (1 Thess. 4:13-18). John states that each believer will receive an incorruptible, eternal body like that of the Lord Jesus, which obviously cannot commit sin (1 Jn. 3:2). Paul affirmed the same truth to the church at Philippi (Phil. 3:20-21).

Having a Christlike body in Heaven means that believers will morally behave as God does forever and they will possess perfect bodies that will never diminish in vitality. There will be no ill thoughts about other people, no crippling bents, no temptations, nor will there be any addictions with which to grapple. God is a holy God, and to dwell in His presence, we will have to be holy too.

Paul states that the appearing of the Lord Jesus is the blessed hope of the Church (Tit. 2:11) and that those who love the Lord's appearing (i.e., living as if the Lord could come back at any moment) will be rewarded for doing so (2 Tim. 4:8). John says that those who live expecting Christ's return will live pure lives, because the Lord is pure and because a believer would not want to be ashamed when He does suddenly come for His people (1 Jn. 2:28, 3:3). So, although believers have not received their resurrection bodies yet, they are to live as though they have!

Since the believer's flesh nature will be eradicated, the present needs and desires of our bodies will cease to exist. There will be no need for air, water, food, rest, sleep, or reproduction. The upshot of all of this is that perfect bodies will not need eyeglasses, wheelchairs, hearing aids, pacemakers, dentures, hormone therapies, pain medications, sleep aids, etc. Doesn't being with Christ in Heaven sound great?

## Resurrection – the Ultimate Victory Over Death (vv. 54-58)

As a result of all that Paul knew to be true concerning Christ's resurrection and the resurrection of believers to be present with Him in glory, Paul welcomed death. Through Christ's victory at Calvary and against all the powers of Hell in His resurrection, the devil's power over Paul's life had been severed; death no longer had any hold on him (vv. 54-57). Christ had punched through death to provide a means of escape for all those in Him (Heb. 2:14-15). Paul knew that if he died, he would be in the Lord's presence and there would be no more trials for him (2 Cor. 5:8).

Verse 59 concisely concludes the apostle's teaching on the resurrection in this chapter. Do not compromise the truth of the resurrection (either Christ's or that of believers in Christ). The glorification of Christians will occur when the Lord returns for those who are His; this is the Church's blessed hope. Therefore, continue abounding in love and good works until we are with the Lord.

# 1 Corinthians Chapter 16

## Conclusion – Instructions and Greetings (vv. 1-24)

The phrase "now concerning" in verse 1 indicates that Paul is addressing another question that the Christians had requested him to answer. This is the fifth time he refers to the contents of their letter to him (see also 7:1; 7:25; 8:1; 12:1). The matter pertained to a collection to meet the needs of the poor saints in Jerusalem. About twelve years earlier, Paul and Barnabas had taken part in a relief effort caused by a severe famine that struck Judea in 44 B.C.; this event had been foretold by the prophet Agabus (Acts 11:27-30, 12:25).

Years later, the conditions in Jerusalem were again such that many Jewish believers were struggling to obtain basic necessities, and Paul was greatly burdened for them. Previously, Paul had informed the Gentile believers in Rome, Galatia, Achaia, and Macedonia that there were impoverished saints in Jerusalem who needed their loving assistance (Rom. 15:25-26; Gal. 2:10). As the gospel message had come from Jerusalem to Gentiles throughout the Roman Empire, Paul felt it was *their duty* to help relieve their distressed brethren in Jerusalem (Rom. 15:27).

It is clear from his later letter to the Corinthians (2 Cor. 8-9) that Paul was concerned they were not preparing their gift as they ought. At this point, the apostle merely responds to their question by providing some wise principles to guide their giving: *"On the first day of the week let each one of you lay something aside, storing up as he may prosper, that there be no collections when I come"* (v. 2). This fourfold exhortation should guide our giving to the Lord also.

First, all believers are to regularly give to the work of the Lord and giving weekly is implied. The early Church settled on a pattern of gathering together weekly on the day of Christ's resurrection, Sunday (e.g., Acts 20:7). Under the Law there were rigid tithes and gifts that were demanded of the Jews, but during the Church Age, believers are not told how much to return to the Lord. So, a tithe (a tenth), as required by the Law, may be a good initial guide for our giving, but love for the Lord and not compulsion is to motivate giving in the Church Age.

Second, *"let each one of you"* means that our giving is a personal matter and should not be publicized (Matt. 6:3). To boast to others about what we give to the Lord means that we are looking for the honor of men rather than the praise of God. Regrettably, the eternal value of such gifts is diminished or altogether lost through vainglory.

Third, "storing up" means that there must be prayerful preparation in deciding how much should be given to the Lord. Our giving to the Lord is a private matter. We should not give what we do not have; otherwise, we are giving what someone else possesses and there is no sacrifice in that.

Fourth, our giving should be proportionate to how God has prospered us. Generally speaking, the Lord does not expect us to give back to Him what is beyond our means. He does expect us to support His work to the degree He has equipped us to do so. The Lord was delighted more with the two mites given by a poor widow than with the more lucrative gift of a self-righteous Pharisee (Mark 12:42). Our giving to the Lord is a good indication of what we truly value. Paul's instructions indicate that the Lord does not expect each of us to contribute the same amount, but He does expect us to give to the work of the Lord willingly and regularly.

> What makes the Dead Sea dead? Because it is all the time receiving, never giving out anything. Why is it that many Christians are cold? Because they are all the time receiving, never giving out anything.
>
> – D. L. Moody

Two important aspects of financial accountability are mentioned in verses 3-4. First, although Paul and the missionary team would help transport the gifts received for the poor saints in Jerusalem, the local church was ultimately responsible for choosing and sending representatives to oversee the distribution of the funds collected (2 Cor. 8:18-19). Second, multiple individuals were involved in transporting and distributing the money received. One person should not be in control of collecting and distributing the Lord's money, but rather *check-and-balance* procedures involving several individuals should be followed to ensure blamelessness. Besides protecting the Lord's money from possible pilfering, the main reason for several individuals being involved with church finances is to keep honest people from being blamed of wrongdoing. The enemy knows that he can cause havoc in a local church through just the suggestion of wrongdoing, even when no sin was committed.

The apostle was writing the Corinthians from Ephesus and he planned to tarry there until the Feast of Pentecost (v. 8; likely the Spring of 56 A.D.). Paul hoped to visit them later that year when he passed through Macedonia (v. 5) and possibly to spend the winter with them (vv. 6-7). This plan did not materialize, a matter that would cause some in Corinth to bring an accusation against Paul later.

Paul did visit Corinth two more times. He came across the Aegean Sea from Ephesus for a brief and painful visit to rebuke the Corinthians (2 Cor. 2:1). After penning *2 Corinthians* from Macedonia, Paul visited Corinth again under more pleasant circumstances (Acts 20:3). He remained there for three months before heading north through Macedonia and then sailing south to Jerusalem where he was eventually arrested.

For the time being, the apostle was going to remain in Ephesus, for the Lord had opened a door of gospel opportunity there (v. 9). Although Satan was constantly opposing his ministry, he realized that Ephesus was where the Lord wanted him to be. This fact should remind us that opposition in ministry is proof that God is empowering what we do, otherwise the enemy would take no notice. Only what God empowers threatens Satan's evil schemes. Service rendered without God's enablement is of no interest to the devil, as what is done in the flesh will ultimately dishonor God anyway.

Paul had sent Timothy to Corinth in order to know of their spiritual state, and to learn how the believers had responded to his epistle. When Timothy arrived, he was to be received without criticism or disdain, for he was a servant of the Lord (v. 10). The Corinthians were also not to hinder his ministry among them or his returning to Paul, but rather they were to assist him (v. 11).

At the Corinthians' request, Paul had urged Apollos to visit them, but it was not a convenient time for him to do so. When a trip became possible, he would come then (v. 12). Apollos did not add a greeting to this letter, so he may have been engaged in ministry at a different location.

Next, the apostle commands the Corinthians to *"watch, stand fast in the faith, be brave, be strong"* and to serve others in selfless love (vv. 13-14). The four verbs in verse 13 are present tense imperatives, but the verbs rendered "watch" and "stand fast" are in the active voice, while "be brave" is in the middle voice, and "be strong" is in the passive voice: God would cause them to be strong, if they chose to be brave while obeying the command to stand fast and remain alert. God is our strength, but we are to be alert to danger; our complacency will eventually result in spiritual failure.

The first souls to be won to Christ in Achaia were those in the household of Stephanas (v. 15). Paul stated earlier that he had baptized the household of Stephanas after they had heard the gospel message and turned to Christ (1:16). Some have used this example to substantiate the practice of water baptizing babies to impart some spiritual blessings. Some teach that this washes away original sin and saves the infant, while others maintain that it makes the infant safe unto salvation at a later date. Neither teaching is found in the Bible, nor is there any example of baptizing infants into the Christian faith in Scripture. The evidence in verse 15 would suggest that no babies were baptized in the household of Stephanas, because all those who had been baptized were devoted to ministry (literally "addicted to" serving), an impossibility for toddlers. (This is one type of *addiction* that pleases God.)

Paul reminds the Corinthians that those set apart for the Lord's work deserved their love and respect, not their criticism and disdain (v. 16). As an example, the three brothers sent by the saints at Corinth to visit Paul in Ephesus had refreshed Paul's spirit (vv. 17-18). It seems likely that they had brought a personal gift to Paul, something the Church at Corinth had not done previously either because of the distance or lack of desire. These men arrived bearing the church's letter (perhaps Chloe's letter also) and though the news received from them was disturbing, these brothers were able to personally comfort Paul. This highlights the benefit of Christian fellowship, especially during sad or stressful situations.

In closing his letter, Paul permits others to add their personal greetings to the Corinthians. Salutations came from the churches in Asia (especially at Ephesus), the brethren with Paul, and also from Aquila and Priscilla, who were known to the Corinthians (they had traveled from Corinth to Ephesus; v. 19). This faithful couple hosted a church in their home at Ephesus.

Paul exhorts believers to greet each other with a "holy kiss" in verse 20. "Holy" is translated from the Greek adjective *hagios*, which is normally translated "holy" or "saint(s)." The Greek noun *philema*, which is derived from the verb *phileo* which means "a brotherly love," is translated "kiss." *Philema* can be any personal greeting which is used to express genuine love in a wholesome (holy) way. The saints at Corinth were to be impartial and blameless in expressing brotherly love to each other and so are we.

Paul takes the pen and signs his own name to the letter as a token of devotion. His name would have been written in large letters, because of his poor eyesight (Gal. 4:15; 6:11). Before concluding the epistle by affirming the grace of the Lord Jesus Christ and his own love to the Corinthians (vv. 23-24), Paul offers this declaration: *"If anyone does not love the Lord Jesus Christ, let him be accursed. O Lord, come!"* (v. 22). The KJV renders "be accursed" as *anathema* and "O Lord, come" as *maranatha*. This verse is a capstone to all that Paul has taught the Corinthians throughout this epistle. One shows love to the Lord Jesus by obeying His commandments (John 14:15, 23), maintaining a holy testimony (1 Pet. 1:16), keeping Him enthroned in one's heart (e.g., Rev. 2:4), and longing to be with Him (1 Jn. 3:2-3). We would do well to abide by this exhortation as well.

# 2 Corinthians

## Background

The city of Corinth was situated some 50 miles west of Athens in southern Achaia. At the time of Paul's writing, Corinth likely had a population of at least 500,000 people, the majority of whom were slaves. Slaves were needed to transport merchandise and supplies between two busy seaports, Lechaeum 1.5 miles west of Corinth and Cenchreae 6 miles east. (Corinth was situated on a four-mile strip of land between these two ports.) Cargo was often transferred on foot from port to port; at times even ships and all were transported overland. This port arrangement made Corinth the main thoroughfare for commerce in southern Greece, and Cenchreae (Corinth's seaport on the Aegean Sea) one of three major Aegean seaports (Thessalonica and Ephesus being the other two).

Because Corinth was a hub for international commerce, it naturally became a hotbed for the most immoral forms of paganism. During the time of Paul's writing, approximately one thousand prostitutes associated with the temple of Aphrodite were roaming the streets of Corinth; consequently, "Corinth" became a byword for what all that was lewd and sensual.

Paul first came to Corinth in the spring of 51 A.D. during his second missionary journey and stayed for one and a half years. While at Ephesus (during his third missionary trip), Paul wrote an epistle to the Corinthians which was not preserved for us in Scripture (1 Cor. 5:9). Apollos was in Corinth at this time; he was sent there by brethren in Ephesus (Acts 18:27). After Paul learned of misunderstandings and additional problems (1 Cor. 1:11, 16:17), he wrote a second letter from Ephesus, which is titled *1 Corinthians* in our Bibles. Paul threatened to come with a rod if the Corinthians did not correct particular problems (1 Cor. 4:18-21). Later, he did sail directly from Ephesus to Corinth for this purpose. He later refers to this visit as "a painful trip" (2:1).

After arriving back at Ephesus, Paul wrote a third letter, which "pained" him (2 Cor. 2:3-4). The Holy Spirit did not retain this letter for us in Scripture. After the riot in Ephesus, Paul traveled to Macedonia where he met Titus returning from Corinth. Titus gave a good report on the Corinthian

Christians, but some still questioned Paul's apostleship (2 Cor. 2:13, 6:5-6). Paul responded by composing a fourth epistle, *2 Corinthians*. Paul made a third trip to Corinth, likely during the winter of 56-57 A.D. and remained there for three months (Acts 20:2-3).

## Theme(s)

In *1 Corinthians*, Paul wrote to transform the behavior of a disorderly group of believers into that which would honor God. Paul emphasized that Christ was their head, that moral integrity was expected of believers, and that they needed to honor Christ by obeying revealed truth concerning Church order and doctrine. The personal themes and content of *2 Corinthians* stand in sharp contrast with the matters dealt with in the former letter.

In *2 Corinthians*, Paul reveals to us his heart and soul for the ministry he had been called to accomplish. He highlights the wonderful benefits of serving the Lord, as well as the value of disappointments, trials, and sufferings in the life of a faithful servant. His final instructions concerning the collection for the saints in Jerusalem was accompanied with teaching on the importance and joy of meeting the needs of others and giving to the Lord. No other Pauline epistle offers such a thorough defense of Paul's apostleship; certainly, Paul's divine calling was proven in fruitful ministry and faithful suffering.

## Keywords

Keywords and phrases include: "comfort," "consolation," "ministry," "glory," "boast/boasting," "truth," "confidence," "reconciled" or "reconciliation," "affliction," "salvation," and "Satan." Notice that various forms of comfort and consolation are mentioned some twenty-nine times in the epistle.

## Date

Second Corinthians was likely written from Macedonia just prior to Paul's third visit to Corinth, late 56-57 A.D.

## Outline

I. Paul's Ministry to the Corinthians (chs. 1-7).
II. Collection for the Saints in Jerusalem (chs. 8-9).
III. Paul's Apostleship Defended (chs. 10-13).

# 2 Corinthians Chapter 1

## Introduction (vv. 1-2)

The opening of this epistle follows the typical pattern of naming the writers of the letter and to whom it is written. First Corinthians was from Paul and Sosthenes, but at the time of this epistle's writing, Paul's spiritual son Timothy is with him, so his name is included. The audience of this letter is more restricted than the previous epistle, being addressed only to the church at Corinth and to believers residing in the region of Achaia, instead of to all who are sanctified in Christ, including the Corinthian believers.

Paul greets the saints with his trademark salutation of extending to them grace and peace from *"God our Father and the Lord Jesus Christ"* (v. 2). It is always so; we must first experience God's grace before we can lay hold of His peace. In the Old Testament, we read of the God of Abraham, the God of Isaac, etc., but He is not referred to in the N.T. by these associations. Rather, since believers are in Christ, God has become our Father.

## Comfort in and Deliverance From Suffering (vv. 3-11)

Paul begins by thanking God for the divine comfort he has received: *"Blessed be the God and Father of our Lord Jesus Christ"* (v. 3). The full revelation and goodness of God is declared to us in God's Son (Heb. 1:1-3). Through experiencing Christ, Paul had received God the Father's peace.

Paul and his ministry companions had suffered many adversities, poverties, and persecutions in fulfilling their God-given callings. Yet, through their difficulties they had become more acquainted with the God of all comfort (vv. 3-4). By identifying with Christ and continuing to walk in faith, they had enjoyed a higher experience with God than they would have without the hardships (v. 5). Paul wanted the Corinthian believers to know God in this way more and more. He wanted them to be comforted in their trials and sorrows by the same consolations of Christ that he had come to appreciate and expect (vv. 6-7). The apostle expresses his confidence that the Corinthians would experience God's comfort as they lived for Christ.

While there are many storms in life that may cause us to mourn and fear, our identification and union with Christ is a special solace for all those who have suffered the sorrows of a God-hating world, or for upholding righteousness, or for identifying with Christ in His rejection. Our English word "comfort" is derived from two Latin roots, *con*, "to be with," and *fortis*, "strong." Literally "comfort" means "to strengthen by companionship."[34] God's infinitely strong arms fully embrace His children with tender mercies from above! The power of Heaven then ushers the downhearted into the secret place of rest and security (Ps. 91:1-2; Isa. 26:3).

Being one with Christ means that everything that comes into our lives also comes into His life. The Lord abandoned the supreme glory of Heaven to be the incarnate man born of a virgin, to live in a sin-cursed world, to endure the contradiction of sinners for thirty-three-plus years, to endlessly serve those in need to the point of exhaustion, to be rejected and betrayed, to lay down His life and to be cursed of God to save others from Hell that they might enjoy the abundant life of God. This is our consolation in Christ during our time on earth – He comes alongside to console and strengthen.

The Lord keenly feels our sorrows and our harsh circumstances. He not only sympathizes with us, He also provides the only kind of comfort that quiets worry and anxiety. We are then able to share our testimonies of comfort to assist those who are going through similar difficulties. Charles H. Spurgeon was known throughout England as a powerful preacher in the nineteenth century, yet during one of his sermons, he said, "I am the subject of depressions of spirit so fearful that I hope none of you ever get to such extremes of wretchedness as I go to."[35] At times, Spurgeon was incapacitated by these fits of depression, yet, he could also testify of how the Lord enabled him to overcome this opposition to fulfill his calling in a marvelous way. Ministries often commence when believers choose to comfort others with the comfort they have received. H. A. Ironside explains:

> Many a saint is permitted to go through deep waters, to pass through severe trial both of body and mind, not only for his own profit, but that he may be the better fitted to be a channel of blessing to his brethren when cast down and in distress. Happy is the saint who is thus subject to the will of God and enabled to be His agent in consoling his discouraged fellows and restoring them, through a ministry received in times of sorrow.[36]

Discouragement is no respecter of persons, and those doing the most for the Lord usually attract more criticism, accusations, mistreatment, and suffering than those superficially identifying with Christ. Paul certainly knew this to be true and provided the Corinthians with information of a life-threatening situation he and the missionary team faced in Asia. Reviewing Church history in the book of Acts, the uproar in Ephesus (Acts 19:23-41) seems to best fit the incident Paul is speaking of, but it is possible that there was another perilous episode in Asia that we know nothing about. Paul left Ephesus after the uproar and went to Macedonia where he met Titus and composed the letter we are reading, before traveling south to winter in Achaia and to visit Corinth (Acts 20:1-3). The timing of the upheaval in Ephesus fits this narrative well.

Regardless of which situation Paul spoke of, he told the Corinthians that he thought it was the end of their earthly sojourn: *"that we were burdened beyond measure, above strength, so that we despaired even of life. Yes, we had the sentence of death in ourselves, that we should not trust in ourselves"* (vv. 8-9a). Paul sensed that their lives were in jeopardy and the situation was so dire, so against them, so unanswerable by human wit and strength that it caused the missionaries to cast themselves completely on the Lord for deliverance. The incredible way that God did save them from certain death caused Paul to praise God for his complete salvation in Christ. In fact, all believers enjoy the same past, present, and future salvation in the Savior: *"God who raises the dead, who **delivered us** from so great a death, and **does deliver us**; in whom we trust that He **will still deliver us"*** (v. 10). Salvation means "to deliver, to rescue, to pardon, to secure, to make safe." All believers in the Church Age enjoy the benefits of this three-tense salvation that delivers, secures, and makes safe.

Through receiving the gospel message, we are born again and receive eternal salvation through the Holy Spirit. Hence, we can rejoice that our souls are saved from the **penalty of sin**, and through the indwelling Holy Spirit we have **power over sin**. Furthermore, we are to anticipate a future day when we (our bodies) will be saved from **the presence of sin**. So, a Christian **has been saved** (John 5:24; Eph. 2:8), **is being saved** (Phil. 2:12; Rom. 8:24), and **will be saved** (Rom. 13:11; 1 Thess. 5:9).

Although our salvation in Christ is not yet fully received, His deliverance in and out of hardships is available for us now through His consolations of grace. God regularly places His children in arduous situations, so that they might learn to trust Him more and have a deeper and higher experience with Him. Thus, earthly tribulations, troubles, sufferings, afflictions, and despair are met with heavenly comfort, endurance, and abounding consolations. Paul accredits the prayers of the saints, including those offered by the Corinthians, as to why God acted so powerfully on their behalf at Ephesus (v. 11).

Given the recentness of this hardship, it is doubtful that the Corinthians would have known what Paul had suffered in Asia. However, the lack of specifics did not stifle their prayers on Paul's behalf. This is a good reminder for us to continue praying for God's servants wherever they may be, whether we know details about their welfare or not. God knows better than we do about every situation faced by other believers, but He so enjoys being called on to exalt His Son's name in human affairs through our intercession.

## Sincerity in Ministry (vv. 12-14)

Paul could not boast about his deliverance in Asia; the situation was out of his control, but God had showed Himself strong in rescuing them. Paul could, however, call the attention of the Corinthians attention to his behavior while serving them. In verse 12, the apostle mentions five characteristics that should be marks of all Christ-centered ministries.

First, Paul had a clear conscience. He had no remorse about his conduct because he served them out of genuine love and concern for their welfare. Second, his ministry was marked by simplicity. All those on the missionary team had the same desire, that God's will be done. Third, their ministry was characterized by godly sincerity. There was no hint of personal gain, just a selfless, giving spirit while serving the Corinthians. Such a disposition keeps the Lord's servants above reproach when they come under the scrutiny of a critical spirit. Fourth, they did not labor according to human wisdom, but under divine guidance. Fifth, their ministry was empowered by God's grace. Spirit-led and Spirit-enabled service is always successful.

Next Paul addresses the integrity of his written ministry. In common with his spoken ministry among them as described above, there were no hidden agendas, false pretensions or motives in his letters, just sincere truth (v. 13). The ultimate goal of Paul's ministry was that both he and the Corinthians could boast of the grace of God together at the Day of the Lord Jesus (v. 14; 11:2; Phil. 4:1; 1 Thess. 2:19-20). This is also called *the Day of Christ*, and speaks of the glorification of believers at the end of the Church Age and the *Judgment Seat of Christ* that immediately follows (1 Cor. 1:8; Phil. 1:10). Not all the Corinthians acknowledged Paul's authority. Nevertheless, he knew that at the Judgment Seat of Christ they would all be rejoicing that he had been the instrument God used to save them. Likewise, he would be rejoicing in them and in the reward that he would receive from the Lord for his faithfulness in winning souls, including the Corinthians.

## Delays Explained and Sparing Shame (vv. 15-24)

Paul explains to the Corinthians about his past and future plans for visiting them (vv. 15-17). He also defends his actions in not having visited them previously (vv. 18-20). The apostle had informed them earlier that he

## 2 Corinthians

wanted to travel through Macedonia and winter with them (1 Cor. 16:5-7), but his plans changed, and the visit did not happen. Paul, still longing to see them, then planned a trip from Ephesus to Corinth (across the Aegean Sea), north to Macedonia, and back south again to Corinth before sailing back to Ephesus (vv. 15-16). This itinerary would have put Paul in Corinth twice, but this plan also changed.

Paul reminds the Corinthians, that he did not follow fleshly wisdom, but was being led in his ministry by the Holy Spirit (v. 17). However, some in Corinth now questioned his authority and integrity, claiming that Paul's word could not be trusted. Paul's *Yes* could not be trusted as a *Yes*, and his *No* could not be taken to mean *No* (v. 18). Regardless, Paul was not talking out of both sides of his mouth. As a servant of God, Paul prayed and planned, but ultimately, he had to obey God's will for his ministry, and God's purposes and designs are never random (v. 19).

In fact, Paul reminds them that God's glory is tied to Him keeping His promises to them: *"For all the promises of God* [the Father] *in Him* [Christ] *are Yes, and in Him Amen"* (v. 20). All the goodness that God wants to bring about in our lives is made possible through Christ and in Him all the promises of God will be fulfilled. Paul's point is that men are not omniscient or omnipotent and are therefore subject to cause-and-effect relationships in time, but that is not the case with God. There is no randomness with God; all that He purposes will happen. We cannot guarantee what we will do tomorrow, but God extends sovereign security over all His affairs, including the believer's salvation. Paul's ministry to the Corinthians was an expression of God's flawless control over his affairs.

All those who can utter *Amen* in response to the gospel message have complete union with and security in Christ. Furthermore, the Holy Spirit anoints believers at conversion with discernment as to what is true and false doctrine (v. 21; 1 Jn. 2:20, 27). The Holy Spirit, Himself, is the seal of the believer's salvation (v. 22). A seal declares ownership and provides security to what is sealed (e.g., a letter). Paul then reminds the Corinthians that the Holy Spirit is given to believers as God's guarantee (i.e., His earnest or pledge to complete what He has started). Consequently, the triune God ensures that all His promises to secure believers forever are *Yes* in Christ.

The chapter closes with Paul informing the saints at Corinth that he was not a dictator, but a God-ordained helper to build them up in their faith (vv. 23-24). God was his witness that he did have sincere motives towards. Yet, he wanted to avoid a sorrowful visit to correct their attitudes, behaviors, and doctrine (2:1). He would rather do that by letter, so that when he did arrive, it would be a mutually joyful, profitable and peaceful experience.

# 2 Corinthians Chapter 2

Forgiveness and Restoration Is Desirable (vv. 1-11)
   This chapter begins with Paul describing a brief, grievous trip he had made to Corinth, and a sorrowful letter he had subsequently written to the assembly (vv. 1-4; 7:8). Given this assumption and synthesizing what we know from other Scripture, the history surrounding these events seems to be as follows: After learning of misunderstandings and additional issues (1 Cor. 1:11, 16:17), Paul wrote a second letter to the assembly from Ephesus (*1 Corinthians* in our Bible). Paul sailed directly from Ephesus to Corinth because serious problems in the assembly were still not resolved; this was a painful visit for everyone (v. 1). Paul then sailed back to Ephesus and wrote a third letter to the Corinthians *"out of much affliction and anguish of heart"* (vv. 3-4). Probably because of the harsh tone and explicit nature of this epistle, the Holy Spirit chose not to preserve it for us in Scripture.
   While contemplating the difficulties that he was forced to address at Corinth, none pained him more than directing the excommunication of a brother who was engaging in fornication with his stepmother (vv. 5-6; 1 Cor. 5:1). Paul knew that if the man remained in the assembly gathering, his sin would degrade the holiness of the entire church. The Corinthians yielded to Paul's admonishment and the man was formally put out of the assembly. This corporate act of discipline isolated the man from other Christians and permitted Satan to buffet him. The goal of this action, which the Corinthians did not understand, was that discipline invoked in love for the Lord and for the wayward, always has the goal of repentance and restoration.
   Apparently, the excommunicated immoral brother had then repented of his sin, but he had not been restored to assembly fellowship because the Corinthian saints had not extended forgiveness and acceptance to him (v.7). Initially, they had been unwilling to uphold the holiness of God, but now they were characterized by hesitation to extend the love and forgiveness of God when it was needed. Hence, Paul encourages the saints to affirm their love to the repentant man and to embrace him again as a brother in the Lord (v. 8). The Corinthians had been submissive to his authority in the previous matter. Paul now urges them to continue to be obedient concerning the restoration of their repentant brother (v. 9).

Believers must both release offenses to the Lord when they occur and extend forgiveness to offenders when they have acknowledged their sin and asked to be forgiven (v. 10; Luke 17:3; Col. 3:13). The Lord Jesus expects us to follow His example of forgiving others; Christians are to be a forgiving people (Matt. 18:21-22, 35). Holding on to past offenses and internalizing anger will result in resentment, and eventually bitterness will take root in the heart. An unforgiving spirit presses down on the heart to cause a loss of joy and fellowship with the Lord and His people. We cannot enjoy fellowship with each other unless all parties are in fellowship with the Lord; believers can only share together what they have from the Lord. A believer who does not repent of sin cannot be in fellowship with the Lord. Consequently, neither can other believers enjoy Christian fellowship with him or her.

In this case, the repentant brother was back in fellowship with the Lord, but the Corinthians did not want anything to do with him. Paul was concerned that Satan would take advantage of this situation to overcome the repentant brother with such immense sorrow that it would cause his eventual downfall (v. 11). Paul reminded the Christians that this was a distinct possibility and warned the believers not to be ignorant of the devil's schemes to make believers unprofitable. Scripture attests to the fact that Satan repeatedly uses the same strategies to oppose the things of God; therefore, believers should be aware of his tactics and not fall prey to them.

## Triumphing in Christ (vv. 12-17)

The historical account of Paul's travels after leaving Ephesus concludes in verses 12-13. After the riot at Ephesus, Paul and the missionary team travelled north to Troas (v. 12). Although Paul was still concerned for the Corinthians, the Lord had opened a door of gospel opportunity in Troas such that Paul was constrained by the Lord to postpone his journey to Corinth. However, after an unknown period of time, Paul, being anxious over the well-being of his spiritual son Titus, resumed his journey (v. 13, 7:6, 13). Given the heightened tension between some at Corinth and Paul at this time, the apostle was unsure of how Titus was being treated by the Corinthians.

Paul's concerns were alleviated when he met Titus in Macedonia. Titus conveyed a good report on the Church at Corinth, though some still questioned Paul's apostolic authority (v. 13, 6:5-6). Paul wrote a fourth letter to answer these concerns, which is *2 Corinthians* in our Bibles.

Although Titus' report encouraged Paul, we are not told exactly what drew him out of his deep emotional distress and caused him to burst forth with high praise and thanksgiving to God, but that is what he did:

> *Now thanks be to God who always leads us in triumph in Christ, and through us diffuses the fragrance of His knowledge in every place. For we are to God the fragrance of Christ among those who are being saved and among those who are perishing. To the one we are the aroma of death leading to death, and to the other the aroma of life leading to life. And who is sufficient for these things?* (vv. 14-16).

Paul borrowed imagery from the Old Testament to express a New Testament truth. The Levitical priests were anointed with holy oil containing fragrant spices. Thus, at all times, and throughout the tabernacle, the fragrance of the holy oil would be enjoyed. In the same spiritual sense, believers in the Church Age are to carry the sweet fragrance of Christ everywhere they go as they perform their priestly duties (vv. 14-15; 1 Pet. 2:5, 9). Believers today are the House of God (1 Tim. 3:15).

The olive oil in the anointing oil represents the work of the Holy Spirit (Zech. 4:2-6), which means believer-priests today can express the sweet moral excellencies of Christ in what they do only by the power of the Holy Spirit. As each believer is controlled by Him, the sweet fragrance of Christ will be powerfully disseminated to all, but as Paul notes, not everyone will appreciate the fragrance of Christ. The lost are able to witness the Lord Jesus through the selfless acts and godly character of believers. As the lost observe divine love, joy, peace, faith, self-control, and humility, they are prompted to take note, breathe in, and ponder the sweetness of the Lord Jesus and the value of His death at Calvary. Some will be repulsed by the message of the cross, but others will be prompted to breathe in again, and some will never desire to inhale anything but Christ again (v. 16).

God had previously told Moses that the priests were to be anointed with olive oil when they were purified by blood and consecrated to the Lord (Ex. 29:7). This undoubtedly symbolizes the initial work of the Holy Spirit at conversion to bring a vile sinner under the power of Christ's blood. Yet, the priests were to be anointed a second time with the fragrant oil before serving in the Holy Place. This represents the ongoing work of the Holy Spirit in the believer's life. Only when He controls us can we disseminate the sweet fragrance of Christ to those who desperately need to consider His message of life. Some will receive this message and obtain life; others find no appeal in the idea that Christ's death could benefit them and so they remain dead.

Paul's ministry was epitomized by a fragrant aroma because it came directly from God, was sincerely done in the sight of God, and centered in the teaching of Jesus Christ (v. 17). Paul was not like the Judaizers, the "so many," who promoted themselves and used Scripture for their own agendas.

# 2 Corinthians Chapter 3

## The Evidence of a Living Epistle (vv. 1-5)

The false teachers, the Judaizers, carried with them letters of introduction from influential Jews in Jerusalem. They had convinced some at Corinth that Paul also needed to have such credentials to be received in the assembly on his next visit to Corinth (v. 1). This request was demeaning to Paul, the one who had led them to Christ, so his response was curt: if they were saved, if they had a testimony of Christ to others, it could only mean one thing – that he had been commended by the Lord to them (v. 2). Paul did not need a written letter of commendation, as the Corinthians, themselves, were a *"living letter"* of God's power at work in their lives, a testimony that all men could read and evaluate.

In fact, the Corinthians were engraved deeply on Paul's innermost affections (v. 3). The existence of the church at Corinth verified that a real work of God had been achieved there; thus, the Corinthians were *"an epistle of Christ."* If Paul were lying about his claim to be an apostle, why would God have blessed his ministry there in such an abundant way? A living letter written by God was more convincing than one penned with ink by men!

Paul did not want the Corinthians to think that he was boasting of himself or his accomplishments, so he was careful to give all the glory to God (vv. 4-5). The missionary team had no sufficiency in themselves; their complete trust was in Christ towards God. They had no wherewithal to do anything for God but through the work of *"the Spirit of the living God."* The *"epistle of Christ"* written at Corinth by God confirmed God's presence among the missionaries, and for that Paul was deeply thankful.

It is clear that Paul had taught them about the importance of local church reception, which should not be confused with the unbiblical practice of local church membership. The practice of reception (usually by letter, but also by the testimony of other believers) introduced new converts or traveling saints to a new church fellowship (Acts 2:41-42, 9:27, 18:26-27; Col. 4:7-8; Rom. 16:1). Reception stresses the privileges and responsibilities within the local church, privileges which are enjoyed, and responsibilities which are carried out, under the authority of the elders in the assembly. Church membership in Scripture relates only to the universal Church and only the Holy Spirit can place a believer into the Body of Christ – the Church.

The unscriptural idea of local church *membership* makes an evaluation of an individual's salvation and extends rights (often in the form of voting) to those inducted. As only the Lord knows the hearts of those who are truly His, *reception* accepts an individual's confession of salvation without making a judgment as to the reality of his or her salvation. The local church is commanded to receive those who have followed Christ's command to be baptized, are sound in life and in doctrine, and who desire to take part in the body-life of the assembly (Rom. 15:7).

## True Ministry Is Spiritual and Glorious, Not Legal (vv. 6-18)

Verse 6 introduces the subject of the "new covenant" which was secured by Christ's own blood to impart spiritual life (Heb. 9:15-28). The new covenant put away the "letter," the "old covenant" (i.e., the Law), which brought only condemnation and death (v. 6). The writer of Hebrews, quoting Jeremiah (Jer. 31:31-34), confirms that it was always God's plan to establish a new covenant with Israel that would offer spiritual life and blessing, not only to the Jewish nation, but also to all people (Heb. 8:7-10).

The Law of God reflected God's holy character to Israel, so it did have a glory associated with it (v. 7). God's commandments were engraved on stones to be preserved for the duration of the Law's stewardship. In contrast to its condemnation of sinners, the Holy Spirit (by the new covenant) gave spiritual life to the condemned. This meant that the new covenant was more glorious than the Law (vv. 8-9). Secondly, the glory of the new covenant is permanent, but the glory of the Law faded away (vv. 10-11). The Law had served its purpose of showing Israel her sin and their spiritual need to be divinely saved (Rom. 3:20; Gal. 3:24). Since the system associated with the Law prepared the way for Christ's advent, and since He came and fulfilled the demands of the Law, the entire Law-related system has been put away and replaced by the New Covenant He established at Calvary (Heb. 8:13).

Paul had already told the Corinthians that God had done a work among them, not through "tables of stone" (the Law), but by His Spirit in their hearts (v. 3). They, as "tablets of flesh," were living testimonies of God's grace. Initially God sent only those He trusted to bring such an important message to the nations; these were Christ's apostles. Paul's ministry centered in sharing this new, life-giving, spiritual message, which was superior to and more glorious than the Law. The fact that God had miraculously blessed Paul's ministry meant that he was a true apostle.

This is why Paul could say, *"since we have such hope, we use great boldness of speech"* (v. 12). Paul had been entrusted with sharing the gospel and had witnessed its power to transform vile sinners into living temples of God. Therefore, he had great boldness in proclaiming the new-covenant message. In contrast, Moses put a veil over his face symbolizing the fading glory of the message he had been tasked to deliver (i.e., the Law).

After being alone with God on Mount Sinai for forty days, Moses returned to the camp carrying the two replacement stone tablets of the Law (Ex. 34). When Moses returned to the camp after receiving the first stone tablets on which God had written the Law, the idolatrous behavior of the people angered him, and he smashed the tablets. However, on this second occasion, the people were patiently waiting for him, and the replacement tablets were delivered as intended. Moses did not realize it, but he soon learned from the reaction of the people that his countenance shone brightly; his face continued to radiate the reflected glory of God. Understandably, the people, and even his own brother Aaron, were afraid to come near him.

When Moses spoke to Aaron and the elders, the people knew it was safe to approach him, but when he was among the people, he covered his face with a veil. However, when he met with God in the tabernacle, he removed it. Did he wear the veil to prevent the people from being anxious, or was there another reason? Paul answers this in verses 13-16.

Moses covered his face, not to make the Israelites more comfortable in his presence, but so they would not notice that the brilliance of his face was gradually diminishing (v. 13). Why was this important? Moses delivered the Law to Israel. However, although it declared God's righteous character, it did not make evident the full measure of God's goodness in addressing and resolving the issue of sin. The Law showed and condemned human sin but did not provide man with power to overcome it. Just as the reflected glory of God faded from Moses' face, the Law also had a diminishing glory.

In time, the Old Covenant (the Law) would be replaced by the New Covenant sealed with Christ's own blood. This truth was conveyed to the Jews when the Lord Jesus presented Himself to them as their Messiah (v. 14). When Christ sojourned among the Jews, He removed the veil that was over the Law in order to show its fading glory. Yet, instead of trusting Him, Israel as a nation refused to remove the veil from their hearts, and nationally they remain in spiritual blindness to this day (v. 15; Rom. 11:7). Only by having an accurate view of Jesus Christ can the true purpose of the Mosaic Law be understood. Jews who read the Law today without seeing Christ are effectively choosing to have their minds veiled with a cloak of deception.

In the unveiling of Moses in the presence of God in the tabernacle Paul observes further illustration of truth in the present dispensation (v. 16). After Israel's rejection of Christ and His crucifixion and resurrection, the message of the new covenant is to be preached throughout all nations. Paul explains that when a person believes in the Lord Jesus the veil of spiritual blindness is removed and the person enjoys fellowship with God. This happens when a sinner, after hearing the gospel message, responds to the conviction and prompting of the Holy Spirit and trusts Christ for salvation (John 16:8-10).

During the Tribulation period, the veil of blindness over the nation of Israel will be removed (Rom. 11:7-12, 25-27). When Christ returns to judge the earth and ends the time of Jacob's Trouble, the purified Jewish nation will worship Jesus Christ as her Messiah (Zech. 12:10; Rom. 9:27). Then Israel will behold the glory of God in Christ with unveiled faces!

In verse 6, Paul told the Corinthians that they had received life by the Holy Spirit. Now we learn that the "Lord is the Spirit" (v. 17). "Spirit" here does not speak of the Holy Spirit, but that Christ is the fulfillment of Old Testament truth – *"the testimony of Jesus is the spirit of prophecy"* (Rev. 19:10). In contrast to the Law that demanded spiritual death, the Lord Jesus is able to give spiritual life. Christ is able to liberate sinners from the bondage of sin and death so they can experience the goodness of God.

Paul concludes this chapter with a lovely devotional thought which should motivate all believers to behold the Lord Jesus more and more through the study of Scripture: *"But we all, with unveiled face, beholding as in a mirror the glory of the Lord, are being transformed into the same image from glory to glory, just as by the Spirit of the Lord"* (v. 18).

While on Mount Sinai, Moses had the wonderful privilege of seeing the Lord's afterglow (a limited view of God's glory; Ex. 33:18-34:29). By immersing himself in Christ throughout the Scriptures, the humblest Christian will be more fully exposed to the glory of God than was Moses in the cleft of the rock. As believers intently examine the Word of God, the Spirit of God unveils the glory of God in Christ with the result that we are being changed into the image His Son. Expectation of the glorious appearing of the Lord Jesus Christ ought to be the longing of the heart of every believer. In the meantime, may we earnestly beseech the Lord with Moses, *"Please, show me your glory."*.

God longs for His children to be like Him in thought and deed (Rom. 8:29). As we keep our faces unveiled before God by confessing and forsaking sin, we gain a greater awareness of righteousness as we pore over the mirror, the Word of God (Jas. 1:23-25) and see ourselves in contrast to God's holiness. By yielding to divine truth, the believer is transformed into deeper hues of Christlikeness. Occupation with the splendor and glory of Christ and submission to the control of the Holy Spirit will truly usher holiness into our lives.

# 2 Corinthians Chapter 4

## Sincere Christ-Centered Ministry (vv. 1-7)

During the Lord's earthly sojourn, He exhorted those listening to His parable, *"Men always ought to pray and not lose heart"* (Luke 18:1). Paul states in verse 1 that though the missionary team was engaged in an arduous ministry, they "did not lose heart" because they had received mercy from above to keep pressing forward. The apostle repeats this declaration in verse 16, but there he adds that God was renewing his inward (inner) man day by day. Paul had learned experientially that if he relied on the strength of his flesh, he would faint, and his joy would dissipate. However, if he continued to draw strength from God through prayers of faith, his spirit would be blissfully invigorated to do what only God could.

For this reason, Paul proclaimed the gospel message without guile or the aid of fleshly craftiness. He preached Christ crucified and did not engage in dishonesty, or the deceitful handling of God's Word, or the preaching of himself (v. 2). Several times in this chapter, Paul mentions his weak human frailty to serve God. Albert McShane observes:

> In no other part of the NT do we have such emphasis put upon the frailty of the human body as here. We have only to collect together some of the expressions employed, such as "earthen vessels" (v. 7), "our mortal flesh" (v. 11), "outward man perishing" (v. 16), or "earthly house of this tent" (5:1), to realize that, if the service of God is being executed successfully, it is not due to the physical strength of the instruments employed in it.[37]

The ministry of this missionary team among the unregenerate was marked by blameless, selfless service; they were not operating in the flesh. This meant that even those who opposed them would have to side against their own consciences to speak ill of Paul and his co-laborers. Deep down, they knew that these men were above reproach and that their message was genuine. This meant that if anyone remained in the darkness of the devil's deception, they did so freely and against the verdict of their own conscience (vv. 3-4).

Practically speaking, gospel work will have the most benefit when executed with Spirit-led power and through a sincere Christ-centered message that speaks to the human conscience rather than to the intellect. Intellectual arguments alone will never cause someone to trust Christ as Savior. Faith is a determination of heart that reaches beyond sensory verification and human reasoning. The human conscience must be reached and brought under the conviction of sin and guilt before conversion can occur. For this reason, Paul felt that he owed it to all men to serve them for Christ's sake and he was determined to preach Christ and not himself (v. 5).

Another reason that Paul refused to preach of himself was that he realized where he had come from, and that if God had not intervened in his life, he would still be lost in the utter darkness of religious deception (v. 6). Paul draws on the Genesis 1 imagery of God causing His light to shine out of darkness to bring life and order to the watery formlessness that existed in the beginning. Before Christ, Paul walked in satanic darkness, and only the divine light of Christ directed him out of this hopeless abyss. Now he enjoyed God's order and peace in his life. How could Paul ever boast of himself, after having previously sought to eradicate Christianity! Gratefully, Paul now knew the truth, and the truth of Christ had set him free (John 8:32)!

Paul then states, *"But we have this treasure in earthen vessels, that the excellence of the power may be of God and not of us"* (v. 7). The "we" continues to represent Paul and the others with him who are preaching the gospel message. The "earthen vessels" speak of their frail, mortal bodies, a common theme in this chapter. Paul's meaning of "this" is a bit harder to discern. Grammatically speaking, the "this" would speak of *"the knowledge of the glory of God in the face of Jesus Christ"* in this verse; this was the light that drew them out of darkness. The "this" then would relate to the gospel message, the treasure, when they were sharing with others.

Common folk in Paul's day did not have the opportunity to store their valuables in secure places like safe deposit boxes and banks. Instead, people hid their valuable possessions in common pots to disguise or hide them from thieves. Sometimes valuables were buried for safekeeping. On the outside, the missionary team members were just common, nearly worthless, clay pots, but the living message they carried within them was eternally priceless. This illustration showed that the power of God was not in the earthen vessels themselves, but in the divine message they were to preach. Accordingly, Paul and his counterparts had nothing to boast about.

## Suffering Now for Glory Later (vv. 8-18)

It was not an easy ministry for which the Lord had chosen Paul for; there was constant opposition, and the threat of persecution and death followed wherever they went. Yet, until Paul had completed his divine calling, he knew that he was invincible in the Lord. So, while there was hardship in the ministry, there was also the evidence of God's sustaining power. Thus, the missionary team was not in despair, nor were they crushed or destroyed by those opposing the message of the gospel (vv. 8-9).

The apex of Paul's paradoxical ministry experience described in verses 8-9 is reached in verse 10. Through the literal death and resurrection of Christ, they possessed the life of Christ, but this required them to die daily in order to live for Christ (1 Cor. 15:31)! They were living testimonies of the power of the very message they were preaching (v. 11). Although they were dying daily to self, and were under constant threat of physical death, Paul could see the gospel message bringing life to the Corinthians. In his estimation made the entire undertaking worthwhile (v. 12).

Obviously, if Paul and the other missionaries did not truly believe the message they were preaching, they would not have been risking life and limb to share it (v. 13). He had witnessed the power of God in his own life and in the lives of many others, therefore Paul could not keep quiet. If he had kept silent and not shared the gospel message in Corinth, there would be no one there to be writing this letter to.

Indeed, there was the possibility that Paul or members of the missionary team might be martyred at any time for their faith. But this did not concern Paul for two reasons. First, God completely controlled their ministry, which meant the timing of their deaths was foreknown by God. As soldiers of the cross, they would triumph until that time. Second, when God did determine that it was time for them to die, being with the Lord in Heaven would fulfill their greatest expectations, for *"to die is gain"* (5:8; Phil. 1:21). Because God raised up Christ from the dead, and all believers are in spiritual union with Him, Paul knew that ultimately all believers, including the Corinthians, would receive bodies fit for Heaven and would be with Christ forever (v. 14). Paul, therefore, was willing to gladly suffer on behalf of the Corinthians; he rejoiced to think of them as part of the heavenly throng that would abound with thanksgiving to the glory of God (v. 15).

This high hope of being with Christ in Heaven invigorated Paul to keep pressing on in his ministry until the Lord called him home: *"Therefore we do not lose heart. Even though our outward man is perishing, yet the inward man is being renewed day by day"* (v. 16). The process of aging gracefully while staying active in ministry is challenging. This is why Solomon encouraged young people to give their best years to the Lord: *"Remember now your Creator in the days of your youth, before the difficult days come"*

(Eccl. 12:1). Throughout life, a person should revere God, obey His commandments, and faithfully serve God. The coming difficult days in this verse refer to the body's deterioration that accompanies old age.

It is natural for older women to fall, for men to slump over with age, and for the elderly to lose their teeth and eyesight. Additionally, they may lose their hearing and often suffer from insomnia, weakened vocal cords, fearfulness, and diminished natural desires (Eccl. 12:3-4). Paul puts the matter this way: the *"outward man is perishing."*

Paul explains that though our physical bodies diminish in ability over time, our inner man (i.e., our spirit) is strengthened through the power of the Holy Spirit. In contrast to a waning, aging body, our union with Christ ensures an endless resource of resurrection power. So, while we may have decreased ability to demonstrate love in our earthly relationships, our union with Christ ensures an increasing capacity to appreciate and demonstrate our devotion to Him.

It is quite amazing that Paul could refer to his jail time, his beatings, being stoned and left for dead as "light affliction." Nonetheless, in the grand scheme of things he understood that all he had patiently endured earned him an eternal weight of glory (v. 17). He realized that God had used these hardships to better him, to declare the gospel message more powerfully, to encourage weaker brethren to do the same, and would give him a greater opportunity to worship the Lord throughout eternity. Therefore, recognizing the temporary nature of suffering and the eternal reality of glory, Paul was determined to live for what was not seen, instead of that which was passing away before his eyes. This is the idea associated with "look" in verse 18.

The Lord remembers our selfless and arduous service and will reward us for it. The Lord is watching. He knows. He cares. He remembers. He will reward appropriately and abundantly. This is why Paul could write: *"For I consider that the sufferings of this present time are not worthy to be compared with the glory which shall be revealed in us"* (Rom. 8:18).

We do not know when Christ will return to remove us to His abode, but He has provided everything that we need until that time. We can be assured that He will not rest until all believers are brought into His full inheritance and eternal rest! Then, we will all be shocked to learn how little we practically appreciated the reality of *"all spiritual blessings in heavenly places in Christ."* Paul had learned to rely on God's grace to accomplish what only He could achieve to receive the reward that only He can give. May we appropriate, in full measure, the grace of God afforded to us now in Christ. An exceeding and eternal weight of glory is worth it!

# 2 Corinthians Chapter 5

### The Ambition of Ministry (vv. 1-10)

Paul continues his discussion from the previous chapter concerning the wonders awaiting believers in Heaven, namely an immortal body. In metaphoric language, the apostle likens our temporary, physical body to a "tent" or an "earthly house" that will be taken down or destroyed (v. 1). He also speaks of the believer's heavenly body as an eternal house that God constructs to clothe or cover the eternal essence of the believer (the human soul). Believers eagerly anticipate receiving this heavenly covering (i.e., eternal bodies fit for Heaven), rather than being eternally naked, so to speak after experiencing death (vv. 2-3).

The earnest expectation of the child of God is not death, which causes the destruction of the earthly body, but rather what follows death, the receipt of a glorified body when mortality will be swallowed up by life (v. 4). God has given believers the Holy Spirit as a guarantee that He will complete the work of salvation that He has begun in them by giving them eternal bodies (v. 5). While we are still in our earthly bodies, however, we are absent from the Lord in Heaven (v. 6). Until the Lord takes us home (by death or through glorification), believers must continue to walk by faith in heavenly truth, not by earthly perceptions of things (v. 7). By death our eternal essence is brought immediately into the Lord's presence (v. 8).

When the Lord saves a repentant sinner, He completely redeems that person's spirit, soul, and body (1 Cor. 6:29; 1 Thess. 5:23). The soul and spirit are immediately delivered from the penalty of sin upon confession of sinfulness and acceptance of the free gift of salvation in Christ (John 5:24). Salvation of the body occurs instantly when raptured from the presence of sin. It undergoes a transformation called glorification that fits it for eternity.

Since all believers must experience the First Resurrection (Rev. 20:6), and one must die to be resurrected, believers must instantly pass through death (if still alive) when glorification occurs. This act of God completes the believer's salvation; the body is transformed and saved at glorification. This renovation will occur for all living believers (simultaneously) at Christ's coming for His Church (1 Thess. 4:13-17). In the twinkling of an eye, that which was corruptible will be incorruptible, and that which was mortal will be immortal (1 Cor. 15:51-52).

The believer's glorified body will be enabled to worship and to please God without any hindrances of the flesh or ills of its previously fallen state. God's offer of salvation is a complete salvation of the whole of person in Jesus Christ! The spirit is saved (Acts 7:59; 1 Cor. 5:5, 6:20), the soul is saved (Matt. 10:28; Jas. 5:20), and the body will be saved (Phil. 3:21). It is in Christ that all man's deepest needs are satisfied.

In summary, an individual's soul and spirit are eternally saved upon trusting the gospel message, while salvation of the body is to be eagerly anticipated in a coming day. This was Paul's blessed hope and his earnest expectation (Tit. 2:13). *"Now is our salvation nearer than when we believed"* (Rom. 13:11). In Christ we are eternally safe and secure, and He provides for our every need.

We have God's assurance that if we die before the saving of our bodies (i.e., at the Rapture of the Church), our spiritual essence will be in His presence. *"We are confident, I say, and willing rather to be absent from the body, and to be present with the Lord"* (v. 8). Given that newly martyred Tribulation Saints are given robes in Heaven but will not undergo resurrection until the end of the Tribulation period (Rev. 6:9, 20:4), it seems likely that these souls are given temporary bodies to enjoy God's abode until such time that they experience glorification. This is likely true also for the souls of saints who are presently with the Lord in Heaven.

Paul then mentions the ultimate motivation for doing our best in serving the Lord Jesus, that whether in life or death, we would please the Lord (v. 9). The apostle affirms that every believer will stand before the Lord to give an account of how he or she lived for Him (v. 10). This is called *The Judgment Seat of Christ*. As every believer stands before the Lord Jesus to be examined, it will be apparent that it is not what we have done for Christ that matters as much as why and how we served Him.

*The Judgment Seat of Christ* is not a judgment of salvation, but one of works. Good works will be amply rewarded. Everything else will be burned up and we will be glad to see it go (1 Cor. 3:11-15)! What was done in truth for Christ (1 Cor. 3:11), done willingly (1 Cor. 9:17), done for the Lord with right motives (Col. 3:23-25) while not seeking the praise of others (Matt. 6:1-5), will be rewarded. The *Judgment Seat of Christ* occurs directly after the Church is taken to Heaven (1 Thess. 4:17; Rev. 22:12).

## The Pure Motives of True Ambassadors (vv. 11-21)

After mentioning the Judgment Seat of Christ in verse 10, Paul reveals his reverential awe for the Lord, spoken of as "terror" (v. 11). The Greek word *phobos* rendered "terror" is normally translated as "fear." Its meaning, which is reflected in the context of the passage, is that which strikes exceeding terror. The idea that in a coming day he would personally stand before the Lord of glory and render an account of all his doings and have all the secrets of his heart revealed thunderstruck Paul's conscience.

This realization motivated the apostle to live a holy life and to engage in ministry with pure motives; this would honor the Lord and also best serve the Corinthians (v. 12). Being sold out for the cause of Christ, Paul would not live a life of duplicity. In saying this, he did not want the Corinthians to think he was commending himself, but rather, by knowing what prompted his sincerity in service, they would boast in him and be more willing to confront those defaming him. Privately, Paul enjoyed high and exhilarating experiences with the Lord, but he did not minister in Corinth with a flamboyant theatrical approach to ministry (v. 13). Such nonsense would naturally appeal to the flesh but not to the human conscience. He sought, rather, to soberly and plainly preach the truth.

The thought of personal accountability before the Lord at His Judgment Seat motivated Paul to live purely, but it was Christ's demonstrated love for him that compelled him to live all out for the Lord: *"For the love of Christ compels us, because we judge thus: that if one died for all, then all died; and He died for all, that those who live should live no longer for themselves, but for Him who died for them and rose again"* (vv. 14-15). Christ's love enabled Paul to genuinely love Christ and others (1 Jn. 4:19). Christ gave His all for us that we might have all the blessings of eternal life in Him; why would we ever not want to live for Him now?

As shown from God's dealings with His covenant people in the Old Testament, He will not tolerate a divided heart in His people. Their religious formalities and idolatry were severely punished. It is impossible to live a holy life for God's glory unless single-hearted devotion guides the way.

Believers in the Church can also forget from where they came. As children of the devil, we were dead in trespasses and sins and enslaved to sin. Similarly, the Lord Jesus wants a spotlessly pure bride for Himself (Eph. 5:27), one that *"abstain[s] from the appearance of evil"* (1 Thess. 5:22, KJV). This is only possible by fully consecrating one's spirit, soul and body for God's purposes by abhorring evil in thought and deed. This requires believers to recall that what once we were in Adam is dead and gone (Eph. 4:22; Rom. 6:6). All that we were before Christ is no more – we died with Christ at Calvary. Because believers have been legally declared dead, they receive a new life – Christ's life through new birth. Now the love of Christ compels us to live daily as He would.

Thus, as Paul looked around, he no longer judged men according to the flesh, but rather by the eternal perspective of whether or not they were in union with Christ (v. 16). There are only two groups of people walking the earth today, those justified in Christ (saints) and those who are not (ain'ts). Those in Christ are no longer children of the devil, no longer dead in trespasses and sins. They are a new creation in Christ, and thus children of God (v. 17). The *Old Man*, all that we were in Adam naturally, positionally died at the cross when Christ died and through Christ's resurrection, we have His life (Rom. 6:6; Eph. 4:22). For Paul, and for us too, this means that we must endeavor to live His life daily and not follow our own ambitions.

God is the essence of life (John 1:3-5); apart from Him there is no life. Sin separated man from God, but through Christ's work of reconciliation, those ruined by sin may be forgiven, cleansed, and brought into communion with God again to experience His life (v. 18). God achieved this life-giving opportunity through Christ. Declaring this message of reconciliation was the pioneering ministry that Christ had assigned Paul to fulfill (v. 19). It is also the message that all believers have been commanded to proclaim wherever God chooses to place them as witnesses for Christ.

Since Christ is seated at the right hand of the majesty on high in Heaven, and all believers are positionally seated with him there (Eph. 2:6), Paul viewed himself and the other apostles (along with all believers) as heavenly ambassadors of Christ on earth (v. 20). Believers are heavenly "ministers of state" in a foreign land. Before ascending back to Heaven, the Lord Jesus charged His followers to be His witnesses throughout the world (Matt. 20:19-20; Acts 1:8). Those who are a heavenly citizenship are to represent Christ's kingdom wherever they have been currently posted (Phil. 3:20).

Christ faithfully declared the name of His Father during His earthly sojourn, and Christians must do the same now to reveal the name of the Lord Jesus Christ to the world. This was Paul's prayer for the new believers at Thessalonica: *"That the name of our Lord Jesus Christ may be glorified in you, and you in Him, according to the grace of our God and the Lord Jesus Christ"* (2 Thess. 1:12). But as Paul instructs Timothy, it is impossible for Christians to display Christ properly unless they are committed to holy living: *"Let everyone who names the name of Christ depart from iniquity"* (2 Tim. 2:19). Those at Corinth had been reconciled to God through the gospel message, but they desperately needed to heed this truth!

To declare the name of Christ is a high honor, but to be associated with His name demands that we live honorably for the One who knew no sin, but became sin for us, that we could be made righteous in Him (v. 21). God punished His Son on our behalf. May we never get over that truth!

# 2 Corinthians Chapter 6

## Supernatural Ministry (vv. 1-10)

The opening verses continue the theme from the previous chapter: Paul and those serving with him were genuine heavenly ambassadors, sincerely pleading with the unregenerate to receive God's gift of reconciliation. God was at work in reconciling men to Himself through Christ, and Paul and the other apostles were legitimately laboring with God to accomplish this (v. 1). Paul then quotes Isaiah 49:8, to affirm that the Corinthian believers had called out to the Lord after being given the opportunity to hear this message of reconciliation, and God had responded by granting them salvation (v. 2).

It is possible that Paul was concerned that there may be some in their ranks (e.g., false teachers) who had not yet humbled themselves and trusted Christ alone for salvation. We gain the sense through this section of Paul's letter that the Corinthians did not appreciate or esteem Paul as they should, especially since it was he whom God had used to save their souls.

Regardless, Paul's point here is that only true ministers of God, with God-like behavior and character, could have declared His Word with the powerful outcome that it had on the Corinthians (v. 3). The conclusion was that Paul and the other missionaries were such ministers. Such a testimony of God's grace, the fruit of the Spirit (Gal. 5:22-23), is possible only through the empowerment of the Holy Spirit. This would help the Corinthians recognize who were the real ambassadors of Christ and who were phonies.

Paul now contrasts himself with the Judaizers who were opposing him and his message. The Judaizers were preaching grace and Law-keeping as the means of salvation, and for their own glory (vv. 14-15). Paul was concerned that these false teachers might turn the Corinthians from the gospel of grace (the message of salvation) to Law-based legalism, which only condemns (Gal. 1:6-9). Paul does not assert his credentials as an apostle at this point. Rather, he highlights the type of hardships a true ambassador of Christ will endure (vv. 4-5) and the type of character qualities that should be evident in a true servant of the Lord (vv. 6-7). He is implying that both aspects were evident in him, but not in those opposing him, his authority, and his message. In other words, what his opposers were saying about Paul was clearly not true, but it was true of themselves.

The apostle poses this argument by grouping what he has patiently suffered into three triplets. First, there were the general trials of tribulations, needs, and distresses (v. 4). Second, he mentions what he has suffered at the hands of his opposers: stripes, imprisonments, and tumults (v. 4). To the Galatians, Paul declared, *"I bear in my body the marks [scars] of the Lord Jesus"* (Gal. 6:17). He describes these marks and other sufferings more explicitly in chapter 12. Third, Paul identifies the hardships associated with his ministry: labors, sleeplessness, and fastings (v. 5). Paul had to labor with his own hands at times to supply his needs. The cares of the churches and the constant threat of persecution weighed heavily on his mind causing him sleepless nights. At times, long hours of ministry and the lack of resources forced Paul to go without food and proper clothing.

Notwithstanding what ambassadors for Christ suffer in ministry, they are to exhibit the power of God as energized by the Holy Spirit in their behavior. Besides these two qualities, Paul mentions several more spiritual evidences to look for: purity, patience, kindness, and selfless love will be evident as the wisdom and truth of God's Word is being declared (v. 6). Finally, true ambassadors for Christ are clad in the armor of righteousness to endure hardships faithfully and honorably for the One they represent (v. 7). The Judaizers did not reflect the character of God or His truth in their message. They had not suffered for the cause of Christ, nor had they benefitted the Corinthians by their erroneous teachings.

To ensure that the Corinthians could discern between a counterfeit ambassador and a true one, the apostle offers nine paradoxes that contrast the natural human response to hardship with how those empowered by the Holy Spirit will behave (vv. 8-10). Despite the evil reports of him being a deceiver who was seeking his own honor, Paul endured the sufferings and hardships of his Christ-promoting ministry joyfully, despite the ever-present threat of persecution and death. True, he was physically poor, but he was spiritually rich. And although his ministry was marked by much turmoil and sorrow, yet he rejoiced in Christ. He was in constant peril, but his life was in Christ, and he knew that not even death could take that away from him.

## Separation and Cleansing Are Necessary (vv. 11-18)

In verse 11, Paul transitions from the contrastive arguments of what a true ambassador of Christ is and is not, to issuing a personal appeal to the Corinthians (even referring to them by name). Paul had always spoken to them in sincere love and desired them to reciprocate the same sentiment to him with unrestricted affections (v. 12). The verb rendered "restricted" in verse 12 is in the passive voice, which means that the Corinthians were permitting things to restrict their expressions of proper love for Paul. As their spiritual father, Paul offers his spiritual children a warning as to how unnatural unions result in misplaced affections (v. 13).

The Corinthians were having close associations with unbelievers (i.e., false teachers and pagans) that were negatively influencing their testimony for Christ and their appreciation for Paul. Unnatural unions with children of the devil are one of the chief reasons Christians fail today. Paul identifies five types of associations in life to beware of:

First, the righteous are to have no close associations with the unrighteous, for their behavior is unholy and unbecoming to those who are to be holy (v. 14). The only safeguard against evil is to remain near the Lord, for *"evil company corrupts good habits"* (1 Cor. 15:33). "The unequally yoked" metaphor is taken from Deuteronomy 22:10, which forbids an ox (a clean animal) from being harnessed with a donkey (an unclean animal) for the purpose of plowing a field. The different natures of the animals meant a disastrous outcome in their association together. Second, what do light and darkness have in common (v. 14)? Darkness is the absence of light, but God, in Christ, is the true light of the world (John 1:5, 8:12), and thus, has no part in the deceptive nature of that which opposes Him and neither should we. Third, Christians follow Christ, the head of the Church, not Belial, the head of paganism (v. 15). Fourth, the message of the Faith is salvation by grace alone, which is opposite to the world's religion of doings (i.e., one can earn Heaven or improve his spiritual existence through personal effort). Hence, believers and the lost have no common faith. Fifth, the believer is a temple of God, but idols, dumb inanimate objects, are abhorrent to God (v. 16).

The devil often lures God's people into unnatural unions with his own children through religious causes and social gatherings, which the Lord cannot attend. These things are valued by churchianity, but not by the Lord. The busy doings of religion are a poor substitute for Spirit-led ministry that counts for eternity! This is what Paul was engaged in, while the Judaizers were self-promoting false teachers who were leading the Corinthians astray.

Therefore, it was absolutely needful that the Corinthians should separate themselves from the influences of worldliness, false teaching, idolatry, and sinful behavior to enjoy fellowship with God (vv. 17-18). God could not commune with them as His children, unless they first chose to separate themselves from the darkness that grieved His heart. John puts the matter this way: *"God is light and in Him is no darkness at all. If we say that we have fellowship with Him, and walk in darkness, we lie and do not practice the truth"* (1 Jn. 1:5-6). God is holy and the Corinthians must also be holy to enjoy full communion with their heavenly Father.

# 2 Corinthians Chapter 7

### The Final Plea for Separation (v. 1)

The chapter break here, as in the last three chapters, is inappropriately placed, and unfortunately severs Paul's flow of thought. The first verse of this chapter is a final appeal to the Corinthians to be separated from all that would defile them. Fornication, which was often associated with pagan practices, not only defiled the body, but also warred against the soul (Prov. 6:32). False doctrine and a numbed conscience cloud good judgment and eventually prompt carnal living. The Corinthians were to mature in holiness in fear of the Lord. The fear of God is the death of all other fears. When believers revere only the Lord, holy living naturally follows.

### Open Hearts and True Repentance (vv. 2-16)

In the last chapter, Paul declared that his heart was wide open to the Corinthians – he had immense love for them (6:12). Accordingly, he asked them to rid themselves of whatever restrained them from opening their hearts to him (6:13-14). Paul had not wronged them or taken advantage of them in any way, so why were they keeping him at a distance and withholding affection (v. 2)? He fondly requests that the Corinthians "make room" for him in their hearts.

The apostle felt such a strong connection with the Corinthians that he was willing to go on together with them in life or in death (v. 3). This declaration of commitment is similar to Ruth's devotion expressed to Naomi, *"Wherever you go, I will go...your people shall be my people, and your God, my God. Where you die, I will die"* (Ruth 1:16-17). It would be hard to find a more sincere expression of one's devotion and loyalty in Scripture – whether in life or death I am completely committed to you.

Paul did not hide his feelings from the Corinthians, nor his boasting of and praise for those he joyfully considered his spiritual children (v. 4). Verse 4 concludes Paul's lengthy discourse (which began at the end of chapter 2) of confirming his love for and confidence in the Corinthians while at the same time interweaving appeals for their love and appreciation for himself.

With this long parenthetical emphasis stressing his blameless conduct, his glorious ambition in ministry, and his enduring sincerity towards them concluded, Paul returns to the subject of his travel itinerary, which he interrupted after 2:13. Paul was mentally distressed over not knowing how the Corinthians had responded to his previous letter and how Titus was faring among them. He had remained in Troas for a time because God had opened a door of opportunity there, but he eventually decided to travel westward to Macedonia. Paul was in much turbulence of spirit in Macedonia, as there were outward conflicts, inward fears, and troubles on every side. Not even the warm hospitality of the Macedonian saints could settle Paul's anxiety (v. 5). But after Titus arrived and delivered a favorable report, many of Paul's concerns were alleviated (v. 6). He was comforted in knowing that the Corinthians had mourned over their past behavior towards him and now had zeal and appreciation for him (v. 7).

Paul labored in the letter known as 1 Corinthians to put the local assembly into godly order. He confronted their personal and corporate behaviors, carnal mindsets, and bad doctrine. He had also sailed across the Aegean Sea to personally confront those who had not heeded his epistle. He followed up this trip with a letter of sharp rebuke, which pained him to write, but was needful for the Corinthians to receive (v. 8; 2:3). Through the beforementioned efforts, the apostle succeeded in making them *"sorry in a godly manner"* (v. 9). After hearing that they had responded well to his rebuke, Paul wrote again to encourage them: *"For godly sorrow produces repentance leading to salvation, not to be regretted; but the sorrow of the world produces death. ...you sorrowed in a godly manner"* (vv. 10-11).

This pattern of cleansing is needful in the lives of all believers, and at times a rebuke will be needful to correct our behavior so that we will repudiate uncleanness. Often, we are grieved in our conscience after doing or saying something without understanding the reason why. Thankfully, through continued exposure to God's Word, seeking the Lord's wisdom in prayer (Jas. 1:5), and the conviction of the Holy Spirit, believers are enabled to better understand what God disapproves of and then to reject it.

The next phase of cleansing is to confess and repent of known failures which have been exposed by God's Word and by which morally awareness has been gained (Jas. 1:21-23). As Paul told the Corinthians, true repentance is repentance that should not be repented of. It is more than telling God, "I know this is wrong, I am sorry – please forgive me." True repentance includes an aspiration to, by the grace of God, not repeat the same sin again.

Scripture cites Esau as an example of what repentance is not (Heb. 12:16-17). Esau was a profane person; though he cried tears of repentance over the loss of his birthright, he did not repent in his heart over his carnal behavior. He was merely sorry that he did not get what he wanted. Esau lived for the moment and did not value the things that God valued. True repentance is more than feeling guilty, feeling sorry that we got caught, feeling sad that things did not work out, being sorry for the consequences of sin, or being grieved about our punishment. Godly sorrow causes a change of mind (repentance) which now agrees with God on the matter of sin, and results in a change of behavior.

As soon as one is conscious of sin, the sin should be confessed – in so doing Christ promises to both forgive and to cleanse the guilty conscience: *"If we confess our sins, He is faithful and just to forgive us our sins, and to cleanse us from all unrighteousness"* (1 Jn. 1:9). Of course, God desires His children to not sin (1 Jn. 2:1) so that He can walk together with them in the light of divine truth (1 Jn. 1:6-7). But when we do sin (choose darkness), there is an immediate solution – His cleansing allows us to again walk with Him in the light. The Christian life then is to be one of ongoing separation from the world while still permitting evangelistic connections with individuals in the world.

Thankfully, there was good evidence that the Corinthians had truly repented of their sinful practices (v. 11). They had a new diligence in the Faith, a greater reverence and fear of God, a genuine longing to see Paul, an increased zeal for the things of God, and they took corrective action against the offender in the assembly (1 Cor. 5).

The vague expressions and pronouns of verse 12 make it difficult to know for sure of whom Paul is speaking. The offender(s) could be the son committing incest or the false teachers speaking against Paul. The one offended could be the father in the former immoral situation or Paul himself if the latter occasion is in view. In any case, Paul wrote the stern letter (i.e., his third epistle, which was not included in inspired Scripture) without selfish motives. Though harsh, it demonstrated Paul's tender care for them in the sight of God, which they now knew and appreciated.

Leaving the matter of correction and repentance, Paul acknowledges the good way in which they had received Titus. The Corinthians had treated him with respect and care, and he had been refreshed by their fellowship (v. 13). The apostle was delighted that his boasting of the Corinthians to Titus had proven to be true (v. 14). Titus had been sent to them with a difficult task, but the way in which the Corinthians had responded to Paul's reproof and had shown respect to Titus was evidence of their love for the Lord. This also increased Titus's affection for them (v. 15). Paul had suffered many anxious days previously, but now, after hearing Titus's report, his full confidence was restored in the believers at Corinth (v. 16).

# 2 Corinthians Chapter 8

### The Generous Example of the Macedonians (vv. 1-8)

Based on Paul's closing accolade in the previous chapter, it is evident that Paul's confidence has been fully restored in the Corinthians. Therefore, he can move on to the next subject to be discussed. Chapters 8 and 9 pertain to the collection of a financial gift for the poor saints in Jerusalem and forms the second of three main divisions in the epistle. Although each section is distinct, the common thread weaving all three divisions together is Paul's planned visit to Corinth. It will be the last time he will speak face to face with the saints there, and the tenor of the visit is pleasant and joyful.

It would be helpful to recall Paul's statement at the end of his previous epistle concerning the gift to be collected for Jewish believers: *"Now concerning the collection for the saints, as I have given orders to the churches of Galatia, so you must do also"* (1 Cor. 16:1). Paul had been delayed in returning to Corinth, which gave the Corinthians more time to prepare their donation. No doubt, Paul wanted to return to Jerusalem with an entourage of Gentile representatives from various churches who were bringing their gifts to Jewish believers as a show of spiritual solidarity.

Paul commences the discussion of the gift by first indicating his camaraderie with them by referring to them as "brethren." True, Paul was an apostle, and had been assigned an important role in the body of Christ, but as far as importance to the Lord was concerned, they were all equals and were working together in a common cause as brethren. The Lord Jesus affirmed this truth to His disciples: *"For One is your Teacher, the Christ, and you are all brethren"* (Matt. 23:8). Christ is Head of the Church and all believers are simply brethren serving Him.

The apostle mentions the generosity of the churches in Macedonia as a good example to motivate the believers at Corinth to properly prepare their gift (v. 1). We know from Acts 16 and 17 that there were churches in the Macedonian cities of Philippi, Thessalonica, and Berea. Gleaning from Paul's letters to two of these churches, we understand that these believers had departed from paganism, were rejoicing in the Lord, were sound in doctrine and had greatly encouraged Paul by their giving spirit (Phil. 4:14-18; 1 Thess. 1:6-10). They were, in effect, laying up treasures in Heaven and offering sweet-smelling sacrifices to God. Although these believers were poor financially and were being afflicted because of the gospel, God had lavished grace on them in such a way that they were able to give willingly and with joy above their natural ability to do so (vv. 2-3). No CPA could explain this type of accounting activity: poverty and affliction, plus grace, equaled abundant joy and liberal giving. It would seem that their giving even exceeded Paul's expectations of them.

The Macedonian believers did not have much, but because of their generous hearts, God enabled them to provide for the saints in Jerusalem far beyond what would have been possible by normal methods and means. This dispels the idea that only the rich can support the Lord's work. Rather than giving out of our abundance, God chooses to wonderfully equip those with willing hearts to accomplish His purposes. This demonstrates that it is His work, not human fancy. This same grace was also available to the Corinthians if they adopted the same spirit of willing generosity that the Macedonian believers had. They were so excited about giving what had been collected that they urgently implored Paul to receive their gift and to ensure its safe delivery to Jerusalem (v. 4).

Why had the Macedonian believers been so willing to give of their resources to support the suffering saints in Jerusalem? The answer to this question is in verse 5: *"They first gave themselves to the Lord."* When saints put themselves on the altar for the Lord, all their energy, time, and possessions come along too. By giving ourselves to the Lord, we naturally want to share with (have fellowship with) other believers to the same degree. Many today resort to fund-raising methods or public solicitations for money to support the Lord's work, but such tactics are foreign to a Spirit-led, Spirit-enabled Church in Scripture. As commonly proclaimed: God's work, done God's way, will never lack God's resources!

Paul informed the Corinthians that he was sending Titus back to them to assist with the collection process, so that all would be ready when he arrived (v. 6). Paul had written to them about the gift the previous year, so there seemed to be some doubt in his mind that the Corinthians had been vigorously preparing their gift (v. 10). Regardless, he did not want to wait for them to get their act together once he did arrive in Corinth (v. 12). He acknowledged that they excelled in spiritual qualities of faith, in spiritual gifts, in sharing God's Word, in diligence, and in love towards Him, so it would be inconsistent for them to be lacking in the virtue of giving (v. 7).

However, Paul wanted them to know that giving had to be from a willing spirit. It could not be commanded (v. 8). Even though he was an apostle, he could only make the Corinthians aware of the need and encourage them to give unto the Lord as He had blessed them and had also impressed the desire for involvement on their hearts. The opportunity would thereby test the sincerity of their love for the Savior. This shows that Paul was more concerned that the Corinthians had the proper motive for giving than about the actual amount they contributed to the relief effort.

## The Giving Example of Christ (vv. 9-15)

Indeed, our selfless sacrifices for the good of others displays God's love in action. Biblical love always begins with genuine sacrifice without any expectation of getting something in return (e.g., John 3:16). With this thought in mind, Paul highlights the greatest example of this type of giving. In exhibiting divine grace, although Christ was rich, He became poor that the Corinthians might become rich in Him (v. 9). Christ willingly forfeited His high status in glory and all the wealth of Heaven to become a lowly Man of poor estate who humbled Himself unto death to suffer for our sins, that we might be restored to God and inherit all things with Him forever.

Contemplating all that the Son of God set aside in glory to be God's Lamb of sacrifice for humanity should prompt us to want to give back to Him whatever we can. If we gave Christ everything we have, and every hour of our lives in service to Him, we still could never repay the debt that He paid on our behalf.

> Majestic sweetness sits enthroned upon the Savior's brow;
> His head with radiant glories crowned, His lips with grace overflow.
>
> He saw me plunged in deep distress, and flew to my relief;
> For me He bore the shameful cross, and carried all my grief.
>
> To Him I owe my life and breath, and all the joys I have;
> He makes me triumph over death, and saves me from the grave.
>
> – Samuel Stennett

Scripture makes it abundantly clear that we cannot out-give God and that when we choose to give to those in need, we are really giving back to the Lord for furtherance of His glory (Prov. 8:21, 19:17). Those giving for such a spiritual outcome will not lack God's favor or provision. For this reason, believers are to work hard, not so that they can squander their extra income on self-seeking thrills and creature-comforts, but so that they can have the ability to help others in need (Eph. 4:28).

Interestingly, the first mention of "riches" in Scripture is found in Genesis 13:2: Abraham returned to Canaan from Egypt with great wealth.

However, this posed a new difficulty, for he and Lot could no longer dwell together because of the abundance of their possessions (Gen. 13:6). What effect do too many accoutrements have on God's people? The result is often strife among the brethren (Gen. 13:7). When brethren strive together, they cease being a testimony for God. When we clutch things tightly, we provide the devil an opportunity to strangle us with them.

How are brethren to consider their possessions? The early Church held the proper view of "equality" and thus maintained and enjoyed unity: *"And the multitude of those that believed were of one heart and of one soul; neither said any of them that any of the things which he possessed was his own; but they had all things common"* (Acts 4:32). These believers willingly gave what they had, so that all the needs of their brothers and sisters in Christ were met and the work of declaring the good news of Christ would not be hindered.

There are two key points about giving to the Lord that Paul wants the Corinthians to understand. First, he was not asking the Corinthians to give what God had not provided (v. 12). Believers should never borrow from others to give to the Lord, as there is no personal sacrifice demonstrated in such a donation, and the Lord has not enabled the activity. This would be giving in the flesh, which results in indebtedness to man and is an affront to God's ability to provide for His own enterprises.

Second, Paul teaches the Corinthians that there should be equality among the brethren (vv. 13-14). If a brother is in need and another brother is able to meet that need, he should readily do so. Paul refers to a historic example of the Israelites gathering manna in the wilderness to illustrate this principle of giving. Though some Israelites gathered more manna than others each morning (except on the Sabbath Day), the outcome was that everyone was completely satisfied with God's provision every day (v. 15).

Equality is not communism. Holding all things in equality is not the same as everyone having equal portions. When God's people properly value God, the things of God and His people, they will enjoy unity; if their focus is shifted to temporal things, they will experience envy, dissatisfaction, and covetousness. It is better to be united rather than to be divided by stuff!

## Trusted Representatives to Distribute the Gift (vv. 16-24)

This section of Scripture highlights the great diligence and accountability that must accompany what is sacrificially given by the saints to the Lord. Not only are such funds to be faithfully secured for the Lord's work, the collection and distribution process is to be governed by procedures that keep the Lord's servants involved above reproach. Years ago, while I was still in engineering, I enjoyed having lunch with a believer who served as a corporate auditor for our company. I asked him how much time he spent investigating fraudulent activities. He replied, "Very little. Most of my time is spent making sure that honest people do not get blamed for wrongdoing. Well-thought-out procedures save the company money and the reputations of valued employees." That should be our attitude with church finances also.

Paul is moved to praise God, because He had put it in the heart of Titus to willingly rise to the challenge of returning to Corinth to ensure that God's provision for the saints in Jerusalem was ready when Paul arrived (vv. 16-17). To ensure blamelessness and security, two highly esteemed, but unnamed, brothers would be accompanying Titus to Corinth for the same purpose (vv. 18-22). One brother, well-known among the churches in the region for his gospel fervor and zeal for the Lord, had been specifically chosen by the churches to represent them in the distribution of their gift.

The second brother, also unnamed, had proven himself diligent in the things of the Lord again and again. As the Greek noun and adjective rendered "because of the great confidence" are singular, it may be that Paul was referring to this brother's confidence in the Corinthians' generosity, rather than the missionary team's confidence in them (v. 22).

Titus would be representing Paul in the matter of completing the collection and the two brothers with him would represent the churches in Macedonia that were involved with the gift (v. 23). Paul asked the Corinthian saints to demonstrate that his boasting in them was not in vain by showing the Macedonian representatives generosity and love (v. 24). In so doing, all the other churches involved with the relief effort would know of their love for the Lord.

Paul's wisdom and wise precautions are evident in the handling of the Lord's money in this passage. First, Titus, who was already known by the Corinthians, was experienced in collecting funds and had proven to be trustworthy (Gal. 2:1, 10; Acts 11:29-30). Second, Paul kept to the work that God had given him to do and was not directly involved in handling the gifts. This kept him from being accused of being motivated by money by his critics. Third, there was a plurality of mature, well-known, proven, and honest servants involved with handling the funds. Each brother had been chosen by the churches to represent them and also had Paul's endorsement. Fourth, these men remained unnamed and served the Lord with humility. The second unnamed man, who worked alongside Paul, could also give a word of testimony to protect Paul's reputation if questioned.

# 2 Corinthians Chapter 9

## Noone Can Outgive God (vv. 1-15)

In a bit of tactful sarcasm, Paul says that it was not necessary for him to remind the Corinthians about supporting the poor saints in Jerusalem, but then he did so anyway (v. 1). The Corinthians had apparently indicated their good intentions of sharing with those in need. Paul had boasted about the believers in Macedonia a year earlier, but the Corinthians had apparently not been proactive in making it happen (v. 2). When the Macedonian believers heard of the Corinthians' exercise to give, it had the effect of rallying their passions to also help the saints in Jerusalem. Hearing of God's love being willingly exercised by His people also prompts other saints to be sacrificial in their giving.

Paul did not want the embarrassment of brothers from Macedonia arriving with him in Corinth at a later date to receive the Corinthian relief donation, only to learn that the Corinthians had been slothful in its preparation (v. 3). This would prove that Paul's boasting in them was not accurate (v. 4). Hence, he was sending Titus and the two unnamed brothers with him to ensure that there was sufficient time for their giving to be with God-led and God-enabled generosity, rather than a last-minute scramble to cobble a gift together in guilt or with a begrudging attitude of duty (v. 5).

Paul shares a general principle concerning giving found throughout Scripture in verses 6-7: *"He who sows sparingly will also reap sparingly, and he who sows bountifully will also reap bountifully. So let each one give as he purposes in his heart, not grudgingly or of necessity; for God loves a cheerful giver."* Nature demonstrates the simplicity of this idea; one must sow to reap of the same. If one chooses to sow little, the return on the investment will also be little, but the opposite is also true. Since everything we have comes from God, both seed and the harvest from the seed, why not fully invest the seed, to obtain much more harvest from the seed (vv. 10-11)? Why be satisfied with the meager provision of the seed when there is so much more that God wants to bestow on us in grace?

Those who give much to God will be liberally enriched, that is, they will reap much abounding grace from God in return for their investment into eternity (v. 8). God may bless with a visible temporal return, but certainly spiritual blessings that have lasting value will be granted. The other benefit of our liberal giving to the Lord is that as the needs of the poor are met by Him, His righteous name is honored by all those witnessing the event (v. 9).

Paul's point is that no believer can outgive God, but He wants our giving to be a joyful free-will act. Giving that is constrained or forced is not a sacrifice pleasing to the Lord. Thus, we may conclude that bountifully giving to the Lord is not limited by one's finances, but rather by one's devotion to God. The widow who gave the Lord two mites, which was all she had, received the praise of God and would also be cared for by Him. Giving exposes what is in one's heart, not how much is in one's pocketbook.

The Greek word rendered "cheerful" in verse 7 is *hilaros.* The English word "hilarious" is derived from *hilaros.* Interestingly, *hilaros* only occurs twice in the New Testament and both incidences relate to giving (Rom. 12:8 is the other). God loves a *hilaros* giver because that is how He gives. Commenting on verse 8, William MacDonald writes:

> Does God really need our money? No, the cattle on a thousand hills belong to Him, and if He needed anything, He would not tell us (Ps. 50:10-12). But our heart's attitude is what is important to Him. He loves to see a Christian who is so filled with the joy of the Lord that he wants to share what he has with others.[38]

God has wonderfully shown us that true giving commences with selfless sacrifice: *"For God so loved the world that He gave His only begotten Son"* (John 3:16). The Lord Jesus affirmed *"to whom little is forgiven, the same loves little"* (Luke 7:47)! In summary, the portion that we return of what we have received from the Lord directly reflects how much we believe we have been forgiven and how much we love Him. Those who have been forgiven much give much, because they love much!

Notice that many of the financial practices of the Church today are not found in Scripture. In New Testament days, there was no collection agency, no forced giving, no personal solicitations, no fund-raising campaigns, only voluntary giving as each person was exercised by the Lord, enabled by the Lord, and in order to show his or her love for the Lord.

The joyful giving of the Corinthians would be a sign of their spiritual maturity, which would result in the saints at Jerusalem praising God on their behalf (v. 12). The Jewish believers would know for certain that the Gentiles had been truly saved through the gospel message of Jesus Christ (v. 13). As a result, the saints in Jerusalem would be prompted to pray for the Gentile believers (v. 14). Paul looked forward to witnessing the outcome of this goodwill gesture by the Gentile believers for their brothers and sisters in Jerusalem. A deep tie of affection, reaching beyond social, cultural, and ethnic barriers would be evident in the Body of Christ.

Paul concludes this section on giving with a sudden exclamation of praise in verse 15. As the apostle had conveyed to the Corinthians all the wonderful truths and blessings associated with sacrificial giving, Paul could not be restrained from praising the greatest Giver of all – God Himself.

> Such was God's original love for man that He was willing to stoop to any sacrifice to save him; and the gift of a Savior was the mere expression of that love.
>
> – Albert Barnes

The word *anekdiegetos* is translated "unspeakable" (KJV) and "indescribable" (NKJV) and is used here to convey the idea that the full nature of God's gift to us (speaking of salvation in Christ; John 4:10; Rom. 5:15) cannot be fully expounded – it is beyond our comprehension! The fact that this Greek word occurs only here in the New Testament is significant; it cannot be compared to any other Scriptural text. This fact only adds to the immeasurability in the application of its meaning. The expression of God's love was so immense in the giving of His Son on behalf of humanity that there just are no words in any language to fully describe it. Man shows us that it is possible to give without love, but God's own behavior proves to us that it is impossible to love without giving.

> The most obvious lesson in Christ's teaching is that there is no happiness in having or getting anything, but only in giving.
>
> – Henry Drummond

The Jewish tithing statutes of the Law were set aside in the New Testament. In the Church Age each believer is required to regularly and proportionately give back to the Lord as God has prospered him or her (1 Cor. 16:2). God makes no demands as to the specific amount we are to give back to Him; rather, we are permitted to evaluate our situation, and to freely express our love and appreciation to Him through giving.

God gave His only begotten Son that we might be reconciled to Him. Christ took our punishment for sin and gave His own life that we might be saved. It is obvious that we cannot out-give God, but we should always give our best in response to His example of sacrificially giving His best. Our giving back to the Lord is a means of expressing: *"Thanks be to God for His indescribable gift!"* (v. 15).

# 2 Corinthians Chapter 10

## Paul's Authority Is Spiritual (vv. 1-6)

The remainder of this epistle, the third and final main section, pertains to Paul defending his apostleship. Although Titus had informed Paul that the Corinthians were repentant, there were lingering questions in the minds of some regarding his apostleship. Paul now assumes a sterner tone and employs significant irony in addressing this important subject. The tenor stands in contrast to the tender language of the preceding seven chapters. Because of this sudden change in intensity, some have suggested that the last four chapters were from a different source, but the common thread throughout the epistle is that Paul is longing and planning to visit Corinth.

The language in verse 1 softens the transition from the gentle tone of chapter 9 to a more confrontational one in this chapter. Paul was pleading with the Corinthians in *"the meekness and gentleness of Christ."* Although addressing a subject dear to his heart and one that was important to the work of God, Paul knows that a servant of the Lord must reflect His character in all things (2 Tim. 2:24). It is good for us to remember that anything done in the flesh cannot please God (Rom. 8:8). We cannot serve the Lord with our fleshly motives or our own strength. It is only what is done in God's will and with His strength that counts for eternity (Gal. 2:20, 5:24).

Some had accused Paul of being a roaring lion in his letters, but a gentle lamb in person (vv. 2, 10). But this was not true; Paul was no coward. Rather, he was hoping that major issues could be dealt with prior to his visit to Corinth, so that it would not be necessary to personally confront anyone. It would be mutually beneficial for everyone if he and those with him could enjoy open fellowship with the Corinthians, rather than having to admonish wrong thinking and disgraceful behavior. Paul was politely warning the Corinthians, "Please do not compel me to prove to you how bold I can be."

Paul candidly admits that he is flesh and blood, physically speaking, but in spiritual power was able to endure the frailties of a mortal body, the hardships of much ministry, and persecution by those opposing his service to God (v. 3). Paul had experientially learned that only by relying on divine resources can victory be ensured against spiritual wickedness in high places:

> *For the weapons of our warfare are not carnal but mighty in God for pulling down strongholds, casting down arguments and every high thing that exalts itself against the knowledge of God, bringing every thought into captivity to the obedience of Christ* (vv. 4-5).

Through having engaged in spiritual battles, Paul knew that the wisdom and strength of the flesh offered no resistance when confronting the enemy of our souls. If the Corinthians forced him to personally rebuke them, it would be with the full authority and power of Heaven, upon which he was accustomed to relying. Paul was well-acquainted with how to deal with rebels and opposers, so anyone resisting Christ's authority in their lives would witness the full vigor of apostolic authority (v. 6).

We learn from a number of Old Testament examples that God's ways are not man's ways for overcoming the enemy. Whether it is Samson slaying a thousand Philistines with the jawbone of an ass, the felling of the walls of Jericho with a shout, or the use of an ox goad to fight men armed with spears and swords, God gives His people spectacular victories with what the world deems feeble and indeed laughable. This was repeatedly done to teach His covenant people not to rely on their strength to conquer their enemies, but rather on His power. The Lord chooses to work this way so that our flesh has no opportunity to glory in His presence (1 Cor. 1:30).

Like Israel, believers in the Church Age must also realize that all our engagements with the enemy are the Lord's battles and that every victory is the Lord's victory. We have no strength against the devil other than what the Lord provides. Thus, we need a supernatural work of God's grace in our lives to pull down the carnal strongholds in our minds and to overcome the enemy's evil tactics and power against us.

Though Paul is speaking to the Corinthians about the threat of being mastered by false teachers (e.g., the Judaizers), the provision of deliverance he mentions has much broader ramifications. John highlights this wonderful principle in his first epistle: *"For whatever is born of God overcomes the world. And this is the victory that has overcome the world – our faith. Who is he who overcomes the world, but he who believes that Jesus is the Son of God?"* (1 Jn. 5:4-5). Though there will be satanic opposition seeking to hinder the work of God in which we are engaged, the solution is before us. In faith, the Israelites daily marched around Jericho until God miraculously delivered the city into their hands. In faith, Shamgar charged against six hundred Philistines with an ox goad. These victories and more were not accomplished with carnal weapons of war but were a divine response to faith and obedience to God's Word.

The application to the Corinthians and to us is that spiritual battles are won or lost depending on what happens between our ears. Believers must continue to stand on the truthfulness of God's Word in thought and deed to identify and resist any solicitation from the enemy to do otherwise (John 15:3; Phil. 4:8). Mental strongholds and bad habits do not get established overnight, nor are they pulled down immediately. Ultimate victory requires much prayer, obedience, and the provision of spiritual power to continue resisting that of which God disapproves and to affirm what pleases him (1 Pet. 4:5-9). If we continue to resist in God's strength, the strongholds in our minds lose their grip and eventually fade away.

## Paul's Authority in Person or by Letter (vv. 7-11)

Paul earnestly desired to enjoy his time with the believers at Corinth rather than wielding divine authority and power to confront his opposers. Having plainly stating what he would do, he would leave the choice up to the Corinthians. Next, Paul addresses the foolishness of the indictment of his critics that he was inconsistent and was therefore untrustworthy. It is utter folly to issue a judgment on a matter without knowing all related facts. (Prov. 18:13). Unfortunately, the Corinthians, being influenced by Paul's accusers were coming to conclusions with only circumstantial information. They were making judgments on the "outward appearance" of things without knowing the truth (v. 7).

Casting doubt on the integrity of God's servants is one of Satan's most used and successful tactics for damaging the reputations of God's people. As a result, the effectiveness of their ministry is often negated or they may be discouraged from engaging in ministry altogether. God forbid that any of us should assist the devil in this evil. All the Corinthians had to do to be assured of Paul's integrity was to examine themselves: If they were saved, it meant that God had empowered Paul's ministry, for God does not use shysters to spread the true message of eternal life in His Son (Phil. 1:15-18).

Paul's God-given authority was for one purpose only – to build up and edify the Body of Christ – the Church (v. 8). Whether through writing letters or speaking for God in person, this was what he was commissioned to do by the Lord Jesus Christ Himself (v. 9). So, despite what the false teachers were saying about his letters being stern and his presence cowardly, there would be nothing but boldness and power if he had to personally confront their foolishness and false doctrine (vv. 10-11).

Clearly, some of Paul's previous written ministry to them had been confrontational, sarcastic, and stern, but that was what was needed to cause a change of heart among the erring believers at Corinth. However, Paul's critics were completely wrong to say that Paul was "weak and his speech contemptible" in person. To behave in such a way would have been a betrayal of his apostolic authority.

## Paul's Authority Has Boundaries (vv. 12-18)

Paul had earlier informed the Corinthians that he did not even judge the value of his own ministry, because he knew that his flesh was biased. Only the Lord can properly judge such things (1 Cor. 4:3). This is his point in verse 12: Teachers cannot judge themselves or others. (The Judaizers were contrasting Paul to others but comparing themselves with themselves.) But teachers must be judged according to the authority of God's Word which expresses His will to us. God had expressed His will regarding Paul's apostolic authority over them, and any boldness in his speech to the Corinthians would be within the confines of that divine decree. Unlike the Judaizers who invaded established churches, Paul did not need to go beyond his ministry boundaries to highlight legitimate reasons to glory (v. 13).

Indeed, Corinth was part of Paul's God-given mission field, and he would execute his rightful authority to bring as much blessing as he could to the region he had been assigned to reach for Christ (v. 14). He was engaging in pioneer missionary work. He was not building on the labors of others before him, nor was he boasting in (taking the credit for) the accomplishments of others (v. 15). Paul had spoken of visiting Rome and Spain, but at present, he understood the furthest reach of his ministry was Corinth (v. 16). Once a lampstand for Christ was securely placed in Corinth, Paul was confident that God would expand his ministry further west.

Paul's determination to remain in the work that God had given him should inspire each of us to engage in "the work of ministry" that we have been assigned by Christ to fulfill in the Body (Eph. 4:12). We will never be more joyful and fruitful on this side of Heaven than when we are using our spiritual gifts in the full measure of faith to fulfill our God-given callings.

Paul had unwillingly been forced to boast of his calling and ministry to confront his opposers, but he is ever mindful that believers are to boast only in the Lord. He had quoted Jeremiah in his earlier epistle to the Corinthians and does so again here: *"He who glories, let him glory in the Lord"* (v. 17; Jer. 9:24; 1 Cor. 1:31). All that matters in our service to Christ is that He receives all our glory! He deserves it! For this aspiration to be realized, we must reckon two things to be true. First, it is only what the Lord thinks about our ministries that matters. Second, it does not matter what others think; they cannot accurately judge the motives, the effectiveness, and the value of what we do. Only the one whom the Lord commends is approved (v. 18)!

# 2 Corinthians Chapter 11

Paul's Warnings Against False Teachers (vv. 1-15)
    The apostle had earlier informed the Corinthians that the flesh was biased and only the Lord could properly judge the value of one's ministry. This meant that it would be wise to refrain from touting one's supposed achievements. However, since the boasting of the false teachers had won over the hearts of the Corinthians, Paul would continue to engage in the folly of boasting, so to speak. So, he asked the Corinthians to put up with his boasting for a wee while longer, but then realized that they would, so it was unnecessary for him to request them to do so (v. 1). It was important that they should know the truth about his ministry instead of being swayed by articulate con-artists who were spinning the truth for their own benefit.
    Paul then revealed three reasons why he knew the Corinthians would tolerate a bit more of his boasting. First, by responding to the gospel message he had unselfishly brought them, they had become a bride in waiting for the Lord Jesus. He, being in effect their spiritual father, greatly desired to present them as a pure virgin bride to their beloved Groom (v. 2; 1 Jn. 3:2-3). For this reason, the apostle had a jealous parental desire to protect the purity of the Corinthians against false doctrine.
    Second, the Corinthians had been saved by the gospel of grace and to depart from single-hearted devotion to Christ to be enslaved by a humanized, works-based religion would cripple their spiritual life (v. 3). Paul returns to the historical imagery of Genesis 3 to express this concern. The false teachers among them were corrupting their understanding of truth in the same manner in which Satan, by the serpent's craftiness, had deceived Eve in the Garden of Eden. These false apostles were attempting to lead the Corinthians away from the simplicity of salvation in Christ alone.
    Third, since the Corinthians were willingly listening to the false teachers, they should extend the same courtesy to Paul. The Corinthians showed poor discernment in listening to the false teachers, for these teachers were preaching another gospel, another Jesus, another spirit. None of what they taught was the truth the Corinthians had received from Paul (v. 4).
    Their spiritual father then issues them a sarcastic reproof: "Why do you listen to them? You should be listening to me." The false teachers had given

them nothing beneficial, but Paul had poured out his own life to bless them.

Paul then explains that he is not inferior to even the most highly esteemed apostles although he realizes that his abilities and behavior may have indicated otherwise (v. 5). To which apostles is Paul referring? It is doubtful that he is referring to the apostles at Jerusalem or even to the "pillars" of the Church residing there (Gal. 2:9).

Paul had been trained at the feet of one of the most prominent Jewish teachers of that time, a Pharisee named Gamaliel (Acts 5:34, 22:3). Paul knew the Law and could do cartwheels and backflips through Old Testament scriptures. He clearly had more academic training in the Law than any of the Galilean apostles appointed by Christ. Nor would any of the apostles at Jerusalem say otherwise in an attempt to demean Paul (e.g., 2 Pet. 3:15-16).

The reference in verse 5 to the "super apostles" best connects with the "he" (v. 4) and the "they" (v. 12) speaking of the *pseudo apostles* being esteemed by the Corinthians. Later, Paul will refer to these as "false prophets," "deceitful workers," "ministers" of Satan, and "fools" (vv. 13, 15, 19). While these false prophets may wax eloquent in speech, they had nothing on Paul who possessed a wealth of scriptural knowledge.

Paul does humbly admit that his speech fell short of the rhetorical sophistication favored by the Greeks of that day, but the use of plain speech was befitting of the simple message of truth that he was commanded to share with everyone (v. 6). No doubt, he could have impressed his audiences with his knowledge, but instead of exalting himself, he sought to preach the necessity of Christ crucified using plain, understandable speech.

For this reason, Paul humbled himself in order to exalt (i.e., to benefit) the Corinthians. He challenges the Corinthians, "Did I commit a sin?" by choosing to live in poverty to more effectively share the riches of God in Christ with them (v. 7). If this was not a sin, then they were wrong to condemn his self-abasing behavior. As explained in an earlier epistle, he was determined to preach the gospel message without charge, so that no one would question his motives for ministry (1 Cor. 9:12-18). His self-sacrificial position stood in sharp contrast to the self-promoting manner of the false teachers. If Paul had asked the Corinthians for money, he would not have been able to use this argument against the false teachers.

Other churches, mainly in Macedonia (Phil. 4:15-18), had supported Paul's missionary work in Corinth, but Paul had neither received, nor did he request, any support from the Corinthians (vv. 8-9). The fact that the Corinthians were giving to the false teachers may suggest that they were not stingy with their finances. Despite their generosity, it may have been that

Paul would not take support from them to ensure that his motives could not be questioned.

Obviously, Paul did not literally rob other churches. The funds he had received from them were given voluntarily and were not recompense for his labor among them. Even when such gifts of fellowship were not available for Paul, he was determined to work with his own hands to supply his own needs. His good work ethic only enhanced his exhortation to others to do an honest day's work for an honest day's wage (2 Thess. 3:7-8).

Paul was a servant of the Lord, who worked for the Lord, and therefore trusted the Lord to provide for all his needs in a way that would best advance the work in which he was engaged. This kind of faith-based service to the Lord is in stark contrast with the employed professionals within Christendom today. God-given ministry was never meant to be a profession to pursue, but rather a calling to perform. Each of us must attend to what we are divinely tasked to do and permit God to do what only He can do – supply all our needs (Phil. 4:19).

Because Paul was speaking the truth as a minister of Christ, he promised to continue doing three activities related to the Corinthians (vv. 10-12). First, he would continue to boast that he was an apostle called to serve the Corinthians, a ministry performed without taking their money. His critics alleged that his absence proved that even Paul knew he was not an apostle. Second, he would continue to love them unconditionally. Third, he would continue his policy of not receiving from them personally, even though the false teachers (e.g., the Judaizers) sought their support. Paul's unselfish style of ministry would therefore be a slap in the face of his critics.

Paul then warned the Corinthians that Satan often transforms himself into an angel of light and his servants into ministers of righteousness because he knows it is easier to deceive God's people in their work than to dissuade them from their purpose:

> *For such are false apostles, deceitful workers, transforming themselves into apostles of Christ. And no wonder! For Satan himself transforms himself into an angel of light. Therefore, it is no great thing if his ministers also transform themselves into ministers of righteousness, whose end will be according to their works* (vv. 13-15).

Paul minces no words about those men the Corinthians were esteeming and giving ear to. They were false apostles and deceitful workers in the service of Satan! These evil men would ultimately receive their eternal punishment in Hell for their deception of men and women by mimicking what was important to God and leading them away from truth.

Many people these days are seeing visions and hearing voices. Paul warns that Satan mimics God's means of declaring revelation to deceive those who desire something beyond what God has already revealed in Scripture (v. 14). During the Apostolic Age, prophecy, visions, dreams, and audible commands were prevalent to express divine revelation. Yet, we must realize that the Lord Jesus is God the Father's ultimate revelation to the world (Jn. 1:1-2, 1:14).

Christ has not left us in the dark concerning truth; He has declared to us the divine revelation needed for salvation, godly living, and bringing Him glory. This revelation was brought by the apostles for us to follow (Heb. 2:3) and is a completed declaration of truth (Jude 3). With this said, God is God, and He can do anything He pleases. However, if the reader does witness some supernatural manifestation, the following checklist should be reviewed to determine the source of the event:

1. All that flows from God will agree with His nature and what He has previously declared as truth in Scripture.

2. Based on the pattern of New Testament Scripture, revelation was conferred only to individuals who had consecrated themselves to holy living (e.g., Joseph, Mary, Simeon, Anna, Stephen, Paul, etc.).

3. Visions from the Holy Spirit will occur when the believer's mind is fully active and not hindered by medications, drugs, fatigue, etc. The opposite is true with evil spirits, as drug abuse is common in satanic rituals.

4. God manifests Himself to those who obey His word and are in communion with Him (John 14:21). For spiritual illumination to be received, our minds must be free of strongholds, otherwise Satan can manipulate our thinking and hinder us from perceiving the truth properly (e.g., Acts 5:1-3).

5. Is the revelation confusing or coercing you to an immediate action? God does not force truth on us in such a way that we are reduced to being mindless puppets. God is patient and wants us to affirm the truth before acting (Rom 14:23).

False prophets plagued Israel throughout the nation's history, and they still infest Christendom today, surmises H. A. Ironside:

> In every age when God has been dealing with His professed people because of their sins and apostasy, there have been such false prophets who have sought to lull the offenders to sleep in a false confidence, assuring them that all is well and there need be no fear of judgment falling upon them. How these prophets abound in Christendom today! With the Judge standing at the door, they continue to cry, "Peace, peace, when there is no peace!"[39]

This problem is compounded by the fact that God's prophets always seemed to be greatly outnumbered by their counterparts. The ministries of Elijah (1 Kings 18), Micaiah (1 Kings 22), and Jeremiah (Jer. 20) serve as good examples. Time and again, God's prophets have suffered greatly for their faithfulness as voices for God among a throng of dissident and hostile people. Because throughout their history the Jews have looked for signs to substantiate their faith, they have invariably fallen into the trap of ignoring God's immutable Word. False prophets can powerfully represent a virtual reality of the truth. Sadly, false brethren and self-ordained prophets, with their overbearing, self-promoting evil practices, continue to plague God's people today.

> Discernment is not a matter of simply telling the difference between right and wrong; rather it is telling the difference between right and almost right.
>
> – C. H. Spurgeon

## Paul's Reluctant Boasting (vv. 16-21)

If the Corinthians thought that Paul was being foolish because of all his boasting, then he asks them to continue thinking that way for a bit longer, for he is not yet finished revealing his full credentials as an apostle of Jesus Christ to them (v. 16). Although it did not follow the Lord's pattern of humility, Paul knew that his boasting would be permitted by them since they were already tolerating the foolish boasting of the false teachers (vv. 17-19).

The difference was that Paul's ministry was one of liberation from the Law and from sin to serve in truth. The false teachers, however, were attempting to enslave the Corinthians into the bondage of humanized religion (i.e., trying to earn God's love and favor through yielding to a prescribed system of doings – legalism; v. 20).

The Corinthians were foolish to listen to those who would rob them of their Christian liberty and who would control them through heavy-handed tactics of intimidation (v. 21). They knew that Paul never resorted to such demeaning tactics to coerce the Corinthians to do anything.

## Paul's Sufferings for Christ (vv. 22-33)

Paul now provides another strong defense to the Corinthians that he is truly an apostle of Christ, namely his willingness to suffer to fulfill his divine calling. His point is that no one in his right mind would willingly suffer what Paul had unless he was absolutely convinced that he had been commissioned by God to do so. Who freely suffers for what he knows is a lie? To this end, Paul reluctantly describes his sufferings for Christ so that the Corinthians will understand he is the real thing, and those negatively influencing them are not.

Paul was a Hebrew, a descendant of Abraham, so the false teachers claiming to be Jews did not have an advantage over Paul (v. 22). Apparently, the false prophets were touting their ethnicity and religious credentials to give validity to their legalistic message. In contrast, Paul rarely spoke of his religious heritage or pedigree because the gospel message conveyed the offer of salvation to both Jews and Gentiles.

Beyond their common ethnicity and knowledge of the Law, Paul had nothing in common with these false apostles. They claimed to be servants of Christ, but it was a false profession. Clearly, they were not devoted to Christ regardless of personal cost, but Paul was. His abundant labors, scars, incarcerations, and near-death experiences proved this point (v. 23).

> It is impossible to be our best at the supreme moment if character is corroded and eaten into by daily inconsistency, unfaithfulness, and besetting sin.
>
> – F. B. Meyer

Five times Paul received thirty-nine stripes from the whip, three times he was beaten with rods, and once he was stoned at Lystra and left for dead (v. 24; Acts 14:19). The Mosaic Law allowed a convicted criminal to receive no more than forty lashes, but the Jews stopped short by one lest they accidentally violate the Law (Deut. 25:3). Paul had been flogged by the Jews five times and had also been beaten with rods by the Greeks three times (e.g., Acts 16:23).

Additionally, Paul had suffered shipwreck three times, once spending a night and a day in the sea before being rescued (v. 25). He had endured the perils of extensive travel, the opposition of false teachers, the discomfort of stocks and prison cells while also frequently suffering from hunger, insufficient clothing, the fatigue of ministry, and the burdens of the churches for which he was responsible to tend (vv. 26-28).

Paul's body bore hundreds of love scars for the Lord Jesus. If stripped of his clothes, he1 would have better resembled a slave than a Roman citizen brought up in an affluent and respected family. Remarkably, when comparing all that he had suffered for the Lord, Paul viewed "his light affliction" as but a momentary and necessary aspect of his service for Christ. Such sufferings could not even be compared to the eternal glory to be revealed in Heaven as recompense for his faithfulness (4:17; Rom 8:18).

> The flesh must be broken. The Lord can use us then, not while it is unbroken. While Paul was writhing under Satan's thorn, he could get some estimate, though not a full one, of what the flesh is as God sees it. When it was broken, and Paul did not know what to do, the Lord came to pour sympathy into the writhing heart of Paul.
>
> – G. V. Wigram

There were things that Paul would continue to brag about, but there were also things in which he would not boast. He would avow his connection with all the saints, but especially those he had led to the Lord (v. 29). He was one with them and when they suffered, he keenly hurt with them. He would also highlight his infirmities (i.e., his sufferings for Christ) for the purpose of validating his apostleship (v. 30).

His sufferings proved his complete devotion to Christ and also that God's grace had sustained him to fulfill his calling as an apostle. He should have died many times, but God had repeatedly delivered him from the jaws of death so that he could continue to fulfill his divine commission. To further substantiate this, Paul calls on the eternally blessed God, the Father of the Lord Jesus Christ, to witness that he is speaking the truth to the Corinthians (v. 31).

Paul will not boast about his accomplishments or abilities, since God was responsible for his achievements, and all his abilities had been given him by God (1 Cor. 4:7). Paul's boasting centered in his weakness, reproaches, and indignities endured for Christ. These are not the kinds of things carnal men brag about. He was determined not to stoop to the self-promoting behavior of the false teachers.

The false teachers did not have scars in their bodies to testify of unreserved devotion to Christ as Paul did. This proved that they were not true apostles. If they were, the devil would have been opposing their message and endeavors, but the absence of evidence of hostility and suffering meant that they were no threat to the devil, but were actually his servants fulfilling his evil, Christ-hating agenda.

F. B. Hole suggests that Paul's example of dedication to Christ, regardless of the cost to himself, is a good test to measure the validity of ministries today, and also to examine the integrity of our service for Christ:

> There are modern religious movements whose main stock-in-trade is the recounting of the wonders they can produce, either in healings, or in tongues, or in the realm of habits and character – "life-changing" as it is called. Of fidelity to Christ, and of suffering for His Name, they have little if anything to say, for it seems non-existent in their scheme of things. They often know quite a lot about high-pressure meetings, and even first-class hotels, but nothing about the labors and perils and infirmities that marked Paul. And as for the rest of us, who do not wish to recount our own doings, successful or otherwise, how little are we like to him.[40]

In what would seem to be an anticlimactic postscript, Paul mentions his humiliating experience in Damascus after detailing his many burdens and sufferings (vv. 31-32). Prior to his conversion and name change, Saul, a Pharisee of Pharisees, zealously and severely persecuted men and women for identifying with Jesus Christ, even consenting to their deaths. He vigorously sought to eradicate this new religious sect called Christianity, which threatened the pure religion of Jewish Law-keeping.

Yet, the newly saved Saul, later called Paul, with even more fervency preached the gospel of Jesus Christ in Damascus and caused quite an uproar in the city, so much so that the governor of Damascus, under Aretas the king, deployed a garrison of soldiers in the city to arrest him (v. 32). Although he did not want to retreat, the brethren in Damascus convinced him to depart with his life while he still could. They let Paul down in a basket through a window in the city's wall so he could safely escape (v. 33).

This was Paul's first *let down*, so to speak, in suffering for Christ and he apparently never forgot the event, nor the guilt he felt for his timid retreat. The fact that Paul would mention this humiliating event in his life after such a powerful testimony of his sufferings for Christ was proof to the Corinthians that he was telling the truth. Would they continue to be deceived by Satan's emissaries or would they honor the one who had selflessly and unpretentiously shared the gospel of truth with them and who bore the marks in his body of God's faithfulness to sustain him as Christ's apostle?

We live in a world marred by sin and immersed in suffering. If there were no God, suffering would be most miserable, for there would be no purpose in it. But for those, like Paul, who accept the call of God in Christ for their lives – suffering fashions trophies of grace in Faith's Hall of Fame.

## 2 Corinthians Chapter 12

### Paul's Vision of Paradise (vv. 1-6)

Paul had just revealed one of his most humiliating ministry experiences (i.e., escaping arrest by being lowered down the Damacus city wall in a basket). Now he will inform the Corinthians of one of the highest honors of his life; he was caught up into Heaven and saw the Lord. The contrast in consecutive stories of being "let down" to the earth and being "caught up" into Heaven is remarkable.

While he realized that it was unprofitable for him to boast, he had not yet finished listing his apostolic credentials, and felt that he must do so to protect the Corinthians from false teachers (v. 1). He will now speak of "visions and revelations of the Lord." As Warren Wiersbe explains, Paul was no stranger to divine visions and revelations:

> Paul saw the glorified Christ on the very day he was converted (Acts 9:3; 22:6). He saw a vision of Ananias coming to minister to him (Acts 9:12), and he also had a vision from God when he was called to minister to the Gentiles (Acts 22:17). During his ministry, he had visions from God to guide him and encourage him. It was by a vision that he was called to Macedonia (Acts 16:9). When the ministry was difficult in Corinth, God encouraged Paul by a vision (Acts 18:9–10). After his arrest in Jerusalem, Paul was again encouraged by a vision from God (Acts 23:11). An angel appeared to him in the midst of the storm and assured him that he and the passengers would be saved (Acts 27:23). Along with these special visions that related to his call and ministry, spiritual revelations of divine truth were also communicated to Paul.[41]

The Lord also extended to Paul the privilege of experiencing a spectacular encounter with Him in heaven, which Paul describes in verses 2-4. Although he initially speaks in the third person, *"I know a man in Christ,"* it is obvious that Paul is the person in the story. The repeated phrase "I know" indicates that he is the one with the intimate knowledge of the situation. Additionally, verse 7 confirms that there was a personal consequence to Paul after this event occurred.

This heavenly encounter happened about fourteen years earlier, which would be approximately 43 to 44 A.D. (v. 2). Given what we know of Church history from Scripture, Paul came to Christ on the road to Damascus about five to seven years after Christ's crucifixion and resurrection (probably 1 to 2 years after Stephen's stoning). This means Paul would have been a believer for about six to seven years when this spectacular heavenly encounter occurred. Paul and Barnabas' commendation to the grace of God by the church at Antioch and their first missionary journey into Asia Minor was likely in the Spring of 48 A.D. (Acts 13:1-4). It seems likely then that this vision or revelation occurred while Paul was in Tarsus (after leaving Jerusalem), but prior to Barnabas' visit to Tarsus to bring Paul to Antioch.

Paul was caught up into the third Heaven (God's abode), but whether he was in his body or out of his body he did not know. That is, he did not know if he had a vision while on the earth (i.e., was still alive) or if he had died and gone to Heaven to see the revelation. If he was out of his body, he did not miss it or need it. This event seems similar to John's experiences on the Island of Patmos when he received the Apocalypse of Jesus Christ.

While in the Lord's presence, Paul *"heard inexpressible words, which is not lawful for a man to utter"* (v. 4). Since Paul could identify specific words being spoken, he must have received the special ability to discern the language of Paradise (this would not be possible for a human otherwise). Such knowledge would have surely made Paul famous back on earth, if revealed, but a spirit of reverence and awe ensured that would never happen. Divine revelation should humble men, not exalt them at God's expense.

When John heard the voices of the seven thunders while being before the Lord in spirit (i.e., revelation by vision), he understood exactly what was said and was about to write down what he heard, but a voice from Heaven prevented him for doing so (Rev. 10:3-4). Later, when John saw the Lamb on Mount Zion, he vividly describes that he *"heard a voice from Heaven, like the voice of many waters, and like the voice of loud thunder"* (Rev. 14:2). In this situation, John heard the voice, but apparently did not understand what was being communicated. Seemingly, there are times that God uses the sensation of sound to inspire awe in those before Him, rather than intelligible communication. However, if God wants to communicate a message, he enables the hearer to understand it. In Paul's situation, mum was the word. He had revealed all that he was going to say about the matter.

Certainly, the Corinthians would be enthralled to read of his visit to Paradise, but that was not Paul's main interest in relaying the story. He was not boasting of the event to capture their admiration by the experience, but rather to point to the physical evidence of this rapturous encounter to further prove his apostleship, namely his "thorn in the flesh" (vv. 5-6). Paul did not want to be esteemed or honored in any way because of his mysterious excursion to Heaven; rather, he wanted the Corinthians to know of his thorn.

## Paul's Thorn in the Flesh (vv. 7-10)

The Lord knows each of us better than we know ourselves (Ps. 139:1-6). He knows our strengths and limitations and what encouragements and challenges are necessary in our lives to accomplish His purposes. God had invigorated Paul by the heavenly scene, but in God's sovereign judgment, He also determined that it would be necessary for Paul to suffer with "a thorn in the flesh" (v.7). This constant affliction would have the benefit of keeping Paul humble before God, dependent on God, and fruitful for God.

We are not told what this thorn was – other than *"a messenger of Satan to buffet"* Paul. The Greek verb *kolaphizo* rendered "buffet" in verse 7 means "to strike." It is a present tense verb which means that God permitted the devil to continually strike Paul with this affliction. This constant attack could only be remedied by God's grace in verse 9. The Greek verb translated "is sufficient" is also a present tense verb. This meant that God's grace was always available to Paul to make him strong enough in the Lord to be an overcomer, though he himself was weak.

The thorn in the flesh was likely a direct result of demonic oppression, which negatively affects believers outwardly. Thus far in the epistle Paul has informed the saints at Corinth of three methods in which Satan attacks people. He …

- Blinds (4:4) – He keeps the lost from seeing Christ and from believing the gospel message; this may include demonic possession.

- Beguiles (11:3) – He deceives believers away from the simplicity that is in Christ to embrace worldliness and to engage in sin. This includes obsessing the believers' minds with evil thoughts (e.g., Acts 5:1-5).

- Buffets (12:7) – He outwardly oppresses believers and afflicts them with infirmities and suffering.

Even though Paul had suffered from this ongoing infirmity for fourteen years, it is noteworthy that he never mentioned it in any of his writings. In time, he seemed to understand that it was a needful provision to make him the most useful to God. But initially, Paul did ask the Lord three times to remove the thorn (v. 8). The Lord responded to Paul's requests, but in a different way than expected: *"My grace is sufficient for you, for My strength is made perfect in weakness"* (v. 9). The Lord's desire for Paul was that he would learn to rely on His grace each and every day despite the limitation. Satan had a devilish message for Paul, but God had a divine provision in response to the devil's attempt to hinder him – abounding, inexhaustible grace. All Paul had to do was to ask for it and rely on it.

Although Paul was disappointed in the Lord's decision, he knew that the Lord knew what was best to keep him humble and dependent on Him. Consequently, Paul accepted his situation and praised the Lord for His grace. He could actually take pleasure in his infirmities because he would be a witness of God's grace in action (v. 10). Rejoicing results from victory over, rather than merely enduring through, our infirmities. Paul would gladly remain weak so that the power of Christ would be more obvious in him. Spiritually speaking, pain's conversion to power is much better for us than the removal of our humiliating weakness. In this sense, the day of small things is the beginning of greater things because God desires to honor His Son's name through our lives. When finite people choose to be small, an infinite God gets so much bigger in the eyes of those who need to see Him!

There has been much speculation as to the nature of Paul's thorn in the flesh. Based on his statement to the Galatians, he evidently had poor eyesight (Gal. 4:15, 6:11). However, this may have been a naturally occurring condition, or a consequence of aging. Paul's thorn may have been something of a different nature altogether. No doubt the thorn remained nameless in Scripture so faithful saints down through the ages could better identify with Paul in their own sufferings and be exercised to fruitfulness also. Whatever it was, it was permitted by the Lord for Paul's benefit. This passage shows us that not all sickness is caused by personal sin, and in God's estimation there is something much worse than our infirmities – the sin of pride. It is much better to be spiritually healthy than physically fit, as God's grace enables effective ministry despite our debilitating hindrances.

Notice that Paul is not rebuked for asking the Lord three times to take away his thorn in the flesh. Neither is there anything wrong with us asking the Lord to relieve our physical suffering. In fact, we are instructed to boldly approach Him in prayer to do so (Heb. 4:15). However, like Paul, we also must understand that the Lord knows what He is doing, and we must trust in His character and in His Word when unwanted hardships are overwhelming and seem meaningless. God has promised not to test us beyond the measure of grace He provides to sustain us through the trial (1 Cor. 10:13), and that all things will work to a greater good in God's purposes for those who love Him (Rom. 8:28). Paul penned both of these promises and was content to rest in them, and so should we.

The Lord delights to demonstrate His power through the weakness of His people (1 Cor. 1:26-31). When men say "not possible," God often does the impossible that He might be known. Human weakness provides a wonderful opportunity for God to add honor to His own name. Great things happen when small people exercise much faith in a big God. Whether it is a teenager taking down a giant with a stone and sling, or a lad's lunch multiplied to feed thousands of hungry people, God specializes in using what is weak and unfit to do the incredible.

## Paul's Boasting Concludes (vv. 11-13)

Paul tells the Corinthians that they were responsible for making him a fool through much boasting. Because he loved them and wanted to protect them from false teachers, they had forced him to lay out his apostolic credentials (v. 11). The Corinthians should have highly regarded Paul, given his past sacrificial care for them, but instead they were willfully listening to his foes malign him. So, instead of them boasting of him to others, Paul was forced to boast of himself to them.

Additionally, all the signs, wonders, and mighty deeds he performed in their presence proved that he was under Christ's authority and not inferior to other apostles (v. 12; Acts 2:22; Heb. 2:1-4). Signs fascinate the intellect in regard to Scripture. Wonders provide shock-appeal to the imagination. Mighty deeds were feats accomplished with supernatural power. The Corinthians had witnessed these by Paul, and it had cost them nothing.

The apostle then offers a sarcastic apology to press his point further (v. 13). Paul had worked as many miracles in their presence as he did at other churches. But there was one area in which they likely felt inferior to other churches – in choosing not to support him. He did not demand their support, but he did deserve it. The false apostles were disdaining Paul as an inferior apostle because he did not receive support like other apostles did.

Regrettably, the Corinthians' deficient support of Paul demonstrated a lack of appreciation for him and his ministry. Did they not value their salvation in Christ and all the teaching that had been received at no cost to them? It is a lesson for all of us to heed. Let us not become so familiar with those who minister to us that we become ungrateful and forget to express thankfulness to God and to them for their selfless service. Treating a servant of God as a servant is a warning sign of an unthankful attitude.

## Paul's Love for the Corinthians (vv. 14-21)

Although the Corinthians had not appreciated Paul as they should, he had abounding love for them and was prepared to visit them a third time in the near future (13:1). Paul had been with them eighteen months during his second missionary journey before returning to Israel (Acts 18:1-18). He had sailed across the Aegean Sea from Ephesus during his third missionary journey for a brief confrontation and then returned to Ephesus (2:1-4).

Paul was not bitter over the matter of financial support, for it was natural for parents to supply the needs of their children and as their spiritual father he had not demanded their backing (v. 14). Hence, Paul would be gladly spent for their edification, though it seemed that the more he sacrificed for them, the less he was esteemed by them (v. 15).

His accusers were making an issue of Paul's apparently deceitfulness in not personally receiving funds from the Corinthians, but then sending an envoy to collect in a roundabout way what Paul was going to receive (v. 16). But Paul was making the needs of others known to them and teaching them (his spiritual children) about the necessity of giving to other believers in need that there might be equality in the Body of Christ.

Paul posed four questions in verses 17-18 with obvious answers (two "no" responses followed by two "yes" replies). The missionary envoy that he sent to them did not personally profit from them, nor did Titus take advantage of them. He and those sent to them walked by the spirit of conviction in what was acceptable behavior before the Lord. The funds being collected were not for himself and would be handled by Titus and representatives from various local churches. These gifts were for the poor saints in Jerusalem. Hence, Paul had not engaged in craftiness and those handling the collected gifts were also blameless in their conduct.

What the Corinthians thought of Paul was not significant compared to what God knew to be true. Everything that he and the missionary team had done for them was motivated by genuine love and for their edification (v. 19). Paul then mentioned a concern that haunted his mind, that when he arrived at Corinth, he would find them in disarray, having regressed from all his previous efforts (as noted in 1 Corinthians) to put away the evils, the disorder, and carnal divisions among them (v. 20). He so wanted to enjoy his time with them in harmonious fellowship, rather than again needing to correct self-seeking, slander, and contentious attitudes, or self-indulgent misuses of the body (e.g., uncleanness, fornication, and lewdness; v. 21).

It is clear from Paul's earlier expression of his trust in them (after hearing Titus' report of their response to his earlier reproof) that this would not likely be the case (7:16). Yet, as their spiritual father, he knew their past propensity to carnal thinking and failings, and did not want to underestimate the negative effect that the false teachers were having on them.

## 2 Corinthians Chapter 13

Final Exhortations (vv. 1-10)
　　Again, Paul affirms that he is about to visit them for the third time (see the 12:14 explanation). Before issuing a warning to the Corinthians, he refers to the Law's requirement that two or three witnesses validate a true testimony in a court of law (v. 1; Deut. 19:15). When Paul did arrive, any sinful behavior in the assembly would be investigated and multiple witnesses would be sought to confirm the facts before church discipline (as executed by the church) would be invoked (v. 2). Paul was not going to be the judge in such matters, but he would ensure that willful sin in the church was properly dealt with under the umbrella of church authority.
　　Some at Corinth were demanding that Paul prove that he possessed the power which as an apostle he claimed to have: *"Since you seek a proof of Christ speaking in me"* (v. 3). Albert McShane explains their request:

> [This] is a statement implying that Christ would be shown to be the speaker and that Paul was merely the instrument He would use; so, by challenging Paul to demonstrate his power, they were, in a sense, demanding Christ to show His. It was one thing to despise Paul as a man, but quite another to despise him as an apostle of Christ, for in despising Christ's representative, they were despising Himself, so in such a situation, Paul has no option but to go to them and give proof of his power; this will convince them that he was not boasting in vain.[42]

　　During Paul's "painful" trip (his second visit to Corinth), he warned false teachers about deceiving the people in regard to his apostleship. He now wrote the same warning and promised not to spare those leading the Corinthians away from the truth. Paul would demonstrate his full apostolic authority to correct those in error or sin (v. 4). Paul mentions the example of Christ to suggest a parallel reality of Christ working in His servants: Christ was crucified in weakness, but now lives in the power of God. Similarly, Christ's servants are inherently weak, but also represent Christ's authority on earth when living in the power of God supplied through Christ.
　　Paul is not questioning the salvation of the Corinthians in verses 5-6. Rather, he is affirming that because God had marvelously saved them

through the gospel of Jesus Christ that he himself had preached to them, it could only mean that he was an apostle of Christ, not a second-rate teacher.

It would be best if the Corinthians dealt with those in sin and error before his arrival. That would put his visit in a more positive light. However, Paul realized that if this were the case, he would be disqualified in the eyes of some as an apostle, because he would not be demonstrating his apostolic authority in a judicial way to ensure that the assembly was in order. In either case, the truth of God would be upheld; the apostles could *"do nothing against the truth, but for the truth"* (v. 8).

If the Corinthians were walking in truth, Paul would be delighted to not act against them, for such behavior would be against the truth. There was no matter of church order, church discipline, or church doctrine in which the apostles were willing to act against revealed truth. Believers cannot properly worship or serve God unless it is in truth and is Spirit-led.

Paul's high hope for the church at Corinth was that they would properly deal with sinful situations in the church (as a result of his letter), rather than him having to come to them to exercise his authority as an apostle to resolve these situations (v. 9). In either event, it would be for their edification, but he preferred to enjoy a visit with them without exercising correction (v. 10).

## The Conclusion (vv. 11-14)

The apostle closes his letter with a benediction requesting that the Corinthian believers push on to maturity, strive for unity, and live in the love of God which brings peace (v. 11). Paul desired them to change their ways and pursue maturity, to receive exhortation with a ready mind, to come into unity by laying hold of the mind of Christ, and to live in peace with one another by avoiding legalism and adhering to sound doctrine.

They were to continue providing indiscriminate and blameless gestures of brotherly love to each other (v. 12; see Rom. 16:16 comments). All the saints with Paul at that time in Macedonia also passed along their greetings (v. 13). Paul closes the epistle by mentioning the ministry of the triune God on our behalf (v. 14). The Father showed His love to us by sending His Son as a sin sacrifice for humanity. Grace is conveyed to believers through Jesus Christ's work at Calvary and His ongoing intercession for us in Heaven. The Holy Spirit brings believers into union with Christ and indwells them to ensure divine communion, power, and guidance are always available.

Paul followed up this letter with a three-month visit to Corinth, during which time he wrote the Roman epistle. Romans 15:23 informs us that Paul's exhortations had been heeded and that he felt he could leave Corinth with a clear conscience and that the saints would press on in Christ.

# Galatians

## Background
Galatia was a region within ancient Asia Minor (modern-day Turkey) that was bordered by Bithynia and Paphlagonia to the north, Pontus and Cappadocia to the east, Cilicia and Lycaonia on the south and Phrygia on the west. This epistle was written to various churches in Galatia. The letter was likely written shortly after Paul and Barnabas returned from their first missionary journey, but before Paul and Silas departed on the second missionary journey. Given the hypocritical behavior of Peter, Barnabas, and other believing Jews towards fellow Gentile believers (2:11-14), the matter of Gentile circumcision apparently had not yet been considered by the Jerusalem Council (Acts 15) which was held in 49 A.D.

Paul and Barnabas had a successful missionary trip in Galatia; many lost souls turned to Christ and several new churches were established. However, not long after they returned to Antioch (the location of their commending assembly), they were informed that Judaizers were trying to influence these new Galatian believers to be Law-keepers. They did not deny that salvation was in Jesus Christ, but taught that believers had to also continue in Law-keeping to maintain their salvation. This was a works-based heresy which attempted to undermine the true gospel message of grace and security in Christ alone. Paul calls the legalizers' message what it was – a false gospel.

Paul pointedly conveys to the Galatians that any gospel message that includes human merit as the basis of *earning* God's favor is not the truth. For this reason, Paul aggressively attacks this error and its perpetrators throughout the epistle. He also provides the Galatian believers with the right spiritual emphasis that will please God – they must walk in the Spirit, not the flesh. To this end, the focus on externals gained the legalizer nothing before God; since it was all of the flesh and for the glory of the flesh.

## Theme(s)
The gift of salvation is bestowed in grace and is received by faith in Christ alone. Paul supplies a defense of his apostleship. The true gospel, not the Law, enables Christian living in the power of the Holy Spirit.

## Keywords
Keywords and phrases include: "law," "faith," "gospel," "circumcision," "just/justified," "curse," "seed," "mediator," "heir(s)," "bondage," "liberty," "flesh," "children," and "accursed."

## Date
A date just before the Jerusalem Council is likely, 48 or early 49 A.D.

## Outline
I. Introduction (1:1-9).
II. Paul Defends His Apostleship and Message (1:10-2:10).
III. Paul Defends the Gospel of Grace (2:11-19).
IV. Justified in Christ by Faith Alone Apart From the Law (2:20-3:24).
V. Believers Have Liberty in Christ (3:25-5:1).
VI. The Life of Faith Is Visible (5:2-6:18).

## Galatians Chapter 1

### Introduction (vv. 1-5)

At the epistle's onset, Paul asserts that his apostolic authority came directly from Jesus Christ and God the Father, who raised Him from the dead (v. 1). He was an apostle – a "sent one" – by Jesus Christ Himself. He was not ordained to be an apostle by any mere human or human agency, but by the risen Christ and God the Father. This also meant that Paul was directly accountable to God for his ministry and not to the other apostles.

True, the church at Antioch commended Paul and Barnabas to the grace of God (Acts 14:23) and were accountable to care for them, but Luke records that it was the Holy Spirit who called them out of the church at Antioch and appointed them to a wider ministry beyond the confines of a local assembly (Acts 13:1-4). Nowhere in Scripture do we find religious organizations "ordaining" individuals to a professional career.

The deity of Christ is clearly affirmed in the opening verse of the letter: Christ being far more than a man, and being equally responsible with God the Father, chose Paul to be an apostle.

Verse 2 identifies to whom the letter is written – "the churches of Galatia." Whether Paul is addressing churches throughout the region or only in the southern part of the province where he and Barnabas had visited (e.g., Antioch, Iconium, Lystra, and Derbe) is debatable. But obviously, the apostles were concerned for those they had witnessed come to Christ and were now in newly established churches in southern Galatia.

The epistle was from Paul and all the brethren with him. We are not told who was with Paul, but whoever they were, they all stood united with Paul in the message of the epistle. Barnabas was apparently with Paul until they both embarked on separate missionary journeys after the Jerusalem Council (Acts 15:36-41). This salutation is streamlined and lacks the warmth of appreciation and thanksgiving that typically marks other Pauline epistles. The apostle did not waste any ink before confronting the crucial matter at hand. Judaizers were negatively influencing the believers in Galatia and this threatened to undermine the gospel work that had been established there.

These legalizers were preaching a Law-keeping gospel message in opposition to what Paul and Barnabas had proclaimed during their missionary trip. They taught that a Christian was saved by grace in Christ Jesus, but that believers had to continue in keeping the Law to maintain their salvation and to earn God's praise. This was a false gospel message and anyone preaching it would be eternally condemned (vv. 6-9).

Paul does apply his standard greeting of grace and peace from God the Father and the Lord Jesus Christ in verse 3. The order of these virtues is purposeful, as there must always be a work of God's grace in our hearts before His peace can reside there. The opportunity to have one's sins forgiven and to be delivered from "this present evil age" (i.e., the moral and religious corruption in the world) is only through Christ. He is the One *"who gave Himself for our sins"* according to the will of God (v. 4). In pondering what God had done to save sinners, Paul cannot go any further without pausing to praise God. He alone deserves all glory and honor forever (v. 5).

## Departure From the True Gospel Message (vv. 6-9)

Paul tells the Galatians that he is shocked by their readiness to accept a false gospel message after having received salvation through faith in Christ: *"I marvel that you are turning away so soon from Him who called you in the grace of Christ, to a different gospel"* (v. 6). It reminds us never to be surprised at how fast and how furiously the devil will attack a true work of God. If Paul had been preaching a false gospel, there would have been no Judaizers knocking on the Galatians' doors so soon after the apostles had departed. Jack Hunter identifies the type of error that the Galatians were committing by listening to the Judaizers:

> Two different words used in v. 6 and v. 7 are translated "another." The first means "another of a different kind"; the second, "another of the same kind." The Galatians were turning to a different gospel which was not the same as Paul preached. It was not that they were placing a different emphasis on certain aspects of the gospel; it was a false gospel, in the words of the NIV, "a different gospel which is really no gospel at all."[43]

The idea of "grace" – God's unmerited favor "in Christ" (v. 6) – is the basis of "the gospel of Christ" (v. 7). The receipt of God's grace for salvation eliminates any opportunity for man to add to what God has completely supplied. The Judaizers were perverting the true gospel of grace with humanized legalism. That message was offensive to God. Such an idea suggests that His Son did not do enough at Calvary to fully save sinners, and man must do something extra to assist God in order to inherit Heaven.

Consequently, these false teachers were causing the new churches in Galatia to be agitated, in turmoil and confusion (v. 7).

The offense of this false message was so egregious that Paul pronounces a curse on anyone preaching it, and for emphasis he repeats the curse twice (vv. 8-9). The true gospel message is completely founded in God's grace. Grace plus a nickel is not grace; it is faulty humanized legalism. Warren Wiersbe summarizes how the Judaizers were identified by the false message that they preached:

> The test of a man's ministry is not popularity (Matt. 24:11), or miraculous signs and wonders (Matt. 24:23–24), but his faithfulness to the Word of God (see Isa. 8:20; 1 Tim. 4; 1 John 4:1–6; and note that 2 John 5–11 warns us not to encourage those who bring false doctrine). Christ had committed the Gospel to Paul (1 Cor. 15:1–8), and he, in turn, had committed it to other faithful servants (1 Tim. 1:11; 6:20; 2 Tim. 1:13; 2:2).[44]

God has only one message of salvation that condemned sinners must believe to be saved – grace through Christ alone. Any other message is a lie from Hell that will keep lost souls on their natural course into Hell. Legalism blinds people from seeing the truth. Even if angelic beings (hypothetically speaking) came to the Galatians preaching a different message than salvation in Christ alone through faith, they were to reject it as heresy (v. 9).

## Paul Defends His Apostleship and Message (vv. 10-24)

In the remainder of the chapter, Paul presents five arguments to prove that his message (saved by grace alone through faith in Christ) came from God and not from man. First, the message that Paul preached was not pleasing to men because it did not originate from a human source. Salvation could not be earned through human effort. God's grace could be received only by faith in Christ alone (vv. 10-11). Biblical Christianity proclaims "done!" We must take God at His Word on the matter of salvation in Christ. In contrast, world religion is a system of self-helps, self-saving, self-enhancing humanistic "doings," which negates the importance of God's gift of grace through Christ. But what can man add to the inexhaustible grace of God to improve its value?

Second, Paul was a Pharisee of Pharisees who before his conversion persecuted the Church aggressively. Obviously, if there were elements of Law-keeping necessary to secure salvation, he would have been cognizant of that fact, but his own knowledge of the Law and the revelation that he had received from God completely repudiated that idea. Additionally, how could he have been so radically converted to a completely new manner of life unless the message he now preached had the power of God associated with it? The fact that he had experienced such a radical switch from being a zealous Law-keeping Jew to a gospel-preaching Christian proved that his message and calling were from God (vv. 12-14).

Third, Paul mentions what happened to him after God's own Son appeared to him on the road to Damacus. Paul had not been discipled by the apostles in Jerusalem; rather, he received his doctrine directly and privately from God in the wilderness (vv. 15-17). By God's grace Paul had been selected as an apostle to the Gentiles even before his birth. Similarly, God informed Jeremiah that he had been chosen to be His prophet even while God was forming Jeremiah in his mother's womb (Jer. 1:5). Knowing God's sovereign purpose for his life, Paul could now recognize how his Jewish upbringing (i.e., learning the Old Testament Scriptures) had prepared him to serve God. His apostleship and message came directly from God.

Fourth, after his conversion in Damacus, God led him into the Arabian desert where He tutored Paul personally. He returned to Damacus and then three years after his conversion traveled to Jerusalem to meet with the other apostles (v. 18). However, in the fifteen days he was in Jerusalem, he was able to privately speak only with Peter and James the half-brother of Christ (v. 19). In the fashion of an oath, Paul affirms that God is his witness and that he is being truthful (v. 20). The point Paul is making is that he had little exposure to the apostles and that fifteen days was not enough time to have learned from the other apostles all the deep mysteries of God in Christ that he as an apostle knew to be true.

Fifth, after this short visit to Jerusalem, Paul journeyed to Syria and Cilicia (v. 21). To further substantiate the fact that he was not taught by the original apostles, Paul notes that his face was unknown to "the churches of Judea" (v. 22). If he had been in Jerusalem for a long period of time to receive training, then he would have been widely known, but that was not the case. The believers in Judea merely knew that a man previously called Saul had brutally persecuted Christians for their faith but was now one of them preaching Christ (v. 23). May we all remember that it is good for us to be "unknown" until God makes Himself known through us.

Paul's testimony caused the believers to praise God for what He had accomplished in his life (v. 24). In contradiction to what the Judaizers claimed, Paul was not promoting a gospel of lawlessness, but rather he was demonstrating in his own life the connection between God's message of grace in Christ and the wonderful outcome of that grace in Christian living.

# Galatians Chapter 2

Apostolic Discussions Before the Jerusalem Council (vv. 1-10)

Before the Jerusalem Council convened, Paul, Barnabas, and a Greek believer named Titus privately met with the apostles in Jerusalem (vv. 1-2). It was at this time that the apostles in Jerusalem affirmed that Paul was proclaiming the truth. We read in verses 6-8 that they did just that. Paul was preaching the same gospel that they preached to the Jews, but Paul had been commissioned by the Lord to preach this message of grace to the Gentiles. There was only one message of truth – grace in Christ alone – but Peter and Paul had different callings in the administration of that message.

The timing of this meeting was fourteen years later than something, but we are not told what that something was. The date of this meeting was clearly after the completion of the first missionary journey (which began in the spring of 48 A.D.; Acts 13-14), but prior to the Jerusalem Council in 49 A.D. (Acts 15). This meant that the unnamed event would have occurred in approximately 35 A.D.

Given what we know of biblical Church history, Paul likely came to Christ on the road to Damascus about five to seven years after Christ's crucifixion. This date would be between 35 A.D. and 39 A.D., depending on which date is used for the events at Calvary. It is plausible then that Paul is referring to the date of his conversion. It seems unlikely that the apostle could be referring to his previous 15-day trip to Jerusalem in 38 A.D. to 42 A.D. (some three years after his conversion), as that would be more like six to ten years previously, not fourteen.

Additionally, Luke records that Paul made a second trip to Jerusalem in approximately 44 A.D. to deliver a relief gift to the poor saints at Jerusalem from Gentile believers (Acts 11:27-30, 12:25). Regardless of what the fourteen years is tied to, the assertion is to show the Galatians that many years had transpired between his first visit to Jerusalem and his visit mentioned in this chapter (apparently Paul's third time to Jerusalem since his conversion). The point is that during this interim he had virtually no exposure to the apostles in Jerusalem, which meant that he had not been taught or influenced by them.

The issue that caused Paul, Barnabas, and Titus to seek out the apostles in Jerusalem is explained in verses 3-4. Certain Jews were teaching that though Gentiles were saved by the Gospel of Christ, they must continue in the Law to maintain their salvation. This meant that Gentile men who came to Christ should be circumcised. Titus, a Greek believer who labored with Paul, was presented as a test case to the apostles. This private meeting appears to be the precursor to the Council of Jerusalem (Acts 15), which was a full-blown convention composed of a large group of apostles and church elders to resolve the matter once and for all.

Thankfully, there was a unified decision among the apostles and elders at the convention; such unity reflects the mind of God in His people. There was no spiritual reason for Titus to be circumcised. As a Gentile, he was never under the Law, so why should he who had been liberated from sin and death by grace, be enslaved by that which only condemns and provides no help for victorious living?

The outcome of the Jerusalem Council thrilled Paul's heart. The foundation of Christian liberty was preserved. The apostle had not been willing to compromise the truth of the gospel message to make peace with the Judaizers (v. 5; 2 Cor. 13:8). He knew that any mingling of the Law with grace to gain or maintain salvation would void the worth of Christ's sacrifice. Only by proclaiming a true message of grace could the Gentiles experience the power of God in salvation through Christ. God used Paul's zealous regard for truth to ensure that Christianity did not become a powerless Jewish sect.

At a first reading of verse 6, it might be thought that Paul was belittling the apostles in Jerusalem, but that was not the case. Rather, he is emphasizing two points. First, Paul had nearly no contact with the apostles in Jerusalem since his conversion, yet, when they did finally discuss the nature and message of Christianity, they were in complete agreement. Truth cannot contradict itself and since the same truth had been committed to all the apostles, they had a united voice in proclaiming the message of truth.

Second, Paul speaks of the apostles as *"whatever they were"* to infer that the apostles in Jerusalem were just brothers in the Lord, and fellow companions and co-laborers with Christ to build His Church. The apostles were not above other believers in the body of Christ intrinsically, though each had a unique ministry in the Church. The authority of the apostles originated with Christ, not each other, so the apostles in Jerusalem had nothing on Paul, so to speak. They were equals in fulfilling their ministry.

Although all the apostles received the same message and same authority from Christ, their assigned ministries were different. For example, it was acknowledged that Peter had been called to preach Christ to the Jews, but

Paul had been called to minister to the uncircumcised (the Gentiles; vv. 7-8). Having come to this realization, the perceived leaders (the pillars) in the church at Jerusalem, James (the half-brother of Christ), Cephas (Simon Peter), and John extended the righthand of fellowship to Paul and Barnabas (v. 9). This act was not any kind of formal ordination, but rather a gesture of love and solidarity. The apostles were rejoicing in the sovereign purposes of God at work in their lives. The apostles in Jerusalem were thankful for the ministries of Paul and Barnabas to the Gentiles, as were they for the gospel work being achieved among the Jews in Judea.

With this said, the apostles in Jerusalem did exhort Paul and Barnabas to teach the Gentiles to remember the poor, which was something they were eager to do anyway (v. 10). Additionally, the Council of Jerusalem concluded that the Gentiles should be taught to abstain from fornication and idolatry, and to avoid stumbling Jewish brethren by eating things which had been strangled (eating meat without draining the blood; Acts 15:19-20). Obviously, fornication and idolatry were against God's moral law for humanity. The subject of meat preparation pertained to relinquishing a personal preference so that Gentile believers would not needlessly stumble Jewish Christians with whom they desired to fellowship.

This directive was not the law of the land, but the counsel of the apostles and elders at Jerusalem to Gentile believers as to conduct that would be profitable in building up the Church (Acts 15:19-29). The outcome of the Council of Jerusalem was sent via letters to the Gentiles. Each group of local believers, after hearing the letter read would then decide the best approach to honor the Lord. Thankfully, the Gentile believers were in full agreement with the conclusions and recommendations of the Jerusalem Council (Acts 15:30-31). What the Spirit of God had shown to be truth to church leaders in Jerusalem was the same truth He had already revealed to all saints. The Jerusalem Council simply affirmed the truth and its application that was most necessary to build up the Body of Christ.

## No Return to Law-Keeping (vv. 11-21)

Not long after the Jerusalem Council, Peter and other Jews came to Antioch and had open fellowship with Paul, Barnabas, and Gentile believers (vv. 11-12; Acts 11:1). Peter even ate with the Gentiles, which was forbidden by the Jewish Law. However, when some staunch Jews from James arrived from Jerusalem, Peter withdrew from fellowshipping with the Gentiles so as to not offend them. Peter was an apostle and one of the chief leaders in the Church, so his behavior had a catastrophic effect on other Jews who were present. Even Barnabas separated from the Greeks (v. 13). The episode exposed a weakness in Peter that was harming the Body of Christ, and Paul would not be silent concerning his "hypocrisy" (literally "play acting"). This superficial display of respect for hardline Jews (in an attempt to keep a false peace with them) degraded God's work among the Gentiles.

Paul saw their actions as a terrible affront to the gospel message which made Jew and Gentile one in Christ (v. 14). Accordingly, he challenged Peter and those siding with him to walk "straightforward" concerning the truth of the gospel. Any mingling of the Law with grace in Christianity would void the worth of Christ's sacrifice. Paul, the apostle to the Gentiles, publicly rebuked Peter, an apostle to the Jews, for his hypocrisy. The incident showed that the apostles were mere men and were not intrinsically above other believers in the Body. Although each had a unique apostolic ministry, they were accountable to each other when correction was needed.

Having rebuked Peter, Paul, now speaking to the larger audience, refutes the idea that Gentile believers were somehow inferior to Jewish believers (vv. 15-19). Justification before God was received through faith alone in Christ and not through the Law: *"that we might be justified by faith in Christ and not by the works of the law"* (v. 16). The Law did not justify anyone because no one could keep it. Paul therefore declares, *"By the works of the Law no flesh shall be justified"* (v. 16). There is absolutely nothing that the flesh can do that will please God (Rom. 8:8). Peter's actions were of the flesh and not of the Holy Spirit; thus, his rebuke was warranted.

The faith in Christ that the Jews and the Gentiles exercised was the same and had the same result – a righteous standing before God and the life of Christ received. Paul then posed two points as to why it would be wrong to think any other way about justification.

First, any behavior that undermines the truth of justification in Christ alone would be slander against Christ. This was the offense that Peter, Barnabas, and other Jews had committed (v. 17). Adding the necessity of Law-keeping to the gospel meant that Christ did not do enough at Calvary to satisfy God's righteous indignation against human sin. Although the Lord declared from the cross that His work of propitiation for human sin was complete, Peter and others were saying by their actions it was not sufficient. This meant that Christ was a liar – a terrible insult against His Person.

Second, if Peter and other Jews had been justified by faith in Christ alone previously, but now were declaring the importance of Law-keeping to maintain justification, then they were sinners in serving Christ (v. 18). Furthermore, the abrupt change in their message of grace alone for salvation to a corrupt message of grace plus Law-keeping in the name of Christ made Him an accomplice to their sin. But Christ was no minister of sin! William

MacDonald puts the matter this way:

> Peter's actions at Antioch, however, seemed to indicate that he was not completely justified, but had to go back under the law to complete his salvation. If this is so, then Christ is not a perfect and sufficient Savior. If we go to Him to have our sins forgiven, but then have to go elsewhere in addition, is not Christ **a minister of sin** in failing to fulfill His promises?[45]

The apostles absolutely could not build on a foundation they had previously destroyed with the truth of the gospel message. Therefore, the sin was not in abandoning the Law, as the Judaizers claimed, but rather in the apostles returning to it. The Law was for the purpose of showing sin (Rom. 3:20), not for obtaining justification before God. Christ, therefore, had to put away the Old Covenant forever by His work at Calvary to establish a New Covenant that offered forgiveness and life with God (Heb. 8:7-13).

Thankfully, God's salvation for every Christian is more than just the forgiveness of sins and being positionally set apart from the world; rather, salvation centers in enjoying Christ and the enabling power of His life (v. 19). The Law condemned and secured death; it did not offer life to the believer. Paul then concisely summarizes the benefit of being fully identified with Christ after being justified through Him:

> *I have been crucified with Christ; it is no longer I who live, but Christ lives in me; and the life which I now live in the flesh I live by faith in the Son of God, who loved me and gave Himself for me"* (v. 20).

The Greek word rendered "crucified" is a passive voice and a perfect tense verb. This means that God is the one who acted on the subject (Paul) in a once-and-for-all-time fashion to accomplish crucifixion. Crucifixion was a public and judicial act that resulted in death! Paul was now in an ongoing position of death since Calvary; this status would continue forever. In fact, all believers have been positionally crucified with Christ. This means that all that we were previously in Adam (i.e., the Old Man) died when Christ died at Calvary (Rom. 6:6-8). One must die before a new life can be received. Hence, when Christ was raised up from the dead, Paul, with all believers, were raised up in the newness of Christ's life (Rom. 6:4).

The word "live" or "lives" occurs four times in verse 20. The idea is that though believers, like Paul, reside in the flesh (i.e., are physically in the world), we must not live after the flesh (i.e., the carnal nature inherited from

Adam). Positionally, all believers have been raised up with Christ and are presently seated with Him in heavenly places (Eph. 2:5-6).

Christ's victory over the world is complete, and we, in Him, are to continue delighting in and declaring that glorious fact day by day: *"These things I have spoken to you, that in Me you may have peace. In the world you will have tribulation; but be of good cheer, I have overcome the world"* (John 16:33). Each redeemed soul has the present opportunity to live out Christ's life by faith; this is *victorious Christian living*! May each of us remember: *"Whatever is born of God overcomes the world. And this is the victory that has overcome the world – our faith"* (1 Jn. 5:4)!

As D. S. Dockery suggests, Paul's logic was so tight on the subject of justification by faith alone that his conclusions were undeniable:

> He answered key objections: Jews do not have to sin in the same gross ways as Gentiles to be sinners (Rom. 1-3). Nor does a message of grace provoke more and more sin (Rom. 6:1-14). Having corrected such common misperceptions, the apostle proclaimed that no one can be justified by God by "the works of the Law," although the law of Moses does play an important role in convincing of "deadness" in sin (Gal. 3:10-25; Rom. 7:7-12). Rather, the only channel of justification is faith in Jesus Christ, and the road of growth in the Christian is also full identification with the death and resurrection of Christ by faith (5:5).[46]

The chapter closes with Paul's resolve to confront any teaching or behavior that would "set aside" the grace of God (v. 21). Promoting justification by any form of Law-keeping would not be tolerated. The meaning of the Greek verb *atheteo* translated "set aside" means "to nullify" or "to make void." Any teaching that adds human doings to what Christ has already done to satisfy God's judicial anger over sin is an affront to Christ. There was no middle ground on this subject matter. Either God's grace was received through Christ by faith or Christ died "in vain." Anyone adding good works to the gospel of Jesus Christ either to obtain, or to maintain salvation, was preaching a false message and would reap God's wrath.

In the first two chapters, Paul shared his personal experiences relating to the gospel, including his calling and his interaction with the Lord, as the format to confront the legalizers. In chapters 3 and 4, Paul will confront the false message of the Judaizers head-on with a doctrinal approach which affirms what justification in Christ meant. In the final two chapters of the epistle, Paul switches to a practical emphasis to show that the Judaizers' message failed to offer believers power to live for God.

# Galatians Chapter 3

### The Doctrine of Justification by Faith (vv. 1-9)

Paul begins this chapter by implying that Jewish legalizers had "bewitched" (deceived) the Galatians from holding on to the true gospel message they had heard from him and Barnabas. The apostle then asked the Galatians, How "did you receive the Spirit?" (v. 2). Was the Holy Spirit received (i.e., were they saved) after exercising faith in the gospel message of Jesus Christ or through Law-keeping? The implied answer, of course, was through trusting Christ alone for salvation.

In fact, Paul considered the position of trusting the Law to produce moral and spiritual maturity to be utter foolishness (v. 3). As expounded in the Epistle to the Romans, the Law only condemned and it gave no power to overcome the flesh nature (Rom. 3:20, 7:7-14). However, through trusting in Christ, the Holy Spirit regenerates believers (Tit. 3:5) and begins the work of sanctification within them to make them Christ-like.

The devil hates and opposes anyone reminding him of Christ, so those who are His and who represent Him in the world, will suffer persecution from those under Satan's control. Had the Galatians suffered for the truth in vain? Paul did not actually think so. He believed that truth would ultimately win out and that the Galatians would reject the teachings of the Judaizers.

Paul provides further evidence that the Galatians had been justified by faith in Christ and not Law-keeping in verse 5. The Galatians had received the Holy Spirit by accepting the gospel message of Jesus Christ, not by the legalizers' message of Law-keeping. God had shown the authenticity of this message by the working of miracles by the same men (the apostles) who were preaching the true gospel message.

To further illustrate the doctrine of justification portrayed throughout Scripture, Paul refers to the key Jewish patriarch Abraham as an example (v. 6). What does Scripture say? Was Abraham justified by faith or by works of the flesh? Because Abraham was justified solely by exercising faith in God's Word, the patriarch could not boast to God of his achievements (Rom. 4:2). Paul quotes Genesis 15:6 to emphasize that God's past dealings with Abraham declared how He would save sinners in the future: *"Abraham believed God, and it was accounted to him for righteousness"* (v. 6). God's

Word was good enough for Abraham; he simply trusted God and believed.

God responded to Abraham's faith by accrediting to him a standing of righteousness. Obviously, God wanted no confusion on this matter of how He would save sinners, for the words "believe," "counted," and "righteousness" all occur for the first time in the Bible in Genesis 15:6. This foundational verse then appears three times in the New Testament: Romans 4:3, Galatians 3:6, and James 2:23. In Abraham's case, what preceded imputed righteousness? His faith. His good works, the outcome of true faith, were demonstrated in Genesis 22, by the willingness to offer up his son Isaac as a burnt offering in obedience to God's command.

The Judaizers' boasted in the fact that they were sons of Abraham, speaking of their ethnicity. However, Paul states that true sons of Abraham follow his example of believing God's Word without insisting on further evidence to do so (vv. 7-9). This meant that people from all nations, not just the Jews, could be blessed through the unconditional covenant that God made with Abraham in Genesis 12:3. Those who would trust in the promised descendant of Abraham to offer them God's blessing – Christ – would be justified before God, but those who sought to be justified by deeds of the flesh, thus rejecting God's offer in Christ, would be cursed.

## The Law's Curse and the Inheritance of Promise (vv. 10-18)

Let us recall that the Law was a conditional covenant between God and the Jews. God revealed a special set of commandments for the Jews to follow in order to please Him. If they obeyed these, they would be justified in His sight and be blessed by Him. While in Egypt, the Israelites had been redeemed by the blood of the Passover Lamb because they exercised faith and obeyed God's Word. But afterwards God taught them through His Law that no one could earn a righteous standing before Him, because no one could keep the Law. Hence, the Law condemned them. The main point in verses 10-12 is that if an individual breaks one part of the Law, he or she is guilty of being a Law-breaker before God and thus deserves His judgment.

Undoubtedly, the Jews at Sinai sincerely wanted to obey all that God had commanded them in His Law, but time would show their utter failure to do so. In the following centuries, Jewish religious leaders added their *Oral Laws* to God's Law, creating an even more cumbersome system of "doings" in an attempt to cleanse their guilty consciences through doing good works. Consequently, all such efforts to justify oneself eventually lead to one outcome – some form of idolatry (i.e., esteeming something or someone more reliable than God for salvation). Jehovah could not tolerate this grievous sin and therefore punished His covenant people by scattering them among the nations, where they largely remain to this day.

Today, the Jewish nation is still held in the bondage of legalism. The Jewish rabbis do not teach that blood sacrifices are necessary to atone for sin, but that repentance, good deeds, and prayer have atoning value and thus replace the animal sacrifices demanded by the Law. But these sacrifices were pictures of the future, once-for-all blood sacrifice of Christ, which would provide complete propitiation for man's sin. Their choice was to live by the Law and die by the Law or to choose Christ, who died to fulfill the Law that they might live in Him (vv. 13-14). Positionally speaking, Christ took the believer's place on the cross; *"He who knew no sin became sin for us."* Christ endured the full judgment of God for sin and by His shed blood redeems believers from the curse of the Law (Col. 2:13-15).

In legal affairs, once a will (a testament) is signed and sealed, it cannot be changed (v. 15). If such careful respect is extended to human covenants, how much more reliable is God's unconditional covenant? The implication is that God's promise to Abraham could not be broken.

Paul states that God's promise to Abraham was to him and to his "Seed" (Christ) not to "seeds" (speaking of his natural descendants; v. 16). The Judaizers were contending that God's promise to Abraham meant they would be blessed because they were Abraham's seed. But Paul declares that would be impossible because the Jews were placed under the conditions of the Law, and only those who fully obeyed its conditions could be blessed by God. In fact, no one could perfectly keep the Law, so the assumptions of the Judaizers were false.

The arrival of the Mosaic Law, some 430 years after God's covenant with Abraham, could not undermine God's promise to bless the Seed of Abraham (v. 17). The Law did not cancel God's covenant with Abraham, but rather upheld its necessity. God's promise to bless all nations was made through Abraham's Seed – Christ. Hence, only by trusting in Christ for salvation can the promised inheritance be received (v. 18).

We receive the promised blessing to Abraham in the same way he did – *"he believed God, and it was counted to him as righteousness."* Abraham was justified before God, through faith in God's Word, not by works. Likewise, we are justified before God, through faith in God's Living Word – Christ – not by doing good works. Thankfully, because Abraham's Seed (Christ) fulfilled all the precepts of the Law, we can, by faith, like Abraham, legitimately receive the blessing promised long ago.

## The Purpose of the Law (vv. 19-25)

Was Paul being negative about the Law? If the Law did not void or add conditions to the Abrahamic covenant as the Judaizers taught, of what benefit was the Law to the Jews (v. 19)? Sin existed in the world from the time of Adam until the Law, but was not imputed as transgression (Rom. 5:13-14). The Law was given to the Jews to show them their sin, and to put them under obligation for sin (Rom. 4:15). The Law had to be stated before God could judicially punish sin as transgression. The purpose of the Law then was to show the Jews that they were a nation of sinners who needed a Savior (v. 24). Spoken to Moses by angels (Acts 7:53; Heb. 2:2), the Law was a temporary covenant to prepare the Jews for the coming Seed (their Messiah). In Him, God would make good all His promises to Abraham.

The covenant God made with Abraham was unconditional and since everything rested on God keeping His word, no mediator of that covenant was needed (v. 20). But not so for the conditional covenant of the Law. A mediator was needed because the Jews, no matter how hard they tried, could not keep their side of the deal. That was what God wanted His covenant people to learn, but instead they created a system of legalism to justify themselves before God.

The Law did not put away God's promises or take their place. If it had been possible to maintain the standard of perfection God demanded in the Law, then salvation could have been obtained through Law-keeping (v. 21). But this was an impossibility, for by the Law all are shown to be guilty of sin (v. 22). Those who understand this and by faith embrace God's only way of forgiving human sin (by Christ's substitutionary death) receive the blessing promised to Abraham. Until this solution (i.e., the Christian "Faith" centered in the death, burial and resurrection of Christ) was revealed, the Law kept the Jewish nation fenced in from knowing how God would righteously deal with sin to confer salvation (v. 23; 2 Cor. 3:7-11).

Paul explains that in the era from Mount Sinai to Calvary, the Law was like a tutor guiding a child into a deeper realization of the truth (v. 24). The purpose of the Law was to show the Jewish nation their sin and to point them to the solution – the Savior, their Messiah – Christ. Obviously, once the child learns all that a guardian has to offer, there is no more need of the tutor (v. 25). Once the Christian faith was revealed and received, believing Jews would no longer be under the constraints of the Law, the tutor.

Failure to draw a distinction between the unconditional covenant which God instituted with Abraham and the conditional covenant confirmed with Moses at Sinai places the Church under the Mosaic Law. Paul adamantly refutes this idea in verses 17-18. The Gentiles were never under the Law, so Paul warns that they should not put themselves under it now (5:3-4). The Law did not cause the Jewish nation to achieve spiritual perfection; it only revealed their imperfections. Those Jews who come to Christ in faith are liberated from the condemnation of the Law and are "free." They are justified and blessed in Christ – the promised Seed of Abraham.

## Sons and Heirs of Promise (vv. 26-29)

All those exercising faith in God's promise of blessing through Abraham's Seed (Christ) not only become children (the seed) of Abraham, but also "sons of God" (v. 26). Until verse 26, Paul has been speaking of the Jewish nation and explaining why God gave them the Law, a conditional covenant that could not grant salvation. They were limited in understanding God's means of salvation until it was revealed in Christ. Paul used the pronoun "we" extensively when speaking of the Jews, but switches to the pronoun "you" in verse 26. Through the end of the chapter, the apostle is addressing both Jewish and Gentile believers who have been justified in Christ and have become the sons of God and heirs of His promises.

But this blessed position in Christ also necessitates responsibility: *"For as many of you as were baptized into Christ have put on Christ"* (v. 27). The expression "baptized into Christ" speaks of our spiritual union with Christ, for all believers are baptized by the Holy Spirit into His Body (1 Cor. 12:13). The "for as many of you" implies "all of you." The phrase "have put on Christ" employs an aorist tense verb in the middle voice indicating that the believers chose for themselves to complete the previous action. This means Paul is connecting their choice of "faith in Christ Jesus" (v. 26) with their choice of displaying their union in Christ through believers' baptism (i.e., water baptism). Salvation is received through believing, but the public confession of Christ through water baptism is the evidence that one has believed (Rom. 10:10). In Paul's day, no true believer would have ever ignored the Lord's command to be baptized.

In Christ, all believers enjoy the same relationship with God, meaning that from a positional standpoint, ethnic, social, and gender distinctions are irrelevant (v. 28). There is one Head (Christ) and His Body (the Church). Since Christ is the Seed of promise in Abraham, all those in Christ are heirs of the spiritual goodness promised to Abraham's seed (v. 29). Hence, believers are the sons of God (v. 26), one in Christ (v. 28), and of Abraham's seed (v. 29). To bring out these wonderful truths, Paul had to discuss three different dispensations (i.e., divinely appointed stewardships given to man):

Vv. 6-9: Promise (relating to Abraham).
Vv. 10-21: Law (relating to the nation of Israel).
Vv. 22-29: Grace (relating to the Church Age).

# Galatians Chapter 4

### Sons and Heirs of Promise (vv. 1-7)

Having highlighted the differences between Law and promise, Paul now contrasts the condition of believers who have received the promise (i.e., Christianity) with that of believing Jews still under Law, but waiting for God's covenant with Abraham to be fulfilled. To illustrate their scattered state in the world while waiting to be gathered to God (John 11:52), Paul likens them to a son who is heir to a family inheritance. Yet, a juvenile does not inherit anything until adulthood is reached. Until then, the son is treated like a slave, in that he is told what to do and what not to do, while guardians care for his person and stewards manage his property (vv. 1-2).

This scenario represents believing Jews who were under the bondage of the Law until Christ established a New Covenant in His blood. This faithful remnant is likened to a son being ordered about by elements of the world (i.e., Jewish religious precepts) without any conscious sense of God being his Father (v. 3). The Jews were the children of Israel and of the patriarchs, but only in the Age of Grace did believing Jews become children of God. Concerning this illustration of the son-heir, Hamilton Smith writes:

> In this respect he is like a servant under bondage, even though he be lord of all. Even so, believers under law were held in a spirit of bondage under principles which mark the world. Every natural man can understand a law which tells us what we are to do, and not to do, and that our blessing depends upon obedience to the law. It is a principle on which the world seeks to regulate all its affairs. It is, however, bondage to the believer, for while binding us down to obey in order to obtain blessing, it gives us no strength to carry out the demands of law. Moreover, it gives no knowledge of the heart of the Father, nor access to the Father – the source of all blessing.[47]

The festivals, offerings, and rituals prescribed by the Law were designed to teach God's covenant people about Him, about their sin, and about His provision of redemption for them in Christ, but these were mere shadows of the coming promise. The Old Testament is full of types and shadows of Christ, but it is only by New Testament truth that their intended meaning is understood. Just as a child learns to identify letters, colors, and objects by looking at pictures of them, these inspired teaching aids were to assist the Jews to better understand the reality of God's blessing to them in Christ, *"when the fullness of time had come"* (v. 4).

When God the Father determined that it was time for the son (the faithful Jew) to enter into his inheritance, he replaced the elementary teaching aids in the Old Testament with the reality of which they had been foretelling – Christ's coming: *"God sent forth His Son, born of a woman, born under the law"* (v. 4). God sent His eternal Son into the world. He was not created, nor was His beginning at His miraculous conception by the Holy Spirit. God's Son entered the world by natural birth and was born a Jew, thus, under the Law.

About seven centuries before the birth of Christ, the prophet Isaiah uttered a delightful prophetic message to foretell the coming of God's Messiah to Israel: *"For unto us a Child is born, unto us a Son is given; and the government will be upon His shoulder. And His name will be called Wonderful, Counselor, Mighty God, Everlasting Father, Prince of Peace"* (Isa. 9:6). The *"For unto us"* supplies the basic premise on which the prophecy rests: the Child born and the Son given would be for Israel. The two initial expressions confirm both the humanity and the deity of the coming Savior, says H. A. Ironside:

> The "child…born" refers to His humanity. He was to come into the world as the virgin's Son. … The "son…given" refers to the Savior's deity. He was born of Mary, but without a human father. The eternal Son of the Father, Christ came from the glory that He had with the Father throughout all the past eternity. The Son was given in grace for our redemption.[48]

The Holy Spirit carefully chose the specific phrases and their order. The Lord was not *"a* child given," nor *"a* son born" – He was the unique child born, because He was the unique Son given. John tells us that the spirit of Antichrist is evident when one denies that God's Son *came* from Heaven to the earth to be born of a virgin (1 Jn. 4:2-3).

There are many today who deny the eternal sonship of the Lord Jesus Christ. But John teaches us that Christ came forth from the Father (John 16:28), and that there was a Father-Son relationship in the Godhead even before the creation of the world (John 17:5, 24). Hebrews 1:2 also states that the Son created all things. God gave His Son (John 3:16), implying that Christ was God's Son before He was given. He did not give one who would become His Son, but one who was already His Son (Isa. 48:16-17; Ps. 40:6-8). Besides verse 4, there are many passages which speak of the Father "sending" the Son; these all imply that Christ existed as God's Son prior to His earthly mission (John 20:21; 1 Jn. 4:10, 14). The Son eternally exists in the bosom of the Father (1 John 1:18) and He alone enjoyed the fellowship of that relationship prior to His incarnation.

Why did the Father send His Son into the world? Answer: *"to redeem those who were under the law, that we might receive the adoption as sons"* (v. 5). Paul includes himself in the pronoun "we" to illustrate that the time to inherit the promises of God (those initially given to Abraham and his seed) had come to the Jewish nation. But how could God righteously provide this wonderful privilege when the Law declared that every Jew was unfit to receive it? The answer to this quandary is that those condemned by the Law must first be redeemed by the sacrifice of God's perfect Lamb. The Son of God became holy humanity so that through His sacrifice, we, being condemned humanity, might become redeemed humanity and sons of God through adoption.

Most of the Jewish nation rejected God's offer, but those who exercised faith in God's promise as did Abraham became sons of God (v. 6). These received "the Spirit of His Son," speaking of the Holy Spirit who placed them into Christ at Pentecost (Acts 2). The indwelling Spirit of God causes believers to realize the dignity of their new position and to be aware of their sonship. Through the Holy Spirit we eagerly and affectionately address God as "Abba, Father." No slave (i.e., no one outside the family) would use such familiar language, but God's intimate children can. Through redemption in Christ, believers are no longer slaves to the Law or to sin, but have been liberated and brought into an eternal relationship with God. Because Christ is heir to all that God has, believers in Christ *"shall inherit all things,"* and each believer will be called "a son" by God (v. 7; Rev. 21:7).

## Paul's Concern for the Galatians (vv. 8-20)

Paul reminded the Galatians, who were mainly Gentiles, that before they knew the one true God, they served false gods (v. 8). While it was true that the Galatians had now learned about the true God, Paul acknowledges that the important part of their relationship with Him is that He knew them.

It is important that believers keep this biblical perspective of our relationship with the Lord, otherwise our intimacy with Him will slip. The only reason we know God and are able to love Him is because we were first known by Him. He initiated sacrificial love and we responded to it: *"But if anyone loves God, this one is known by Him"* (1 Cor. 8:3). *"We love Him, because He first loved us"* (1 Jn. 4:19). Thankfully, the security of our relationship with God rests in the fact that He knows us. Though we may temporarily forget the Lord, it is impossible for Him to forget us. And thankfully, He loves us too much to permit us to stray very far from Him.

Under the influence of the Judaizers, the Galatians were turning from the truth to another form of bondage – legalism. The weak and beggarly elements of Law were meant to reveal God's plan of reconciliation in Christ to the Jewish nation (v. 9). Why, after knowing the truth, and being brought into a living relationship with God as His sons, would anyone want to trade that privilege for observing *"days and months and seasons and years"* (v. 10)? The Jewish Sabbath rituals and national feasts were to point the Jews to God's solution for their sin – Christ, so why trade the fulfillment of these things for the mere shadow of what they foretold?

Religiosity is a poor substitute for experiencing God through biblical Christianity. The danger of prizing a religious calendar is that involvement in superficial observances obscures what is truly sacred to God, and the tendency is to ignore God and live according to our own desires on non-special days. Paul was greatly concerned for the Galatians and was wondering if he had labored among them in vain (v. 11).

As Gentiles, the Galatians were not under the Law, but Paul being born a Jew was subject to the Law from birth. Paul fondly appeals to the Gentile Galatians as "brethren." Since being in Christ he had become like them, not under the Law. In fact, the Gentiles had never been under the Law, and Paul encourages them to ignore the Judaizers who wanted to put them under the bondage of the Law. Paul says that he and the Galatians are in the same state – free from the law! (v. 12). Paul was not pleading with the Galatians to return to the truth because he was personally offended by their behavior, but rather out of concern for where the Judaizers were leading them – away from God and into bondage.

Paul then recalls that when he first arrived to share the good news of Jesus Christ with them, he was suffering (in his flesh) with an infirmity (some suggest malaria) that greatly weakened him (vv. 13-14). Yet, God used him mightily to preach the truth and the Galatians loved and respected him for doing so. Despite his infirmity and simple speech, the Galatians did not reject the apostle. Rather, because he was the Lord's messenger, they received him with the honor befitting a heavenly messenger (an angel).

We are not told the nature of Paul's infirmity in the flesh, but he did apparently struggle with poor eyesight (v. 15). The Galatians were so appreciative of Paul sharing the gospel with them that had it been possible, they would have given Paul their own eyes as an expression of thankfulness. But where was that sentiment now? What had changed the Galatians' appreciation for Paul? He was still Christ's messenger. His message had not changed. Paul was still contending for the truth of salvation in Christ alone. So, if they now considered him as their enemy, undoubtedly they were holding to a dangerous doctrine that would eventually ruin them (v. 16).

The Judaizers were up to "no good"! Paul realized that they were zealously courting the Galatians in an attempt to cut them off from him and from the truth he taught (v. 17). False teachers seek followers, rather than encouraging believers to follow Christ (2 Pet. 2:18). Such self-serving ideology contrasts with the motivation of true servants of God, who, like John, seek to magnify the Lord Jesus in whatever they do (John 3:30).

Although Paul was their spiritual father, he did not mind other servants of the Lord influencing the Galatians, as long as it was in Christ-centered truth (v. 18). If we serve others with pure and honest motives, being warmly esteemed by those we serve would be appreciated and appropriate. That is what Paul desired from the Galatians, whether he was with them in person or not.

By addressing them as "little children" he was reminding the Galatians that he was the one who labored among them to lead them to Christ (v. 19). Yet, he was experiencing the pangs of childbearing again for them, not for their conversion, but that Christ would be formed in them. Christlikeness is God's high goal for all believers (Rom. 8:30; Eph. 4:13). Paul knew that if the Galatians would fully embrace the truth, the Holy Spirit would cause them to reveal the moral excellence of Christ in their thinking and behavior.

The exact meaning of verse 20 is difficult to ascertain. No doubt Paul would have rather been with the Galatians in person to address these crucial issues. He was anxious as to their spiritual condition and how they would respond to his forthright letter. If Paul had been with them, he would have known their response to his challenge, and hopefully, he would have been able to change the tenor of his message from concern to that of joy.

## Bondage or Freedom (vv. 21-31)

The word "law" appears twice in verse 21 but has two different connotations. The first occurrence refers to those who were seeking holiness by Law-keeping, while the second reference to "the law" speaks of the Old Testament Law books (Genesis through Deuteronomy). Paul is inferring that those seeking justification through Law-keeping do not really understand what the Law demanded.

Paul borrows an Old Testament story to illustrate the negative aspects of choosing the bondage of Law-keeping over liberty in Christ. He reminds the Galatians that two sons were born to Abraham. Ishmael was born first of the bondwoman Hagar, then Isaac was born of Sarah, a freewoman (v.

22). God had promised Abraham and his wife, Sarah, a natural son after he arrived in Canaan. However, after some ten years without a child, Sarah convinced him to take her handmaiden Hagar as a concubine in order to provide a son for Abraham on her behalf. In a moment of weakness, Abraham obeyed the voice of his wife, rather than trusting the promise of God, and Ishmael was conceived in Hagar through human effort. Genesis 21 records that Sarah later bore Abraham a son, Isaac, and nursed him in her old age, just as God had promised (v. 23).

Paul uses the two women to represent two covenants: Hagar, the Law (the Old Covenant), and Sarah, the New Covenant founded in grace (vv. 24-25). The Law of bondage was given at Mount Sinai and was later ratified as the law of Israel in Jerusalem, but the capital city of those justified by faith in the new covenant is the Jerusalem above. It is from there that grace descends (v. 26). This heavenly Jerusalem is home to all true believers, Jew and Gentile, which, to the praise of God, fulfills Isaiah's prediction quoted in verse 27. The barren woman (Sarah) through God's promise of a son received many more children (Jews and Gentiles) than the woman (Hagar) who had a husband received through the operation of the flesh.

Isaac and Ishmael depict the two results of the beforementioned covenants, as each son assumes the character of his mother. Consequently, the sons are different in birth (v. 23), in disposition (v. 29), and in their inheritance (v. 30). By choosing to trust in God's promise (salvation in Christ), all believers become like Isaac, the child of promise (v. 28). Furthermore, Isaac inherited all that Abraham had (Gen. 25:5), and sons of God will co-inherit all things in Christ (Rev. 21:7).

Ishmael symbolizes the energy of the flesh to seek God's blessing apart from His promise. Those operating in the flesh will always persecute those born again of God through promise, just as Ishmael oppressed Isaac long ago (v. 29). F. B. Hole addresses the practical implications of Paul's illustration for those living in the Church Age.

> The proud orthodox Jew might rightly boast that according to the flesh he was a true-born son of Isaac. Yet in a spiritual sense he was only a son of Ishmael and in bondage under the schoolmaster. True the schoolmaster regime came first, and later came the promise, which materialized in the advent of the Son of God. But that only confirmed the type, for Ishmael came before Isaac. The type was further confirmed by the fact that it was the proud Jews who persecuted the humble Christians (v. 29).[49]

God's miraculous solution to a barren couple's problem was not to change Ishmael; it was the birth of Isaac. The strife of the flesh against what is of the Spirit could only end in one way – the bondwoman and her son had to be cast out (v. 30). Only by yielding to the truth and experiencing spiritual rebirth can believers enjoy liberation from the bondage of the flesh (v. 31; Tit. 3:5). Justification through Law-keeping is nothing but self-imposed bondage. This flesh-motivated attempt to obtain justification insults God, for it rejects His offer of full salvation through the death, burial, and resurrection of His Son.

Speaking of the Sarah and Hagar illustration from Genesis 21, J. G. Bellett contrasts God's working in the dispensations of Law and Grace:

> And further, he shows that the time was now fully come, when the Lord had ripened all His dispensational actings up to this very point of casting out the bondwoman and her son (vv. 1-7). Nothing could be more perfect than a warrant thus delivered, thus verified, thus sealed, and thus countenanced, if I may so speak, by God's own acts. The apostle, therefore, with full ease, and conscious authority, finds himself in company with Sarah in Genesis 21. As she then knew her right, without leave from her husband or apology to anyone, summarily to demand the expulsion of Hagar and Ishmael from the house, so does Paul here.
>
> He shows what the modern or mystic Hagar is – that it is the religiousness of mere nature, or a system of observances and ordinances, either imposed or revived by man in the churches of the saints – that formality of days, and months, and times, and years, which genders the spirit of bondage, and hinders the formation of Christ in the soul, and that spirit of liberty which He ever brings with Him. And the expulsion of this Hagar, this bondwoman, from the house of Abraham, or the churches of the saints, he demands with as full, unsparing decision as ever Sarah demanded the casting out of Hagar the Egyptian and her mocking child (Gal. 4:8, 5:12).[50]

God's miracle solution to a barren life is eternal life received by new birth, not a "makeover" of the old nature, which is loathsome to God. The birth of Isaac did not improve Ishmael, but it did bring out his hidden opposition to the child of promise begotten by God.

Ishmael was the son of a bondwoman (a slave), illustrating that naturally, we are slaves to sin with no hope of deliverance. Regeneration, however, implants life (the very divine nature of God) within those earthen vessels who accept His offer of salvation through Christ (John 1:12-13). No new spiritual birth means no spiritual life, no spiritual fruit for God, and no Heaven or eternal inheritance to enjoy (John 3:3).

# Galatians Chapter 5

Freedom in Christ (vv. 1-6)

The first verse introduces a new subject and provides a thematic capstone for the entire epistle, *"Stand fast therefore in the liberty by which Christ has made us free"* (v. 1). The previous chapter closed by stating that those justified in Christ are positionally set free from the bondage of Law-keeping. Seeking justification through Law-keeping is nothing more than self-imposed slavery. No one can earn freedom by working for it; we must be set free by God's grace through Christ to be free. But, our freedom in Christ is not without responsibility, for believers have a new Master to serve out of love and appreciation. Thus, in this chapter, Paul shifts the focus from the *position* of believers in Christ to their *practice* in living for Christ.

Three main points are emphasized: First, believers are exempt from the necessity of circumcision (vv. 2-6). Second, liberty in Christ allows believers to fulfill the Law (vv. 7-15). Third, those in liberty must "walk in the Spirit" (v. 16), be "led by the Spirit" (v. 18), and "live in the Spirit" (v. 25) to please God (vv. 16-26). Having been set free by grace, Paul, speaking as an apostle to them, implores the Galatians to stand (i.e., to live a life) consistent with their liberated position. People cannot profit from Christ's offer of liberation until they cease from trying to earn their freedom by Law-keeping (e.g., relying on one's circumcision to impress God; v. 2).

Those relying on circumcision to be justified before God remain debtors to keep the whole Law and thereby stand condemned before God (v. 3). Those who live by the Law shall die by the Law (3:10). Those who count on circumcision (or any activity, for that matter) to earn God's favor have ensured that Christ's work at Calvary is of no benefit to them (Rom. 4:3-5).

Additionally, Paul states that those who pursue Law-keeping as a means of enhancing their righteousness suffer severed fellowship with Christ and have "fallen from grace" (v. 4). Obviously, living a respectable and moral life apart from Christ will never earn Heaven, but the context would indicate that Paul is speaking to believers who thought that legalism would perfect righteousness in them. Thus, verse 4 is not talking about Christians in sin (sin is not mentioned) and supposedly lose their salvation, as some assert. Rather, Paul is speaking of those *"who attempt to be justified by law."* As

F. B. Hole explains, as soon as someone chooses legalism to perfect what only God can achieve through Christ, he or she has "fallen from grace":

> He [a person who has "fallen from grace"] takes up a ground before God which practically makes Christ of no effect to him. The words "fallen from grace" are sometimes wrongly used as though they meant that a believer who once stood in the grace of God has now been ejected from it by God because of his bad behavior. The point of the passage is rather that anyone who has once taken up his position before God in grace, as these Galatians had, and then abandons it *in his own mind and consciousness* for law has had a bad fall. To step off the grace platform on to the law platform involves a descent that amounts to a fall, for the one is far lower than the other. In the case of a true believer being entangled thus, the fall, we repeat, is in his own mind and consciousness. God's grace and the relationship established by grace remain the same, for *"the gifts and calling of God are without repentance"* (Rom. 11:29).[51]

Those who have not received salvation in Christ are not in Him, and therefore remain condemned before God, no matter what they "do" (John 3:18). Consequently, the idea that someone can receive Christ as Savior and then perfect holiness through Law-keeping is offensive to God.

In contrast to those in verse 4, "we" (liberated Christians like Paul), "by faith," are eagerly waiting for the day when our righteous standing in Christ will be fully displayed in all that we do (v. 5). This event is called glorification and occurs when Christ returns for His Church (1 Jn. 3:2-3; 1 Thess. 4:13-18). True faith has the visible evidence of the Holy Spirit working in a believer's life, for He will display the love of God in action (v. 6). On the other hand, circumcision (denoting Law-keeping) does not provide anyone with any power or hope for the future. Circumcision contributes nothing with respect to the matter of a righteous standing before God, nor is it instrumental in enabling a believer to better live for Him.

## Love Fulfills the Law (vv. 7-15)

Paul tells the Galatians that they started well in running for Christ because they obeyed the truth, but someone had tripped them with false doctrine (v. 7). The doctrine of legalism did not originate with God and therefore should not be added to guide Christians into service for God (v. 8). The Law demands strength from those who have none and then curses those who do not *keep the Law*, while Christ gives strength to those who have none and rewards those who *fulfill the Law*.

To illustrate how the false doctrine of the Judaizers had adversely affected the Galatians, Paul refers to their false teaching as leaven and a little leaven is sufficient to leaven an entire lump of dough (v. 9). Likewise, false doctrine has a mushrooming effect that can spread throughout the local church if unchecked. This does not mean that every believer in the assembly will be corrupted by the false doctrine, but it will affect the character of the assembly as a whole. In 1 Corinthians 5, Paul used this illustration to refer to the negative effect of unaddressed moral evil in a local assembly.

A little error, a little sin, a little humanism inevitably leads to more of the same if not eradicated. Thankfully, just as the invisible heat of an oven kills the influence of leaven in the dough, so the invisible power of the Holy Spirit works to mortify what offends God in the believer's life. For this reason, Paul had confidence in the Lord that the Galatians, in the Spirit, would reject the false teachers who were hindering their spiritual growth, and that God would also punish those spreading false doctrine (v. 10).

Apparently, the Judaizers had convinced the Galatians that Paul taught the necessity of circumcision, perhaps because Paul had Timothy, who was born to a Greek father and a Jewish mother, circumcised (v. 11; Acts 16:3). Young Timothy joined Paul during his second missionary journey. His circumcision permitted the missionaries to speak to Jews about Christ. Timothy's circumcision was not to earn justification, which would have been contrary to the message of liberty in Christ they were proclaiming. Paul's point is that if he were really preaching the necessity of circumcision, as the Judaizers affirmed, why was he being persecuted and hounded by them wherever he went (e.g., Phil. 3:2)? In other words, the response of the Judaizers towards Paul proved that he was not preaching their message.

The lost considered the preaching of the cross for salvation as foolishness (1 Cor. 1:18) and the legalist considered the preaching of the cross as a deficient message without Law-keeping. Paul was being persecuted by both for preaching Christ alone for salvation and sanctification. Why would he preach such a message unless it was true? There was no personal gain for him in preaching Christ crucified for sinners.

Although Paul was suffering now for preaching the truth, he knew the legalizers would not escape God's wrath for spreading their heresy (v. 12). But in the meantime, Paul wished that these legalizers would use their sacred circumcision knives and "cut themselves off." If this statement is taken literally, Paul was saying he wished these false teachers would castrate themselves with their own ceremonial knives. In a bit of irony, he is suggesting that this action would take the bite out of them. However, it seems more likely that Paul is simply expressing a figurative desire that the false teachers be completely cut off from influencing the Galatians.

The apostle was teaching the Galatians that Christian liberty and not legalism should guide their conduct. To eliminate any confusion on this matter, the apostle clarifies what liberty should and should not be used for in verses 13-15. Liberty maintains the glory of God as a focus, serves others in genuine love, and ensures spiritual flexibility in personal growth and service. Christian liberty should not be used as an opportunity to stir up the flesh, which leads to sin that causes division within the body of Christ and hinders the lost from believing the gospel. Believers cannot truly love others if they are exalting themselves by living in the flesh. Demonstrating genuine love towards others is only possible when walking in the Spirit.

The Judaizers were focused on Law-Keeping, but Paul affirms that God was interested in believers fulfilling the Law by loving their neighbors (v. 14; Rom. 13:8-10). Expressing selfless love to a neighbor fulfills the Law. This can only happen after a person has been regenerated and possesses the love of God to share with others. Keeping the Law included not stealing from others, but fulfilling the Law was more than just not stealing, it also required giving sacrificially to others. The Law is fulfilled in sacrificially giving to others, not just in refraining from taking from them. It is by this type of love for others that the world will know a true disciple of Christ. Law-keeping does not produce this kind of love among believers because sacrificial love originates with God. No wonder the Galatians were in conflict with each other.

## Walking in the Spirit (vv. 16-26)

Paul begins this section with a categorical statement: *"Walk in the Spirit, and you shall not fulfill the lust of the flesh"* (v. 16). What does it mean to walk in the Spirit? First, notice that it is the opposite of living in the bondage of legalism (v. 1) and in the license of the flesh (v. 13). The Holy Spirit and our carnal flesh (as controlled by our fallen nature from Adam) have nothing in common (v. 17). Each wants to control our behavior (what we walk after), the former for God and the latter for whatever we crave.

Paul says that *"if you are led by the Spirit, you are not under the law"* (v. 18). Believers cannot be led by the Spirit if they are depending on Law-keeping for justification. The Holy Spirit would never lead those already justified in Christ to seek an alternate self-help means of justification

As Paul explains in Romans 7:7-9, the Law revives sin in our members and appeals to the energy of the flesh. When we are told not to do something, our flesh nature just wants to do it all the more. Paul provides an overview of four types of sins that are produced by our fallen nature:
- Sexual sins (v. 19): Adultery, fornication, uncleanness, licentiousness.

- Religious sins (v. 20): Idolatry, sorcery.
- Social sins (vv. 20-21): Hatred, strife, jealousies, unrighteous wrath, selfish ambitions, dissensions, heresies, envy, murders.
- Personal sins (v. 21): Drunkenness, wantonness, and the like (i.e., many others could be named).

Those who continue practicing these works of the flesh will not inherit the kingdom of God (v. 21; 1 Cor. 6:10-12; Eph. 5:5; Rev. 21:8). Those who are born of God will be grieved over sin and will loathe continuing in sin (1 Jn. 3:9). Believers on this side of glory are not sinless, but neither are they to practice sin. In fact, as Christians grow in Christ by walking in the Spirit, they will sin less. Those who identify with Christ but continue in sin are deceiving themselves. If Christ was in them, they would be the most miserable people on earth in such active rebellion against Christ.

The only means for a believer to have victory over the sinful impulses of the flesh is to walk in the illumination, the enablement, the guidance, the instruction, and power of the Holy Spirit (v. 16; Rom. 8:11-13, 13:14). When believers choose to be in fellowship with God by walking in the truth as guided by the Holy Spirit (1 Jn. 1:6-7), the fruit of the Spirit will be evident in their lives. To walk after the flesh is to break fellowship with God. He is holy and cannot walk in the darkness (in sin) with us.

Believers walking in the Spirit will exhibit the character of God in what they do. Paul identifies the homogeneous nature of these godly virtues as "fruit," not "fruits" of the Holy Spirit: *"But the fruit of the Spirit is love, joy, peace, longsuffering, kindness, goodness, faithfulness, gentleness, self-control. Against such there is no law"* (vv. 22-23). These nine character qualities represent the way a holy God behaves all the time and every time. All that God does is motivated by who He is. No one character quality diminishes another in His behavior. Rather, all aspects of His holy essence are always satisfied in what He does. Even when a righteous God must judge rebellion, He is still slow to anger, quick to forgive, and His love and mercy temper His judgments. This is the kind of Christlike behavior that God desires to see in all His children.

The Lord Jesus told His disciples that only good trees bear good fruit, and, likewise, that bad trees produce according to their nature (Matt. 7:17). His point was that a true believer is known by his or her fruit in the same way that *"a tree is known by its fruit"* (Matt. 12:33). Apple trees do not produce pears; they bear only apples. This means that true Christians will be characterized by the fruit of the Spirit, not by works of the flesh.

The qualities of this fruit relate to three categories of associations: Love (sacrificial Christlike giving), joy (delighting in Christ), and peace (having the mind of Christ). These pertain to **our union with Christ**. Longsuffering (patience), gentleness (kindness), and goodness (doing beneficial acts) relate to **our interaction with others**. Faithfulness (loyalty and fidelity), meekness (gentleness and humility), and self-control (having mastery over desires) are **in relationship to ourselves**. Paul says, *"Against such there is no law."* Laws are established to restrain human sin and punish the guilty, so there would be nothing in these God-produced character qualities that would demand any action by law.

The Holy Spirit longs for us to experience the love, joy, and peace of Christ in our lives. These eternal qualities are found only in God. The Holy Spirit also enables us to be patient, kind, gentle, longsuffering, forgiving in our interactions with others. We want to show others the goodness of God that we ourselves are experiencing. The Holy Spirit also wants us to be full of faith, and to keep our carnal nature in check. All that we do and say should be guided by meekness and self-control.

The deeds of the flesh, such as those listed in verses 19-21, are in opposition to what God wants exhibited in the believer's life. If believers choose to engage in carnal behavior, the indwelling Spirit of God is grieved and quenched (Eph. 4:30; 1 Thess. 5:19). As believers, we do not want the Holy Spirit to oppose what we do, but rather to enable and control all that we do. This necessitates keeping short accounts with God, confessing sin, and asking for forgiveness as soon as we are aware of it (1 Jn. 1:9).

When the Holy Spirit is not in control of the believer's thinking and behavior, the flesh nature will reign. The lusting of our fallen flesh is in direct conflict with the holy nature and operations of God; thus, a constant state of war exists in the believer's members. There is nothing in the old nature that can please God (Rom. 8:8). Only when our bodies are under God's control do we have the capacity to please Him.

This battle will continue on the personal level until each believer experiences death or glorification. In Heaven we will never have to suffer another stinking thought, carnal appetite, ungodly word, or selfish deed. The battle will continue on all fronts until God removes all evil from His presence in a future day. Nevertheless, in Christ and through the Holy Spirit we can be more than conquerors today (Rom. 8:37)!

Paul states an identification truth in verse 24: *"All those who are Christ's have crucified the flesh with its passions and desires."* The aorist tense and active voice of the verb rendered "have crucified" would indicate that the subject *"All those who are Christ's"* (i.e., those in Christ) completed an action in the past. What is something that everyone has done to become one with Christ? We have affirmed that we are condemned sinners and that through repentance and confession of faith in Christ we stand with God against ourselves to receive His gift of salvation in Christ.

Paul's point is that a believer in the Lord Jesus Christ has, by believing, declared that previously, in the flesh, he was spiritually dead in trespasses and sins. Moreover, those in Christ have agreed with God that their flesh nature was offensive to Him and had nothing acceptable to offer Him. This declaration at conversion is the meaning of *"crucified the flesh with its passions and desires."* Hamilton Smith summarizes this declaration of faith: "The true Christian position is that we accept the cross of Christ as the judgment of God upon the flesh, in order that we should no longer live by the flesh but 'by the Spirit.'"[52]

God's solution for believers to overcome the flesh's impulses begins by understanding the positional truth of our co-crucifixion with Christ (Rom. 6:6). In Adam, we were *"made subject to vanity"* (Rom. 8:20). At the cross, the Old Man, the man in Adam, the man that we once were, the man who was dominated and controlled by the flesh, died with Christ. The purpose of crucifixion was to end a life, though death itself would occur some hours or days later. From God's perspective, believers have been crucified with Christ so that their craving flesh will eventually die (i.e., there should be a diminishing influence of the old nature in believers as they mature in Christ). Dying by crucifixion is a slow and agonizing process, but it is necessary so that believers can please God as they ought.

Paul exhorts the Galatians, and us too, that since we have received eternal life in Christ by the Holy Spirit, we must live this new life in the power of the Holy Spirit (v. 25). Spiritual life in Christ should exhibit spiritual power. Verse 25 concludes Paul's charge to walk in the Spirit and also introduces a new subject. That is, how to practically live for God having received new life in Christ. Beginning with verse 26, the apostle provides a number of practical helps and exhortations for Spirit-enabled, godly living.

In the final verse, Paul exhorts us to avoid three attitudes if we are to walk in the Spirit and be fruitful for God. First, since Christians have their boast in Christ alone, they should therefore avoid conceit (i.e., having an empty or deceptive opinion of ourselves). Second, believers should not provoke one another to anger by imposing their personal standards of conduct on other believers or interjecting unwanted opinions into their affairs. Third, those who are Christ's should not envy one another (i.e., we should not be driven by desire for what belongs to another. Rather, we should give thanks to God for what we have).

# Galatians Chapter 6

## Our Life in Christ Blesses Others (vv. 1-10)

The apostle launches into a string of exhortations to assist the Galatians in living for Christ in the freedom He grants. The first charge is, *"Brethren, if a man is overtaken in any trespass, you who are spiritual restore such a one in a spirit of gentleness, considering yourself lest you also be tempted"* (v. 1). Perhaps Paul was equipping believers who had not been tainted by legalism to confront and restore those who had. Warren Wiersbe observes that a legalist has no interest in bearing other people's burdens. Rather he adds to the burdens of others (Acts 15:10):

> This was one of the sins of the Pharisees in Jesus' day: *"For they bind heavy burdens and grievous to be borne, and lay them on men's shoulders; but they themselves will not move them with one of their fingers"* (Matt. 23:4). The legalist is always harder on other people than he is on himself, but the Spirit-led Christian demands more of himself than he does of others *that he might be able to help others.*[53]

Believers cannot truly help a sinning brother or sister unless they are first humble in the Lord, innocent of the offense themselves, have pure selfless motives, and are dedicated to obeying His Word. Only with this attitude can the work of correction and restoration be effective. Those who are truly spiritual will in this way restore a fellow brother or sister who has been overtaken by a trespass (i.e., sin; this is more than just a fault or personal offense). This is especially important, if the one engaged in restoring another was the one wronged by the errant believer.

Next, the Galatians are charged to *"bear one another's burdens, and so fulfill the law of Christ"* (v. 2). Deuteronomy 15:11 reads, *"For the poor will never cease from the land; therefore, I command you, saying, 'You shall open your hand wide to your brother, to your poor and your needy, in your land.'"* Although not a command for Christians today, this verse does highlight what God deems as fitting conduct for His people in all ages, that is, to rally around and help each other during times of distress. On this point William Kelly writes:

There are difficulties, trials, sorrows; there are things in the shape of infirmity; there are circumstances of the most variedly painful nature that press upon the children of God. Now, if we wish to show our value for the saints, opportunity need not be lacking. *"Bear ye one another's burdens, and so fulfill the law of Christ."* Stoop down, and take up that which your brother groans under. The Ten Commandments may not demand it, but so you will fulfill the law *of Christ*. This is the law for us Christians. It is not a question of the law of Moses, because although that was the law of God, and always must be the measure with which God deals with the natural man, He is dealing here with those who were living in the Spirit, and the law at Sinai was never given to the spiritual man, but to a fleshly people, even to Israel.[54]

It is Christlike to *"bear one another's burdens."* The Greek verb *bastazo* rendered "bear" means "to carry" and the noun *baros*, translated "burdens," implies a crushing load. There are times in life when we may be unexpectedly buried by a crushing load. It is at those times believers must readily support each other. For example, the early Church cared for their poor widows (Acts 6:1; 1 Tim. 5:3-5). Early believers did not value their possessions (of which they were merely God's stewards) more than each other (Acts 4:32). As a result of this loving unselfishness, all the Lord's people were wonderfully sustained: *"nor was there anyone among them who lacked"* (Acts 4:34). God forbid that we, who have received so much goodness in Christ, should *"oppress one another"* by withholding our temporal possessions from our brethren in need (Lev. 25:14, 17).

Paul reminds us that we are all of like passions, and if it were not for the grace of God, each of us would be capable of doing the most hideous works of unrighteousness (v. 3). Realizing this should keep us broken before the Lord. It should pain us to confront another's sin. If we gain any personal satisfaction in the process, then we have the wrong attitude!

A different type of load is spoken of in verses 4-5: *"But let each one examine his own work, and then he will have rejoicing in himself alone, and not in another. For each one shall bear his own load."* The word "load" in verse 5 is derived from the Greek word *phortion* and closely resembles the bearing of a soldier's backpack. It is used here to speak of the daily duties that we are assigned and expected to bear for the Lord. This represents our daily assignments in service to the Lord and no other soldier of the cross is to take over those duties from us. So let us do what we know we must do for the Lord and be ready to help those being overwhelmed by a crisis.

The next apostolic exhortation pertains to blessing (i.e., sharing of good things) those who have taught us God's Word (v. 6). The New Testament indicates that Church workers were supported by the Lord and were not employed by local churches. Serving the Lord is not a career to be chosen, but a heavenly calling to be fulfilled! God enables the worker's ministry and is responsible for supporting them financially (Phil. 4:10-19; Col. 4:17). Since He most often accomplishes this through His people, Paul emphasizes that those spiritually blessed by ministry have a "duty" to support those who blessed them (Rom. 15:27).

Paul then applies sowing and reaping principles (vv. 7-8) to faithful service and rewards (vv. 9-10). Those who sow to the flesh will reap corruption and those who sow to the Spirit will reap life: *"Do not be deceived, God is not mocked; for whatever a man sows, that he will also reap. For he who sows to his flesh will of the flesh reap corruption, but he who sows to the Spirit will of the Spirit reap everlasting life."*

There are three inescapable laws of the harvest associated with carnality and spiritual life. First, we reap what we sow: if we sow to the flesh, we reap corruption, but if we sow to the Spirit of God, we reap a spiritual harvest which God will reward. Second, we reap later than we sow. If we sow to the flesh corruption may continue for a long time thereafter, but if we sow to the Spirit a beneficial and eternal spiritual harvest is reaped. Third, we reap more than we sow. The results of sowing to the flesh are much more devastating than what we could ever imagined. Likewise, our eternal reward for sowing to the Spirit will greatly exceed what we can ever comprehend.

For this reason, Paul charges the Galatians: *"And let us not grow weary while doing good, for in due season we shall reap if we do not lose heart. Therefore, as we have opportunity, let us do good to all, especially to those who are of the household of faith* (vv. 9-10). While it is certainly possible to grow *weary in* the Lord's work, we never want to be *weary of* it. The Lord's servants can give out only what they receive from the Lord themselves. So, if physical exhaustion and emotional anxiety continue to characterize our service to the Lord – there is something wrong! Either we are serving as we should, but in the power of the flesh, or we are not serving as we should by the power of the Spirit.

It is important to accomplish the work God assigns, regardless of how we feel about the nature of the work, or about doing it. Paul encourages us to be especially motivated to serve those in the Body of Christ (Eph. 2:19; 1 Tim. 3:15) – *"let us do good to all"* (v. 10). Those who faithfully serve the Lord now, despite expense, hardships and persecutions, will be amply rewarded in due season at the Judgment Seat of Christ. Then, all of the labor and warfare associated with our earthly sojourn will be over.

## Conclusion (vv. 11-18)

In closing the epistle, Paul picks up the pen and writes the final verses in his own hand (v. 11). Typically, he dictated his epistles to a scribe, and then wrote the closing himself (Rom. 16:22; 1 Cor. 16:21; Col. 4:18; 2 Thess. 3:17). Some have suggested that Paul wrote the entire epistle to the Galatians to stress the significance of avoiding legalism and living in the liberty that Christ offers. However, all Scripture is God-breathed and the one who actually penned the letters (an apostle or a scribe working with an apostle) is not important to the validity of Scripture. It seems more likely that Paul wrote only the final section by his own hand or he would have mentioned the matter earlier in the letter. Apparently because of poor eyesight he needed to write in large letters (4:15).

The apostle again rebukes the "many" who "make a good showing in the flesh" through circumcision, rather than preaching the truth of the cross of Christ and suffering for doing so (v. 12). Under the Law, the Jews were bound to circumcise their male infants eight days after birth. The mark of circumcision was given to Abraham and his posterity as a reminder of the covenant God had entered into with the Patriarch and his descendants (Gen. 17). The Law given at Sinai through Moses to the Jews was theirs exclusively. Its precepts and regulations were not given to the Gentile nations (Acts 15:10).

This is why Paul exhorts the Galatians not to give ear to the Judaizers. These legalists were teaching that salvation was by grace through Christ, but that a believer had to also continue keeping the Law to maintain his or her salvation. As the Galatians had never been under the Law, it was irrational for the Judaizers to place them under its bondage now, especially since the Law only condemned (as no one could keep it) and it provided no assistance in living for Christ.

The circumcision insisted upon by the Judaizers did nothing to assist them in keeping the Law. Neither could it contribute any benefit to Gentile believers in serving Christ (v. 13). The legalists were wearing the badge of the Law (i.e., circumcision) without feeling guilty about breaking the Law's commands. Circumcision was the easy part – the rite was performed by a rabbi when they were babies as a result of their parents' obedience, not theirs. The legalists did not fully obey the Law which meant they were guilty before God, circumcised or not. Keeping only one part of the Law did not make a person spiritual in the sight of God. Accordingly, Paul concludes that the only reason the legalists wanted the Gentiles circumcised was so they could boast in their influence over them.

Therefore, Paul used the strongest language he could muster to assert that when a person has trusted in the gospel of Jesus Christ thereby becoming a new creation, he could never again embrace legalistic religion or worldly secular ideologies. The believer's boast is exclusively in the means of his or her salvation, that is, through the finished work of the Lord Jesus Christ on the cross (v. 14).

Paul puts the matter this way: *"the world has been crucified to me, and I to the world."* The Greek verb rendered "crucified" is in the imperative mood, passive voice, and perfect tense. This means that Paul could not boast of anything but the cross of Christ, since through it, the power of God had carved him out of the world forever. Spiritually speaking, he could never again be part of an anti-God system that hates Christ. Christ's cross is like a sharp knife that cuts believers out of that which is dead and makes them alive forever in Christ.

In the dispensation of the Church Age, physical circumcision or uncircumcision provides no spiritual benefit (vv. 15-16). The system of the Law and the gift of grace cannot be combined to transform condemned sinners into new creations in Christ. Only those who are in Christ will enjoy God's peace and mercy. The point of the parable told by the Lord Jesus concerning a new patch on an old wine skin is that no religious system is capable of joining together the Law and grace. Each has a distinct purpose – he former to expose sin; the latter, God's means of offering salvation to all (that takes effect in the lives of all who believe).

To silence his critics, Paul offers one final proof of his apostolic authority and that the message he preached was from God – the many scars that he bore in his body (v. 17). Satan hates the message of Jesus Christ and, as the Lord promised, His servants will suffer for preaching it (John 15:18-20). The Judaizers were touting their circumcision as a symbol of true spirituality, but they did nothing to obtain that mark. Conversely, Paul had an abundance of marks in his body that spoke of his personal dedication to Christ. There was really no comparison between the visible faithful testimony of the apostle and the hidden claims of these false teachers.

The tragic departure from the truth by many of the Galatians caused the apostle to conclude his epistle without any of his typical affectionate pleasantries. Despite the restraint of his customary warmth, Paul earnestly desired that the grace of God would be with them. His closing remark not only conveys that aspiration, but also summarizes the theme of his epistle to the Galatians: *"Brethren, the grace of our Lord Jesus Christ be with your spirit. Amen."* The grace of God is able to overcome the world's opposition to the true message of salvation and sanctification through the Lord Jesus Christ!

# Ephesians

## Background

Ephesus, on the western coast of Asia Minor (modern-day Turkey), was one of three major seaports of the Aegean Sea (Thessalonica and Corinth being the other two). Its busy port made Ephesus one of the leading commercial centers in the Roman Empire. A good portion of the commerce and paganism of that day related to the worship of the great Ephesian goddess Artemis. In fact, so many people had turned from idols to worshiping Christ in Ephesus that the silversmith Demetrius, whose business was manufacturing and selling idols, stirred up a citywide riot while Paul was there during his third missionary trip.

Ephesians is one of four epistles written during Paul's first imprisonment in Rome which commenced approximately 60 A.D. and lasted about two years. Paul was under house arrest during much of this time but had much more liberty to engage in ministry than during his second Roman imprisonment a few years later, which culminated in his death. Drawing from Luke's account of Paul's journeys as recorded in Acts, Paul dedicated a total of about three years ministry time to Ephesus, meaning that he spent more time there than anywhere else before his imprisonments.

Paul had worked diligently in Ephesus, taking the gospel message house to house as well as preaching in public (Acts 20:20). By God's grace, a church testimony was established. The kindred spirit of Paul and the Ephesian believers is clearly witnessed in Paul's farewell to the Ephesian elders at Miletus, where much sentiment and affection were mutually displayed in their parting (Acts 20:36-38). Paul's familiarity with and appreciation for the saints at Ephesus gird the epistle with a warmth well-suited to declaring the timeless mysteries of God accomplished in Christ.

## Theme(s)

Mysteries concerning the Body of Christ: The Church (composed of Jews and Gentiles) sitting with Christ in heavenly places, walking with Him in humble service, and standing fast in Him by the Holy Spirit against Satanic opposition.

## Keywords

Keywords and phrases include: "mystery," "grace," "love," "spirit," "spiritual," "walk," "fellowship," "one" (speaking of unity), "peace," "power," "understanding," "will" (as in God's will), "fullness," and "in Christ" (as related to blessings in Christ).

## Date

Ephesians was written during Paul's first Roman imprisonment in 60-61 A.D. It was likely the first of four prison epistles written during Paul's incarceration.

## Outline

The first three chapters concentrate largely on doctrine: the heavenly wealth that believers have in Christ; positional truth is stressed. The last three chapters focus on duty: instructing believers how to live the heavenly enriched life now; practical service is stressed. Someone composed the following poem to colorfully express the doctrinal flow of Ephesians:

> What we *were* by nature.
> What we *are* by grace.
> What we *will* be in glory.
> And how it all took place.

I. Introduction (1:1-2).
II. The *Wealth* a Christian possesses in Christ (1:3-3:21).
III. The *Walk* a Christian maintains with Christ (4:1-5:33).
IV. The *Warfare* a Christian withstands through Christ (6:1-20).

# Ephesians Chapter 1

## Introduction (vv. 1-2)

The letter to the Ephesians commences with the same type of salutation found in other Pauline epistles to churches. The author is stated: Paul (v. 1). The Latin root of Paul's name means "little" and this lowly demeanor typified his strenuous service to the Lord; he considered himself to be "the least of all saints" (3:8). His authority as an apostle (a "sent one") of Jesus Christ by the will of God is affirmed. The addressees of the epistle are the saints gathered in the church at Ephesus, and more generally "the faithful [believing ones] in Christ Jesus," indicating a much wider audience.

Because these believers had been justified in Christ (i.e., they had been declared positionally righteous in Christ by God; Rom. 4:21-25), Paul refers to them as "saints" (v. 2). Obviously, Paul is addressing living people on earth, not the deceased who had been given some special heavenly status by humanized religion. In short, all who have trusted Christ and have been regenerated by the Holy Spirit have an eternal and righteous standing before God (2 Cor. 5:21). Scripture often refers to Christians as "saints" (Col. 1:12; Jude 3). Accordingly, Paul typically addressed his epistles to the saints gathered together at some particular locale (e.g., 1 Cor. 1:2; Phil. 1:1).

Continuing his salutation, Paul declares *"grace to you and peace from God our Father and the Lord Jesus Christ"* (v. 2). This is Paul's trademark greeting and is word for word how he saluted the Romans and the Corinthians (Rom. 1:7; 1 Cor. 1:3). *Grace* was a greeting that the Greeks commonly used, while Jewish believers traditionally referred to the blessing of *peace* to convey a how-do-you-do.

## To the Praise of His Glory (vv. 3-14)

It is important to have a dispensational view of Scripture to better understand the mysterious truths that Paul reveals in this epistle. The kingdom gospel message the Lord Jesus and His disciples preached throughout Israel offered a literal, political, earthly kingdom to the Jewish nation. It was not received by the Jews because they rejected the spiritual requirements necessary to enter into it, namely, repentance and spiritual renewal in Christ. Instead, Israel crucified her Messiah, God's Lamb, according to God's providential plan (1 Pet. 1:19-20). Throughout most of the Old Testament era the Jews longed for, expected, and fought for a kingdom. Their motivation was based in God's promise to them of a land inheritance, enshrined in a covenant between God and Abraham (Gen. 15).

Consequently, God's promises to Israel have an earthly focus, but Christ's promises to the Church are for a heavenly inheritance. Paul writes: *"Blessed be the God and Father of our Lord Jesus Christ, who has blessed us with every spiritual blessing in the heavenly places in Christ"* (v. 3). Christians, from God's perspective, are citizens of Heaven who are representing Him on earth (Phil. 3:20). God is not stingy. He has made available to those who are in Christ "every spiritual blessing" (the untold wealth of Heaven) equipping them to accomplish this ambassadorial task.

In the Church Age, believers do not labor for a *place* of rest as Israel did, and still does. Instead, our rest and inheritance are in a *Person* – Christ in the heavenly places. This is why Paul could pray for fellow believers, *"The Lord of peace Himself give you peace in every way"* (2 Thess. 3:16). Christ is the believer's inheritance and resting place. The blessing and effectiveness of the heavenly possessions granted to the believer in Christ are practically experienced as he exercises faith and obedience while actively engaged in spiritual conquest energized by the resurrection power of the Lord Jesus Christ. In Christian experience, the portion of the spiritual inheritance possessed and enjoyed by believers is directly related to their personal familiarity with the Lord's gracious and holy character.

The Lord does not bestow such things as power and authority lightly. These are received in measure and in accordance with the believer's capacity to retain each gift of grace in faith, love, and humility. To be the steward of that which cannot be managed with wisdom would surely result in a worse outcome than not having that possession at all. Believers have different spiritual gifts, callings of ministry, talents to serve, and developed maturity in Christ. This means that each of us has different and varying capacities to receive and retain resurrection power as a spiritual possession (Phil. 3:10-16). Instead of living like paupers, may each believer lay hold of the vast heavenly resources that are available in Christ!

To lay hold of our spiritual possessions in heavenly places, believers must travel along an unencumbered path of righteousness, although the flesh will constantly attempt to block the way and encumber the believer with detours of disobedience to the Lord. The flesh must therefore be fought, beaten, and driven out of the way again and again. This is how believers experience and benefit from their spiritual blessings in Christ. The enemy must be engaged and defeated in the Lord's strength.

The phrases "in Christ" (v. 3) or "in Him" are significant in the epistles of the New Testament. The phrase "in Christ" generally speaks of the blessings believers have because of their position in Him, while the phrase "with Him" centers on timeless identification truths with respect to what Christ accomplished for us concerning our salvation. "With Christ" addresses how the Father sees us in relationship with His Son (e.g., seated with Him in heavenly places; 2:6). In verses 3, 4, and 6, we learn that believers are "blessed" in Christ, "chosen" in Christ, and "accepted" in Christ. *Echaritsen,* rendered as "accepted," is rendered "highly favored" in Luke 1:28. In Christ, the believer enjoys the fullness of divine favor and complete acceptance with God.

Moreover, the expression "in the heavenly places," mentioned five times in the epistle, is vital to the thematic development of Paul's message. With Christ in Heaven is where our spiritual blessings reside (v. 3). This is where Christ is enthroned (v. 20) and where we are presently enthroned with Him (2:6). It is from this high vantage point that God is using the Church to teach the angels about His manifold wisdom (3:10). Believers can only triumph over spiritual wickedness in high places by resting in Christ where He is enthroned representing the highest place of Heaven's authority.

The sectional construction of verses 3-14 is for an important emphasis. Paul inserts a note of praise, for example, "for the praise of His glory," in verses 6, 12, and 14 to create three divisions, each pertaining to the role of the Godhead in our salvation. In verses 2-6, the will of God the Father is expressed in the overall plan to save and bless the condemned. In verses 7-12, it is the redemptive work of Christ for the condemned, in the will of the Father, that is paramount. In verses 13-14, we see the witness of the Holy Spirit to secure those Christ has redeemed and who God the Father is determined to bless through adoption is declared.

In verse 4, we learn that God the Father chose us in Christ for a purpose before anything was created, namely, to be a holy people with a blameless standing before Him. According to the Father's will and for the praise of His glory, we are made positionally acceptable to Him in Christ and are therefore predestined to be fully *son-placed* as the ultimate goal of our salvation (vv. 5-6). Albert Leckie suggests that God's choice to bless redeemed sinners includes the elements of sphere, time, and purpose:

> Paul acquaints us with the *sphere* [a medium], *time* and *purpose* of God's choice. The sphere was "in Christ": the choice of the individual was in Christ and not because of anything in the individual. The time was "before the foundation of the world" (see also John 17:24; 1 Pet.

1:20): before the world was made and time commenced and man had been introduced or sin had entered. The purpose was "that we should be holy and without blame before him in love." While the thought of "before him" anticipates the future, yet all of this is now true in essence of the saints of God. What the church will be on that great day when Christ presents it to Himself (5:27), so each child of God is in essence now and will be eternally before the face of God.[55]

The key words that Paul chose to express God's profound plan of salvation are important. The Greek verb *exelexato,* rendered "He chose" or "He has chosen" (v. 4), speaks of specific purposes (choices) in time that God will accomplish to ensure the greatest opportunity to bless those son-placed in Christ. Examples include selecting Christ (1 Pet. 2:6), the selection of Christ's disciples including Judas (John 13:18, 15:16), and the formation of the Church (Eph. 1:4). Warren Wiersbe observes that biblical election (God's choosing) is always "unto something":

> God chose us even before He created the universe, so that our salvation is wholly of His grace and not on the basis of anything we ourselves have done. He chose us *in Christ*, not in ourselves. And He chose us for a purpose: to be holy and without blame. In the Bible, election is always *unto* something. It is a privilege that carries a great responsibility. Does the sinner respond to God's grace against his own will? No, he responds because God's grace makes him willing to respond. The mystery of divine sovereignty and human responsibility will never be solved in this life. Both are taught in the Bible (John 6:37). Both are true, and both are essential.[56]

"Having predestinated" (vv. 5, 11) is derived from *proorisas*, and means to "mark out beforehand." "Predestination" expresses the determination of God, based on his foreknowledge before time began, to complete "the adoption of sons" for all believers. His predetermination guarantees that all things will work out to ensure all believers are conformed to the moral image of Christ (Rom. 8:29) and will inherit all that is Christ's (Rom. 8:17; Rev. 21:7). Predestination is God's plan that bridges His foreknowledge (before He created anything) with the enduring results of what He desires and will accomplish in eternity on behalf of all believers. Ultimately, God will share His eternal love with "a holy and without blame" people who will be with Him! By grace, God chose to make us suitable to Himself and for His good pleasure; He predestinates believers to the relationship of sons.

Thus, "the adoption of sons," translated from *huiothesian*, represents the ultimate goal of the believer's salvation – to be fully son-placed (Gal. 4:5).

Only an adult son receives his full inheritance and governing authority (Col. 3:24). While salvation of the soul occurs by trusting in the gospel message of Christ, the benefits and blessings of that salvation are not fully entered into until the believer's body has been redeemed and transformed into a glorious body (v. 14). Believers receive bodies fit for Heaven at the Rapture of the Church (1 Cor. 15:51-52) and come into their full inheritance when Christ obtains His (Rom. 8:14-15). Then believers will rule and reign with Christ (2 Tim. 2:12). Adoption, here, speaks of what God does for believers.

Another key concept associated with God's salvation prerogative is His "foreknowledge," which is derived from the Greek *prognosis* (Rom. 8:29; 1 Pet. 1:2). God's foreknowledge permits Him the ability to design the plan of salvation before time, with all the facts, possible permutations of events and outcomes in time at hand. As cause-and-effect relationships, man's failures, and Satan's evil doings are all foreknown by God, nothing can foil His purposes, or the end goal of blessing faith-exercising individuals through Christ. God's predestined plan of salvation in Christ begins with His foreknowledge and concludes with son-placement of believers. Many sovereign choices in time are necessary to ensure the sonship of believers in God's eternal design.

One of these sovereign choices was the predetermined death of His Son at Calvary (1 Pet. 1:18-20). Only by the shed blood of Christ can guilty sinners be forgiven, redeemed, and cleansed to enjoy the riches of God's grace in Christ (v. 7). God's plan of complete salvation that He purposed in Christ was previously hidden, for if the devil had understood what God was accomplishing at the cross, he would not have crucified the Lord Jesus (1 Cor. 2:8-9). But after Christ's resurrection, the mystery of God's will, that was fostered in wisdom and prudence for His good pleasure, was revealed in the gospel message of Jesus Christ (vv. 8-9). The New Testament epistles then reveal to us the vast implications of what God had previously kept secret before time began.

It is regrettable that much needless division in the Body of Christ has occurred in debating the mysterious aspects of our salvation, which God alone fully understands. While Christians have differing opinions about the work of the Holy Spirit necessary to bring a sinner to repentance and receive Christ in faith, clearly that divine work (illumination, conviction, etc.), whatever it may be, rests with God. The Church has been tasked by Christ to be witnesses for Him in the world (Acts 1:8) and to share the gospel message throughout the world (Matt. 28:19-20). Therefore, we should permit God to do what only He can do, and we should be doing what we are commanded to do. Arguing about what we cannot fully understand now is a waste of time. It keeps us from obeying what we are supposed to do, which then hinders the fruitfulness that God demands in our lives. If the devil can keep us busy arguing about non-essentials, he wins!

As before mentioned, verses 7-12 speak of Christ's role in our salvation. He is the one who redeemed us by His own blood, forgave us our offenses (v. 7), and then went to Heaven to secure our inheritance in Himself (v. 11). In modern terms, we might say that Christ through legal adoption and redemption brought us into His family, then wrote us into His *Last Will and Testament*, died to put it into force, and then rose from the grave to be our Advocate in Heaven to ensure every detail will come about.

Verse 10 speaks of the latter event, that is, when believers come into their inheritance. It occurs in a future dispensation (a stewardship or an economy of truth revealed to man by God) that will mark the fullness of time when Christ gathers all that is His to Himself and His inheritance is received. This is the goal of God's salvation for us that was predestined in Christ before time began. Those who are redeemed by Christ will have an inheritance with Christ. Paul applies the pronoun "we" in verses 11-12 to note that the Jews received this opportunity before the Gentiles did. The realization of the believer's sonship will occur during the millennial reign of Christ on earth – the Kingdom Age. When Christ comes into his inheritance and rulership, so do we in Him.

After Paul speaks of the wonderful blessings that those who have been redeemed by Christ have in Him, the apostle highlights why Christ still has His Church in the world: that we *"should be to the praise of His glory."* Paul mentions this idea three times in this narrative (vv. 6, 12, 14). Why is the Church not in Heaven with Christ? The main reason we remain on the earth is to show the goodness of Christ to others – to make Him look good – to be the praise of His glory. When Christ determines that this work is complete, He will come to receive His Bride and return to Heaven with Her.

Through our spiritual sanctification, the Lord gets more glory from us as we become more like Him (Rom. 8:29). Believers should sin less with spiritual maturity (Rom. 6:1), though sinless perfection will not be achieved until we experience glorification at His coming (1 Jn. 3:2-3). To be *the praise of His glory*, believers must be marked by righteous living. Nearness to Christ enables us to experience Him and permits us to express His glory. God the Father desires that we would honor His dear Son. This should prompt us to consider what we do and say, and to stay near to the Lord.

Although the securing work of the Holy Spirit that Paul speaks of in verses 13-14 is true for all Christians, Paul switches from speaking to Jewish believers (including himself in the "we"; vv. 11-12), to addressing Gentile believers ("you"; vv. 13-14). By doing so, Paul is supplying a preface for his teaching in chapters 2-3, as to how Gentile believers will obtain an inheritance with Jewish believers. Thus, Paul speaks of "our" inheritance in verse 14, as both redeemed Jews and Gentiles have an inheritance in Christ.

There are a number of one-time acts that the Holy Spirit accomplishes at a believer's conversion. Spiritual baptism, indwelling, anointing, cleansing, regeneration, and the bestowing of spiritual gifts are some, to name a few. Also, the Holy Spirit seals and secures the new believer by taking up permanent residency within him or her (v. 13). The Holy Spirit Himself, is God's guarantee that He will finish what He has started (v. 14). In a coming day, the Lord Jesus will return to claim His purchased possession that was previously redeemed by His blood (1 Cor. 1:6-9).

This eternal seal is likened to the wax seal placed on a letter or scroll in ancient times. Such a seal protected and secured the letter from being opened, and it also indicated who the originator and owner of the letter was. In some cases, seals were used to indicate approval of a contract or an agreement. Through the sealing ministry of the Holy Spirit, the believer is both approved of and secured in Christ forever!

## Praying for Comprehension (vv. 15-23)

Paul offers two prayers on behalf of the Ephesians in the epistle (vv. 15-23, 3:13-21). Paul first prays for their enlightenment and *comprehension* concerning Christ and their understanding of all the riches that are found in Him. The Church will be strong or weak depending on her concept of God and her awareness of what she has in Christ. In his second prayer, he prays for their *apprehension* of Christ – that the Ephesians would be compelled to pursue Christ with their whole being and look earnestly for His coming.

In verses 15-16, Paul revealed why he was motivated to pray for the Ephesians and to praise God for their authentic testimony. First, he was prompted to praise God for their good testimony, which was marked by faith in action and by demonstrating God's love to others. Second, he acknowledged that as he gave thanks to God for them, he was also inspired to pray for them. Although he did not know their specific needs, he knew that they would be more fruitful and joyful if God granted them further illumination *in the knowledge of Christ*.

Paul asked the Lord to give the Ephesians the spirit of wisdom and a greater personal understanding of Christ (v. 17). The apostle wanted them to have a deeper experiential and devotional knowledge of God, and to better comprehend how "the Father of glory" had resurrected and highly exalted "the Son of Man" in Heaven (Acts 7:55-56). A loving heart rises above one's intellect to appreciate what Christ has achieved and to honor Him the way that the Father desires us to. This is why the apostle asked the Lord to enlighten the eyes of the Ephesians' *dianoia*. *Dianoia* is the mind (the heart of the heart, so to speak). Paul desired that all the feelings, knowing, and desire of the Ephesians would swell up towards Christ.

The apostle wanted them to know more about three particular spheres of divine revelation. First, of what *"the hope of His [God's] calling"* was in them (v. 18). This is different than *"the hope of your [believer's] calling"* which Paul addresses later (4:4). That calling speaks of the believer's destiny to be morally conformed to Christ through glorification (Rom. 8:29), and then to be fully son-placed to receive an eternal inheritance. This will occur after the Church has been raptured and is with Christ in His kingdom. The hope of God's calling in verse 18 speaks of God's desire for His sons to be before Him and in His love forever (vv. 4-5).

Second, Paul prayed that they would be aware of the riches of the glory of God's inheritance in (or among) the saints (v. 18). In verse 14, Paul spoke of the Holy Spirit securing the believer's inheritance yet to be possessed, but in verse 18, the inheritance is still with God (as it has not been given yet). When bestowed (when believers are son-placed), God will display the riches of His glory in His saints. Believers in Christ are God's own special people (1 Pet. 2:9; Tit. 2:14) and will inherit all things with Christ. The believer will rule and reign with Christ on the earth during the Millennial kingdom (2 Tim. 2:12).

Third, Paul prayed for them to experience the exceeding great power that "the Father of glory" demonstrated in Christ's resurrection and exaltation (vv. 19-20). The Greek word *dunamis* is rendered "power"; it is also the basis for our English word "dynamite." The Greek word *energeia* (from where our English word "energy" is derived) is translated "worked" in verse 20. The second word "power" is derived from *ischus* and speaks of God's inherent strength. It is combined with "mighty" from *kratos* to speak of a force superior to all others. All this to say that the exceeding power and energy exerted by God to raise up Christ from the grave to the heights of Heaven will also save and preserve the saints of God unto glorification (vv. 20-21). The Church has all spiritual blessings in heavenly places in Christ, and desperately needs the manifestation of resurrection power today.

The Lord Jesus Christ is the head of the Church and the center of her Body-life (vv. 22-23; Col. 1:18). Paul refers to Psalm 8:6 to affirm that God the Father has placed Christ above all powers, all principalities, all dominions. The Lord Jesus has a name to be valued above all others; He is the King of kings and Lord of lords. God the Father is honored when the

Church worships and adores His Son in accordance with His divine essence and His exalted position (John 5:22-23).

Regrettably, the truth of Christ's headship is distorted by unbiblical behaviors such as having elected church officials and maintaining denominations and centralized headquarters that rule over local churches. The ideological ideas that formed these organizations initially define what, or who, is important to them. Instead, under Christ's authority as Head, believers are to gather in autonomous groups (local churches) according to His order for His Body (1 Cor. 14:23, 33).

Some identify themselves by a particular doctrine (e.g., the Baptists), or by a form of church government (e.g., the Presbyterians), or by evangelistic methods (e.g., the Methodists), or a person (e.g., Lutherans). Others gather under the focus of spiritual gifts, social cliques, schooling preferences and family ties. Scripture does uphold the doctrines of believer's baptism, spiritual gifts, plural church oversight, and differing evangelistic methods, but we do not gather to these things; we gather in the name of Christ. To come together for any other reason is to ignore our Head and to supplant His centrality in the meeting.

Paul informs us that not only do all believers compose the Body of Christ, but that He, as the Head of that Body, will return to gather all those who are His to Himself. Then, all believers, in His presence, will forever enjoy the *"fullness of Him who fills all in all."* William MacDonald writes:

> This simply means that the church is the complement of Christ, who is everywhere at one and the same time. A complement is that which fills up or completes. It implies two things which when brought together constitute a whole. Just as a body is the complement of the head, so the church is the complement of Christ. But lest anyone should think this implies any imperfection or incompleteness in Christ, Paul quickly adds, **the fullness of Him who fills all in all**. Far from His needing anything to fill up any lack of completeness, the Lord Jesus is Himself the One **who fills all in all**, who permeates the universe and supplies it with all that it needs.[57]

In His essence, as God, Christ is completely self-sufficient. But from a relationship perspective, Christ is not whole without His bride. Hence, believers are to eagerly long for the fruition in God's timing, of all that in faithfulness Christ has achieved. The Lord Jesus Himself waits with blissful anticipation to be with His glorious bride and to establish His eternal kingdom (Isa. 53:11). Until summoned home by the call of the archangel, may each believer count on the faithfulness of God to enter into His rest.

# Ephesians Chapter 2

### Saved by Grace Through Faith (vv. 1-10)

In the previous chapter, Paul highlighted the spiritual *possessions* believers have in Christ in heavenly places through redemption and adoption. In this chapter, he addresses the spiritual *position* believers have in Christ through regeneration. Previously, Paul spoke of the Church as Christ's own Body, but in this chapter, the Church is a spectacular Temple that He is building, composed of both Jews and Gentiles.

Death, generally speaking, in the Bible implies some type of *separation*. Either physical death, when the body and soul separate, or spiritual death, speaking of our spiritual separation from a holy God because of sin. Paul affirms that we were all born spiritually dead as a consequence of Adam's sin, but once an individual trusts the gospel of Christ, the Holy Spirit regenerates and implants eternal life within that individual. He or she is given life as a new creation in Christ (v. 1).

Both the unregenerate and believers are described as children (sons) in Scripture. Paul has already explained that believers in Christ are sons of God waiting to receive their full inheritance. In this chapter, the apostle describes the unregenerate as "sons of disobedience" (v. 2). Elsewhere those who are not children of God are referred to as "children of the devil" and "children of wrath" (1 Jn. 3:10; Col. 3:6). In contrast, believers are called "children (sons) of God," "children of light," "children of obedience," and "children of Abraham (i.e., of faith)" (5:8; Rom. 8:16; Gal. 3:7, 26; 1 Pet. 1:14). The former describes those who follow the devil in rebellion against God, while the latter speaks of those who honor God by abiding in Christ.

Before regeneration, believers followed the devil, walking according to secular ideologies, and gratifying the passions of our fallen nature (v. 3). We were dead in trespasses and sins and enslaved by these three masters, but through Christ we were liberated to serve Him. Yet, this does not mean that we are not vulnerable to the evil influences of our old masters: the devil, the world, and the flesh. Although we are not enslaved to them anymore, they still seek to master us.

Most of us have seen a drum major or majorette lead a marching band down a spectator-lined street during a parade. In your mind's eye, picture

Satan as a drum major who is leading a group of disorderly zombies down a wide way. This mob of ruffians follows their leader wherever he goes and does his bidding with uncanny fervency. These walking corpses eat his food, behave like him, walk like him, listen to his music, and enjoy his entertainment. The members of this band proudly engage in lying, stealing, blasphemy, and all sorts of lascivious behavior as they march along. Bang! Pound! Bam! The drums of rebellion sound. The cadence both energizes and enrages their rebel ranks. Where is this unruly mob headed? Their leader knows, but most of those following him have no idea that they're on a one-way trip to the Lake of Fire, a place created by God to punish Satan and his fallen angels (Matt. 25:41).

The devil's main ambition is to lead as many as possible of those who bear the image of God away from Him and the salvation He offers. As Satan knows his doom is sealed (Rev. 12:12, 20:10), he is determined to lead as many as possible into Hell's eternal flames (Rev. 13:15, 19:20-21). This parade imagery pictures man's natural state in the world. God can have no fellowship with these children of the devil in the zombie band, as their allegiance, though at times unwittingly rendered, is to His archenemy.

One of the most awe-inspiring expressions in Scripture is found in verse 4, *"but God."* Found forty-two times in our Bibles "but God" normally identifies an incredible feat of God's grace in response to man's desperate need for it: *"But God demonstrates His own love toward us, in that while we were still sinners, Christ died for us"* (Rom. 5:8) and *"But God, who is rich in mercy, because of His great love with which He loved us, even when we were dead in trespasses, made us alive together with Christ (by grace you have been saved)"* (vv. 4-5). Humanity was dead in trespasses and sins, *but God* found a way to resolve our hopeless spiritual condition by grace in Christ. Be thankful for this little phrase "but God" in Scripture; without it there would be no joy in this life and no hope for a future one.

Because of God's immense love and mercy, He made those who were dead to Him alive together "with Christ" (v. 5). Believers did nothing to merit this work of God; His salvation is received by grace alone. The phrases "in Christ" or "in Him" (v. 3) or "with Him" or "with Christ" (v. 6) are significant in the epistles of the New Testament. The phrase "in Christ" generally speaks of the blessings that believers have because of their position in and union with Christ. The phrase "with Him" centers on timeless identification truths of what Christ has accomplished for us concerning our salvation. "With Christ" addresses how the Father sees us in relationship with His Son. We were made alive and were raised up with Him, and presently are seated with Him in heavenly places (vv. 5-6).

Every believer is eternally hidden with Christ (Col. 3:3). God views the believer, outside of time, with Christ in every accomplishment and blessing of redemption: crucifixion (Rom. 6:6), death (2 Tim. 2:11), burial (Rom. 6:4), revived (made alive; v. 5), risen (v. 6), seated in Heaven (v. 6), living (Rom. 6:8), glorified (Rom. 8:17), reigning (1 Cor. 4:8), and inheriting (Rom. 8:17). Through understanding these "identification truths" we gain a sense of security and cease fearing separation.

So vast is our salvation in Christ that Paul suggests that it will require all eternity for God to reveal to us what has been accomplished on our behalf: *"That in the ages to come He might show the exceeding riches of His grace in His kindness toward us in Christ Jesus"* (v. 7). This means that there is so much more of the Savior to learn than what has already been revealed to us in God's Word about Him. Indeed, there is much more truth to come, but we simply cannot comprehend it now. Nonetheless, during our earthly sojourn, we must search Scripture to know Christ more intimately.

Paul pauses to affirm that salvation in Christ Jesus is in no way earned. Rather, it is received because God is "rich in mercy" (v. 4), "great in love" (v. 4) and is determined to show His "kindness" (v. 7) towards us by demonstrating "the exceeding riches of His grace" (v. 7). *"For by grace you have been saved through faith, and that not of yourselves; it is the gift of God, not of works, lest anyone should boast"* (vv. 8-9). The word "saved" (referring to salvation) means, "deliverance, rescue, security, safety, and soundness." As shown in 2 Corinthians 1:10 and Hebrews 9:24-28, our salvation in Christ has three tenses: delivered from the penalty of sin (past), deliverance from the power of sin (present), and will yet deliver from the presence of sin (future).

Once a person is born again by an *act* of God, his or her soul is eternally saved from the penalty of sin. The believer thus becomes a child of God and that relationship is secure in Christ. In a practical way, the Lord is transforming believers into holy children; He is delivering them from the power of sin. A lifetime of refining trials, testing, and exposure to the Word is necessary for this *process* of God to take place. The Lord will return to the air and snatch all believers up into His presence, thus saving them from the presence of sin. Each believer's body will be transformed into an incorruptible, sinless, and Christ-like body. Believers will morally behave like Christ forever. The saving of the body is a one-time *act* of God. Hence, a believer has been saved, is being saved, and will be saved, but the entire process from start to finish is accomplished in grace through faith (Rom. 1:17).

Some have cited verse 8 as a proof-text for the idea that "faith" is strictly a "gift" from God and no one can be saved unless God chooses them for this gift. But the Greek text contradicts that idea. There is no specifically-stated antecedent for "gift" in this context. However, one can be inferred: the gift is the **salvation** that is implied by the verb "saved." Grammatically speaking, there is no parsing agreement between "faith" and "gift." Faith (*pisteos*) is in the feminine gender (as is "grace"), while "that" (*touto*) and "gift" (*doron*) are in the neuter gender; therefore, the "gift" is not speaking of the "faith" to believe, but rather the gift of salvation received in grace by believing.

Some have objected to this argument, contending that the verb rendered "saved" is masculine, thus it cannot be the antecedent of "gift." While it is true that the Greek verb "saved" is masculine, the verbal construction found here used in connection with a neuter pronoun "this" requires that the antecedent must also be neuter, thus "salvation" is understood to be the gift, not "faith." This, of course, is in perfect harmony with Paul's declaration elsewhere that the "gift of God is eternal life" (Rom. 6:23).

Some Bible translations render verse 8 "by grace you have been saved" (NKJV), while others, like the KJV, declare "by grace you are being saved." So which rendering is correct? Actually, in the English, it requires both aspects to express what two Greek verbs are expressing about our salvation in Christ. The verb *este* is a present tense verb that conveys the action of "you are being." The second verb, sozo, is a perfect tense verb acting as a participle to describe that we are a "having been saved" people. This verb is in the passive voice, to indicate that the previous action of God has brought forth this enduring consequence. Hence, the believer in Christ has been saved and is being saved.

Next, Paul tells us the outcome of this type of salvation is solely based in grace: *"For we are His workmanship, created in Christ Jesus for good works, which God prepared beforehand that we should walk in them"* (v. 10). In Psalm 139, David acknowledged that God not only knew everything that he would do before he did it, but He also knew his thoughts afar off. God is omniscient and omnipresent, which ensures that He knows all things within and outside of time. God knew what we would do, what we would say, and what we would think, even before we were created. Foreknowing our choices and steps in time, God has predestined good works for us to do for His glory and for our reward. Although man cannot work to earn salvation, good works are a needful testimony to the salvation which has been received from God in grace through faith (Jas. 2:17).

Because time poses no limitations on God, He foreknows our failures and our obedience, which permits Him to preordain specific works for us to accomplish. This is why Peter exhorts Christians to *"make your election sure,"* and Paul instructs us to *"walk in the works that God has foreordained."* Only by the empowerment of the Holy Spirit can we have such a testimony for Christ! Accordingly, Paul says that each believer is God's workmanship. "Workmanship" is rendered from the Greek word *poiema*, from which we also derive our English word "poem." Literally, then, each believer is a unique poem of God's grace to express the beauty and loveliness of Christ. What God conveys through us pleases Him and results in blessing and joy for us, but that which is of carnal motives and pride does not honor Him and results in our sorrow and suffering.

God's work will be accomplished by one means or another. If we are hesitant because of weak faith, He is faithful to enhance our faith, usually by involving those with faith in His purposes. Such individuals will then receive the reward that we might have earned for eternity. Deficient faith has many consequences. May God help us when our faith is weak to do those good works which He has graciously predetermined for us to walk for His glory.

## Jew and Gentile Become One in Christ (vv. 11-22)

Paul now reveals another great mystery: how the uncircumcised (the Gentiles), who were without God and Christ, and hence without any covenantal promises or hope in the world, were brought near to God through the blood of Christ (vv. 11-13). God, in His mercy, permitted the Gentiles to come into the good of the New Covenant as a second benefactor of His promise to bless Abraham's descendants. Gentiles can enter into the blessing of this covenant only by following Abraham's example of trusting God's Word by faith; in this way, they become spiritual descendants of Abraham and are able to partake of the spiritual blessings promised to his descendants (Rom. 4:11-17).

Through the New Covenant, God is able to righteously justify sinners, if they trust Christ alone for salvation (Rom. 4:23-25). Those who do so receive the gift of the Holy Spirit (John 14:16-17; 1 Cor. 12:12-13). Thus, through the gospel of Jesus Christ, those who were not God's people (the Gentiles) can become His children (Rom. 9:25-26).

How was this incredible feat accomplished? In Christ, Jew and Gentile are made one, the wall of partition (legal separation) demanded by the Mosaic Law was torn down; therefore, Christ "Himself is our peace" (v. 14-15). Christ's work of propitiation at Calvary put away the Old Covenant which resulted in animosity between the Jews and Gentiles. But the New Covenant established in Christ's own blood permits peace between Jews and Gentiles because in Christ both have peace with God: *"Therefore, having been justified by faith, we have **peace with God** through our Lord Jesus Christ"* (Rom. 5:1).

Pronoun usage in this section is extensive and Paul includes himself in these pronouns in various ways for emphasis. Albert Leckie summarizes the pronoun usage and applications in verses 11-22:

> In vv. 11–13 Paul addresses himself to the Ephesians as believers who were formerly Gentiles in the flesh: "ye [plural you] being in time past Gentiles in the flesh" (v. 11), "ye [plural you] were without Christ" (v. 12), "ye [plural you] who sometimes were far off" (v. 13). In vv. 14–18 Paul views both Gentile believers and Jewish believers as one (vv. 14, 15, 16). The "you" and "them" of v. 17 have become "our" and "we" (vv. 14, 18). Both are made one (v. 14), both are reconciled (v. 16), and both have access (v. 18). In vv. 19–22 Paul reverts to the Ephesian Gentile believers, employing as in vv. 11–13 the second person pronoun "ye" [plural you] (vv. 19, 22).[58]

The Greek word translated "peace" is *eirene*. It is derived from a verb meaning to "bond together." It literally means to "be made at one again," as reflected in Acts 7:26 when Moses sought to make two quarreling Israelites *"at one again." Eirene* is almost always translated "peace" in Scripture, but on rare occasions it is rendered "rest," "quietness," and "at one again." In this application, then, Romans 5:1 means that we are "one again" with God when we believe the gospel message – this is the saving of the soul. We are reconciled to God through the cross of Christ (v. 16).

During His earthly ministry, the Lord Jesus taught: *"Other sheep I have, which are not of this fold* [the Jewish fold.] *Them also I must bring, and they shall hear My voice; and there shall be one fold* [the Christian fold] *and one Shepherd"* (John 10:16). In the dispensation of the Church Age, *"There is neither Jew nor Greek, there is neither bond nor free, there is neither male nor female: for you are all one in Christ Jesus"* (Gal. 3:28). Consequently, Christ is our peace (v. 14), He accomplished our peace (v. 15), and He came to preach the message of peace to us (v. 17).

This message of peace is what the angels delivered to the shepherds watching over their sheep one night near Bethlehem. The initial angelic herald declared: *"I bring you good tidings of great joy which will be to all people. For there is born to you this day in the city of David a Savior, who is Christ the Lord"* (Luke 2:10-11). Afterwards an entire angelic choir appeared to praise God: *"Glory to God in the highest, and on earth peace, good will toward men"* (Luke 2:13). Having peace with God in Christ means that all past religious, social, and ethnic barriers have been removed, such that all embracing this truth enjoy peace with each other.

He has made the two (Jew and Gentile) as one in a "new man" (v. 15). This new body (v. 16) is called the Church. Reconciliation of Jews and Gentiles was possible because in Christ all are reconciled to God. Through Christ, those who had the Law and were near to God (i.e., the Jews) and those without the promises of God who were far away from God (i.e., the Gentiles) have access to God through the Holy Spirit who placed them in the Body of Christ.

Although the Jews had distinct privileges as God's covenant people and were ceremonially near to God, morally speaking, they were no different than the Gentiles. But in Christ, peace was secured. Therefore, Gentiles were no longer strangers and foreigners to the goodness of God. They had been brought near to God in the same way as the Jews – in Christ. Because both Jew and Gentile were one in Christ, they both enjoyed full access to God the Father (v. 18). Through the Holy Spirit the opportunity of continuous communion, prayer, worship, and provision can be enjoyed.

This "new man" and "one body" that Paul refers to is called the Church, the temple of God, the dwelling place of God, a spiritual house, and the house of God (vv. 19, 21; 1 Cor. 6:19-20; 1 Pet. 2:4-6; 1 Tim. 3:15). In Scripture, the members of this Body are called believers, disciples, Christians, brethren, living stones, priests, fellow citizens, and the household of God (v. 19; Acts 5:14; 9:26, 11:26; Col. 1:2). This new Temple of God created by the Holy Spirit is not physical, but spiritual in nature (v. 22).

The foundation for this mysterious temple is the gospel truth as declared by the Apostles (v. 20; Heb. 2:3-4). Before His crucifixion, Christ declared that on the "rock" of Peter's confession that He was the Christ, the Son of the Living God, He would build His Church and the gates of Hades would not prevail against it (Matt. 16:18).

Christ is the Cornerstone of the Church. His is the admired foundational cornerstone that aligns and gives strength to the building that rests on Him, because we are being built up "in" Him. Through His example and Word, He morally aligns the living stones (saved souls; 1 Pet. 2:6) who are being added to His Body and then supports them with abounding grace (v. 21).

All may appear bleak and ominous on any given day, but Christ's primary work today is to build His Church, the dwelling place of God on earth, and nothing is going to prevent that – end of story (v. 22)!

# Ephesians Chapter 3

### Paul's Stewardship of Grace (vv. 1-13)

The phrase "for this reason" in verses 1 and 14 provides a natural division in this chapter. The former section addresses the stewardship of Paul's ministry, while the latter portion contains Paul's second prayer for the Ephesians and a doxology. Paul interrupts his discourse concerning the mysterious spiritual temple that God was building to explain his own stewardship in this activity. Because the Ephesians had come to Christ and had been taught by Paul, they already knew something of his ministry (vv. 1-2). Regardless, Paul affirmed more explicitly how he had been personally tasked by Christ Jesus to take His message of peace and unmerited kindness to the Gentiles. As an apostle, Paul had become a willing prisoner of Christ and was thus bound to honor Christ's decree for his life.

A steward is someone appointed to administer the affairs of another and Paul wanted to be found faithful in *"the dispensation* [or stewardship] *of the grace of God"* (1 Cor. 4:2). Although we are not called to be apostles today as Paul was long ago, all believers have this same stewardship of grace that Paul received. We too have been commanded to be Christ's witnesses and messengers of grace throughout the world (Matt. 28:19-20; Acts 1:8).

As foretold by the prophets, God sent His beloved Son to plead with Israel to repent and be restored to God, but the Jewish nation rejected Him and had Him put to death. As Paul explained in the previous chapter, the offer of grace in Christ has been presented to the Gentiles who through faith have been brought into the commonwealth of blessing promised to Israel. As a result, Gentile believers were now bearing spiritual fruit to God. This is what God wanted from Israel, but having rejected Christ, the opportunity was given to those who were not God's covenant people (Rom. 9:25).

A dispensation describes an economy of truth that God reveals to individuals or a people which puts them under a stewardship. If obeyed, then the recipients of the promises of God will be blessed, but if rejected, God is justified in judging rebellion. The "dispensation of the grace of God" pertains to the Church Age which began at Pentecost (Acts 2) and will conclude with "the fullness of the Gentiles" (Rom. 11:25) when Christ returns to remove His Church from the earth (1 Thess. 4:13-18).

How God would fulfill His covenant promise to Abraham to bless his seed and all families of the earth through him was an unrevealed truth to any previous generation of people (Gen. 12:3). Paul refers to this sacred secret as *"the mystery of Christ"* (v. 4). This term refers to the outcome of Christ's redemptive work, the union of Jews and Gentiles with Christ to form His spiritual Body, with Him being the Head (v. 4). Paul wanted the Ephesians to understand the importance of this divine mystery.

God chose to reveal this hidden agenda directly to Paul first (v. 3), then to the apostles and prophets by the Holy Spirit (v. 5). Notice that "the mystery of Christ" was not an Old Testament reality that was hidden, but a revealed New Testament reality to be understood – the Church did not exist before Pentecost (1 Cor. 12:13; Col. 1:26). Through the preaching of the apostles and prophets and by the illumination of the Holy Spirit, those receiving their message would also be able to understand this mystery (vv. 8-9). Lastly, Paul wrote of these truths so that the Ephesians and subsequent generations of believers everywhere would be able to read about and understand what God had accomplished in Christ on their behalf (vv. 2-4).

In Christ, Gentiles would become a second benefactor of the New Covenant established with Judah and Israel (Heb. 8:8). Through trusting the gospel message, Jews and Gentiles would be fellow members in Christ's Body and fellow heirs to the unconditional blessings God promised to Abraham as obtained in Christ (v. 6). It was by this same message of grace that God powerfully worked in Paul's life and not only saved him, but also made him a minister of the gospel of grace (v. 7). Paul realized that because he had previously persecuted the Church, he was the least of the saints, and most unworthy of receiving God's grace and the privilege of revealing "the unsearchable riches of Christ" to the Gentiles (v. 8).

Previously, this good news message had been a mystery, that is, a truth tucked away deep in the vast recesses of God's mind before time began, but now had been revealed at the appropriate time in accordance with God's sovereign purposes. Paul had a twofold stewardship; he was called to preach the gospel to the Gentiles (vv. 7-8) and to enlighten believers as to how the mysteries of God in Christ were being worked out on their behalf (v. 9).

If Satan (who influences and controls worldly leaders to do evil) had understood what God was going to accomplish through Christ's death and resurrection, Satan would not have crucified Jesus Christ (1 Cor. 2:7-8). So, God kept His plan of salvation a mystery until after Christ's work of redemption and His resurrection were complete. But now, the God of Heaven wanted to reveal what had been previously concealed so that everyone could *"see what is the fellowship of the mystery"* (i.e., could share in and rejoice in what God had accomplished through Christ).

The angels watched and praised God when the foundations of creation were laid (Job 38:7), but they did not know that, even then, God had a deep secret in His heart. Before He created Adam from the dust of the earth – God had already preplanned the death of His Son (1 Pet. 1:19-20). The holy angels must have gasped as they watched God's Son tortured by feeble humans, who then nailed Him to a cross to kill Him. Heaven was silent; no command to rescue Jesus Christ was given. For hours, the holy angels observed the Son of God in flesh struggling to breathe while wretched humans insulted and mocked Him. Only God knew about the work of redemption being accomplished on humanity's behalf at Calvary. It is no wonder, then, when speaking of the sufferings and glories of Jesus Christ, Peter says, *"things which angels desire to look into"* (1 Pet. 1:12).

Today ("now"), God is demonstrating His wisdom and power to principalities (rulers) and powers (authorities) in heavenly places through His temple on earth called the Church (v. 10). Mere humans possessing the life of Christ and indwelt by the Holy Spirit are confounding Satanic opposition – all of which was according to God's masterfully executed plan, His *purpose of the ages* (v. 11). On this point, Hamilton Smith writes:

> Creation was the most perfect expression of creatorial wisdom, but in the formation of the Church God's wisdom is displayed in every form. Before the Church could be formed, God's glory had to be vindicated, man's need met, sin put away, death abolished, and the power of Satan annulled. The barrier between Jew and Gentile had to be removed, Heaven be opened, Christ be seated as Man in the glory, the Holy Spirit come to earth, and the Gospel be preached. All this and more is involved in the formation of the Church. These various ends could only be attained by the all-various wisdom of God, wisdom displayed, not only in one direction, but in every direction.[59]

God created time, and in time God reveals His sovereign purposes, so that all creation will be in awe of Him. Through the Church, the unregenerate witness the awesome nature of God and His capacity to do the unbelievable in His people, who, naturally speaking, can do nothing to please Him. In the previous chapter, Paul unveiled divine mysteries concerning Christ's Body, the Church. But before going further, he inserts a parenthetical statement about his divine stewardship in the first thirteen verses of this chapter. Now we learn why. Paul wanted the Ephesians to understand that heavenly realms were learning about the greatness of God through what He was displaying in the Church.

They, with Paul, were a part of God's spiritual temple on earth, and through Christ had bold access to the throne of Heaven – the control center of the Universe (v. 12). Through Christ, God has become our heavenly Father, meaning that we, with reverential awe, may eagerly approach Him with unhindered access and without fear (Heb. 4:16). Moreover, if we petition Him in faith and in integrity, we may be confident that He will listen to and act favorably in response to our requests (1 Jn. 5:14).

The "therefore" in verse 13 explains what Paul hoped to accomplish through explaining "the mystery of Christ" that had been entrusted to him. The Ephesians were not to lose heart, or be discouraged about his imprisonment, which had been for their benefit. Rather, they were to rejoice in what God was accomplishing through his ministry – Christ was building His Church. To this end, the Ephesians had witnessed the manifold wisdom and glory of God. Given what God had been achieving by Paul's ministry, they should view his imprisonment as a glory (a triumph), not as a disgrace.

Paul had sought to encourage the Ephesian believers by making them aware of his divine stewardship. This ministry included taking the message of grace to the Gentiles (v. 2) and then expounding the deep mysteries of what God was accomplishing in Christ (v. 3). Paul affirmed that both Jews and Gentiles composed Christ's Body – the Church (v. 6). This meant that both Jews and Gentiles were coheirs to the inheritance secured in Christ (v. 6); that Gentiles, being previously estranged from God, could now become His sons and receive *"the unsearchable riches of Christ"* (v. 8); that through the Church, God was displaying His supreme wisdom and power to all realms of authority (v. 10); and that He had purposed in eternity past to accomplish all of this (v. 11). What an encouraging mystery indeed!

## A Prayer of Apprehension (vv. 14-21)

The phrase *"for this reason"* connects back to chapter 2 and completes Paul's parenthetical explanation of his mystery stewardship that began in verse 1. In the first two chapters, the apostle explained to the Ephesians what they were by nature and what they had become through their union in Christ. They had been dead in trespasses and sins, and were spiritually impoverished, but in Christ, they were spiritually rich and were declaring the glory of God. In chapter 1, Paul prayed that the Ephesians would receive further spiritual illumination in comprehending Christ. He bows his knees again to *"the Father of our Lord Jesus Christ"* to pray that those of the family of God at Ephesus would apprehend Christ (vv. 14-15) – that is, to fully appreciate and practically enjoy the benefits of their union with Christ. Paul knew that as believers better comprehend Christ, they gain a greater opportunity to apprehend His Life and experience resurrection power. To this end, Paul prayed for the Ephesians.

First, the apostle asked that God would bless them by strengthening the inner man according to the riches of Christ's glory (v. 16). The inner man receives power from the Holy Spirit (2 Cor. 4:16) while exercising faith in the Lord and delighting to do His Word (Rom. 7:22). A rich man might give a trifling amount "out of his riches" to assist someone in need. Not so with the Lord, He gives "according to His riches." He lavishes upon us that which is proportional to His infinite wealth! We honor the Lord by requesting Him, in faith, to do what seems impossible to us. This behavior demonstrates that we truly know God's character and attributes.

Second, Paul prayed that Christ "may dwell" in their hearts by faith (v. 17). Paul previously addressed the Ephesians as "saints" so he is not praying for them to believe the gospel message to be saved. Christ takes up residence within a repentant sinner at his or her conversion (through regeneration; John 14:20). This had already happened for the Ephesian believers. Nor is Paul talking about the possibility of Christ leaving the believer, but rather how much Christ feels at home within the believer (Rev. 3:20). The aorist verb rendered "may dwell" has the idea of Christ, by a once-for-all action taking up residence in the believer's heart. Kenneth Wuest's expanded translation puts it this way, "to settle down and feel at home." Paul was praying that the Ephesians would have an ever-deepening experience with Christ. It is through continued dependence on Christ without distraction and by submission to His will that we enjoy deepening communion with Him.

Third, Paul requested that they might know the love of Christ and then be "rooted and grounded" in that love (v. 17). For a tree to survive and thrive, it must drive its roots deep into the soil; this provides both stability against threatening wind and access to the nutrients and moisture necessary for growth. Maintaining unhindered communion with Christ permits the believer to be deeply rooted in His love. Those believers deeply rooted in Christ's love will also be able to weather life's storms and grow in Him to maturity. Ongoing meekness, humility, selflessness, and kindness in one's life are manifestations of receiving love from beyond this world.

Fourth, it was desired that the Ephesians *"may be able to comprehend with all the saints what is the width and length and depth and height –"* (v. 18). The aorist verb translated "may be able" builds on the previous aspirations: Being strengthened by the Holy Spirit in the inner man, permitting Christ to be settled in one's heart by faith, and being established in Christ's love leads to more fully comprehending "the mystery of Christ" through experience (v. 4). We normally describe physical things by three dimensions (height, width, and length), but Paul uses four dimensions (width, length, depth, and height) and an incomplete sentence (there is no subject), to infer that what "all the saints" should know of God's mystery in Christ is beyond our full grasp to comprehend presently. Nonetheless, we should yearn to know more of it.

Fifth, the apostle requested that they would *"know the love of Christ which passes knowledge; that you may be filled with all the fullness of God"* (v. 19). Such "fullness" comes through growing in our knowledge of Christ through practical experience. Like the Shulamite bride in the Song of Songs who speaks more about her beloved to others than speaking to him directly, we can shortchange our opportunities to be more deeply drawn into Christ's presence. If our hearts were more open to who the Lord Jesus is, we would be much less satisfied with merely talking about Christ. Rather, we would earnestly plead with Him, "draw me nearer, dear Lord."

The human mind cannot fathom this supreme experience, yet the heart engages to know more of Him. In the ages to come, believers will be forever learning about *"the exceeding riches of* [God's] *grace and His kindness towards us in Christ"* (2:7) and of *"the love of Christ"* (v. 19). Yet, Paul urged the Ephesians to learn and appreciate all they could of the mystery of Christ, for this is the means of enjoying His abundant life now.

> There will always be as much horizon before us as behind us. And when we have been gazing on the face of Jesus for milleniums, its beauty will be as fresh and fascinating and fathomless as when we first saw it from the gate of Paradise.
>
> – F. B. Meyer

## Doxology (vv. 20-21)

The general format of the Pauline epistles to churches is to present foundational doctrines first and then exhort believers on how to live based on what he has just taught them. In this epistle and in the letter to the Romans, a doxology marks this transition point between the believer's *position* in and *practice* for Christ (e.g., end of Romans 8).

While praising God, Paul tells the Ephesians to remember that Christ is able to accomplish about much more than they could ever imagine or even ask for (v. 20). The power of the Holy Spirit within an obedient believer is not restricted. Christ desires that God, through the submission and faithfulness of His Church, might receive glory forever and ever! (v. 21). May each of us continue to count on God for what only He can do. Our heavenly Father desires to honor the name of His dear Son and our prayers of faith provide Him opportunities to do just that.

# Ephesians Chapter 4

## Walk Worthy of the Lord (vv. 1-3)

The first three chapters of this epistle addressed the believer's heavenly calling in Christ; the last three chapters pertain to walking worthy of this calling while on earth. Having revealed how Jews and Gentiles have become one in Christ and are mutual heirs in Him, Paul now explains the practical implications of this spiritual union. In short, our union with Christ should prompt us to display Him in all we do. Paul uses the word "walk" to epitomize this idea. Hence, to be counted as a "prisoner of the Lord" was an honorable way to walk worthy of his calling in Paul's estimation (v. 1).

The word "walk" is used in a metaphorical sense throughout the Bible to speak of a certain course of life or one's conduct in life. Ephesians chapters 4 and 5 contain the most densely clustered occurrences of the word "walk" in the New Testament (found six times in these chapters). Believers in Christ receive a new walk – a new lifestyle (i.e., the way that Christ's life should be lived out; v. 17).

Ponder Paul's medley of exhortations concerning the walk of the believer. We are to walk worthy of our calling in Christ (v. 1), in love, as Christ did (5:2), as children of light (or truth; 5:8), and circumspectly and in wisdom (5:15). We are not to walk the way the Gentiles do in the vanity of their minds, or as fools (5:15), or in the way we formerly did in darkness (5:8). Thankfully, we have God's Word to tell us exactly what conduct He expects from us. When we yield to the Word of God and the Spirit of God, we walk as God desires us to: *"Walk in the Spirit, and you shall not fulfill the lust of the flesh"* (Gal. 5:16-17). Paul then describes the behavior of a believer being controlled by the Holy Spirit (vv. 2-3):

- Lowliness: Genuine humility that is cognizant of our own nothingness and elevates the interests of others above our own.

- Meekness/gentleness: This is power in control and submits to God's work in our lives without a rebel attitude.

- Longsuffering: A spirit of patience even during long, difficult circumstances.

- Bearing with one another: Showing love to those who hurt, irritate, or disturb us.

- Safeguard unity: Believers are to safeguard the unity that the Holy Spirit maintains in the Body by living peaceably with each other.

When believers are in communion with the Lord, they will be in fellowship with each other and be able to better serve the Lord together. Believers are to *"keep the unity of the Spirit in the bond of peace"* (i.e., be at peace with each other) – *"the unity of the faith"* will be obtained later when in glory (v. 13). The Holy Spirit is the only One who can create unity in the Church, and believers are the only ones who through carnal behavior and impure thinking can destroy that unity. If we are not in fellowship with God, it will be impossible for us to be in fellowship with each other or to serve the Lord in a cooperative way. His peace and blessing will be missing in all we attempt to do.

The Holy Spirit draws together all believers in Christ, equips them to serve each other, and lubricates the Body with grace, so to speak, so that the Body's moving parts do not generate too much friction! In local churches where believer-priests are sitting in the premises instead of standing on the promises, there is minimal friction because there is little activity.

## Walk in Unity (vv. 4-6)

The Lord Jesus alluded to the importance of unity while addressing His Father in prayer (John 17:21-23). In fact, the unity of believers in the world is to be a direct reflection of the glorious oneness of the Godhead. To the Ephesians, Paul mentions seven unities to be appreciated by all believers, as they endeavor to keep the unity of the Spirit:

*There is one body and one Spirit, just as you were called in one hope of your calling; one Lord, one faith, one baptism; one God and Father of all, who is above all, and through all, and in you all* (vv. 4-6).

We enjoy these same aspects of Body unity today. First, there is one Body (v. 4). Paul often described this incredible spiritual oneness that the Church enjoys in Christ: *"For by one Spirit we were all baptized into one body – whether Jews or Greeks, whether slaves or free – and have all been made to drink into one Spirit"* (1 Cor. 12:13). The Church is composed of all believers from all different ethnic backgrounds over the entire Church Age. This spiritual temple is still being constructed, and when the last believer is added to the Body, then Christ will return for His Church.

Second, there is one Spirit (v. 4). The third person of the Trinity is fully God and thus omnipresent, omniscient, omnipotent, immutable, and eternal. He does what is needed to honor Christ and indwells all believers forever.

Third, there is one hope (v. 4). That is, to be with and like Christ and to share in His glory forever. For the Church, this occurs at the Lord comes for His bride, which we often refer to as the Rapture (or "the catching up") of the Church from the earth into glory.

Fourth, there is one Lord (v. 5). The Gentiles worshipped many gods and lords (1 Cor. 8.5), but Christians understand that there is only one God, the Creator and Sustainer of all things. The Lord Jesus Christ is the centerpiece of Heaven and is to be the object of the Church's attention and affection. He is our Lord and Savior and we are to serve Him faithfully.

Fifth, there is one faith (v. 5). There is only one body of divine doctrine that has been entrusted to the Church. God revealed it to the apostles first, who then by divine inspiration penned Scripture to preserve the basis of the Christian faith (Heb. 2:3; Jude 3).

Sixth, there is one baptism (v. 5). Since the spiritual bond of Jew and Greek in "one body" was addressed in verse 4, baptism here likely speaks of the profession of Christ's Lordship by both Jewish and Greek believers in water baptism. Else, the idea of spiritual baptism would be redundant.

Seventh, there is one divine Father (v. 6). God the Father is "above all" (the supreme Ruler of all), "through all" (accomplishes His sovereign purposes throughout creation), and "in you all" (He is omnipresent in His creation). Instead of magnifying our differences, believers should strive for unity by appreciating all that we have in common with each other in Christ.

The Lord affirmed the oneness and equal standing of all believers when He told His disciples, *"But you, do not be called 'Rabbi'; for one is your Teacher, the Christ, and you are all brethren"* (Matt. 23:8). Christians are identified by biblical names such as Christians, believers, saints, and brethren. No denominations, cliques, or separate followings should be found in the Body of Christ. Paul asked the Corinthians who were bestowing honor on various preachers instead of following Christ, *"Is Christ divided?"* (1 Cor. 1:13). Identifying with anyone or any organization instead of Christ is completely unbiblical. Harry A. Ironside's response to the question as to what denomination he belonged stresses this point. He answered, "I belong to the same denomination that David did," and then quoted Psalm 119:63, *"I am a companion of all them that fear Thee and of them that keep Thy precepts."*[60]

In the practical sense, Christian fellowship (i.e., what we share together in the commonwealth of Christ) is dependent on how much we determine we have in common with other believers. While it is true that we will not be able to have the same degree of fellowship with all believers, we should strive to walk as far as possible with all who have been redeemed by the precious blood of Christ. So often believers cast others aside because of some difference in thinking, although in fact, they have more in common than matters upon which they disagree. This wrong mindset hinders the fellowship Christ wants the members of His body to enjoy.

The fact of the matter is that the saints will not agree on everything on this side of glory (v. 13). Once in God's presence, we will discover that none of us had it all right. Coming into true, and eternal unity of the Spirit with all Christians will be one of the purest blessings of Heaven. Until then let us strive to walk as far as we can with other believers. Unfortunately, such fellowship will be limited by matters of sound morality and doctrine.

## Walk as Equipped by God (vv. 7-16)

Although the Body is composed of many members all sharing the previously mentioned unities, there is also diversity and individuality within the Church. Both the gifted individuals given to the Church by Christ (v. 11) and the spiritual gifts given to all believers by the Holy Spirit (1 Cor. 12:11) will uniquely equip and enable each believer for a specific work of ministry within the Body (v. 12). Each believer is a unique trophy of God's grace and each believer has a unique function in the Body of Christ. The Lord chooses the calling of each believer to perform in the Body and then enables him or her to fulfill their assigned ministry (v. 7; Rom. 12:6).

In this section, we also learn that Christ has given gifts to His Church for the purpose of wider Body edification. Paul borrows Old Testament imagery to convey the idea that Christ shares with His Church the gifts He received following His magnificent victory at Calvary: *"When He ascended on high, He led captivity captive and gave gifts to men"* (v. 8). This verse is drawn from Psalm 68:18, but with modifications to imply a different focus, for the one ascending (returning to Heaven triumphantly) is not merely receiving gifts for Himself, but as the victorious Man, is freely bestowing them to other humans (*anthropos*), not angels. Given the five minor and two major variations Paul applies to Psalm 68:18, Harold W. Hoehner suggests:

> "...that Paul was not quoting one particular verse of the psalm but rather that he was summarizing all of Psalm 68, which has many words similar to those of Psalm 68:18. The essence of the psalm is that a military victor has the right to give gifts to those who are identified with him.

Christ, having captivated sinful people by redeeming them, is Victor and gives them as gifts to the Church.[61]

This means that the Church did not exist in the Old Testament times as some claim, for it would have been a spiritually gift-less and Spirit-less reality. Christ did not send the Holy Spirit, nor did He receive the spoils of His victory, until after His resurrection (John 16:7).

A similar scenario to Psalm 68 is conveyed in song of Deborah and Barak recorded in Judges 5. There we read, *"Arise, Barak, and lead your captives away"* (v. 12) and in verse 30, that the victorious Jews were *"finding and dividing the spoil."* It was common in ancient times for the victor of a battle to display the conquered captives before a celebrating crowd of peers, who also received a portion of the spoils taken from the enemy, the difference here is that Barak did not descend from Heaven first to engage the enemy, nor could he lead his conquered captives back to Heaven, but he could merely take them away. Additionally, there is nothing that the enemy has that Christ wants, other than the redeemed souls who were previously under the enemy's authority.

Christ descended from Heaven to the lowest parts of the earth (Phil. 2:6-8), conquered Satan and death (John 12:31), and then ascended to the highest station in Heaven – *"that He might fill all things"* (vv. 9-10; 1 Cor. 15:28; Phil 2:9). There are at least three explanations of who the captives are that He is leading in His triumphal procession Heavenward. First, He is making an open show of the Satanic opposition that opposed him but was defeated at Calvary (John 12:31; Col. 2:15). Paul has already explained that Satan opposed Christ's resurrection; regardless, God exalted Him far above all principalities and dominions (1:19-21). Albert Leckie favors this understanding:

> He "led captivity captive" in His triumphal ascension when He led captive those whom He conquered at Calvary (Col 2:15) as He passed through their domain. The gifts He gives are trophies of Calvary's defeat of those forces that would seek to impede the work of God.[62]

Second, Christ is leading Heavenward those who were previously His enemies (those under Satan's rule) but were liberated from sin and death through believing the gospel (John 12:32; Rom. 5:9). This idea best captures the ancient custom of parading prisoners from a defeated army after victory was achieved, but in this case the captives are cheering too. Hamilton Smith holds this view: "So Christ has triumphed over all the power of Satan, and having delivered His people from the power of the enemy, He is exalted on high and gives gifts to His people."[63] J. N. Darby favors this idea, but also includes aspects of the former view:

> The people of God were captives of Satan; Christ has triumphed over Satan, and has led him captive, and has brought along with Him the Church delivered from his chains. Satan was the master, and Christ gains the victory over the strong man and delivers the Church. Having delivered it from the power of Satan, He can communicate to us this same power which gains the victory over Satan. God has set this power of victory in man, in order that it may energize.[64]

Third, it seems likely that Christ's spirit went to Abraham's bosom (a holding place of faithful disembodied spirits; Luke 16:19-31; Acts 2:31) prior to His resurrection. *Sheol*, the realm where disembodied spirits reside in the Old Testament is equivalent to *Hades* in the New Testament, but *Sheol* sometimes also includes the broader idea of the grave. The Lord identified two compartments of this holding place for the departed dead: one a pleasant place for the faithful called *Abraham's Bosom* and one a place of torment for the souls of the wicked, referred to as *Hades* (Luke 16:22-23).

We know from Matthew 27:52-53, that some of the saints in Abraham's Bosom experienced resurrection after Christ's resurrection. Apparently, the souls who were in Abraham's Bosom departed with the Lord and accompanied Him to Heaven. James Vernon McGee holds this view:

> He led captivity captive, which refers, I believe, to the redeemed of the Old Testament who went to paradise when they died. Christ took these believers with Him out of paradise into the very presence of God when He ascended.[65]

While this may also be another meaning of *"He led captivity captive"* in verse 7, it is noted that these Old Testament saints would not be receiving gifts to edify the Body of Christ on earth – they went to Heaven.

The Lord certainly did not descend into Hell to be further judged by God for our sin, as some teach. Just before His death, the Lord Jesus declared that His propitiatory work for sin was "finished" (John 19:30). Wherever the Lord is – is paradise, and that is where the soul of the repentant thief who died with Christ went after his death (Luke 23:43). In the Church Age, as soon as believers die, their souls go to be with the Lord in Heaven. They wait with Him there until experiencing their part in the first resurrection (i.e., glorification; 2 Cor. 5:8; Rev. 20:6). With Christ's payment for sins finalized at Calvary, there is no need for faithful souls to be kept in Abraham's Bosom any longer.

The reference to "the lower parts of the earth" may be understood in two ways. First, David refers to his mother's womb as "the lower parts of the earth" (Ps. 139:15). The Son of God departed from the majestic splendor of Heaven and through the power of the Holy Spirit was conceived in Mary's womb (an incredibly humble setting for the Lord of Heaven). He was then born as the baby Jesus nine months later.

Second, the reference speaks of a tomb or grave (Ps. 63:9; Matt. 12:40). After finishing the work at Calvary, Christ's body was placed in a tomb, until raised up three days later (Acts 2:30-34). While both views are true, the latter idea more sharply highlights the dichotomy between the highest glory in Heaven and the lowest place a human can go while on earth – the grave (perhaps including *Sheol*), to convey the willing self-abasement of the Lord Jesus to achieve victory.

Christ, the Victor, bestows the heavenly gifts (redeemed people he has gained who were previously possessed by the enemy) to enable those who are His to be victorious during their earthly sojourn and pilgrimage Heavenward. Paul identifies five specific types of individuals (gifts) that He has bestowed on to the Church: *"And He Himself gave some to be apostles, some prophets, some evangelists, and some pastors and teachers"* (v. 11). Then the apostle explains why Christ has given these various individuals to the Church: *"for the equipping of the saints for the work of ministry, for the edifying of the Body"* (v. 12). Every believer has a work of ministry, the benefit of which will bless the entire body.

Apostles were "sent ones" that were commissioned personally by the Lord and were given special authority by Christ to do signs and wonders (Heb. 2:4). The apostles were men who led the Church in its infancy, until church elders were in place for each local assembly. The last mention of the apostles having a leadership role in the affairs of the Church is recorded in Acts 16:4. The apostles provided the Church with the foundational doctrines of the Faith (Heb. 2:3). Once Scripture had been God-breathed and canonized, the ministry of the apostles was complete (1 Cor. 13:9-10).

The prophets spoke for God to the saints until Scripture was canonized; this would involve both private (Acts 21:9) and public ministry. The prophets also checked the validity of what was being preached in the Church to ensure accuracy (1 Cor. 14:29-32).

Evangelists equip saints to evangelize, often through personal example. It is a misconception to think of evangelists primarily as soul-winners. While it is true that evangelists have a passion for souls and are bold in

*Revealing Heaven's Secrets*

sharing the gospel message, their primary task is to stir up and equip the Body of Christ to fulfill the Great Commission. All believers are to be witnesses for Christ (Acts 1:8), and evangelists help those of us who are not evangelists to faithfully and effectively evangelize others.

Pastors are those who shepherd God's people. Many church elders would certainly be included in this gifted group, but it also would include others that shepherd God's people in various ministries who are not elders.

It is noted that there is no article ("some") in front of teachers, meaning that Greek grammar would connect "pastors" and "teachers" as being the same, but as Bill Mounce explains, not necessarily the same individual:

> The question is whether "pastors and teachers" designate one spiritual gift or two. One interpretation sees them as one gift and point to the use of the article. It is repeated before all the other gifts, but when it gets to the last two, there is only one article that governs both nouns. Grammatically, this signals a change and expects us to see that "pastors and teachers" form a unit that is set off from the preceding series. There can be no debate on this point; this is just plain Greek grammar. The question is the precise nature of the "unit." The use of a single article with multiple plural nouns indicates a single unit, but it does not necessarily mean the two nouns are identical. This same construction occurs earlier in 2:20 and joins "apostles" and "prophets," but these are not identical gifts. Hoehner suggests that the distinction is that the prior gifts are expressed in an itinerant ministry and the latter two are gifts for a local ministry.[66]

While this understanding is reasonable, it is observed that not all teaching ministries are of a localized nature, whereas pastoral ministries typically are. Obviously, those who shepherd God's people must be apt to teach, but not all teachers prompt the personal accountability and encouragement required in pastoral care. Those who shepherd God's sheep are uniquely equipped to guide believers in the way they should go. Accordingly, the pastor-teacher gift is needed in localized ministry, but a broader instructive ministry within the Church is needed too. Just as the apostles engaged in itinerant work to teach the foundational doctrines of the Faith to a wider audience; itinerant teachers are needed to reaffirm and explain these previously revealed truths.

Teachers are those who expound truth and exhort others to follow it, both in word and in deed (they live out what they teach). Teachers affirm doctrine and its proper application in living a life pleasing to the Lord.

It is important to understand the distinction between those Christ gives to the Church as shepherds and those who will be recognized as elders in various local churches. Two Greek words are used in the New Testament to identify those men who hold an office of leadership in their respective local churches: *presbuteros* (elder) and *episkopos* (overseer). *Presbuteros* and the related word *presbuterion* are used seventeen times to speak of church elders. *Episkopos* (and its verb form) is used six times in the New Testament to address the "overseers" (again referring to church elders). These two words (including their verb forms) relate to a church position which was not given at spiritual rebirth, but gained as a result of spiritual maturity, divine calling, and public recognition. A man may serve as a *presbuteros* and *episkopos* in one church, but if he relocates, he may not be an elder in another church.

A third word, *poimen,* is normally used to speak of the shepherding work in which both elders and non-elders engage. Thus, the pastoral gift that Paul is speaking of in verse 11 remains within the recipient throughout his entire lifetime, regardless of where he may take up residence. The gift *poimen* cannot be equated directly with the office of elder, though certainly many elders will have this spiritual gift. It is noted that the only instances in which *poimen* is used in the New Testament to describe a specific person are when it is applied to the Lord Jesus. He is the Good *Poimen* (John 10:11), the Chief *Poimen* (1 Pet. 5:4), and the Great *Poimen* (Heb. 13:20).

The Lord Jesus gave individuals, such as evangelists and teachers, as gifts to the Church *"for the equipping of the saints for the work of ministry"* (v. 12). Every believer in the body of Christ has a work of ministry to engage in, the benefit of which will bless the entire Body. The Lord demonstrated by the care for His own disciples that mentoring others for the kingdom is not accomplished through training programs. One does not become, for example, an evangelist by completing an accredited program resembling that of secular professions. Evangelism is a gift, not a profession.

At regeneration, each believer receives a spiritual gift (or gifts) from the Holy Spirit for the purpose of building up the Church (1 Cor. 12:4, 11). Every believer has been called by God to perform a specific function within the Church. A believer's effectiveness in this service will depend on his or her spiritual maturity and the development and use of his or her spiritual gift(s). As believers rightly use their spiritual gifts, they equip others in the Body to do ministry, which then passes the original blessing along to other believers in order to further edify the body.

Visualize for a moment several children standing perfectly still in a wading pool while another child jumps into the pool. The resultant wave glides across the surface of the water and eventually bounces off every child in the pool. Each time the wave comes in contact with a child, it is also reflected back across the pool, eventually making contact with every other child in the pool, and so on. This wave-motion phenomenon illustrates how the initial edification of one member in the Body equips other members to minister to the Body; the blessing then continues to the entire Body.

The outcome of such body-life enables individuals to reach their full potential in Christ and fulfill God's sovereign purpose for their lives. For example, though the evangelist is skillful in reaching the lost for Christ, his main ministry to the Church is to equip and to stir up others within the Body to evangelize wherever God has placed them as a testimony. The result is that, in a collective sense, the Church is stimulated and enabled to obey the great commission (Matt. 28:19-20).

Beneficial Church body-life is enjoyed as each member learns and practices sound doctrine while also learning how to properly use his or her spiritual gifts. Scripture supplies a foundation of truth for each believer to live out and practical sanctification occurs when he or she yields to it. Inevitably, all believers will suffer failure; conviction, correction, and reproof are God's means for restoring the wayward to righteous living. The Holy Spirit and other believers will assist in this ministry. God-honoring service becomes more feasible with maturity.

Next, Paul expresses his desire for the Ephesians to *"no longer be children, tossed to and fro and carried about with every wind of doctrine, by the trickery of men, in the cunning craftiness of deceitful plotting,"* but to push forward to maturity (v. 14). The Church is to be occupied with three main ministries in Christ's absence: the upward ministry of *exaltation*, the inward ministry of *edification*, and the outward ministry of *evangelism*. These three important ministries of the Church can be summarized by the short slogan: "Lift up, build up, and reach out." Or the *Exaltation* of God, the *Edification* of believers, and the *Evangelism* of the lost.

If an assembly has great worship, but no evangelism, in time they will die out. If a church engages in evangelism, but neglects discipleship, the babes in Christ will tend to be blown to and fro with every wind of doctrine. Many will eventually leave the church to find one better suited to their comfort level. If a local church has tremendous teaching but fails to stimulate new believers to love and honor the Lord, those being discipled will not have the right motive for service, nor will they be inclined to flee sin. Those who do not grow in their love and appreciation for Christ will not live for Him. Even if they know the truth, they have no reason to make personal sacrifices for it.

The inward ministry centers in the *edification* of all believers. The Bible likens this ministry to that of a shepherd (John 21:15-17; Acts 20:28-31; 1 Pet. 5:1-3). The Lord commissioned His disciples to teach those responding to the gospel message all the things that they had been taught by Him (Matt. 28:20). Believers in the early Church readily taught new disciples what they knew to be true, by referring them to His Word (Acts 2:42, 4:2, 5:42, 11:26, 13:1, 20:35). Believers are to engage in this important ministry: *"Preach the word! Be ready in season and out of season. Convince, rebuke, exhort, with all longsuffering and teaching"* (2 Tim. 4:2). Teaching, reproof, instruction, and correction through the use of God's Word is absolutely necessary to refine believers' characters in such a way as to make them profitable unto good works (2 Tim. 3:16-17). The need for discipleship ministries in the Church is paramount today.

Yet, doctrine alone is insufficient to guide believers in proper conduct, a work of grace in the heart is also required: *"Knowledge puffs up, but love edifies"* (1 Cor. 8:1). Love and grace must temper our actions to ensure the edification of others. Separation among believers will occur when divine truth is embraced and false doctrine is shunned (2 Thess. 3:6).

With that stated, it is understood that not all division is profitable. If love does not guide one's activities, isolation of the members within the body of Christ will occur over minute points of disagreement, the result of which will hinder the work and growth of the Church. Just as grace and truth are inseparable aspects of Christ's character (John 1:14), the believer should not invoke one quality without the other. On this point, Paul commands, *"But, speaking the truth in love, may grow up in all things into Him who is the head – Christ"* (v. 15). The challenge, then, is to have fellowship with all believers to the degree that sound doctrine and sound living allow.

The Greek word translated "equipping" in verse 12 is the noun *oikodomen*, which means "building" or "edifying." All believers should engage in Spirit-led ministry that edifies the Body of Christ in love (v. 16). As previously stated, all believers are equipped with spiritual gifts to serve and edify the body of Christ. Only when all believers use their spiritual gifts with the full measure of faith that God gives will the Church be fully functional (Rom. 12:3; 1 Pet. 4:10). All believers have been equipped to worship Christ and to serve each other in Christ.

## Walk Not as Gentiles (vv. 17-32)

Next, the apostle challenges the believers at Ephesus to exhibit the behavior of Christ in all their actions. This meant that they could not live as they did before as spiritually blind, vain-thinking, pagan Gentiles (vv. 17-18). They were insensitive to God's voice, and the natural behavior of their fallen natures produced lifestyles characterized by lasciviousness, uncleanness and greed. They had not learned this from Christ, for His character and behavior were completely different (vv. 19-20).

Since the Ephesians had been instructed by the Lord (through His Word), they knew what He expected (v. 21). Therefore, through the power of the Holy Spirit they were to imitate Christ ("put Him on," so to speak) in their speech and deeds (vv. 22-24). In this world the believer is to project an accurate display of Christ-like character. This enables the lost to see what Christ is truly like (holy, kind, gentle, meek, merciful, true, etc.) so that they will want Him too.

This means that believers must desire to be controlled by the Holy Spirit and not their lusting flesh, Only then are the deeds of the flesh mortified and fellowship with God maintained: *"If by the Spirit you put to death the deeds of the body, you will live"* (Rom. 8:13). By doing so, we put on the *new man* that we are in Christ! The believer has been positionally crucified with Christ (Rom. 6:6) so that his or her craving flesh will ultimately die (i.e., by maturing in Christ, the old nature loses its control over the believer).

This means that believers must endeavor to behave as Christ would in all matters of life. If the believer has put on Christ, He is the one to be seen. This means abstaining from sinful behavior, such as lying (v. 25). Lying to and deceiving others is an affront to the truth, and thus to the God of truth (Ps. 31:5). Solomon reminds his son that there are seven things God hates: a proud look, a lying tongue, murder, devising wicked schemes, a swift inclination to do mischief, a false witness, and those who sow discord among God's people (Prov. 6:16-19).

Lying is never permissible for the child of God. Rather, believers are to speak the truth in love, or be silent and entrust the consequences of either of these honorable responses to the Lord (v. 15). When things go wrong, we should not go wrong with them! The belt of truth is spiritual armor that should be worn by believers at all times (6:14). The moment that we start to flavor or spin the truth, to deceive others or make ourselves look good, we cease to accurately represent the Lord. There is nothing done in the flesh that pleases God (Rom. 8:8).

Many relationships have been damaged and much personal harm has resulted from anger-motivated, fleshly behaviors such as rage and resentment. Anger is often thought of as an undesired and hostile behavior, but this notion is flawed on two counts. First, anger is an emotion, not a behavior, though it often incites behavior. Secondly, circumstances exist that require anger-motivated behavior to accomplish good (e.g., upholding the indignation of God concerning evil or releasing our offenses to God).

Therefore, anger should not be thought of as an evil emotion – it is the wrong choices actualized when one is angry that are harmful.

If one chooses to uphold the righteousness of God when angry, as tempered by His goodness, then God is honored (v. 26). But anger is a powerful emotion that equips our bodies to respond to abnormal situations. Therefore, it must have a present righteous purpose or it must be extinguished. If not, holding on to anger will eventually lead us into sin and we will permit the devil to use us in his agenda (v. 27).

The apostle addresses the sin of stealing next (v. 28). It is good for us to remember that whatever we have at present was given to us by God; therefore, we are to have a humble approach towards the stewardship of our possessions (1 Cor. 4:7). Paul exhorted the Ephesians that, rather than stealing from others as they may have done before they were saved, they instead ought to work hard to supply their own necessities and then to assist those in need.

Let us not think so highly of ourselves and our possessions that we are not willing to assist others with what God has graciously placed in our stewardship. Furthermore, we are to labor for our necessities and to have the ability to assist others in need. We are not to labor more to indulge our flesh with frivolous luxuries and extravagances. These only tend to strangle the spiritual man and pull his heart away from the Lord.

Work hard, consume little, give much and let all be to Christ!

– Anthony Norris Groves

The believer's speech must also reflect the character of Christ. Paul has already challenged the Ephesians to speak the truth in love (v. 15), but now he warns against corrupt speech and encourages them to only speak for the purpose of edifying and imparting grace to others (v. 29). We are not to resort to malicious flattery, spiteful words, sarcasm, jabs, etc., but are to speak the truth in love when a response is necessary.

Obedience to the next exhortation is paramount to exhibiting Christ-like behavior: *"Do not grieve the Holy Spirit of God, by whom you were sealed for the day of redemption"* (v. 30). Wrong thinking and behavior grieves the Holy Spirit and quenches His full activities within the believer (1 Thess. 5:19). Submission and holy behavior result in Spirit filling (5:17-18) which enables the believer to pour out the blessings of God to others in a way that only God can. Believers are to be God's channels of blessings.

It is essential for believers to learn the mind of Christ so they will be motivated by Christ-like compassion, humility, and wisdom in the circumstances of life. This ensures that the Holy Spirit will not be hindered from operating in the believer's life, thus allowing the infusing power of God to pass through the believer as electricity passes through wire.

One of the chief ways the Holy Spirit is grieved is through ungodly responses when others offend or wrong us. For this reason, Paul charges the Ephesians: *"Let all bitterness, wrath, anger, clamor, and evil speaking be put away from you, with all malice"* (v. 31). As previously mentioned, anger is an emotion, not a behavior. Anger can serve God or serve the flesh and the devil (v. 26). Scripture identifies four main outlets in which our anger will manifest itself. Two of these behaviors are God-honoring, while the remaining two lead to sin. Two behaviors are Spirit-controlled and two are flesh-motivated. We will cover the latter first.

First, there is *rage* or "blowing up": In verse 31, it is called *wrath*, as derived from the Greek word *thumos*. Rage is violent, an expression of uncontrolled anger, a work of the flesh with visible harm. It is sometimes referred to as *Open Aggression* and is "a self-preserving stand for personal worth, needs, and convictions at someone else's expense." Rage doesn't think; it vents in order to satisfy selfish need.

Second, there is *resentment* or "clamming up": The Greek word *orge* is rendered *anger* in this verse. Resentment represses feelings of anger, which then smolder and ultimately seek covert revenge. Often it is social etiquette that forces us to repress expressions of rage and to choose resentment as a more acceptable form of venting anger. Denying the existence of angry feelings or suppressing them results in resentment and eventually bitterness.

Third, there is *righteous indignation* or "lifting God up." Indignation sacrifices selfish interest in order to intensely and actively pattern God's own abhorrence of sin. As an example, the Lord "was much displeased" with His disciples for forbidding children to come to Him (Mark 10:14). The Greek verb translated "was much displeased" means "to have indignation" towards. The Lord was righteously angry with His disciples.

Fourth, there is *release* or "giving anger up." The word *charizomai* is often rendered "forgiving," as in verse 32. *Release* determines to not take revenge for an offense, but is determined to suffer loss and simply entrust the outcome to the Lord. It waits patiently for the opportunity to extend forgiveness when the offending party confesses sin (Luke 17:3). Until such time, the matter remains in the background of one's thinking. The main word rendered "forgive" in the Gospels is *aphiemi* and means "let be." Yet, in the epistles, we learn of how we have been forgiven by God through Christ; thus, we are to release offenses to God, rather than to take no action.

Rather than permitting our bitterness and resentment to destroy us and others, Paul exhorts, *"And be kind to one another, tenderhearted, forgiving one another, even as God in Christ forgave you"* (v. 32). The Greek word *charizomai* is found twenty-four times in the New Testament. It is translated as various forms of "forgive" fourteen times. Interestingly, only two of these fourteen references are found in the Gospel accounts (both are contained in one parable in Luke 7); the remaining occurrences are contained in the epistles. *Charizomai* means "to bestow a favor unconditionally or to freely give." It expresses the type of unconditional *releasing* attitude a Christian should maintain when offended by others. To freely release the matter means that one does not seek revenge, vengeance or become resentful.

The mechanics of forgiveness are mainly addressed in the Gospel accounts and are associated with a different Greek word *aphiemi*, which means "to send away" and by implication "let it be – take no action." For example, Matthew 18:15-18 informs us how to go about problem resolution with others, while Luke 17:3 instructs us to not *declare* personal forgiveness until the offending party has repented.

> Forgiveness on the part of God always has a judicial basis, not an emotional basis, and represents an attitude of God based upon the satisfaction of His righteousness in some way.
>
> – John F. Walvoord

Why did the Holy Spirit mainly use *aphiemi* in the Gospel accounts and *charizomai* in the epistles to speak of forgiveness? Apparently because the epistles better express the proper motive for forgiveness: *"Forgiving one another, if anyone has a complaint against another; even as Christ forgave you, so you also must do"* (Col. 3:13).

In view of the believer's immense debt of sin that has been forgiven because of Calvary, we must be ready to forgive those who offend us. This will free us from being in bondage to bitterness and enable us to pray for those who despitefully use us. The unresolved matter is, thus, immediately left in the Lord's hands. This liberating activity allows believers to move an offense into the background of their thinking and not keep it in the foreground. The unresolved issue, though not forgotten, does not rule one's daily life, for it has been entrusted to Christ.

When the offending individual does confess his or her wrongdoing, we have already been well prepared to personally declare the matter forgiven. In light of the huge debt that we have been forgiven, we must be willing to forgive what are, in comparison, the petty offences of others.

# Ephesians Chapter 5

Walk Worthy of the Lord (vv. 1-7)
The "therefore" in verse 1 forms a logic statement connecting 4:32 and 5:1 together. Since God has forgiven our sins through Christ, as children of God, we are to imitate our heavenly Father's example of forgiveness by releasing the offenses of others against us. God's children are to live up to the family name, so to speak. Paul is in the midst of a three-chapter dissertation on what it means to practically put on Christ and how to walk in Him. Believers are not to walk as fools (v. 15), the way they formerly did (v. 8) as Gentiles walking in mental vanity (v. 17). Rather, believers must walk as children of light (v. 8), and in love, as Christ did (v. 2).

The Lord Jesus promised that if we obey His commandments, He will manifest Himself to us in deeper fellowship (John 14:21). To walk with the Lord, we must be in agreement with Him on the matter of sin, for *"can two walk together except they be agreed?"* (Amos 3:3). Surely, light has no communion with darkness. Thus, may each of us walk with God according to divine truth and in moral integrity.

The work and worth of the Lord Jesus was previously typified through the Levitical offerings and sacrifices in order to point the Jews to their Messiah. Christ willingly sacrificed Himself in submission to His Father's will. Because this offering was not forced but a choice, it was considered a sweet-smelling aroma to God, like the burnt offering, the meal offering, and the peace offering in the Levitical system.

Likewise, when we willingly follow Christ's example and we offer to God living sacrifices in the Holy Spirit's power, this is a sweet fragrance before Him in Heaven. This was Christ's example, in contrast to sons of disobedience who earn for themselves the wrath of God. Offering ourselves to God as living sacrifices means serving others in lowliness and meekness rather than pursuing our own interests and the impulses of the flesh. These remind our heavenly Father of His own Son's goodness and faithfulness.

As God's children, we receive our Father's blessing and care while walking in the light with Him. He also expresses His love towards His children through parental reproof when we wander from the path of righteousness (Heb. 12:6). Accordingly, Paul warns, *"Be imitators of God, as dear children"* (v. 1). Peter puts the matter this way, *"as obedient children, not fashioning yourselves according to the former lusts in your ignorance"* (1 Pet. 1:14). The Lord Jesus said, *"the Son can do nothing of Himself, but what He sees the Father do; for whatever He does, the Son also does in like manner"* (John 5:19). If we are to walk with God and make Him glad, we must follow Christ, the perfect example (John 8:12).

The Lord Jesus affirmed God's design for marriage which is a covenant between one biological man and one biological woman until death separates them (Matt. 19:4-6). This is the pattern to which the apostles, church elders, and deacons adhered (1 Cor. 9:5; 1 Tim. 3:1-12); consequently, there are no examples of Christians engaging in polygamy, open-marriages, or homosexual relationships in the New Testament. There are, however, many warnings and prohibitions against fornication (v. 3). Jude includes a history lesson in his warning: *"Even as Sodom and Gomorrah, and the cities about them in like manner, giving themselves over to fornication, and going after strange flesh, are set forth for an example, suffering the vengeance of eternal fire"* (Jude 7). Any sexual relationship other than between a husband and a wife is referred to in Scripture as fornication. This is why Paul says *"to avoid fornication, let every man have his own wife"* (1 Cor. 7:2). Fornication then includes adultery, pre-marital unions, homosexuality (e.g., sodomy), bestiality, etc. Under the Law, any Jew engaging in these sexual sins was to be put to death (Lev. 20:10-13), with the exception that those engaging in pre-marital sex were to marry (Deut. 22:29).

In the New Testament, God's standard for sexual behavior is unchanged (1 Cor. 6:9-11, 18; 1 Thess. 4:3; Rev. 21:8). The only difference is that capital punishment for sexual sins is not demanded by God for the Church. Because such sins are offensive to God, Paul warns believers to avoid uncleanness, covetousness, and filthiness (vv. 3-4). Uncleanness would include looking at impure pictures or suggestive material. Covetousness would be lusting to satisfy one's sexual appetites outside marriage. Filthiness would be engaging in dirty jokes, foolish talk, coarse jesting, or puns with sexual overtones. Fornication is such a serious sin that believers are not to even joke about it. Active fornication is evidence of an unconverted soul, who will not go to Heaven (v. 5).

Many arguments are offered by the devil's children to justify fornication as an acceptable lifestyle in our day. They argue that integrity and chastity are old-fashioned ideas that we have outgrown. Yet, history indicates that societies eventually collapse when they lust after pleasure and sport instead of integrity and virtue. Paul warns the Ephesians not to listen to those who are subject to God's wrath or to be partakers with them in sin (vv. 6-7).

## Walk in Light as a Child of God (vv. 8-14)

Rather than walking in darkness with children of the devil destined for wrath, believers are to walk in the light with God as children of light (i.e., revealing the truth and righteousness of God). In doing so, the Holy Spirit produces the fruit of truthfulness, righteousness, and goodness in the believer's life, which is well-pleasing to God (vv. 8-10). Not only are believers not to have fellowship with the unfruitful works of darkness, but their lives should expose what is displeasing to God (v. 11). Walking in the light is more than not committing sin. It is a testimony that reproves without leniency that of which God disapproves.

For example, Jacob did nothing after hearing that his son Reuben had slept with Bilhah (Jacob's concubine; Gen. 35:22). Jacob did not reprove his son's sin. Rather, he waited to the end of his life (some forty years later) to announce the consequences of Reuben's behavior (Gen. 49:4). During that interim, his silence excused the sin. Furthermore, Paul states that believers are not to even speak about that which God loathes in a way that makes light of it or glamorizes it (v. 12).

If the light of our testimony does not confront the darkness of sin, something is wrong (v. 13). Silence condones sin! William MacDonald explains why believers cannot be silent spectators of unrighteousness:

> When innocent people are being led off to gas chambers, ovens, and other modes of execution – when unborn babies are destroyed in abortion clinics – it is inexcusable to stand by and not seek to rescue them. It is also useless to plead ignorance. As Dante said, "The hottest places in Hell are reserved for those who in a time of great moral crisis maintain their neutrality."[67]

Our society is in great moral crisis! Those who would side with God cannot be silent against social depravity; we must seek and love good while shunning and confronting evil. The light of Christ within must shine outwardly to guide the lost out of darkness to the Savior! Our lives should be a powerful sermon to those who are dead in trespasses and sin: *"Awake, you who sleep, arise from the dead, and Christ will give you light"* (v. 14).

## Walk in Wisdom (vv. 15-21)

The urgency of this light-bearing ministry necessitates that each believer must *"walk circumspectly, not as fools but as wise, redeeming the time, because the days are evil"* (vv. 15-16). As Moses and Aaron learned, one of the devil's tactics to rob God of the worship He deserves is to keep His people so busy that they have no time for Him. After Pharaoh received

God's command to release the Israelites so that they could worship Jehovah, the king surmised that his slaves had too much time on their hands if they were thinking about an extended holiday in the desert. His remedy for this perceived inefficiency and idleness was to command the Jews to *"get to their burdens"* and he increased their workload *"the same day"* (Ex. 5). Not only would the Jews have to perform their existing duties, but they now also had to scavenge for their own straw to produce bricks. Pharaoh's solution to Moses' and Aaron's request was to keep the Jews so busy they would have no time to think about getting alone with their God.

The same tactic is used today by Satan to divert the Lord's people from spending time alone with their Savior and from serving Him. The world system that Satan controls devalues the things of God and exaggerates the value of what is temporary and sensual. Consequently, undiscerning believers have been deceived into forsaking the best for that which may be permissible, but which steals their available time. What is Satan's strategy? Christians can have their religion, but I (Satan) will not allow them to have any time to enjoy and serve their Savior.

Many families have allowed the teen culture of our day and its associated busyness to rule the home. Much time is expended transporting children to "fluff of life" activities. Dads are beguiled into working more to financially support the extra amusements of their children. As a result, not only do many families have no time to be a family, but they also have no time to wholeheartedly pursue the Lord. The home thus loses its appeal as a safe haven, and a place of significance and importance to the children. The lack of family devotions and family time together is devastating to family unity and promotes the isolation of its members. The way in which we use our time speaks frankly of our love for the Lord. We cannot *buy back* time per se, but we can *buy up* opportunities to serve God. Let us have no regrets later for how we spend our lives now.

It is paramount that each of us know *"what the will of the Lord is"* rather than trying to live for Him in ignorance (v. 17). "The will of God" and the related phrases "the Lord's will," "the Lord will," and "Your will" occur thirty-four times in the New Testament. Nineteen times the sovereign plan of God to accomplish a distinct purpose is in view. There are four references to the will of God being done or that it shall be done, and seven references to believers doing God's will. Scripture further declares that the expressed will of God should be understood, and three times it is specifically declared for all believers to know.

The term relates to a sovereign God accomplishing His purposes in time, whether it be through a specific event, or in conforming the behavior and attitudes of believers to be like those of His Son. Several times in Scripture "the will of God" refers to the overall holy behavior all believers should exhibit. For those aspects of God's will which are not fully revealed, the believer learns to trust God's guiding hand. In this way, God works on our attitudes and motives, and refines the quality of our faith.

As an example, God is *"long-suffering towards us, not willing that any should perish"* (2 Pet. 3:9). How can God desire something, but yet not force it to happen? It is an unfolding of His foreknowledge and predestined blessings in Christ which are guaranteed to benefit those who, in time, repent and receive His Word. God, in a way that we cannot fully understand, weaves together the infinitely numerous thoughts, decisions, and actions of human beings to achieve His purposes in ways that are fully in accord with His perfect will. Thankfully, we don't have to completely understand the mind of God to obtain His blessing; God simply wants us to trust Him for what cannot be fully understood and to obey what He has revealed to us.

For those aspects of God's will which are clearly revealed, the believer learns to yield to the Lord – our conduct is brought into alignment with His will. This pleases God and promotes Christ-likeness, which will be the ultimate outcome of our salvation (Rom. 8:29).

Paul instructs believers to *"be not unwise, but understanding what the will of the Lord is"* (v. 17) in order to *"prove what is that good, and acceptable, and perfect, will of God"* (Rom. 12:2). Consequently, Paul exhorted the believers at Colosse, *"stand perfect and complete in all the will of God"* (Col. 4:12). Knowing, yielding to, and demonstrating the will of God is the goal of the Christian life. In summary, we are *to learn* the revealed will of God (Ps. 143:10) and *to delight* in doing it (Ps. 40:8).

What is God's will for all Christians? The following behaviors are the expressed will of God for all believers (this is not an exhaustive list):

1. Serve and please the Lord instead of men (6:6).
2. Do not be conformed to the world (Rom. 12:2).
3. By well-doing put to silence the ignorance of foolish men (1 Pet. 2:15).
4. Abstain from fornication (1 Thess. 4:3).
5. In everything give thanks (1 Thess. 5:18).
6. Suffer for well doing, rather than for evil doing (1 Pet. 3:17).
7. Do not be controlled by the lusts of the flesh (1 Pet. 4:2).

A true believer will long to know the will of God and then do the will of God. Love for the Lord Jesus Christ prompts obedience: *"If you love Me, keep My commandments"* (John 14:15). The believer is challenged to live for and invest into eternity. John wrote, *"And the world passes away, and the lust thereof: but he that doeth the will of God abides forever"* (1 Jn. 2:17). All that is of this world is going to vanish someday and only what is done for Christ has lasting value. May each of us know and yield to the revealed will of God. It is the only way to experience Christ and to please God during our earthly sojourn.

Paul's next exhortation is associated with accomplishing this goal: *"And do not be drunk with wine, in which is dissipation; but be filled with the Spirit"* (v. 18). While the use of wine is not prohibited in Scripture, its abuse is. Drunkenness is consistently forbidden. Paul exhorts believers not to be controlled by excess wine, but rather be controlled by the Holy Spirit. The Greek verb *pleroo* is rendered "be filled" and means "to have influence or control over." In moderation, the fruit of the vine may stir up joy, but if abused, it certainly will control behavior. Both the Holy Spirit and wine can be permitted to have influence within us that unnaturally affects our behavior. Paul is not suggesting that believers get more of the Holy Spirit through being filled by Him, but rather that He would get more of us. Both alcohol and the Holy Spirit can cause us to behave abnormally. The former promotes folly, the latter only what pleases God.

It would be impossible for a believer to be filled with wine (controlled by the effects of alcohol) and also be filled with the Holy Spirit. In truth, besides alcohol, there are a host of things we can permit access into our lives which negatively influence our thinking. How can the Holy Spirit fill us up if we have allowed our minds to be flooded with things that do not have God's approval? If we are pursuing selfish or carnal lusts, or have strongholds of envy, pride, or bitterness in our hearts, what room is there for the Holy Spirit to add His goodness? We cannot be filled by Him if we are already full of ourselves. In response to His conviction, we must yield to Him that He might empty us of self, and so that we might experience His control. F. B. Hole writes: "The contrast is between what is fleshly and what is spiritual. We are to decline what excites the flesh that we may know the power of the Spirit. When thus filled we can offer the sacrifice of praise."[68]

As the believer submits to the known will of God, the Holy Spirit responds by filling that individual and equipping him or her for service with divine power. Through the Spirit's "filling" believers are able to enjoy the fullness of His presence. Submission leads to Spirit-filling, which results in usefulness and fruitfulness. Without Spirit-filling we can do nothing to please God. This truth is clearly witnessed in the dawn of the Church Age (Acts 1:4 with 1:12 and 2:1-4; Acts 4:23-32; Acts 6:9-10 with 7:55; Acts

9:6 with 9:17). As submission leads to Spirit-filling resulting in fruitfulness, the believer is commanded to *"be filled with the Holy Spirit"* (v. 18).

Next Paul highlights several evidences of Spirit-filling in the believer's life. First, Spirit-filled believers should be *"Speaking to one another in psalms and hymns and spiritual songs, singing and making melody in your heart to the Lord"* (v. 19). Psalms are the inspired poems from the book of Psalms. Hymns ascribe worship, praise, and thanksgiving to God, but their lyrics are based on Scripture, rather than being directly inspired. Spiritual songs have edifying lyrics which prompt believers to aspire to deeper devotion to God, to affirm godly living, and to yearn to be with Christ.

Paul wrote something similar to the church at Colosse (Col. 3:16) to convey the truth that our singing is to reaffirm Scriptural truth and to worship and praise God. Regrettably, the Church accepts error more readily through music than through preaching, and Satan knows it! Understanding that music is a powerful medium in which to convey both our thoughts to God and of God to each other, let us be careful to ensure that our songs are doctrinally and contextually sound and that the composition does not stir up the flesh to carnal behavior or thinking. Rather, *"making melody in your heart to the Lord"* means the Holy Spirit stirs up joyful admiration for the One about whom we are singing!

A second indication of the Spirit-filled life is a spirit of thankfulness. How is it possible to offer God thanks *for all things*, when much of what we suffer in our sin-cursed world is distasteful, harsh, unjust, and sometimes deadly? The idea of verse 20 is not just to find something in a bad situation for which to thank God for, but to actually appreciate His sovereign care, even when it does not seem reasonable to do so (also see 1 Thess. 5:16-18).

We may not feel like being joyful or thankful after a particular hardship, but we must do so. Later, we will be glad that we did (Phil. 3:15-16)! If we feel we cannot be strong, we can still choose to rejoice in Christ. When we do so, we will find that strength will come. Daniel was in a life-threatening ordeal but chose to give thanks to God (Dan. 6:10). Afterwards he was promoted and his God was exalted throughout the Persian Empire. Choosing to offer God thanks in arduous times shows that we know His character and attributes, and count Him faithful. This provides an opportunity for God to exalt Himself. When things go wrong, do not go wrong with them. Rather, rejoice in the One who will right all wrongs.

Third, Spirit-filled believers willingly submit to other believers (v. 21). Christ is Head of the Church, and all believers are His servants. This means that no believer can adopt an attitude of superiority over another. In fact, the writer of Hebrews instructs us to *"exhort one another daily"* (Heb. 3:13) in an effort to keep each other from doubting God's Word and from engaging in conduct that would be displeasing to the Lord. Although God assigned an order to the exercise of His authority on earth (e.g., in the church and in the home), believers understand that they are under Christ's authority. Therefore, they gladly submit to each other as unto Him.

## Marriage – Christ and the Church (vv. 22-33)

One of the most powerful testimonies of changed lives is the presence of Christ's love and authority in the home. Through the remainder of the chapter, Paul reveals what a God-honoring marriage looks like and the proper attitudes and roles of husbands and wives to achieve what is being modeled by Christ's own relationship with His Bride – the Church. Although most of the exhortations in this section are to husbands, Paul begins this discussion by first addressing wives: *"Wives, submit to your own husbands, as to the Lord. For the husband is head of the wife, as also Christ is head of the church; and He is the Savior of the body"* (vv. 22-23).

Submission to order includes dependence on the authority over us. God funnels blessings from Heaven through proper channels of authority. All of us are under some authority. Since the days of Noah, this has been His tool for teaching human submission to Himself. The Church is dependent upon Christ for provision and blessing and she is to willingly submit to His authority in all things. A wife is to be dependent upon her husband to provide for her needs and to protect her. Her husband is her head, just as Christ is Head of the Church (v. 24).

The term "head" (e.g., 1 Cor. 11:3) refers to someone who has authority and, thus, the one to whom subjection is to be yielded. Biblical headship includes three main spheres of authority: church order, home order, and civil order. If the maximum blessing of God is to be obtained and experienced, those exercising God's delegated authority in each sphere must be doing so in complete submission to His divine authority.

In Home Order, wives are to be submissive helpers and are to respect their husbands' authority (Gen. 3:16; Col. 3:18). The deepest need of the man is to be respected, whereas the deepest need of a woman is to know that she is significant and secure in her husband's love. Positionally, the wife is equal to her husband, yet God has given the husband authority over the wife in the marital relationship. It was God who designed and initiated the marriage relationship in Genesis 2:23-24, therefore, His rules apply. The Lord Jesus confirmed that God's order for marriage had not changed (Matt. 19:5-6). Warren Wiersbe summarizes God's plan to bless the home:

God does all things "decently and in order" (1 Cor. 14:40). If He did not have a chain of command in society, we would have chaos. ... True spiritual submission is the secret of growth and fulfillment. When a Christian woman is submitted to the Lord and to her own husband, she experiences a release and fulfillment that she can have in no other way. This mutual love and submission creates an atmosphere of growth in the home that enables both the husband and the wife to become all that God wants them to be.[69]

Next, Paul exhorts husbands, *"Husbands, love your wives, just as Christ also loved the church and gave Himself for her"* (v. 25). It has been said that "an ideal wife is any woman who has an ideal husband" and "a good husband makes a good wife." Just as woman was fashioned from and for man, biblical manhood advocates biblical womanhood. For a wife to enjoy the full and essential qualities and blessings of femininity she must firstly understand the divine purpose for which she was created. Then, her husband must satisfy her intrinsic needs, and she must be sustained by God's grace for the strenuous responsibility of being a help, fitted for her husband. In God's design, woman was created to be a helper for man. Man was created to satisfy her needs, thus assisting her to fulfill her God-given role.

Using Christ's relationship with His Church as an example, Paul defines what genuine love for one's wife looks like (vv. 25-30). In God's design for the family, the husband is to lead, provide, protect, and shepherd his family and love his wife in the following biblical ways. First, the husband is to be a *stable* head (i.e., leader; vv. 22-24). His decisions are to be consistent, just, wise, and spiritual in nature. He should not be prone to emotional outbursts, frivolous expenditures, or carnal appetites. Christ is a stable Head!

Second, the husband *sacrificially* serves his wife, just as Christ gave himself for His Church (v. 25; Col. 3:19). God created the woman to be a love-responder. Generally speaking, husbands who love their wives in this fashion will have wives who both respect their authority and want to reciprocate the Christlike love they have received. The Church responds to the love it receives from Christ by returning that love, for we love God because He first loved us (1 Jn. 4:19). The husband is commanded to sacrificially give to his wife, just as Christ gave Himself for the Church.

Third, the husband is to have a *sanctifying* ministry (vv. 26-27). The husband is to promote his wife's spiritual growth through applying the Word of God, just as Christ cleanses the Church through Scripture. This would include using the Word for both encouragement and to promote God-honoring conduct. But husbands must have "clean hands and a pure heart" before assisting their wives to have the same.

Fourth, besides her spiritual needs, the husband is to *satisfy* the emotional and physical needs of his wife, just as Christ nourishes and cherishes His Church (vv. 28-30). The requirement for a church elder is literally to be *a one-woman man* and this is a good pattern for all married men to follow (i.e., one's relationship with his wife is above reproach and reflects God's best design for marriage; 1 Tim. 3:2). Such a man is to be morally blameless in his marriage. This means no sexual misconduct, no inappropriate touching with anyone, no meetings with females alone, and no pornography or lascivious behavior (Prov. 5:15-20; Eph. 5:3-4).

The marriage covenant sanctifies and protects the sexual union of a man and a woman, but it does not condone what is inappropriate, unnatural, harmful, or offends the conscience (Deut. 23:17; Rom. 14:23; Heb. 13:4). Biblical love is shown by a husband attending to his wife's needs first.

Fifth, the husband is to provide his wife *security* (v. 30). Paul refers to the relationship of Christ and the Church to stress his point of secure oneness in marriage. Believers amazingly become spiritually one with Christ through the New Covenant (v. 31). A man and woman "become one flesh" (a one-person relationship; Gen. 2:24) through the marriage covenant, which is then consummated by their sexual union. The husband is to ensure his wife is secure in his love, just as the Church, the body of Christ, is secure in Him. The woman has a deep need for security (i.e., she needs to know that her husband has eyes only for her) and significance (i.e., she needs to feel important to and appreciated by her husband).

The word "submission" is not popular in our modern society, but submission to God-ordained authority is absolutely necessary to please God and receive His blessing. Biblical submission to authority has two main ingredients. First, there is obedience. A wife is to obey her husband's leadership decisions, just as the Church is to obey Christ's direction (v. 24; John 14:15). The wise husband will listen to his wife. Information given respectfully is not a lack of submission; rather, it is needful. Gathering the necessary facts on a matter before making a decision is just good leadership!

Second, there is respect (v. 33). A wife is to respect her husband's God-given *position* of authority. The army says, "Salute the uniform, not the man." A husband may be a poor leader, but God's order of authority should still be honored. The deepest need of the man is to be respected and a wife would do well to fulfil that need for her husband in assisting him to become the man God wants him to be. Verse 33 supplies a concise summary of how to have a God-honoring marriage: Wives are to respect their husband's authority, as unto the Lord, and husbands are to follow Christ's example and selflessly love their wives.

# Ephesians Chapter 6

### Parents and Children (vv. 1-4)

In the previous chapter we learned that the Spirit-filled life is one of submission to other Christians and to the authorities that God has placed over us. We recognize that submitting to God's order and will for our lives enables us to be joyful in Him and profitable for Him. Continuing the subject of *Home Order*, Paul transitions from the husband-and-wife relationship to that of parents and children.

Paul instructs children to honor and obey their parents *"in the Lord"* (vv. 1-3). The Greek word translated "children" in verse 1 is *teknon,* which means "that which is derived of another" (i.e., children are derived from their parents). Age is not implied, meaning that the application of the word is not limited to small children. A different Greek word, *paidion,* is used to speak of infants and small children. Therefore, children should always respect and honor their parents regardless of how old they are (v. 2). Of course, when children marry and have children of their own, the new parents become accountable to do what is God-honoring for their own family.

The stipulation phrase, *"in the Lord,"* implies children are to serve their parents as unto the Lord in matters of righteousness, but not in matters of sin. For example, in the case of Korah, some of his sons refused to follow their father into rebellion against Moses and Aaron, and most importantly the Lord, and thus escaped the divine judgment which completely wiped out the rebels (Num. 16). They disobeyed their father in order to follow God's expressed will, which had been clearly shown to them.

Paul mentions the promised blessing tied with children obeying this commandment: *"that it may be well with you and you may live long on the earth"* (v. 3). In general, those who despise authority and are rebellious usually reap the consequences of their carnality and die earlier or at least live lesser lives than if blessed by God. A child not corrected would be socially miserable and a nuisance to society. His sinful ways and rebellious manner would probably lead him into an early grave. Samson, Absalom, and Eli's sons are examples of such. However, a child who practices obedience is much more likely to live a happy and prosperous life.

After admonishing children to obey their parents, the fifth of the Ten

Commandments, Paul admonishes fathers, *"Do not provoke your children to wrath, but bring them up in the training and admonition of the Lord"* (v. 4). Fathers are never to abuse their leadership role in the family, for God will hold them accountable (e.g., 1 Pet. 3:7). Albert Leckie explains the grammar in the text to affirm the divine accountability that Christian fathers have to raise up spiritual children for God:

> "Fathers" (*pateres*) may be translated "parents," but this would not be consistent with the context. In v. 1 "parents" is the translation of *goneis*, and in v. 2 "father and mother" (*patera ... mētera*). It would appear that the apostle is thinking not only of the particular responsibility of the father, but of a peculiar danger: "... provoke not to wrath" (*parorgizō*, to anger, noun in 4:26 "your wrath"). Children obey; fathers exercise necessary self-control so that by not continually looking for faults, nor showing relish and hastiness in correction, nor personal bad example, they do not provoke to anger.[70]

Whenever God gives authority, there is always accountability to Him (e.g., Heb. 13:17). Hence, fathers are to train their children for the Lord, for He desires a "godly offspring," not just reproduction (Mal. 2:15). Children do not naturally know the way they should go; they must be shown what God expects through a godly example (Prov. 22:6).

In a coming day every man will give an account to God for any abuse or neglect of his wife and children. During a Bible study with a group of young men, I asked how fathers might provoke their children to wrath. These were a few of the ways that were suggested: Being physically, sexually, emotionally abusive. Being overbearing, not acknowledging achievements, fault-finding or having a critical spirit, showing favoritism, exhibiting hypocrisy, reminding children of past failures, not being sensitive to needs or feelings, failing to keep promises, controlling, and reliving his life through his children.

The word "training" or "nurture" (KJV) in verse 4 is derived from the Greek word *paideia*. The word "chastise" comes from the same Greek root word as *paideia, paideuo,* meaning "to train by disciplinary punishment." Pilate employs *paideuo*, meaning "to chastise," just prior to the Lord's crucifixion: *"I (Pilate speaking) will therefore chastise Him, and release Him"* (Luke 23:16). In summary, *nurture* or *training* includes a broad range of educational methods, which also includes the provision "to train by pain."

It is the measured response of the parent towards a child who has ignored instruction – measured in that it applies justice according to the previously stated order; measured also in that it considers influences which may have adversely affected the child's judgment. Under-measured chastisement mocks justice and will effectively undermine the weight of parental instruction. If the punishment is too harsh or undeserving, it will depress the child or provoke him or her to wrath. Nurturing supports instruction – the disciplinary rod is never without reproof (Prov. 22:15)!

The Greek word *nouthesia* is rendered "admonish," which means "to put in mind" or "to call attention to a subject matter by giving a mild rebuke or warning." A caution or gentle reproof is given by parents as they witness their children heading toward forbidden territory. If a child is young and learning boundaries, use admonition.

Christian parents must know the Lord and His Word to properly teach their children to know and love Him too. The Bible should never be neglected in the home, but rather should be the rulebook for all family matters. A Christian family is not a household of Christians, but a Christian household. It is more than Christ dwelling within the hearts of family members; it is a family that is pursuing the heart of God. If the Bible is not at the center of family life and all home affairs, that home cannot be called a true Christian home.

## Masters and Servants (vv. 5-9)

It is estimated that about 120 million people lived within the Roman Empire at the time Paul wrote this epistle and that about half of these subjects were slaves. Although the Bible does not endorse slavery, it does place limits on its practices. For example, under the Law, a Jewish slave was to be released after six years of service, or at the fifty-year Jubilee if it occurred prior to the six-year tenure (Lev. 25:39-42; Deut. 15:12). Being a nation of liberated slaves, the Jews were not to enslave each other, but servitude was permissible for matters such as settling outstanding debts or fulfilling judicial penalties.

As Christianity spread through the Roman Empire, both slaves and masters were becoming Christians and fellow brethren in Christ. This created a difficulty, as all those in Christ should mutually love, respect, and serve each other, but slavery did not permit such social liberty. Hence, Paul supplies wisdom for how both believing masters and slaves should behave towards each other to honor the Lord (vv. 5-9; Col. 3:22-25). In principle, these exhortations are prudent for employer-employee relationships, which is a type of indentured service.

Slaves were to be obedient to and respectful of their human masters as unto Christ (v. 5). This meant that slaves were to serve faithfully, even when their masters were not watching, since the Lord always observed them (v. 6). *"Whatever you do, do it heartily, as to the Lord and not to men"* (Col. 3:23). Faithful service rendered with a proper attitude to the Lord pleases Him and will be rewarded (vv. 7-8). Masters were to remember that they also had a Master in Heaven to whom they were accountable for the treatment of slaves in their care (v. 9). Masters were to be just and fair, and not overbearing or cruel in executing their leadership (Col. 4:1).

## Christian Warfare (vv. 10-20)

Paul revealed several mysteries of God (previously concealed truths about Christ and His Church) in his epistle to the Ephesians. The apostle wanted them to finish well, so first he taught them to "sit" with Christ in heavenly places (chs. 1-3), and then about the necessity to "walk" with Him in holiness (chs. 4-5). He concludes by telling them how to "stand" strong in the Lord against spiritual wickedness (ch. 6).

**The Believer's Position in Christ.** To "sit" in the heavenly places (2:6) means to rest in our identification with Christ. Sitting means no strain on the legs (no walking or standing): We are to rest in faith without expending fleshly energy. Christ usually waits until we rest in Him before acting to rescue us from our difficulties.

**The Believer's Life in the World.** To "walk" has two aspects: First, it means to complete (i.e., *walk in*) what God has divinely arranged for us to do (2:10). Second, and the more common application, walk means to "order one's behavior." We are not to walk like we did before (4:17), but rather as selfless, cross-bearing children of light (5:8). This is a life worthy of our union in Christ.

**The Believer's Attitude Towards the Enemy.** To "stand" means we are to resist and withstand satanic powers in high places (vv. 11-14). Gospel work is offensive in nature because it must confront sin, but the focus of Ephesians 6 is how to withstand satanic attack.

To war against spiritual wickedness in heavenly places, we must rely on an authority higher than that of the enemy, thus the paramount importance of the priestly ministry of Christ. This means that believers must use all the spiritual armor that God supplies (vv. 13-17) and approach Christ in heavenly places to receive the resources required to "stand" against darkness and wickedness. Only then can we *"be strong in the Lord and in the power of His might"* (v. 10).

The epistle reaches its thematic crescendo at verse 11. Paul has spoken of the believer's position in Christ and the blessings associated with that union (Eph. 1-3). He has taught that the believer's union with Christ demanded an appropriate walk (lifestyle) that would honor Christ (Eph. 4-5). In Ephesians 6, Paul identifies the spiritual battle that wages on for those in Christ. We war against spiritual wickedness in heavenly places. Paul wanted the believers to *stand* strong against this powerful enemy. But they needed to understand the particulars of the *sit-walk-stand* process he detailed in his epistle, and so do we.

The Ephesians were to stand against demonic forces that oppose Christ in the world. Paul mentions "to stand" three times and "to withstand" or "to resist" once in verses 11-14. Christ defeated Satan at the cross, and believers are to continue the victory already achieved at Calvary by resisting the enemy. Watchman Nee explains:

> Christ's warfare was offensive; he gained the victory over the devil at the Cross. Our warfare is mostly defensive – we war against Satan only to maintain and consolidate the victory which Christ has already gained – we hold what Christ has gained against all challenges. If we fight with the concept of gaining a victory, then we lose the battle at the onset. The Christian walk and warfare draw their strength from sitting before God and resting in Him. Satan's objective is to move us from the perfect ground of triumph, thus our armor is essentially defensive.[71]

To withstand such a powerful enemy, spiritual wickedness in high places, the believer must rely on the One who resides in the highest place and be strengthened in Him. Kenneth Wuest translates verse 10 this way: "Be constantly strengthened in the Lord and in the active efficacy of the might that is inherent in Him." The believer is not dependent on *trying* to gain victory in his own strength in the circumstances of life, but on maintaining Christ's victory in life's circumstances by *trusting* Christ in heavenly places (i.e., depending on His strength, not ours). Again, Watchman Nee writes:

> No Christian can hope to enter the warfare of the ages without learning first to rest in Christ and in what he has done, and then through the strength of the Holy Spirit within, to follow him in a practical, holy life on earth. If he is deficient in either of these, he will find that all the talk about spiritual warfare remains only talk; he will never know its reality. Satan can afford to ignore him, for he does not count for anything.[72]

So, believers are to stand, that is, take up a resistive opposition to Satan and spiritual wickedness on the triumphant ground of Christ. We must be energized through prayer and clad with spiritual armor to stand. Verse 13 does not primarily address the matter of standing in victory daily, although every day until the Rapture is the evil day (day = period) in which the believer must stand. Rather, it speaks of the believer's ability to stand in every instance of conflict in any day until the Rapture.

Paul begins to identify the spiritual armor provided by the Lord for believers: *"Stand therefore, having girded your waist with truth, having put on the breastplate of righteousness"* (v. 14). Being a prisoner in Rome, Paul would have been quite acquainted with how a Roman soldier was dressed and equipped (Acts 28:16). He then applies what is a familiar scene as an illustration to teach about the spiritual armor provided for all believers. The Greek narrative on the subject (vv. 14-18) is composed of two separate statements initiated by the imperative verbs rendered "stand" in verse 14 and "take" in verse 17.

Satan's voice is recorded only three times in Scripture (Gen. 3; Job 1-2; Matt. 4). This would seem to indicate that he is more likely to use subtle approaches to work his evil agenda rather than employing a direct assault. Satan's subtle devices are not always obvious. This is why the first three pieces of armor should be worn at all times. Notice that "having" is connected with the belt of truth, the breastplate of righteousness, and feet shod with the gospel. However, when the enemy's activity is more obvious, we must "take" and put on every piece of armor supplied by God for protection. Believers should be wearing the whole armor of God in such spiritual confrontations.

"Take" and "taking" is connected with the latter three pieces of spiritual armor. Thus, God permits Satan to test believers to prove or refine them. This has the effect of making us more dependent upon Him, and as a result, more fruitful for Him (Jas. 1:12-13; Job 1:6-12). This is an ongoing process, meaning that the believer should always be appropriately spiritually equipped with the belt, the breastplate and the proper footwear.

*Having* **girded your waist with truth**: Roman soldiers wore a long square tunic which could be pulled up and tied to prevent hindrance of their movement. This action speaks of the readiness that believers are to have with the truth at a moment's notice. The soldier's sword hung on his belt. In the same way truth undergirds all of the believer's spiritual armor. But we cannot be ambassadors of truth if we are entangled by worldly affairs (2 Tim. 2:4) or if we are corrupted by hypocrisy (Col. 2:4). This involves more than just knowing doctrine. The belt of truth readies the inner man by controlling his thoughts and affections based in the truth. Hamilton Smith writes:

The first piece of armor strengthens the inner man and regulates our thoughts and affections, rather than our conduct, speech and ways. Oftentimes we make great efforts to preserve a correct outward demeanor towards one another while, at the same time, careless as to our thoughts and affections. If we are to withstand the wiles of the enemy, we must commence by being right inwardly. The Preacher warns us as to what we say with our lips, as to what our eyes look upon, and as to the path our feet tread, but first of all he says, "Keep *thy heart* more than anything that is guarded" (Prov. 4:23-27).[73]

The Roman breastplate was composed of a solid piece of metal that was formed in the shape of a man's chest with a second piece of fitted metal for his back. The front and back components were held together by leather straps. The breastplate protected the soldier's vital organs from blows from swords or penetration by spears or arrows. This piece of armor was to be worn at all times.

Spiritually speaking, **the breastplate of righteousness** covers a pure heart and speaks of maintaining holy conduct at all times. G. V. Wigram suggests that we have the breastplate of righteous on properly when we choose to walk in the world as Christ did:

> *"Having on the breastplate of righteousness."* Christ has walked through the world and left the marks of His feet, and we are to walk as He walked, to like what He liked, and to dislike what He disliked. If I do this it will be a perfect covering for me. Verse 15. I should connect that as much with "having done," and "standing," as with walking. Both "the peace of God," connected with your emptying your heart out before God, and the "God of peace" from your walking with God (Phil. 4:6-9), both enter in here as giving rest and quietness to the soul.[74]

Believers must keep short accounts with the Lord concerning confession of sin and also seek to maintain a pure walk before Him. Righteous living provides a blameless testimony which will limit accusatory attacks. Believers dedicated to holy living will enjoy a strong defense against the accusatory blows of the enemy. Believers walking hand in hand with Christ are invincible and immortal until their work on earth is done.

Next, Paul speaks of the believer's spiritual footwear: ***"And having shod your feet with the preparation of the gospel of peace"*** (v. 15). The Roman soldier wore sandals fitted with hobnails on the bottom to ensure sound footing. This provision was especially helpful when a legion put their shields into various formations to protect each other from a bombardment of arrows and darts, or when the enemy attempted to push through their shield barrier. Just as the Roman sandals provided firm footing, believers are to stand firm in the peace of the gospel while in enemy territory (i.e., the world's unrest and wickedness). F. B. Hole describes what it means for believers to have their feed shod with the preparation of the gospel:

> In a normal way we hardly think of shoes as being in the nature of armor, yet inasmuch as it is with our shoes that we continually come into contact with the earth, they take on that character from the Christian standpoint. If our contact with earth is not right, we shall be vulnerable indeed. What does "the preparation of the gospel of peace," mean? Not that we should be preparing the way of the gospel in an evangelistic sense (though to do that is of course very desirable) but that we ourselves should come under the preparation which the gospel of peace effects. If our feet are shod in this way, we shall carry the peace of the Gospel into all our dealings with men of this world, and be protected ourselves in so doing.[75]

This means that believers need to be ready at a moment's notice to be faithful witnesses for Christ (Acts 1:8) and to patiently use Scripture in whatever way necessary to convey the truth of the gospel in word and in deed (2 Tim. 4:2; 1 Pet. 3:15-16).

The next piece of spiritual armor is identified in verse 16, **the shield of faith**: *"Above all, taking the shield of faith with which you will be able to quench all the fiery darts of the wicked one."* While some Roman shields were made of metal, the more widely used shield *thureon* was a thick piece of leather covered wood of about two-and-a-half by four feet in size. The leather was treated to make it fire resistant. This type of shield was heavy, weighing about twenty pounds. The shield was capable of stopping fiery darts, spears, and arrows. The shields could be connected together or overlapped to form a wall or ceiling, or both, depending on the type of protection needed. This also ensured that retreat was not an option. The soldiers were safer staying and working together to create an impenetrable barrier in the face of the enemy.

Paul states that the shield of faith is needed to extinguish the fiery darts of the wicked one. The darts speak of demonic suggestions and enticements. The enemy can discourage us by planting doubts in our minds, or stimulating mental strongholds such as greed or bitterness, or causing anxiety over what we cannot control, or by deceiving us concerning the truth (Acts 5:3; 2 Cor. 11:14-15; Col. 2:4).

As spiritual armor for the believer, the shield represents trusting in the Lord for protection against the adversary. Soldiers of the cross are to stand firm on biblical truth and not withdraw from it. There are times when we all suffer from weak faith. Doubts and discouragement come in like a barrage of flaming darts. At such times, those who are strong in faith can rally around the fainthearted and protect them from further attack with their own shields of faith. Like a Roman legion, believers who engage the enemy together provide encouragement and protection for the whole group.

The Roman shield was too heavy to carry around every moment of the day, but as soon as a threat was observed, the shields were quickly taken up and readied for action. Spiritually speaking, believers must be watchful and immediately ready to take up their shields of faith when an obvious attack is looming. Believers gathered for prayer and resting in God's truth and promises pose an impenetrable fortress against the fiery darts of the enemy.

Next, Paul exhorts believers to *"take **the helmet of salvation**, and the sword of the Spirit, which is the word of God"* (v. 17). As mentioned previously, the verb "take" in this verse is in the imperative mood (it is not another participle), thus dividing the believer's armor into two groups of three pieces. The Roman soldier's helmet, shield, and sword were heavy equipment. It was not necessary to wear the helmet, hold up the shield, and have one's sword drawn every moment of the day. However, these were to be accessible to take up quickly if it was obvious that a battle was imminent. For all other times, the belt, breastplate, and shoes were adequate protection.

The Roman helmet protected against the heavy broadsword which was swung like a bat by horse-mounted cavalry. The broadsword was used with the intention of removing the head of an enemy soldier. Likewise, the devil wants Christians to lose their heads when opposed by him. Hope invigorates the soldier in adversity, and believers have the assurance of ultimate victory and eternal safety in God's presence (Rom. 8:31). Because Christ has already defeated Satan at Calvary, we know that our destiny is secure in Him. Accordingly, we are to wear the helmet which is *"the hope of salvation"* (1 Thess. 5:8). The matter of destiny is settled. The eternal Christ is in and with the believers no matter how difficult our circumstances are in this present life.

Effective spiritual warfare requires: First, maturity and training; we are on active duty and in the Lord's school. Second, we must be committed to holy living to ensure that we remain in fellowship with Him. Third, we must maintain full reliance on the Lord Jesus Christ. All beneficial spiritual exercise begins when we rest in Him who is seated in the heavenly places. The helmet speaks of our security in Christ.

"Spirit" is in the genitive case in relationship to "sword" in verse 17, meaning that the sword originated with the Holy Spirit – it is His sword. **The sword of the Spirit** is the Word of God used in the power of the Spirit. The sword could be used for offensive or defensive warfare. However, the context of this text highlights its defensive use.

God's Word properly applied is able to cut to the heart, or more specifically, the human conscience (Heb. 4:12). The sword in verse 17 is the *machaira*, which was a six- to eighteen-inch two-edged sword used in hand-to-hand combat. It was sheathed and attached to the soldier's belt. The Greek word rendered "word" is *rhema*. The word *logos* is more often translated "word" in Scripture and is used to speak of a general concept or the full ramification of something. However, *rhema* is used to convey the idea of a specific thought or application. Spiritually speaking, then, Paul is instructing believers to rightly know Scripture and by the power of the Holy Spirit precisely apply it to a specific situation.

The example of the Lord Jesus in the wilderness countering every attack by Satan with precise application of quotations of God's Word from Deuteronomy (Matt. 4:1-11) demonstrates Paul's point. Ownership of a physical copy of the Bible does not in itself mean that we possess a spiritual sword. Rather, we must know Scripture, accurately discern its meaning, and so that the Holy Spirit can enable us to call to mind an appropriate passage to wield in any given situation.

To use their spiritual armor effectively, Paul charges the saints to always be praying in the Spirit and to be watchful (v. 18). Harold Hoehner observes that the Greek participles describe the tenacity that good soldiers must have:

> The manner in which a soldier takes up these last two pieces of armor is suggested by two Greek participles: "praying" and "being alert." When the enemy attacks – and on all occasions – Christians are to pray continually in the Spirit (i.e., in the power and sphere of the Spirit; Jude 20). With all kinds of prayers and requests suggests the thoroughness and intensity of their praying. And like reliable soldiers, they are to be keeping alert, literally, "in all persistence."[76]

In the Church Age we are invited to lift up our needs, cares, and burdens to the Lord (1 Pet. 5:6-7). Sincerely casting onto the Lord by prayer those things pressing down on our hearts is initially a laborious task, but ultimately results in abiding peace.

Prayer is work, and believers must leave strength and time for effectual praying. If we fail to pray, we will fall in spiritual battle. The objective of prayer is not to shift our loads so that we can better shoulder them (that would be an exhausting waste of time), but to release our burdens to the Lord to deal with as only He can. However, we must remember that groaning in prayer is not the same as grumbling or complaining to God about our difficulties (Rom. 8:22-27). The latter behavior reveals something lurking within us that inhibits praying in the Spirit (Eph. 6:18). The hindrance may be a rebellious spirit, doubt, some level of distrust, or perhaps dissatisfaction with the Lord. We can escape these snares by candidly and genuinely lifting up our burdens to our caring Savior.

Grammatically speaking, prayer and alertness are tied together with the use of the helmet and the sword. God's armor is not given to make us independent of Him. It can only be rightly used in the spirit of dependence upon its Giver. We must pray always "in the Spirit." Nee writes:

> Prayer in Christ's name unleashes the power, the authority, of His name in three ways: Preaching of the gospel, our warfare, and in our asking. We must be careful to invoke Christ's name on what is confirmed to be divine in purpose, per the word, and completely dependent on Him.[77]

Our spiritual armor is only effective when the power of God is working on our behalf. The proper defense against Satan is not our money, fame, organization, wit, or intellect, but in using *all* the spiritual armor (resources) that is provided for us by God.

In verses 19-20, Paul explains that he was a prisoner of Jesus Christ before he was a prisoner of Rome (Rom. 1:1). Shortly after his conversion, Paul had been made aware of the ministry that Christ was calling him to complete (Acts 9:15-16). He was an ambassador of Christ called to declare Christ and the mysteries of the gospel to the Gentiles.

## Conclusion (vv. 21-24)

Paul informed the Ephesians that he was sending to them a beloved brother and faithful minister named Tychicus (v. 21). He would deliver Paul's letter to them, and also letters to the saints at Colosse and to Philemon (along with a newly converted runaway slave named Onesimus). Tychicus would inform them about the specifics of Paul's situation and be a comfort to them (v. 22).

Paul closes the epistle with a farewell extending peace and love with faith to the brethren from God the Father and the Lord Jesus Christ (v. 23). In the final verse, Paul expresses his desire that God's grace would fully enable all those who sincerely love Christ to serve Him faithfully (v. 24).

# Philippians

## Background

Philippians is one of four epistles written during Paul's first imprisonment in Rome, commencing in approximately 60 A.D. and lasting about two years. Paul was under house arrest and had much more liberty to do ministry than he was allowed during his second Roman imprisonment a few years later. According to the book of Acts, Paul journeyed to Philippi, a Roman colony situated in Macedonia just north of the Aegean Sea, during his second missionary journey. Philippi was where Paul and Silas witnessed the first European converts to Christ – Lydia and her household.

After casting out a spirit of divination from a servant girl, Paul and Silas were arrested, severely beaten, and imprisoned without a trial as commanded by the magistrates. While securely bound in the inner prison, the two evangelists began to sing praises to God. An earthquake then occurred, which freed Paul, Silas, and the other prisoners from their bonds and cells. The jailkeeper, knowing that he would be put to death if any of his prisoners escaped, sought to take his own life. Paul cried out to him not to do so and the keeper responded by asking how to be saved. In short order, he and his household heard and believed the gospel message and afterwards were baptized. The Church at Philippi was a direct outcome of suffering saints rejoicing in the Lord Jesus Christ.

It is unlikely that Paul spent more than a couple of months at Philippi before departing shortly after being arrested and beaten. However, the Philippians' deep love for Paul is evident in their giving spirit in support of him and his ministry. Indeed, the very purpose of the epistle was to acknowledge a gift of support from the church. The epistle is practical and personally endearing. Paul's deep appreciation for the saints of Philippi is apparent throughout the letter.

## Theme(s)

Suffering with and for Christ brings joy. The practical implications of the Christian experience.

## Keywords

Keywords and phrases include: "Christ," "in Christ Jesus," "joy/rejoice/glad," "mind/minded/likeminded", "think/thinking/thought," "you all," "knowledge," and "know/known/knowing."

## Date

Philippians was written during Paul's first Roman imprisonment. As Paul infers that his case should be decided soon (1:12-13, 19, 23, 26), it is likely Philippians was written near the end of his first Roman imprisonment: 61 to early 62 A.D.

## Outline

Dan Krusich offers the outline on the left, while Warren Wiersbe provides the one on the right:

| | |
|---|---|
| Suffering for Christ (chp. 1) | Singleness of Mind (chp. 1) |
| Serving Christ (chp. 2) | Servant Mind (chp. 2) |
| Seeking to know Christ (chp. 3) | Spiritual Mind (chp. 3) |
| Standing with Christ (chp. 4) | Secure Mind (chp. 4) |

# Philippians Chapter 1

## Introduction (vv. 1-2)

The letter to the Philippians commences with the same type of salutation that is found in other Pauline epistles to churches. The author is stated, Paul (v. 1). As Timothy was with Paul in Rome at this time and was known by the Philippians, his name is also included in the salutation. This did not mean that Timothy assisted Paul in drafting the letter.

Paul refers to himself and Timothy as bondservants. According to the Mosaic Law, a Hebrew slave was to be released after six years of service, or at the fifty-year Jubilee if that occurred before the six-year tenure was served, unless the slave desired to remain with his master for life (Lev. 25:39-42). Paul and Timothy had made such a commitment to serve Christ. Hence, Paul often referred to himself as a bondservant to express his own love for and lifelong devotion to Jesus Christ.

To the Philippians, Paul makes no assertion of his apostleship in the letter's introduction as the saints at Philippi were completely settled on that subject. In fact, the overall tenor of this letter is warm and positive. There are no doctrinal corrections and only a few exhortations found within the epistle. In thanking the Philippians for their past financial support of his ministry, Paul conveys an attitude of joy throughout the epistle.

The apostle employs five different Greek words which are translated as "joy" and "rejoice" (in various forms) for a total of eighteen times (plus one occurrence of "gladness"). He also mentions "Christ" thirty-seven times in this epistle, while the "mind" is spoken of ten times. The phrase "in Christ Jesus" is found seven times. The connection of these keywords and phrases suggests that a believer can have joy in any circumstance if he or she chooses to rejoice in the Lord Jesus Christ. Paul was a prisoner in Rome, but he had chosen to rejoice in Christ and therefore retained his joy despite this hardship.

Because these believers had been justified in Christ (i.e., they had been declared positionally righteous in Christ by God; Rom. 4:21-25), Paul refers to them as "saints" in Christ Jesus located at Philippi (v. 2). All who have trusted Christ and have been regenerated by the Holy Spirit have an eternal and righteous standing before God (2 Cor. 5:21). The epistle is addressed to the church at Philippi. Scripture informs us that Philippi was a city governed by pagan practices, licentious living, unjust rulers, and that the people were in opposition to the teachings of Christ (Acts 16:16-24; Phil. 1:28-29, 3:17-19). Paul saw Philippi as a great mission field!

The church at Philippi was well established, having appointed both elders and deacons to serve the local church. Two Greek words are used in the New Testament to identify those men who hold the same office of spiritual leadership in their respective local churches: *presbuteros* (elder; 1 Acts 14:23; Tit. 1:5) and *episkopos* (overseer; Acts 20:28; 1 Tim. 3:1-2). An overseer and church elder were the same person (Acts 17:28; 1 Pet. 5:1-2).

Unfortunately, the KJV and NKJV render *episkopos* as "Bishop" which reflects the Anglican influence on the KJV translation several centuries ago (i.e., the Church of England already had Church bishops at that time); however, the literal meaning of *episkopos* is "overseer." These two words (including their verb forms) relate to a church position which was not given at spiritual rebirth, but was gained as a result of spiritual maturity, divine calling, and public recognition. Deacons are appointed by the local church to assist the elders in the functional operations of church body-life (Acts 6:3-6; 1 Tim. 3:8-13).

Continuing his salutation, Paul declares *"grace to you and peace from God our Father and the Lord Jesus Christ"* (v. 2). This is Paul's trademark greeting and is word for word how he saluted the Romans and the Corinthians (Rom. 1:7; 1 Cor. 1:3). *Grace* was a greeting that the Greeks commonly used, while Jewish believers traditionally referred to the blessing of *peace* to convey a how-do-you-do.

## Prayers of Thanksgiving (vv. 3-11)

Paul was overwhelmed with thankfulness to God for what He had accomplished in Philippi. For this reason, the apostle could always pray for the Philippians with joy (vv. 3-4). Although he did not know their specific needs, he was prompted nevertheless to pray for them often, as God knew exactly what was necessary to edify and protect the Philippian believers.

Please notice the phrase "you all" in verse 4. Paul uses words and phrases such as "you," "you all," "together," and "one spirit" several times in this chapter to indicate that he will be addressing the theme of productive church body-life throughout the epistle.

Verse 5 introduces the purpose of the epistle: to acknowledge the generosity of the church at Philippi to support Paul's ministry, that is, their "fellowship in the gospel." The Greek word *koinonia* is rendered "fellowship" and conveys the idea of "sharing" or "partnership." The

Philippians could not go with Paul into the mission field, but they could co-labor (partner) with him in the cause of Christ by praying for him and financially supporting him. We learn later (4:15-16) that the Philippians were the only church to financially support Paul while he labored in Europe during his second missionary journey, and they did so repeatedly from the time the assembly was first formed.

Notice the prevalence of the word "gospel" in this chapter: the "fellowship of the gospel" (v. 5), "the defense and confirmation of the gospel" (v. 7), "the furtherance of the gospel" (v. 12), "the defense of the gospel" (v. 17), "the gospel of Christ" (v. 27), "striving together for the faith of the gospel" (v. 27). "The conflict for the gospel" is also implied in verse 30 (see 1 Thess. 2:2). The apostle's emphasis in chapter 1 is that believers need to have one mindset during their earthly sojourn – all that is done is to accurately represent Christ and His message to the world.

Next Paul expressed his confidence that the Lord would, at the day of Christ, complete the good work of salvation He had already begun in the Philippian saints (v. 6). All believers are to eagerly wait for the day of His coming, the moment when He will be personally revealed to His Church (1 Cor. 1:7). This event, which includes the *Judgment Seat of Christ*, is referred to by Paul as *"the Day of our Lord Jesus Christ"* or *the Day of Christ*, or *the Day of the Lord Jesus* (v. 1, 10, 2:16). *The Day of Christ* is not to be confused with *the Day of the Lord*, an Old Testament term that speaks of divine judgment on the earth but is used in the New Testament to speak of the Tribulation period, the millennial reign of Christ, the destruction of the earth, and the Great White Throne Judgment (1 Thess. 5:1-11; 2 Pet. 3:10).

The apostle knew that at the Day of Jesus Christ, both he and the Philippians would be partakers of God's grace, for their salvation in Christ would be complete by the saving of their bodies (v. 7). Until that time, whether in chains or not, Paul was committed to his twofold calling in Christ: the *"defense and confirmation of the gospel."* He would defend the gospel against unregenerate critics and confirm its mysterious truths to better edify believers.

The gospel both overthrows its foes and strengthens its friends!

– W. E. Vine

In verse 8, Paul expresses his deep love and appreciation for the saints at Philippi – *"greatly I long for you all with the affection of Jesus Christ."* No one could love the Philippians more than Christ, so Paul likens his affection for them to that of the Savior's love for them.

It is at this juncture that Paul exhorts the saints at Philippi: *"And this I pray, that your love may abound still more and more in knowledge and all discernment"* (v. 9). Paul similarly exhorts the church at Thessalonica: *"The Lord make you to increase and abound in love one toward another, and toward all men, even as we do toward you"* (1 Thess. 3:12), an exhortation he repeats in 1 Thessalonians 3:9-10.

Interestingly, Paul also characterized the church at Thessalonica as a group of saints who really loved each other (1 Thess. 1:2-3, 3:6), but then exhorted them to increase in their love for each other (1 Thess. 5:8). Paul's exhortations show us that believers can never love each other too much. The believer should never be satisfied with his outward expression of God's love. God is love, and the more we love others, the more we will demonstrate Him to a lost world (John 13:35). God's love is irresistible and we all need to abound in His love more.

Paul reminds the Philippians in verse 10 that it is possible to perform well outwardly, but within have wrong motives, sinful desires, and poor attitudes towards others. These are a beam in the eye and hinder true service (Matt. 7:3-5). Abounding love is not self-centered. Selfless sincerity makes deception a forgotten ill of the past.

Submitting to Christ's Word and example permits the Holy Spirit to produce fruit (not fruits) of the Spirit in our lives. There are many kinds of God-honoring deeds the Holy Spirit enables us to do, but all of these reflect the entire holy character of God. In verse 11, Paul refers to this outcome as *"being filled with the fruits of righteousness."* The Greek verb translated "being filled" is in the perfect tense and passive voice, indicating that the Holy Spirit always acts through a righteous life to produce what will bring honor and glory to God. Anything done in the flesh does not please God (Rom. 8:8). Rather, God is pleased and honored by all that Christ achieves in those declared righteous through the power of the Holy Spirit.

## Preaching Christ (vv. 12-18)

To encourage the Philippians, Paul wanted them to understand something about his time in prison: *"But I want you to know, brethren, that the things which happened to me have actually turned out for the furtherance of the gospel"* (v. 12). God was working through Paul's arduous situation to accomplish a greater good for the honor and glory of His own name. This is also what the Lord did when Paul and Silas first visited Philippi years earlier. What often appears to us to be unfortunate is actually God accomplishing His sovereign purposes.

*Philippians*

It was at Philippi that Paul and Silas witnessed the first European converts to Christ – Lydia and her household. After casting a spirit of divination out of a servant girl, Paul and Silas were arrested, severely beaten, and imprisoned without a trial as commanded by the magistrates. While securely bound in the inner prison, the two evangelists began to sing praises to God. Then, a timely earthquake freed Paul, Silas, and the other prisoners from their bonds and cells. The jailkeeper, knowing that he would be put to death if any of his prisoners escaped, sought to take his own life. Paul cried out to him not to do so and the jailer responded by asking the two missionaries how he could be saved. In short order, he and his household heard and believed the gospel message and afterwards were baptized.

The church at Philippi was formed from a nucleus of suffering saints rejoicing in the Lord Jesus Christ. It is therefore not surprising that Paul teaches that even during the most dismal of situations there is always a way to escape from depression. Believers are called to rejoice – *rejoicing is a choice*.

Though a prisoner in Rome, the apostle focused his mind on the great things God had accomplished through his imprisonment: First, the soldiers who formed the praetorian guard (they protected Caesar's palace and perhaps the entire praetorium) knew why Paul was imprisoned in Rome – because of his testimony for Jesus Christ (v. 13). Second, timid brethren (i.e., those positionally "in Christ") had become bold in preaching the gospel of Jesus Christ (v. 14). Third, even though some believers were preaching out of envy, strife, and selfish ambition, Paul could still rejoice that they were preaching Christ (vv. 15-16). These latter saints had the right message, but the wrong motive for serving and the wrong goal of trying to discourage Paul by doing so. What is done in the flesh ruins everything.

Nevertheless, Paul's spiritual rejoicing defeated their fleshly efforts. Paul would not let anyone steal his joy: *"Christ is preached; and in this I rejoice, yes, and will rejoice"* (v. 18). He was called to defend the gospel, and given his imprisonment, the best method of accomplishing that task was to faithfully rejoice in Christ (v. 17). Instead of becoming depressed by setting his mind on the loss of his personal freedoms and spiteful saints, Paul was determined to rejoice in and be thankful for all that God was doing.

If Paul had focused his thoughts on his difficulties, he would have been overcome with despair. Instead, he chose to concentrate on the positive outcomes of his suffering: *"The things which happened to me have actually turned out for the furtherance of the gospel."* This reflects Paul's single-mindedness. Regardless of the circumstances in which he found himself, his one desire was to preach Christ to further the spread of the Gospel. He did not see his difficulties as stumbling stones. Instead, he saw them as stepping stones into greater gospel opportunities. In this epistle, the *single mind* of chapter 1 leads to the *servant mind* of chapter 2, and then to the *spiritual mind* of chapter 3, so that we can enjoy the *secure mind* of chapter 4.

Because Paul was not defeated by the harshness of his situation, but triumphed over it through faithful rejoicing, he could legitimately exhort the Philippians to follow his example: *"Rejoice in the Lord always. Again I will say, rejoice!"* (4:4). Satisfaction, full joy, and contentment are only found in the Lord – knowing and experiencing Him makes life worth living.

Whether we are confronted by intense opposition, daily suffering, or the disappointing regression of the Church, we must learn to trust and rejoice in the Lord. In such times of distress, may we too recall Nehemiah's charge to his distressed fellow countrymen: *"The joy of the Lord is your strength"* (Neh. 8:10). Rejoicing is a choice and it is a command (1 Thess. 5:16). Indeed, Paul was bound, but God's Word was not constrained by Paul's situation. Holding to the truth while rejoicing in God revives the heart of the redeemed and opens the way for God to perform the spectacular in our lives!

It is both a great privilege and our duty to rejoice in our blessed Savior. To rejoice in Christ when everything around us shrieks of despair shows Him that we really know Him and that we trust in Him at all times.

## Living Christ (vv. 19-26)

Paul refers to the certainty of his "deliverance" in verse 19. This may refer to Paul's certainty that God's grace would lift him above the dreadful attempts of envious preachers to make his life bitter, or it may be one of several instances in which he confidently anticipates imminent release from prison (see also v. 26, 2:23). Since Paul accredits this outcome to the Philippians' prayers on his behalf, the latter explanation seems correct, especially since the Philippians would not have known about the envious preachers.

Because the other three prison epistles do not mention the idea of Paul's imminent release, it is likely that the letter to the Philippians was the last prison epistle to be written. How encouraging it must have been for the Philippians to hear that their prayers had made the difference in Paul's suffering. In fact, Paul prayed that their rejoicing in Christ would be even more abundant when they saw Paul again. This would confirm to them that Christ had answered their prayers on Paul's behalf (v. 26).

However, Paul had the mindset that he was going to glorify Christ in every situation, regardless of favorable or ominous circumstances. At present, Christ sits at the right hand of His Father in Heaven. Paul was determined to boldly magnify Christ through his Spirit-filled testimony, and so he viewed his body as a telescope through which to bring Christ closer and make Him visible so that others might see and appreciate Him. (v. 20).

Whether in life or even by suffering unto death, this was his single ambition in his earthly sojourn: *"For to me, to live is Christ, and to die is gain"* (v. 21). The verb rendered "to die" is in the aorist tense, meaning that Paul was not thinking about dying per se, but its outcome – death. Clearly, execution was not far from the apostle's thinking, but even death did not matter because afterwards He would have "gain" – He would be with Christ.

Paul lived each and every day in the anticipation of being imminently brought into the presence of Christ (Tit. 2:13). But though he yearned to be with the Lord, as long as the Lord had work for him to do, he would gladly remain where the Lord placed him to perform it. That is, he would "live in flesh." He had no choice in that matter (vv. 22-23). There is no article before the word *sarx* translated "flesh," so Paul was clearly speaking of living in his body, not according to his inherited nature from Adam. He was torn between two deep yearnings in his soul – to be with Christ after death (a gain for him), and his desire to remain on earth to build up the Church (a gain for others; v. 24). Either way, there was gain to be had in Christ.

Paul understood that his ministry was needful for the edification of the Philippian believers (v. 25). Thus, he pressed onward until the Lord would call him home, either through death or through glorification at Christ's coming for the Church. This is the pattern of life that all believers should follow. If the Lord did permit Paul's release from prison, the Philippians would have even more to rejoice about when he visited them again (v. 26).

## Serving and Suffering for Christ (vv. 27-30)

Whether Paul was released from prison in the near future or not, the Philippians were to remain faithful. Their conduct should be worthy of the gospel, and they should strive together in unity for the cause of Christ. This would delight Paul's heart (v. 27). Believers in a local church cannot labor together effectively in the gospel until spiritual unity characterizes their testimony. The unity of believers is to reflect God's triune essence to others (John 17:21-23).

Suffering patiently for the cause of Christ is a proof of perdition to the unregenerate but a token of salvation to believers (v. 28; 2 Thess. 1:5). One of the thieves crucified with Christ was motivated to repent having observed Christ's patient suffering. Suffering patiently while relying on God's grace is a supernatural testimony to the lost. Nonetheless it is a consolation to the believer that he or she is truly a child of God. William MacDonald suggests that: "Fearlessness in the face of persecution has a twofold meaning. First, it is an omen of destruction to those who fight against God. Secondly, it is a sign of salvation to those who brave the wrath of the foe."[78]

Praying for those who persecute you is a demonstration of God's control of your will and it also safeguards the mind. It is a defense against bitterness and being overwhelmed by sorrow.

History records the intense persecution of the Church by the Roman Empire, but not as well documented is the impact of the patient suffering of the early Church on specific leaders in the empire. When Pliny was governor of Bithynia (about 110 A.D.), he wrote a letter to the Roman Emperor Trajan to ask why Christians were being exterminated, then added:

> I have been trying to get all the information I could regarding them. I have even hired spies to profess to be Christians and become baptized in order that they might get into the Christian services without suspicion. Contrary to what I had supposed, I find that the Christians meet at the dead of night or at early morn, that they sing a hymn to Christ as God, that they read from their own sacred writings and partake of a very simple meal consisting of bread and wine and water (the water added to the wine to dilute it in order that there might be enough for all). This is all that I can find out, except that they exhort each other to be subject to the government and to pray for all men.[79]

Not only is patient suffering for the cause of Christ testimony to the lost of the supernatural resources of the believer, but Paul informed the Philippian and Thessalonians saints that it was proof of their salvation.

Paul then describes the marks of believers who are controlled by the Holy Spirit in verses 29-30. They are not afraid of the enemy, nor do they quit because of cowardice. Rather, they willingly suffer for Christ's sake. The Lord never promised His disciples a life of happiness and ease. To the contrary, He assured them that trials and suffering were necessary to properly represent Him to those who hated Him (John 15:18-20). Yet, the Lord did promise them that despite hardship, they could enjoy His abiding peace and joy: *"In Me you may have peace. In the world you will have tribulation; but be of good cheer, I have overcome the world"* (John 16:33).

The Philippians knew firsthand that this mindset characterized Paul's ministry. There were some at Philippi who had witnessed how he had bravely and joyfully suffered for Christ years earlier (Acts 16). It was a powerful testimony that had brought them to the Savior. The church in Philippi began when Paul and Silas chose to rejoice after being beaten and jailed for proclaiming Christ's message of hope.

# Philippians Chapter 2

## Unity Through Humility (vv. 1-4)

In this chapter, the apostle shifts his focus from the necessity of having the single mind of magnifying Christ in chapter 1, to assuming the lowly, servant mind of Christ. Paul begins by making a personal request of the Philippians. The "if" in verse 1 does not express doubt; it is the beginning of a logic statement. That is, since there is consolation in Christ, the comfort of His love, fellowship with the Holy Spirit during times of affliction, and the benefit of His merciful deliverance, a deep oneness should mark the church at Philippi. Paul's joy would be full if they were all walking together in unity, by having the same love for each other and being like-minded.

What does it mean to be like-minded with other Christians? Believers do not, naturally speaking, think alike, so Paul suggests we need a different mindset – we need the mind of Christ. The only way that believers can enjoy the same love is if it is Spirit-generated love that focuses our attention on one Person (Christ). Focusing less on ourselves and more on Christ naturally draws His people together. Paul wanted the Philippians to be of one accord. That is, being united in soul and willing to fight for unity, not uniformity. All this would be possible if the believers at Philippi would adopt the cooperative and lowly mind of Christ.

All the disunity and contention within the Church today is the result of our pride in one form or another. Nothing good can come from pride! This is why Paul admonished the believers at Philippi to follow Christ's example of selfless humility: *"Let nothing be done through strife or vainglory; but in lowliness of mind let each esteem others better than themselves"* (v. 3; KJV). As R. C. Chapman attests, the best defense against the destructive nature of pride is to follow the Lord's lowly example of selfless obedience:

> In 1 Corinthians 15:28 we read: "Then shall the Son also Himself be subject," and in Revelation, "The throne of God and of the Lamb." Christ is forever the Shepherd and forever the Lamb, and it is the lowly or little Lamb, the diminutive being used. There is an infiniteness in the lowliness of the blessed Lamb, and He is now at the utmost of His lowliness. Satan took upon himself the form of a master, being created a servant; instead of serving in obedience, he would be lord, and "the condemnation of the devil"

is in his self-will; he chose to take to himself what belonged only to God. What a rebuke to the devil the exaltation of the Son of God will be to all eternity – a mirror in which to see his own folly! Acquaintance with the Cross of Christ brings me to nothing! Let any thought of self-exaltation be to me as a serpent; I have nothing to do but to kill it![80]

Strife is the devil's way to get one's way, but lowliness permits God to judge legitimate wrongs His way and in His timing. How do we know this is true? Vengeance (i.e., justified wrath for sin) is the Lord's alone (Rom. 12:19). Only He can rightly dispense wrath to humble the proud heart (Job 40:11-12). Moreover, the wrath of man does not work the righteousness of God (Jas. 1:20). This is why David asked the Lord to vindicate him and judge his oppressors. He reckoned that God was more able to judge his oppressors than he ever could through strife (Ps. 35:1, 23-24).

Paul highlights the threefold behavior of believers who possess the mind of Christ in verses 3-4. First, they do not exalt themselves before others through selfish ambition and conceit. Second, they are determined to assume the low place and esteem others better than themselves. Third, they own the interests of others and do not put their own interests ahead of the necessities of others. In summary, the mind of Christ is a selfless, sacrificial, serving disposition toward others. Believers need this humble self-abasing attitude in order to properly serve each other as Christ would (v. 5).

## The Humiliation and Exaltation of Christ (vv. 5-11)

Paul addresses the mind or its attitude (thinking) twelve times in this epistle, but the main focus of this matter is in this chapter. Paul speaks of four individuals who exhibited the lowly servant mind introduced in verses 3-4: Christ (vv. 5-11), Paul himself (vv. 17-18), Timothy (vv. 19-24), and Epaphroditus (vv. 25-30). The supreme example of a lowly, selfless servant, the Lord Jesus Christ is spoken of first:

> *Let this mind be in you which was also in Christ Jesus, who, being in the form of God, did not consider it robbery to be equal with God, but made Himself of no reputation, taking the form of a bondservant, and coming in the likeness of men. And being found in appearance as a man, He humbled Himself and became obedient to the point of death, even the death of the cross* (vv. 5-8).

Christ, being the very essence of God, divested Himself of the legitimate right to be honored as God, and took upon Himself a form in which His divine glory was hidden. He did not clutch the glory His divine

*Philippians*

personage deserved, but chose to humble Himself to a low position to serve others through personal sacrifice.

This willful humbling of Himself as the Son of God was typified long ago in the High Priest's attire on the Day of Atonement. The High Priest had two sets of priestly garments. On the annual feast of the Day of Atonement, he was to exchange his garments of *"glory and beauty"* (Ex. 28:2) for the simple white linen outfit and miter (Lev. 16:4). Then he was permitted to sprinkle animal blood on the Mercy Seat to atone for Israel's sin that year. In type, this activity pictures the Holy One (Luke 1:35, 4:34) who willingly put aside His glorious appearance, left Heaven, and came to earth as God's holy sacrifice to suffer death to provide propitiation for human sin (1 Jn. 2:2). The obvious difference between the type and antitype is that Aaron's beauty came from his priestly garments, but the glory of the Lord Jesus emanates from His very person. Aaron's beauty and glory lasted only as long as he lived and wore the priestly garments, but Christ is the *"Lord of Glory"* (1 Cor. 2:8) from eternity past and will be forevermore.

The Greek verb in verse 6 is present, not aorist tense: Christ, the Lord of Glory, *"being in the form of God"* chose to humble Himself. This is in contrast to the Greek verbs in verses 7 and 8 which are in the aorist tense to indicate completed actions. God is essential to Himself alone and therefore cannot change the essence of who He is and always will be (Mal. 3:6). The Greek *morphe*, rendered as "form" in verses 6 and 7, may mean a literal "shape" or, in the figurative sense, the "nature" of something. Warren Wiersbe clarifies how *morphe* is used figuratively in these verses:

> "Form of God" has nothing to do with shape or size. God is Spirit (John 4:24), and as such is not to be thought of in human terms. When the Bible refers to "the eyes of the Lord" or "the hand of the Lord," it is not claiming that God has a human shape. Rather, it is using human terms to describe divine attributes (the characteristics of God) and activities. The word "form" means "the outward expression of the inward nature."[81]

Because Christ *"existed in the form of God,* [and] *did not regard equality with God a thing to be grasped"* (v. 6; NASB), He chose to lower Himself to take on a different form, the form of a lowly servant (v. 7) in contrast to the form of almighty God (v. 6). The nature of position, not personal essence, is being stressed in the transformation from the higher to the lower form. The verb *genomenos* in verse 7, translated "made Himself," is an aorist tense verb in the middle voice, indicating that the Lord chose and caused Himself to become what He was not before. This is the same verb in verse 8, that is rendered "and became" – Christ willingly chose obedience unto death!

There are various erroneous teachings concerning the person of Christ. Some say Christ was not fully God, nor fully man. Others teach that Christ became some hybrid creature, a created being between God and man, but neither God nor man. This view, commonly held among many cults today, is one that Paul confronts in the book of Colossians. Yet others see a "schizophrenic" Jesus, someone with a dual personality who switches back and forth in personality and natures. Christ is not diminished deity added to a human personality. God literally and personally became a human, without emptying Himself of any divine attributes (John 1:14).

One of the erroneous theories of Christ's personage is derived from the Greek noun *kenos* (v. 3, 16, 17) and the verb *kenoo* (v. 7). It is called the "Kenosis Theory." Both these word forms convey the idea of "emptiness" or "to empty." This teaching claims that the Son of God somehow laid aside His divine attributes and self-consciousness to become human. Yet, Christ became flesh to sacrifice Himself at Calvary. We do not empty something by adding to it! **The Kenosis Theory is a stool with four erroneous legs:**

- Christ had no divine attributes when he became a servant.
- Christ was the exact counterpart of the first Adam.
- Christ was a human, just like us in every aspect.
- Christ was tempted in His flesh just as we are.

But as we shall soon see, each of these propositions is false. First, let us consider Paul's declaration of Christ's deity while being in human form: *"Great is the mystery of Godliness. God was manifest in the flesh"* (1 Tim. 3:16; KJV). Christ was fully man, but He had a unique human nature, different from our nature. Because there is no definite article in the Greek before the word "flesh," this verse is better rendered, as John Darby translates it, *"God has been manifested in flesh."* God was manifest "in flesh," not "in the flesh." The Lord Jesus was veiled in flesh (Heb. 10:20), He was made flesh (John 1:14), but He was not *in* the flesh – the nature of His flesh did not rule Him; it served Him. His flesh had not been invaded by the corruption of sin.

Paul explains the difference: *"For what the law could not do in that it was weak through the flesh, God did by sending His own Son in the likeness of sinful flesh"* (Rom. 8:3). The same Greek word *homoiomti*, translated as "likeness" in this verse, is also applied in verse 7, which states that Christ *"was made in the likeness of men."* The word "likeness" in both verses means "resemblance" or "form." Humanly speaking, Christ's form was that of a man, but He was more; He also possessed a divine nature. The Lord looked like everyone else, but He didn't act like everyone else. His life was unique, for *"in Him is no sin"* (1 Jn. 3:5); He *"knew no sin"* (2 Cor. 5:21); and He *"did no sin"* (1 Pet. 2:22).

Speaking of Christ, the writer of Hebrews declares the matter frankly, *"who being the brightness of His* [God's] *glory, and the express image of His* [God's] *person, and upholding all things by the word of His power, when He had by Himself purged our sins, sat down on the right hand of the Majesty on high"* (Heb. 1:3). It was needful for Christ to be veiled in flesh, or mankind would have been consumed by the direct presence of Almighty God. The veil of flesh allowed the perfect moral glory of God to shine out to the world. When you looked upon the Lord Jesus, you would see the form of a man, with the character of God shining through.

Second, Christ, the Last Adam, was not an exact counterpart to the first Adam. Christ was fully human but had a different spiritual nature than Adam. According to Ecclesiastes 7:29, Adam was made "upright" or "innocent." Until Adam sinned, he reflected the character of God, for he bore God's image and likeness (Gen. 1:26). Adam was God's representative in creation before the fall of man (Heb. 2:6-8). After Adam had sinned, he no longer bore the likeness of God, but his own likeness (Gen. 5:3). The Last Adam, Christ, was not just *innocent humanity,* as was Adam; He was *holy humanity* (Luke 1:35). Indeed, *"for in Him dwells all the fullness of the Godhead bodily"* (Col. 2:9). Nowhere in Scripture do we read of Adam being "holy." God was not in Adam, but *"God was in Christ reconciling the world to Himself"* (2 Cor. 5:19).

Third, although fully human, Christ is not of the same type of humanity that you and I are. Adam, Eve and Abel came into being on the earth in three different ways (i.e., from the ground, from Adam's rib, and through procreation). The Lord Jesus came into the world conceived by the power of the Holy Spirit and born of a virgin. Nevertheless, each was fully human, possessed of body, soul, and spirit. Christ, as holy humanity, had a different spiritual makeup than all other humans.

When Adam sinned, he made a transition from *innocent humanity* to *condemned humanity* and was cursed by God. Everyone coming from Adam is also condemned (Rom. 5:12-14). Through the obedience of Christ came the offer of grace, forgiveness, and restoration (Rom. 5:15-21). Those who respond to Christ's gospel become *redeemed humanity* and wait to become *glorified humanity* at Christ's return to the air (1 Thess. 4:13-18). What Adam lost is fully restored through the Last Adam, the Lord Jesus.

Fourth, Christ was not tempted in His flesh the same way that you and I are. Christ, as *holy humanity*, could not sin, for there was nothing in Him that would respond to sin; His essence was repulsed by sin and loathed its working. Hebrews 4:15 states that Christ was tested, but not in sin as you and I are. There was no sin in Him – he was tested "sin apart" (J. N. Darby). Hence, Christ can sympathize with believers concerning their external solicitations to sin, but not with the wantonness desires of their lusting flesh.

Some have suggested that the external solicitations of Satan upon the Lord Jesus provoked in Him a moral struggle. This is not the case. How could the Father, looking down from Heaven, declare, *"This is My beloved Son, in whom I am well pleased"* (Matt. 3:17) if the Lord was struggling internally with thoughts of sin. As John declared, the Lord Jesus was, not might have been, *"The Lamb of God who takes away the sin of the world!"* (John 1:29). The Father never questioned the impeccability of Christ – only Satan and men do that – He was blameless and perfect, the only acceptable substitutionary sacrifice for man's sin.

Scripturally speaking, the word "temptation" has different meanings depending upon the context of the related passage. The word *peirasmos*, normally translated "temptation" in the KJV, may also be rendered as "trial" or "testing." *Peirasmos* means "to demonstrate the proof of something," either by suffering through a holy trial or enduring an evil solicitation. Holy trials are those tests that originate with God for our edification and perfection. Unholy temptations, though allowed by God, do not originate with Him. Rather these solicitations to sin comes from Satan and his domain of influence in the world.

Christ was externally solicited by the devil to do evil although it was not possible for Him to sin. It is flawed thinking, to suggest that He had "forbidden desires" He had to suppress to exhibit God-honoring behavior. Lusting in the flesh comes from the fallen nature we inherited from Adam, and not from God (1 Jn. 2:16). Apart from three instances in the New Testament (Luke 22:15; Phil. 1:23; I Thess. 2:17) "lust" has a negative connotation. The underlying stimulus for such lust is dissatisfaction with our circumstances (i.e., God has wrongly limited us in some way). In contrast to our first parents in Eden, the Lord Jesus, being God, was never prompted to think or act beyond the boundaries of contented holiness.

The intercessory activity of the Lord Jesus outlined in Hebrews 2:17 and 4:15 highlights His sympathy for our frailties in the face of satanic opposition and for our suffering for upholding righteousness. However, He does not sympathize with the sin which results from submission to temptation. He cannot relate to the latter, but He can fully sympathize with our sufferings related to enduring the contradiction of sinners, living on a sin-cursed planet, and being rejected and despised for righteous living. We cannot venture to the throne of grace and expect sympathy for the sin that is within us; rather, we are to detest it, and yearn for it to be mortified. God's Spirit and Word do this, like a javelin piercing through the evil beast within.

In summary, Christ is not diminished deity added to a human personality, but the true and personal God taking on humanity. By that unprecedented act of divine condescension God, in the person of the Lord Jesus Christ, exhibits the selfless human attitude that ought to be evident in all believers. The Kenosis doctrine has no Biblical basis. It undermines the impeccability of Christ's divine nature and is an erroneous teaching that needlessly divides the Lord's people.

Having described Christ's departure from Heaven to become God's sinless human sacrifice for humanity's sin, Paul now speaks of Christ's exaltation for His faithfulness. God the Father reverses the depths of Christ's humiliation and suffering to exalt His Son to the heights of Heaven:

*Therefore, God also has highly exalted Him and given Him the name which is above every name, that at the name of Jesus every knee should bow, of those in Heaven, and of those on earth, and of those under the earth, and that every tongue should confess that Jesus Christ is Lord, to the glory of God the Father* (vv. 9-11).

In a future day, the words of the Lord Jesus Christ will be proven true: *"My judgment is just"* (John 5:30) and *"The Father judges no one, but has committed all judgment to the Son"* (John 5:22). Only a just and impartial Judge can uphold the righteousness and holiness of God in rewarding and condemning others. Paul declared that we will all answer to the just Judge: *"For it is written: 'As I live, says the Lord, every knee shall bow to Me, and every tongue shall confess to God.' So then each of us shall give account of himself to God"* (Rom. 14:11-12). The Lord will reward believers at His Judgment Seat and will also punish the wicked at His Great White Throne (Rev. 20:11-15). On that day, no one will argue with His justice!

The Greek verb translated "should confess" in verse 11 is in the middle voice, which means those being judged will confess on their own behalf that Jesus Christ is Lord. If they were forced to do so, the verb would be in the passive voice. The majesty of Christ will be so spectacular at the Great White Throne that even the most evil people in human history will fully agree that He is Lord. In a coming day everyone will proclaim that Jesus Christ is Lord! Those who previously embraced Him as Savior will gladly do so for eternity, but those who rejected Him in life will bring honor to

Him in the second death (Rev. 20:11-15).

## Working Out Your Salvation (vv. 12-16)

Notice that Paul does not say "work for" your salvation in verse 12. Rather, he is instructing the Philippians to "work out" how they should properly live for Christ. This imperative verb is in the middle voice, meaning that the believers should immediately engage in this action on their own behalf. We can do nothing to earn God's favor. We must simply trust Christ's work at Calvary for salvation (Eph. 2:8-9). Legalism teaches that although a person is saved by grace through faith, he must then continue to keep the Law to maintain that salvation. God is holy. He therefore wants His children to reflect the family image (1 Pet. 1:16). This means that the believer must build his faith on the truth which is the Word of God, and seek direction from the Lord through prayer. In the process of living a holy life, as God is holy, godly counsel from mature believers can also be beneficial.

Teaching younger believers to work out their salvation is extremely important. It provides them with tools for life in the discernment of wise and godly behavior. We neither want the immature in faith to be pulled into the world's religion of *doing*, nor into the world's pleasure of *indulgence*. Even in Paul's day the undertow of these spiritual ills was apparent. The churches of Galatia were being pulled towards legalism – "I must do to please God," while the Corinthian church's motto was, "Christ died for all our sins – let's party." The world's religion says "do," but biblical Christianity says "done." The world's pleasure proclaims, "Live for the day and for the moment – enjoy life," but Christ says, *"whosoever will lose his life for My sake, the same shall save it"* (Luke 9:24). In this way a Christian maintains an abiding joy in life.

The Lord wants us to be wise, to do good, and to avoid foolish and wrong behavior. To accomplish this, we must build our lives on the foundation of His teachings and not on secular wisdom (Matt. 7:24-25). The child of God is to discern between what is holy and what is evil, what is wise and what is foolish. What is holy and wise should be obeyed. What is evil and foolish should be shunned.

Discernment between right and wrong behavior depends upon knowing the demands of Scripture. Discerning between what is wise and what is foolish is depends on knowing God's commandments, warnings, principles, promises, and the "lessons learned" from personal narratives in Scripture. In fact, the Lord addressed the matter of being wise and not foolish more often than the matter of what is right and what is wrong, though the latter would be included in what is wise and foolish. Gaining discernment of what is wise and what is foolish requires prayer, study, the godly counsel of others, and the leading of the Holy Spirit in our lives. This is how God works in the believer to develop the willing desire to do what pleases Him. (v. 13).

In verses 3-5, Paul instructs the Philippians to have the mind of Christ: They should not exalt themselves, but willingly take the low place and elevate the needs of others above their own. In verses 14-16, the apostle provides some practical examples of how that may be accomplished.

First, true Christlike service is performed without complaining, grumbling, and arguing with others (v. 14). It is natural for our carnal flesh to want others to esteem us as important, and we usually feel affronted if that does not happen. How do you feel when you are not recognized by others for an achievement for which you diligently labored? It is also natural for us to minimize others to make us feel significant. For example, how do you respond when people treat you like a servant when you have freely shown kindness to them? If we have the mind of Christ (i.e., possess genuine humility), we will not be offended in either situation. In fact, the possibility of being offended would never enter our minds.

Second, believers may be recognized and honored by others for humble, diligent service, but such accolades should not be sought after. Genuine, selfless service to others is given without thought to one's self or to what others may think. This type of ministry will keep the children of God blameless (above reproach) and harmless (viewed as non-threatening) to the unregenerate (v. 15). This means that if we are grumbling and complaining while serving or hoping that we will be recognized by others for what we are doing, we are not really serving the Lord, but ourselves (Matt. 6:2). As worldlings readily recognize their own selfish behavior, the believer's opportunity to display behavior which is not of the world is lost when we act like the unregenerate, rather than the way Christ would.

To be a light in the world (a testimony) for Christ, believers must hold fast to the words of life (Christ's teachings; v. 16). Those who genuinely do so, can expect rejoicing and reward at the Day of Christ (i.e., the Judgment Seat of Christ). Paul would also be rejoicing on that day with the Philippians, for the reality of his ministry in them would be fully displayed. Anticipating that glorious outcome excited the apostle (v. 17).

## Paul's Humble Example (vv. 17-18)

Paul supplies three more examples of individuals who rendered Christ-like service to others: himself, Timothy, and Epaphroditus. Speaking of himself, Paul says that he was like a drink offering being poured out on the sacrifice and service of the faith of the Philippian saints (v. 17). Christ's humble sacrifice at Calvary is the basis of acceptance for all other offerings of personal sacrifice to God. Paul was following Christ's example and expending himself for the good of others. Likewise, what the Philippians offered to God while having the mind of Christ would also please God. This meant that they and Paul could rejoice and be glad in how they were refreshing God's heart with offerings that reminded Him of His Son.

## Timothy's Humble Example (vv. 19-24)

Paul told the Philippians that he would send Timothy to them shortly to encourage them (Timothy may have carried the letter we are reading), and to learn of their condition (v. 19). Timothy would then supply a report of the assembly's spiritual condition to Paul. Paul was Timothy's spiritual father, and the apostle states that there was no other man as likeminded with him as Timothy (v. 20). Consequently, there was no question in Paul's mind that he would be properly cared for by the Philippians when he arrived.

Paul could attest to Timothy's proven character. He had the mind of Christ and thus would seek their interests and not his own. Timothy had learned that the greatest use of his life was to expend it for Christ. Only then would he gain something that would outlast his own life and count for eternity. Paul was temporarily delaying Timothy's departure from Rome, until he had learned about the outcome of his appeal to Caesar. He was hoping to send good news to the Philippians about his release.

## Epaphroditus' Humble Example (vv. 25-30)

In chapter 4 we learn that Epaphroditus was from Philippi and had been sent by the Philippian assembly to deliver a message and a gift to Paul (v. 25, 30, 4:18). He had decided to stay with Paul and to serve him for an unknown period of time. Many saints will not visit prisons to encourage those in chains for preaching Christ, but Epaphroditus was not one of those individuals. Paul's expressions of endearment for Epaphroditus are touching: *"my brother, fellow worker, and fellow soldier"* (v. 25).

While serving Paul, Epaphroditus became very ill. Twice, Paul states that he almost died from this illness (vv. 27, 30). To further underline his humility mind, Paul says that though he was quite ill, Epaphroditus was concerned that the Philippian saints would be worrying about his frail condition (v. 26). Paul was thankful to God for healing Epaphroditus, for in doing so, He bestowed mercy on both of them. Although he was greatly appreciated, Paul was sending Epaphroditus back to them (perhaps with Timothy) and the Philippians were to receive him with gladness and esteem him as one who had hazarded his life in service to Christ (vv. 29-30).

# Philippians Chapter 3

## Paul's Warning Against Legalizers (vv. 1-3)

It might seem as if Paul is wrapping up his letter to the Philippians by the word "finally" in verse 1. However, the literal meaning of the Greek word *loipon* translated "finally" means "as for the rest." It is used here to refer to a topic that yet needed to be addressed (e.g., 1 Cor. 7:12). As Paul uses this same word again in 4:8, it is evident that he still had much to say to the Philippians. The apostle also affirms the value of repetition in teaching others (v. 1). It is "safe" for us to hear truth again and again. This causes us to review what Scripture actually declares so that, over time, we do not drift by assuming we accurately remember what God's Word says.

The apostle then warns the church at Philippi against Jewish legalizers who were perverting the gospel by mixing Law with grace (v. 2). He refers to these false teachers as "dogs," "evil workers," and "of the mutilation." The latter expression is a sarcastic term describing the legalizers' insistence in requiring the circumcision of Gentiles who had trusted in Christ. These legalizers were like a pack of wild dogs, who had previously been snapping at Paul's heels wherever he went. His epistle to the churches in Galatia some twelve years earlier also warned new converts not to be influenced by these false teachers. This shows that, even years after the Council of Jerusalem, there were those who would not heed the apostles' doctrine of salvation by grace in Christ alone and who were seeking to lead people from the truth into a works-based religion.

These false teachers taught that Gentiles who trusted in Christ for salvation must also keep the Law to maintain their salvation. This included the requirement of male circumcision. In contrast to this false doctrine, Paul reminds the Philippians that it is not the physical act of circumcision that is important to God, but circumcision of the heart (v. 3). The Jews were required by the Law to circumcise their sons on the eighth day after birth, but the New Covenant secured by Christ's blood put away the first covenant that God had made with the Jews at Sinai (Heb. 8:8-13). That covenant was a conditional covenant and since the Jews never kept their end of the agreement it was impossible for the Old Covenant to save anyone; it only condemned the guilty (Rom. 3:20).

Spiritually speaking, the circumcised life is one that worships God, rejoices in Christ and has no confidence in the flesh (v. 3). Believers under the Holy Spirit's control do not permit the flesh to rule their behavior or thought life. True worship to God must be in truth, Spirit-led, Christ-centered, and without any human focus or flesh appeal.

## Paul's Past (vv. 4-11)

If anyone could have possibly boasted of his personal efforts to earn God's favor, it would have been Paul. He was a Jew, one of God's chosen people on earth, and from the tribe of Benjamin, as was Saul, Israel's first king. Paul was a high-profile Jewish leader, a Pharisee. He was blameless in the law. This did not mean that he was sinless in respect to keeping the Mosaic Law, but that any infractions had been properly atoned for per the Law. Additionally, Paul was zealous for God, as shown by his earlier persecution of the Church (vv. 4-6). William MacDonald summarizes the credentials in which Paul once boasted as: "pride of ancestry (v. 5a); pride of orthodoxy (v. 5b); pride of activity (v. 6a); pride of morality (v. 6b)."[82]

From a Jewish perspective, Paul was the cream of the crop, the best the Jewish nation had to offer. But after Paul encountered Jesus Christ on the road to Damacus, everything changed. He learned that all of his religious accomplishments did not impress God one bit. It was all accomplished in the flesh and thus a had achieved nothing of spiritual value (v. 7):

> *But what things were gain to me, these I have counted loss for Christ. Yet indeed I also count all things loss for the excellence of the knowledge of Christ Jesus my Lord, for whom I have suffered the loss of all things, and count them as rubbish, that I may gain Christ* (vv. 7-8).

Paul likened all that he thought was important in his life before knowing Christ to "dung" or "rubbish" (i.e., manure). The Greek word translated "count" in verse 8 is a present tense verb in the middle voice. This means that Paul continually counted for himself (in his own estimation) that all his past religious achievements and all that the world was still offering him was worthless in contrast to knowing and living for Christ. God had declared Paul righteous in Christ through faith and that is what caused him to be accepted before God – "accepted in the Beloved" (v. 9; Eph. 1:6). When we adopt this type of spiritual mindset, we realize that feeding on what the world offers for sustenance is like choking down putrid cow pies with a ludicrous smack of enjoyment. "Barf!" the spiritual man exclaims.

Bragging about our secular feats is like calling attention to piles of dung we have sculpted into award-winning figurines and set on pedestals for all to admire. Apart from Christ, what we do in this world is completely worthless. No matter how good it looks on the outside, it is still putrid to God (Isa. 64:6). What is done in Christ is for His glory, not ours (1 Cor. 1:31). Manure is neither the food nor the prize of the child of God.

Believers are called to be nourished by God's Word, to be empowered by His Spirit, and to do His will. They are not to be controlled by sin. Paul knew that this was only possible by identification with Christ: *"That I may know Him and the power of His resurrection, and the fellowship of His sufferings, being conformed to His death"* (v. 10). What did Paul mean by wanting to "know" Christ? Sydney Maxwell answers this question:

> In the phrase "that I may know him" the verb "know" (*ginōskō*) is in the aorist tense denoting a definite experience. W. E. Vine says the word indicates not mere knowledge, but recognition involving appropriation. This is something beyond the fact of being found in Him. It rather stresses the thought of experimental acquaintance. Paul yearns to know deeper communion with Christ and for a greater insight of His person.[83]

This means that Paul earnestly wanted to suffer as Christ suffered and to die a martyr's death as Christ did, and then like Christ, to experience the power of resurrection. Paul wanted to experience everything that would cause him to enjoy deeper intimacy with Christ. Perhaps Paul was thinking of Stephen's stunning and intimate vision of Christ in Heaven just prior to being stoned by the Jewish Sanhedrin (Paul had consented to Stephen's death; Acts 7). Paul would not be satisfied with a superficial life. He wanted to know Christ more through experiencing Him, even if it meant his death. This is how the expression, which is derived from one verb, a present participle in the passive voice, "being conformed to his death" must be understood. Paul wanted his life to be spiritually characterized by all the ramifications of the Lord's own death. Ruth declared this type of attitude to her mother-in-law Naomi, *"where you die, I will die"* (Ruth 1:17). Paul was expressing his complete dedication and faithfulness to Christ unto death.

In Christian experience the measure of the inheritance presently enjoyed is directly related to the extent to which each believer has experienced the Lord's gracious and holy character. The Lord does not bestow such things as power and authority lightly. These are received in measure and in accordance with the believer's capacity to retain each gift of grace in faith, love, and humility. To be endowed with that which cannot be managed in wisdom would surely result in an outcome more detrimental than if it had never been received. Believers have different spiritual gifts, callings of ministry, talents to serve, and maturity in Christ. This means that each of us has varying opportunities to receive and retain resurrection power in Christ.

The phrase "if by any means" in verse 11 must be interpreted given the context of the passage. Paul was not doubting his own resurrection, but rather was counting the cost of suffering for Christ until his work on earth was complete. The Rapture of the Church, about which he had previously written the Corinthians and the Thessalonians, may not occur during his lifetime. That did not matter to the apostle since Paul was willing to suffer trials and persecutions for the cause of Christ until the Lord took him home. Paul was determined to labor for Christ until Christ determined that his work was complete. May we all remember that in Christ, we are immortal and invincible on earth until He calls us to Himself.

## Paul's Present (vv. 12-16)

The chief apostle to the Gentiles proclaimed, *"Not that I have already attained, or am already perfected; but I press on, that I may lay hold of that for which Christ Jesus has also laid hold of me"* (v. 12). Paul affirms His desire to know Christ more and to further experience His resurrection power. Paul admitted that, in this regard, he was not "already perfect." He was not speaking about receiving a perfect body through resurrection, rather, that he had not apprehended all that was available to him in respect of experiencing Christ (Eph. 1:3) and being morally conformed to Christ (Rom. 8:29). Therefore, Paul was determined to keep pressing forward to obtain all that could be possessed in and of Christ now.

To move forward and Heavenward in the cause of Christ meant that Paul must forget his past failures (though learning from them) and his previous accomplishments in the flesh (vv. 5-7, 13). It is wise to learn from our mistakes, but past failures should not hinder Christians from persistently moving upward in their heavenly calling. Falling is a normal part of learning to walk properly. Falling does not make a saint a failure. Rather, failure is not getting up in grace to finish the race. Moreover, let us not glory in our past triumphs as these can be a snare to our feet. To Paul, moving forward meant that he must leave the past behind to serve Christ with zealous love while being made conformable to the image of his Savior through testing and suffering.

In Paul's spiritual race illustration, the strategy of the Christian race is to maintain a consistent, God-honoring life day after day so as to maximize our capacity to serve Him and to finish the race well. The verb rendered *"reaching forward to"* (v. 13) is in the middle voice and conveys Paul's intense desire to *"press toward the goal"* (v. 14). He was like a runner leaning towards the tape stretched across the finish line. The apostle aspired to pursue and to please Christ until the end of his race. Believers may grow weary *in* God's work, but they should never grow weary *of* His work, if they truly believe that Christ is waiting for them at the finish line.

In writing to the Corinthians, Paul informed believers that they do not compete against each other (1 Cor. 9:24-27). In fact, God has given each believer gifts and abilities to fulfill a specific calling. Each has a unique race to finish. Every believer in the Body of Christ has a divine calling and a work of ministry to complete (Eph. 4:12). Hence, each believer races against himself to keep a stride ahead of his own flesh. Through the power of the Holy Spirit believers are able to mortify the lusts of the flesh for what is outside of God's will. This permits believers to be unhindered while running their personal races.

Paul then speaks of *the goal* of his race, which is to reach the finish line of his earthly sojourn (either his death or the rapture of his body to be with Christ). He also describes why he is running for the Lord, *"for the prize of the upward call of God in Christ"* (v. 14). The prize refers to the rewards to be received at the Judgment Seat of Christ and also being in Christ's presence. The entire race from start (his conversion) to finish (his death or rapture) is described as this *upward call*. This encompasses all that God wanted to accomplish in Paul's life to honor His Son's name – salvation, sanctification, good works, moral conformity to Christ, etc.

Although the Philippians were to follow Paul's example of pressing onward and upward in God's calling for them in Christ, the apostle realized that younger saints may not understand what he was talking about. Those lacking maturity were to press forward in obedience in what they knew to be true, spiritual maturity and blessing would come (vv. 15-16). The word "perfect" in verse 15 speaks of mature Christians, who should have the same vision of suffering and dying for the Savior that Paul had just shared.

Paul prayed that those who did not have this mindset would obtain it. He urged the less mature believers to be busy for the Lord immediately. It was not a matter of delaying service until a certain level of knowledge was gained. Rather, it was a matter of immediate obedience to the present understanding of truth, and as a result of the Lord's blessing in the midst of service, experiencing a growing knowledge of and intimacy with the Lord. God grows ministries as He grows people. In the interim, we should be faithful to what we know God has asked us to do and long for what is yet to come. We tend to focus on what is visibly spectacular, but God is interested in our character and how faithful we are to mundane obligations. Those who are faithful in the little things will receive greater opportunities from God.

Indeed, there are many spiritual blessings in heavenly places to be obtained in Christ (Eph. 1:3), but God is wise to grant only that portion which we can both receive and retain today. We are to thank God for what has been received, while at the same time continuing in conquest and requesting from Him a greater portion of His riches in Christ. May believers bless others with their possessions already received while continuing to rest in the Lord and increasing their capacity to receive more spiritual blessings.

This was Paul's passion and why he could gladly associate preaching Christ with suffering for Christ. He knew this mindset would permit him to further know Christ and experience Him in ways that he had not previously known. May this be our passion also.

## Paul's Future (vv. 17-21)

Paul instructed the Philippians to follow his example in pressing on to maturity in Christ (v. 17). This was the means of living Christ's life to the fullest. Regrettably, some had professed Christ out of selfish self-interest. They were not true believers but enemies of the cross of Christ (v.18).

Those in 1:18 were true believers preaching Christ with the wrong motives. The legalizers in vv. 1-2 were not saved, but truly believed the message they were preaching. However, those identified in verse 18 were using the gospel as a cloak to cover their carnal appetites, while they profited from gullible believers. These con-artists valued transient things like food and drink more than God's truth and blessing. Truly *"their god was their belly"* (v. 19). Self-promotion and self-gratifying behavior by a supposed gospel preacher is a telltale sign of spiritual abnormality.

With tears, Paul warned the Philippians not to give ear to these enemies of Christ. Paul endured much sorrow because of the harm to believers, to local assemblies, and to the Church in general, caused by such enemies of the cross. These antinomians would eventually be cast into the Lake of Fire to suffer eternal damnation in Hell.

Having completed his warning against those who oppose God to gain personal liberties (vv. 18-19), Paul returns to the important upward calling that all believers must maintain in verse 20. In contrast to the wicked who will suffer forever in Hell, believers are destined to be with Christ forever in glory. Philippi was a Roman Colony formally established when Octavian became Emperor of Rome in 27 B.C. As a result, the Philippians enjoyed privileges, protection, and status as Roman citizens away from Rome.

Paul uses their civil situation to make a spiritual appeal. The Philippians were to be heavenly-minded because that is where their true citizenship resided (v. 20). Believers are at present seated with Christ at the right hand of God the Father in Heaven (Eph. 2:6). This position in Christ ensures that all Christians are citizens of Heaven. Just as it was important for the names of babies born in Philippi to be registered on legal records, all those born again in Christ have their names in the Lamb's Book of Life.

Until Christ removes His Church from the earth, believers form a heavenly colony on earth. This is why Paul refers to believers as "ambassadors for Christ" (2 Cor. 5:21). Our citizenship is in Heaven, but we have the opportunity to represent Heaven's interests on earth now until He recalls all His ambassadors home. "We look for" is derived from a middle-voice verb implying that believers should have an earnest desire to be with Christ. Elsewhere John and Paul speak of this blessed hope:

> *Looking for the blessed hope and glorious appearing of our great God and Savior Jesus Christ* (Tit. 2:13).
> *To wait for His Son from Heaven, whom He raised from the dead, even Jesus who delivers us from the wrath to come* (1 Thess. 1:10).
>
> *We know that when He is revealed, we shall be like Him, for we shall see Him as He is. And everyone who has this hope in Him purifies himself, just as He is pure* (1 Jn. 3:2).

In recognition of Christ's imminent return for His Bride, may believers be heavenly-minded to accomplish earthly good, rather than merely existing on earth and waiting to be raptured from their responsibility.

While salvation of the soul occurs by trusting in the gospel message of Christ, the benefits and blessings of that salvation are not fully entered into until the believer's body has been redeemed and transformed into a glorious Christlike body (v. 21; Eph. 1:14). Thankfully, believers will receive bodies fit for Heaven at the Rapture of the Church (1 Cor. 15:51-52).

The Lord Jesus prophesied His own resurrection (John 2:19-21) and later showed His resurrected body to His disciples (Luke 24:40). He told them that He was not a spirit, but flesh and bone (Luke 24:37-39). He then ate some fish and honeycomb in their presence (Luke 24:42). By showing the nail prints in His body to the disciples, the Lord Jesus was demonstrating that His new body retained features of the old body that had been nailed to a cross. Stephen later reported seeing the Lord at the right hand of God in Heaven (Acts 7:55-56). Christ is the firstfruits from the dead, thus giving hope of glorification to all believers (1 Cor. 15:20).

By the same power that God is able to subdue all things to Himself, believers are guaranteed eternal, glorious Christlike bodies which will never wear out or degrade, and will always declare the moral glory of Christ!

# Philippians Chapter 4

### Beneficial Exhortation (vv. 1-3)

How can we reprove others in such a way that it is received without offense or creating doubt about our motives? When a behavior needs to be reproved, such corrections should be done in person. Because written reproof restricts communication to a factual level, it rarely accomplishes its intended purpose. Face-to-face interaction is best when offenses need to be addressed or a word of correction is required (Matt. 18:15). If this is not possible, video or phone calls are the next best alternative, so that the one receiving the reproof can see our love and sense sincerity in the tone and inflections of our voice.

John had to address difficult topics in both his second and third epistles, but on the more sensitive matters he refused to write. He preferred to address those matters in person (2 Jn. 12; 3 Jn. 13). Face-to-face communication is by far the best format for approaching difficult issues and we should not permit cowardice to keep us from doing what we know is best for others. It is important to pray about exhorting others before we engage in the activity. If we wait on the Lord for the right timing, He will assist us in speaking what is needful. Often, He permits these opportunities to arise naturally and unforced during casual personal interactions.

Paul demonstrates a lovely three-step technique to exhort two women in the church at Philippi. Euodia and Syntyche were bickering with each other and causing disunity within the church.

First, Paul began with a positive address: *"my brethren, dearly beloved and longed for, my joy and crown."* Paul uses tender language to affirm his love for and familiarity with the two women to be exhorted. They, with the other Philippians, were Paul's joy and would be his crown at the Judgment Seat of Christ. Without a preexisting love-relationship between believers, exhortation is rarely willingly received.

Second, the apostle identified the issue and the solution: *"I beseech Euodia, and beseech Syntyche, that they be of the same mind in the Lord."* Notice that Paul did not play favorites in addressing a mutual problem; he "implores" each of them separately to heed his reproof and to change their behavior. Paul also enlisted another person, his "true companion" (likely

Epaphroditus who was laboring with Paul in Rome at the time), to help these sisters resolve their differences and provide accountability for monitoring their progress – *"help these women"* (Phil. 4:3). Sometimes we need a wise third party to help us navigate around our own carnality.

Third, Paul concluded his exhortation with another positive statement, mentioning that both of these sisters labored with him in the gospel and *"whose names are in the book of life."* These sisters had assisted Paul previously in the cause of Christ and he looked forward to spending eternity with them in Heaven. This technique of sandwiching reproof between positive affirmations is a good pattern for us to follow in exhorting others. Exhortation is to be a normal part of our Christian experience (Heb. 3:13).

## Enjoying the Peace of God (vv. 4-9)

Rejoicing in God and giving Him thanks during arduous situations declares our confidence in His character and promises. This is why Paul charged the Philippians to *"Rejoice in the Lord always!"* (v. 4). Moreover, they were to be governed by a spirit of patient moderation in their day-to-day circumstances.

The same Greek word translated "gentleness" in verse 5 is used to identify a spirit of patience and gentleness that church elders must possess while shepherding God's sheep (1 Tim. 3:3). The idea is that those enjoying God's peace are not given over to emotional vacillations resulting from their circumstances because they realize that the Lord's coming is imminent (v. 5). Believers who are settled in the hope of Christ's coming will also enjoy settled emotions. We must remember that this is not the real world. Believers are merely aliens waiting to be taken to their real home.

The meaning of "anxiety" is to be pulled in different directions at the same time, and the idea of "worry" is to be strangled. Anxiety and worry are the principal thieves of the believer's joy. Yet, we cannot be robbed of God's peace if we choose to rejoice in Him instead of seeking satisfaction and happiness in favorable circumstances. The prophet Isaiah tells us that this is how we can enjoy God's *"perfect peace"* of mind: *"You will keep him in perfect peace, whose mind is stayed on You, because he trusts in You. Trust in the Lord forever, for in YAH, the Lord, is everlasting strength"* (Isa. 26:3-4). Nearness to God is the greatest defense against depression and the best means of promoting a stable mind.

> Worry does not empty tomorrow of its sorrow. It empties today of its strength.
>
> – Corrie Ten Boom

> Anxiety does not empty tomorrow of its sorrows, but only empties today of its strength.
>
> – Charles Spurgeon

True peace is found in God alone. William Kelly reminds us that "strength depends upon what passes between our own souls and God, who in His gracious and vigilant care watches over His saints individually."[84] Each saint must personally appreciate Christ and rest in Him to do what is appropriate and right each day. To accomplish this, we must heed Paul's exhortation to the saints at Colossi, *"Set your affection on things above, not on things on the earth"* (Col. 3:2).

If we are anxious about anything, we have a remedy: *"Be anxious for nothing, but in everything by prayer and supplication, with thanksgiving, let your requests be made known to God"* (v. 6). If the issue is not worthy of being released into the Lord's care, then it is certainly not worth fretting over. We either must pray about or forget about such things, for it is a waste of time and energy to agonize over things we cannot change by worry. To rejoice in Christ and to give Him thanks in all things demonstrates that we really believe who He says He is, and that we implicitly trust Him!

> We would worry less if we praised more. Thanksgiving is the enemy of discontent and dissatisfaction.
>
> – Harry Ironside

> Why worry when you can pray? Trust Jesus; He'll be your stay.
> Don't be a doubting Thomas; rest fully in His promise.
> Why worry, worry, worry when you can pray?
>
> — Unknown

The Lord Jesus not only made peace with God on our behalf (Rom. 5:1), He now offers us His serenity – the peace of God (v. 7). The Greek word translated "peace" is *eirene*. It is derived from a verb meaning to "bond together." It literally means to "be made at one again," as reflected in Acts 7:26 (KJV) when Moses sought to make two quarreling Israelites *"at one again."* *Eirene* is almost always translated "peace" in Scripture, but on rare occasions it is rendered "rest" and "quietness." Believers must permit the Lord's rest and peace to flow into our souls so that we may enjoy His tranquility despite our circumstances.

In application, Romans 5:1 means that we are "one again" (have peace) with God when we believe the gospel message. This is the saving of the soul. However, verse 7 refers to the saving of the mind which is achieved when we are "one again" with Christ in His thinking, affections, and attitudes (this is the outcome of John 16:33). This is how we secure a guard of peace for our hearts and minds *"which surpasses all understanding"* (v. 7).

It is impossible to convey God's peace to others unless the believer personally possesses His peace. Being one again with Christ brings peace to the soul. If we are fretful, we should ask ourselves, "In what respects is my thinking not one with Christ?" Only by *"looking to Jesus, the author and finisher of our faith"* (Heb. 12:2) can we demonstrate His peace in such a way that the lost will want it too.

The mind is to be strengthened in the same way that the muscles of our body are – through exercise and proper diet. Paul provides the Philippians, and us too, with a wholesome dietary menu that is sure to enhance the vitality of the believer's thought life (vv. 8-9). If we are going to expose our minds to violence, pornography, filthy language, course jesting, and extravagant indulgences, the heart will readily be conformed into a stagnant cesspool of carnal ambitions. *"For as he thinks in his heart, so is he"* (Prov. 23:7). Physically we are what we eat, but spiritually we become what we think on.

When a believer feeds on (thinks upon) what is corrupt, it must lead to a full harvest of corruption (Gal. 6:6-7). It will be realized long after the initial seeds were sown that the repercussions were far more devastating than could have ever been imagined. The nude images that a man tucks away in his mind earlier in his life can be used by Satan to stir up dissatisfaction with his own wife years later. We choose our sin and God chooses the consequences of our sin, but the painful aftermath of sin is never worth what we thought we might temporarily enjoy outside of God's will.

Thankfully, we have peace with God through Christ's finished work at Calvary, but to enjoy God's peace Paul says that we must train our minds to feed on a proper spiritual diet. Posed as questions, these virtues are:

Is it true – genuine, real, and reliably transparent?
Is it noble – worthy of respect and honorable?
Is it just – righteous and faultless?
Is it pure – unmixed wholesomeness and high moral character?
Is it lovely – admirable and appreciated by others?
Is it of good report – or of good repute?

These six patterns of thought are virtuous (of moral excellence) and praiseworthy (deserving of commendation). All that goes through the eye and ear gates should first pass the Philippians 4:8 filter! It is the only way to enjoy the presence of the God of peace. While Scripture records believers praying at various times, Paul is encouraging us to follow his example and develop an atmosphere of prayer by enjoying the ongoing presence of Christ through faithful obedience and submission (v. 9).

## Learning Contentment (vv. 10-13)

Remembering that God is sovereign over all things will defeat feelings of jealousy and discontent. God is in control and everything is as He allows it. Nothing occurs in creation, including our trials, which does not first pass over His desk, so to speak. It was through this attitude that Paul learned contentment during periods of lack or during times of blessing (v. 10).

At this moment you have exactly as much money as God wants you to have. If He wanted you to have more, your bank account would show it. The reason He has not bestowed more monetary blessings on you is that you do not need it, or you would be a poor steward of it, or He is teaching you lessons concerning budgeting and giving. The Lord knows what He is doing, and what He does serves our best *interest*. So let us appreciate what we have, assess our present condition with a spiritual mindset, adjust where we lack, and accept everything as from the Lord. Let us, like Paul, learn to be content in whatever state we find ourselves (v. 11).

The Greek verb rendered "learned" in verse 12 is *memuemai* and is drawn from the root *mueo* which means "to initiate into the mysteries" or "to learn the secret." Paul's circumstances (whether lacking or abounding) did not affect his abiding joy in Christ, because he had been ushered into the secret of God's presence which the world could know nothing about. Under the shadow of God's wing, so to speak, there is rest, peace, and power that no one can take away from us unless we forfeit these blessings ourselves through worry and anxiety. For this reason, Paul knew that he would be completely victorious in Christ in any situation in which God placed him. Hence, he had confidence that he could do all things through Christ who continually strengthened him (v. 13). G. C. Willis summarizes Paul's humble disposition that allowed him to be infused with God's power:

> What wonderful words to come from a man in prison, one who was apparently in most abject circumstances, and in no small danger: one who was unable to do anything, as men would say. But faith speaks according to God, and the one who could do nothing, in the judgment

of others, is the very one who could say he had strength for all things; not in himself, truly, but in the One empowering him. The word translated "empowering" is the word from which we get *dynamite* and *dynamo;* what mighty power is expressed in each of those words: but the One who empowered Paul was mightier than all dynamite and all dynamos. He is the One who could say: *"All power is given unto Me in Heaven and on earth."* And *therefore,* we are to go into all the world and preach the Gospel. And it is because all power is given unto Christ that we may take up Paul's language and say: "I have strength for all things in the One empowering me."[85]

Learning the power of godly contentment will keep our covetousness and impure jealousy in check. King Saul, even after understanding that the kingdom had been promised to David, was lifted up in pride and jealousy. Saul could not accept God's sovereign rule or the just punishment he received for his own blunders. We will never be able to enjoy God's peace until we willingly step down from that imaginary throne of self-rulership.

> The labor of self-love is a heavy one indeed. Think whether much of your sorrow has not arisen from someone speaking slightingly of you. As long as you set yourself up as a little god to which you must be loyal, how can you hope to find inward peace?
>
> – A. W. Tozer

If we truly understand that we have exactly what God wants us to possess, what room is there for envy and covetousness in our thinking? Haggai told the nation of Israel that because they were dwelling in their nice paneled houses while God's house remained unfinished, He had blown their assets away to cause them to lack. His point: sometimes lack is God's way of getting our attention, especially if the matter is one of disobedience.

Let us remember God's past goodness and faithfulness and that at all times He is good and does good (Ps. 119:68). If you have done all that you can and still have legitimate lack, humbly petition Him for help, but remember that your joy is not in temporal things. It is in the eternal Christ.

## God Supplies All Our Needs (vv. 14-19)

Paul informed the saints at Philippi that they were the only church to share with him after he departed from Macedonia during his second missionary journey (v. 15). Afterwards, they sent Paul two more gifts while he was in Thessalonica (v. 16). Another gift from Philippi is referenced in

Paul's letter to the Corinthians (2 Cor. 11:9), and then another gift was received from them during Paul's first Roman imprisonment (v. 14).

Paul acknowledges that there had been a gap in their giving to him, but he attributed this to their lack of opportunity, perhaps because he had been a prisoner in Rome and in Caesarea for several years (v. 10). This is a good example for us to follow. If we do not know the facts about a particular situation, we do well to think positively about the other believers involved, or at least to give them the benefit of the doubt until we know the truth. Paul was not seeking a gift from the Philippians, per se, but he was excited that they were bearing spiritual fruit to God (v. 17). Indeed, their sacrifice to God on Paul's behalf was a pleasing, sweet-smelling offering to God (v. 18). Paul not only loved the Philippians, but he also rejoiced greatly in them and in their eternal reward for investing in his gospel ministry.

After recognizing the giving spirit of the saints at Philippi, Paul noted that, not only would they receive a heavenly reward for their generosity, but God would replenish their resources on earth to satisfy all their needs: *"My God shall supply all your need according to His riches in glory by Christ Jesus"* (v. 19). "My God" is Heaven's Banker. "Shall supply all your need" is the requested value of the bank draft. "According to His riches" speaks of Heaven's resources – the bank's assets. "In glory" is where the bank is located. "By Jesus Christ" is the authorizing signer of the bank draft.

Those who are united with Christ are greatly blessed because of that union and will not lack resources to worship and serve the Lord. However, we should remember that it is not the lack of resources that hinders our ability to honor the Lord, but the extent to which we serve our own interests rather than devotedly serving the Lord with what we have received from Him. May our steadfast devotion affirm, *"now to our God and Father be glory forever and ever"* (v. 20).

## Conclusion (vv. 20-23)

In closing, Paul affirms a good Christian principle of fellowship (v. 21): Greet all God's people with the same Christian love. We should not be partial regarding those to whom we show kindness and respect (Jas. 2:1-4).

Paul concludes his letter by passing along greetings from the believers who were with Paul in prison and from the local saints, especially from those in Caesar's household. Though Paul was restrained in body, the message he preached was not. The gospel message had even penetrated into wicked Nero's palace with its saving power. In the final verse, Paul expresses his desire that God's grace would fully enable all those who sincerely love Christ to serve Him faithfully (v. 23).

# Colossians

## Background

Colossians is one of four epistles written during Paul's first imprisonment in Rome, commencing in approximately 60 A.D. and lasting about two years. Paul was under house arrest and had much more liberty to minister than he would be allowed during his second Roman imprisonment a few years later. Apparently, the gospel was brought to Colosse by a believer named Epaphras who lived there (1:7). Paul confirmed that he had not visited that city previously (Col. 2:1).

It is likely that the epistles of Colossians and Philemon were written at roughly the same time, since Tychicus was to deliver both and return the runaway slave Onesimus (now a believer) to his master Philemon in Colosse. There is no mention of Paul's possible release from prison, as in his epistle to the Philippians. Apparently, he had already been in Rome for some time, so the epistle was likely written in the middle portion of his first Roman imprisonment.

The main threat to the Church at Colosse was Gnosticism. *Gnosis* means "knowledge" and the Gnostics prided themselves on special knowledge. They claimed to have more superior information on spiritual matters than Paul possessed. Although we do not know exactly what the Gnostics were teaching, their message was undermining truths concerning Christ's humanity and deity. In general, the Gnostics denied the complete unity of His deity and humanity. Some believed Christ to be a hybrid creature between God and man, while others suggested that there was a separation of His humanity and deity just prior to the crucifixion. By demeaning His deity, Gnosticism undervalued Christ's divine attributes and His redemptive work at Calvary.

Paul sets the matter straight by explaining the glories of Christ's person and work. He silences the Gnostics by telling them that in Christ is all true knowledge and spiritual life, so if people want to understand and experience spiritual things, they must come to Christ. Besides the danger of Gnosticism, there were also some at Colosse who were promoting legalism (i.e., salvation in Christ by grace plus Law-keeping). Paul also confronts this erroneous teaching (2:18-23).

*Revealing Heaven's Secrets*

## Theme(s)
"The preeminence of Christ." "Hold fast to Christ, not human traditions or philosophies."

## Keywords
Keywords and phrases include: "mystery," "with Christ Jesus (or with Him)," "power(s)," "knowledge," "truth," "head," "firstborn," "created," "wisdom," and "put on/put off."

## Date
Colossians was likely written during the middle part of Paul's first Roman imprisonment: 61 A.D.

## Outline
I. Introduction With a Prayer of Thanksgiving and for Protection (1:1-14).
II. The Preeminence of Christ as Creator and Head of the Church (1:15-23).
III. Declaring Christ's Sufficiency and Supreme Wisdom (1:24-2:23).
IV. The Practical Demands of a Believer's Position in Christ (3:1-17).
V. Living Out Christ's Life in the World (3:18-4:6).
VI. Paul's Co-laborers and Final Instructions (4:7-18).

# Colossians Chapter 1

## Introduction (vv. 1-8)

The letter to the Colossians commences with the same type of salutation found in other Pauline epistles to churches. The sender is stated, Paul (v. 1). Additionally, his authority as an apostle (a "sent one") of Jesus Christ by the will of God is also affirmed. In his letter to the Philippians, Paul did not assert his apostolic authority as there was no challenge to it at Philippi, nor was there any doctrinal error in that church to be confronted by apostolic authority. That was not the case at Colosse.

The addressees of the epistle are specifically *"the saints and faithful brethren in Christ"* gathered in the church at Colosse (v. 2). However, it was understood that the truths contained in this epistle would also be profitable for other saints in the region. For example, after this letter was read at Colosse, it was to be read by the church at Laodicea (4:16).

Because the believers at Colosse had been justified in Christ (i.e., they had been declared positionally righteous in Christ by God; Rom. 4:21-25), Paul refers to them as "saints" (v. 2). Scripture often refers to Christians as "saints" (v. 12; Jude 3). Accordingly, Paul typically addressed his epistles to the saints gathered together at some particular locale (e.g., 1 Cor. 1:2; Phil. 1:1). The term "brethren" indicates that all those born again in Christ have become children of their common heavenly Father.

Continuing his salutation, Paul declares *"grace to you and peace from God our Father and the Lord Jesus Christ"* (v. 2). This is Paul's trademark greeting and is word for word how he saluted the Romans and the Corinthians (Rom. 1:7; 1 Cor. 1:3). *Grace* was a greeting that the Greeks commonly used, while Jewish believers traditionally referred to the blessing of *peace* to convey a how-do-you-do.

Paul was prompted to frequently pray for the Colossians after learning of their faith in Christ (vv. 3-4). There is no evidence in Scripture that Paul ever visited the city of Colosse, although he did become acquainted with a number of saints from that city: Onesimus (4:9), Epaphras (4:12), Philemon, Archippus, and Apphia (Philem. 1-2). Although Paul had not personally labored in Colosse, he was abundantly thankful to God after hearing from Epaphras the response of many in that city to the gospel. These now all had their hope in Heaven (v. 5). Paul wanted the Colossians to know they were not an isolated work of God, but that the gospel of Jesus Christ was bearing much fruit to God throughout the Roman Empire (v. 6).

Epaphras may have come to Christ during Paul's three-year stay at Ephesus (during his third missionary journey) and then returned to Colosse. Epaphras was a faithful minister of Christ who shared *"the grace of God in truth"* with those at Colosse, and some responded to it (v. 7).

Although they had not directly heard the gospel from an apostle, Paul confirms that they had believed the true gospel message as evidenced by their genuine love in the Spirit for the Lord and for others (v. 8) – *"Everyone who loves is born of God and knows God"* (1 Jn. 4:7). Regeneration is a work of the Holy Spirit (Tit. 3:5), yet the Holy Spirit is not referred to again in this letter. Regrettably, as the letter progresses, it becomes obvious that the Colossian saints were being influenced by other things such as evil doctrines and seducing spirits (2:4-8).

## Paul's Prayer (vv. 9-14)

Having expressed his thanksgiving to God for the Colossian believers, the apostle offers intercession on their behalf. Paul will pray for their spiritual awareness, their walk (a worthy testimony), their spiritual power, and for them to maintain a thankful spirit (vv. 9-11). The words "all," "fully," and "every" in his prayer indicate Paul's desire that the Colossians would experience Christ and His life to the fullest extent possible.

The paramount reason to study Scripture is to learn what God reveals about Himself. Knowledge that "puffs up" is not the goal, but rather awareness of God's greatness which prompts us to fall on our faces in wonder and awe before Him. For this reason, Paul regularly prayed that the Colossian believers would be *"increasing in the knowledge of God,"* for he knew such knowledge would lead them into spiritual wisdom, strength, and fruitfulness. Having experienced the grace of God (v. 6), the Colossians should desire to increase in the knowledge of God also (v. 9). Spiritual growth and fruitfulness occur by apprehending and yielding to God's will.

Paul knew that as the believers experienced Christ in this way, they would also benefit from His reviving power. Whenever a believer's understanding of Christ slips, or his or her desire to know Him more intimately wanes, something is very wrong. Understanding who Christ is, and what He has done and will do, promotes our spiritual vitality. Most of our doubts and anxieties arise from a diminished view of God's true nature and of the power of His gospel message centered in His Son.

Note the progression in Paul's prayer from the knowledge of God to the wisdom of that knowledge (v. 9), to the outworking of both in fruitfulness, which then leads to further knowledge of God (v. 10). Not only were the believers to know the truth of Scripture, but they were also to grow in wisdom (the practical application of understood truth).

This dynamic of practicing and experiencing the truth to learn wisdom was evident in the life of the Lord Jesus. Though He was full of truth (John 1:14), yet He increased in wisdom and favor with God (Luke 2:52) and learned obedience by doing God's will for His life (Heb. 5:8). Experiencing the truthfulness of God's Word is also necessary in the believer's life. Tribulations, for example, practically test our faith and work into our faith a quality of patience that could not be achieved otherwise (Jas. 1:3). Generally speaking, this is why the Lord changes His people before He changes their circumstances.

Increasing in the true knowledge of God translates into being strengthened by His glorious power (v. 11). It is only by God's help that believers have the capacity to be patient and longsuffering with a joyful and thankful disposition while enduring hardships. William MacDonald identifies the distinct benefits of a patient and longsuffering disposition:

> The difference between **patience** and **longsuffering** has been defined as the difference between enduring without complaint and enduring without retaliation. God's grace has achieved one of its greatest objects in the life of the believer who can suffer patiently and praise God in the midst of the fiery trial.[86]

As the Greek verb *eucharistountes,* rendered "giving thanks" in verse 12, is *plural,* it is not Paul giving thanks, but the Colossians who were to give thanks to their heavenly Father. He had delivered them out of the power of satanic darkness, had adopted them as His sons, and predestined them to receive a heavenly kingdom and inheritance in Christ (vv. 12-13; Eph. 1:11). The *"Son of His love"* not only acknowledges that Christ is the object of His Father's love, but that the Son is also the revealer of His Father's love to others, for *"God is love"* (1 Jn. 4:8).

By trusting in the gospel message, the Colossians had been snatched out of Satan's kingdom of darkness, hate, and death to become saints in the kingdom of Christ, which was full of divine light, love, and life. By trusting in the gospel, the Colossians had been redeemed by the blood of Christ and received the forgiveness of their sins (v. 14). Although they had not heard the gospel directly from an apostle, it was the power of the message that was critical, not the one who shared it. Paul thanked God that the Colossians had experienced the full power of the gospel message of Christ.

## The Preeminence of Christ (vv. 15-19)

The Gnostics prided themselves on human knowledge and intellectual arguments. However, Paul wanted the Colossians to be filled with the knowledge of God's will, with wisdom and spiritual understanding concerning Christ and then be renewed in the inner man by that knowledge. What was Paul's message for those being influenced by Gnosticism? That Jesus Christ is fully God in human body. Therefore, if anyone wants to gain true knowledge, he or she must go to its source – Christ (v. 19). He possesses all wisdom, knowledge, and power.

In verses 15-19, Paul identifies several supreme qualities of the Lord Jesus that should be appreciated by the Colossians and by us too. These relate to His relationship with His heavenly Father (v. 15), His relationship with His creation (vv. 16-17), and His relationship to His Church (v. 18).

**He is the image of the invisible God** (v. 15; John 14:7-9): Paul is stressing the divine relationship of Christ; the Son is like the Father. The word "image" here means likeness through relationship; the Son is like the Father (Christ is the express image of the Father; Heb. 1:3). God was displaying Himself visibly to humanity through His Son, who was also His representative, replacing Adam who failed to represent Him perfectly.

**He is the Firstborn of creation** (v. 15): Christ was not the first act of creation by the Father as some teach. Rather, "Firstborn" speaks of Christ's honored position over creation. He has the place of sovereignty and rules over His creation. The word does not speak of physical birth or created origin (e.g., Luke 2:7), but a position of superiority and authority held by the firstborn son in the family or clan (e.g., Ps. 89:27).

**He is the Creator and Sustainer of all things** (vv. 16-17): *"He is before all things, and in Him all things consist."* There was nothing created that was not created by Christ and He continues to sustain all created things. Speaking of Christ, God's eternal Word, John states that *"All things were made through Him, and without Him nothing was made that was made"* (John 1:3). All things were created by the Son in accordance with the will of His Father and through the power of the Holy Spirit. Hence, the essence of all life is in Jesus Christ. Apart from Christ there is no life.

**He is the Head of the Church** (v. 18; Eph. 1:22-23): Christ alone has authority over His Church. He is the center of her attention and worship.

**He is the Eternal God** (v. 18; John 1:1): The Lord Jesus existed before time and was the beginning of all things. John refers to Him as the Almighty God who is "the first and the last," "the alpha and the omega," and "the beginning and the end" (Rev. 1:8, 11). And yet, the Lord said, *"I am He who lives, and was dead, and behold, I am alive forevermore"* (Rev. 1:18).

Incarnate God, Christ, gave up His life that we might have life in Him.

**He is the Firstborn from the dead** (v. 18; 1 Cor. 15:20-21): Christ was the first man to experience glorification; He is the firstfruits of the first resurrection (the resurrection of the just). He is glorified humanity presently sitting on the throne of God in Heaven (Rev. 3:21). When He comes into His kingdom, He will have His own throne (Heb. 1:8).

**He has preeminence over all things** (v. 18; 1 Cor. 15:24-28): Christ is sovereign and Lord over all His creation. *"He who is the blessed and only Potentate, the Lord of lords and King of kings"* (1 Tim. 6:15).

**He possesses the fullness of the Godhead** (v. 19; Col. 2:9): He is fully God, not diminished deity! *"For in Him dwells all the fulness of the Godhead bodily"* (2:9). The gnostics taught that Jesus Christ was less than God and therefore was a limited resource of wisdom, but Paul declares His divine superiorities for appreciation by all. The Father never demeans His Son. Only ignorant men disdain the Lord Jesus by not acknowledging His authority, position, and rulership as God.

Those with a low estimation of God's Son will ultimately live defeated lives because they will also underestimate the strength of the devil and the danger posed by his cunning devices. These spiritually despondent souls fall prey to the wiles of the enemy, and then both fail to learn from their disappointing experiences, and how to rise up in grace to victory. It is one thing to know that Christ is omnipresent and omnipotent, but it is quite another to fully trust in His abiding presence, wisdom, and power when one is suffering terribly for doing what is right.

## Christ's Work of Reconciliation (vv. 20-23)

Because Christ was fully God, He was able to reconcile all things to Himself and by Himself through redemption (v. 20). The Greek verb translated "to reconcile" in verse 20 means "to be restored to a right relationship or standard." When God's representative on earth, man, fell prey to the devil's solicitations in Eden, that which man enjoyed with God on earth was ruined. Satan introduced sin into God's perfect creation. God could not have a corrupt head ruling over a perfect creation, so the earth came under God's judgment. Thankfully, in a coming day, Christ will return to the earth and restore creation to its full potential (Rom. 8:19-23).

Through trusting in the gospel message of Jesus Christ, individuals are spiritually born again to become children of God and to be eternally one with Christ. Christ applies His own blood to redeem the body and soul of the repentant sinner (1 Cor. 6:20; 1 Pet. 1:18-19). This permits the condemned to be completely reconciled to a holy God (2 Cor. 5:18-19). This is only possible because God was completely satisfied with the propitiatory work for human sin achieved by Christ at Calvary (Heb. 2:17).

Not only were we once alienated from God – we were His enemies – but through Christ, repentant sinners are justified and positionally declared to be holy and without blame in God's sight (v. 21): *"For if when we were enemies we were reconciled to God through the death of His Son, much more, having been reconciled, we shall be saved by His life"* (Rom. 5:10). This reconciliation was made possible because Christ *"in the body of His flesh through death"* suffered on our behalf (v. 22). Christ, taking our place, died on the cross in a real human body. He did not suffer as a spirit being, as the Gnostics claimed, but as the Son of Man and the Last Adam.

After affirming the wonderful truth of reconciliation, the apostle poses a challenge: If the Colossians were truly saved by the gospel that they first heard through Epaphras, then they must continue in the power of that message (v. 23). Paul is not questioning the salvation of the Colossian believers (he has already affirmed that), but he is warning them not to drift from what they know to be experientially true: "If you are saved, do not listen to the Gnostics." Paul employed similar logic with the Corinthians: "If you are saved, that means that God has endorsed my ministry as an apostle among you" (2 Cor. 13:5-6). He was not questioning their salvation, but affirming that their salvation was proof of his divine apostleship.

Salvation is secured in Christ alone (John 10:28-29), but true salvation is also characterized by perseverance. Those who truly know Christ and have experienced His life through the gospel continue in that truth.

Paul uses hyperbole to dramatically convey how the gospel had radically spread throughout the Roman Empire in such a short time – as having been *"preached to every creature under Heaven"* (v. 23). But not all men had yet received the message of reconciliation in Christ. This was God's appointed ministry for Paul and there was still much work to do.

## The Apostle's Stewardship and Concern (vv. 24-29)

Not only was Paul tasked to preach the gospel, but he was also chosen to reveal its mysteries to the Church. Paul informed the Colossians of this divinely given stewardship (vv. 24-25). A steward is someone appointed to administer the affairs of another. Despite the affliction associated with this ministry, Paul wanted to be found faithful in revealing to the Church the mystery of *"the dispensation of the grace of God"* (1 Cor. 4:2).

A dispensation describes an economy of truth that God reveals to individuals or a people, which puts them under a stewardship. If obeyed, then the recipients of the promises of God will be blessed, but if rejected,

God is justified in judging rebellion. The "dispensation of the grace of God" pertains to the Church Age which began at Pentecost (Acts 2) and will conclude with "the fullness of the Gentiles" (Rom. 11:25) when Christ returns to remove His Church from the earth (1 Thess. 4:13-18).

How God would fulfill His covenant promise to Abraham to bless his seed and all families of the earth through him was a truth not revealed to any previous generation of people (v. 26). Paul refers to this sacred secret as *"the mystery"* (v. 26) or *"the mystery of Christ"* (Eph. 3:4). This term refers to the outcome of Christ's redemptive work, the union of Jews and Gentiles with Christ to form His spiritual Body, with Him as the Head. Paul was called to be a special minister of God to reveal this previously hidden truth (i.e., this divine mystery) *"to His saints."*

God chose to reveal this hidden agenda directly to Paul (Eph. 3:3), then to the apostles and prophets by the Holy Spirit (Eph. 3:5). *"The riches of the glory of this mystery among the Gentiles"* and its future outcome, *"the hope of glory,"* are *"Christ in you* [the Gentiles]" (v. 27). Christ had reconciled Gentiles to God, had become one with them and was coming back for them. *Hope* speaks of having present joy in God's future promises. The Church is to hope in Christ's imminent return (Tit. 2:13).

This mystery of Christ was not an Old Testament reality that was hidden, but a revealed New Testament truth to be understood. The Church did not exist before Pentecost (1 Cor. 12:13). Through the preaching and writings of the apostles and by the illumination of the Holy Spirit, those receiving their message would also be able to understand this mystery (Eph. 3:8-9). Jews and Gentiles had become one with Christ in His Church!

God had bestowed on Paul a great privilege in revealing the mystery of Christ, but there was also a tremendous responsibility attached to his ministry. As all believers are called to be witnesses for Christ in the world (Matt. 28:19-20; Acts 1:8), we also share the responsibility of revealing to others what Paul has revealed to us about Christ – *"Him we preach"* also.

If we truly understand what God has accomplished in Christ on our behalf, we will also exude the fervency exhibited by Paul with respect to his apostolic stewardship. Paul sought to use every opportunity to warn mankind of the coming judgment and then to teach the mysteries of Christ to those who received Him and who would ultimately be with Him forever (v. 28). If we have this type of passion for the lost, then we will witness the mighty power of God working through us to save souls (v. 29). Like Paul, we also have a stewardship. All believers are required to faithfully preach and teach God's Word. Everything else necessary to bring sinners to salvation and to maturity in Christ is God's business (John 6:29, 37, 44)!

# Colossians Chapter 2

### Christ Is the Fountainhead of Wisdom (vv. 1-3)

At the end of chapter 1, Paul spoke of his deliberate striving through gospel preaching and discipleship to present mature believers to Christ. In this chapter Paul speaks of his engagement in another spiritual conflict, that of fervently praying for the believers at Colosse and Laodicea (v. 1). As Paul had not visited Colosse previously, this touching gesture both indicates Paul's love for Christ and those who are His, and the intensity of the spiritual warfare raging against gospel work and the building of the Church.

The Colossian believers were being pressured by Gnostics to think less of Christ and to gain wisdom through human reasoning. Given this dangerous influence, Paul prays for the believers with respect to four matters (vv. 2-3). First, he desired *"that their heart may be encouraged,"* that is, strengthened against the dangers of the Gnostic teachers. The Greek word rendered "may be encouraged" is *paraklethosin* which means "to call to one's side." It may mean "to supply comfort" or "to exhort or admonish" depending on the context. The latter meaning best fits Paul's efforts here.

Second, he desired that the believers would be *"knit together in love."* Paul knew that Christians could not properly love each other unless they loved the Lord according to revealed truth. As the Colossians loved the Lord and each other, a strong defense against satanic attack would be forged.

Third, he prayed that they would gain *"the full assurance of understanding."* It is by exercising faith in God's Word that a believer understands and experientially knows Scripture to be true (John 6:69). More understanding of truth results in more conviction to live for Christ.

Fourth, Paul prays that the Colossians would gain *"the knowledge of the mystery of God"* (1:16-19): To know that Christ is the Son of God and the Head of the Church of which all believers are members is the wonderful mystery of which Paul speaks. If this is known, then believers will be prompted to request from the Father, in Christ's name, all that is needed to further know Him and please Him. This idea confronted the Gnostics' worldview as they sought wisdom and understanding by unbiblical means. It was Christ who possessed *"all the treasures of wisdom and knowledge"* and yet they were demeaning Him through their self-derived wisdom.

## The Dangers of Human Philosophies and Legalism (vv. 4-8)

In verses 4-8, Paul warns the Colossians of three primary tools Satan uses to hoodwink Christians into wrong thinking. First, he uses "enticing words" (v. 4). This speaks of clever presentations and persuasive speech to lure and ensnare the ignorant and foolish. Second, *"philosophy and empty [vain] deceit"* draws those fascinated by intellectual arguments into accepting exalted human reasoning as fact. Third, "the traditions of men" refers to man-made rules and laws that compromise sound doctrine and Church order. There were many legalists in Paul's day preaching the necessity of Law-keeping to be a true Christian. Even today, the devil commonly uses emotionalism, intellectualism, and legalism to lure believers from the truth, thus ensuring their fruitlessness for God.

In spiritual matters, there is nowhere else to go for understanding than to Christ, for in Him are the vast treasuries of divine wisdom and knowledge. However, as evidenced by his deceitful work in Eden, Satan constantly works to cast doubt in the minds of men as to the validity of God's revealed Word. Not only does the first question in the Bible belong to the devil, but so does the first effort to deceive: *"Then the serpent said to the woman, 'You will not surely die'"* (Gen. 3:4). He added the word "not" to what God had said to change the meaning of God's decree. Satan spoke of physical death. God spoke of spiritual separation from Himself. Adam and his wife believed the devil. Every cemetery is proof that God told the full truth and that Satan is a liar.

The Greek verb *paralogizomai* in verse 4 is rendered "should deceive" and is in the middle voice, meaning that believers should choose for themselves to not be deceived. *Para* means "around" or "near" and *logizomai* is an accounting term which means "to account" or "to reckon." *Logizomai* is the Greek word repeatedly used in Romans 4 to explain the doctrine of justification. Believers are declared righteous in Christ because God has *credited* their personal account with His righteousness. All this to say that the word "deceive" means "to put near or around the truth."

This is what Satan does. He puts what he wants us to believe near God's revealed truth to entice us to move away from it. Paul states what the devil wants to achieve concerning believers by deception: First, to rob us of godly order (which results in chaos) and prevent us from having steadfast faith in Christ (v. 5). Second, to impede us from walking in the truth of Christ (v. 6). Third, to ensure that we are not rooted in and built up in truth (v. 7). Fourth, to restrain us from abounding with thanksgiving to God (v. 7).

Just as the Colossians had trusted Christ for salvation alone, they should understand that He was also sufficient for all aspects of the Christian life.

They were to learn of Him, draw strength from Him, and follow His perfect example. Christ is absolute truth. Therefore, our faith must rest on the foundation of Christ alone. The verb "rooted" in verse 7 is a perfect tense and passive voice participle which indicates that at their conversion the Colossians were like a tree being firmly rooted in Christ by God. This eternal grounding has an enduring result ensures that they will have the stability and strength to endure threatening satanic gales and the storms of life. Being so grounded, believers become immovable if by faith we hold to the truth and do not fall prey to enticing secular reasoning. God strengthens those who want to learn more of Him and of His gracious purposes. The devil cannot overcome those who are rooted in God's Truth (1 Pet. 5:8-9)!

As mentioned previously, the first question in the Bible belongs to the devil (Gen. 3:1). His question to Eve in Eden was for the purpose of planting doubt in her mind concerning the validity of God's Word and the rightness of His character. "Did God really say?" "Is it fair for God to limit you in this way?" Satan then presented a half-truth to the woman – "You shall not surely die" and mankind acted on the wrong half. Satan is never more dangerous than when he has a Bible in his hands. This is why Paul exhorts the believers at Colosse to have a faith fully grounded in Christ and His teachings: *"Beware lest anyone cheat you through philosophy and empty deceit, according to the tradition of men, according to the basic principles of the world, and not according to Christ"* (v. 8). This is the only way to not be deceived by a wise and cunning enemy.

Satan rarely presents outright lies. Rather, he depends upon a series of blurry deceptions to gain a footing and to wreak havoc within the Church. Satan deceptively places the error he wants us to believe near the truth. In doing so He seeks to entice believers to depart from what God has already declared to be truth. This is deception.

## Completeness in Christ (vv. 9-13)

The Gnostics were influencing the Colossians through human philosophy and secular reasoning to adopt a degraded view of Christ, but Paul wanted them to know that the fullness of God dwelt bodily in the Lord Jesus. He is the head of all principality and power (vv. 9-10). Thomas Bentley explains Paul's choice of words to further assert Christ's divinity:

> *Theotēs* ("Godhead") is a word quite different in meaning from *theiotēs* ("divinity," Rom 1:20), because the latter describes the quality of God whereas the former looks at the essence of God. There dwells in Christ not certain aspects of God but the totality of God's attributes, powers

and glories. This is conveyed in the term "all the fullness" by which Paul asserts there can be no sharing of His divine power and majesty with other beings, such as angels or the like.[87]

Clearly then, Jesus Christ is the ultimate source of all true knowledge and wisdom. It also meant that because the Colossians were one with Him, they were fully complete and secure in Him. God never lacks anything, so being One with Christ ensured that the Colossians would have everything they needed to enjoy an abundantly fruitful life for Him.

Having warned of the dangerous philosophies of the Gnostics, Paul turns his attention to another spiritual threat against the church at Colosse – Legalism. The Judaizers taught that male circumcision was essential for the Greeks to maintain their salvation in Christ. Conversely, Paul states that the only cutting off of the flesh that mattered to God was that resulting from spiritual circumcision in Christ ("accomplished without hands"). This had the benefit of putting away the sins of the flesh from the believer's body (v. 11). "You were circumcised" is derived from an aorist verb to indicate that at their conversion the Colossians were circumcised in Christ. This meant that they no longer were to be ruled by their flesh, but could now through the power of the Holy Spirit, bear fruit to God through Christ.

Besides being circumcised in Christ, Paul reviewed several other identification truths so that the Colossians would understand how God now viewed them in Christ. They had "died with Christ" (v. 20), had been "buried with Christ" (v. 12), had been "made alive together with Christ" (v. 13), and had been "raised up (resurrected) together with Christ" (v. 12). There are only two groups of people in the world today: those in Christ and those who are not in Christ. In Christ is life and outside of Christ is death.

From God's perspective, all those who have trusted Christ and have been born again by the Holy Spirit are one with His Son forever. Positionally speaking, He views all believers as having died with His Son, having been buried with His Son, and having been made alive and resurrected with His Son. At present, all believers are seated with Christ in heavenly places (Eph. 2:6), and although believers have not yet been glorified in time, God speaks of believers as already glorified in Christ (Rom. 8:30; because Christ has been glorified and we are in Him).

To live the circumcised life, which cuts off and puts to death the deeds of the flesh, believers must reckon these identification realities as true: Who we were in Adam (i.e., the Old Man) legally died at Calvary. Now, because of the union of the believer with Christ, he is a new man and alive in Him. This means that the believer is able to live for Christ instead of the flesh.

## Liberation in Christ (vv. 14-17)

The Law demanded a judicial penalty of death for its violators. Christ, God's sinless, perfect Lamb, took the death sentences of all the condemned (i.e., *"the handwriting of requirements that was against us"*), nailed it to His cross and then suffered God's wrath for humanity's sin (v. 14). How encouraging it is to know that believers will never be judged for our crimes against God because He has already executed the judgment for our sin on His Son (Rom. 5:9).

Additionally, this nailing to the cross of written ordinances announced the end of the Old Covenant (the Mosaic Law) and all of its ceremonial obligations (Heb. 8:13). Although the Law was still holy and just in revealing man's sin (Rom. 7:12-14), the Jews were no longer under it.

As Christ foretold a few days before His crucifixion (John 12:31-33), He would defeat Satan and his hordes of evil angels through His work at Calvary. Satan thought he was winning, but he had no idea what God was accomplishing through Christ to save humanity. If he had, Christ would not have been crucified (1 Cor. 2:7-8). But God's sovereignty was demonstrated at Calvary, when Christ *"having disarmed principalities and powers, He made a public spectacle of them, triumphing over them"* (v. 15).

The verb rendered "having disarmed" is in the middle voice to indicate that Christ completed this action on His own behalf and for His own glory. Not only was Satan defeated at the cross, but a public display of Christ's victory was again witnessed in His resurrection. All the powers of Hell opposed this event (Eph. 1:21-22), but the power of God was triumphant over the enemy, and the prince and power of the air (Satan) could only watch the victorious Christ rise up through his domain.

Having upheld the supreme relevance of Christ's work at Calvary, Paul warned the Colossians to not value superficial religious things that would cause them to devalue Christ's redemptive work or His lordship over them (vv. 14-23). He reminded them that feasts and festivals under the Law were foreshadows of Christ that anticipated His coming. These were therefore abolished by Christ's work at Calvary: *"Regarding a festival or a new moon or Sabbaths, which are a shadow of things to come, but the substance is of Christ"* (vv. 16-17). These observances had served their intended purpose by foreshadowing aspects of Messiah's coming. Now that He had come, the shadows of things did not matter anymore.

One of the best examples of these shadows is found in the Feasts of Jehovah. The seven Feasts of Jehovah provide an exceptional prophetic blueprint of God's means of reconciling the nation of Israel to Himself forever. Every aspect of this blueprint centers in the work of Christ. The four Spring Feasts of Jehovah prophetically typify Christ's death, burial, resurrection, and the beginning of the Church Age. The Church Age is represented by the gap between the spring and autumn feasts. (This also relates to the interval between Daniel's 69$^{th}$ and 70$^{th}$ weeks; Dan. 9:24-27.) The autumn feasts speak of Israel's future acknowledgement of Christ as Messiah, their restoration to Him, and the blessings of His Millennial Kingdom on earth. The autumn feasts prophetically pertain only to Israel.

It was not the Old Testament shadows of things to come that mattered, but rather, the One of Whom they spoke – Christ. He is the "substance" of the Old Testament types and shadows (v. 17).

## The Danger of Mysticism (vv. 18-19)

Paul warned the Colossians to not be fooled by the false humility of mysticism. For example, a man might think he is too lowly a creature to approach God directly and, therefore, choose to worship God by honoring His angels instead. Such thinking was not true humility, but foolishness: It is *"a form* [a profession] *of godliness, but denying its power"* (2 Tim. 3:5). The man in the illustration, far from demonstrating humility before God, is *"intruding into those things which he has not seen, vainly puffed up by his fleshly mind"* (v. 18).

The Law prohibited the worship of angels or anything else in God's creation but God Himself (Ex. 20:3-4). Because it was forbidden, the Jews would never worship angels, but as Norman L. Geisler points out, Satan tricked them and the Gentiles into embracing the doctrines of fallen angels and their mystical nonsense:

> Legalism is the teaching inspired by fallen angels (1 Tim. 4:1) who as "elemental spirits" (Gal. 4:3) would bring men into slavery by their mystical meditations. These legalistic mystics dwell on what they have seen (in visions), which Paul called "idle notions." ... Far from being humble, such a person's unspiritual mind (literally "the mind of the flesh"; v. 19) is puffed with pride in his visions.[88]

In Paul's day, many subserviently worshipped the Greek gods or various pagan deities who were not real. Others honored the heavenly angels or dead religious people. Some today vainly petition dead saints, instead of obeying the Lord's command to supplicate the Father in His name for their needs (John 15:16). Humble, sincere reverence for that which is false does not give it credence!

Paul's point was that revering anyone other than the One who possessed all knowledge and power was not honoring to God. Rather, individuals should be *"holding fast to the Head,"* the One who was causing His Body, the Church, to grow and thrive (v. 19). To worship Christ as something less than He is, is not worship, but an insult. There is no value in such religiosity.

## The Danger of Asceticism (vv. 20-23)

No doubt the Gnostics were promoting the elementary principles of humanized (world) religion in their message (v. 20). However, given his rebuke in verses 21-23, Paul probably had the more zealous Judaizers in mind. These legalists wanted to put the Colossian believers under the yoke of Law-keeping, even after they had been liberated in grace by the gospel of Christ. But Paul reminds the Colossians that having died with Christ, they were also dead to any humanized religious thinking, including the idea that self-denial (according to human regulations) would somehow please God (v. 20). *"Do not touch, do not taste, do not handle," which all concern things which perish with the using – according to the commandments and doctrines of men"* (vv. 21-22). Hinduism and Buddhism promote self-torture and self-denial as marks of holiness, but outside of being in Christ, there is nothing man can do or not do that will earn God's favor.

We cannot earn God's love or increase His esteem for us by "doings." The Christian is *"accepted in the Beloved"* (Eph. 1:6) – end of story. There is nothing a believer can do to persuade God to love him or her more than He already does. His love is unchanging and has already been fully displayed for us at Calvary (Rom. 5:8).

We have all encountered legalistic types who want to impose their stern lists of dos and don'ts upon us, which is none other than the world's religion of good works under a Christian disguise. Although Paul confronted legalism numerous times, perhaps his candid language to the saints at Colosse best captures his disgust for those promoting it. Let us beware of the same trap!

Paul closes the chapter by revealing the true message and motives of the legalists. Their teachings are the doctrines of men, not from God (v. 22). Their teachings have an attractive appearance because they appeal to the flesh, but they are void of true wisdom. Their message is "self-imposed religion" that is fostered in self-righteous pride. Deprivation of the body has *"no value against the indulgence of the flesh"* (v. 23). What is of the flesh will never mortify the flesh. Only God's Word and God's Spirit can accomplish that (Rom. 8:13). The self-reformation of humanized religion only makes men worse, but a spiritual love-relationship with Christ makes men better.

# Colossians Chapter 3

## Our Position and Practice (vv. 1-4)

The best way to prevent the Colossian believers from slipping into the deceitfulness of intellectualism or the pitfalls of legalism, mysticism, and asceticism was for them to set their minds on heavenly things in Christ.

In the two previous chapters, Paul affirmed Christ's supremacy over all creation. He is the omnipotent Creator and Sustainer, the Savior of mankind, and Lord over all. Because all the fullness of the Godhead bodily dwells in Christ (2:9), He alone is the ultimate source of knowledge, wisdom, peace, and grace, and of access to the Father. Paul reminds the Colossians of their blessed union with Christ. Because they were one "with Christ," they were complete "in Him."

In the final two chapters of the epistle, Paul profoundly affirms that our identification with Christ should motivate us to holy living. Our *position* in Christ (what God has done) should motivate our *practice* (how we should behave). Verses 1-3 form the transition between these two important subjects. Paul intertwines what God has done in Christ (our position) with what we should do (our practice) in Christ. Salvation is God's doing, but living out our salvation is our responsibility made possible by God's grace.

| **Positional Truth** | **Practical Truth** |
|---|---|
| Raised with Christ | Seek those things which are above |
| Died with Christ | Set your mind on things above, not on earthly things |
| Life hidden with Christ | |

F. B. Hole summarizes from an identification standpoint what was gained for the believer through the crucifixion, burial, death, and resurrection of Christ:

> The counterpart to our identification with Christ in His death is our identification with Him in His resurrection. The effect of the one is to disconnect us from man's world, man's wisdom, man's religion. The effect of the other is to put us into touch with God's world and with all that is there. ... As risen with Christ, then, we are lifted into His heavenly interests and permitted to seek them while still on earth. ...

> How little do we go about as those who are risen with Christ into another region of things, and that a heavenly one! How much do we get our minds clogged with earthly things![89]

Through spiritual birth, believers become one with Christ. This eternal union is held together by God Himself. In response to what God has done on our behalf in Christ, we must set our minds on things He deems important and not on what is temporal. Our sole purpose in life is to please Christ and exalt Him by living out His life to the fullest (Eph. 1:12).

Sometimes believers can become so preoccupied with all the things in the world that oppose Christ that they forget the importance of being occupied with Him who has already overcome the world. Attacking atheists, agnostics, or religious people will not win them to Christ. Rather, we are *"raised up with Him"* to extol Christ through our preaching and testimonies.

It is when we choose to exalt Christ, and not ourselves, before men, that the lost will come to cherish Him too. The soul who is in love with Jesus Christ will undoubtably be a good witness for Him! We are to continue with this type of mindset until Christ descends to the air for His Church, and removes her from the earth. Then we will *"appear with Him in glory"* (v. 4; 1 Thess. 4) and ever be with the Lord (2 Cor. 5:8; 1 Thess. 4:13-18).

## The Old Man Died – The New Man Lives (vv. 5-17)

To properly represent Christ on earth, those who are His must not engage in the sinful behaviors that formerly marked them as children of the devil and sons of disobedience destined for God's wrath (vv. 6-7). Rather, through spiritual power "our members" (i.e., our lusting in the flesh) that cause us to sin must be "put to death": *"fornication, uncleanness, passion, evil desire, and covetousness, which is idolatry"* (v. 5). To engage in these (and the like) strengthens the old nature within us, but Paul says that the deeds of the Old Man (who we were in Adam) must be put off (v. 9).

Positionally speaking, the Old Man died at Calvary when Christ died, but his influence is still within us. Unrighteous anger (resentment and bitterness), wrath (rage), malice (revenge), blasphemy (railing and reviling), filthy language (shameful speech) are all behaviors of the old nature that should not be in the believer's life (v. 8). The ungodly longings of the flesh should not be strengthened through sinful behavior or by wrong thinking. Rather these should be starved so that they lose their strength and can be completely "put off" from the believer's conduct. If not fed, these ungodly longings lose their hold on the believer's life and die out more quickly, although ultimate freedom will not be achieved until glorification.

As an illustration of this truth, imagine for a moment that you lived in Paul's day and had a good friend who had been sentenced to death by a Roman magistrate. Your friend is being publicly crucified and is suffering terribly. Would it be reasonable for you to carry a stepladder to his location and climb up the ladder to spoon-feed your friend hot chicken noodle soup? "Eat this; it will give you strength and make you feel better." No, your friend is going to die. That is the end goal of crucifixion – so enabling him to endure his suffering in the flesh even longer is a disservice to your friend. We have been positionally crucified with Christ, so that the power of the lusting flesh in our lives will also die. Engaging in sin only feeds and strengthens what is destined to die and just adds misery to life.

Mortification and gratification are the only two things the flesh understands. The only spiritual recourse in dealing with the lust of the flesh is to deal it a deadly blow and to keep on mortifying it every day. This is God's will for every believer.

Additionally, the Colossians were to *"put on the new man,"* that is, they were to live up to the holy image of the One who had made them into new creations (v. 10). Scripture affirms the Christlike behavior that we are to pattern in our minds so that it will become the spiritual norm in representing Christ. All that we do in this world should project an accurate display of Christ's character. This enables the lost to see what Christ is truly like (holy, kind, gentle, meek, merciful, true, etc.) so that they will want Him too.

This means that believers must want to be controlled by the Holy Spirit and not their lusting flesh. Only then are the deeds of the flesh mortified and fellowship with God maintained: *"If by the Spirit you put to death the deeds of the body, you will live"* (Rom. 8:13). By doing so, we put on the *new man* that we are in Christ! The believer has been positionally crucified with Christ (Rom. 6:6) so that the craving flesh will ultimately die (i.e., by maturing in Christ, the old nature loses its control over the believer).

This process of living for Christ is the same for all believers on this side of glory for in the Church there is no distinction of race, gender, or social status. Jews and Greeks, barbarians (e.g., the Scythians) and refined people, slave and free are all one with Christ. This is the meaning of *"Christ is all and in all"* (v. 11). All believers are in Christ and one with Christ.

Only "the elect of God," those who are holy and beloved in Christ will receive eternal salvation in Him. Until our earthly sojourn is over, those who are in Christ are to reveal the captivating holy character of their altogether lovely Savior. Just as one might choose to put on an outer garment, Paul exhorts the believers at Colosse to put on the lovely character and disposition of Christ so that all can appreciate Him: *"Put on tender mercies, kindness, humility, meekness, longsuffering; bearing with one another, and forgiving one another..."* (vv. 12-13).

*Tender mercies* speak of extending compassion to those who are undeserving. Generally speaking, *grace* is getting what we do not deserve and *mercy* is not getting what we do deserve. Showing compassion to those who are responsible for their own ruin and suffering is the heart of God. *"Mercies"* is grammatically plural to indicate that we should be well marked by this behavior.

*Kindness* speaks of a willing and selfless disposition to help others and show them goodwill. It is similar to grace in this respect for it longs to exhibit unmerited favor to others.

*Humility* tramples down one's own pride and assumes the low ground in respect to others – esteeming them better than oneself.

*Meekness* is power in control. It is the strength to allow oneself to experience undeserved injustice or hardship without retaliation.

*Longsuffering* speaks of the ability to exhibit patience and not strike back when passions are provoked to do otherwise. It willingly and joyfully suffers long despite offenses.

> Humility is perfect quietness of heart. It is to expect nothing, to wonder at nothing that is done to me, to feel nothing done against me. It is to be at rest when nobody praises me, and when I am blamed or despised. It is to have a blessed home in the Lord, where I can go in and shut the door, and kneel to my Father in secret, and am at peace as in a deep sea of calmness, when all around and above is trouble.
>
> – Andrew Murray

*Bearing with* or *forbearing one another* means to have a longsuffering disposition towards the peculiarities and bents of others that might be irritating. What does it mean to be "bearing (or forbearing) with one another"? William MacDonald answers this question:

> Bearing with one another describes the patience we should have with the failings and odd ways of our brethren. In living with others, it is inevitable that we will find out their failures. It often takes the grace of God for us to put up with the idiosyncrasies of others, as it must for them to put up with ours. But we must bear with one another.[90]

*Forgiving one another* is to have an unconditional releasing spirit even when there is an active offense that would otherwise warrant a complaint.

This does not mean we tell the offender that we forgive him, but rather that we release the matter to the Lord to deal with. That permits us to extinguish our anger over the issue and to think rationally about how to handle the situation. Could it be an opportunity for me to edify the offender by bringing the offense to his attention, or should I just let it go and say nothing? The latter choice is wise if the offense is not a pattern of behavior but an offhand comment or random act. It is foolish to declare forgiveness to someone if they have not confessed their sin (this condones sin) and it is wrong to not do so if someone has repented and has asked to be forgiven (Luke 17:3).

Paul also provides the motive for having a releasing spirit when wronged: *"Bearing with one another, and forgiving one another, if anyone has a complaint against another; even as Christ forgave you, so you also must do"* (v. 13; Eph. 4:32). Given all that we have done against the Lord and yet have been forgiven, we should be eager to show God's forgiveness to those who have repented of wrongs against us. After such an issue has been properly resolved, it should not be revisited. God is slow to anger, but quick to forgive and we should be also (Ps. 145:8). Through the power of the Holy Spirit, Christ's love draws those who previously had nothing in common into intimate communion with each other. This is why believers are to be forbearing of one another and have a forgiving spirit towards each other. While forbearance is slow to take offense, when we have put on the love of Christ, forgiveness is quick to let it go.

This is why believers must put on love which is the bond of perfection (v. 14). Just as wearing a belt holds things up or together, love binds all these Christlike virtues together to bless. Love energizes these virtues so that the spiritually mature person reflects Christ in all behavior. Through the power of the Holy Spirit, Christ's love draws into intimate communion with each other those who previously had nothing in common. This is why believers are to be forbearing of one another and are to have a spirit of forgiveness towards each other.

The Lord Jesus not only made peace with God on our behalf (Rom. 5:1), but He now offers us His serenity, the peace of God (Phil. 4:7). The Greek word translated "peace" is *eirene*. It is derived from a verb meaning to "bond together." It literally means to "be made at one again," as reflected in Acts 7:26 (KJV) when Moses sought to make two quarreling Israelites *"at one again."* Eirene is almost always translated "peace" in Scripture, but on rare occasions it is rendered "rest" and "quietness." Believers must permit the Lord's rest and peace to flow into our souls so that we may enjoy His tranquility despite our circumstances. This is what Paul means by letting the peace of God rule in our hearts with a spirit of thankfulness (v. 15).

It is impossible to convey God's peace to others unless the believer personally possesses His peace. Being one with Christ brings peace to the soul. If we are fretful, we should ask ourselves, "In what respects is my thinking not one with Christ?" Only by *"looking to Jesus, the author and finisher of our faith"* (Heb. 12:2) can we demonstrate His peace in such a way that the lost will want it too.

In verse 16 Paul highlights the importance of thoroughly internalizing God's Word so that it may direct all of life's affairs according to wisdom. Furthermore, Spirit-filled believers should be *"teaching and admonishing one another in psalms and hymns and spiritual songs, singing with grace in your hearts to the Lord."* Psalms are the inspired poems from the book of Psalms. Hymns ascribe worship, praise, and thanksgiving to God, but their lyrics are based on Scripture, rather than being directly inspired. Spiritual songs are edifying and aspiring lyrics that prompt deeper devotion to God, affirm godly living, and cause believers to yearn to be with Christ.

Paul wrote something similar to the church at Ephesus (Eph. 5:19) to convey the truth that our singing is to reaffirm Scriptural truth and to worship and praise God. Regrettably, the Church accepts error more readily through music than through preaching, and Satan knows it!

Understanding that music is a powerful medium in which to convey our thoughts to God and of God to each other, let us be careful to ensure that what we are singing is doctrinally and contextually sound and that the composition does not stir up the flesh to carnal behavior or thinking. Rather, *"singing with grace in your hearts to the Lord"* means the Holy Spirit stirs up joyful admiration for the One about whom we are singing!

Paul exhorts the Christians at Colosse to consider every aspect of their conduct and speech as an approval or disapproval of the name of Jesus Christ. *"And whatever you do in word or deed, do all in the name of the Lord Jesus, giving thanks to God the Father through Him"* (v. 17). Each believer functions as an ambassador of Christ on earth (2 Cor. 5:20). We are to represent the Lord and conduct His affairs on earth in a manner which honors Him. Believers are Christians, or *Christ-ones*. Warren Wiersbe speaks to what it means to bear the name of the Lord Jesus as a Christian.

> The name of Christ, then, means *identification:* we belong to Jesus Christ. But His name also means *authority.* ... The President's name signed to a bill makes it a law. In the same way, it is in the name of Jesus Christ that we have the authority to pray (John 14:13-14; 16:23-26). Because Jesus Christ is God, and He has died for us, we have authority in His name. All that we say and do should be associated with the name of Jesus Christ. By

our words and our works, we should glorify His name. If we permit anything into our lives that cannot be associated with the name of Jesus, then we are sinning. We must do and say everything on the authority of His name and for the honor of His name. Bearing the name of Jesus is a great privilege, but it is also a tremendous responsibility.[91]

It is a great honor to be intimately associated with the name of Jesus Christ, but as Paul declares, it also entails responsibility: *"that the name of our Lord Jesus Christ may be glorified in you"* (2 Thess. 1:12). Believers filled with God's Word and with His Spirit will be joyful, thankful, profitable servants who wonderfully represent Christ in the world.

## The Christian Home (vv. 18-21)

One of the most powerful testimonies of changed lives is the presence of Christ's love and authority in the home. Paul's exhortations to the Colossians are brief in comparison to his teaching on the same subject to the Ephesians (Eph. 5:22-33). To the Ephesians, the apostle reveals what a God-honoring marriage looks like and the proper attitudes and roles of husbands and wives to achieve what is being modeled by Christ's own relationship with His Bride – the Church. To the Colossians, Paul merely summarizes the key points of what was shared with the Ephesians.

Paul begins by first addressing wives: *"Wives, submit to your own husbands, as is fitting in the Lord"* (v. 18). The phrase, *"as is fitting in the Lord"* is understood by the parallel exhortation in Ephesians 5:22, *"as to the Lord."* The word "submission" is not popular in our modern society, but submission to God-ordained authority is absolutely necessary to please God and receive His blessing. Biblical submission to authority has two main ingredients. First, there is obedience. A wife is to obey her husband's leadership decisions, just as the Church is to obey Christ's direction (John 14:15). The wise husband will listen to his wife; since information given respectfully is not a failure to submit; rather it is needful.

Second, there is respect (Eph. 5:33). A wife is to respect her husband's God-given *position* of authority. Submission to order includes dependence on the divinely appointed authority over us. God funnels blessings from Heaven through proper channels of authority. We are all under some authority and God teaches us submission to Himself through the authority structures that He puts in place.

The Church is dependent upon Christ for provision and blessing, and she is to willingly submit to His authority in all things. Similarly, a wife is to be dependent on her husband for protection and to provide for her needs.

Her husband is her head, just as Christ is head of the Church (Eph. 5:24). Therefore, she is to show respect to Christ by submitting to her husband's authority (i.e., in all things that honor the Lord).

Next, Paul exhorts husbands, *"Husbands, love your wives, and do not be bitter toward them"* (v. 19). To the Ephesians, Paul points to the model husbands are to follow: *"just as Christ also loved the church and gave Himself for her"* (Eph. 5:25). For a wife to enjoy the full extent of the God-given blessing of her femininity, she must comprehend the divine purpose for which she was created, her husband must be satisfying her essential needs of importance and significance, and she must be sustained by God's grace for the strenuous responsibilities God has assigned her. In God's design, woman was created to be a helper for man, and man was created to satisfy her needs, thus assisting her to fulfill her God-given role.

Using the example of Christ's relationship to His Church, Paul defined for the Ephesians the indispensable attributes of a husband's love for his wife (Eph. 5:25-30). A husband is to be a stable, sacrificial, sanctifying, satisfying, and secure head of his wife, just as Christ is to the Church. Just as Christ is not bitter against the Church for her imperfections, husbands should not be bitter against their wives for imperfect attitudes and behaviors.

By demonstrating genuine love and through prayer, husbands can assist their wives to become all that God intends for them to be. Likewise, through respect and prayer, wives can assist their husbands to become what God desires them to be. In God's design for the family, the husband is to lead, provide, protect, shepherd his family and love his wife. The wife is to respect and obey her husband's authority as unto the Lord.

Paul instructs children to *"obey your parents in all things, for this is well pleasing to the Lord"* (v. 20). The apostle adds the phrase *"in the Lord"* to this command in his letter to the Ephesians (Eph. 6:1). The stipulation phrase, *"in the Lord,"* implies children are to serve their parents as unto the Lord in matters of righteousness, but not in matters of sin.

The Greek word translated "children" in verse 20 is *teknon*, which means "that which is derived of another" (i.e., children are derived from their parents). Age is not implied, meaning that the application of the word is not limited to small children. A different Greek word, *paidion*, is used to speak of infants and small children. Therefore, children should always respect and honor their parents regardless of how old they are (v. 2). Of course, when children marry and have children of their own, the new parents become accountable to do what is God-honoring for their own family.

After instructing children to obey their parents, Paul admonishes fathers, *"Do not provoke your children, lest they become discouraged"* (v. 21). Fathers are never to abuse their leadership role in the family for God will hold them accountable (e.g., 1 Pet. 3:7). Whenever God gives authority, there is always accountability to Him (e.g., Heb. 13:17). Hence, fathers are to train their children for the Lord, for He desires a "godly offspring," not just reproduction (Mal. 2:15).

Children do not naturally know the way they should go. They must be shown by godly example what God expects (Prov. 22:6). Much more encouragement than correction and reproof is needed to accomplish this goal, otherwise children will become discouraged (i.e., give up on trying to please their parents). In a coming day every husband and father will give an account to God for any abuse or neglect of his wife and children.

## Servants and Masters (vv. 22-25)

It is estimated that the Roman Empire had a population of approximately 120 million when Paul wrote the Colossian epistle. About half of the population were slaves. Although the Bible does not endorse slavery, it does place limits on its practices.

As Christianity spread throughout the Roman Empire, both slaves and masters became Christians and fellow brethren in Christ. This created a difficulty, since believers in Christ were required to mutually love, respect, and serve each other, but slavery did not permit such social liberty. Hence, Paul supplies wisdom for how believing masters and slaves should behave towards each other to honor the Lord (vv. 22-25). In principle, these exhortations are prudent for employer-employee relationships, which is a type of indentured service.

Slaves were to be obedient to and respectful of their human masters as unto Christ and in the fear of God (v. 22). This meant that they were to serve faithfully, even when their masters were not watching, since the Lord whom they served always observed them (v. 23). Faithful service rendered with a proper attitude to the Lord pleases Him and will be rewarded (v. 24).

At the Judgment Seat of Christ (2 Cor. 5:10; Rom 14:10-12), every believer will receive or lose rewards for works done on earth. There will be no partiality shown by the Lord, wrongs will be set right, and deeds accomplished in Christ's strength and for His glory will be rewarded (1 Cor. 3:11-15). Therefore, let us not be self-serving, self-exalting, and Church-harming children of God. But rather, may we remember Paul's exhortation: *"whatever you do, do it heartily, as to the Lord and not to men, knowing that from the Lord you will receive the reward of the inheritance; for you serve the Lord Christ"* (v. 24).

# Colossians Chapter 4

## The Believer's Life and Speech (vv. 1-6)

The chapter break here is unfortunate because the first verse of chapter 4 pertains to the subject of masters and slaves from the previous chapter. Masters were to remember that they also had a Master in Heaven to whom they were accountable for the treatment of slaves in their care (v. 1). Masters were to be just and fair, and not overbearing in exercising their leadership.

As in the final chapter of his first letter to the Thessalonians, Paul concludes with a rapid volley of godly-living exhortations as he begins to bring the letter to a close. He has addressed how the Christian life should be exhibited in marriage, parenting, and with respect to social distinctions. Now Paul conveys various general principles that all saints should consider.

Believers are to be earnest in praying to God while maintaining a spirit of thanksgiving (v. 2). Paul specifically asked them to pray that he would have an open door of opportunity to speak as he ought to others about the mystery of Christ (vv. 3-4). Thankfully, although Paul was in prison, the gospel message was not chained or limited in any way.

Paul's exhortation to *"walk in wisdom...redeeming the time"* in verse 5 is reminiscent of his charge to the Ephesians. Given the importance and urgency of gospel ministry, believers must *"walk circumspectly, not as fools but as wise, redeeming the time, because the days are evil"* (Eph. 5:15-16).

The satanically controlled world system belittles the things of God and exaggerates the value of that which is temporary and sensual. Consequently, undiscerning believers have been deceived into forsaking the best for that which may be permissible, but which steals their available time. What is Satan's strategy? "Those Christians can have their religion, but I will not allow them to have any time to enjoy and serve their Savior." The way in which we use our time speaks frankly of the quality of our love for the Lord. We cannot *buy back* time per se, but we can *buy up* opportunities to serve God. Let us have no regrets later for how we spend our lives now.

Next Paul challenges the Colossians to have wise and edifying speech, *"Let your speech always be with grace, seasoned with salt, that you may know how you ought to answer each one"* (v. 6). To be effective comforters and counselors, we must follow the Lord's example, otherwise we will be like Job's "miserable comforters" to others. John writes of the Lord: *"We beheld His glory, the glory as of the only begotten of the Father, full of grace and truth"* (John 1:14). The Lord Jesus exhibited perfect balance of character. Everything He did and said was full of grace and truth.

Just as grace and truth are inseparable aspects of the Lord's character, believers must also maintain this equilibrium. Our speech must be gracious and seasoned with salt. If it is not necessary to say, or cannot be said in love, or is not true, then the Lord would not have us say it. This is particularly important if the person with whom you are speaking is suffering.

Thomas Bently summarizes the complementary exhortations of the apostle to godly living in verses 2-6:

Be constant in your speaking to God – our asking (v. 2a)
Be careful in your speaking to man – our answering (v. 6a)

Let your asking be mixed with the grace of gratefulness (v. 2b)
Let your answering be seasoned with grace of considerateness (v. 6b)

Pray for open doors for the Word (v. 3)
Plead for opportunities for the work (v. 5b)

That I may know how to witness (v. 4)
That you may know how to walk (v. 5a)[92]

## Conclusion (vv. 7-18)

Tychicus was a beloved brother, a faithful minister to Paul, and a fellow servant in the Lord (v. 7). It appears that he apparently was to carry the letters from Paul to the Church at Colosse and to Philemon and also to escort Onesimus, a runaway slave who had come to Christ, back to Philemon, who was also from Colosse (vv. 8-9). Paul asked Tychicus to encourage the hearts of the Colossian saints by informing them of his condition in prison. He also assigned Tychicus the task of returning to him in Rome with news about the Colossian assembly.

It is observed that although the ministry of faithful Tychicus is described by Paul, the apostle only refers to Onesimus' faithful character and calls him a beloved brother in the Lord. We gather that Onesimus had stolen some things from his master Philemon before running away (Philem. 18-19). Paul was sending Onesimus to Philemon to make right the previous wrong and he requested that Philemon receive Onesimus back as a brother in the Lord who would now be a profitable servant. Under Roman law, Onesimus could have been executed for his crimes, but Paul sought a solution beneficial for all concerned parties and one that would honor Christ.

The Colossians knew Onesimus and his history. They were probably surprised to hear that he was with Paul and had become a Christian. Before Onesimus could be used in ministry for the Lord, he first had to be properly restored to one who owned him as a slave, and who exercised authority over him. Repentance for sin and restitution for wrongs on the part of Onesimus, and the extension of forgiveness by Philemon, would accomplish this purpose. This is a good reminder for us to remain in good standing with those in authority over us, to right our wrongs and to pursue holiness, so that we too may serve the Lord in fruitful ministry.

> Whatever "call" a man may pretend to have, if he has not been called to holiness, he certainly has not been called into ministry.
>
> – Charles Spurgeon

Paul was not alone in prison (vv. 10-14). Besides Tychicus and Onesimus, there were several other *"fellow workers for the kingdom of God"* who were with Paul. Paul mentions his Jewish countrymen first: Aristarchus (a fellow prisoner; Acts 19:29), John Mark (who earlier abandoned Paul on his first missionary journey) and Justus (vv. 10-11).

Epaphras (a Colossian himself) not only served Paul, but labored in prayer for the saints at Laodicea, Hierapolis, and Colosse to *"stand perfect and complete in all the will of God"* (vv. 12-13). Luke, the beloved physician, who had accompanied Paul during many of his missionary treks, was also with Paul in Rome (v. 14). Demas, who later deserted Paul during his second imprisonment, was also with Paul at this time (2 Tim. 4:10).

The apostle asked the saints at Colosse to pass along his greetings to the saints at Laodicea and to Nymphas and the assembly that met in his home, apparently in Colosse (v. 15). After this letter was read to the saints at Colosse, it was to be read by the brethren at Laodicea. Similarly, a letter which had been sent to the Laodiceans was to be read in Colosse (v. 16). There may have been two church meetings gathering in homes in Colosse, the home of Nymphas (v. 15) and the home of Archippus (Philem. 2).

Archippus was exhorted to be a good steward of the ministries and abilities God had given him (v. 17). God has preordained the nature of our individual ministry in the Church and has uniquely equipped us to fulfill His will (1 Cor. 12:4-11; Eph. 4:12). Accordingly, we should all endeavor to bring God glory by doing what we have been created to do. This was also Paul's exhortation to Timothy (1 Tim. 4:12-13; 2 Tim. 2:1-3).

Paul takes the pen in his own hand to close the letter and asks the Colossian believers to remember his bonds and to pray for him (v. 18).

# 1 Thessalonians

## Background

Thessalonica, located in Macedonia, was one of three major seaports on the Aegean Sea (Corinth and Ephesus being the other two). The population at this time is estimated to have been 200,000. Most citizens were native Greeks, but some Romans and Jews also lived there. The Medo-Persian Empire fell to the Greeks in 330 B.C. and Thessalonica was built 15 years later in 315 B.C. by Cassandra, a general under Alexander the Great.

Cassander married Thessalonica, the half-sister of Alexander, after whom he named the city. Cassander is one of the four Greek generals who are featured in Daniel's prophetic record (chs. 7, 8, 11). Upon Alexander's death, each general received a fourth of his empire. After conquering the world in only four years Alexander died at the age of 32. In 42 B.C. both Anthony and Octavian (later called Caesar Augustus) granted the city "free" status. This allowed the inhabitants to live their daily routines without much Roman influence. In fact, no Roman soldiers were garrisoned there.

During Paul's second missionary journey, Paul and Silas traveled to Thessalonica from Philippi, where they had been severely beaten. The timing of this visit was likely late 50 A.D. From the record in Acts, we learn that Paul preached on three consecutive sabbaths in a synagogue (Acts 17:2), before being driven out of Thessalonica by persecution. However, Paul may have been in Thessalonica a brief time before he began speaking publicly in the synagogue, since he was there long enough to engage in the craft of tent-making and to see a church begin (2:9; 2 Thess. 3:8). Acts affirms that some Jews and Greeks came to the synagogue, and some wives of prominent Thessalonian citizens were saved through Paul's teaching.

Paul, Silas, and Timothy were forced to leave Thessalonica after a riot broke out in which Jason's home was assaulted (the mob was looking for Paul). Jason was apprehended by the mob and taken to the civil authorities. He was accused of harboring Paul's missionary team who were leading a revolt against Caesar.

Paul, Silas, and Timothy then traveled to Berea, and Paul later went on to Athens alone. As there was an opportunity in Athens for the gospel, Paul sent for Silas and Timothy. Shortly after they arrived in Athens, Paul sent

Timothy back to Thessalonica to check on the church's welfare. Silas returned to Philippi on a similar errand while Paul remained in Athens alone. He then traveled to Corinth. First Thessalonians was written by Paul from Corinth shortly after Timothy returned from Thessalonica. What better way to encourage believers suffering great persecution than to speak about the coming of the Lord for His Church. There is a mention of this wonderful event in each of the five chapters. In this letter, Paul also refutes the notion, claimed by those opposing the gospel message, that he ministered the gospel for profit.

## Theme(s)
"The Day of Christ" speaking of the Rapture of the Church and the Judgment Seat of Christ to follow.

## Keywords
Keywords and phrases include: "hope," "day" (mainly speaking of "the day of Christ"), "your faith," "glory," "joy/rejoice," "patience/patient," "comfort," "sanctification/sanctify," "Lord," "night," and a number of related words such as: *distress, affliction, suffering,* and *tribulation.*

## Date
Since Gallio (Acts 18) was not appointed proconsul of Achaia until 53 A.D. and he ruled in favor of Paul near the conclusion of Paul's 18-month stay at Corinth, it is likely this epistle was written in 51 A.D., shortly after Paul's arrival in Corinth.

## Outline
I. Introduction (1:1).
II. The Faith, Hope, and Love of the Christian Life (1:2-10).
III. The Ministry, Walk, and Reward of the Lord's Servant (ch. 2).
IV. The Testing and Refining of "Your Faith" (ch. 3).
V. The Sanctified Walk and Blessed Hope of a Believer (ch. 4).
VI. The Model Walk and the Day of the Lord (5:1-24).
VII. Conclusion With Final Blessings and Admonitions (5:25-28).

# 1 Thessalonians Chapter 1

Introduction (vv. 1-4)
The letter to the Thessalonians commences with the same type of salutation that is found in other Pauline epistles to churches. Paul's name is stated as the originator of the letter, and since Silas and Timothy were with him in Corinth at that time, he also includes their names (v. 1). Timothy had just returned from Thessalonica with favorable news about the new church. There is no assertion of Paul's apostolic authority in the introduction since the Thessalonians did not dispute it and doctrinal reproof was not required.

The epistle is addressed to the company of believers who composed the new local church in Thessalonica which was *"in God the Father and the Lord Jesus Christ"* (v. 1). Continuing his salutation, Paul declares *"grace to you and peace from God our Father and the Lord Jesus Christ"* (v. 2). This is Paul's trademark greeting and is word for word how he saluted the Romans and the Corinthians (Rom. 1:7; 1 Cor. 1:3). *Grace* was a greeting commonly used by Greeks, while Jewish believers traditionally referred to the blessing of *peace* to convey a how-do-you-do.

Paul was prompted to frequently pray for the Thessalonian believers and to thank God for them (v. 2). Persecution had forced the missionary team to leave Thessalonica shortly after a church was planted. Paul would have preferred to remain and instruct them more fully in the doctrines of the Christian faith, but the citywide riot cancelled that opportunity. Regardless, God had protected what was His, and the saints at Thessalonica were flourishing despite fierce opposition from the devil.

God the Father was completely aware of the reality and vibrancy of their spiritual life in Christ. It was also evident to Timothy who observed the genuineness of their faith during the fact-finding mission he had completed for Paul. Paul commends them for three Christian virtues: their *"work of faith, labor of love, and patience of hope in our Lord Jesus Christ"* (v. 3).

*Faith* is a living trust in God's Word without verifying proof. Faith is first exercised on hearing the gospel and is strengthened as a believer grows in Christ. True faith is evidenced by good works (Jas. 2:17). At the Lord's coming believers will be made perfect and the need for faith will cease.

*Love* is the present selfless and sacrificial outworking of God's own kindness and grace in the believer's life. Love will continue forever. Thus, it is the greatest virtue (1 Cor. 13:13).

*Hope* fervently and joyfully anticipates the fulfillment of God's promises. At Christ's coming for His Church, hope will be complete, since believers will be with Him forever and will have all things in Him.

Paul's tenderness towards the Thessalonians is conveyed by the endearing term "beloved brethren" (v. 4). He refers to them as "brethren" fifteen times in the epistle. All who are born again in Christ have a heavenly Father in common and are thereby "brethren."

Although the saints at Thessalonica were suffering for their faith, Paul wanted them to understand their security in Christ – their "election by God" (v. 4). Election generally speaks of God's specific choices to accomplish His purposes in time. God's sovereign choices ensure the performance and completion of the plan of salvation for mankind which in foreknowledge He devised before creation, and which predestines those who are in Christ to receive an eternal inheritance as mature sons. Paul knew that the Thessalonian believers were in Christ by the way they had chosen to live for Christ after responding to His gospel. Accordingly, they were destined to receive all the blessings of salvation in Christ.

With all the facts at hand, including, by His foreknowledge, every possible permutation of the consequences of human and angelic choices since creation, God has marshalled the events of the ages to accomplish His plan of redemption for mankind. This is why Peter exhorts believers to *"make your call and election sure"* (2 Pet. 1:10) and Paul says, *"walk in the works that God has foreordained"* (Eph. 2:10). Knowing our position in Christ and what God is achieving on our behalf by Christ, believers are to be willing participants in His plan of redemption. This is what the Thessalonians were doing. Their persistent faith in Christ despite opposition was proof of their election (i.e., that they were in Christ).

## The Christian Life: Turn, Serve and Wait (vv. 5-10)

The evidence that Paul and the missionary team were men of God proclaiming His message of life was witnessed in the conversion of the Thessalonians themselves. They did not just hear the gospel message but chose to obey it. They had experienced regeneration by the power of the Holy Spirit (v. 5). Paul then assured the Thessalonians that because they had followed the example of himself and his colleagues despite suffering affliction, it was evidence that they were truly in Christ (v. 6).

The work of the Holy Spirit in the saints at Thessalonica was obvious for all to see, as they were bravely enduring persecution with tenacious inner joy (v. 7). Even before Timothy returned to Corinth with his report on the saints at Thessalonica, stories of their victorious faith had already spread within Macedonia and as far south as Achaia. Thus, Paul did not need to tell others about their faithfulness. News of their victorious testimony for Christ had already been published throughout the region (v. 8).

The apostle was delighted to hear that the previous evangelistic labor of his team in Thessalonica had, encouragingly, been fruitful. Those who heard and obeyed the gospel *"turned to God from idols"* and were serving God despite hostility from those who would not heed the gospel (v. 9).

The message of God's salvation is inclusive in its application. It is offered to anyone who will believe it (Rev. 22:17). However, it is simultaneously exclusive in nature, for trusting in any other message brings eternal judgment (Gal. 1:6-9). God is *"not willing that any should perish but that all should come to repentance"* (2 Pet. 3:9), but a seeking sinner must repent and trust Christ alone for salvation (Luke 13:3; Rom. 10:9).

Repentance means that we agree with God that we are sinners deserving of His judgment with the result that we turn away from all that we ever thought would earn us Heaven, and by faith cling to what will – Christ. One who is truly repentant is deeply grieved over personal sin and yearns to turn from iniquity (Jer. 8:6). Those who repent and turn must turn to that which is an effective solution for their sin. They must believe the gospel of the Lord Jesus Christ. This is what the Thessalonians did. They turned to God from idols. Their salvation was evident in that, despite being persecuted for their faith, they continued to serve the true God. They were the real thing!

Paul mentions The Day of Christ in one way or another in each chapter of this epistle. The first reference to Christ's coming for His Church is in verse 10: *"To wait for His Son from Heaven, whom He raised from the dead, even Jesus who delivers us from the wrath to come."* Paul describes more specifically how Christ will return from Heaven to the air to remove His Church from the earth in chapter 4. At present, Christ is seated on His Father's throne, but when He returns to the earth, He will establish His own throne from which He will rule over the nations (Rev. 3:21; 20:4).

As shown by the experience of the Thessalonian saints, the Church is not exempt from suffering for Christ. Yet, the Church is exempt from ever experiencing divine wrath (Rom 5:9). *"For God did not appoint us to wrath, but to obtain salvation through our Lord Jesus Christ"* (5:9). Thus, the Church must be in Heaven before Christ opens the first seal on the scroll to begin the Tribulation period (Rev. 6:1). The Thessalonians were both following God and faithfully serving Him despite hardship, and they were to wait in joyful anticipation of Christ's return to take them to Heaven.

# 1 Thessalonians Chapter 2

### Paul's Conduct (vv. 1-12)

The apostle was delighted that the Thessalonians had duplicated his testimony of living for Christ despite enduring persecution (v. 1). He and Silas had been severely beaten and unjustly jailed in Philippi just days before arriving in Thessalonica (v. 2). Not deterred by what had happened in Philippi, the missionary team boldly proclaimed the gospel at Thessalonica, which resulted in some there responding to its message.

It was important for the Thessalonians to realize that how they lived should validate what they said. Using their own testimony in Thessalonica as an example, Paul describes the pattern of behavior believers should exhibit to effectively share the gospel with the unregenerate (vv. 3-10):

- Must be sincere; no impure motives, trickery, or deceit while preaching the gospel (v. 3).
- Must preach to please God, not men, for God tests our motives (v. 4).
- Must not use flattering words or use the gospel to promote one's own agenda or as a secret means of getting rich (v. 5).
- Must not seek personal glory while serving the Lord (v. 6).
- Must be gentle and diligent in caring for new Christians (v. 7).
- Must be willing to be poured out in ministry (i.e., to do what is necessary to benefit others despite the personal consequences; v. 8).
- Must not charge others for preaching the gospel to them; this ensures one's motives will not be questioned (v. 9).
- Must be holy and blameless in conduct to limit false charges (v. 10).

Paul uses different metaphors in this chapter to describe his ministry to the Thessalonians: He was like a nurse (v. 7), a laborer (v. 9), and a father (v. 11). As their spiritual father, Paul exhorted his children to follow his example and *"walk worthy of God who calls you into His own kingdom and glory"* (v. 12). Being children of a holy God and part of His kingdom (although presently invisible on earth) they were to be holy.

Paul gives us a good pattern to follow in discipling those who profess Christ. First, there should be consistent tender care, *"just as a nursing mother cherishes her own children"* (vv. 7-8). Just as a newborn is not expected to function as a school-age child, or a teen, or an adult, so, spiritual growth in a new convert requires time, care, and patience. Second, we are to expend ourselves to commit the truth to reliable people who will be faithful to teach others what they have learned (2 Tim. 2:2).

Striking the balance between these two ideas is one of the challenges of discipleship. Those who profess Christ as Savior will require tender care and regular feedings of the sincere milk of the Word (i.e., the rudiments of the Christian faith; Heb. 5:12; 1 Pet. 2:2). Initially, the milk of the Word is necessary to encourage growth, yet, in time, maturity must result.

Spiritual maturity is evidenced by a deepening devotion to Christ, being a witness for Him, spending time in Bible study and prayer, repentance, forsaking sin, and faithfully attending church meetings. When engaged in discipling individuals or small groups, those who have made a false profession of faith and the apathetic can absorb time and distract from fulfilling the Great Commission. Hence, after a few months, it would be wise to commit these to the Lord (with an open invitation for renewed interest) and move on. If the devil can keep us busy entertaining his goats, instead of feeding and caring for God's sheep, he will!

## True Conversion (vv. 13-16)

Thankfully, the Thessalonians were neither lethargic nor negligent in absorbing God's Word and declaring it to others. For this Paul was grateful (v. 13). Humanized religion cannot produce love-motivated, self-sacrificing passion for God that will hold to the truth and share it with others regardless of personal cost, but faith in God's Word does. In fact, the Thessalonians' zeal for God reminded Paul of the early days of the Church Age when the apostles and new Jewish converts shared the gospel message in Jerusalem and Judea and willingly suffered while doing so (v. 14).

After mentioning his countrymen, Paul briefly pauses to indict the stiff-necked religious pride of Judaism, which has opposed God's messengers of truth throughout history (v. 15). His faithful prophets in the Old Testament were persecuted and murdered. Eventually God spoke directly to the Jews in the Person of His Son, the Lord Jesus Christ, but they nailed Him to a cross. Since that ultimate, belligerent act of rebellion, the Jews continued to persecute God's messengers of truth, and even thought that they were pleasing God for doing so. Paul knew all about this reckless religious pride, as it had motivated his own heart until his conversion en route to Damascus.

Paul's message, that Jews and Gentiles alike could be saved and blessed by God, was infuriating to the hard-hearted Jewish zealots (v. 16). Judaism in Paul's day was still characterized by the same rebellious features that had marked previous generations of Jews. They, in effect, had their religious cup unabashedly filled up with the measure of their sins. Before being stoned to death, Stephen courageously accused the Jewish Sanhedrin: *"You stiff-necked and uncircumcised in heart and ears! You always resist the Holy Spirit; as your fathers did, so do you"* (Acts 7:51).

God had been longsuffering with the Jewish nation, but time was running out. Paul announced that divine wrath was coming *"upon them to the uttermost."* It is debatable whether Paul was speaking of the centuries of war and desolations determined against Israel until a final refined Jewish remnant will be restored to God in the Kingdom Age (Dan. 9:26-27), or specifically of the destruction of the temple and Jerusalem in 70 A.D. (Matt. 24:3). Regardless, God would heap terrible retribution on His covenant people for centuries of rebellion, and for crucifying His Son.

## Paul's Yearning to Visit (vv. 17-20)

Persecution had forced Paul and the other missionaries to prematurely leave Thessalonica (Acts 17:1-4). Paul did not want the new Christians to think they were abandoned like orphans. He had them in his heart and in his prayers. Paul yearned to visit them again, but Satan had hindered him from returning to Thessalonica more than once (v. 18).

Paul most often received specific direction from the Holy Spirit about his ministry, both where to go and where not to go (e.g., Acts 16:6-10). At other times God permitted satanic opposition to direct Paul's travel and to remind him to be completely dependent on divine grace (2 Cor. 12:7-10).

The chapter closes with Paul affirming his love and admiration for the saints at Thessalonica. They were his "crown of rejoicing" (v. 19). The thought of the Thessalonians being in glorified bodies with Paul before the Lord Jesus Christ in Heaven filled the apostle with great joy (v. 20).

The *Judgment Seat of Christ* is where the believer's works will be judged for reward or burned up (1 Cor. 3:11-15). Eternal glory has a weight to it (2 Cor. 4:17) that gives the believer an appreciation of Heaven and the ability to reflect Christ's glory. Our clothing in Heaven reveals our rewarded righteous acts (Rev. 19:8). Some saints will shine brighter than others (1 Cor. 15:41-42). Others may be ashamed (1 Jn. 2:28). While Paul was likely speaking of the evidence of God's glory in the Thessalonian saints in verses 19-20, there does appear to be a soul-winner's crown given at the Judgment Seat of Christ (v. 19; Phil. 4:1). *"He who wins souls is wise"* (Prov. 11:30).

# 1 Thessalonians Chapter 3

## Timothy's Ministry at Thessalonica (vv. 1-10)

After the riot in Thessalonica, Paul, Silas, Timothy, and others left that city for Berea (Acts 17:5-10). But after Jews from Thessalonica learned that Paul was in Berea, they traveled there to stir up opposition to his preaching. Fearing for his safety the brethren sent Paul away, but Silas and Timothy remained in Berea. Paul was escorted to Athens. After seeing an open door of ministry in Athens, Paul asked his Berean escort to instruct Silas and Timothy to join him immediately (Acts 17:11-15).

While Paul was alone in Athens, he delivered a powerful message on Mars Hill that revealed *The Unknown God* to the Athenians (Acts 17:16-34). Some in Athens did turn to Christ. Shortly after the missionary team was reunited in Athens, Paul could stand it no longer; he had to know how the new believers in Thessalonica were doing. Timothy was tasked with assessing their condition and helping to establish them in their faith. He was to remind them that persecution was a normal aspect of the Christian life (vv. 2-3). Timothy went to Thessalonica, Silas traveled to Philippi on a similar errand, and Paul remained alone in Athens, then traveled to Corinth.

Although Timothy was a younger man, he was a dear brother in the Lord and a fellow laborer with Paul in the gospel. He had already won Paul's confidence as a true minister of God. Paul, familiar with the hardships of identifying with Christ, did not want the new believers in Thessalonica to be overcome by hostility. He did not sugarcoat the ramifications of following Christ. The saints had witnessed the abusive treatment to which the missionary team had been subjected, and since they too had received Christ, they could expect similar persecution (v. 4).

Paul was following the example of the Lord Jesus who plainly informed His disciples of the cost of discipleship (Luke 14:25-27; John 15:18-21). The Lord wanted those who would follow Him to count the cost of doing so, lest they fall away later into a worse spiritual condition and bring disdain on His name. Likewise, Paul wanted the Thessalonians to stand fast when the devil opposed their witness for Christ. Paul knew that Satan would tempt them to give up their faith – "following Christ is not worth the cost" (v. 5).

While in Corinth, Paul anxiously awaited Timothy's report (v.7), and when he came, he gave a heart-warming account of the condition of the Thessalonians. The believers were steadfast in faith and in love and standing fast in the Lord. This news thrilled Paul's heart; he felt like he could breathe again (v. 8). What does it mean to stand fast in the Lord? James and Peter tell us standing fast in Christ means that believers must humble themselves, rest in Christ's strength alone, and obey His Word (Jas. 4:6-8; 1 Pet. 5:6-9). Trees that have deep, intertwined roots are able to withstand powerful storms. Likewise, believers weather winds of adversity by having deep faith in the Lord and by being intertwined with others of like mature faith.

The phrase "your faith" occurs five times in this chapter and expresses the genuineness of the Thessalonians' salvation. In verse 6, for example, Paul affirms that the proof of *their faith* was being declared by their love to others and by their affection towards him (they even wanted to see him again). Moreover, *their faith* encouraged Paul in his own sufferings, as he realized that his labor among them had not been in vain (vv. 7-8). Also, although Paul had been praying for them night and day, he realized that they needed more teaching to grow and mature in *their faith* (v. 10). Paul very much wanted to visit them again to accomplish this goal, but in the meantime, he was rejoicing in them and thanking God for them (v. 9).

## Paul's Prayer for the Thessalonians (vv. 11-13)

Paul prayed that God would permit him to return to Thessalonica to better equip the saints to serve Christ (v. 11). This was granted, and Paul did visit Thessalonica again during his third missionary journey (Acts 20:4).

The apostle also prayed that God would enable the saints to have an ever increasing and abounding love for each other (v. 12). In their approach to ministry among the Thessalonians the missionaries exhibited ample evidence of such sacrificial love. Paul had previously commended the labor of love of the Thessalonians saints (v. 6, 1:2-3). Although the church at Thessalonica was thriving in the midst of persecution, Paul exhorts them to love each other more. Believers should never be satisfied with the degree to which the love of God is expressed through them. There is always room for growth in this grace. Can a husband love his wife too much? No, he will never love his wife perfectly as Christ loves the Church (Eph. 5:25). There will always be room to abound more and more in love.

Lastly, Paul prayed that the hearts of the Thessalonian believers would be established *"blameless in holiness before our God and Father at the coming of our Lord Jesus Christ with all His saints"* (v. 13). Exercising sacrificial love in revealed truth results in *practical* holiness, but those in Christ have *position* of holiness and blamelessness before God forever.

# 1 Thessalonians Chapter 4

### A Call to Purity (vv. 1-8)

The "finally" in verse 1 does not mean that Paul is closing his letter. The Greek word *loipon*, meaning "moreover" or "furthermore," is often used by Paul in his epistles to introduce a new subject. The apostle previously addressed the topic of the Christian's walk (2:12), but revisits the subject twice in this chapter (vv. 1, 12). Believers are to have a lifestyle marked by complete dependence on Christ and obedience to His commands (v. 2). Such a testimony exhibits Christlike behavior to the lost. This mindset is pleasing to God and must be maintained for believers to bear fruit to God.

Pagan rituals among the Gentiles in Paul's day often included various sexual perversions. God designed sexual pleasure to enhance a covenantal marriage relationship, not for casual carnality. It was important then that the marital relationships of the saints should reflect God's will for His people, and not mirror the pagan norms of Thessalonian society. God is holy and He demands holiness from His children (i.e., those having the Holy Spirit; vv. 7-8). This meant that the Thessalonians were to possess ("to acquire for one's self") their own bodies in purity and were not to defraud each other by committing fornication (i.e., adultery) with the wife of another man.

Dear reader, if you want God's will for your life, you must abstain from fornication and any associated sensual uncleanness (v. 3). Fornication is any sexual union outside of the bounds of the marriage covenant between a biological man and a biological woman (Matt. 19:4-9; 1 Cor. 7:2). Not only is fornication a sin against God, it is an offense against one's own body (1 Cor. 6:18) and also defrauds the other guilty party. The Lord will severely judge such debauchery. Unrepentant fornication is evidence against someone having received eternal life in Christ, as all those actively engaging in the sin will suffer judgment forever in Hell (Eph. 5:5; Rev. 21:8).

Besides discussing the Christian's "walk" twice in this passage, Paul uses the Greek word *hagiasmos* (in various forms) four times in eight verses to describe the state of purity that believers must maintain to walk with the Lord. In the context of sexual purity, believers are to have *holy* and *sanctified* lives which are literally "set apart" to worship God. This means that believers are not only to refrain from fornication, but also from lusting after anything outside of God's will for His people.

Paul states that those who look on others committing fornication with approval know that they deserve God's wrath (Rom. 1:32). It is this *looking* at sexual perversions to achieve pleasure that has become a scourge to our society and has led to many broken marriages and homes. Not only should believers abstain from fornication, neither should they derive pleasure by watching others engage in immorality.

Since both are derived from the same root word, *pornography* and *porneia* ("fornication") are closely associated in meaning. *Porneia* is used in the New Testament to address all forms of sexual impurity and wanton behavior. The word initially meant "to act the harlot" but later evolved to mean "to indulge in unlawful lust." *Porneia* describes various types of sins: pre-marital sex (1 Cor. 7:1-2), physical adultery (Matt.19:9), any form of unchaste conduct (1 Cor. 6:13, 18), prostitution or harlotry (Rev. 2:20-21), homosexuality (Jude 7), and spiritual adultery (Rev. 14:8, 17:4). Interestingly, when sins are listed in the New Testament, fornication normally tops the list (1 Cor. 5:11; Col. 3:5).

## A Call to Order (vv. 9-12)

Paul again acknowledged the "brotherly love" the Thessalonians exhibited to each other and to other believers in Macedonia, yet he exhorted them to abound in this love more and more (vv. 9-10). To this end, Paul provides them with three nuggets of practical counsel (vv. 11-12).

First, believers should aspire *"to lead a quiet life"* (v. 11). Christians should not seek the admiration of others but should quietly serve and lovingly appreciate fellow believers. A quiet, orderly life demonstrates a wise and secure mind, and selfless love displays the heart of God.

Second, a Christian is *"to mind your own business"* (v. 11). A "busybody" is someone who inserts his own interests into the interests of others. Believers, on the other hand, are to regard the interests of others as more important than their own (Phil. 2:4).

Third, the Thessalonians were to labor with their hands to supply their needs. Apparently, some were so excited about the Lord's return that they decided to quit working. Yet, this meant that they were taking advantage of the generosity of others. Christians are not to be parasites, but mutual supporters of the communal good in the Body of Christ (2 Cor. 8:13-14).

To work for an honest day's wage and to provide for the needs of one's family would be a good testimony to the unregenerate (v. 12). The Thessalonians would not be in need if they did so. Neither would they, because of a chaotic lifestyle, hinder the lost form considering Christ.

## A Call Home (vv. 13-18)

Paul did not want the saints at Thessalonica to be ignorantly sorrowing over believers who had died (v. 13). Rather, he asserted that the death and resurrection of the Lord Jesus should transform their grief into hope: Just as He died and rose again, so God will raise the bodies of deceased saints from the grave at Christ's coming (vv. 14-15). The Thessalonian saints possessed this wonderful hope in contrast to the hopelessness of unbelievers (vv. 14-15; John 14:3). Those who have "fallen asleep" refers to believers who had already died. There is no such thing as *soul sleep*, since disembodied spirits are fully conscious after death (Luke 16:19-31; Rev. 6:9-11). The souls of dead saints are with the Lord while awaiting their glorification (2 Cor. 5:8).

Although the dead will be raised first when the Lord comes, immediately thereafter living saints will also be quickly caught up to meet Him in the air (vv. 15-17). This event, "the catching up" (or "the Rapture") of previous dead and living saints in Christ all happens in a brief moment of time (1 Cor. 15:51-52). The resurrection and glorification of the saints is part of "the First Resurrection" of which Christ is the firstfruits (1 Cor. 15:20, 23). Since all believers have a part in the First Resurrection (Rev. 20:6) which occurs in several stages (Rev. 20:4), and since there must be death before resurrection, it may be that believers who are alive at the coming of the Lord Jesus to the air, instantly pass through death (Heb. 9:27) when glorification occurs. This act of God completes the believer's salvation; the body is transformed and saved for all eternity at glorification.

The Lord shall descend into the clouds to meet His Church in the air. With a shout, like a voice of a trumpet (Rev. 4:1) and an archangel, Christ will summon, and snatch away from the earth all Church Age saints who will instantly receive their glorified Christ-like bodies (v. 16; Phil. 3:21). Assurance of the imminent return of Christ, and the divine promise that believers will "always be with the Lord" were welcome comfort for the Thessalonians. They are no less comforting for every saint who has suffered for the cause of Christ since the dawn of the Church Age (vv. 17-18).

Because Christ suffered the full extent of the judicial wrath of God for human sin, those who receive forgiveness by trusting Christ are eternally sealed by the Holy Spirit (Eph. 1:13). Thus, the Church will never suffer divine wrath, she is rescued from earth before the outpouring of God's wrath in the Tribulation period begins (1:10; Rev. 3:10). Christians will be removed from the earth before God refines and restores His covenant people to Himself during the Tribulation period (Rom. 11:25). Christians are to wait for the imminent return of Christ. At that moment, they shall be instantly glorified and translated from the earth to ever by with the Lord.

# 1 Thessalonians Chapter 5

The Day of the Lord (vv. 1-11)

The Greek expression *peri de* rendered *"but concerning"* is often used by Paul to introduce a new subject (v. 1, 4:9, 13). Here, Paul transitions from The Day of Christ (4:13-18; the Rapture of the Church) to The Day of the Lord (God's judgment on the wicked). Because the Church will not be on the earth during the Tribulation period, it was not necessary for Paul to write much about *"the times and the seasons,"* referring to The Day of the Lord.

Just before He ascended to heaven the disciples asked the Lord when He would restore the kingdom to Israel. His response included a phrase referring to times and seasons later used by the Apostle Paul: *"It is not for you to know times or seasons which the Father has put in His own authority"* (Acts 1:7). Christ focused the attention of the disciples on the immediate task of world evangelization (Acts 1:8). Information about times and seasons was in the Father's control and was not to concern them.

Similarly, the primary interest of the Apostle was to inspire and equip the Thessalonian saints to live for Christ in the midst of hardship due to persecution. Since he had previously taught them as much as they then needed to know about times and seasons, he declined to expand upon the subject at that time. Old Testament prophets spoke much about the Day of the Lord, thus a subject familiar to the Jewish believers. Yet, Paul's interest was to prepare the believers for the Day of Christ about which nothing was known until revealed by God, primarily through Paul, in the Church Age.

The Day of the Lord is an Old Testament term that speaks of occasions when Jehovah intervened in a visible and powerful way to judge the wicked on the earth. This meaning continues into the New Testament where it speaks of the Tribulation period (vv. 2-8) and the Millennial Kingdom. Peter foretold that the Day of the Lord would conclude with the destruction of the earth at the end of the Kingdom Age (2 Pet. 3:10). This event will be followed by the *Day of God*, often referred to as the *eternal state* (2 Pet. 3:12).

Paul explains that the wicked will not be expecting God's judgment. It will come *"as a thief in the night. For when they say, 'Peace and safety!' then sudden destruction comes upon them"* (vv. 2-3). This judgment will be worldwide, sudden, destructive, inevitable and inescapable. The distress of that time is compared to the distress of a woman enduring labor pains.

The "thief in the night" imagery or similar language is used five times in the New Testament to convey the thought that the coming of the Lord Jesus to judge the wicked will be sudden and unexpected (e.g., Matt. 24:42-43; Luke 12:42-46; 2 Pet. 3:10). Just as a thief does not publicize his intention to break into a house, neither will the wicked realize that wrath is coming until it is too late. The "thief" idiom is never applied to believers who are to be watching and waiting for the Lord's imminent return.

For this reason, Paul explained to the Thessalonians that they would not be on earth during the Day of the Lord, referred to in verse 4 by the expressions "in darkness" and "this Day." Believers will not be overtaken by the Day of the Lord when it arrives unexpectedly like a thief, because they will not be in their earthly homes. Instead, they will already be dwelling with Christ in eternal light. Christians are "sons of light" and "sons of the day" and will be taken up to be with Christ in Heaven before The Day of the Lord begins (v. 5). T. Earnest Wilson clarifies what Paul meant by the expression "sons of light":

> "Sons (*huioi*) of light" is a common Hebrew idiom. A man is said to be a son of any influence which dominates or determines his character. In the OT we read of "sons of Belial" (Judg. 19:22), and in the NT of "sons of thunder" (Mark 3:17); Barnabas is called "the son of consolation" (Acts 4:36).[93]

The Lord Jesus said, *"I am the light of the world"* (John 8:12) and *"I am the way, the truth, and the life, no one comes to the Father, except through Me"* (John 14:6). Christ was God's Message and Messenger. He was the embodiment of divine light (truth) to the world. Hence, those who hear and trust His message become "sons of light." These who have come out of the world's darkness into Christ's light must continue to walk in His light to represent Him in the world (Eph. 5:8; 1 Pet. 2:9; 1 Jn. 1:7).

Because of Christ, *sons of light* are no longer *"of the night nor of darkness"* which speaks of Satan's present domain and the coming Tribulation period (v. 5). Because believers do not know when they will be removed from the world prior to the coming darkness, they are not to behave like the spiritually destitute residing in the night (i.e., the unregenerate in Satan's domain). Rather, Christians are to be alert, watchful, and soberminded (v. 6). The extensive use of pronouns and allegory in verses 2-8 poses some difficulty in determining of whom and what Paul is speaking.

The following key is suggested:
"They," "them" = non-believers;
"You brethren", "we", "you," "us" = believers;
"Darkness," "wrath," "sudden destruction" = Tribulation period;
"The night" = Satan's domain;
"Light" = God's revelation of truth;
"The day" = God's domain (Heaven, excluding the verse 4 reference);
"Sleeping," "drunkenness," "of the night" = behavior of the lost;
"Watching," "sober," "of the day" = behavior of believers.

Sons of the day, believers, are not to live lethargic, distracted lives, but as sons of light in a dark world marked by spiritual rebellion and indifference to the things of God (v. 7). In the natural world it is normal to sleep at night, but in the spiritual realm sons of the day are continually alert to darkness and mindful of spiritual things associated with darkness. Believers are to be waiting for the Lord's return, while living sober-minded lives characterized by faith, hope and love (v. 8, see discussion of 1:3).

In verse 9, Paul again categorically states that the Church will not go through the "darkness," referring to the Tribulation period: *"For God did not appoint us to wrath, but to obtain salvation through our Lord Jesus Christ."* He previously exhorted the Thessalonians: *"To wait for His Son from Heaven, whom He raised from the dead, even Jesus who delivers us from the wrath to come"* (1:10). As shown by the testimony of the Thessalonians, the Church is not exempt from suffering for Christ. However, she is exempt from experiencing divine wrath (Rom. 5:9). God's wrath is against wickedness, not against His redeemed (Zech. 12:8-9).

Because Christ died for us, whether awake (alert) or asleep (slumbering), believers are guaranteed to *"live together with Him"* forever (v. 10). The expression *"whether we wake or sleep"* in verse 10 does not relate to Paul's doctrine about The Day of Christ (the Rapture of the Church) in chapter 4, but instead, of spiritual alertness in contrast to non-believers who slumber in such things. The Greek words used in verse 10 more closely track with the words and meanings of chapter 5 than chapter 4.

The Greek root verb *gregoreo* rendered *"we wake"* in verse 10 is translated *"let us watch"* in verse 6. Furthermore, the Greek root verb *katheudo* rendered "sleep" in verse 10 is also used in the same way in verses 6 and 7 to convey a meaning of "being settled in the world and insensitive to divine truth." A different Greek verb, *koimao*, translated "are asleep," refers three times to death in 4:13-15. Thus, Paul affirms that whether believers live vigorously or lethargically for the Lord, each of them is in Christ and He will return to gather to Himself all who belong to Him.

*1 Thessalonians*

Being in Christ secures our salvation, but how we live for Christ will be properly assessed at the Judgment Seat of Christ. The Thessalonians saints, who were suffering for Christ, were to comfort each other by regularly recalling this truth (v. 11).

## Eschatology Overview
### Periods to Come
1. The Tribulation period: Daniel's 70th week (Dan. 9:27) = the Time of Jacob's Trouble (a 7-year period; Jer. 30:7). It begins the Day of the Lord (2 Thess. 2).
2. The Millennial Kingdom (Rev. 20; Isa. 11). Also, part of the Day of the Lord (2 Pet. 3:10).
3. The Eternal state (Rev. chs. 21-22). The Day of God (2 Pet. 3:12).

### Events to Come
1. Church is raptured home, the Judgment Seat of Christ, the Marriage of the Lamb (4:13-18; 2 Cor. 5:10; Rev. 19:7-8).
2. Remnant of Jews refined and completely gathered in Israel (Ezek. 39).
3. Christ returns to the earth to destroy the Beast (including his army) and the False Prophet; Satan is put into a bottomless pit (Rev. 19:1-20:3).
4. Christ will judge the nations (Dan. 12:7-12; Rev. 19:21). During this 75-day period the Earth is also cleansed (Dan. 2:35, 44-45). The Judgment of Nations = separating the sheep and the goats (Matt. 25:31-46).
5. God judging the fitness of surviving Jews to enter and possess the land promised to Abaraham (Ezek. 20:33).
6. Christ rules the nations for 1000 years on a restored Earth (Rev. 20:1-6).
7. Satan's final assault against God and his destruction (Rev. 20:7-10).
8. The Great White Throne Judgment of the wicked (Rev. 20:11-15).
9. A New Heaven and New Earth are created (Rev. 21:1-2).

**GOD'S SALVATION FOR ISRAEL AND THE CHURCH**

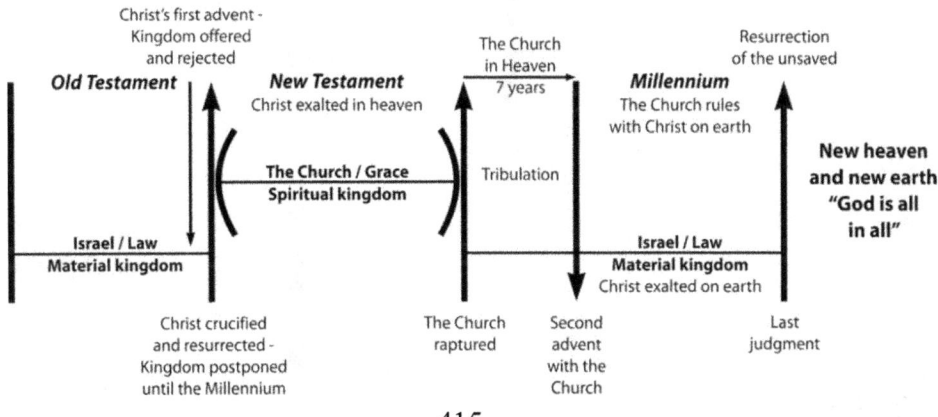

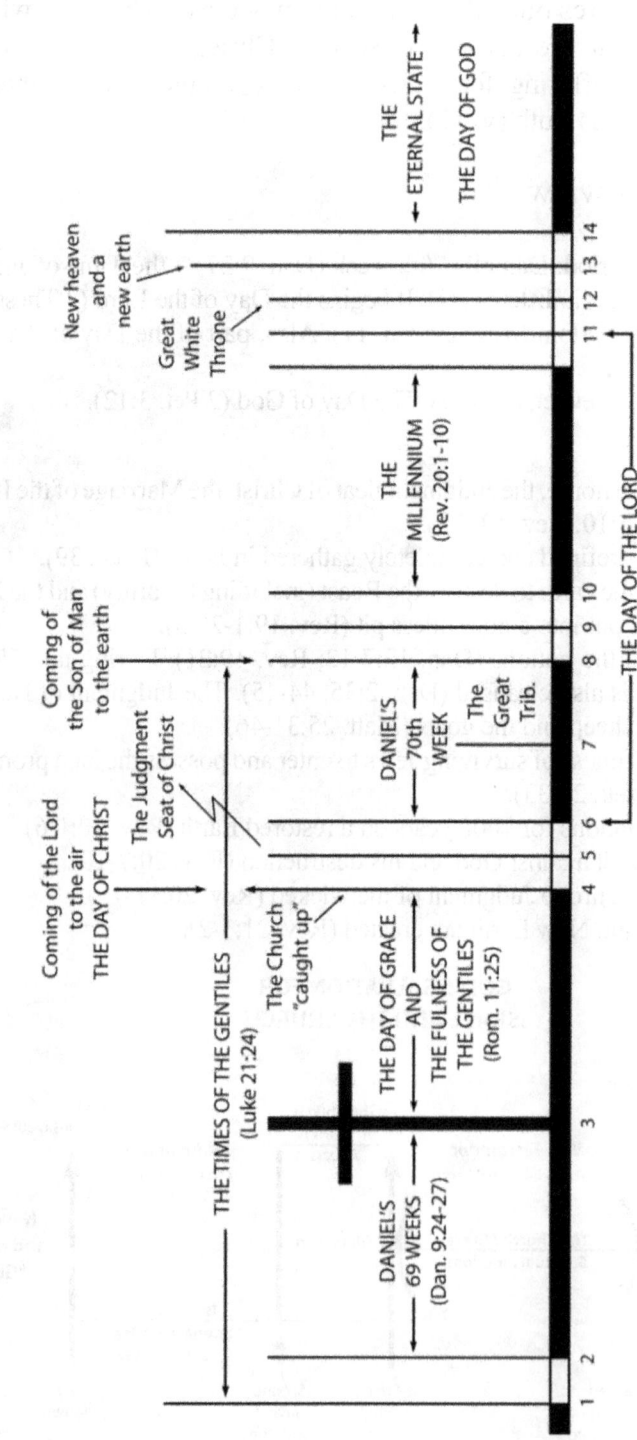

## Final exhortations (vv. 12-22)

As in the apostle's epistle to the Colossians, Paul closes his letter with a series of pithy exhortations to inspire the Thessalonians to maintain a holy walk before the Lord and a blameless testimony in the world.

First, the church elders laboring among them were to be highly appreciated, respected, and loved for the important shepherding work they undertook (vv. 12-13). Some within the church, because they thought the Lord's return was immediate, had apparently stopped working and had become busybodies and freeloaders (v. 11; 2 Thess. 3:10). It seems likely that the church elders at Thessalonica had rebuked these unruly saints and it had not been well received.

Shepherding God's people is a critical but arduous ministry that is often unappreciated. God's sheep can glare, wander, kick, bite, be standoffish, and downright stink, but they are God's sheep, and those in love with the Savior will also desire to love His sheep. Church elders representing the Lord's character and care should be encouraged and loved by all whom they serve (Heb. 13:7, 17, 24). The sheep should obey their elders as unto the Lord, and thereby live peaceably with other saints.

Second, Paul gave a fourfold exhortation in verse 14: *"Now we exhort you, brethren, warn those who are unruly, comfort the fainthearted, uphold the weak, be patient with all."* If the *unruly* (literally, those "out of rank") are not corrected, their behavior will rob the assembly of peace and ruin its testimony in the community. As just mentioned, the church elders had such a challenge in the assembly at Thessalonica.

Paul also encouraged the Thessalonians to *"comfort the feebleminded, support the weak."* Often the faith of others is needed to strengthen the fainthearted (e.g., Heb. 11). Hence, not only is the "shield of faith" a necessary part of a believer's spiritual armor, but it can also be used to assist others to stand fast in the faith (Eph. 6:16). Roman soldiers used a leather-covered, wooden shield which could be overlapped with the shields of other soldiers to create an impenetrable wall and ceiling against incoming darts and arrows. There is strength in numbers, and the faith of the many can "pull up" those wobbly-kneed saints who tend to be weak in faith, or those suddenly overcome by crushing circumstances (Gal. 6:2). If infused with God's grace, we will have the wherewithal to *"be patient with all."*

Third, Paul writes: *"See that no one renders evil for evil to anyone, but always pursue what is good both for yourselves and for all"* (v. 15). It is important to rejoice in the Lord and to pray for help during arduous times, but if you are being overcome by people problems, resort to the spiritual weapon of love. The more you are hated – the more you should love. In

God's timing, many oppressors have learned that God's love is irresistible.

Fourth, Paul urges the Thessalonians to *"rejoice always"* (v. 16). This is the shortest verse in the Greek New Testament, but one of the most important. Joy removes the burden. God's family should be a cheerful family, meaning we all must contribute to the atmosphere of joy. There is no room for *a doom and gloom* attitude. *"Yet if anyone suffers as a Christian, let him not be ashamed, but let him glorify God in this matter"* (1 Pet. 4:16). As a believer chooses to rejoice in the Lord in the midst of a dire situation, God often glorifies Himself by working a miraculous solution to end the trial. Paul's purposeful rejoicing after being beaten and jailed at Philippi is a good example (Acts 16).

Fifth, the saints were to "pray without ceasing" (v. 17). *"Pray without ceasing"* does not mean we must constantly be uttering prayers. The Greek word *adialeiptos* here means "constantly recurring," not "continuously occurring." It would be impossible to pray twenty-four hours a day, seven days a week. But it is possible to have an actively recurring prayer life. To "pray without ceasing" means to stay in contact with God in such a way that our praying is like a long conversation with short pauses; we never sense a break in conversation. The believer should pray at regular times (e.g., to confess sin, to make intercession, to seek grace in a time of need), but the Lord should never be far from our thoughts at any time.

Sixth, the charge *"in everything give thanks; for this is the will of God in Christ Jesus for you"* is given (v. 18). Why are we to give thanks in all things? Because *"we know that all things work together for good to them that love God, to them who are the called according to His purpose"* (Rom. 8:28). This means that we have exactly what the Lord intends that we should have. Does a critical spirit keep you from thinking positively about what God is doing? We usually cannot change the reality of our hardship, but we can change our perception of it. A thankful spirit demonstrates to God that we really do trust Him to do what is best and honoring to His own name in every situation. A thankful spirit and critical mind cannot exist together.

Seventh, the Thessalonians were exhorted, *"do not quench the Spirit"* (v. 19). Sin quenches and grieves the Holy Spirit (Eph. 4:30). Because the verb is in the present tense and imperative mood, the phrase could easily be translated "stop quenching the Spirit." *Wuest's Expanded Translation* reads, "Stop stifling and suppressing the Spirit"! The Holy Spirit is likened to a flame (Isa. 4:4; Rev. 4:5). He warms our hearts, enlightens our minds, and empowers the believer's spirit, but He can be resisted (Acts 7:51).

It is the effectual working of the Holy Spirit that Paul warned against hindering or even snuffing out. Although the Holy Spirit is always present in the believer, when the believer chooses to sin, it is as if he or she has thrown a wet blanket over His energizing capacity. Submission leads to Spirit filling, which results in usefulness and fruitfulness. Thus, the believer is commanded to *"be filled with the Holy Spirit"* (Eph. 5:18).

Eighth, a compound exhortation is given, *"Do not despise prophecies. Test all things; hold fast what is good"* (vv. 20-21). These two verses cannot be separated from each other: To despise prophecy (God's declared Word) would prevent spirit-filling by the Holy Spirit and squelch our overall spiritual growth. Before the Scripture was supplied to the Church by the apostles, there were prophets who immediately declared the Word of God in the local assembly and also tested the validity of what was said (1 Cor. 14:26-32). Paul was telling the believers at Thessalonica not to neglect studying, understanding, meditating on, and memorizing God's Word.

The Greek *dokimazete* rendered "test" is a present tense imperative verb that commands believers to actively "examine in order to approve" everything that relates to us. But we cannot *"test all things,"* to determine what is truth or deception, without first knowing what God's Word says. Blatant wickedness besieges the heart of rebels, but there is no reason that subtle deception should ensnare saints. Deceit is often carefully combined with something acceptable. Consequently, much discernment is required in daily conduct, or the believer will certainly fall prey to the enemy's trickery and craftiness. There is no reason to be deceived, so leave nothing to chance.

Ninth, Paul challenges the Thessalonians to *"*abstain from every form of evil"* (v. 22). The KJV renders this verse, *"Abstain from the appearance of evil."* As we read in verse 23, the believer's spirit, soul and body should be fully consecrated to God. This means that we must abhor evil in thought and deed. The matter hinges on the believer's understanding that, positionally, what he was in Adam is dead. It died on the cross when Christ suffered and died on our behalf (Rom. 6:6; Eph. 4:22). All that we were before Christ is no more. We died with Him at Calvary. Because believers have legally been declared dead, we receive a new life – His life. We must now endeavor to live His life in practice and not follow our own ambitions (2 Cor. 5:14-17). Such a lifestyle will center in holy living, so that the unregenerate cannot legitimately accuse the believer of wrongdoing.

## A Final Blessing and Admonition (vv. 23-28).

Paul's chief aspiration for the Thessalonians is expressed in verses 23-24: *"Now may the God of peace Himself sanctify you completely; and may your whole spirit, soul, and body be preserved blameless at the coming of our Lord Jesus Christ. He who calls you is faithful, who also will do it."*

Through Paul, the Holy Spirit acknowledges man's physiological design of spirit, soul, and body. The spirit is *God-conscious* and refers to the innermost area of our being – the "inner man." The body is *flesh and world-conscious*. It is the lowest part of our essence and forms the physical part of our being. Between these two components dwells the soul. The soul is *self-conscious* and comprises intellect, emotions, personality, and will.

Through the five senses the soul interacts with the physical realm and through the spirit the soul connects with God. The soul is a bridge, a window, a medium, set between the body and the spirit. When a believer is in fellowship with God, the Holy Spirit has freedom to commune with man's spirit which transmits godly thoughts to the soul. This in turn exercises the body to conform to the Spirit's rule and to be a vessel of honor.

The spirit cannot act directly upon the body without the medium of the soul. Thus, the will of man can choose to ignore his spirit and follow the baser desires of the body. God created the soul of man as a mediator with power to influence the whole man, giving him discernment and the enablement of his will to choose to pursue the spiritual rather than the natural world. The soul of man includes his heart, will, and mind. The mind is the intellectual and cognitive center of the soul and ultimately determines the direction the soul will follow.

The bulk of scriptural exhortation is not focused on the soul or the heart, but on the mind. The mind must be "transformed" (Rom. 12:2) to "form" a pure heart (Ps. 51:10). A pure heart serves to "conform" (Eph. 6:5-8) our will to God's will. The mind is the locale between the physical and spiritual realms where spiritual battles are won or lost. The mind frames the soul's will and emotions. If a believer truly wants the Holy Spirit to have free access to his or her soul, the mind must make holy choices.

To bear fruit for God, we must yield to the leading, convicting, equipping, and enabling work of the Holy Spirit. But, regardless of each believer's progress in practical sanctification, Christ will gather all believers to Himself and present them blameless before God after their glorification.

In closing, Paul reminds the Thessalonians to pray for the missionary team, and to show impartial love to all believers (vv. 25-26). The Greek noun *philema*, which is derived from the verb *phileo* which means "a brotherly love," is translated "kiss." *Philema* can be any personal greeting which is used to wholesomely express genuine brotherly love. It does not necessarily mean a literal "kiss." The idea is to express genuine affection to, and for, believers that is void of any lustful intention. This type of expression will vary among cultures. Lastly, Paul blessed the Thessalonians and requested that his letter be read to everyone (vv. 27-28).

# 2 Thessalonians

## Background

Thessalonica, located in Macedonia, was one of three major seaports on the Aegean Sea (Corinth and Ephesus being the other two). The population at this time is estimated to have been 200,000. Most citizens were native Greeks, but some Romans and Jews also lived there. The Medo-Persian Empire fell to the Greeks in 330 B.C. and Thessalonica was built 15 years later in 315 B.C. by Cassandra, a general under Alexander the Great.

Cassander married Thessalonica, the half-sister of Alexander, after whom he named the city. Cassander is one of the four Greek generals who are featured in Daniel's prophetic record (chs. 7, 8, 11). Upon Alexander's death, each general received a fourth of his empire. After conquering the world in only four years Alexander died at the age of 32. In 42 B.C. both Anthony and Octavian (later called Caesar Augustus) granted the city "free" status. This allowed the inhabitants to live their daily routines without much Roman influence. In fact, no Roman soldiers were garrisoned there.

During Paul's second missionary journey, Paul and Silas traveled to Thessalonica from Philippi, where they had been severely beaten. The timing of this visit was likely late 50 A.D. From the record in Acts, we learn that Paul preached on three consecutive sabbaths in a synagogue (Acts 17:2), before being driven out of Thessalonica by persecution. However, Paul may have been in Thessalonica a brief time before he began speaking publicly in the synagogue, since he was there long enough to engage in the craft of tent-making and to see a church begin (3:8; 1 Thess. 2:9). Acts affirms that some Jews and Greeks came to the synagogue, and some wives of prominent Thessalonian citizens were saved through Paul's teaching.

Paul, Silas, and Timothy were forced to leave Thessalonica after a riot broke out in which Jason's home was assaulted (the mob was looking for Paul). Jason was apprehended by the mob and taken to the civil authorities. He was accused of harboring Paul's missionary team who were leading a revolt against Caesar.

Paul, Silas, and Timothy then traveled to Berea, and Paul later went on to Athens alone. As there was an opportunity in Athens for the gospel, Paul sent for Silas and Timothy. Shortly after they arrived in Athens, Paul sent

Timothy back to Thessalonica to check on the church's welfare. Silas returned to Philippi on a similar errand while Paul remained in Athens alone. He then traveled to Corinth. First Thessalonians was written by Paul from Corinth shortly after Timothy returned from Thessalonica with a good report. The Thessalonian saints were remaining strong despite persecution.

Apparently, not long after Paul sent his first letter to the Thessalonians, it was reported to him that the saints there had receive a forged letter in his name (2:2). This counterfeit epistle claimed that the Christians there had missed the Lord's coming and were now in The Day of the Lord. Since the saints were already suffering persecution for the name of Christ, it was likely devastating to hear that their suffering would become even more severe because they were in the Day of the Lord (1 Thess. 5:2-8). So, Paul quickly wrote a second letter to correct the phony one and to provide more eschatological insights concerning the Lord's future judgment of the wicked and His second advent to the earth to establish His earthly kingdom.

## Theme(s)
"The Day of the Lord."

## Keywords
Keywords and phrases include: "day," "your faith," "glory," "everlasting," "always," "truth" (vs. the "lie"), "patience/patient," "Lord," "tradition(s)," "come/coming," "unruly," and "command/commandment."

## Date
Since Gallio (Acts 18) was not appointed proconsul of Achaia until 53 A.D. and he ruled in favor of Paul near the conclusion of Paul's 18-month stay at Corinth, it is likely that this book was written in 51 A.D. (within a few months after arriving in Corinth).

## Outline
I. Introduction (1:1-4).
II. Comforting the Persecuted (1:5-10).
III. The Day of the Lord (2:1-17).
IV. Obey the Word; Deal With the Disorderly (3:1-15).
V. Conclusion and Benediction (3:16-18).

# 2 Thessalonians Chapter 1

## Introduction (vv. 1-2)

The second letter to the Thessalonians commences in much the same way the first epistle did. Verses 1-2 are identical in both letters. The originator was Paul, but since Silas and Timothy were still with him in Corinth, he also included their names (v. 1). The epistle is addressed to all the believers in the local church at Thessalonica.

Paul again extends his trademark greeting of grace and peace to the saints and affirms that both blessings come from God the Father and the Lord Jesus Christ. Apparently, a forged letter purporting to come from Paul had been received by the Thessalonian church. Undoubtedly the consistency of the wording in both of Paul's letters would have helped the saints to distinguish between the genuine and the false.

## Paul's Thanksgiving (vv. 3-4)

As in the first epistle, Paul acknowledges the abounding love of the Thessalonians towards each other and their steadfast faith in the Lord (v. 3). Because both these spiritual qualities were growing profoundly, Paul was moved to continually praise God on their behalf. Notice Paul's order of the spiritual virtues in verses 2-3: divine grace must be received before we can enjoy God's peace, and our divinely-rooted faith must grow so that we might better display His love to others. Especially commendable was the faith of the Thessalonian saints which was enabling them to patiently endure persecution and tribulation in Christ's name (v. 4). By recounting their faithfulness to others, Paul wanted the Thessalonians to know how they had encouraged Christians elsewhere to live for Christ.

## God's Righteous Judgments (vv. 5-12)

Suffering patiently for the cause of Christ is to the unregenerate, a proof of perdition (Phil. 1:28) and to believers, "evidence" of salvation (i.e., God's righteous work in them; v. 5). The observance of Christ's patient suffering at Calvary is what caused one of the thieves crucified with Him to repent. Suffering patiently while relying on God's grace is a supernatural testimony to the lost. On the other hand, it is a consolation to the believer that he or she is truly a child of God (1 Pet. 4:12-14).

If the Thessalonians were not truly saved, they would not have continued to go on with Christ despite immense suffering. Their tenacious faith was proof that they were "worthy of the kingdom of God." It was also proof of the reality of their salvation. Salvation is received by grace through faith (Eph. 2:8), but true faith does not stand alone. It is accompanied by good works (Jas. 2:17 20). The Thessalonians exhibited genuine faith!

In verses 6-9, Paul provides two reasons why God permits His people to be persecuted for their faith. First, those who oppress His people prove their allegiance to the devil and thus their fitness to be judged by a righteous God (v. 6). Second, those who patiently suffer persecution for Christ's sake validate their faith and thus their fitness to rule and reign with Christ in His coming kingdom (v. 7). Paul then promised the Thessalonians that every act of injustice and undeserved affliction by their persecutors against them would be judged by Christ. The judgment of the wicked living on earth will occur at His second advent to the earth. Then, all the wicked throughout world history will be judged at the Great White Throne judgment (Rev. 20).

Because He is just and righteous and also omniscient, omnipresent, omnipotent, eternal, and immutable, no unforgiven offense against Him will escape His retribution. In a coming day, believers will enjoy rest in Christ's presence either after death or at their glorification when the Church is raptured from the earth (2 Cor. 5:8; 1 Thess. 4:13-18). Then, after the Tribulation period, Christ (with His saints following) will return to the earth to vindicate His name and allot vengeance to those who deserve it (v. 8).

The phrase "in flaming fire" refers to the awesome glory and power that will be displayed by Christ at His second advent. He will exact terrible judgment on all those who rejected His offer of salvation. These are those who did not know God and who chose to oppress those who did (Matt. 24:27; Rev. 19:11-21). Then, all believers will eternally enjoy God's peace and be free from the oppression of those who challenged His authority.

By their evil works (including oppression of God's people; Rev. 20:11-13) and their rejection of salvation in Christ the ungodly prove their fitness for divine judgment. These rebels will *"be punished with everlasting destruction from the presence of the Lord"* in the Lake of Fire – Hell (v. 9; Matt. 25:41-46; Rev. 20:14-15).

Everlasting destruction does not mean annihilation but endless torment of the wicked away from God's presence. For example, the Antichrist and the False Prophet will be cast into the Lake of Fire after the Battle of Armageddon at the end of the Tribulation period (Rev. 19:20). A thousand years later, the devil will join them: *"The devil, who deceived them, was cast into the lake of fire and brimstone where the beast and the false prophet are. And they will be tormented day and night forever and ever"* (Rev. 20:10). Hell is where sinners eternally serve their sentence for sin and their rejection of Christ. It is a place where the worm never dies (it is putrid), and where the resurrected wicked wail and gnash their teeth, suffering in total darkness and unquenchable fire (Mark 9:44-46; Luke 3:17; Jude 13).

Christ will be glorified by His creation one way or another, either by exercising His authority and power to judge those who reject His rule, or by extending grace to those who humble themselves and accept His offer of salvation, which cost Him His life. Therefore, on vindication day (at His second advent to the earth) the Lord Jesus Christ will *"be glorified in His saints and to be admired among all those who believe"* (v. 10). William MacDonald explains the meaning of this statement:

> He [Christ] will be admired among all those who believe. Amazed onlookers will gasp as they see what He has been able to do with such unpromising human beings! And this will include the Thessalonian believers too. Because they had received and believed the testimony of the apostles, they would share in the glory and triumph of that Day, namely, the Day of the Revelation of Jesus Christ.[94]

In the previous verses the apostle described the glorious calling of God's people to represent His Son to a lost world. All those who live for Christ will suffer persecution (2 Tim. 3:12), but those who willingly go on with Christ despite suffering for Him prove themselves fit to rule with Him in His kingdom (v. 11). Paul prayed that the Thessalonians would live in such a way as to be counted worthy of this heavenly calling.

Paul reveals the primary goal of the Christian faith in verses 11-12: to walk worthy of our calling in Christ; to experience the work of faith in power; to accomplish God's good pleasure such that the name of the Lord Jesus Christ will be glorified. Believers are only on planet Earth for one purpose – *"for the praise of His glory"* (Eph. 1:12). The chief aspiration of every Christian should be to magnify Christ in all that we do (Phil. 1:20). That is, to make Him look good no matter what! Likewise, those magnifying Christ will also be glorified in Him on His vindication day.

Through Christlike believers the unregenerate are able to witness the beautiful and gracious character of Christ, whether through suffering for Him or serving in His name. Believers are to reflect the moral glory of the Lord Jesus Christ in all they do. However, Paul reminds us that this is only possible by *"the grace of our God and the Lord Jesus Christ"* (v. 12).

# 2 Thessalonians Chapter 2

The Day of the Lord (vv. 1-12)

In his first epistle, Paul spoke five times of Christ's imminent coming for His Church (e.g., 1 Thess. 4:13-18) and of the Day of the Lord (i.e., the Tribulation period which would follow the Rapture of the Church; 1 Thess. 5:1-5). Shortly after receiving Paul's first epistle, rumors and confusion occurred about what Paul was teaching concerning these events. Additionally, someone had apparently written a letter in Paul's name informing the suffering saints at Thessalonica that they had missed Christ's coming (the Rapture) and were now in The Day of the Lord. Paul wrote this epistle to correct this erroneous teaching and rectify the problem.

Understanding the correct context of verse 1 is crucial in understanding Paul's meaning in the verses that follow: *"Now, brethren, concerning the coming of our Lord Jesus Christ and our gathering together to Him, we ask you"* (v. 1). Some translations (e.g., KJV) have inserted a "by" (which is not in the Greek text) in front of "our gathering," and other translations (e.g., RV) have rendered *huper* as "touching" (meaning "about" or "on behalf of") to indicate that Paul is talking about two events, the first, The Day of the Lord, and the second, The Day of Christ (the Rapture of the Church).

The NKJV translates *huper* as "concerning" and the KJV as "by" to convey the idea that Paul was talking about a single event in verse 1: the coming of the Lord Jesus to gather His Church to Himself. Paul's appeal at the end of verse 1 then makes perfect sense. On the basis that the Rapture of the Church occurs prior to The Day of the Lord, the Thessalonians should not think that they were in The Day of the Lord.

Besides this translation difficulty in verse 1, there is a textual disparity in verse 2 between the majority manuscripts from which the KJV and NKJV are drawn from as compared to the Critical Text derived from the Alexandrian codices. For example, the NIV is based on the Critical Text and reads "asserting that the day of the Lord has already come," while the NKJV reads "as though the day of Christ had come."

Most textual differences between the Critical and Majority Texts are not significant, but the one in verse 2 is important. Scripture must interpret Scripture and the clear context of the passage affirms that the Majority Text

*Christos* or "Christ" is incorrect, while the Critical Text *Kyrios* or "Lord" is correct. An additional difficulty is asserting the correct meaning of the Greek verb *enesteken* translated as "has already come" (NIV), or "had come" (NKJV), or "has come" (NASB), or "is at hand" (KJV). *Enesteken* is a perfect tense verb only found here in the New Testament. The idea of "is now present" seems to best express Paul's thought in verse 2.

The correct understanding would be that the Thessalonians should not think that they were in The Day of the Lord (i.e., that it was then present). The text is not saying that they should not think that The Day of Christ had come and gone. T. W. Smith provides this textual overview of verse 2:

> There is no hesitation in condemning the rendering "as that the day of Christ is at hand" [KJV] as contrary to all the oldest authorities, so states Alford. The correct reading is "the day of the Lord," and "is at hand" should read "is already come" (or "is now present"). The importance of these amendments ... emerge when it is understood that whilst the day of Christ and the day of the Lord run parallel for almost the same period of time [i.e., The Day of the Lord begins on earth, just after The Day of Christ that takes the Church to Heaven concludes], the former concerns believers and Heaven, the latter (contextually) speaks of unbelievers and earth.[95]

Paul's main emphasis in verses 3-12 is to affirm that the Thessalonians could not be in the Tribulation period (The Day of the Lord), since Christ had not yet returned to remove His Church from the Earth. He then uses the Greek word *proton* to introduce the first of two consecutive events which must happen prior to the onset of The Day of the Lord. First, Christendom will fall away from sound doctrine, and second, the Man of Sin, the Antichrist, will be publicly revealed (vv. 3-6). At that time, the Church was in its vibrant infancy and doctrinal purity marked the Apostolic Age. There was no widespread apostasy and clearly the Antichrist had not appeared on the world scene. Hence, the Thessalonians were not in The Day of the Lord.

The first sign Paul mentions of the coming Tribulation period is *apostasy*. The word Greek *apostasia* (apostasy), meaning "a departure" or "defection," is found only twice in the New Testament. It is rendered "falling away" in verse 3. Paul later informed Timothy what this widespread defection from sound doctrine would look like (1 Tim. 4:1-3; 2 Tim. 4:2-5). Towards the end of the Church Age, the "professing church" will be marked by people leaving sound doctrine and listening to seducing spirits and doctrines of demons. They will speak hypocrisy with a seared conscience. They will follow their lusts and seek teachers who will preach to them what they want to hear. For example, some will forbid marriage, while others will have dietary prohibitions. At present, we are witnessing a large-scale departure by Christendom from scriptural Church order and sound doctrine.

Concerning the second sign that The Day of the Lord was nearing, Paul states what the Man of Sin, the Son of Perdition (the Antichrist; 1 Jn. 2:18), will do on earth after he receives his authority (Rev. 6:1-2). He will promote the Abomination of Desolation that the prophet Daniel foretold, and that Christ affirmed would happen (Dan. 7:8; Matt. 24:15). The Antichrist, standing in the Jewish temple, will stop the sacrifices and claim to be God (v. 4). Before the Jewish sacrifices can be stopped by the Antichrist, they must start again (offerings have not occurred since the temple in Jerusalem was destroyed in 70 A.D.). The Lord Jesus addressed this same prophetic subject with His disciples just a few days before His crucifixion (Matt. 24).

The Lord taught that one sign of the proximity of His return to the earth to judge the wicked would be that the fig tree (i.e., religious Israel) will again shoot forth leaves after a long winter season of deadness (Luke 21:29-31). Leaves must precede fruit, but the fig tree will bear no fruit until the spiritual rebirth of the nation occurs in the latter days of the Tribulation (Joel 2:12-32). Of what do the new leaves speak? This is likely a reference to the revival of the old sacrificial system by the Jews. This event may occur just prior to or just after the commencement of the Tribulation period.

When Israel is spoken of as a fig tree in Scripture, the metaphor relates to the religious element of Israel, which often was fruitless for God (Jer. 8:13; Matt. 21:19-21). This reality, which characterizes Judaism today, was identified during an event in the life of the Lord Jesus (Luke 13:6-9). After preaching for three years to the lost sheep of Israel and just before Calvary, Christ cursed the fruitless fig tree. Less than forty years later, Jerusalem and the temple were destroyed, and the Jews have not sacrificed since. The Old Covenant was replaced by the New Covenant, sealed with Christ's blood, and God would not permit the Jews to continue in what was now obsolete.

Before the Antichrist can desecrate the Jewish temple and put a stop to animal sacrifices at the midpoint of the Tribulation period, there must be a temple and the Jews must be sacrificing again. This religious formality could commence just prior to the Tribulation period. The Lord said that the generation that witnessed this event would also see His second coming (Luke 21:32). It is worth noting that the Temple Institute in Jerusalem has already recreated the temple vessels and furnishings and has performed "educational" animal sacrifices in anticipation of this historic event.

> Rabbi Yisrael Ariel [a leader of the Temple Institute in Jerusalem] has stated that everything is now ready for recommencement of the

sacrificial system. All that remains is for the government of Israel to give them the permission to go onto the Temple Mount and perform the sacrifice. While Israel does control the Temple Mount, it is administered by the Islamic Waqf of Jordan, and the Israeli Police generally prohibit any action that might cause contention with the Muslims.[96]

All is set for the Jews to begin offering sacrifices to Jehovah at any time. The generation that sees this occur will also see Christ's second advent.

Paul notes that he had previously taught these truths to the saints (v. 5). Yet, the subject of eschatology is not easily grasped, especially by those young in the faith, so the apostle revisited the subject.

The apostle then affirmed that the Antichrist could not be revealed until that what was restraining him would be removed (vv. 6-7). Paul uses the neuter Greek verb *katechon* in verse 6 to speak of the restraint or holding back of Antichrist until the moment appointed by God. He uses the same verb in verse 7, but with the masculine gender. Thus, it is translated as a person who is hindering: *"He who now restrains."* Who on earth can hinder the "mystery of lawlessness" (i.e., rebellion against God) until such time that the Antichrist is to be revealed? That which is of the flesh will never restrain sin, but the Holy Spirit by His empowering presence in believers can, and will, do so (John 16:8-10; Rom. 8:8-14).

Although the text does not state that the Holy Spirit is the Restrainer, verse 7 does describe what the restrainer does. He is actively restraining, and will continue to restrain, until it is the right moment for Him to withdraw His restraint. John reminds us that the One within believers is more powerful than anything the devil can muster against them: *"for greater is He that is in you, than he that is in the world"* (1 Jn. 4:4). In the same way that the Holy Spirit suddenly appeared on Earth at Pentecost to form the Church, His empowering presence will suddenly be taken away when Christ removes His Church from the Earth.

Until the restraining influence of the Holy Spirit is removed, the Man of Sin cannot receive authority or come into power during the Tribulation period (v. 8; Rev. 13:7). The Man of Sin in this text is clearly the Antichrist. John speaks of him being destroyed by Christ at the Battle of Armageddon, thus ending his reign (v. 8; Rev. 19:11-20).

When the Pre-Tribulation Rapture of the Church occurs, every Spirit-indwelt believer will be removed from the Earth. While the Holy Spirit will still be omnipresent and active, His special influence in the world through indwelt saints will be removed. He will continue to convict men of sin and their need for a Savior while the Kingdom Gospel is being preached during the Tribulation period (Matt. 24:14). However, the saints who were confronting evil by preaching the gospel of grace (1 Cor. 15:3-4) and performing Spirit-enabled deeds will no longer be present. One can only imagine the chaos that will envelop the world after all Spirit-indwelt saints are snatched away and the Man of Sin appears with satanic power to work signs and lying wonders to deceive the masses (v. 9). John describes some of the feats by which the Antichrist and False Prophet will then deceive the world (Rev. 13:5-7, 11-15, 19:20).

Verses 10-12 are a solemn warning to those who have heard the gospel message of Jesus Christ during the Church Age, but have chosen to continue in unrighteousness, reject the truth, and refuse to be saved (v. 10). If these individuals are alive when the Tribulation period begins, the Holy Spirit will apparently no longer influence them to repent, but rather *"God will send them strong delusion, that they should believe the lie"* (v. 11). The verb *pempsei* rendered "will send" is in the active voice, meaning that God is doing this action, not just permitting it to happen.

Similarly, Israel was in a state of unbelief when they rejected and crucified Christ. God responded by giving them over to a state of spiritual blindness which they had chosen by their constant unbelief (John 12:40). The Jewish nation will remain in this state of unbelief throughout the Church Age (Rom. 11:7, 25). Having been given over to delusional blindness, those previously rejecting the gospel will believe the lie of the Antichrist and hence will perish with him. Thomas L. Constable surmises:

> The "powerful delusion" (v. 11) that God will bring on these individuals [the gospel rejectors] in particular suggests that few if any then living on the earth will be saved after the Rapture. This seems to be a special judgment from God that will occur at this one time in history.[97]

On this point, William MacDonald writes: "From this passage it seems that those who hear the gospel in this Age of Grace but who do not trust Christ will not have another opportunity to be saved after the Rapture."[98] Regrettably, those who rejected the truth will believe the lie, take the mark of the beast, and follow the Antichrist into rebellion against God and into Hell. Because they chose to have pleasure in lawlessness rather than receive the truth and be saved (v. 12), God will honor their choice.

Sunrises occur so frequently that we often do not appreciate their beauty. Yet, if you were waiting out the night alone in a jungle, you would have a much deeper appreciation for those welcome hues of morning bliss in the eastern sky. It is for this reason that Christ likens Himself to *"the bright and morning star"* (Rev. 22:16) which is most visible in the eastern sky just before dawn. Focusing on Christ instead of the spiritual darkness that surrounds us inspires hope for the coming glorious day.

Scripture describes predawn events of His coming in order to encourage those who are watching and waiting for Him. This was Paul's desire for the Thessalonians, and for us too. Dark times will precede the curtain call of the Church Age, yet believers are promised that their *Bright and Morning Star* shall appear. He shall come for His beloved at the dawning of the Day of the Lord, and then the *Sun of Righteousness* (Mal. 4:2) shall rise in His full fury and flood the earth with His glory!

## Paul's Thanksgiving and Prayer (vv. 13-17)

In contrast to the judgment of the wicked (who did not love the truth; vv. 10-12), Paul praises God for the complete salvation of the Thessalonians who had obeyed the gospel. The apostle then summarizes the past and future aspects of their salvation in verses 13-14:

God chose them (v. 13): God's election (choices in time) is based on His foreknowledge (1 Pet. 1:2) and permits the believer to ultimately partake of His divine nature and be Christlike. Such observable evidence proves the reality of the believer's election in Christ (2 Pet. 1:4-10).

God set them apart (v. 13): Here, Paul is not speaking of the ongoing refining work of the Holy Spirit in the believer's life after salvation is received (1 Thess. 5:23), but the sanctifying work of the Holy Spirit to bring a lost sinner to salvation in Christ (John 16:7-11; 1 Pet. 1:2).

God called them (v. 14): What was necessary for the Thessalonians to receive salvation in Christ? They had to hear the gospel call and respond to it in faith to receive forgiveness of their sins (Rom. 1:16; 10:14-17).

God gave them glory (v. 14): God's plan to save sinners began with His foreknowledge before creation and concludes when He fully son-places (adoption) all those in Christ into the riches of His glory. At the First Resurrection (i.e., glorification), all believers will receive eternal Christlike bodies and share in Christ's glory forever (Rom. 8:20, 13:11; Rev. 20:4-6).

God makes choices in time to accomplish His predestined plan to save repentant sinners through Christ. This plan was devised by His foreknowledge and will sanctify and glorify all believers in Christ forever.

Hence, the Thessalonians were to hold to the truth (i.e., the traditions of the apostles; v. 15). Paul is not speaking of developed Church traditions, but of the spoken and written apostolic revelation from God that had been delivered to the Thessalonians. Paul then confirmed the love and grace of Christ towards them and prayed that they would hold to truth, and that their words and works would be founded in grace and in the truth (vv. 16-17).

# 2 Thessalonians Chapter 3

### Let Us Pray for Each Other (vv. 1-5)

The apostle passed along three prayer requests to the Thessalonians in verses 1-2. First, that the gospel message would *"run swiftly"* (i.e., that it would spread rapidly). Second, that God's Word would continue to go forth in power as it had in Thessalonica. Third, that God might grant them deliverance from *"unreasonable and wicked men"* (v. 2). This would include those blinded by pride and those who oppressed the saints who were preaching the gospel, *"for not all have faith."* The latter group included staunch, Law-keeping Jews who opposed Paul at Corinth (Acts 18:5-6).

These prayer appeals encapsulate much of what the New Testament Church prayed for when they came before the throne of grace to beseech the Lord for help. Christians asked for renewed boldness to preach the truth and that God would deliver or sustain those who were suffering for doing so (e.g., Acts 4:29-31, 12:5, 12).

However, Paul did not want the Thessalonians to be overly focused on the faithless ones opposing the gospel (v. 2), but rather, on the faithful Lord Jesus who would give them the victory (v. 3). He was able to establish and guard them from the attacks of the evil one. Paul then expressed his confidence that the Thessalonians would continue to walk in the apostle's doctrine as commanded (v. 4). Paul then asked the Lord to provide them with a deeper experience of His love and to enable them to better exhibit Christ's patience (v. 5). When God's love permeates the believer's heart, the character of Christ will be exhibited in all that he or she does.

Paul's charge and prayer confirmed that the Thessalonians were safe in Christ and that He would supply them with sufficient grace to weather the storms of life, to reject the solicitations of the devil, and to press on despite the attacks of wicked people.

### Dealing With the Unruly (vv. 6-15)

In verses 6-15, Paul instructed the believers in how to handle unruly saints who were threatening the order and peace of the Church at Thessalonica. Some in the church were using the truth of the Lord's imminent return as an excuse to stop working. As a result, they were failing to provide for the needs of their families (vv. 10-11). These freeloaders were sponging off believers who understood that Christ's return was *imminent*, but not necessarily *immediate*. In his first epistle, Paul had scolded these unruly saints to get back to work and had charged the church elders to also warn them to do so (1 Thess. 4:11, 5:14).

To correct this irresponsible conduct, Paul instructed believers to withdraw from these disorderly saints (i.e., limit personal fellowship with them; v. 6). The Thessalonians were to obey Paul's *command* in this matter and to follow the industrious example of the missionary team while with them. Although Paul had a full plate of apostolic ministry, when necessary, he still engaged in tent-making to provide for his needs (v. 7; Acts 18:3).

The apostle engaged in long hours of ministry for the Lord, but without being a burden to others. This was the example the Thessalonians should follow (v. 8). Although Paul acknowledged that he had a right to be supported by those who had benefitted from his ministry, he chose not to claim that right lest his motives for service be brought into question (v. 9).

To remain above reproach in his ministry, Paul was content to provide for himself as required with his own hands. The apostle was practicing what he had previously taught: *"If anyone will not work, neither shall he eat"* (v. 10). If it is necessary to eat to live, then work to eat. Using a bit of sarcasm, Paul refers to these unruly, non-busy saints as "busybodies" (v. 11).

A busybody is someone who injects their own interests, rather than the Lord's concerns, into your interests. Such presumptuous behavior within a local church harms body-life and leads to disunity and division, and often spoils what is important to the Lord. At such times a purifying action is needful to remedy the problem. Paul acknowledges this mysterious truth of Church body-life: *"For none of us lives to himself, and no one dies to himself"* (Rom. 14:7). *"And if one member suffers, all the members suffer with it; or if one member is honored, all the members rejoice with it"* (1 Cor. 12:26). Hence, we should never think that our personal sins do not have ramifications for others. The choices we make today affect our family members, our local churches, and indeed all the brethren.

As a sanctified Body gathered to the Lord, the local assembly should completely avoid those who have been warned but continue to be disorderly (vv. 11-15), divisive (Rom. 16:17), or contentious (Tit. 3:9-11). Heresy causes needless division among God's people and often results from out-of-balance thinking (e.g., majoring on a minor or on one truth to the exclusion of the fuller truth). *"Cast out the scorner, and contention will leave; yes, strife and reproach shall cease"* (Prov. 22:10). The purpose of this shunning is to help the shunned person see that he is out of fellowship with God, and therefore out of fellowship with His people. This remedy is motivated by love, not pity. The saints must do what is best for the unrepentant individual.

Only those who are walking close to the Lord will be able to clearly discern issues of sin and have the mind of the Lord to handle such deeply troubling situations (Gal. 6:1). We must have a spirit of meekness and humility to restore those in sin, but without condoning what is wrong or being adversely influenced by those who are in the wrong. As believers, we need the collective strength of all believers walking with the Lord. So, thank the Lord when someone has both the spiritual sense and courage to tell you when you have gone your own way. Otherwise, how would you know?

Moreover, Paul instructs the Thessalonians to *"work in quietness and eat their own bread"* (v. 12). God established work as a normal part of human existence before the fall of man (Gen. 2:15). Therefore, we should appreciate the opportunity to labor to provide for our needs. However, we should not glory in our work for it is not an end in itself but it supplies an opportunity to advance the Great Commission and glorify Christ. Further, it prevents us from burdening others to supply our needs. It is human nature to indulge the flesh, to flirt with the world, and to intrude into other people's affairs when we have "spare" time. Keeping busy in the Lord's work and laboring with our hands protects us from the dangers of idle time.

The Christian race begins with a profession of Christ, but in time true converts are revealed by loyalty despite hardship. Hence, the Thessalonians were exhorted to not grow weary in well doing – *keep on keeping on* (v. 13)! The Lord said, *"To him who overcomes I will give to eat from the tree of life, which is in the midst of the Paradise of God"* (Rev. 2:7). While overcoming does not secure salvation it does prove its validity.

If some in the assembly would not heed Paul's commands by apostolic authority, then they were to be avoided (v. 14). This social shunning would hopefully make unruly believers aware of their sin, feel the shame of it, and change their ways. This action was to be taken by individuals who were aware of the situation. Thus, the unruly were still to be considered brothers in the Lord while being shunned, and not as "heathen" who do not know the Lord (Matt. 18:17). Yet, if the offender continues in sin and is causing harm to the assembly a corporate act of excommunication may be required.

## The Closing Benediction (vv. 16-18)

Paul asks the Lord to bless the Thessalonians with His peace in all their affairs and that they would enjoy His presence (v. 16). Paul closes his letter by picking up the pen and adding his trademark benediction in his epistles: *"The grace of our Lord Jesus Christ be with you all. Amen"* (vv. 17-18).

# 1 Timothy

## Background

Timothy's mother, Eunice, and his grandmother, Lois, were Jewish (2 Tim. 1:5) and his father was Greek (Acts 16:1). It seems likely that the gospel ministry of Paul and Barnabas at Lystra during their first missionary journey had directly or indirectly led to young Timothy's conversion. While publicly preaching the gospel at Lystra, Paul healed a crippled man (Acts 14:8-10). Perhaps, Timothy, his mother or his grandmother had heard Paul's message. Timothy and Paul first met during Paul's second visit to Timothy's hometown of Lystra (Acts 16:1-2). At that time, Timothy was already a believer in the Lord and well-spoken of by the believers at Lystra. He joined the missionary team and accompanied Paul on the remainder of the second journey into Macedonia and Achaia. He would become one of Paul's most trusted disciples and co-laborers.

The biblical evidence suggests that Paul endured two distinct Roman imprisonments, since Paul was able to visit Troas, Corinth, and Miletus after release from his first incarceration (2 Tim. 4:13, 20). At the time 1 Timothy was written, Paul was between his first and last imprisonments. It is generally believed that Paul was becoming more aware of his impending demise at the hands of Nero when he penned this epistle. He realized he might not have another opportunity to impart advice and counsel to Timothy, his spiritual son, the man he considered most likeminded with respect to care of the saints (Phil. 2:20).

Paul had invested three years of ministry in Ephesus and in his absence, he directs and encourages Timothy to protect and edify the Ephesian saints. Besides the personal encouragement to Timothy, the epistle elaborates on the treatment of believing widows, church leadership, deacons, and the elderly, and how masters, youth, and, in general, all believers should behave in the body of Christ.

## Theme(s)

"Church Order." "The Faithful Ministry of God's Servant."

## Keywords

Keywords and phrases include: "good," "fight," "this is a faithful saying," "doctrine," "elder/bishop (overseer)," "deacon," "fables," "guard," "blameless," "heed," "Savior," "charge," and "content/contentment."

## Date

Likely written in 64 A.D. (perhaps from Greece), just before Paul's second Roman imprisonment.

## Outline

I. Introduction and the Value of Sound Doctrine (1:1-11).
II. Paul's Charge to Timothy (1:12-20).
III. Creation Order: Gender Roles (2:1-15).
IV. Church Order: Elders and Deacons (3:1-16).
V. A Good Minister Heeds and Lives Out Sound Doctrine (4:1-16).
VI. Specific Instructions for Widows and Elders (5:1-25).
VII. Beware of False Teachers and Be Godly With Contentment (6:1-21).

# 1 Timothy Chapter 1

## Salutation (vv. 1-2)

Paul opens his epistle to Timothy by stating that his apostleship had been received by a direct command from the Lord Jesus Christ, a matter that Church history bears out (Acts 9). Paul was an apostle, a "sent one" by Christ to preach the gospel to the Gentiles (Acts 9:15-16). This assertion would remind Timothy that Paul had not been appointed by men to his ministry, nor did he choose it as means of a livelihood. As mentioned later, Timothy also had a God-appointed ministry to perform. It is God who chooses our callings in the Body of Christ and equips us to do all that He wants accomplished for His honor and glory.

In reference to believers, the apostle next mentions that the Lord Jesus Christ is our Savior (by the commandment of God) and He is our hope (v. 1). This meant that the Lord was alive, and so believers could be assured of His return for them and that they would forever be with Him (1 Thess. 4:13-18). The title "Savior" appears twenty-four times in the New Testament. Ten of those references are in Paul's epistles to his spiritual sons Timothy and Titus. These men were called to a difficult ministry, so the apostle wanted them to keep their spiritual focus on their life-line to Heaven, their Savior, Jesus Christ, while they waited for His return.

Paul's salutation to his spiritual sons Timothy and Titus deviates from his traditional trademark greeting in his epistles to churches, in that he extends to them the additional aspect of God's mercy with His grace and peace (v. 2; Tit. 1:4). No doubt Timothy and Titus would appreciate the mercy of the Lord in fulfilling their difficult ministries.

The reference to Timothy being *"a true son in the faith"* may indicate that Paul had a part in leading Timothy to the Lord during his first visit to Lystra with Barnabas (Acts 14). However, Luke indicates that Paul and Paul's spiritual qualities were also evident in Timothy, Paul's disciple. Timothy was a true spiritual descendant of the Apostle (Acts 16:1-2).

The modifier "true" seems to indicate that Paul was referring to the quality of Timothy's character which had matured since he professed Christ. Timothy was exhibiting all the spiritual and moral qualities of Paul, his teacher, and thus was a true spiritual descendant of the apostle (Phil. 2:19-

20). Similarly, all those who exhibit Abraham-like faith in God's Word are referred to as sons of Abraham (Gal. 3:7-9).

First and Second Timothy and Titus are often referred to as the "Pastoral Epistles" but the Greek word *poimen,* typically rendered "shepherd" or "pastor" (once), is never found in these epistles. Paul does provide helpful counsel on how to shepherd God's people, but neither Timothy or Titus held any kind of clerical position in the Church or in any local church. They were not ordained "bishops" in the Church, as uninspired subscripts in the older versions of the KJV Bible suggest, but were engaged in itinerant ministry. Paul does instruct his spiritual sons as to the practical truths that should be taught to the churches to maintain Christ-honoring order in the local assembly, in the home, and while interacting with the unregenerate in the daily affairs of life.

## Confronting False Teachers (vv. 3-11)

Paul had been in Ephesus with Timothy and left him there while he went into Macedonia (v. 3). He instructs Timothy to exhort the brethren to continue in sound doctrine for godly edification while avoiding unprofitable distractions, such as focusing on fables and endless genealogies (v. 4). Some were using the Patriarchal genealogies along with heretical gnostic ideas, and applying their fanciful speculations to the Church Age. Obviously, such humanized fantasies are not found in Scripture. Some cults today (e.g., the Mormons) continue to emphasize the importance of such things.

The Greek verb *prosechein,* rendered *"give heed to"* in verse 4, means "to turn towards" something. The implication here, with the conjunction *mede* (rendered "nor"), is that Timothy was not to turn his mind to unprofitable discussions, but instead, to remain focused on that which was most important, the teaching of sound doctrine. The more we understand the truth, the easier it will be to spot what is phony. Learning more about what is wrong does not necessarily enhance knowing what is right.

> Federal agents don't learn to spot counterfeit money by studying the counterfeits. They study genuine bills until they master the look of the real thing. Then when they see the bogus money, they recognize it.
>
> – John MacArthur

The apostle then contrasts true and false teachers in verses 5-7. False teachers are motivated by greed, pride, money, etc., but the motivation and power of Timothy's ministry was to be genuine love from a pure heart, a

*1 Timothy*

good conscience, and untainted faith. These godly virtues reveal the true nature of the gospel message. "Having strayed" in verse 6 is derived from the Greek verb *astochesante* meaning "to deviate from." Because the false teachers had deviated from the truth, they also swerved away from these honorable evidences of resting in the truth. But to turn away from something means that one must also "turn aside" (*ektrepo*) to something else. The false teachers turned from the truth to unprofitable talk and vain jangling (v. 6). In contrast, Timothy's ministry was to avoid the dangerous pitfalls of these legalists by focusing on what would produce spiritual fruit and demonstrate the power of the gospel.

The issue was not that the Law was bad; in fact, it was good, holy, just, and spiritual (v. 8; Rom. 7:12-14), but the Law must be used "lawfully." Regrettably, these so-called Law-keeping teachers did not recognize the purpose of God's Law. God gave His covenant people His Law at Mount Sinai to show them their sinfulness in contrast to His holiness (Rom. 3:19-20). The purpose of the Law was to convince them that no matter how hard they tried, they could never perfectly keep God's Law. Consequently, no one can approach God through personal effort and doing good. In verses 8-11, Paul supplies examples of behaviors condemned by God's Law:

a. Lawless and insubordinate (v. 9): By denying God's authority over them, these rebels had created in their minds a god of higher authority, thus breaking the first and second of the Ten Commandments.

b. Ungodly, sinners, unholy, and profane (v. 9): By engaging in conduct that violated God's Law, God's name was being treated with contempt and disdain, thus breaking the third and fourth Commandments.

c. Murderers of fathers and mothers (v. 9): Disrespect of parents or neglecting their care was willful violation of the fifth Commandment.

d. Manslayers (v. 9): Murderers violated the sixth Commandment. This may include harboring hatred towards others (Matt. 5:22).

e. Fornicators and Sodomites (v. 10): Engaging in sexual relations outside of a marriage covenant between a man and a woman. This includes pre-marital sex, adultery, homosexuality and any other perversion prohibited by the seventh Commandment. Lusting in the heart for what is not lawful leads to these sins (Matt. 5:28).

f. Kidnappers (v. 10): Those who participate in the slave trade. Stealing people from their families broke the eighth Commandment.

g. Liars and perjurers (v. 10): Those who bear false witness, or twist and deny the truth, break the ninth Commandment.

h. Any other behavior that is contrary to sound doctrine and, thus, affronts the gospel message of Jesus Christ (vv. 10-11): Lusting for what is beyond God's will is prohibited by the tenth of the Ten Commandments. Believers must live out sound doctrine (i.e., remain in God's will) to represent Christ properly to the lost (Tit. 2:1).

Even if someone had a perfect day without sin, what would make up for offenses against God on every other day? The purpose of the Law was to show man his sin, to cause him to acknowledge his guilt before God, and to point him to God's only solution for sin – to be justified in Christ by faith (Gal. 3:24). Consequently, *"the Law is not made for a* [self] *righteous person"* (v. 9). Rather, it reveals God's holiness to cause awareness of sin. The Law is not dead (it actively reveals sin), but judicially speaking, believers have died to the Law (Rom. 7:4). This is how one uses the Law *lawfully*.

## Thankful for God's Grace (vv. 12-17)

Perhaps his mention of the zealous legalists to be confronted by Timothy in Ephesus reminded Paul of his own religious roots. Paul thanked the Lord Jesus Christ for calling him into gospel ministry and for enabling his service in response to his faithful obedience (v. 12; 1 Cor. 9:16-17). He was especially thankful to receive God's mercy and for the opportunity to please Christ, given the destructive nature of his former religious pride in which he had ignorantly blasphemed the Lord (v. 13).

As a Pharisee and Jewish zealot he arrested Christians, and saw them tried and put to death for what he felt was heresy against the Law. In so doing, he showed his disdain for Jesus Christ (Acts 9:1-2; Eph. 3:8; 1 Cor. 15:9). Nevertheless, since his conversion on the way to Damascus, he had faithfully obeyed the Lord Jesus despite suffering for doing so. As a result, he had experienced the exceeding goodness of Christ through many years of traveling hardships, staunch opposition, dreadful sufferings, and never-ending ministry to the Church (v. 14).

When Paul considered from where he had come and how Christ was now using him, he could adamantly avow: *"This is a faithful saying and worthy of all acceptance, that Christ Jesus came into the world to save sinners, of whom I am chief"* (v. 15). This is the first of five *"faithful sayings"* in the epistles to Timothy and Titus. Two of these statements include the additional phrase *"worthy of all acceptance"* (v. 15, 4:9). Verse

15 summarizes what Scripture declares concerning the Son of God's mission to earth as God's salvation Messenger and Message to condemned humanity; hence, this is obviously a "faithful saying."

That Christ *"came into the world"* means that He already existed prior to His incarnation in Mary's womb. Paul is affirming that God, the Creator of all things, personally came to the earth (Col. 1:16-17). As John elaborates more fully, any view that denies that the Son of God came from Heaven as incarnate Christ is the spirit of antichrist (1 Jn. 2:22, 4:2-3). Anyone who will not believe that Christ is the great "I Am" will perish in sin (John 8:24).

Having considered his formerly hopeless and miserable state and the heights of Heaven from which Christ came to save him, Paul declared that among sinners he was the foremost or chief of all. The Greek adjective *protos*, meaning "first" (in time) or "chief" (in rank), is combined with the present tense verb *eimi* to convey Paul's humble assessment of himself at that time. He was not saying that he was merely once a sinner, or that he had been the worst sinner, but even after years of faithful service, he felt that he was still undeserving of the grace that had been shown to him. From Paul's perspective, he was *"the least of the apostles"* (1 Cor. 15:9) and *"less than the least of all saints"* (Eph. 3:8).

The word "sinner" is generally associated with those who are actively living out the nature of Adam apart from Christ. Since Scripture does not address those justified in Christ by this title of condemnation, it is likely that Paul's present tense affirmation is more speaking of *time* (first) instead of *rank* (chief). Thus, he is implying his own salvation early in the Church Age as "a pattern" for the future salvation of *"those who are going to believe on Him* [Christ] *for everlasting life"* (v. 16). On this point, James Allen writes:

> While the RV "as chief" echoes the word of v. 15, the AV "first" may more accurately combine the two thoughts [of time and rank] …in the word *prōtos*. Not only would one who headed the line of sinners become a pattern of salvation but he would be the representative of a great host of "the ones coming to believe" (literal). There would be many throughout the subsequent centuries who would experience what he had experienced.[99]

In this respect, F. B. Hole suggests that Paul becomes a "pattern man":

> Not only a pattern *of* mercy but a pattern *to* believers. He exemplifies and shows forth the truth in its practical workings in the hearts and lives of the people of God. It is because of this that again and again in his epistles he calls upon his converts to be followers of himself.[100]

Additionally, Paul was the firstfruits of the nation of Israel brought to God through Christ. The apostle acknowledged this truth in Romans 11:1. His own salvation in Christ was one of five evidences presented in Romans 11 to prove that God was not finished with the Jewish people.

The way in which Paul obtained mercy in Christ was also "a pattern" of God's longsuffering means to save the Jewish nation in a future day. Reviewing Paul's conversion story recorded in Acts 9:1-6 illustrates his meaning. Israel's future conversion at the end of the Tribulation period occurs at Christ's Second Advent to the earth (Zech. 12:10-13:1, 14:4; Rev. 1:7). Likewise, on the road to Damacus, Paul actually saw Christ at the moment of his conversion. Paul's conversion pictures Israel's future acceptance of Christ as their Messiah when He appears to rescue them from the Antichrist. Hence, Paul's own salvation as the firstfruits of the Jewish nation foreshadowed the national Jewish harvest to come.

After contemplating God's abounding goodness to him through Christ, he cannot contain himself any longer, but bursts into a doxology: *"Now to the King eternal, immortal, invisible, to God who alone is wise, be honor and glory forever and ever. Amen"* (v. 17). "Glory" is derived from the Greek word *doxa*, which is where we get the English word "doxology." This is the first of three doxologies in the epistle.

To Christ, the King of ages, Paul would render honor and glory for all ages to come. Hamilton Smith writes: "Paul, when zealous for the law, was simply a man of the present age, seeking to maintain the age of the law. God is the 'King of the ages' who is acting in sovereign grace for His own glory throughout the ages of ages."[101]

As declared in the Song of the Lamb, sung by the redeemed in Heaven during the Tribulation period, the Lord Jesus Christ is *"Lord God Almighty"* and the *"King of the saints"* (Rev. 15:3). Paul's doxology emphasizes Christ's deity and authority: He is self-existent and thus incorruptible. He will never decline. He is invisible, distinct from and above His creation. Being divine, Christ alone is the source of all wisdom and deserves all the honor and the glory of His creation.

## Fight the Good Fight (vv. 18-20)

Paul now returns to the charge given to Timothy in verses 3-5 to confront false teachers (v. 18). Prophetic declaration had confirmed that Timothy's ministry at Ephesus was to rebuke false teachers. He was to remember these prophecies and be a good soldier who continued to engage the enemy in spiritual warfare, battle after battle. The Greek verb root *strateuo* is in the middle voice, and meant that it would be good for Timothy to choose on his own behalf to *"wage the good warfare."* A good soldier is one who does not get entangled by the cares of life, *"that he may please him who enlisted him as a soldier"* (2 Tim. 2:4). Timothy was not to please himself, rather Christ who enlisted him to be a soldier of the cross.

In contrast, two men, Hymenaeus and Alexander, are given as examples of those who did not engage in good warfare. Hymenaeus was not a common name and is probably the same man Paul refers to in his second epistle to Timothy who was propagating erroneous teachings (2 Tim. 2:17). There are four different Alexanders mentioned in Scripture, so although this man was probably known to the Ephesians, we cannot be sure that it is the same man mentioned in 2 Timothy 4:14.

These two men, evidently believers, shipwrecked their testimonies for Christ through theological error. Faith and a good conscience go together. Where one is absent, the other will be missing (v. 19). Even if we preach the truth accurately, but do not allow God's Word and the Holy Spirit to direct us into the secret life of godliness in Christ, we can suffer the same fate as these men.

"Having rejected" (*aposamenoi*) means to "deliberately thrust away." For preaching false doctrine, these two men, by apostolic authority were turned over to Satan for chastening. Excommunication of believers in sin was an act conducted by local churches, not by apostles (1 Cor. 5), but Paul did have God's authority to confront false doctrine and those who by teaching it blasphemed the Author of Truth. The purpose of this action was for them to learn, which extends, in principle, the opportunity for them to repent and return to the truth. This means chastisement for doctrinal error is in view and not condemnation for apostasy.

What does it mean to blaspheme and can a believer blaspheme God? Blasphemy is the act of disdaining God through speech and conduct. It is the absence of reverence for, and active irreverence towards, the Lord. When other people are present, it is conduct that causes them to think less of God. Although a true believer would not openly blaspheme the Lord in speech (1 Cor. 12:2-3), the same is accomplished through ungodly behavior. That is, disdain can be brought upon the Lord's name through ungodly actions (6:3-4; Prov. 30:9; Matt. 26:74). Paul was once a blasphemer, but through Christ, he obtained mercy for his past offenses against God (v. 13).

Men blaspheme what they do not know.

– Blaise Pascal

# 1 Timothy Chapter 2

## Pray for All Men (vv. 1-7)

This chapter begins with a fourfold exhortation concerning prayer. Paul knew the political situation in Rome was deteriorating. In July 64 A.D., likely just after this letter was written, Rome was burned by wicked Nero and Christians were being blamed. Both Timothy and those he taught were to be faithful to pray to God on behalf of *"all men"* (vv. 1-2).

"All men" is rendered from *anthropos*, which speaks of all humanity. Paul is not limiting his statement only to males. Certainly, prayer should be offered for kings and all in authority, no matter how evil they may be. The Apostle then speaks of four types of prayer to be offered on behalf of others:

a. Supplications: *Deesis* means a prayer or petition that presents specific needs to God.

b. Prayers: *Proseuchas* means "to draw near to God." In deep reverence we earnestly intreat the only One who is able to meet our need.

c. Intercessions: *Enteuxis* conveys the idea of having an intimate conversation with God to present the specific needs of others to Him.

d. Giving of thanks: *Eucharistias* expresses gratitude and thanksgiving for what God has done and blesses Him for who He is.

To behave with godliness and reverence while committing all things to prayer, especially during times of social upheaval, is a lifestyle that is good and acceptable to the Lord (v. 3). Although not all men will choose God, Paul highlights God's attitude towards the lost in verse 4. He is patient and longsuffering, wanting all men to repent and to trust in Him for salvation (2 Pet. 3:9). God does not delight in punishing the wicked, but His holy and just character demands that He must (Ezek. 33:11).

In verses 5-6, the apostle acknowledges that there is but a single means for condemned sinners to be reconciled with a holy God: *"For there is one God and one Mediator between God and men, the Man Christ Jesus, who gave Himself a ransom for all, to be testified in due time."* A prophet represents God to man and a priest represents man to God. The Greek word for mediator in verse 5, *mesites*, describes someone who is a go-between, or a reconciler who instigates peace between two opposing parties. This is what Christ, the God-Man, does for repentant sinners. Since His holy sacrifice on Calvary paid the ransom for all human sin (Heb. 2:9; 1 Jn. 2:2), Christ is able to restore to God all who will believe, enabling them to have peace with God and endowing them with the peace of God.

Paul then uses his own salvation and calling to demonstrate that God desires all men to be saved (v. 7). As a religious Pharisee persecuting the Church, not only was he the most unlikely person to receive salvation in Christ, but then Christ commissioned him as an apostle to preach the gospel to the Gentiles. God was not content that only Jews should be saved by Christ's work at Calvary. Rather the gospel was to go out from the Jews in Jerusalem to all nations (Acts 1:8). Paul was being faithful to his calling. He was preaching the true message of faith and truth to the Gentiles.

## Roles of Christian Men and Women (vv. 8-15)

The Greek word translated "men" in verses 1, 2, and 5 is *anthrōpos* and speaks of humanity. In verse 8, Paul switches to the masculine word *aner*, which has an article, hence, Paul is speaking of "the males." Paul instructs men (not women) *"to pray everywhere while lifting up holy hands."* The lifting of hands while leading God's people in prayer followed the practice of Jewish priests and kings (Lev. 9:22; 1 Kgs. 8:22). The lifting of holy hands to the Lord was an action that portrayed dependency (open needy hands) and transparency (the request of a pure heart; Ps. 24:4). On this point, Hamilton Smith writes:

> The Apostle is speaking of public prayer, and on such occasions the title to pray is restricted to men. ... Praying in public is not confined to elders, or to gifted men, for prayer is never treated in Scripture as a question of gift. It is men that are to pray and the only restriction is that a right moral condition is to be maintained. Those who lead in public prayer are to be marked by holiness, and their prayers are to be without wrath or reasoning. The man that is conscious of unjudged evil in his life is in no condition to pray.[102]

Paul then instructs women to wear discreet attire, to not call attention to themselves by elaborate hairdos or other superficial means (e.g., jewelry and expensive clothing), and to express godliness in doing good works (vv. 9-10). When gathered together, the sisters were not to lead, nor distract or stumble others by an outward show, but rather were to obey God's order for the genders by being submissive helpers. John Phillips summarizes Paul's teaching in verses 9-10 to believing women on the subject of modesty:

> Paul taught that women should avoid immodesty and "adorn themselves with modest apparel." The word translated "adorn" primarily means "to arrange, to put in order." Our English word *cosmetic* is derived from it. The corresponding noun refers to "a harmonious arrangement of things" and came to signify the world and the universe as divinely set in order. The word for *modest* means "orderly," or well-arranged. The word for *apparel* points to the flowing outer garment worn by kings and the members of the nobility. In summary, Paul conveys the idea that a woman should dress in ways becoming to a Christian. No room exists for immodesty on the one hand or flashy display on the other. Paul was too wise to go into details; he simply stated the principle.[103]

Obviously, women are to dress modestly and engage in godly conduct beyond the church meetings, just as men are encouraged to lead in prayer "everywhere." Clearly, Paul's instructions had a wider application than just when all the saints were gathered in one place for meetings of the church. William MacDonald explains that informal gatherings are also in view:

> Wherever a mixed group of Christians is gathered together for prayer, it is the men and not the women who should lead in this exercise. ... Neither is a woman to have authority over a man. That means that she must not have dominion over a man, but is to be in silence or quietness. ... The latter part of this verse is by no means limited to the local assembly.[104]

James Allen also addresses this subject by answering the question, "Where are the believers to pray?"

> "Everywhere" (AV) is better translated in RV by "in every place." ... He is simply saying "wherever it is you are meeting" (e.g., a rented hall, Acts 19:9, and believers' homes, Rom 16:5; 1 Cor 16:19; Col 4:15; Philem. 2). Neither "place of worship" in common speech nor "consecrated building" is either authorized by or contemplated in the NT (see Acts 17:24). The first mention historically of any special building being used for church gatherings does not come until the close of the third century when NT simplicity had been widely abandoned.[105]

Paul is addressing situations in which Christians might gather (for prayer, for Bible studies, for ministry events, etc.). For informal gatherings (when the entire church, with elders, have not come together), men should lead in teaching and in prayer, but in such settings, women could read Scripture, contribute thoughts to the study, and ask questions. Women are to be "settled down" and be in "quietness," the meaning of *hesuchia* rendered "in silence" in verses 11-12, and speech which does not assert leadership in the presence of men is permitted.

However, when the local church is gathered in one place, women are not to have any leading voice but are to "keep silent" (the meaning of *sigao* ensures that she is not to disrupt the male speaker in any fashion; 1 Cor. 14:33). In other words, there should never be a time when someone might think a woman was leading the assembly meeting. However, *sigao* does not mean total silence because both men and women should be participating in group singing and congregational *amens* (1 Cor. 14:16). Israel followed the same pattern when they came before the Lord in the Old Testament. God's order for the Church cannot be compromised but we should be as gracious as possible for unique occurrences. A distraught sister sharing an urgent prayer request is not going to kick God off His throne!

God's *home order* imposes no limitations on wives, mothers, or daughters praying or sharing scriptural thoughts with other family members. Hence, it can be difficult to discern proper spiritual etiquette for the audible participation of a sister in informal gatherings which include the presence of brothers who are not immediate family members. The standard of behavior appropriate for a particular set of circumstances may be determined by asking the question, to whom would I go if there was a problem? Should the answer be, to the head of the home, then *home order* applies. Thus, women could ask and answer questions, read Scripture, etc., but they should not have a leading role in the gathering. Similarly, if the answer is, the elders of the church, then *church order* applies. Yielding to Church Order is the safest approach, but is also the more restrictive.

We live in days in which the devil is relentlessly trying to undermine the rudiments of God's *creation order* in Genesis 1, including, "What is gender?" and "What is marriage?" Regrettably, many naming Christ today are falling prey to humanism which attempts to erode God's purposes. In 1 Corinthians 11, Paul explains how, in *creation order*, that which is created by another, or is created out of another, becomes the glory of the source: God created man from the dust of the ground, thus man represents God's glory. God created the woman from the side of the first man, thus the woman symbolizes man's glory. And the woman's long hair originates from her and is therefore her glory (1 Cor. 11:7). As William Kelly concludes, what originates from another should not rule over the originator (vv. 13-14):

> The apostle had already laid down most salutary principles in 1 Corinthians 11:1-16, where he had deduced that the man is woman's

head, and that the head uncovered became him, as the covered head became her. He is called of God to public action, she to be veiled, for man is not from woman but woman from man, though neither is without the other in the Lord, while all things are of God.[106]

God created both genders for specific purposes. He created the male to sacrificially lead and the female to submissively help. Humanity naturally devalues God and His purposes, but to preclude believers from doing so He has assigned a visible salute (symbolic actions) for the Church. This salute reminds us of His sovereignty and creation order (1 Cor. 11:3-7).

Paul demonstrates that the man is responsible in God's order to lead the woman by pointing to the order in which the man and the woman were created. First the man, Adam, and then from a portion of Adam's side, the woman. (v. 13; Gen. 2:21-23). Hence, she is identified as "woman," meaning that which came from the man. It was only after the Fall that the woman received the proper name, Eve. Furthermore, with respect to man's leadership role in relation to the woman, Paul provides evidence from the Fall of man in the Garden of Eden. Having been deceived by the devil to transgress God's prohibition concerning eating from the Tree of the Knowledge of Good and Evil the woman enticed Adam to also sin against God (v. 14). Paul states that Adam was not deceived; rather, he rebelled against God by an act of his will. Since God had made Adam head in the marriage relationship, He held Adam, not the woman, accountable for the transgression (Rom. 5:12-14).

Men and women will have the fullest lives when they yield to and rely on God for His best. While some saints will serve the Lord in singleness, most will marry. For those couples blessed with children, a wife will find the most satisfaction in helping her husband reach his potential (Gen. 2:18), nurturing her children (v. 15), and keeping her home a safe haven (Tit. 2:4).

The home is the woman's delegated sphere of authority (1 Tim. 5:14). But Paul's promise of "salvation" or "deliverance" is extended only to those who *"continue in the faith, love, and holiness, with self-control"* (i.e., those living for Christ). These sisters convey Christlikeness to their husbands, their children, and to all who enter their homes.

In the home, the wife is spared from being exposed to defiling filth and temptations. This protected refuge enables her to engage in the natural work that God has given her to accomplish as a wife and mother. This is the idea of being "saved in childbearing." Clearly, many women have tremendous abilities to do well in secular professions, but whenever we shun God's best plan for our lives, we will ultimately lose His blessing also.

# 1 Timothy Chapter 3

## Recognizing Church Elders (vv. 1-7)

The second "faithful saying" in the epistle affirms that those who desire to shepherd God's sheep are doing a noble work for the Lord: *"This is a faithful saying: If a man desires the position of a bishop, he desires a good work"* (v. 1). The Darby translation better captures the meaning of the text: *"The word is faithful: if any one aspires to exercise oversight, he desires a good work."* *Ei tis* is neuter and should be rendered "if any" or "if anyone." However, in the specific examination criterion given in verses 2-7, the gender is masculine, and only a man can be the husband of one wife. Only males were to be recognized as elders (always plural in the New Testament).

The male gender is to represent the glory of God in the Church (1 Cor. 11:4-7); thus, only men were chosen by Christ to be apostles, only men served as church elders (v. 2), as church deacons (vv. 11-12), and only the men were to lead in prayer and teach publicly (2:8-9; 1 Cor. 14:34-35).

It must be observed that verse 1 does not address the office of a church overseer (*episkopos*). Rather, the Greek word *episkopes* that appears in verse 1 speaks not of the office, but of the function of the office. Accordingly, Darby renders it "to exercise oversight." Unfortunately, most Bible translations speak of the church office of overseer (elder), rather than the important work of overseeing God's sheep.

Two Greek words are used in the New Testament to identify those men who hold a leadership position in the local church: *presbuteros* (elder; Acts 14:23; Tit. 1:5) and *episkopos* (overseer; Acts 20:28; 1 Tim. 3:1-2). *Presbuteros* and the related word *presbuterion* are used seventeen times to speak of church elders. This word is also used to speak of an older man (1 Tim. 5:1). *Episkopos* (with its verb form) is used six times in the New Testament to address the "overseers" (again referring to church elders). An *overseer* and *elder* were the same person (Acts 17:28, 20:17, 28; 1 Pet. 5:1-2). Unfortunately, the KJV and NKJV render *episkopos* as "bishop" which reflects the Anglican influence on the KJV translation several centuries ago (i.e., at that time the Church of England already had a hierarchical clergy system with bishops towards the top of the hierarchy).

There are two "desires" mentioned in verse 1. The first "desire" is derived from the verb *oregomai*, which means "to stretch one's self out in order to grasp something," like a sprinter stretching out for the tape across the finish line of a race. Because it is in the middle voice, it speaks of an internal desire that God places in an individual's heart to do the work. The second "desire" is derived from the verb *epithymei* which means "to turn on a thing" with intense focus, similar to coveting or lusting after something.

Verse 1 reveals the divinely-implanted desire a man must have to properly shepherd God's people. The idea is that the man who, out of pure motives, aspires to do the important work of oversight, is impelled by the inward prompting of God the Holy Spirit. If God has not called a man to shepherd God's sheep, he may do so anyway, but it will be drudgery to his soul and the sheep will know it. Younger men should avoid being formally involved in assembly oversight until they have had an opportunity to grow in maturity. However, if they are being raised up by the Holy Spirit (Acts 20:28), eventually they will want to assume this solemn responsibility. Those who are being raised up by the Holy Spirit will already be seen to be shepherding the Lord's people well before being recognized for oversight. It is the work, not the title that is crucial to the work.

Some have rejected the idea of recognizing church elders after the end of the Apostolic period of the Church. How then would the saints be able to obey the biblical commands to obey and respect elders in the assembly? To do so requires that there must be recognized elders, and that the saints know who they are (Heb. 3:7, 17). Moreover, it was the Holy Spirit who chose men for assembly oversight, not the apostles (Acts. 20:28). The apostles merely recognized those whom the Holy Spirit had already chosen.

The New Testament process of appointing elders is much the same as the process observed in the Old Testament in anointing David as king in Israel (2 Sam. 5:1-3): First, the people recognized that David had been chosen by God to shepherd the nation. Second, they recognized that David was actively shepherding the people even when Saul was king. Third, David was recognized by everyone and anointed king. There was a *divine call*, an *internal call*, and then a *recognized by all* process to anoint David king.

Similarly, the Holy Spirit chooses men from among the local flock to be elders (they are not to be hired in; Acts 14:23, 20:28). In verse 1 Paul asserts that such men will have an internal desire to do the work. Verses 2-7 provide the moral and spiritual criteria for recognizing men chosen by God, and who will already naturally be exercising a shepherding ministry among the Lord's people. Just as Titus was to guide the appointment of elders by this process on the island of Crete, Timothy needed to be equipped to do the same at Ephesus, or wherever the Lord directed him in ministry.

*1 Timothy*

Before reviewing the moral and spiritual criteria for recognizing church elders, we should realize two important things. First, the verb tenses in this section are in the "present" tense, meaning that the characteristics are not qualifications but ongoing qualities to be displayed in elders. The idea of qualification means fitness at a particular moment of time. However, an elder will be disqualified from office in the event that he ceases to display the requisite moral and spiritual attributes.

Second, an elder is not a perfect man, but he should be characterized by perfect qualities. The chief component of blamelessness should be evident in all aspects of an elder's life, but it does not mean that he is infallible or invincible. Paul provides the following qualities to recognize in those men whom God has chosen to be elders in the local church. The Greek root words for each quality help to better understand Paul's meanings (vv. 2-3):

**Blameless** (*anepilemptos*): Used as a negative participle signifying unaccused, and by implication irreproachable. The idea here is that an elder is "above reproach or accusation in character." He is unrebukable.

**Husband of one wife**: One wife modifies the noun "husband," meaning that an elder is to literally be "a one-woman man" or "a one-wife husband." This requirement would prohibit a polygamist from being recognized as an elder. If married, the elder must reflect God's best design for marriage, that is, a one-man-and-one-woman relationship. In application, the elder must be morally blameless in the conduct of his marriage. Holy living will be evident in the routine affairs of life, but especially so in the home.

**Temperate** (*nephalios*): This word means to be "sober-minded" or figuratively, to be circumspect. It only occurs two other times in the New Testament and is translated "sober" in both. An elder must not be rash in behavior or prone to debilitating excesses; he must be *level-headed*.

**Sober-minded** (*sophron*): The idea is to be "safe (sound) in mind," or self-controlled (moderate) in one's opinions or passions. *Sophron* is also translated "discreet," "sober," and "temperate." The elder uses discretion in handling people problems and is temperate in his use of authority.

**Of good behavior** (*kosmios*): The English word "cosmetics" is drawn from this word and includes the idea of "something put in order." An elder must be "orderly." The word is also translated "modest." It is found only one other time in the New Testament, where women are instructed to wear "modest" apparel (2:9). Elders must be respectable and sensible in conduct.

**Hospitable** (*philoxenos*): This word literally means "fond of guests." All saints are to be given to hospitality (Rom. 12:13; 1 Pet. 4:9). Yet an elder recognizes the value of shepherding work that can best be accomplished in the private setting of his home. Elders are raised up from among the sheep

(Acts 20:28) and are to remain among the sheep (1 Pet. 5:2-3).

This closeness highlights two important aspects of shepherding work. First, it allows the shepherd to observe the attitudes and behavior of believers to provide timely exhortation, encouragement, and, as necessary, reproof. Second, this transparent relationship allows the sheep to observe the elder's godly character, selfless motives, and ability to properly teach the Scripture. Hospitality provides an excellent opportunity to shepherd God's people. Accordingly, elders must *"be given to hospitality."*
Hospitality demonstrates Christian love to others in the home. Whether ministering, restoring, refreshing, or shepherding the Lord's people or serving strangers, hospitality is a huge blessing to others.

**Able to teach** (*didaktikos*): *Didactic* means to be "instructive." The elder must know, handle, and wisely apply the Word of God to correct, reprove, exhort, and encourage others. He rightly uses Scripture in love to impart knowledge and wisdom that promotes spiritual growth, and to detect and confront the spread of false doctrine (Tit. 1:9).

**Not given to wine** (*me paroinos*): The literal meaning of this word is "not staying near wine." *Me paroinos* occurs only one other time in the New Testament (Tit. 1:7) and is rendered the same way. This is not a prohibition against drinking wine, but the requirement does prohibit its abuse, or the abuse of any substance, for that matter. An elder cannot be preoccupied with or overindulgent in drinking wine. To shepherd God's people, he must be filled with the Holy Spirit, not controlled by something else.

**Not violent** (*me plektes*): An elder is not to be "a striker" or literally one who is "ready to give a blow." An elder cannot be hot tempered, prone to emotional outbursts, or quick to attack others. John Darby translates *me plektes* as "not addicted to contention."

**Not greedy for money** (*me aischrokerdes*; not in the Critical Text): This is a negative participle meaning "without covetousness or greedy ambitions." An elder is not motivated by wealth; he is satisfied with an honest income. He does not love or pursue money through foolish means, such as gambling, high risk-taking, and get-rich-quick schemes.

**Gentle** (*epieikes*): This word means "appropriate or mild." *Epieikes* is translated "gentle," "moderate," and "patient." The elder is to be kind, gracious, gentle, forbearing, yielding, amiable, and understanding.

**Not quarrelsome** (*amachos*): The KJV renders this word as "not a brawler." The idea is that an elder is not contentious; he does not argue or debate with others for emotional stimulation, but rather abstains from unprofitable discussions that do more harm than good.

**Not covetous** (*aphilargyros*): An elder does "not love money." An elder is not motivated by wealth in doing what is just, honest, and appropriate. The elder loathes the willful display of money and its lustful pursuit.

**One who rules and cares for his own house well**: Paul speaks of two important aspects. First, "rule" is drawn from *proistemi*, which means "to stand before in example and practice" (vv. 4-5). He practices what he teaches his children. His children willingly yield to their father's authority because his example makes it advisable to obey, his proven wisdom makes it natural to obey, and his unquestionable love makes it a delight to obey.

Second, with tender interest, he "cares for" his family. The Greek verb, *epimeleomai*, is used only one other time in the New Testament, to describe the care of the injured man by the good Samaritan (Luke 10:34-35). If a man cannot lead and provide for his own house, neither will he be able to oversee the church. This disqualification pertains to children living in the home. Adult children are accountable to the Lord for their own actions.

Next, Paul addresses two limiting factors to consider in recognizing elders in verses 6-7. First, he must not be a novice (i.e., not a new convert or young in the faith). The limitation has a warning associated with it: lest he be puffed up in pride. Spiritual maturity takes time and patience. There can be no rapid advancement to leadership in God's economy. The natural consequence of ignoring the warning is that the prideful person will be brought low. Satan was brought low when he was lifted up in pride. God resists the proud, but gives grace to the humble.

Second, an elder must have a good testimony in the community since he represents the local assembly and is under constant public scrutiny. The consequence of failure in this matter is firstly that the elder will *"fall into reproach"* (v. 7). The warning pertains to a loss of public testimony and the resultant stain on the name of Christ. Further, he will fall into *"the snare of the devil."* Spiritual leaders are a special target of the devil (e.g., Nehemiah, Peter, and Paul). If elders engage in activities in which Christ would and could not be present, they should not be surprised if the devil shows up to ensnare them in sin thereby bringing shame on Christ's name.

## Recognizing Church Deacons (vv. 8-13)

Having supplied helpful guidance in recognizing elders, those men chosen by the Holy Spirit to shepherd a local assembly, Paul turns his attention to the office of deacon. Acts records the appointment of seven *deacons* (literally "servants") in the church at Jerusalem in the early days of the Church Age. Deacons were selected by the assembly (after affirming the moral and spiritual criteria provided by the apostles; Acts 6:1-6). They were then confirmed by the church leadership for a specific church ministry.

In contrast, elders are chosen by the Holy Spirit (Acts 20:28) and then are to be confirmed by the saints in the local church. Elders were responsible to care for the flock (feeding, protecting, leading, etc.) entrusted to their care by God (1 Pet. 5:3). Deacons were appointed as needed to assist the elders by performing delegated tasks. Elders are essential to the maintenance of proper body-life in the assembly. Conversely, deacons may not be required in every assembly. The moral and spiritual requirements of a deacon are similar to those of an elder with the exception that a deacon did not have to be an able teacher of God's Word (v. 2; Tit. 1:9). The following criteria guides the appointment of deacons (vv. 8-13):

**Reverent** (*semnos*): The idea is that deacons must have dignity and an honorable character as demonstrated by their words and deeds.

**Not double-tongued** (*me dilogous*): Deacons must speak without spinning or distorting the truth. There must be consistent reporting of the facts concerning their ministry to eliminate confusion and possible distrust.

**Not given to much wine**: This constraint is similar to the limitation placed on elders, except not quite as stringent in that the word "much" is added. Whereas elders were *not to stay near wine*, the emphasis for deacons is *no excess wine*. Neither elders nor deacons were to be controlled by wine or any substance that would taint their public testimonies and impair their cognitive abilities in properly serving the Lord.

**Not greedy for money** (*me aischrokerdes*): This is the same word used to disqualify a man from being recognized as an elder. Elders and deacons must be satisfied with laboring with their hands for a just and honest income. They should not be involved in foolish or scandalous pursuits to make money or in squandering what the Lord has supplied for legitimate needs.

**Holding the mystery of faith with a pure conscience**: Obeying sound doctrine guards against greed, being double-tongued, and drunkenness.

**First tested and found blameless**: Before a man is recognized as a deacon, he must have demonstrated blamelessness and faithfulness in completing previously assigned tasks (1 Cor. 4:2). *Dokimazo*, rendered "tested," speaks of passing metals through fire to validate their quality. Likewise, consistent faithfulness through fires of adversity verifies valuable character to God. No one should be entrusted with the administration of the Lord's money unless they have first been proven to be faithful and above reproach in their own financial affairs (2 Cor. 8:22).

**Having reverent, non-slanderous, temperate, and faithful wives.** Verse 11 has been interpreted in various ways. As a deacon had to be the husband of one wife, the apostle is not suggesting that there should be female deacons in the local church. The lack of an article (i.e., "their" is implied) preceding *gunaikas* (women or wives) causes some translation difficulty. However, *hosautos* (rendered "even so") is used to introduce a new comparison not a new class of things) with what has just been outlined. That is, the character of elders, the character of deacons and the character qualities of the wives of deacons. It is evident that it is the wives of deacons that are spoken of in verse 11 and not a third church office, for it would be strange to introduce a third office of female deacons and then return to finish addressing the second office of male deacons (v. 12).

Thus, if married, a deacon must have a faithful wife who can assist him in performing his assigned duties. Like her husband, she has to be reverent (*semnos*), not a slanderer (*me diabolos* – not speaking like the devil), sober or temperate (*nephalios*), and faithful (*pistos*) in all things to which she puts her hand. Such a wife would be a tremendous blessing in helping her husband fulfill various aspects of ministry, especially when a woman's presence would add comfort and accountability to the situation.

**Husband of one wife**: The requirement to literally be "a one-woman man" or "a one-wife husband." This requirement was the same for elders and would prohibit a polygamist from being recognized as a deacon. If married, the deacon must reflect God's best design for marriage, that is, a one-man-and-one-woman relationship. The deacon must be morally blameless in conduct in his marriage.

**One who rules his children and his own house well**: The English word "rule" in derived from the Greek word *proistemi*, which was also used in verses 4 and 5 in relationship to the elder's home. It means "to stand before in example and practice." A deacon practices what he teaches his children. His children willingly yield to their father's authority. If a man cannot lead his own house, neither will he be able to serve in the house of God. This disqualification pertains to children living in the home. Adult children are accountable to the Lord for their own actions.

Paul closes this section on the appointment of deacons by stating that those who serve well will *"obtain for themselves a good standing and great boldness in the faith which is in Christ Jesus"* (v. 13). In reviewing the account of the first deacons appointed in Acts 6, we see, in the examples of Philip and Stephen, deacons who obtained a good standing and great boldness in the faith. Because they faithfully served Christ in Jerusalem as deacons, the Lord broadened and further empowered their ministry. Philip became an itinerant evangelist and Stephen an able teacher of God's Word. *"He who is faithful in what is least is faithful also in much"* (Luke 16:10).

## Conduct in the Church (vv. 14-16)

Paul hoped to soon be reunited with Timothy in Ephesus. However, if he was delayed, he wanted his spiritual son to know how believers should conduct themselves in the House of God (vv. 14-15). This includes how elders and deacons, and their wives should behave in performing their appointed duties. It was good that Paul provided Timothy these insights, as there is no evidence that the apostle rejoined Timothy in Ephesus.

Paul's next statement is not limited to elders, deacons, or their wives. Paul charges all believers (not just Timothy) as to how they should behave in *the House of God*. The Household of God refers to the saints themselves (Eph. 2:19). Early believers continued in activities such as teaching, prayer, fellowship, and the Lord's Supper (Acts 2:42). But there is a definite article before the word "fellowship" in verse 42. Thus, believers are to enjoy one specific fellowship – their communion with Christ. The Church is God's instrument to teach all those who witness its behavior that God is Holy. Indeed, *the Church of the living God is the pillar and ground of the truth*.

Paul closes the chapter by declaring an indisputable fact pertaining to the Lord Jesus Christ and the ministry to which he and Timothy were called to: *"Great is the mystery of godliness: God was manifested in the flesh, justified in the Spirit, seen by angels, preached among the Gentiles, believed on in the world, received up in glory"* (v. 16). The *mystery of godliness* relates to the incarnation of the Son of God to fulfill His redemptive mission on earth on behalf of humanity. Christ is fully man, but He is holy humanity untainted by sin. This differs from our nature which was initially innocent, but by Adam's rebellion became condemned humanity.

Because there is no definite article before "flesh." This verse is better rendered, *"God has been manifested in flesh."* God was manifest "in flesh," not "in the flesh." The Lord Jesus was veiled in flesh (Heb. 10:20). He was made flesh (John 1:14), but was not in the flesh. The nature of His flesh did not rule Him; it served Him. The Lord was holy humanity (Luke 1:35).

The Lord Jesus was justified in Spirit. The Holy Spirit justly declared the glory of Christ in incarnation, baptism, transfiguration, resurrection, and ascension (e.g., Matt. 3:15-17; Rom. 1:4). Christ was *"seen by angels"* at His birth, when tempted by Satan, while praying in Gethsemane, at His resurrection, and ascension (Matt. 28:2). He was preached to the Gentiles as part of the Great Commission to take the gospel message to the uttermost part of the world (Acts 10:34; Rom. 10:18). He was received up into glory to the right hand of God the Father in Heaven. Hence, in addition to His intrinsic glory and moral glory, Christ, through faithful obedience, has acquired a positional glory (Luke 24:51-53; Heb. 1:3).

# 1 Timothy Chapter 4

### The Coming Apostasy (vv. 1-5)

The phrase *"the Spirit expressly says"* does not mean that only some of Paul's writings were divinely inspired. Rather, Paul is adding emphasis to that which he is about to declare, namely, that in the future day many will depart from biblical Christianity. (v. 1). The *"latter times"* refers to a period after the Apostolic Age, but before the close of the Church Age. Paul often refers to "the faith" in his letters to Timothy. This phrase relates to the central body of truth given to the Church by apostolic authority (Jude 3).

Paul informed the church at Thessalonica that this widespread apostasy by the *professing* Church must occur before the Antichrist is revealed in the Tribulation period (2 Thess. 2:3). To *"depart from the faith"* meant that many identifying with Christ in name only would withdraw or revolt in such a way that God-inspired truth would be replaced by demonic deception. In the end time, false teachers speaking *"lies in hypocrisy"* will abound.

The word "hypocrisy," derived from the Greek word *hypokrisis*, was used to describe someone acting on the theatrical stage. These actors often wore masks to hide their true identities, allowing them to pose as someone that they were not. Cults today often claim family values, social benefits, and moral good deeds but regardless of how benign they appear to be, they are founded in false doctrine. Literature picturing a peaceful family or tranquil earthly scenes is standard, but Christ is not present in any of it because He is truth and cannot be present in a lie. The explosion of false cults began about 1830 A.D. and was followed by a surge of New Age Religions in the 1960s. These continue to deceive the masses to this day.

These "latter day" deceivers will be so given over to demonic deception that lying will no longer bother their consciences. Having any part of one's body *"seared with a hot iron"* (literally "cauterized"; Darby) would result in widespread nerve damage with a loss of functionality and sensitivity. These false teachers will be so given over to demonic doctrines that they will become numb to the truth and their own guilt before God.

Although many false teachings will be circulating at the curtain call of the Church Age, Paul highlights two erroneous doctrines that will then be evident at that time. First, some will proclaim that it is wrong, or at least less than spiritual, to marry. This, despite the fact that in creation God instituted marriage for the well-being of family life (v. 3; Gen. 2:18-25). Under the pretext that celibacy is a more spiritual lifestyle, false teachers will undermine the importance of the ideal human relationship instituted by God to promote human companionship and procreation (Gen. 1:28). The writer of Hebrews proclaims, *"marriage is honorable"* (Heb. 13:4).

We live in days in which the devil is relentlessly trying to erode the rudiments of God's Genesis 1 creation order. Just as he deceived the woman in Eden with subtle questions, so he implants questions, such as the following today, as subtle devices to trap the unwary: What is life? What is the origin of life? What is gender? What is marriage? What is work? Regrettably, many who identify with Christ today fall prey to the undercurrent of humanized religion which craves to reverse God's designs.

Second, Paul stated that in the latter days, to enhance spirituality, some will forbid the eating of certain foods or perhaps any food, for extended periods of time (vv. 3-5). Some contemporary religious movements forbid consumption of meat, and yet God sanctioned the killing of animals to provide meat as a human dietary provision (Gen. 9:2-3; Lev. 11; Acts 10:14-15). The Lord affirmed that it was not what went into the mouth, but what came out of it (a reflection of the heart) that defiled a person (Matt. 15:11).

An individual conscience, rather than any legalistic dietary laws, should guide what we eat (Rom. 14:14, 23). When *"those who believe and know the truth"* pause to thank God for the food He has provided, we can be sure that by what we ingest He will strengthen our bodies to serve Him. False teachers fail to do this because they do not heed the truth. Giving God thanks for what we are about to eat reminds us that we are to constantly acknowledge our dependence on Him for every aspect of life.

## Serving Christ Despite the Coming Apostasy (vv. 6-16)

Given the coming apostasy, Timothy and every teacher of God's Word should remind the saints of the fundamentals of the faith to prevent them from being tricked by false teachers (v. 6). Additionally, *"a good minister of Jesus Christ"* must himself be *"nourished in the words of faith."* It is noteworthy that the word "pastor" (*poimen*) is not used in Paul's letters to Timothy. Yet, the concept of being a faithful "minister" of the Lord (v. 6) who "serves" others appears often (3:10, 13, 6:2; 2 Tim. 2:24). Timothy was to be a servant engaged in faithful ministry to the Church although he did not hold any form of church office. Paul's letters to Timothy and Titus are better labeled "Ministerial Epistles," rather than "Pastoral Epistles."

Sound doctrine is not just simply head-knowledge; it is to be lived out in the believer's life every day (Tit. 2:1). Hence, Timothy was not to waste time refuting silly fables. Instead, he was to ignore them and be exercised to godliness according to sound doctrine (v. 7). Just as exercise is profitable to the physical body, deeply contemplating, rightly knowing, and living out God's Word is profitable for edifying the spiritual man (v. 8). However, because the body is temporal and bodily exercise has a limited benefit *"for the life that now is,"* doing that which would strengthen the eternal inner man is far more beneficial for *"that which is to come."*

Living out Christ's life now in resurrection power is a foretaste of the eternal bliss and joy to come in Christ's presence in Heaven and is therefore a *"faithful saying and worthy of all acceptance"* (v. 9). This is the third such statement in the epistle and it gives parenthetical approval to the precept in verse 8. This is the believer's calling in Christ, which means that laboring in sorrow and suffering reproach is inevitable in the Lord's work (e.g., Jer. 20:18). Yet, saints must see past these things to the eternal reality.

As Paul explains in Romans 8, the believer's eternal inheritance can be realized only after a season of suffering during our earthly sojourn (v. 10). Those who are Christ's will gladly live for Him, despite the fact that this invites the world's hatred and persecution (John 15:18-20). Paul told Timothy that all who live godly for Christ will suffer persecution (2 Tim. 3:12). But the apostle also explains that the joy, the fellowship in Christ, and the purification that results from undergoing righteous suffering will more than compensate for all the ills endured for Him in this world.

Every believer will enjoy the Lord in eternal bliss and glory, but some will appreciate the heavenly experience more than others. Paul knew the tie between suffering for Christ now and reigning with Him later. When Paul weighed all his troublesome experiences against his future with Christ, he concluded: *"For I consider that the sufferings of this present time are not worthy to be compared with the glory which shall be revealed in us"* (Rom. 8:18). As shown through the Lord's own example of living for God, suffering precedes glory, and this is honorable to God (1 Pet. 2:20-24). The Lord is watching and He knows the quality of our work and will reward it abundantly in a coming day (Heb. 6:10-12; 1 Pet. 4:12-14).

If believers hope *"in the living God, who is the Savior of men, especially to those who believe,"* then the disappointing world of passing things will have no ill effect on our spiritual joy and faithfulness. William MacDonald explains what Paul means by God being *"the Savior of all men"*:

> **God** is **the Savior of all men** in the sense that He preserves them in the daily providences of life. But He **is** also **the Savior of all men** in the

sense pointed out previously – that He has made adequate provision for the salvation **of all men**. He is the Savior of **those who believe** in a special way because they have availed themselves of His provision. We might say that He is the potential Savior of all men and the actual Savior of those who believe.[107]

It was with this mindset that Timothy was to live out his days on earth and was to inspire other Christians to do the same by sound doctrine (i.e., by being a good example of what he taught others from Scripture; v. 11).

Assuming that Timothy was about eighteen to twenty years of age when he joined Paul during his second missionary journey in 50 A.D. (Acts 16:1-4), Timothy would then have been in his mid-thirties. This meant that Timothy would probably have been significantly younger that most of the Ephesian "elders" to whom he would be ministering. Hence, Paul exhorts his spiritual son, *"Let no one despise your youth"* (v. 12).

Paul was not instructing Timothy to assume a superior attitude over the saints among whom he was serving, but neither was he to allow someone to disparage the value of his teaching because of his age. The best way to accomplish this was for Timothy to be a godly example to all believers. Such a lifestyle would minimize opportunities for accusations against him that might cast doubt on the integrity of his ministry. A blameless testimony disarms the devil. In verse 12, Paul commends several spiritual disciplines to Timothy. These of course, are also vital for us.

**In word**. To properly edify others, a believer's speech should always be in truth, in love, and be necessary (Eph. 4:15, 29).

**In conduct**. The demeanor and behavior of believers is to reflect Christ's character in all that we do. Our walk and not just our talk is in view.

**In love**. Believers must be motivated by the love of Christ in all they do (i.e., to declare His love to others and our love to Him by obedience).

**In spirit**. Believers are to have a sound mind which exhibits the excitement and power of knowing and pursuing the Lord Jesus Christ.

**In faith**. Believers are to trust God and constantly live out true doctrine.

**In purity**. Believers are to be morally clean in action and in character.

While serving the Lord at Ephesus, Timothy was to encourage the saints "to reading" the Scripture, and "to exhortations" and "to doctrine" (teachings) of the Scripture. As there is an article before all three of these activities, each was distinct and important for wholesome spiritual growth.

Next, Paul exhorts his spiritual son to not neglect the ministry to which he had been called, and for which he had been equipped: *"Do not neglect the gift that is in you, which was given to you by prophecy with the laying on of the hands of the eldership"* (v. 14). In the early days of the Church

Age, the apostles laid their hands on Jews and Samaritans who had believed the gospel message so that they might receive the Holy Spirit (Acts 6:6, 13:3). This act showed Jews and Gentiles that there was only one gospel, one Spirit, and one Church. Following the pattern of the Old Testament, the laying on of hands in the New Testament was also used for consecration to a particular ministry (e.g., elders, ministers, deacons, etc.; v. 13, 5:22; Acts 13:3). There is no example of apostles imparting spiritual gifts to others by the laying on of hands; the Holy Spirit accomplished this (1 Cor. 12:11).

Paul reminded Timothy that his ministry had been identified by apostolic authority. Consequently, it was not to be neglected (v. 14). As he progressed in holiness and exercised his spiritual gift, he would benefit personally, and there would be greater ongoing benefit to the Church. Later, Paul exhorted, *"I remind you to stir up the gift of God which is in you through the laying on of my hands. For God has not given us a spirit of fear, but of power and of love and of a sound mind"* (2 Tim. 1:6-7).

It is evident that Timothy had answered the call to salvation, the call to sanctification, and the call to service. Paul told the church at Philippi that there was no other man as likeminded with him as Timothy. Accordingly, there was no question in Paul's mind that Timothy would properly care for them when he arrived (Phil. 2:20). Timothy had learned that the greatest use of his life was to expend it for Christ, for only then would he gain something that would count for eternity. This realization motivated Charles Spurgeon to write this letter to his son concerning the importance of missionary work:

> I should not like you, if meant by God to be a missionary, to die a millionaire. I should not like it, were you fitted to be a missionary, that you should drivel down to a king. What are all your kings, all your nobles, all your diadems, when you put them together, compared with the dignity of winning souls to Christ, with the special honor of building for Christ, not on another man's foundation, but preaching Christ's Gospel in regions far beyond.[108]

Timothy was to meditate on all that his spiritual father had admonished him to consider so that the stamina of a sanctified life would appear to everyone (v. 15). He was to especially *heed* and *continue in* sound doctrine because in doing so would save himself from the pitfalls of fleshly lusts and satanic entrapments (v. 16). His conduct and teaching would inspire others to follow his example, thus also saving them from the power of sin.

Like Timothy, all believers are called to holy living, to spiritual maturity, and to faithful service. These aspects cannot be separated from each other. Believers will accomplish their ministry within the Body as they continue to grow spiritually in holiness, and to exercise their spiritual gifts.

# 1 Timothy Chapter 5

## Proper Care and Respect of Various Believers (vv. 1-16)

At Ephesus, Timothy would be serving a broad spectrum of believers, young and old, men and women, and saints from different ethnic and social backgrounds. In the local assembly, as in any family, respect is warranted for differences in age and gender. This chapter supplies counsel in handling these various personal interactions.

As a younger man, it would be natural for Timothy to get impatient with older men who might not react as quickly or in the way he would appreciate; regardless, he was to respect them as fathers (v. 1). Likewise, older women were to be treated with tender care as he would his mother (v. 2). Timothy, being a spiritually-minded man, would naturally attract the attention of unmarried believing women, but Timothy was to treat his spiritual sisters with the same wholesome respect he would have for a natural sister (v. 2). His conduct with younger women was to be blameless and above reproach.

At the time that this letter was written, it was common for younger women to marry older established men, and because the life expectancy of a laboring man was fairly short there were many widows among the population. Showing kindness to needy orphans and widows is upheld throughout Scripture as a behavior well-pleasing to the Lord. However, there needed to be a practical assessment of the matter since not all Christian widows needed to be supported by the Church. For example, younger women could work with their hands to provide for their needs.

In verses 3-16, the apostle provides counsel for determining if a woman *"is really a widow"* ("a widow indeed" KJV), that is, a widow truly deserving of financial support from the Church (v. 16).

- The widow has no relatives to take care of her (v. 4). Piety begins at home, and children and grandchildren are to repay "their parents." The Greek word translated "their parents" is *prognonois*, which means "forebearers" (i.e., their ancestors; see 2 Tim. 1:3).

- The widow lives alone, is given to serving the Lord, and only has the Lord to look to for support (v. 5).

- The widow is a pure woman, not having a luxurious or self-gratifying lifestyle (this would obviously include lascivious behavior; v. 6).
- The widow must be a believer as evidenced by a blameless life (v. 7).
- The widow not having family support must be sixty years of age or older and have been a faithful wife to one man (v. 9).
- The widow not having family support, must be known for her previous good deeds during the days of her prosperity (such as hospitality, nurturing children, and selflessly serving others), which was again proof of her sincere faith (v. 10).

Paul suggests that a widow *"who lives in pleasure is dead while she lives"* (v. 6). This speaks of engaging in behavior which is outside of God's will; such works have no value to God (Luke 15:24; Rev. 3:1). Hence, a believer may be physically alive, but out of fellowship with God. Despite having eternal life, his behavior appears as one who is spiritually dead. This is why John states that a true believer does not *continue* in sin (1 Jn. 3:9).

The apostle also has strong words for those who do not properly care for those in their own house. Their actions make a mockery of the Christian faith which is characterized by the demonstration of selfless love (vv. 8, 16). Even the heathen care for those in their own family, so when a Christian neglects to provide for and protect those in his own family (including his widowed mother or mother-in-law), it shames the name of Christ.

Younger widows were not to be placed on a list to receive long-term support from the church for three main reasons. First, Paul surmises that natural sexual and maternal urges may cause younger widows to seek remarriage, instead of serving the Lord in singleness (vv. 11-12).

Remarriage to a believer would be completely acceptable (1 Cor. 7:39), but to abandon Christ's care for her in widowhood by seeking marriage out of mercenary motives would dishonor the Lord. This offense would be even worse if the widow were to marry a non-believer for sensual or financial reasons. Some commentators suggest that Paul had in mind a widow who made an untruthful promise to remain unmarried and serve the Lord for the sole purpose of taking financial support from the church. However, this seems doubtful and is certainly devoid of biblical and historical support.

Rather, it is suggested that the young widow's offense is not towards the church for a broken pledge, but to Christ, for misplaced devotion. That is, the widow had *cast off her first faith.* Her previous loyalty to and sufficiency in Christ had been replaced by a lower and earthly affection. It was not that she had renounced her faith in Christ, but she had forgotten the

Object of her first love and in whom she had security. In doing so she would come under judgment, just as the Lord threatened the church at Ephesus for the same offense (Rev. 2:4). Thus, eternal condemnation of the widow is not in view in this scenario. William Kelly clarifies what was entailed in the *casting off of first faith*:

> The young widows are judged according to their relationship to Christ. They of all perhaps might have been expected from their personal experience of sorrow to feel that the time is straitened, and that the fashion of this world passes (1 Cor. 7:29-31). But they lose sight of Christ and His dealings with them and look out for themselves. Instead of seeking to please Him, they wax wanton against Him, and cannot rest without a return to that estate which had just closed for them. Nothing of vows or of office appears here, but what became a younger widow looking for Christ, as all saints are called to wait for Him.[109]

The second reason why younger widows were not to be on the church's support list is explained in verse 13. If the Church supported younger widows, then there would be no necessity for them to work with their hands to provide for themselves. Such idleness could result in these women becoming gossipers and busybodies as they wander from house to house.

The third reason it was preferrable for younger widows to remarry and not be a financial burden to the Church was so that they could fulfill the natural ministry for which God created the woman. That is, to be a companion to her husband, to bear and nurture children, and to keep an orderly home (v. 14; Tit. 2:4). The home is her sphere of authority. If she manages the home well, she prevents Satan from gaining an "opportunity" (literally, a military term meaning "a beachhead") to cause disorder and frustration that could result in the breakdown of the household.

Paul notes that if a younger widow does not remarry or if she rejects God's will for her life, she may abandon her faith altogether, as some in Ephesus had apparently already done (v. 15). When we do not rest in God's best we ultimately end up with less. God always gives His best when we leave the choice with Him.

Paul hoped that these instructions would assist the church to properly care for widows deserving support. Adhering to his instructions would also reduce the possibility that church fellowship, and the spiritual growth of saints would be hindered by carnal thinking. The Body of Christ should willingly support "widows indeed." Extended family should not neglect the care of their widowed loved ones. Younger widows, if possible, should seek to remarry (v. 16).

## Proper Care and Respect of Church Elders (vv. 17-25)

The remainder of the chapter pertains to church elders. The apostle states, *"Let the elders who rule well be counted worthy of double honor, especially those who labor in the word and doctrine"* (v. 17). "Who rule" is derived from the Greek verb *proestotes*, a participle, and conveys the meaning of "standing before" in rank and by implication, in practice, hence *lead by example*. As church elders have equal authority, the idea is that those who are "first among equals in leading" are deserving of double honor.

Honor would certainly mean respect, but also financial compensation (e.g., Matt. 15:4-6). This would certainly be appropriate for those elders who devote themselves to studying and teaching God's Word so as to properly nurture God's people. There would be an obvious investment of time by an elder to accomplish this important work, which means a loss of opportunity for him to labor to provide for his family's needs. Accordingly, such servants should willingly be compensated (e.g., Gal. 6:6).

Paul supplies two Scripture references to further substantiate why elders who lead well, especially those laboring in doctrine, deserve financial support. First, he quotes Moses who stressed the fair and kind treatment of beasts of burden: *"You shall not muzzle an ox while it treads out the grain"* (Deut. 25:4). An ox that was serving its master by trampling stalks of grain on the threshing floor in preparation for winnowing should be permitted to eat some of the stalks. Likewise, those laboring for the kingdom of God were worthy of financial support from those who had benefitted from their preaching (v. 18; 2 Cor. 9:9-10).

Second, Paul quotes Christ's teaching that a laborer is entitled to a portion of the fruit of his labor (Luke 10:7). Although elders might not work in a vineyard or on a threshing floor, they are entitled to compensation for their labor in preparing and sharing from God's Word that which is necessary to edify and protect His saints.

Besides financially caring for church leaders, Paul also states that they should be protected from gossip, slander, and unjust criticism: *"Do not receive an accusation against an elder except from two or three witnesses"* (v. 19). The devil, the world system he controls, and our flesh nature oppose the things of God (Gal. 5:17). We also realize that *"the wrath of man does not produce the righteousness of God"* (Jas. 1:20). Believers should want to edify each other, not cause harm by operating in the flesh for personal gain. Those who lead God's people will be special targets of the enemy and of unruly saints, so they need to be zealously protected by God's people.

Because the devil hates Christ and seeks to destroy His Church, elders, who represent Christ's authority in the assembly, must be protected.

Believers are to not even listen to an accusation about a church elder unless there is irrefutable evidence available from reliable witnesses (v. 19). To do so simply permits the devil to mess with the minds of the saints, and we do not need his influence for we tend to easily think negatively about others. However, if there is a legitimate matter of sin, the situation is not to be hidden (even if there is repentance); it must be made public (v. 20). Congregational rebuke of an elder who has failed, reinforces in the minds of the saints the standard of holy conduct expected by God of His people. It makes it evident that He is no respecter of persons in addressing matters concerning sin in the body of Christ.

Just as God the Father, the Lord Jesus Christ and the elect (holy) angels are associated only with righteous judgments, Paul charges Timothy to operate according to the same high standard (v. 21). While executing his ministry and especially in handling matters of sin, Timothy was to show no partiality or prejudice in judgment. Many churches have been harmed because prominent family members or relatives of elders were treated with leniency instead of receiving just consequences for sins committed. God does not behave this way, and neither should His people.

Next, Paul instructed Timothy to not be hasty in recognizing church elders and perhaps others for particular ministries. *The laying on of hands* during the Church Age followed the Old Testament practice of publicly identifying those who were being consecrated for service (e.g., Num. 8:10). Men of unknown character, despite their portfolios and business experience, should never be recognized for a ministry or a church office. Let us not appoint unfamiliar, untested men to positions of responsibility.

Verse 23 seems to be disconnected from the verses before and after on the proper care and protection of church elders. But perhaps Paul was anticipating that Timothy's difficult ministry in Ephesus or constant exposure to contaminated drinking water would adversely affect his stomach, causing him gastro-intestinal problems. Regardless, Paul counseled his spiritual son to drink a little wine to settle his stomach.

The final two verses of the chapter link back to the warning in verse 22. All men will be judged eventually (believers and unbelievers). Timothy, and we too, can be fooled into recognizing a man as an elder, but in time, God's people will see his true character. Paul's exhortation is wise. By not making quick judgments in such matters, in the end fewer mistakes are made.

It is good to remember that any man who has been truly called by God will be engaged in shepherding God's people whether or not he has been publicly recognized as an elder. It is best to wait to recognize such a servant until it is blatantly obvious to all that this man is God's provision for us.

# 1 Timothy Chapter 6

## Bondservants and Masters (vv. 1-2)

Although the Bible does not endorse slavery, it does place limits on its practices (Lev. 25:39-42; Deut. 15:12). As Christianity spread through the Roman Empire, slaves and masters were becoming Christians and brethren in Christ. This created a difficulty, since believers in Christ should mutually love, respect, and serve each other, but slavery did not permit such social liberty. How should believers who were slaves behave? What attitude should they have towards unbelieving masters who were often brutal?

Paul offers wisdom to answer these questions in verses 1-2. Slaves were to honor those in authority over while laboring with faithful dignity as unto the Lord. Godly submission is learned through a proper response to authority. Willing obedience was a good testimony to slave masters of the grace of God in the lives of slaves. Slaves who had believing masters were not to think negatively of them, for they all were positionally one in Christ (Gal. 3:28). Social standing does not affect spiritual standing.

## False Teachers and the Love of Money (vv. 3-10)

In verse 3, Paul makes it clear that knowing and yielding to *"wholesome words"* (i.e., sound doctrine) produces godliness in the life of a believer (2 Thess. 3:6; Tit. 2:1). Sound doctrine is not merely head knowledge. It must be lived out. This meant that false teachers could easily be spotted, since their lack of godliness meant that the doctrines that they were teaching were flawed (Matt. 7:15-20; 2 Pet.2:1-17).

Such men know nothing about spiritual life because they are blinded by pride (v. 4). Instead of spending time searching for what is important to God, they waste time debating minor points, preferences, and unresolvable issues for the sake of promoting themselves. Their wrangling does not promote godly living. Rather, it stirs up their flesh to envy and strife. They rail and have evil suspicions concerning others. Although destitute of the truth, these corrupt men are proficient in the sue of religious jargon and in using social hot buttons for their personal financial gain (v. 5). Paul warns Timothy to withdraw from anyone who is using gospel ministry for personal profit.

Rather than being negatively stirred up by those hoping to profit by living in the flesh, Paul exhorts Timothy to be content (satisfied) with living a simple and godly life: *"Godliness with contentment is great gain"* (v. 6). Wealth, itself, does not corrupt good character, but yearning for the carnal gratifications it offers does. Paul says it is better to have a contented mind settled in godliness than to pursue a satisfaction that wealth can never provide.

> When wealth is lost, nothing is lost; when health is lost, something is lost; when character is lost, all is lost.
>
> – Billy Graham

All that we have is from the Lord and is given to us to enjoy life by living for Him (1 Cor. 4:7): *"We brought nothing into the world, and it is certain that we can carry nothing out"* (v. 7). The Lord is faithful to provide for our necessities, but pursuing more than this leads to discontentment and to complaining against God. The Greek word *skepasmata* in verse 8 is translated "clothing" but has a broader meaning of "a covering." Hence it includes both clothing for the body and shelter from the elements. Believers are to be content with the necessities of life (i.e., food, clothing, and shelter). They are not to strive to be rich but are to pursue God in personal holiness.

Sadly, many people are neither content nor thankful for God's provision for them. They often covet money and err from the faith (v. 9). If we value things, we will foolishly abuse people, but if we value people, we will wisely use things. If God wanted us to have more than we have, He would gladly give it to us. God wants us to have that which is best for us: *"Every good gift and every perfect gift is from above, and comes down from the Father of lights"* (Jas. 1:17). Being thankful for God's provision defeats the temptation to be dissatisfied (Phil. 4:11-12).

Paul suggests that every ungodly deed we can imagine has been pursued for the love of money (v. 10). The root of this sin seems to be dissatisfaction, with selfishness and pride trailing close behind. When we are not content with what we have, we murmur against God. Murmuring is muttered, vague complaints of which God is fully aware. Complaining results when we look backwards (comparing where we are to where we came from) and downward (with an earthly appraisal), instead of gazing Heavenward (trusting in God's character) and forward (with expectation as to what He will do). Going through life while looking backward and downward leads to discontent and sorrow, while gazing Heavenward and forward (i.e., walking with God), fills the soul with joyful confidence about tomorrow.

## O Man of God, Fight the Good Fight (vv. 11-16)

Only twelve men in the Old Testament, four of whom are unnamed, are identified as a "man of God." Timothy is the only servant of the Lord referred to by that name in the New Testament (v. 11). However, the Greek word for "man" is *anthropos* meaning "humanity." This means that all believers become *men and women of God* if they permit Scripture *to thoroughly equip them for every good work* (2 Tim. 3:16-17).

Timothy was a young man of high character and faithfulness. Paul yearned that he would continue to be an example of godliness imitated by others. Paul highlights three traits that should characterize "a man of God." First, he should flee from the captivating influences of riches, fame, and materialism (v. 11). Second, he should seek those virtues that please God: righteousness and godliness speak of Godward devotion; faith and love are inward qualities, while patience and gentleness are outward expressions of character. Third, Timothy was to *"fight the good fight of faith, lay hold of eternal life"* (v. 12). Timothy was to hold fast to the Christian faith, without compromising any truth. Paul's three imperatives to Timothy are: *keep on* fleeing worldliness, *keep on* pursuing truth, *keep on* fighting for the faith!

Timothy was to continue in his God-chosen calling and in accordance with the longstanding testimony of his confession of faith witnessed by many since he first professed Christ as Savior. As Paul taught the Thessalonians, a consistent testimony of the life of Christ is evidence of eternal life (2 Thess. 1:4-5). True faith presses on through life's sorrows and trials exhibiting godly conduct. Just as Christ held the course of His ministry to completion and maintained a good confession to the end (v. 13), Paul charges Timothy before God the Father and Christ Jesus to do the same.

The believer is to faithfully finish his course in life. His spiritual battles are over when he passes into the presence of Christ from this world, either through death, or by His "appearing" to take His bride (v. 14; 2 Tim. 4:8).

In Paul's final doxology, he describes the One who will judge and reward the believer's works on The Day of Christ (vv. 5-16). The Lord Jesus Christ is the only Potentate, King of kings, and Lord of lords (Rev. 17:14). He is the immortal and immutable God who holds pure truth in Himself; to Him be honor and everlasting power. Noone in the flesh (inherited from Adam) can approach Christ in His dazzling glorified state and live. The holy brilliance of His person and presence is unapproachable (Ex. 33:17-23).

## Instruction to the Wealthy (vv. 17-19)

Having just taught that *"godliness with contentment is great gain"* and having warned that seeking to be rich often invites unchecked lust that results in a shipwrecked testimony, in verses 17-19 Paul provides an additional exhortation for those who are already rich.

It is not a sin to be rich, for God alone is the Giver of everything, However, a prideful, self-sufficient trust in wealth to the exclusion of God to resolve personal problems or to indulge in worldliness, is sin (v. 17). That which we possess is exactly what God wants us to have. It has been given for the purposes of serving Him, helping others, and providing for our basic necessities. If our needs are satisfied, we are to labor to provide help for others in need (Eph. 4:28). Regrettably, many wealthy believers have accumulated much stuff that is strangling their spiritual lives. The familiar adage, *"Use it up, wear it out, make it do, or do without"* is a good one for all believers to adopt during their earthly sojourn.

The Lord Jesus used the parable of the *Unjust Steward* in Luke 16 to instruct His audience with respect to a proper attitude towards riches. A steward was caught embezzling his master's wealth. Knowing that he would soon have to give an account of his actions and would then lose his job, he settled many of his master's accounts for less than the debtors owed. He hoped that by this course of action he would gain the favor of the debtors, who would then be inclined to show him kindness later. The Lord did not commend the steward for his crookedness, but for his forward thinking.

The Lord observed that the unregenerate are often better than God's people at investing for the future. Hence, He exhorts us to *"make friends for yourselves by unrighteous [money]"* while secular riches still have value. In other words, be future thinking by investing present assets for eternity because a day will come when they will have no ability to earn anything of real value. Paul's charge to the wealthy is to not trust in riches but use what God has given so that you can be rich in good works by benefitting others who are in need (v. 18). In doing so, the life of Christ is exhibited, and a "good foundation" is laid up forever (i.e., eternal reward in Heaven; v. 19).

## Final Charge – Guard the Faith (vv. 20-21)

At this juncture, Paul did not know if he would ever see Timothy again or have another opportunity to write to his spiritual son. His parting charge is a summary of what he has already written. Timothy was to guard with his life the doctrinal truth he had been taught, and avoid being sidetracked into unprofitable confrontations with those spewing idle babblings (v. 20). These false teachers professed to have knowledge, but they had actually strayed from the truth, the doctrines of the Faith given by apostolic authority.

Paul ends his tender, but forthright letter to Timothy with his trademark closing, "Grace be with you" (v. 21).

# 2 Timothy

## Background

Timothy's mother, Eunice, and his grandmother, Lois, were Jewish (2 Tim. 1:5) and his father was Greek (Acts 16:1). It seems likely that the gospel ministry of Paul and Barnabas at Lystra during their first missionary journey had directly or indirectly led to young Timothy's conversion. While publicly preaching the gospel at Lystra, Paul healed a crippled man (Acts 14:8-10). Perhaps, Timothy, his mother or his grandmother had heard Paul's message. Timothy and Paul first met during Paul's second visit to Timothy's hometown of Lystra (Acts 16:1-2). At that time, Timothy was already a believer in the Lord and well-spoken of by the believers at Lystra. He joined the missionary team and accompanied Paul on the remainder of the second journey into Macedonia and Achaia. He would become one of Paul's most trusted disciples and co-laborers.

The biblical evidence suggests that Paul endured two distinct Roman imprisonments, since Paul was able to visit Troas, Corinth, and Miletus after release from his first incarceration (4:13, 20). At the time 1 Timothy was written, Paul was between his first and last imprisonments. After Paul's second arrest, he penned his second epistle to Timothy. Paul's situation was now serious – most of his friends had abandoned him and he was on trial for his very life. The great fire of Rome in July of 64 A.D. was blamed on the Christians (though Nero himself was likely the culprit); this ushered in a new wave of persecution against the Church.

*Second Timothy* is the last of the known writings of Paul. It is a letter filled with personal exhortations and encouragements to his spiritual son Timothy. He was to hold to the Word of God and be faithful to the ministry God had given him to accomplish, regardless of the personal cost.

## Theme(s)

Despite affliction, hold to the truth. Various final charges to Timothy.

## Keywords

Keywords and phrases include: "Life/live/living," "remember/remembrance," "that day," "faith," "first," "Scripture/Word (God's)," "truth," "endure," "suffer," "persecutions," "affliction," "ashamed," "sound," "doctrine," and "commit."

## Date

Likely written in 67 A.D., during Paul's second Roman imprisonment and just prior to his execution by Nero.

## Outline

I. Introduction (1:1-2).
II. Paul's Charge to Timothy (1:3-18).
III. The Faithful Servant – God's Choice Vessel (2:1-26).
IV. Holding to the Word in Perilous Times (3:1-17).
V. The Faithful Servant Has a Faithful Lord (4:1-18).
VI. Closing (4:19-22).

# 2 Timothy Chapter 1

## Salutation (vv. 1-2)

Paul opens his epistle to Timothy by stating that his apostleship had been received by a direct command from the Lord Jesus Christ, a matter that Church history bears out (Acts 9:15-16). This assertion would remind Timothy that Paul had not been appointed by men to his ministry, nor did he choose it as means of a livelihood. It is God who chooses our callings in the Body of Christ and equips us to do all that He wants accomplished.

In reference to believers, the apostle next mentions that the Lord Jesus Christ is our Savior and He is our hope (v. 1). This meant that the Lord was alive, and so believers could be assured of His return for them and that they would forever be with Him (1 Thess. 4:13-18). The title "Savior" appears twenty-four times in the New Testament. Ten of those references are in Paul's epistles to his spiritual sons Timothy and Titus. These men were called to a difficult ministry, so the apostle wanted them to keep their spiritual focus on their life-line to Heaven, their Savior, Jesus Christ.

Paul's salutation to his spiritual sons Timothy and Titus deviates from his traditional trademark greeting in his epistles to churches, in that he extends to them the additional aspect of God's mercy with His grace and peace (v. 2; Tit. 1:4). No doubt Timothy and Titus would appreciate the mercy of the Lord in fulfilling their difficult ministries.

The reference to Timothy being *"a true son in the faith"* may indicate that Paul had a part in leading Timothy to the Lord during his first visit to Lystra with Barnabas (Acts 14). However, Luke indicates that Paul and Paul's spiritual qualities were also evident in Timothy, Paul's disciple. Timothy was a true spiritual descendant of the Apostle (Acts 16:1-2).

The modifier "true" seems to indicate that Paul was referring to the quality of Timothy's character which had matured since he professed Christ. Timothy was exhibiting all the spiritual and moral qualities of Paul, his teacher, and thus was a true spiritual descendant of Paul (Phil. 2:19-20).

## Timothy's Faith and Godly Heritage (vv. 3-5)

Before any final charges are bestowed on Timothy, Paul first pauses to give God thanks (v. 3). This is the response of true faith to a good God who always achieves good out of what is seemingly bad (Rom. 8:28). Paul's situation was bleak, he was in prison and mostly alone, and the Roman empire was brutally persecuting Christians. Many believers had already been put to death and Paul was in line to follow their course into glory.

Despite the ominous situation, Paul thanked God both for calling him into the ministry and for enabling him to accomplish it with a pure conscience. Many of Paul's Jewish forefathers had also proven a similar loyalty to God through obedience and devoted service. Like Paul, their hope was to be resurrected and to stand before God forever (Acts 23:6, 26:6).

Next, Paul informed Timothy that he greatly desired to see him again and had constantly remembered him in his *"prayers night and day."* At their last parting, perhaps when Paul was arrested, Timothy had wept for his mentor. It was a scene that deeply impacted Paul, and one he was not soon to forget (v. 4). Timothy's response reminds us that if we lack compassion for others, we will lack also passion in sharing the love of Christ with them.

Whether he would see Timothy again before his execution seemed doubtful, but just remembering Timothy's sincere faith brought Paul great joy (v. 5). It was the same quality of faith that the apostle knew to be in his Jewish mother Eunice and grandmother Lois, who had come to Christ before Timothy. His father was a Greek and not saved, as Paul makes no mention of his father's faith. Timothy's godly life shows how much a mother's faith and sacrifice in the home count for eternity.

## Exhortations to Faithfulness (vv. 6-18)

Next, Paul exhorts Timothy to be faithful to his spiritual calling in Christ, a matter he previously addressed in his first epistle to Timothy: *"Do not neglect the gift that is in you, which was given to you by prophecy with the laying on of the hands of the eldership"* (1 Tim. 4:14). Following the pattern of the Old Testament, the laying on of hands in the New Testament consecrated someone to a particular ministry (e.g., elders, ministers, and deacons; v. 13, 5:22; Acts 13:3). There is no example of apostles imparting spiritual gifts to others by the laying on of hands. The Holy Spirit performs this task (1 Cor. 12:11). Timothy had received *"the gift of God"* (v. 6).

Paul reminded Timothy that his ministry had been identified by apostolic authority. Therefore, it should not be neglected: *"I remind you to stir up the gift of God which is in you through the laying on of my hands. For God has not given us a spirit of fear, but of power and of love and of a sound mind"* (vv. 6-7). As Timothy progressed in holiness and exercised his spiritual gift, there would be greater ongoing benefit to the Church and also to Timothy personally. Believers who are in fellowship with the Lord and walking in the good of their callings are invincible until their service for Christ is complete. Thus, there is no reason to fret over or fear anything.

Given that Paul was staring martyrdom in the face, his charge to Timothy to be strong and to have a sound mind was all the more significant. Our fear of death and judgment is removed by Christ's work at Calvary (Rom. 8:15; Heb. 2:15). Having been made one with Christ by the Holy Spirit, we experience the fullness of God's love which dispels all fear and enables us to love in ways that we never could before (1 Jn. 4:18-19). Despite suffering for Christ, believers understand that this is their calling in Christ and is for God's glory and their edification, strengthening, and maturing (1 Pet. 5:10). Reminiscing on these truths results in a sound mind!

In the remainder of the chapter, Paul acknowledges that the gospel of Jesus Christ has differing consequences for various people. Believers, who faithfully share the gospel message, will suffer affliction and persecution (vv. 8, 15; John 15:18-20). Believers who are ashamed of the truth and those who do not share the gospel (like Phygellus and Hermogenes) will suffer shame at Christ's appearing (vv. 12-15; 1 Jn. 2:28). For the unregenerate, the gospel offers a choice of receiving eternal life with God, or of remaining spiritually dead and being separated from God forever (v. 10; John 5:24).

Paul reminds Timothy that God's plan of salvation in Christ was predetermined before the foundations of the world were laid, that is, before time had any meaning (v. 9; 1 Pet. 1:20). At God's set time, Christ, God's Messenger and Message, appeared on the earth to abolish physical death and to offer eternal life to those who are dead in trespasses and sins (v. 10). By God's grace alone, they are been saved through Christ and given a holy calling as priests to serve before God forever (1 Pet. 2:5).

Having already spoken of Timothy's gift and calling, Paul acknowledged his own assigned role in furthering God's kingdom on earth; he was *"a preacher, an apostle, and a teacher of the Gentiles"* (v. 11). Knowing that he was secure in Christ and would ultimately appear before Christ at His Judgment Seat ("that Day"), until then Paul would gladly suffer for Christ in the provision of grace and mercy given to him (v. 12).

Timothy was not to be ashamed of the gospel or of those who were suffering for proclaiming it (like Paul). Rather, he was to partake of the afflictions associated with holding to the truth (as received from Paul) while displaying the love of God through the power of the Holy Spirit (vv. 13-14).

Paul then commends and blesses Onesiphorus from Ephesus who had traveled to Rome and diligently searched for him. He was not afraid to visit Paul in prison and to refresh the apostle, as he had done earlier (vv. 16-18).

# 2 Timothy Chapter 2

### Exhortations to Endurance (vv. 1-13)

Paul encourages Timothy, his beloved son in the faith, to be courageous and tenacious in accomplishing his ministry in the strength endowed by God in grace (v. 1). The Greek verb *endynamou* rendered "be strong" is a present tense imperative in the passive voice, meaning that Timothy was to "keep on being empowered" by Christ's grace. This would enable him to impart the doctrines of the faith that he had learned from Paul to faithful men who were to pass them along to the next generation of disciples (v. 2).

Verse 2 contains four generations of disciples: Paul, Timothy, "faithful men," and those whom the faithful men would teach. The Lord's plan to build His Church has always been to preach the gospel throughout the world and to teach all to those who respond to the gospel all that Christ taught. (Matt. 28:19-20). Yet, Paul provided some practical counsel to Timothy on how to best invest his time in ministry. New converts require special care (1 Thess. 2:7), but as time passes, their maturity and fruitfulness should be evident. Timothy was not to waste time with those who were negligent in learning and living sound doctrine. If Satan can keep us busy with his people, he will do so to keep us from attending to those who need our help.

Being in the final days of his life, and having run his race and finished his course, Paul sought to inspire Timothy to do the same. The apostle employs seven similes in this chapter for that purpose. Timothy is described as a son (v. 1) and was to be like: a soldier (vv. 3-4), an athlete (v. 5), a farmer (v. 6), a worker (v. 15), a cleansed vessel (v. 21), and a servant (v. 24). The soldier, athlete, and farmer form the first triad of exhortative analogies. Each profession has unique obligations and associated rewards.

First, Timothy was to be a good soldier who does not get encumbered by worldly affairs so that he may please Christ, his Commander (vv. 3-4). Likewise, we, as soldiers of the cross, are to remain on active duty and not to be entangled with the cares of this world. The Greek verb rendered "entangles" is *empleketai* which means "to be entwined with." While its tense indicates an ongoing activity, the verb's passive voice infers that the affairs of life are acting on the soldier. This means that the Christian soldier is not the one pursuing worldly activities. Rather, they are pursuing him intent on ensnaring and incapacitating him. An alert soldier defends against such attempts. This can be problematic, as initially, that in which we engage may seem harmless, but in time we become mastered by it. The reward of the soldier is to receive praise from the one who enlisted him.

Second, Timothy was to compete like a rule-abiding *athlete* (derived from the verb *athle*) to finish his race, lest he be disqualified (v. 5). To compete against the flesh requires discipline, self-control (to live purely), endurance, obedience to the rules (Word of God), and beating the flesh into submission to run one's best (1 Cor. 9:24-27). Failing to run in this fashion eventually results in a shipwrecked life and being a castaway (i.e., being unusable in the Lord's work until restoration occurs). The reward for running well is victory and an imperishable crown received from the Lord.

Third, Timothy was to imitate a hardworking farmer who tills the soil and sows seed to later enjoy the reward of a good harvest (v. 6). The farmer works hard, with the expectation of a harvest, and is the first one to enjoy the fruit of his own labor. The first exhortative triad that Timothy was to heed was to encourage him to endure as a soldier, to faithfully finish his race as an athlete, and to work diligently as the farmer (v. 7).

Moving on from these similes, the apostle reminds Timothy of the Lord Jesus and His great example of faithfulness. To receive Heaven's praise and reward, He endured suffering and sorrow (v. 8). James R. Baker writes:

> It is important to note that the conjunction "that" is not in the original text and should be omitted; thus, the exhortation is not to recall facts about Christ but rather to remember, or keep in mind, the person Himself. "Remember" is in the present tense and is in the form of a command. Having spoken in varied ways of the hardship, discipline and suffering which precedes the time of reward, the apostle now reminds Timothy that the highest example is seen in "Jesus Christ."[110]

Christ chose to suffer in righteousness unto death for the unrighteousness of others, but God raised Him up from the dead and highly exalted Him for His faithful obedience to doing His Father's will (Phil. 2:10-12).

Christ crucified, buried, and raised up from the dead to justify sinners was Paul's gospel message, and it is ours too (1 Cor. 15:3-4). It was for preaching this truth that Paul was a prisoner of Rome, but the message itself could not be constrained by iron chains (v. 9). Paul gladly endured the suffering associated with his calling to preach the gospel so that all who responded to its message would be saved (i.e., those foreknown to God and chosen in Christ, these would have their names written in the Lamb's Book of Life before the earth was created (v. 10; Rev. 17:8, 20:15).

The fourth of five "faithful sayings" in Paul's letters to Timothy was:

*For if we died with Him, we shall also live with Him. If we endure, we shall also reign with Him. If we deny Him, He also will deny us. If we are faithless, He remains faithful; He cannot deny Himself* (vv. 11-13).

Positionally speaking, all believers are one with Christ forever. From God's perspective we have died with Christ and have also been raised up with Him and are now seated with Him in heavenly places (Rom. 6:3-8; Eph. 2:6). Just as Christ exhibited faithfulness unto death, this is also expected of those who are in Christ. Just as Christ was rewarded and honored for His faithfulness, so shall all believers be rewarded who follow His example of enduring, even unto death if necessary. No doubt this promise has inspired those facing martyrdom for Christ through the ages.

Proclaiming His name and suffering for His name go hand in hand; these realities cannot be separated. Those who do not go on with the Lord are not His; therefore, He is not obliged to claim them as His redeemed: *"If we **endure**, we shall also reign with Him. If we **deny** Him, He also will deny us"* (v. 12). The Lord explained this connection to His disciples on the eve of Calvary. He told them that the world hated Him and would hate them also, and informed them that they would be persecuted by the world, for *"all these things they will do to you for My name's sake"* (John 15:21).

Paul then reminded Timothy that God is faithful to His character and His Word: *"If we are faithless, He remains faithful; He cannot deny Himself"* (v. 13). We have the Lord's promise, despite our failings, to bring us safely through to glorification in Christ, which completes our salvation (Phil. 1:6, 3:20-21). Verse 12 speaks of habitually denying (i.e., disowning) the Lord, whereas verse 13 speaks of our brief lapses of faith while journeying Heavenward in Christ (such as Peter's failure to identify with Christ at Calvary).

Speaking to His disciples, the Lord said, *"Whoever **denies** Me before men, him I will also deny before My Father who is in Heaven"* (Matt. 10:33). Paul also wrote, *"If indeed we **suffer** with Him, that we may also be glorified together"* (Rom. 8:17). The Greek verb for "denies" in Matthew 10:33 comes from the root word used in verse 12 for "deny." The verb tense is in the present tense for "endure," and "deny" (v. 12), "denies" (Matt. 10:33), and "suffer" (Rom. 8:17), meaning that a true believer is characterized by going on with Christ no matter the cost. Persistence through hardship is evidence of salvation in Christ. An apostate is known by ongoing denial of Christ after first professing the truth. Habitual denial is proof that one is not saved, thus Christ will (future tense) deny such a person on judgment day.

Many in the early church were so enthralled with Christ that they considered it a great privilege to suffer for His sake. In doing so, they were enabled to more closely identify with the Lord. This was Paul's desire, to know Christ more deeply through suffering for Him: *"That I may know Him and the power of His resurrection, and the fellowship of His sufferings, being conformed to His death"* (Phil. 3:10). The assurance of God's Word gave the apostles hope for the future and joy while suffering for their Savior.

Hence, the Lord's disciples faced death with the same hope and joy that their Savior did, and so can we. Aegeas crucified Andrew, Peter's brother, for his faith in Christ. Seeing his cross before him, Andrew bravely spoke, "O cross, most welcome and longed for! With a willing mind, joyfully and desirously, I come to thee, being the scholar of Him which did hang on thee: because I have always been thy lover, and have coveted to embrace thee."[111] Andrew could approach his cross with expectancy and joy, because he had watched the Lord Jesus do the same at Calvary. *"He who overcomes shall inherit all things, and I will be his God and he shall be My son"* (Rev. 21:7-8). True believers shall reign with Christ and inherit all that He has!

## Approved and Unapproved Vessels (Servants) (vv. 14-16)

Not only was Timothy to remember these things and refuse to strive about words to no profit (which ruins opportunities to share Christ with the lost), he was to remind those he taught of the same truths (v. 14). Paul continues by identifying more "to dos" and "not to dos" concerning a believer's handling of God's Word in verses 15-19.

To prevent ourselves from embracing false doctrines, and to present ourselves to God "approved," believers must rightly divide Scripture (v. 15). Through the systematic study of Scripture (i.e., using Scripture to interpret Scripture), one is able to determine the "big picture" truth of God's purposes. A believer should not engage in unprofitable discussions (e.g., profane arguments and vain babblings), especially when the lost are in earshot (v. 16). These debates tend to energize the flesh and often needlessly dividing believers and causing disrespect for Christ's name.

False teachers, who oppose sound doctrine, will always be divisive and be marked by unChristlike behavior (1 Tim. 6:3-4). False doctrine produces that which opposes God in every aspect, including words, deeds, and character. That which is of the flesh cannot please God (Rom. 8:8). This means that rightly dividing Scripture and standing on the truth, no matter what, will eventually result in suffering for Christ. The apostle could attest to this fact many times throughout his years of ministry.

As an example, Paul mentions two men, Hymenaeus and Philetus, who had *"strayed concerning the truth, saying that the resurrection is already past"* (vv. 17-18). In the energy of the flesh, their false teachings had spread like cancer in a healthy body and had "overthrown the faith" of some believers. Perhaps they were teaching that spiritual rebirth in Christ was the only resurrection there would be, and so believers should not hope in a bodily resurrection in which believers receive bodies fit for Heaven.

Or perhaps these bogus teachers were echoing the false doctrine being propagated at Thessalonica. That is, that Christ had already come for the Church and the resurrection of the just was past. Whatever they were preaching, it was false and had stumbled some believers in their faith – "Why live and suffer for Christ, if He has already come for His Church?" "If there is no future resurrection, then this is as good as it is going to be on earth, so we might as well settle in." Phygellus and Hermogenes (1:15) chose to not identify with Paul and his teachings to avoid being shamed. However, Hymenaeus and Philetus, being unregenerate, had no remorse in swerving (erring) from the truth and leading others astray by false doctrine.

Despite what these two men taught, the foundation of truth that God laid in the beginning was unaffected; His word and purposes are timeless and immutable (v. 19; Heb. 6:18). Hence, those in Christ are sealed in Him forever – *"He knows those who are His."* And one of the proofs that someone is truly Christ's, and not merely a Christ-professor, is that he or she is determined to depart from iniquity and to be separate from those who will not. Harry A. Ironside asserts that this is the meaning of Christian faith:

> Faith says, "Let the evil rise as high as it may – let lawlessness abound, and the love of many wax cold – let all that seemed to be of God in the earth be swallowed up in the apostasy – nevertheless God's firm foundation stands, for Christ has declared, 'Upon this rock I will build My Assembly, and the gates of Hades shall not prevail against it'"! But this brings in responsibility. I am not to go on with the evil – protesting, perhaps, but fellowshipping it still – though it be in a reserved, halfhearted way. I am called to separate from it. In so doing I may seem to be separating from dear children of God and beloved servants of Christ. But this is necessary if they do not judge the apostate condition.[112]

As Paul has often stressed, those holding to sound doctrine are able to represent Christ in word and deed; those who do not, cannot.

With Hymenaeus and Philetus, and many other perverse preachers in mind, Paul further illustrates the dangers and consequences of false teachers to the Church. It is observed that there is no definite article preceding *megalei oikia* rendered *"a great house"* (v. 20). Obviously, the *house* here is not the same as *"the house of God"* – the Church (1 Tim. 3:15). If there were an article, then we would read *"the great house"* and conclude that Christendom was likely in view. Regardless, if Paul is using a great house in Ephesus containing many vessels as a simple object lesson or figuratively speaking of Christendom (which contains all those identifying with Christ, whether truly saved or not), the application is really the same.

Vessels are articles available for service, but Paul refers to them as *people* in his analogy. This great household includes vessels of gold, silver, wood, and clay which are used for various tasks, some were for honorable functions and others, more abhorrent (v. 20). Some commentators associate the gold and silver vessels as being believers, and the wood and clay with mere professors in Christendom, but that is not Paul's point in verse 21. It is not the material of the vessel or how it is used that is critical; the Master will determine that part. What is crucial is that the vessel be clean and available to be used now, when and where the Master determines.

For example, it would be acceptable, depending on the venue, to serve food to house guests on either a silver platter or a paper plate, but both must be clean. No one wants to eat off a filthy plate. A toothbrush is not a glamorous household item, but it serves an important function if clean. As Harry A. Ironside elaborates, it is willing separation and sanctification by the living vessels that Paul is emphasizing to Timothy in the parable:

> The vessels are seen to be *persons*. And just as valuable plates might stand uncleansed and dirty with a lot of kitchen utensils waiting to be washed, and then carefully separated from the vessels for baser uses, so Timothy (and every other truly exercised soul) is called upon to take a place apart, to "purge out himself" from the mixed conditions, that he may be in very deed "a vessel unto honor, *sanctified*, and meet for the Master's use, prepared unto every good work." ... And so it is with the man of God who has thus purged himself out from what is opposed to the truth and the holiness of God. He is sanctified, or separated, and in this way becomes "meet [available] for the Master's use."[113]

False teachers were filthy plates and could not be used by the Lord to accomplish anything that would honor Him in service. However, Christ is pleased to use believers who have consecrated themselves to holy living and the truth. The unregenerate, unclean false teachers were vessels of wrath who fit themselves for destruction because they rejected the truth (Rom. 9:22). Christ will receive honor from these vessels by their condemnation.

To be a vessel fit for the Master's hand one must shun false doctrine and sanctify oneself by choosing to study and obey God's Word (v. 22). Believers should associate with those who are following truth, and purifying themselves from sin. When believers make the choice to flee ungodliness, empty themselves of pride, and submit to God's will, they become vessels available for God's sovereign use. The Holy Spirit responds by filling them with divine power and equipping them for service (Acts 4:23-32). No matter how favorable or unpleasant the task that we are called to do, Christ will honor those who faithfully do His bidding.

> Oh, to be but emptier, lowlier, mean, unnoticed and unknown,
> And to God a vessel holier, filled with Christ, and Christ alone.
> Naught of earth to cloud the glory, naught of self the light to dim,
> Telling forth His wondrous story, emptied to be filled with Him.
>
> – Francis Bevan

Not only did Paul want Timothy to be a cleansed vessel fit for the Master's use, he also wanted his spiritual son to be wise and effective as *a servant of the Lord* (vv. 23-24). This meant that he was to avoid foolish arguments founded in ignorance. Such disputes would only stir up strife without resolution and Timothy should not risk losing his godly temperament. Rather, any discussions with those opposing the truth were to be held on God's turf, so to speak, of spiritual humility and patience.

If flesh combats flesh, nothing good can result. However, a servant of the Lord not acting in the flesh just might convince errant teachers of something more powerful than the flesh and cause them to repent of their heresy (v. 25). By accessing the grace of God in this way, the servant of Lord frees others from the snare of the devil (false doctrine) and from working with him any further to oppose God (v. 26).

The character of the servant of God is as important as what that servant does. The servant of the Lord represents Christ in character and conduct. This is why God does not use filthy vessels (speaking of those in sin or spreading false doctrine) to represent His Son. In contrast, God uses vessels of mercy (sanctified believers) to proclaim His glory (Rom. 9:23).

What was Paul's message to his beloved son Timothy in his second trilogy of similitudes? He was to be *a worker* who labored diligently to rightly divide God's Word (v. 15), *a cleansed vessel* that shunned false doctrine and youthful lusts (v. 21), and a gentle and meek *servant* of the Lord who sought for opportunities to recover those who were caught in Satan's snare of false doctrine.

# 2 Timothy Chapter 3

## Perilous Times and the Coming Apostasy (vv. 1-13)

Still pondering the *"great house"* analogy of many vessels, many of which were unclean, the apostle informs Timothy what the condition of the professing church will be *"in the last days"* (v. 1). This phrase is versatile and context must determine its specific meaning. For example, in Hebrews 1:2, *"in these last days"* speaks of Christ's first advent. False teachers existed when Paul was writing to Timothy, for the apostle instructs him *"from such people turn away"* (v. 5). However, Paul is looking beyond the Apostolic Age to the era just before the Rapture of the Church by telling his mentee that during the last days, *"perilous times will come."* Both the Lord and Paul alluded to increasing deception, wickedness, and sorrows just prior to the beginning of the Tribulation period (Matt. 24:3-8; 2 Thess. 2:3).

The Greek word translated "perilous" in verse 1 is also rendered as "fierce" in Matthew 8:28 where it describes the demon-possessed man in the country of the Gadarenes. The latter times (or seasons) of the Church Age will be extremely powerful and wicked days – "perilous times" indeed!

Paul states that before the Antichrist is revealed, the professing church will fall away from sound doctrine (2 Thess. 2:3-5). Paul has already shown that when sound doctrine is not lived out, the worst of man's degenerate nature is witnessed, and such will be the case before the curtain call of the Church Age. Therefore, it should be no surprise that even those who have previously identified with Christ in name, behave in much the same way as the heathen (vv. 2-5), who do not know God. The flesh is flesh, and when our flesh is not under God's control, the worst that is within us emerges.

The Greek word *anthropos* rendered "men" in verse 2 speaks of humanity, not the male gender. In verses 2–5, Paul identifies nineteen traits that will characterize the general behavior of mankind during the latter days of the Church Age. William MacDonald supplies this list of synonyms for each behavioral characteristic:

> **Lovers of themselves** – self-centered, conceited, egotistical.
> **Lovers of money** – greedy for money, avaricious.
> **Boasters** – braggarts, full of great swelling words.
> **Proud** – arrogant, haughty, overbearing.

**Blasphemers** – evil speakers, profane, abusive, foulmouthed, contemptuous, insulting.
**Disobedient to parents** – rebellious, undutiful, uncontrolled.
**Unthankful** – ungrateful, lacking in appreciation.
**Unholy** – impious, profane, irreverent, holding nothing sacred.
**Unloving** – hard-hearted, unnaturally callous, unfeeling.
**Unforgiving** – implacable, refusing to make peace, refusing efforts toward reconciliation.
**Slanderers** – spreading false and malicious reports.
**Without self-control** – men of uncontrolled passions, dissolute, debauched.
**Brutal** – savage, unprincipled.
**Despisers of good** – haters of whatever or whoever is good; utterly opposed to goodness in any form.
**Traitors** – treacherous, betrayers.
**Headstrong** – reckless, self-willed, rash.
**Haughty** – making empty pretensions, conceited.
**Lovers of pleasure rather than lovers of God** – those who love sensual pleasures but not God.[114]

Towards the end of the Church Age many people will give lip service to Christ without any commitment to obey His word or to live for Him. Christianity will become *Churchianity* and the vast majority of those identifying with Christ will be pseudo-religious, but not born again and their proud, self-focused, wanton, and rebel behavior will prove this to be true. These have *"a form of godliness but denying its power"* (v. 5). Paul commands Timothy to have nothing to do with these self-deceived fakers.

On Judgment Day, the Lord said that there would be many who know things about Him and have done works in His name who will be eternally condemned because they did not obey God's will for them (Matt. 7:21-23). These people did not repent and receive Christ as their Savior when they had the opportunity, but continued in humanized religion which denies the necessity of spiritual rebirth and spiritual life in Christ.

In the latter days, these unregenerate spiritual-wannabes will be easy prey for false teachers. Without Scripture and the Holy Spirit to lead them into the light of truth, Satan's workers will deceive them to believe his lie. No matter how much they learn while residing in satanic darkness, they will never be drawn into the light to know the truth (v. 7; 1 Cor. 1:18; 1 Jn. 1:6).

False teachers coming *ek touton,* "out of this kind" (i.e., from the former group who have *a form of godliness*), are likened to slithering serpents *"who creep into households and make captives of gullible women loaded down with sins, led away by various lusts"* (v. 6). The Greek word rendered "gullible" is speaking more of instability than a lack of intelligence.

The threat may be from false teachers embedded in Christendom or from canvassing cult members. Many modern cults, in pretense, identify with the name of Christ, but they deny His Word, diminish His attributes, and lessen His importance as Savior by promoting a *good-works* message for salvation. Often these ambassadors of deception visit during the day when God's appointed protector of the home is absent, and the stress of caring for one's children is at its highest. They slither in and secretly take the gullible captive. Edward Dennett states that these individuals are "one of Satan's most dangerous subtleties," and then explains why:

> If he [Satan] can succeed in open opposition to the truth, he will not conceal himself, but if this door of antagonism is closed, he will transform himself into an angel of light. It was so in Paul's days, and it is especially the case at the present moment. Professing Christians would scarcely be led away by the open exhibition of Satanic power, but how many are seduced by it because outwardly it is an imitation of the divine. …There is not a single operation of the Spirit of God, nor a single form of His working, that Satan does not imitate. His counterfeits are around us on every hand, within and without.[115]

We would not have known the identities of Pharaoh's magicians who withstood Moses and Aaron in Egypt long ago, if Paul had not recorded their names in verse 8: *"Now as Jannes and Jambres resisted Moses, so do these also resist the truth: men of corrupt minds, disapproved concerning the faith; but they will progress no further, for their folly will be manifest to all, as theirs also was"* (vv. 8-9). Paul used Jannes and Jambres as an object lesson to illustrate how people having a form of godliness resist truth. Obviously, these sorcerers defied Moses, but in what way did they have a form of godliness in doing so? C. H. Mackintosh answers this question:

> The mode in which "Jannes and Jambres withstood Moses" was simply by imitating, as far as they were able, whatever he did. We do not find that they attributed his actions to a false or evil energy, but rather that they sought to neutralize their power upon the conscience [of those present], by doing the same things. What Moses, did they could do, so that, after all, there was no great difference. One was as good as the other. A miracle is a miracle. If Moses wrought miracles to get the people out of Egypt, they could work miracles to keep them in; so where was the difference?

> From all this we learn the solemn truth that the most satanic resistance to God's testimony in the world is offered by those who, though they imitate

the effects of the truth, have but "the form of godliness," and "deny the power thereof." Persons of this class can do the same things, adopt the same habits and forms, use the same phraseology, profess the same opinions as others. If the true Christian, constrained by the love of Christ, feeds the hungry, clothes the naked, visits the sick, circulates the Scriptures, distributes tracts, supports the gospel, engages in prayer, sings praise, preaches the gospel, the formalist can do every one of these things, and this, be it observed, is the special character of the resistance offered to the truth "in the last days" – this is the spirit of "Jannes and Jambres."[116]

In the same way that Jannes and Jambres withstood Moses, so will these self-loving, pleasure-seeking counterfeit teachers "resist the truth." After being tested, they were found *unapproved*, the idea of "corrupt" minds (v. 8). In contrast, the man of God is shown *approved* by adhering to Scripture (2:15). They may embrace *the form of godliness* for social acceptance, but they will always hate the power of what it stands for because that would require self-denial, self-sacrifice, and becoming like Christ through the power of the Holy Spirit. Nothing doing – too high a personal cost.

Thankfully, believers today do not have to be deceived by the Janneses and Jambreses of the world. Besides His Word, God has provided a safeguard for believers so that they should not be deceived by the ensnaring arts of Satan's workers. John instructed the believers, *"Believe not every spirit* [teacher]*, but test the spirits whether they are of God"* (1 Jn. 4:1-4). He also informed them of an anointing they had received at spiritual rebirth, which would lead them into the truth of all things (1 Jn. 2:20-21).

Thus far, Paul has introduced three pairs of men who have had differing and wrong responses to the truth. First, Phygellus and Hermogenes (likely believers) were *ashamed of* the truth and of Paul, a preacher of truth (1:15). Second, Hymenaeus and Philetus (of the unregenerate) *had swerved* (erred) from the truth and were preaching false doctrine (2:17-18). Third, Jannes and Jambres *resisted* the truth by reproducing it through deception to keep people from knowing and believing the truth.

In contrast to these who had been ashamed of, erred from, and resisted the truth, Timothy had "carefully followed" Paul's teachings, and his devout pattern for life. Paul's honorable character and tenacity in ministry despite persecution was a good pattern to follow (v. 10). Only those holding to sound doctrine can demonstrate the *"faith, longsuffering, love and perseverance"* of Christ in ministry. As Paul's case studies have shown, false doctrine can never produce that which is truly from God.

During the second missionary journey, Timothy had witnessed how Paul suffered in Antioch, Iconium, and even in Lystra, Timothy's hometown, where Paul was stoned and left for dead (v. 11). "Persecution" is derived from the verb meaning "to pursue." Many rejecting Paul's message pursued him with the intent of killing him, but the Lord had delivered Paul out of their hands. Paul suggests that his example is the normal pattern for the Christian life: *"Yes, and all who desire to live godly in Christ Jesus will suffer persecution"* (v. 12). Paul affirms that if believers live to serve Christ, suffering is to be expected.

Dear believer, do not expect anything less and you will not be disappointed. Prepare your mind for the struggles ahead, and do not get bogged down in self-pity or grapple with despair when the forecasted storms of life arrive (1 Pet. 1:13). As the apostles repeatedly demonstrated, suffering patiently for Christ results in an inner joy that the enemy cannot take away (Acts 5:40-42, 16:23-25). Paul told the saints at both Philippi and Thessalonica (who were being persecuted for their faith) that suffering patiently was evidence (a proof) of their salvation.

If you are an evangelist faithfully sharing the gospel message, a preacher who shares the full counsels of God, or a shepherd who faithfully uses God's rod to lead, comfort, and correct, then you already know that you will suffer for doing what God wants you to do. If we do anything for the Lord, we should expect to be misunderstood, criticized, slandered, and oppressed.

Many of our failures can be attributed to having the wrong view of what we experience in our wilderness journeys. If new converts would realize that they are destined for disappointment, hardship, and persecution because of their identity in Christ, then every provision of God's grace in the wilderness would be answered with joyful praise. But if new believers begin their pilgrimage Heavenward expecting ease in the world, the coming relentless adversities will be overwhelming.

From this perspective, the *Prosperity Gospel* message often preached today will always appeal to the flesh. However, those desiring the benefits of the cross but denying its demands will eventually be disappointed (Luke 9:23-26). Those who try to live with one foot in the world and one in the church will eventually experience failure.

Every Christian who righteously suffers for the cause of Christ will be rewarded: *"If we suffer, we shall also reign with Him"* (2:12; KJV). Indeed, though believers are destined for trouble, we should not despair. Just as Paul did not want Timothy to be surprised by the growing depravity of evil men and spiritual impostors, neither should believers today be overwhelmed by what we know will characterize the last days of the Church Age (v. 13).

Rather, Timothy was to press on in the truth, "the Holy Scriptures," that he had been taught throughout his life, first beginning in the home when he

*Revealing Heaven's Secrets*

was a child (vv. 14-15). Knowing God's truth and yielding to it in faith makes believers wise to experience the wonders of His full salvation.

Paul tells us that all Scripture is literally God-breathed. The Holy Spirit has preserved what God wanted to be in our Bibles from His originally inspired words given to the original apostles long ago (v. 16). In the next chapter, Paul writes, *"Preach the word! Be ready in season and out of season. Convince, rebuke, exhort, with all longsuffering and teaching"* (4:2). Teaching, reproof, instruction, and correction, as directed by God's Word, are absolutely necessary to refine character in such a way as to make believers profitable unto good works (v. 17).

*Doctrine* teaches us to understand the mind of God. *Reproof* speaks to our conscience and confronts wrong behavior. *Correction* means to straighten what is bent. We all have character bents that need to be corrected for us to stand morally upright. *Instruction* in righteousness refers to a wide range of training tools that reveal the gap between what I am and where I should be. *Doctrine* teaches sound thinking, while *correction* straightens erroneous thinking. *Instruction* approves holy behavior and *reproof* confronts wrong behavior. Knowing and obeying the Word of God saves us from being defiled and delivers us from the world's deceptive influences.

The Greek word translated "instruction" in 2 Timothy 3:16 is *paideia*, which means "education or training; disciplinary correction." In the NASB, *paideia* is rendered as "training," while the NIV translates it as "being thoroughly equipped." *Paideia* is rendered "the training" in Ephesians 6:4, *"Fathers ... bring them up in **the training** and admonition of the Lord."* *Paideia*, therefore, means "education or training, which includes disciplinary correction." The latter aspect of this training is clearly brought out in Hebrews 12, where four times *paideia* is translated as "chastening." Just as parents are to train up their children in the way they should go (Prov. 22:6), Christians are required to train younger believers in the way of righteousness (i.e., holy character) by rightly applying God's Word.

The passion of all believers should be that the lovely character of Christ, his joyful disposition, steadfast morality, and genuine care for others, would be revealed to the world through us. As exemplified in the lives of Paul and Timothy, knowing and living out sound doctrine produces this quality of spiritual life in Christ. Such believers are sanctified vessels fit for the Master's hand. But those who resist the truth and choose to abide in darkness can only mimic what is spiritual, but without its true power. The character of what is produced in our lives is the evidence of what is within. Yielding to truth enables enjoyment of the life of Christ. Resisting the truth results in moral failure and God's judgment (e.g., John 3:36).

# 2 Timothy Chapter 4

Preach the Word (vv. 1-5)

Paul begins to draw his letter to a close with one final solemn charge to Timothy. He does so in the sight of God the Lord Jesus Christ, to remind Timothy that as surely as Christ will return to establish His kingdom, so He will judge every sinful deed committed by the living and the dead. Just as everyone in Christ's Kingdom will be subject to His rule, so every wicked soul will be subject to His judicial wrath.

How was Timothy to respond to this inescapable truth? He was to...

*Preach the word! Be ready in season and out of season. Convince, rebuke, exhort, with all longsuffering and teaching. For the time will come when they will not endure sound doctrine, but according to their own desires, because they have itching ears, they will heap up for themselves teachers; and they will turn their ears away from the truth, and be turned aside to fables* (vv. 2-4).

Paul had already foretold of a time during the latter days of the Church Age in which the professing church would not hold to sound doctrine but would prefer to listen to teachers who preached what they wanted to hear. Paul did not know when the Church would be raptured, but he did know that this apostasy would crescendo just prior to that event (2 Thess. 2:3).

This meant that Timothy needed to be ready to confront such deception, so Paul sought to equip his spiritual son with deception-fighting tools (v. 2).

First, Timothy was to use God's Word and not high-minded humanized arguments to confront false teaching. Scripture was to be at the center of his teaching, correcting, and rebuking ministry.

Second, he was to be diligent in the proper use of Scripture in his ministry. This conveys the idea of urgency, preparedness, and continued diligence in season and out of season (i.e., whether there were convenient opportunities or less opportune times, including afflictions).

Third, those in doctrinal error were to be rebuked and corrected.

Fourth, Timothy was to exhort with all longsuffering and doctrine: Those who were doing well were to be encouraged to continue to do so. All reproving, rebuking, correction, and exhortation was to be done with patience and by divine instruction. Timothy must be emboldened to preach God's Word and to confront the sin without regard to religious status or social rank. Sin is sin regardless of the who the guilty party is, and it must be confronted with a spirit of humility and by the authority of God's Word.

Paul then explained why Timothy was to preach the Word. In the last days of the Church Age many who profess to know Christ will *"turn their ears away from the truth"* (v. 3). These will not endure sound doctrine, but will follow silly fables, the doctrines of demons, and will seek teachers who will preach what they want to hear (v. 4). These *religious* people will pursue lust with a dull and seared conscience, and be ensnared by legalism (e.g., touch not, taste not, marry not) to self-qualify as holy (1 Tim. 4:2-4).

In contrast, Timothy was to be alert, to keep a cool head during turbulent times, to do the work of an evangelist, and to fulfill his calling (v. 5). Given the wicked days in which we live, this is good counsel for all believers.

## Paul's Final Farewell (vv. 6-8)

Seeing Christ's superb example and knowing the boundless provision of His grace, Paul was determined to finish well. In anticipation of his soon departure to be with Christ (i.e., his execution), he could say: *"I am already being poured out as a drink offering, and the time of my departure is at hand"* (v. 6). Levitical priests poured out drink offerings over the lambs to be burnt on the bronze altar before the Lord (Num. 28:7-8). Paul, as a believer-priest, had willingly poured out his life in service to Christ, God's Lamb who had sacrificed Himself for Paul (v. 6). God had answered Paul's prayer: *"That I may know Him and the power of His resurrection, and the fellowship of His sufferings, being conformed to His death"* (Phil. 3:10). To identify with Christ in His rejection must be the aspiration of all believers!

Paul had *"fought the good fight, I have finished the race, I have kept the faith"* (v. 7). After his conversion, Paul had no regrets. He had fought the good fight, had finished the racecourse (the ministry) assigned to him, and had protected the truth, "the faith" which had been committed to him.

Christ is presently working with all believers on earth (Mark 16:19-20); in the future, His Church will be with Him in Heaven. His forever abiding presence with us is certain, though our intimacy with Him each day depends on our desire for it. With His exaltation looming, Christians are to live each day in the anticipation of *"that Day"* speaking of Christ's coming for His Church – *The Day of Christ* (v. 8). On that day, Christ will judge the value of each believer's works (1 Cor. 3:11-15) and eternal rewards (crowns) will be given to His faithful servants. There is a special reward, *"the crown of righteousness,"* bestowed on those who joyfully and faithfully live in expectation of His imminent return.

In the twinkling of an eye, what was corruptible will become incorruptible, and what was mortal will become immortal (1 Cor. 15:51-52), and believers will be caught up into the air to ever be with the Lord (1 Thess. 4:13-18). The believer's glorified body will be able to worship and please God without any hindrance from its previous fallen state.

Paul had one hope (Eph. 4:4), one earnest expectation, the *blessed hope*: *"Looking for the blessed hope and glorious appearing of our great God and Savior Jesus Christ"* (Tit. 2:13). While this may include aspects of Christ's future kingdom, the believer's faith and hope finish their course at Christ's coming for the Church (the Rapture), yet love will continue forever (1 Cor. 13:8, 13). Those who truly have the hope of glory purify themselves now (1 Jn. 3:2-3). The Lord is pure and saints having the blessed hope will want to be found living in purity when He suddenly returns from Heaven.

## Paul's Final Requests and Closing Remarks (vv. 9-22)

We learn in the final verses of this epistle that Paul had largely been abandoned during the final days of his second imprisonment. The apostle longed to see his spiritual son Timothy one final time before his earthly departure, although there is no evidence that such a meeting ever occurred.

Regardless, the apostle requested that Timothy travel to Rome as soon as possible (before winter; vv. 9, 20). He was not to sail to Rome directly, but rather to travel through Macedonia and across the Adriatic Sea. Timothy was to *pick up* John Mark en route to Rome and bring the cloak that Paul left at Troas with Carpus. He also asked that his books (probably papyrus scrolls of Paul's letters and studies) and his parchments (likely leather copies of Scripture, perhaps also Christ's recorded teachings; vv. 11, 13).

Paul knew that his days were numbered, but his final requests to Timothy indicate what he valued at the end of his life: God's Word, the people of God, and the mere necessities of life needed to do God's work.

Barnabas, the son of consolation, had taken his nephew John Mark, who had abandoned Paul and Barnabas during their first missionary journey, with him to Crete about twenty years earlier (Acts 15:39-40). Thankfully, the younger man had been restored to faithful service, and Paul gladly acknowledged that it would be profitable for his ministry to have John Mark assist him in Rome. This is a good reminder that in the Lord's work failures are only final if we make them so. When we fall, the Lord desires us to learn from our mistakes, to get up in grace, and press on in our heavenly calling.

Paul mentions the names of several individuals in verses 10-20. Demas, once a co-laborer with Paul, had now forsaken the apostle in his hour of need. He loved the world and did not want to suffer the reproach of Christ with Paul. This did not mean that he was not a true believer or that he had denied the faith. Rather, Demas chose to live as a worldling instead of joining with Paul in suffering for Heaven. Demas went to Thessalonica (v. 10). Crescens went to minister in Galatia (v. 10). Titus, Paul's spiritual son, helper, and messenger, went to Dalmatia (formerly Yugoslavia; v. 10).

Luke, the beloved doctor, the writer of Luke and Acts, accompanied Paul on many of his journeys and was one of Paul's few companions at the time this epistle was written (v. 11). Tychicus was a scribe for Paul and delivered his epistles. He was also Paul's traveling companion; but he was then in Ephesus (v. 12). Carpus lived in Troas, and had probably been hospitable to Paul during his travels (v. 13). Alexander the coppersmith had relentlessly opposed the gospel and ill-treated Paul, but the Lord would repay Alexander for his hostility to the truth on Judgment Day (vv. 14-15).

Prisca and Aquila had labored with Paul in tent-making and also hosted church meetings in their home at several locales. They cared for and taught Apollos in Ephesus (v. 19). The household of Onesiphorus was in Ephesus where they had been hospitality to Paul. Onesiphorus was not ashamed of Paul's chains and traveled to Rome to encourage the suffering apostle.

Erastus remained in Corinth, and was a prior traveling companion of Timothy in Macedonia (v. 20; Acts. 19:22). Trophimus, being sick had been left at Miletus (v. 20). Eubulus, Pudens, Linus, and Claudia were likely brethren at Rome who had deserted Paul, but he politely listed their names.

Paul provides Timothy with a brief update of his legal efforts to be acquitted and released from prison. At his initial hearing, no one stood with Paul but the Lord. Although alone, Paul was not bitter about his situation as shown by his request that the Lord not judge those who had forsaken him (v. 16). Rather, Paul was thankful to have received the Lord's help in responding to the charges against him, and that the Lord had chosen to preserve his life a bit longer. This meant that the Lord was not finished with Paul. Indeed, we have this letter to appreciate because of this short reprieve.

Before his first hearing, the apostle thought that he might be immediately executed, but God delivered Paul *"out of the mouth of the lion"* (poetically describing the place of death; v. 17). Paul expresses his thankfulness to God and his appreciation for more time to serve the Lord. The apostle is confident that, through Christ, he will be empowered to honor his Savior in his remaining days and that he will be eternally preserved to rule and reign with Christ in His kingdom (v. 18). Paul's final words to his beloved son were to affirm that the presence and grace of Christ would enable him to do all that he had written (vv. 21-22).

# Titus

## Background

Titus was Greek by birth (Gal. 2:1). Since Paul refers to him as his spiritual son (1:4), it is likely that Titus first heard the gospel message through Paul's preaching, or at least Paul was instrumental in discipling him as a young convert to Christ. Titus was the object lesson of the Jerusalem Council (Gal. 2:1-3; Acts 15) which concluded that Gentile believers did not need to be circumcised or to adhere to the Law to be received by Christ or to be preserved in Christ. Law-keeping did not result in or maintain one's salvation, which was completely founded on grace in Christ.

Titus is not mentioned in the book of Acts, but his name appears in four of Paul's epistles. From 2 Corinthians we learn that he was sent by Paul to Corinth to assess how the Church fared after receiving Paul's *sorrowful letter* rebuking some in that Church (2 Cor. 7:6-14). Titus, with two other men, were put in charge of the collection being made in Achaia and Macedonia for the poor saints in Jerusalem (2 Cor. 8:6, 16, 23). Paul also sent him to Dalmatia, a region formerly known as Yugoslavia until the 1990s (4:10).

The only biblical account of Paul being in Crete was when the ship carrying him to Rome as a prisoner briefly harbored at Fair Havens, on the south side of the island (Acts 27:8). Since Luke accompanied Paul during many of his later years of ministry, he would have certainly been aware of such a visit to the remote isle and recorded it in the book of Acts.

Piecing together various biblical accounts of Paul's journeys, it is likely that Paul and Titus visited Crete after his first Roman imprisonment. Paul left Titus in Crete (v. 5) and sailed to Ephesus, where he left Timothy to address an issue of doctrinal error in the assembly. Leaving Timothy in Ephesus (1 Tim. 1:3-4), Paul sailed across the Aegean Sea to visit Philippi (Phil. 1:26). Lastly, he traveled southwest across Macedonia to Nicopolis, where he planned to stay throughout the winter. The apostle hoped that Titus would again join him there (3:12).

There were approximately one hundred cities on the island of Crete at this time, and many had local churches. Titus was to ensure that men who were already actively shepherding in the assembly would be properly recognized as church elders. This epistle records the final instructions of the older missionary to this younger servant of the Lord.

## Theme(s)
"Church Order," "Sound Doctrine is Lived Out," "Good Works."

## Keywords
Keywords and phrases include: "doctrine," "elder/bishop," "blameless," "works," "sober-minded," "sound," "hope," and "foolish."

## Date
Likely written in 64 or 65 A.D., perhaps from Macedonia, just before Paul's second Roman imprisonment. As the content is similar to 1 Timothy, both epistles were probably written at about the same time.

## Outline
I. Introduction (1:1-4).
II. Characteristics and Duties of a Church Elder (1:5-16).
III. Living Sound Doctrine (2:1-15).
IV. Maintain Good Works (3:1-11).
V. Closing (3:12-15).

# Titus Chapter 1

## Salutation (vv. 1-4)

Paul refers to himself as both a bondservant and as an apostle of Jesus Christ in verse 1. According to the Mosaic Law, a Hebrew slave was to be released after six years of service, or at the fifty-year Jubilee if occurring before the six-year tenure was served. The slave could choose to remain with his master for life (Lev. 25:39-42). For this choice, the slave's ear was punched through with an awl and he was thus marked as a bondservant for life. Hence, Paul often referred to himself as a bondservant to express his own love for and lifelong commitment to the Lord Jesus Christ.

Paul was also an apostle, or "sent one," of Jesus Christ to minister "the gospel of God" (Rom. 1:1). Those responding to this truth were God's elect, as evidenced by ongoing faith that produced godly living (v. 1). Moreover, all who receive eternal life in Christ have the hope of abiding with God forever (John 5:24; 1 Thess. 4:17) in glorified bodies (1 Cor. 15:51-52), as He has promised. God cannot lie!

In Paul's salutation in 2 Timothy, we read of a similar declaration of the believer's hope: *"according to the promise of life which is in Christ Jesus"* (2 Tim. 2:1). The promise of eternal life in Christ is the believer's blessed hope (2:13). At regeneration the believer's soul is saved (3:5), but salvation is not complete until the body is transformed and made fit for Heaven at Christ's coming for His Church (2:13; Rom. 13:11).

The apostle states that "in due time" God revealed His marvelous program of eternal life, which He had predetermined to accomplish in Christ before time began (v. 3). The Old Testament is full of types and shadows of what God would achieve in Christ (e.g., Gen. 3:15), but it is only by New Testament truth that their intended meaning is understood. Just as a child learns to identify letters, colors, and objects by looking at pictures, these inspired teaching aids were to assist the Jews to better understand the reality of God's blessing to them in Christ, *"when the fullness of time had come"* (Gal. 4:4). Now that Christ had come and completed God's redemptive provision for humanity, the gospel message was to be broadcast throughout the world (Matt. 28:19-20). God desires as many as possible hear the message of eternal life and be saved; whosoever will may come to God and taste and see that He is good (2 Pet. 3:9; Rev. 22:17).

Paul referred to Titus as *"a true son in our common faith"* (v. 4). Like Timothy, Titus was both faithful to the Lord and much appreciated by the apostle. Because Titus exhibited all the spiritual and moral qualities of Paul, his teacher, the apostle considered Titus his spiritual descendant. Similarly, all who exhibit Abraham-like faith in God's Word are referred to as sons of Abraham (Gal. 3:7-9).

Paul's salutation to his spiritual sons Timothy and Titus deviates from his traditional greeting in his epistles to assemblies. To Timothy and Titus, he extends a measure of God's mercy in addition to His grace and peace (v. 4; 1 Tim. 1:2). God's abundant mercy would be appreciated in their arduous ministries of caring for God's people and in combatting false doctrine.

## Recognizing Church Elders (vv. 5-9)

Paul left Titus at Crete to encourage the churches on that island to recognize the elders whom the Holy Spirit had already appointed for each local assembly (v. 5; Acts 20:28). There is no God-honoring instance of one man overseeing a local church in the New Testament. Rather, just the opposite was true. The oversight of each local gathering was to be plural in nature. God revealed a similar leadership structure for Israel to follow in Numbers 11:16-25. He was to rule over them as their God, but there were also to be seventy elders who would oversee His people by enforcing His written Law.

God's model for Church order is similar to the one given to Israel: Christ is head of the Church and elders are to oversee local churches. As with Israel, the men who led a local church were normally referred to as "elders." The New Testament clearly indicates that a plurality of qualified men was to share the spiritual leadership of a local church:

- There were elders in the church at Jerusalem (Acts 15:6, 22).
- The sick were instructed to call for the elders of the church (Jas. 5:14).
- Paul and Barnabas recognized "elders in every church" on their missionary journeys (Acts 14:23).
- Peter refers to the elders at particular local churches (1 Pet. 5:1).
- Paul instructed Titus to appoint elders in every city (i.e., every church).
- There were elders at the church at Ephesus (Acts 20:17, 28).
- Paul mentions that there were elders (overseers) and deacons in the church at Philippi (Phil. 1:1).

Elders (a plurality of godly men) are to govern each assembly; they are to pastor those whom God puts into their care, though they may not have received the pastoral spiritual gift (Eph. 4:11). All the elders of a meeting have equal authority, but they do not necessarily have equal gifting or the same spiritual gifts – this is what brings strength and balance to a plurality of church leadership. Elders serving in unity with the mind of Christ is a lovely picture of a triune God at work! In God's design, the male gender is to represent God's glory in the Church (1 Cor. 11:4-7), thus only men were chosen by Christ to be apostles, only men served as church elders (v. 6), and as church deacons (1 Tim. 3:11-12), and only the men were to lead in prayer and teach publicly (1 Cor. 14:34-35; 1 Tim. 2:8-9).

Two Greek words are used in the New Testament to identify those men who held a leadership position in their local church: *presbuteros* (elder; v. 5; Acts 14:23) and *episkopos* (overseer; v. 7; Acts 20:28; 1 Tim. 3:1-2). An *overseer* and *elder* were the same person (Acts 17:28; 20:17, 28, 1 Pet. 5:1-2). Unfortunately, the KJV and NKJV render *episkopos* as "bishop" which reflects the Anglican influence on the KJV translation several centuries ago (i.e., the Church of England already had Church Bishops at that time).

Some have rejected the idea of recognizing church elders after the Apostolic Age was complete. But how then would saints be able to respect and to obey the elders in their assembly, if they do not know who they are (Heb. 3:7, 17)? Moreover, it was not the apostles who chose men for church oversight, the Holy Spirit accomplished that task (Acts 20:28). The apostles merely recognized those whom the Holy Spirit had already chosen. Verses 6-9 provide helpful moral and spiritual criteria for churches throughout the Church Age to recognize those whom God had chosen to lead His people.

The New Testament process of appointing elders is much the same as the process that was used in the Old Testament for anointing David king over Israel (2 Sam. 5:1-3): First, the people recognized that David had been chosen by God to shepherd the nation. Second, they recognized that David was actively shepherding the people even when Saul was king. Third, David was recognized by everyone and anointed king. There was a *divine call*, an *internal call*, and then a *recognized-by-all* process to anoint David king.

Similarly, the Holy Spirit chooses men from among the local flock to be church elders (they are not to be hired in; Acts 14:23, 20:28). Paul affirmed that such men will have an internal desire to do the work (1 Tim. 3:1). Then we have the moral and spiritual criteria in the epistles of 1 Timothy 3 and Titus 1 to publicly recognize those whom God has chosen and whom we see doing shepherding work among us. Titus was to guide the appointing of elders by this process on the island of Crete.

Before reviewing the moral and spiritual criteria for recognizing church elders, we should realize two important things. First, the verb tenses in this section are "present" tense, meaning that the characteristics are not qualifications, but are ongoing characteristics to be displayed in elders. Qualification has a one-time connotation of fitness, but if an elder ceases to display these required attributes, he is disqualified from the office.

Second, an elder is not a perfect man, but he should be characterized by perfect qualities. The chief component of blamelessness should be evident in all aspects of an elder's life, but it does not mean that he is infallible or invincible. Paul provides the following qualities to recognize those men whom God has chosen to be local church elders. The Greek root words are noted for each quality to better discern Paul's meanings (vv. 6-9):

**Blameless** (*anegkletos*): This character trait for elders tops the list of evaluation criterion in both 1 Timothy 3 and Titus 1. This word means unreprovable, unaccused, or blameless. The idea is that an elder is "above reproach or accusation in character." Paul repeats the same word in verse 7 to emphasize the necessity of an elder being unrebukable.

**Husband of one wife**: One wife modifies the noun "husband," meaning that an elder is to literally be "a one-woman man" or "a one-wife husband." This requirement would prohibit a polygamist from being recognized as an elder. If married, the elder must reflect God's best design for marriage, that is, a one-man-and-one-woman relationship. In application, the elder must be morally blameless in the conduct of his marriage. Holy living will be evident in the routine affairs of life, but especially so in the home.

**Having faithful children**: The parallel requirement in 1 Timothy is *"one rules his own house well, having his children in submission with all reverence"* (1 Tim. 3:4). The word "rule" in this verse is drawn from *proistemi*, which means "to stand before in example and practice." Such a man practices what he teaches his children. His children willingly yield to their father's authority because his example makes it advisable to obey, his proven wisdom makes it natural to obey, and his unquestionable love makes it a delight to obey. The idea here is that if a man cannot lead and provide for his own house, he will not be able to oversee the church either. The joyful countenance of a man's wife and the discipline of his children are two visible evidences of a man with godly character and sound leadership!

Parents are responsible for sharing the gospel message with their children, but the Holy Spirit is the only One who can convict them of sin and woo them to Christ to be saved. So "having faithful children" does not mean that all children have come to Christ, but rather, if a man has children, they must respect and honor their father's authority in the home – *"children in submission with all reverence"* (1 Tim. 3:4). Such children must not be accused of dissipation (i.e., wasting money on wanton pleasures) and insubordination (i.e., disobedient and unruly). This disqualification pertains to those children living in the home. Adult children are accountable to the Lord for their own actions.

**A steward of God:** The requirement of blamelessness is repeated a second time and is associated with divinely entrusted stewardship. Does the potential elder identify with what is important to God? Is he careful to be a good administrator over God's affairs assigned to him? Does he feel the weight of responsibility in being directly accountable to God, knowing that he must be under authority to have authority? A self-interested, self-willed man who is an authority unto himself should not be recognized as an elder.

**Not self-willed** (*me authade*): This limitation conveys the meaning of "self-pleasure." An elder must be others-focused in ministry, instead of being driven by self-interests. To shepherd God's people properly, the mind of the Good Shepherd must be displayed: *"Let nothing be done through selfish ambition or conceit, but in lowliness of mind let each esteem others better than himself. Let each of you look out not only for his own interests, but also for the interests of others"* (Phil. 2:3-4).

**Not quick-tempered** (*me orgilon*): *Orgilon* only appears here in the New Testament, so we cannot compare other texts to discern how the word is used. Its meaning is to be quick-tempered, *short-fused,* so to speak. God is slow to anger (Ps. 145:8), and an elder must likewise keep his passions under control to create an atmosphere that will contribute to the best outcome in stressful situations. The spiritual man realizes that *"the wrath of man does not produce the righteousness of God"* (Jas. 1:20).

**Not quarrelsome** (*amachos*): The KJV renders this word as "not a brawler." The idea is that an elder is not contentious; he does not argue or debate with others for the emotional stimulation, but rather abstains from unprofitable discussions that do more harm than good.

**Not given to wine** (*me paroinos*): The literal meaning of these two words is "not staying near wine." *Me paroinos* only occurs one other time in the New Testament (1 Tim. 3:3) and is translated the same way. This is not a prohibition against drinking wine, but the requirement does prohibit its abuse or the abuse of any substance, for that matter. An elder cannot be preoccupied with or overindulgent in drinking wine. He must be filled with the Holy Spirit to shepherd God's people, not controlled by something else.

**Not violent** (*me plektes*): An elder is not to be "a striker" or literally one that is "ready to give a blow." An elder cannot be hot-tempered, prone to emotional outbursts, or quick to attack others. John Darby translates *me plektes* as "not addicted to contention."

**Not greedy for money** (*me aischrokerde*): This is a negative participle meaning "without covetousness or greedy ambitions." An elder should be satisfied with a just and honest income; he does not love or pursue money through foolish means, such as gambling and get-rich-quick schemes.

**Hospitable** (*philoxenos*): This word literally means "fond of guests." All saints are to be given to hospitality (Rom. 12:13;1 Pet. 4:9). Yet an elder realizes the importance of shepherding work that can best be accomplished in the private setting of his home. Elders are raised up from among the sheep (Acts 20:28) and are to remain among the sheep (1 Pet. 5:2-3).

This availability highlights two important aspects of shepherding work. First, it allows the shepherd to observe the attitudes and behavior of believers to provide timely exhortation, encouragement, and, as necessary, reproof. Second, this transparent relationship allows the sheep to observe the elder's godly character, selfless motives, and ability to properly teach the Scripture. Hospitality provides an excellent opportunity to shepherd God's people. For this reason, elders must *"be given to hospitality."* Hospitality demonstrates Christian love to others in one's home. Whether ministering, restoring, refreshing, or shepherding the Lord's people or serving strangers, hospitality is a huge blessing to others.

**A lover of what is good** (*philagathon*): In general, an elder is a lover of goodness, whether in character or deed. Likewise, his own behavior and speech reflects what is good; thus, his actions mark a clear division against what does not have the Lord's approval.

**Sober-minded** (*sophron*): The idea is to be "safe (sound) in mind," or self-controlled (moderate) in one's opinions or passions. *Sophron* is also translated "discreet," "sober," and "temperate." The elder uses discretion in handling people problems and is temperate in his use of authority.

**Just** (*dikaion*): This word implies that an elder will have an impartial, righteous disposition in dealing with others, that has God's approval.

**Holy** (*osion*): An elder is a man who is not defined by sin and maintains a pure disposition towards God that is free from wickedness.

**Self-controlled** (*egkrate*): An elder must not be prone to debilitating excesses; he is mindful of what is lawful and appropriate and maintains proper bodily discipline. David E. West provides this helpful insight into the meaning of this prohibition:

> The Greek word is not used elsewhere in the NT; literally it means "one in control of strength," and so describes the overseer's ability to control his desires and appetites: he must demonstrate that he is temperate in all things. There is a distinction between "sober" and "temperate"; a sober man is moderate in the enjoyment of what is lawful, whereas a temperate man refrains from that which is unlawful and harmful.[117]

Towards others, the elder is just; towards God, he is holy; towards himself, he is to be self-controlled.

**Holding fast the faithful word:** The elder must know, handle, and wisely apply Scripture to correct, reprove, exhort, and encourage others. He rightly uses God's Word in love, to impart knowledge and wisdom that promotes the spiritual growth in others and to detect and confront the spread of false doctrine (v. 9). For this reason, those young in the faith (i.e., a novice in the Scripture) should not be recognized as elders (1 Tim. 3:6).

## Confronting False Teachers (vv. 10-16)

In verse 10, we learn why it was necessary for elders to hold fast to God's Word (v. 9). There were many who were insubordinate, idle talkers, deceivers and legalizers who had infiltrated the gatherings of believers on the island of Crete. The New Testament church meetings permitted believer-priests to use their gifts as enabled by and ordered by the Holy Spirit for the purpose of offering worship to God and for the edification of the saints (1 Cor. 14:23-26, 33-35). *"Where the Spirit of the Lord is, there is liberty"* (2 Cor. 3:17), but when the flesh controls what is meant for God, nothing is accomplished that will please Him (Rom. 8:8).

This is what was occurring on Crete; many of the churches were marked by unruly behavior and unprofitable speech. False teachers were going from house to house subverting the truth for financial gain. This disorderly and destructive behavior had to be stopped and those perverting the truth had to be confronted by those who knew God's Word (v. 11).

Just addressing this serious situation would have been difficult enough, but Titus also had to confront an ungodly culture while trying to promote order, truth, and godliness in the church. Even Epimenides, a Cretan poet and philosopher living in the sixth century B.C., harshly characterized his own countrymen as liars, evil beasts, and lazy gluttons (vv. 12-13). Paul was confirming that not much had changed in six centuries. The Cretans were compulsive liars and indulged in all sorts of wild passions and forms of wickedness. But despite their gross depravity, the gospel of Jesus Christ was saving the Cretans and through the power of the Holy Spirit was transforming them into the moral likeness of Christ.

Paul charges Titus as to what he must do: *"Therefore rebuke them sharply, that they may be sound in the faith"* (v. 13). The propagation of *"Jewish fables and commandments of men"* was stumbling some in their faith and must be stopped (v. 14). It was not necessary for Paul to identify what these Jewish speculations, ritualistic observances and rites were; it all was humanized religion being added into the Christian faith without a scriptural basis. Paul addressed the same issue at Colosse: *"These things indeed have an appearance of wisdom in self-imposed religion, false humility, and neglect of the body, but are of no value against the indulgence of the flesh"* (Col. 2:23). For example, Christians would be more spiritual if they did not eat pork or gave a tithe to God, per the Law.

Titus was not to remain quiet; he was to use sound doctrine to sharply rebuke the Cretans so that the mouths of those propagating false doctrine would be stopped and those in the faith would be edified (vv. 11, 13). Although Timothy did not have to confront the Cretans, Paul gave him similar counsel in dealing with the evil beasts at Ephesus who were preaching heresy (1 Cor. 15:32; 2 Tim. 4:2).

But who are the "they" that should be built up in the faith as a result of rebuking the "them" in verse 13? Commentators have various opinions on this verse's application. Some claim the "them" and "they" refer to the false teachers who were deceived believers who needed to be brought back to biblically-based behavior. While this view is possible, Paul does refer to these as "unbelieving" and "defiled" in verse 15, which better describes the behavior and state of the unregenerate than of believers. Conversely, if Paul were merely addressing questionable matters of ceremonial Law being practiced in the church (which is the context of the passage), then an application towards Christian liberty would be possible.

Other commentators believe that unbelieving false teachers were to be rebuked, so that believers being deceived by them would be built up in their faith. Yet, rarely does Scripture command believers to rebuke the unregenerate. But rebuke is needed to recover believers from sin and deception and restore them to sound faith and life (1:9, 2:15; 1 Tim. 5:20).

Grammatically speaking, "Cretans" in verse 12 is a plural masculine accusative noun, which directly relates to the pronoun rendered "them" in verse 13. "They" is the inflected pronoun represented in the verb *hygiainosin*, which means to "be whole, be healthy, and be sound." This means that "them" and the "they" both refer directly back to the noun "Cretans." The Greek verb *elegche* rendered "rebuke" means "to convict, to expose, and to refute." The adjective *apotomos* translated "sharply" implies "decisive and abrupt sharpness." Putting this all together, Paul was telling Titus: "You know how the Cretans are prone to chase wild ideas. Shepherd the Cretan believers diligently and relentlessly so they may be doctrinally sound."

The proverbial saying that Paul supplies in verse 15 must be interpreted from this context: The propagation of Jewish fables and commandments of men in the church must be challenged. *"To the pure all things are pure, but to those who are defiled and unbelieving nothing is pure; but even their minds and conscience are defiled"* (v. 15).

The context is not addressing blatant sin or what the Bible condemns, but the choosing and forcing unbiblical ideas on others as a measure of spirituality. What is of the flesh cannot please God (Rom. 8:8), so when unbiblical behavior is promoted in the church, disorder and contention result instead of edification. On this point William MacDonald writes:

> Let it be clearly understood that this verse has absolutely nothing to do with things that are sinful in themselves and condemned in the Bible. ... Paul has *not* been speaking about matters of clear-cut morality, of things that are inherently right or wrong. Rather, he has been discussing matters of moral indifference, things that were ceremonially defiling for a Jew living under the law but that are perfectly legitimate for a Christian living under grace. The obvious example is the eating of pork. It was forbidden to God's people in the OT, but the Lord Jesus changed all that when He said that nothing entering into a man can defile him (Mark 7:15). In saying this He pronounced all foods clean (Mark 7:19). ... When he says: **"To the pure all things are pure,"** he means that to the born-again believer all foods are clean, **but to those who are defiled and unbelieving nothing is pure**. It is not what a person eats that defiles him but what comes out of his heart (Mark 7:20–23). If a man's inner life is impure, if he does not have faith in the Lord Jesus, then nothing is pure to him.[118]

Some have taken the application of Paul's proverb out of context and transformed it into an absolute: "As a believer, I am pure, therefore all things that I access as pure are permissible for me to engage in." But all things are not pure despite of what we think about them. Scripture determines what is right and wrong behavior. This verse cannot be used to justify sin!

The false teachers professed to know God, but their deeds did not give any evidence to validate their profession. Rather, their abominable and disobedient behavior disqualified them from doing anything that could please God (v. 16). Only God knows who is truly saved, but believers are to examine the works of those professing Christ to determine what their interaction with them should be (Matt. 7:18-20). Believers can only share Christ's fellowship with those who are in fellowship with Him, and those who are not must be reproved and avoided (e.g., 1 Cor. 5:11). These Judaizers were undermining the truth of the gospel, stumbling Christians in their faith, and dishonoring the name of Christ. They had to be stopped!

# Titus Chapter 2

## Sound Doctrine to Be Demonstrated in the Church (vv. 1-15)

The apostle instructs Titus to teach those *"things which are proper for sound doctrine"* (v. 1). Verse 1 presents the theme of the entire epistle. Doctrine (teaching) is not merely a head knowledge of the truth, but it is to be demonstrated in a blameless life. God's Word is living and powerful and is to have its way with those who have been born again in Christ (Heb. 4:12). What we know to be truth is to be reflected in all that we say and what we do. This godly manner of life stood in sharp contrast to the false teachers whose conduct denied the true reality of the faith.

Paul then supplies life-promoting doctrine for various gender and age groups to consider in order to have a good testimony of Christ in their lives. The apostle first speaks to **the older men** and identifies six character traits to be evident in their behavior (v. 2):

**Sober** (*nephalios*): *Nephalios* means to be "sober-minded" or figuratively, to be cautious and temperate. Older men were not to be rash in behavior or prone to debilitating excesses; they must be *level-headed*.

**Grave** (*semnos*): A grave man is an honorable man – he is balanced in judgment, honest, and not controlled by hasty speech, substances or the love of money. His motives are pure, and his behavior is blameless.

**Temperate** (*sophron*): The idea is to be "safe (sound) in mind," or self-controlled (moderate) in one's opinions or passions. *Sophron* is also translated "discreet," "sober," and "temperate."

**Sound in faith** (*hygiaino pistis*): This trait implies having wholesome and healthy faith that expresses optimism, thankfulness, and opinions free from any mixture of error, cynicism or bitterness. Such a man is not blown to and fro by winds of doctrine; he knows God's Word and is consistent.

**In love** (*agape*): Older men are to express sacrificial and tender love to others. This is only possible when one possesses a lowly mind that esteems others better than oneself (Phil. 2:3).

**Patient** (*hupomone*): This word has the meaning of "cheerful endurance, constancy, and patient continuance." One of the greatest assets to a man is a tenacious character that relies upon the Lord for direction and grace and is longsuffering with others.

Next, Paul conveys the character traits that should be admired in **older women** of the faith. Paul also addresses the ministry that older women should not neglect in verse 3:

**Reverent in behavior** (*hieroprepes katastema*): This is the only time that the Greek word *hieroprepes,* translated *"reverent in"* occurs in the New Testament. A spiritual woman will passionately aspire to holy living. Holiness is not just not sinning; it is a mindset of being blameless, an attitude that loathes wickedness, and a heart that is determined to remain in the center of God's will. Holiness demonstrates reverence for God.

**Not slanderers** (*me diabolos*): Older women were not to be engaged in malicious gossip and slander. The Greek word *diabolos,* translated "devil" 34 times in the New Testament, is applied here. Literally, "devil," which is not a proper name, means "slanderer." Slander (*dibbah*) means "to defame or give an evil (unrighteous) report." In Paul's estimation, older women were prone to jump to conclusions without all the facts and then deliberately and ungraciously share these presumptuous judgments with others. Such behavior, at best, distorts the truth concerning the guilty and at its worst defames and defrauds the innocent. God is not glorified in either case.

**Not given to much wine**: Believers are not to be controlled or mastered by substances; they are to be controlled by the Holy Spirit (1 Cor. 6:12; Eph. 5:18). Why did Paul exhort the older women and not others concerning the abuse of alcohol? Perhaps, being at home, there was more opportunity, and if her children were grown, there would be less accountability.

**Teachers of good things**: What good things were the older women to teach? They were commissioned to teach and admonish younger women how to be better wives, mothers, and keepers of the home (v. 4). For discretion and because experience is a great teacher, the older women, not Titus, were to assist the younger women in these matters. The older sisters had a wealth of practical knowledge in domestic affairs to pass down to the younger women. Such instruction would lessen the possibility of a new wife and mother needlessly repeating the past mistakes of others. Younger women should seek friendships with spiritually-minded older women; the result will enhance personal growth in performing domestic responsibilities.

The older women were to teach good things from Scripture and from their experience to admonish the younger women to be faithful in their God-given roles in the home. The verb *sophronizo* is rendered "admonish" and means "to restore one to his or her senses and to make sound in mind." Older women can help settle younger women in their roles as a wife and mother. After addressing this important ministry of the older sisters, Paul identifies the qualities of character and of service that should mark **younger**

**women** (i.e., young wives and mothers; vv. 4-5).

**To love their husbands:** This is the only time in the New Testament that the word *philandros* occurs; it means to "be fond of or affectionate to." A husband is commanded several times in Scripture to sacrificially love his wife (e.g., Eph. 5:25-33), while the wife is to learn to be warm, kind, and friendly towards her husband. Clearly, the husband is to be like Christ and be the initiator of love in the relationship. As he loves his wife as Christ loves the Church, feelings of love will naturally well up within her. She will reciprocate these feelings back to her husband who initiated love, in the same way the Church naturally responds to Christ's love (1 Jn. 4:19).

William MacDonald suggests some practical ways that wives can demonstrate love and respect to their husbands as godly helpers:

> By acknowledging his headship in the home, by making no major decisions apart from him, by keeping an orderly home, by paying attention to personal appearance, by living within their means, by confessing promptly, by forgiving graciously, by keeping the lines of communication always open, by refraining from criticizing or contradicting her husband in front of others, and by being supportive when things go wrong.[119]

**To love their children:** *Philoteknos* is found only here in the New Testament, and speaks of the maternal fondness a mother is to have for her children. It seems strange that Paul would have to exhort young women to be friendly and kind towards their children, for the mother-child relationship is a strong natural bond. But there is a difference between providing for the temporal needs of a child and adequately preparing them to serve the Lord.

True maternal love is marked by an active prayer life that empowers a mother to properly teach, discipline, and encourage her children Heavenward. A spiritually-minded mother will be available to spend time with her children, to know them, and to assist them in overcoming life's difficulties and their own character weaknesses. The excitement of going to a ballgame is temporary, but children's appreciation for parents who assist them in overcoming lingering impediments ensures abiding endearment.

**Discreet** (*Sophron*): This Greek word appeared in verse 2 with the same inflection; it was rendered as "temperate" there and as "discreet" in verse 5. The characteristics of self-control, self-discipline, and prudence are paramount traits of a godly woman.

**Chaste** (*hagnos*): Chaste implies "clean" in the figurative sense. Scripturally speaking, it means "modest, pure, innocent, and clean." In view is sexual purity. It refers to faithfulness to one's husband, a clean thought-life, wearing modest attire, and innocent responses. The chaste woman sees no value in reading romance novels or in watching inappropriate movies and soap operas. Her love and her mind are pure, undefiled, and innocent.

**Keepers at home** (*oikourgos*): *"Keepers at home"* does not mean a wife can never leave the home, but her desire and primary ministry is at home, rather than elsewhere. The literal meaning of this phrase is that she is "a guardian at home." Wives and mothers are to be gatekeepers in the home; they keep out bad attitudes, elements that taint, and whatever might defile the household. They maintain an orderly home so that Satan cannot establish a base of operation within it to cause chaos (1 Tim. 5:14).

**Good** (*agathos*): The psalmist proclaims of God, *"You are good, and do good"* (Ps. 119:68). Goodness is an attribute of God, and all His doings are good. He is not selfish, but gracious and generous to others. A spiritual woman will be good to others. She will be given to hospitality, to assisting the needy, to encouraging the brokenhearted; she will live to serve others.

**Obedient to their own husbands**: Obedient means to submit to or be respectful of her husband's God-given authority in the home. *"Wives, submit to your own husbands, as to the Lord"* (Eph. 5:22). If wives choose not to adhere to God's order of authority in the home (i.e., they will not submit to their husbands as unto the Lord), then God's name is blasphemed.

Lastly, Paul states that **young men** should maintain various character qualities to properly reflect Christ in their lives (v. 6). Paul shifts to specific exhortations for Titus to consider in verse 7, but these would be profitable for any young man involved in ministry for the Lord to heed also:

**To be sober-minded** (*sophroneo*): This is the verb form of *sophron*, which has already appeared in verses 2 and 5. Paul highlights the need for all God's people, regardless of age or gender, to have self-control, self-discipline, and discretion. *Sophroneo* exhorts young men to have moderate behavior and to make sound judgments. A spiritual man controls himself under stress and when spoken ill of. He does not resort to teasing, jabbing, or sarcasm to promote himself or to put others down (Jas. 1:26; 3:2).

**Be a pattern of good works** (v. 7): Titus was to influence his peers to foster godly behavior consistent with sound doctrine. Hence, Titus was to teach them doctrine from Scripture and then exemplify what he was teaching by a pattern of good works. Titus was to practice what he taught. He also had a high-profile ministry which necessitated that he must have impeccable character, a blameless life, and a pattern of good works.

Young men should be given to good works, whether in ministry or as providers for themselves and their families. A good work ethic is necessary and proper: *"But if any does not provide for his own, and especially for those of his own household, he has denied the faith, and is worse than an unbeliever"* (1 Tim. 5:8). A godly man sticks with tasks and jobs until finished; he does not give up easily, nor is he a professional tumbleweed. He does not acquire debt through poor judgments or laziness.

**In doctrine** (*en didaskalia*): Titus must be in Scripture to learn sound doctrine and live it out (v. 1; Prov. 2:1-2; 2 Tim. 2:15). A spiritually-minded man will search out Scripture and seek godly counsel before acting on something important. He will be in God's Word daily and passionately desire to obey what God has for him.

**Showing integrity** (*adiaphthoria*): There was to be no corruption in what Titus taught the younger men from Scripture or through his example.

**Reverence** (*semnotes*): Titus' teachings must be dignified.

**Incorruptibility** (*aphtharsia*): Titus was to be known for his genuineness and for holding to the truth in purity, no matter what.

**Sound speech** (*hygies logos*): Sound or whole speech is streamlined to reflect the truth, such that people cannot take exception to it. Rambling down "rabbit trails," or telling jokes, or venturing into political topics and other secular oddities provide opportunities for someone to take issue with something said. Then the speaker has to waste more time addressing what should have never been voiced in the first place.

Although the Bible does not endorse slavery, it does place limits on its practices (Lev. 25:39-42; Deut. 15:12). As Christianity spread through the Roman Empire, both slaves and masters were becoming Christians and brethren in Christ. This created a difficulty, as all those in Christ should mutually love, respect, and serve each other, but slavery did not permit such social liberty. How should believers who were slaves behave? What attitude should they have towards unbelieving masters who were often brutal?

Paul gives wise advice to his spiritual sons, Timothy (1 Tim. 6:1-2) and Titus in verses 9-10 to answer these questions. Slaves were to honor those in authority over them and to labor with faithful dignity and good fidelity as unto the Lord. This meant that they were not to answer their masters disrespectfully or to steal from them (v. 9). We learn submission through authority and willing obedience was a good testimony of the grace of God in one's life. Slaves that had believing masters were not to think of them negatively, for masters and slaves were all positionally one in Christ (Gal. 3:28). Social standing does not affect spiritual standing.

Verse 11 does not teach that there is the universal salvation of all men, but rather, *"the grace of God that brings salvation"* is available to all men through Christ. *"The Lord is not slack concerning His promise, as some count slackness, but is longsuffering toward us, not willing that any should perish but that all should come to repentance"* (2 Pet. 3:9).

Those coming to Christ for salvation realize that by grace they are a new creation in Christ and must live out His life. What they were in Adam is positionally dead, but they are now alive in Christ. Hence, Christians are ambassadors of Christ and citizens of Heaven (Phil. 3:21) and must turn away from ungodliness and worldly lusts in order to represent the righteous and godly character of Christ to those sojourning with them in the world (v. 12). This duty is to continue until each believer is with the Lord through death or by the Rapture (2 Cor. 5:8; 1 Thess. 4:17).

As pilgrims, who belong where they are going, and as strangers, who do not belong where they are, believers are to live expectantly for Christ's imminent return to the air to remove them from the earth to Heaven. Paul refers to this event as *"the blessed hope and glorious appearing of our great God and Savior Jesus Christ"* (v. 13). As there is only one article in the latter phrase, Greek grammar confirms that our great God is Jesus Christ!

The word "hope" in the New Testament is extensively used to speak of the Rapture of the Church. Afterwards, *hope* disappears, for the promise is realized (1 Cor. 13:8-13). Thus, there is only *"one hope"* for the Church (Eph. 4:4). Meditating on this hope provides joy during dark days and promotes holy living now (1 Jn. 3:2-3). Certainly, the Church will rejoice with Christ when He vindicates His name at His second advent (Rev. 19:11-21), but chronologically speaking, the Church's hope is for the imminent coming of her Bridegroom (2 Cor. 11:2). F. B. Hole summarizes the matter:

> The glory will be the fruition of all the hopes that grace has awakened. It may well be that, by *the blessed hope*, the Apostle indicated the coming of the Lord for His saints ... if so we have both His coming *for* and His coming *with* His saints set before us as our hope in verse 13.[120]

Paul then reminds Titus to exhort believers to pursue godly living. The blood of Christ is intended to not merely redeem lost people, but to purify and set them apart as a holy people fit for God's use (v. 14). God's redeemed and purified people should therefore be zealous for good works!

All that Paul had written in the previous verses was to be taught and lived out by Titus. He was commissioned to teach, exhort, rebuke, and encourage godly living that would be pleasing to Christ in the Cretan believers. Titus was not to be bashful or apologetic in performing this ministry. He was not to permit his young age, his Gentile ethnicity, or his personal limitations to interfere with his divinely assigned task. Having the full authority and power of God, he was to be bold in ministry, and not to permit anyone to despise him in performing it (v. 15).

# Titus Chapter 3

Exhortations for the Church (vv. 1-11)
In this chapter, Paul issues several exhortations to Titus concerning godliness, starting with his relationship with authority. Submission to God-ordained authority (when it is not acting against His revealed truth) is critical to obtaining God's blessing and to being a testimony of God's grace in our communities (v. 1). Believers must willingly obey laws and yield their personal rights as necessary for the good of others to honor God in society.

Believers are not to be contentious people, but peaceable. They should not be gossipers or slanderers, knowing that unjust and unneeded talk can do irreparable damage to one's name and testimony (v. 2). What is said about others should be true (based on the facts), stated gently (in the spirit of genuine love and concern), and only voiced if necessary to prevent others from being hurt and for the good of the subject (Eph. 5:15, 29).

Verse 3 describes what a believer was by nature, verses 4-7 define what the believer possesses by grace, and verse 8 describes the practical benefits of salvation. Before conversion, we were foolish, disobedient, carried away by lust, void of truth, living for pleasure, and governed by envy and resentment (v. 3). Mercifully, the love of God appeared in Christ, who suffered in the sinner's stead that grace might be offered to humanity (v. 4).

True believers, those who trust Christ alone for salvation, undergo cleansing and regeneration and are implanted with Christ's life (vv. 5-6). Prior to trusting Christ as Lord and Savior, we do not have the ability to please God. In fact, our flesh nature directly opposes God in thought and deed (Rom. 5:10, 8:7). The believer needs a new nature that longs to please God and perform His will (Rom. 8:5-6). This new nature is received from God at conversion by the cleansing and regeneration of the Holy Spirit.

This cleansing does not mean that all the sinful tendencies, addictions, and bad character qualities are removed from believers at their conversion. But the purifying work of the Holy Spirit at that time will affect their thinking towards such things. They will not desire or be able to enjoy sin as they once did. In some cases, addictions will be overcome instantly, but in others, the believer will struggle to overcome what he or she now detests.

The cleansing away of old attitudes and the implanting of new ones will prompt believers to learn to rely on the power of the Holy Spirit to overcome the conduct they now know displeases God. Regeneration is the implanting of a new life and a new order of living. Conversion results in a new creation. David Gooding summarizes these works of the Holy Spirit at conversion:

> The washing of regeneration is an initial experience of salvation which holds two ideas. First, it is a washing, a cleansing away of evil and polluted things. In the second place it is regeneration, the positive implanting of a new life, and order of living. The Holy Spirit washes us by bringing us to see the wrong and evil in our sinful attitudes and desires. He makes us feel their uncleanness, and leads us to repent of them and repudiate them. More deeply than that, He brings us to see that, in spite of all our efforts to improve ourselves, we cannot eradicate these evil powers within us: we need a Savior. We cry in the secret of our heart: *"O wretched man that I am! Who shall deliver me? For all too often the good things I want to do, I don't do; and the bad things I don't want to do, I do"* (Rom. 7:15-25). And He brings us to the point where we are prepared for all the changes of lifestyle that we must be willing to accept, if we receive Christ from now on as Savior and Lord of our lives.[121]

Those who are justified in Christ are able to experience the renewing power of the Holy Spirit on an ongoing basis. The Holy Spirit enables believers to live for Christ, and to also experience the joy of God's love. They also have the assurance of being joint-heirs with Christ (Rom. 8:16-17) and the secure hope of dwelling with God forever (v. 7).

Titus was to constantly affirm these truths to guard his own mind against discouragement during disappointing times in his ministry (v. 8). Those who had professed Christ were to remember that the validity of their profession would be proven by their continuing in good works. To disassociate good works from one's salvation was an unprofitable doctrine: *"Faith by itself, if it does not have works, is dead"* (Jas. 2:17). Salvation in Christ is received by grace through faith, but faith never stands alone; it has good works alongside. Works prove the reality of what someone truly believes and this is a *"faithful saying"* (an important doctrine) to remember.

In verses 9-11 Paul provides helpful insights both in identifying and dealing with heretics in the church. A heretic does not necessarily promote false doctrine, but his unbalanced focus on particulars causes division among God's people. For example, a heretic might major on a minor which is unprofitable (i.e., foolish disputes, genealogies, and striving about the Law; v. 9). Or a heretic might focus on one truth to the exclusion of the full truth (e.g., spiritualizing Scripture or twisting its context to elevate the importance of a particular teaching). A heretic might forward certain political or social views while ignoring scriptural insights on such matters.

Heretics often have hobbyhorse topics which they relentlessly *ride* to sway people to their position. These pet topics usually have nothing to do with how to live more effectively for Christ. The heretic exalts himself by promoting what does not matter, he wastes the time of the saints, and exhausts them to the point of causing division among God's people (v. 10).

Titus was to work with the church elders in dealing with this dangerous threat to church unity. Heretics were to be warned twice and then expelled from the church fellowship if they did not repent of their behavior (v. 10). Anyone who professes to know Christ, but continues to do what harms the Body of Christ sins against Christ. Such a person is warped in his or her thinking (v. 11). Having been warned, anyone continuing to harm the saints for self-promoting reasons would be self-condemned in their conscience.

Many of the Lord's people tend to argue about things that have little or no bearing on what is important to God. Paul told Timothy to avoid such arguments because they tend to needlessly divide the Lord's people. How do Christians benefit by foolish disputes concerning genealogies, humanized traditions, or matters of Christian liberty? The Lord reproved the Pharisees for majoring on the minor aspects of the Law and neglecting the more important and profitable aspects (Matt. 23:23). We too must be careful not to seize on one tenet of scriptural truth while ignoring all that God reveals in His Word to be obeyed. The truth is in the whole!

## Closing Remarks (vv. 12-15)

Sometime after Paul's first imprisonment, he sailed to Crete with Titus. After a period of time, Paul left Titus at Crete and went on to Ephesus. His plan was to ultimately journey to Nicopolis in southwest Macedonia. After he arrived at Nicopolis, Paul would send one of two messengers, Artemas or Tychicus, to Titus (v. 12). Titus was then to depart Crete with his escort and come to Nicopolis, where Paul planned to winter (probably in 65 A.D.).

Apparently, Zenas (a lawyer) and Apollos were on their way to see Titus. They were likely carrying the letter to Titus that we are reading. Paul seemed concerned that the Cretans might be stingy with sharing their funds and hospitality with these men (v. 13). Titus was to ensure that they were properly cared for and that their financial needs for traveling were met (v. 14). By attending to the needs of others in this way, the Cretan saints were bearing fruitful works which testified that they had received grace in Christ.

Paul's final words to Titus were to affirm that the presence and grace of Christ would enable him to do all that he had written (v. 15).

# Philemon

## Background
A slave named Onesimus had run away from his master Philemon, who lived in Colosse. Onesimus traveled as far as Rome before hearing the gospel message and trusting Christ as Savior. After making contact with Paul in prison, he was under conviction to return to his master and make amends for the wrong he had done. Apparently, Onesimus had stolen from his master before fleeing Colosse (vv. 11, 18).

Tychicus was to accompany Onesimus back to Philemon and to hand-deliver this letter. Paul intercedes for Onesimus and asks Philemon to receive Onesimus as if he were Paul himself. Onesimus was now a brother in Christ and, thus, would live up to his name and be a "profitable" servant.

Paul instructs Philemon to forgive Onesimus and to lay any personal losses connected with his offense to Paul's personal account. Given Paul's plea for restoration, the spiritual debt Philemon owed Paul (vv. 19-20), and the love Philemon was known for (vv. 5-7), it is not likely that Philemon charged Paul for what Onesimus had stolen, but rather forgave him the debt.

## Theme(s)
A Forgiving Love Ensures Restoration.

## Keywords
Keywords and phrases include: "love/love's sake," "receive him," "saints," "profitable/Onesimus," "unprofitable," and "me/mine/myself."

## Date
Likely written during the mid-portion of Paul's first Roman imprisonment (approximately 61 A.D.).

## Outline
I.  Introduction (vv. 1-3).
II. The Character of Philemon (vv. 4-7).
III. Intercession for Onesimus (vv. 8-21).
IV. Closing (vv. 22-25).

# Philemon

## Introduction (vv. 1-3)

In addressing Philemon, Paul refers to himself as a prisoner of Christ Jesus. True, Paul was a prisoner at Rome, but as indicated in other epistles, he considered himself a lifetime bondservant of Christ (v. 1). Timothy was with Paul at this time, so he included his name in the salutation.

Philemon's name means "affectionate" and he lived up to his name, for Paul calls him his *"beloved friend and fellow laborer."* Paul also salutes Apphia, likely Philemon's wife, and Archippus, possibly Philemon's son. Archippus was a fellow soldier of the cross and hosted a church meeting in his home at Colosse (v. 2). Churches commonly gathered in homes during the early years of the Church Age (e.g., Rom. 16:5; Col. 4:15).

Continuing his salutation, Paul declares *"grace to you and peace from God our Father and the Lord Jesus Christ"* (v. 3). This is Paul's trademark greeting and is his usual salute to saints elsewhere (Rom. 1:7; 1 Cor. 1:3).

## The Character of Philemon (vv. 4-7)

The apostle frequently prayed for Philemon and praised God for his love and faith towards Christ, which was shown by his care of other believers (vv. 4-5). Philemon shared his faith with others through good works (v. 6).

Paul acknowledged that Philemon had refreshed the hearts of many saints, which caused the apostle to offer joyful thanks to God (v. 7). In love for Christ, the Holy Spirit refreshes the saints through us, but if our love for Him grows cold, the flesh will prompt disunity and declension in the saints.

## Intercession for Onesimus (vv. 8-21).

Paul reveals the purpose of his letter in verse 8. As an apostle, he could have commanded Philemon to forgive and receive the repentant runaway slave Onesimus, but Paul desired to accomplish more than just righting a wrong. Paul desired that Philemon's love for Paul and not an apostolic command would prompt restoration. That would create a positive situation for Onesimus in relationship to his master, whereas Philemon receiving Onesimus by command might create a miserable environment for the slave.

So Paul, as an imprisoned older man deserving of Philemon's sympathy, appeals to Philemon (v. 9). Paul then intercedes for Onesimus, a runaway slave who had traveled as far as Rome before meeting Paul in prison and hearing the gospel (v. 10). After trusting Christ as Savior, Onesimus came under conviction for his behavior and wanted to return to his master and make amends for the wrong he had done, Apparently, Onesimus had stolen from his master before fleeing Colosse (v. 18).

Onesimus' name means "profitable," so Paul uses a play on words to inform Philemon that his previously *unprofitable* servant would now be *profitable* to him – he would be a better servant than before (v. 11). He was lost for a season, but now was a brother in Christ forever (v. 16). Therefore, Paul was sending "his own heart" (speaking of Onesimus) back to Philemon and asking that he receive his newly saved slave, Paul's son in the faith, as if he were receiving Paul himself (v. 12). Tychicus was carrying Paul's letter to the church at Colosse, and also escorting Onesimus to Philemon.

Paul desired that Onesimus remain with him in Rome to assist him, but he knew that the offense must be dealt with first (v. 13). Although a believer, Onesimus was still Philemon's property. Paul knew that Philemon would probably approve of Onesimus ministering to him, but he would not infringe on Philemon's authority without his permission (v. 14). Such presumption would taint the beauty of Philemon's kindness without his consent.

Moreover, Paul asked Philemon to forgive Onesimus and to lay any losses he had suffered by him to his account (v. 18). Whether or not Paul wrote the entire letter or not is unknown, but Paul picked up the pen at this point and signed his name to formalize his commitment to pay the debt (v. 19). Paul then reminded Philemon that he now enjoyed eternal life because Paul had shared with him, without cost, the message of Christ.

Given Paul's personal plea, the spiritual debt Philemon owed Paul, and Philemon's love for the Lord and Paul, we may safely assume that Philemon did not charge Paul for what had been stolen. Rather, Philemon forgave the debt and received Onesimus as a brother in the Lord, as if he were the apostle himself (v. 17), and the Lord Jesus Himself (Matt. 25:40). Knowing Philemon, Paul was confident that he would do this and more and that his heart would be refreshed by Philemon's gracious response (vv. 20-21).

## Closing (vv. 22-25)

Optimistic of his release, Paul asked that Philemon prepare a guest room for him (v. 22). It is unknown if Paul ever traveled to Colosse, but Philemon was ready for him nonetheless! Paul closed his letter by imparting grace and passing along greetings from Epaphras (a fellow prisoner), and fellow laborers: Mark, Aristarchus, Demas, and Luke (vv. 23-25).

# Endnotes

1. William MacDonald, *Believer's Bible Commentary* (Thomas Nelson Publishers, Nashville: 1989) op. cit., p. 1679
2. F. B. Hole, *Romans*, STEM Publishing; Rom. 1: https://stempublishing.com/authors/hole/NT/ROMANS.html
3. L. M. Grant, *Romans*, STEM Publishing; Rom. 2: https://www.stempublishing.com/authors/grantlm/ROMANS.html#a2
4. Bruce, F. F., *Romans: An Introduction and Commentary, Vol. 6* (InterVarsity Press; Downers Grove, IL; 1985), pp. 101–102
5. Charles Stanley, *The Epistle to the Romans*, STEM Publishing; Rom. 3: https://stempublishing.com/authors/stanley/Romans.html#a3
6. C. H. Mackintosh, *Genesis to Deuteronomy* (Loizeaux Brothers, Inc., Neptune, NJ; 1972), p. 389
7. Warren Wiersbe, *The Bible Exposition Commentary* Vol. 1 (Victor Books, Wheaton, IL; 1989), Rom. 5:12-14
8. F. B. Hole, *Romans*, op. cit.; Rom. 5
9. Oswald Sanders, Spiritual Lessons, (Moody, Chicago, IL; 1975), pp. 112-113
10. C. H. Mackintosh, *Numbers*, STEM Publishing; Num. 21: http://stempublishing.com/authors/mackintosh/Pent/NUMBERS0.html
11. J. G. Bellett, *Thoughts on Romans*, STEM Publishing; Rom. 7 https://stempublishing.com/authors/bellett/Rom6_8.html
12. Charles Ryrie, *So Great Salvation* (Victor Books, Wheaton, IL; 1989), pp. 59-60
13. J. N. Darby, *Romans*, STEM Publishing; Rom. 7 https://www.stempublishing.com/authors/darby/MISCELLA/33016E.html
14. E. J. Young, *The Book of Isaiah*, (Eerdmans Publishing Co., Grand Rapids, MI; 1965), Isa. 65
15. Fred Stallan, *What the Bible Teaches*: Romans (John Ritchie LTD, UK; 1998), p. 250
16. W. E. Vine, *Isaiah, Prophecies, Promises, Warnings* (Oliphants Ltd., London and Edinburgh; 1946), Isa. 65
17. Fred Stallan, op. cit., p. 284
18. William MacDonald, op. cit., p. 1732
19. F. B. Hole, *Romans*, op. cit.; Rom. 13
20. Warren Wiersbe, op. cit., Rom. 14:10-12
21. Charles Stanley, op. cit. *The Epistle to the Romans*, Rom. 14
22. Jack Hunter, *What the Bible Teaches: 1 Corinthians* (John Ritchie LTD, UK; 2015), pp. 7-8
23. William MacDonald, op. cit., p. 1748
24. Hamilton Smith, *What the Bible Teaches: 1 Corinthians*, STEM Publishing; 1 Cor. 2: https://stempublishing.com/authors/smith/CORINTH1.html#a2
25. F. B. Hole, *Isaiah*, STEM Publishing; Isa. 64: https://stempublishing.com/authors/hole/Art/ISAIAH.html

26 Randy P. Amos, *The Church* (Henrietta, NY); no date
27 William MacDonald, op. cit., p. 1773
28 Warren Wiersbe, op. cit., 1 Cor. 9:24-27
29 Jack Hunter, op. cit., p. 107
30 C. H. Mackintosh, op. cit., Num. 8
31 Jack Hunter, op. cit., p. 146
32 Darren Carlson, *"When Muslims Dream of Jesus"* (International Mission News; May 31, 2018): https://www.thegospelcoalition.org/article/muslims-dream-jesus
33 Ronald Gregor Smith, *Secular Christianity* (Collins, England; 1966), p. 103
34 H. A. Ironside, *Isaiah* – Revised Edition (Loizeaux, Neptune, NJ; 2000), p. 255
35 Warren Wiersbe, op. cit., 2 Cor. 1:7
36 H. A. Ironside, *Notes on the Book of Ezra* (Shiloh Christian Library, no date); pp. 5-6
37 Albert McShane, *What the Bible Teaches: 2 Corinthians* (John Ritchie LTD, UK; 2015), p. 283
38 William MacDonald, op. cit., p. 1854
39 H. A. Ironside, *Ezekiel* (Loizeaux, Neptune, NJ; 1949), p. 82
40 F. B. Hole, *2 Corinthians*, STEM Publishing; 2 Cor. 11: https://stempublishing.com/authors/hole/NT/2CORINTH.html#a11
41 Warren Wiersbe, op. cit., 2 Cor. 12:1-6
42 Albert McShane, op. cit., pp. 396-397
43 Jack Hunter, *What the Bible Teachers: Galatians to Ephesians* (T. Wilson & K. Stapley eds.), (John Ritchie LTD, UK; 2000), p. 15
44 Warren Wiersbe, op. cit., Gal. 1:8-10
45 William MacDonald, op. cit., p. 1879
46 D. S. Dockery, *The Pauline Letters* in *Holman Concise Bible Commentary* (Broadman & Holman Publishers, Nashville, TN; 1998), p. 570
47 Hamilton Smith, *The Epistle to the Galatians*, STEM Publishing; Gal. 4:3: https://www.stempublishing.com/authors/smith/Galatians.html
48 H. A. Ironside, *Isaiah* – Rev. ed. (Loizeaux, Neptune, NJ; 2000), p. 57
49 F. B. Hole, *Notes on Galatians*, STEM Publishing; Gal. 4: https://www.stempublishing.com/authors/hole/Art/Notes_on_Galatians.html
50 J. G. Bellett, *Galatians*, STEM Publishing; Gal. 5: https://stempublishing.com/authors/bellett/Gal_word.html
51 F. B. Hole, op. cit., Gal. 5
52 Hamilton Smith, op. cit., Gal. 5:24-26
53 Warren Wiersbe, op. cit., Gal. 6:1
54 William Kelly, *Lectures on the Epistle of Paul the Apostle to the Galatians*, STEM Publishing; Gal. 6:3: https://www.stempublishing.com/authors/kelly/2Newtest/galatian.html
55 Albert Leckie, *What the Bible Teaches: Galatians to Ephesians* (T. Wilson & K. Stapley eds.), (John Ritchie LTD, UK; 2000), p. 110
56 Warren Wiersbe, op. cit., Gal. 1:4
57 William MacDonald, op. cit., p. 1915

# Endnotes

58 Albert Leckie, op. cit., p. 122
59 Hamilton Smith, *Ephesians*, STEM Publishing; Eph. 3: https://stempublishing.com/authors/smith/EPHESIAN.html
60 E. Schuyler English, *H. A. Ironside, Ordained of the Lord* (Loizeaux Brothers Inc., Neptune, NJ; 1976). p. 132
61 Harold W. Hoehner & Dallas Theological Seminary, *The Bible Knowledge Commentary: An Exposition of the Scriptures NT* (Victor Books, Wheaton, IL; 1983-1985), p. 634
62 Albert Leckie, op. cit., p. 132
63 Hamilton Smith, op. cit., Eph. 4:8
64 J. N. Darby, *Notes on the Epistle to the Ephesians*, STEM Publishing; Eph. 4: https://stempublishing.com/authors/darby/EXPOSIT/27002E.html#a4
65 James Vernon McGee, *Thru the Bible*, Vol. 5 (Thomas Nelson Pub. Nashville, TN; 1983), p. 253
66 Bill Mounce, *For an Informed Love of God: "Pastors and Teachers, and the Article (Eph. 4:11),"* Friday, October 10, 2008 https://www.billmounce.com/monday-with-mounce/pastors-and-teachers-and-the-article-eph-4-11
67 William MacDonald, op cit., p. 852
68 F. B. Hole, *Leviticus*, STEM Publishing; Leviticus 10: F. B. Hole, http://stempublishing.com/authors/hole/Pent/LEVITICUS.html
69 Warren Wiersbe, *The Bible Exposition Commentary,* op. cit., Vol. 2, p. 142
70 Albert Leckie, op. cit., p. 157
71 Watchman Nee, *Sit Walk Stand* (Gospel Literature Service, Bombay, India; 1957), ch. 3
72 Ibid.
73 Hamilton Smith, op. cit., Eph. 5:14
74 G. V. Wigram, *Lectures on the Epistle of the Ephesians*, STEM Publishing; Eph. 6: https://stempublishing.com/authors/wigram/MEM1414.html
75 F. B. Hole, *Ephesians*, STEM Publishing; Eph. 6 https://stempublishing.com/authors/hole/NT/EPHESIAN.html#a6
76 Harold W. Hoehner, op. cit., p. 644
77 Ibid.
78 William MacDonald, op cit., p. 1964
79 P. L. Tan, *Encyclopedia of 7700 illustrations* (Bible Communications, Garland TX; 1996, c1979)
80 R. C. Chapman, *Robert Cleaver Chapman of Barnstaple*, by W. H. Bennet (Pickering & Inglis, Glasgow, Scotland; no date – 1st ed.), pp. 125-126
81 Warren Wiersbe, *The Bible Exposition Commentary,* Vol. 2 (Victor Books, Wheaton, IL; 1989), Phil. 2:6
82 William MacDonald, op cit., p. 1972
83 Sydney Maxwell, *What the Bible Teaches, Philippians* (T. Wilson & K. Stapley eds.), (John Ritchie LTD, UK; 2000), p. 218

84 William Kelly, *Isaiah - Exposition*, Part 2, STEM Publishing; Isa. 26: http://stempublishing.com/authors/kelly/1Oldtest/ISA_PT2.html#a1
85 G. C. Willis, *Philippians*, STEM Publishing; Phil. 4: https://www.stempublishing.com/authors/GC_Willis/GCW_Philippians4.htm
86 William MacDonald, op. cit., p. 1992
87 Thomas Bentley, *What the Bible Teaches, Colossians* (T. Wilson & K. Stapley eds.), (John Ritchie LTD, UK; 2000), p. 316
88 Norman L. Geisler & Dallas Theological Seminary, *The Bible Knowledge Commentary: An Exposition of the Scriptures NT* (Victor Books, Wheaton, IL; 1983-1985), p. 679
89 H. B. Hole, Colossians, STEM Publishing; Col. 3: https://stempublishing.com/authors/hole/NT/COLOSSIA.html#a3
90 William MacDonald, op. cit., p. 2011
91 Warren Wiersbe, op. cit., Gal. 3:17
92 Thomas Bentley, op. cit., p. 368
93 T. Earnest Wilson, *What the Bible Teaches, 1 Thessalonians to Titus* (T. Wilson & K. Stapley eds.), (John Ritchie LTD, UK; 2000), p. 54
94 William MacDonald, op. cit., p. 2052
95 T. W. Smith, *What the Bible Teaches, 1 Thessalonians to Titus* (T. Wilson & K. Stapley eds.), (John Ritchie LTD, UK; 2000), p. 104)
96 Prophecy News, "Temple Institute Performs 'Educational Passover Sacrifice" by Chris Perver; April 10, 2012, http://www.prophecynews.co.uk/index.php/temple-mount/1919-temple-institute-performs-educational-passover-sacrifice
97 Thomas L. Constable & Dallas Theological Seminary, *The Bible Knowledge Commentary: An Exposition of the Scriptures NT* (Victor Books, Wheaton, IL; 1983-1985), p. 721
98 William MacDonald, op. cit., p. 2056
99 James Allen, *What the Bible Teaches, 1 Thessalonians to Titus* (T. Wilson & K. Stapley eds.), (John Ritchie LTD, UK; 2000), pp. 188-189
100 F. B. Hole, *1 Timothy*, STEM Publishing; 1 Tim. 1: https://stempublishing.com/authors/hole/NT/1TIMOTHY.html
101 Hamilton Smith, *1 Timothy*, STEM Publishing; 1 Tim. 1: https://stempublishing.com/authors/smith/1TIMOTHY.html
102 Hamilton Smith, op. cit., 1 Tim. 2
103 John Phillips, *Exploring the Pastoral Epistles: An Expository Commentary*, (Kregel, Inc., Grand Rapids, MI; 2004), p. 70
104 William MacDonald, op. cit., p. 2083
105 James Allen, op. cit., pp. 201-202
106 William Kelly, *1 Timothy*, STEM Publishing; 1 Tim. 2: https://stempublishing.com/authors/kelly/2Newtest/1timothy.html
107 William MacDonald, op. cit., p. 2093
108 William MacDonald, *True Discipleship* (Walterick Pub., Kansas City, KS; 1975), p. 56

[109] William Kelly, op. cit.; 1 Tim. 5: https://stempublishing.com/authors/kelly/2Newtest/1timothy.html
[110] James R. Baker, *What the Bible Teaches, 1 Thessalonians to Titus* (T. Wilson & K. Stapley eds.), (John Ritchie LTD, UK; 2000), p. 336
[111] W. Grinton Berry, editor, *Foxe's Book of Martyrs* (Power Books, Old Tappan, NJ; no date), p. 9
[112] Harry A. Ironside, *Holiness: The False and the True* (Loizeaux Brothers, Pub. New York, NY; no date), p. 75-76
[113] Ibid., pp. 74
[114] William MacDonald, op. cit., p. 2120
[115] Edward Dennett, *Exodus*, STEM Publishing; Ex. 7: Edward Dennett; http://stempublishing.com/authors/dennett/EXODUS1.html
[116] C. H. Mackintosh, *Genesis to Deuteronomy* (Loizeaux Brothers, Inc., Neptune, NJ; 1972), p. 174
[117] David E. West, *What the Bible Teaches, 1 Thessalonians to Titus* (T. Wilson & K. Stapley eds.), (John Ritchie LTD, UK; 2000), pp. 407–408
[118] William MacDonald, op. cit., pp. 2138–2139
[119] Ibid. p. 2140
[120] F. B. Hole, *1 Titus*, STEM Publishing; Tit. 2: https://stempublishing.com/authors/hole/NT/TITUS.html#a2
[121] David Gooding, *In the School of Christ* (Gospel Folio Press, Grand Rapids, MI; 1995), p. 30

*May We See Christ – An Old Testament Journey* is a sequential study of Scripture containing 366 two-page devotions (758 pages). Besides the plain language of the Old Testament, God has employed a variety of types, symbols, and allegories in a complementary fashion to teach us about His Son. With the light of New Testament truth and the illuminating assistance of the Holy Spirit, we are able to understand and appreciate these fascinating Old Testament pictures. All of God's written Word speaks of Christ to some degree as He is the main emphasis of Scripture. Accordingly, the best reason to embark on this one-year journey is to more clearly see, know, and love Christ. May the Lord richly bless your daily contemplations of the Savior as you expectantly peer into God's oracles and witness the glory of His Son. — Warren Henderson

*A New Testament Journey*

# May We Serve Christ!

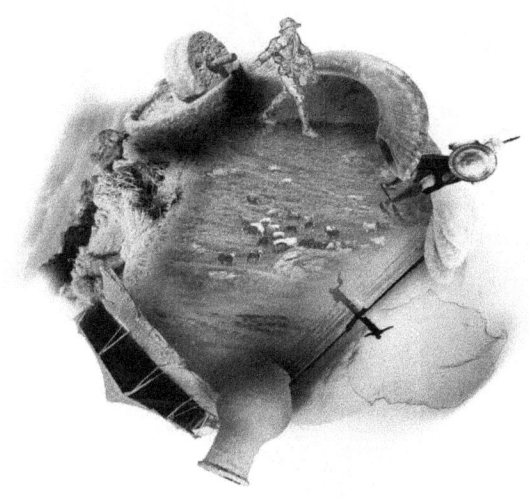

## WARREN HENDERSON

At this moment, each of us is as close to the Lord Jesus Christ as we desire to be. Our patient Savior is always ready to assist anyone genuinely seeking Him and desiring to serve Him in his or her appointed capacity and calling. Through His Word and His Spirit, God aids a true seeker every step of the way into a deeper knowledge of Himself and His purposes. *May We Serve Christ? – A New Testament Journey* draws practical application from Scripture to convict, to confront, and to encourage us to *"press toward the goal for the prize of the upward call of God in Christ Jesus"* (Phil. 3:14.). There is a Savior to know, a work to do, a calling to be fulfilled, a race to run, and a higher experience with God to be enjoyed! — Warren Henderson